W9-CPE-193

DATE DUE

Prevention and Control
of Aggression
(PGPS-123)

Pergamon Titles of Related Interest

PERGAMON GENERAL PSYCHOLOGY SERIES
EDITORS
Arnold P. Goldstein, *Syracuse University*
Leonard Krasner, *SUNY at Stony Brook*

Prevention and Control of Aggression

Center for Research on Aggression
Syracuse University

Arnold P. Goldstein, Director

Pergamon Press

New York   Oxford   Toronto   Sydney   Paris   Frankfurt

Pergamon Press Offices:

U.S.A.   Pergamon Press Inc., Maxwell House, Fairview Park,
                          Elmsford, New York 10523, U.S.A.

U.K.   Pergamon Press Ltd., Headington Hill Hall,
                          Oxford OX3 0BW, England

CANADA   Pergamon Press Canada Ltd., Suite 104, 150 Consumers Road,
                          Willowdale, Ontario M2J 1P9, Canada

AUSTRALIA   Pergamon Press (Aust.) Pty. Ltd., P.O. Box 544,
                          Potts Point, NSW 2011, Australia

FRANCE   Pergamon Press SARL, 24 rue des Ecoles,
                          75240 Paris, Cedex 05, France

FEDERAL REPUBLIC   Pergamon Press GmbH, Hammerweg 6,
OF GERMANY   D-6242 Kronberg-Taunus, Federal Republic of Germany

Copyright © 1983 Pergamon Press Inc.

Library of Congress Cataloging in Publication Data

Main entry under title:

Prevention and control of aggression.

    (Pergamon general psychology series ; 122)
    Includes index.
    1. Aggressiveness (Psychology)--Prevention.
2.Violence--Prevention. I. Syracuse University.
Center for Research on Aggression. II. Series.
BF575.A3P73   1983   302.5′4   83-2152
ISBN 0-08-029375-1

Printed in the United States of America

This book is dedicated to an idea—
   That aggression is not inevitable, that the constructive in
   human relations can prevail.

Contents

Preface

Child abuse, spouse abuse, school vandalism, juvenile delinquency, assault, murder, terrorism, and violence in its other diverse individual and collective expressions remains a societal problem of the first magnitude. The price of such aggression in pain, unhappiness, money, and unrealized aspirations is immense. The need for effective interventions designed to respond constructively to this state of affairs is urgent. In this spirit, the Syracuse University Center for Research on Aggression was organized in 1981 to stimulate, conduct, and disseminate applied research on the multiple causes of aggression, its effective prevention and control, and the development of prosocial alternatives to such antisocial behavior.

The Center for Research on Aggression is a broadly interdisciplinary group, whose academic members—all interested in the study of aggression and its reduction—are affiliated with a wide array of university departments: Psychology, Sociology, Education, Special Education, Religion, Public Communications, Nonviolent Conflict and Change. To help concretize the substantial Center emphasis upon applied research, an advisory board was constituted of community agency directors and policy implementers whose organizations and responsibilities directly bore upon aggression and aggression control concerns.

The Center's goals, its academic disciplines, and applied emphases are thoroughly reflected in its first joint scholarly effort, the present book. The authors are primarily members of the Center and their Syracuse University collaborators. Our aspiration in planning and writing this book has been to offer a thoughtful, comprehensive, and research-stimulating presentation of major avenues for preventing aggression, controlling its occurrence, and stimulating prosocial alternatives to it. Our largely applied emphasis appropriately dictated that both potentially effective interventions and relevant (especially evaluative) research be our dual focus—an aspiration largely realized in the chapters which follow.

Recent decades have been marked by the "discovery" of domestic violence in the United States. While long a closet phenomenon, the women's movement and heightened social, medical, and legal concern in the 1960s and 1970s led to greatly increased awareness of the frequency of child abuse and spouse abuse in the American home. This heightened awareness has, fortunately, stimulated a large amount of clinical and empirical research interest regarding both cause and cure. Keller and Erne in chapter 1, "Child Abuse," and D. Goldstein in chapter 2, "Spouse Abuse," examine in considerable depth both traditional and newly innovative approaches to the prevention and control of such domestic violence. In both instances, their evaluative scrutiny and future-oriented recommendations loom as particularly valuable advances to our thinking and planning. It is noteworthy that both chapters underscore a comprehensive model of both causality and intervention, stressing—as is stressed elsewhere throughout this book—the complexity of aggression's antecedents and, therefore, the need for equally complex interventions.

Harootunian and Apter, in chapter 3, approach their topic—the prevention and control of school violence—from an explicitly ecological or systems perspective. School violence, they propose and carefully illustrate, will yield most readily when interventions utilized are implemented simultaneously with the target youngsters involved, their teachers, the school's administration, and such out-of-school influences as parents, local community, and the larger society. The authors do us the great service of broadening our perspective, and underscoring still further that the complex and multidetermined phenomenon called aggression requires for its reduction equally complex and multidimensional intervention combinations.

Violent acts committed by adolescents occur in all contexts, not merely schools, as Glick's examination of the juvenile delinquency intervention literature makes clear. He provides us, in chapter 4, with an historical perspective on this persistent social problem; reviews the major theories of causation; and, stressing again our prevention and control theme, places special emphasis upon describing a series of model intervention programs. As is true for many of the evaluative appraisals in other domains of concern to aggression prevention and control, the juvenile delinquency intervention literature consists far more of anecdotal, impressionistic reports than of careful, systematic evaluation. This early investigative stage also characterizes most of the "evaluations" for the model programs singled out by Glick. We take these where they are, namely pregnant leads and promising paths to follow. We strongly second Glick's stance, and hope that their more complete empirical scrutiny will follow.

Chapter 5, by Morokoff, deals with the topic of rape. This chapter seeks to present diverse perspectives on the meaning of rape, the several theoretical formulations employed to explain it, and the numerous strategies utilized toward its reduction. Thus, rape is examined from a legal-definitional perspective, as seen and experienced by both victim and offender, as a social statistic, and in terms of attitudes of the population in general. Morokoff uses this band of often divergent viewpoints, combined with prevailing theoretical explanations of rape, relevant cross-cultural research findings, and laboratory studies of sexual arousal and aggression to provide us with a much deeper, truly comprehensive understanding of this particularly virulent expression of overt aggression. Her equally insightful approach to rape prevention urges (1) the refutation of the many myths surrounding the topic of rape through public education, (2) greater investment in psychological and social research seeking to identify the means by which sexual aggression is taught, and (3) political efforts to enhance both the power and prestige of women in American society.

Mazur, in chapter 6, takes us in a somewhat different direction. His particular concern is one especially important facet of the domain more broadly describable as the physiology of aggression. Focusing primarily upon possible hormonal antecedents of overt aggression, Mazur addresses three questions: (1) Is there a physiological basis for the broadly reliable observation that males are more aggressive than females? (2) Is aggression in males associated with levels of testosterone? (3) Is aggression in females related to stage of the menstrual cycle? Mazur's careful, systematic examination of the empirical evidence bearing upon these questions is a model of scientific reasoning and scrutiny. His conclusions are interesting in their own right, and most certainly relevant to this book's overriding aspirations. But the chapter may well be most valuable as an examplar to those concerned with yet other dimensions of the physiology of aggression, especially for its implicit guidelines regarding how one ought optimally to proceed when considering, evaluating, weighing, and finally drawing tentative conclusions from a body of scientific evidence. The reader will note that Mazur's chapter is brief, in comparison for example with the one which follows. Both chapters, however, rather comprehensively address the central issues in their respective domains, illustrating the relative unevenness in the amount of ongoing work in diverse aggression-relevant topic areas.

Behavior modification approaches to aggression prevention and control constitute our next focus. A. P. Goldstein, in chapter 7, describes a broad array of aggression-relevant behavioral interventions, their research base, and their optimal sequencing and combinations. Important for the goals of prevention and control, means for encouraging appropriate, prosocial alternative behaviors are given companion emphasis along with techniques for reducing inappropriate, antisocial behaviors. This chapter also deals in some depth with a theme of prime relevance to the many other types of interventions described in other chapters, namely the ethics of efforts to predict, prevent, control, and substitute alternatives for aggressive behavior.

The prevention of aggression by the encouragement and utilization of prosocial alternatives to it is the explicit or implicit theme of the three chapters which then follow. Such preventive efforts, as is made clear, can occur in a diversity of contexts—school, mass media, and the larger community. Zimmerman devotes chapter 8 to a thorough explication of Kohlberg's approach to moral education—its context, rationale, procedures, and contents. Most central to our theme, she carefully examines the nature of the complex relationship between moral reasoning and moral behavior and, especially with reference to chronically aggressive persons, helps us toward a beginning understanding of both the promise and limitations of such educational interventions as a means toward enhancing prosocial behavior. Comstock, in chapter 9, carefully traces the history of media violence and its purported effects on individual behavior. Both relevant political opinion and empirical research are examined, including Comstock's own significant contribution to the latter. Going beyond the immensely important but global conclusion that such effects reliably occur, he draws upon evidence discerning when, with whom, and under what circumstances media violence influences individual behavior to draw implications for the prevention and control of violence which are well worth serious consideration and dissemination.

Beyond the real and potential contributions to prosocial behavior which the educational establishment and the mass media may provide, Katz and Uhler, in chapter 10, examine nonviolent action as an important alternative to aggressive behavior. Nonviolent action is a widely used but grossly underpromoted approach to the prevention and control of aggression, a stance hopefully corrected in part by its inclusion and explication here. Katz and Uhler share with us the history of nonviolent behavior; describe its principle theories, guidelines, and methods; and provide two in-depth illustrations of their successful utilization.

Chapter 11 deals with terrorism, an especially flourishing manifestation of aggression in recent years. The Braungarts place terrorism in historical context, examine its social and psychological roots, describe its diverse and often complex motivations, and cast it in clearer perspective by reporting its current levels and global trends and patterns. They deepen our understanding of its "why, where, by whom, toward what ends" still further in their penetrating discussions of perpetrators, terrorist strategies and tactics, and its use as a political weapon. Clearly, terrorism is a difficult phenomenon to fully understand, and even more difficult to prevent and control. Prevention and control efforts, as the Braungarts elucidate, have been diverse and of very mixed success. International legal efforts, gun traffic control, the use of intelligence information, Special Weapons and Tactics (SWAT) team utilization, and, especially, skilled negotiation are chief among the several prevention and control responses popularly used. Each are carefully described and evaluated by the authors. In all, this chapter provides a comprehensive and enlightening picture of modern terrorism in all its manifestations and societal ramifications.

In our final chapter, by A. P. Goldstein and Keller, we seek especially to look to the future. Many agenda must be addressed—in the street, in the school, in the laboratory, in government offices—if the prevention and control of aggression is to move more fully from aspiration to reality. We seek in this chapter to highlight but a few aspects of this agenda for the future, stressing in particular domains and methods of inquiry we feel to be especially promising for real-world fruition. A particularly important, and remarkably ignored, domain of relevant inquiry concerns the prediction of aggression. Investigations seeking to identify, validate, and cross-validate predictive criteria have been surprisingly infrequent and disappointingly unsuccessful. With very minimal exception, our predictive tools are weak and grossly unsatisfactory. Building generously upon the seminal work of Monahan, the authors seek in this chapter to make clear where the field of prediction now (barely) stands, wherein lies its major deficiencies, and what are some of the major investigative directions beckoning those wishing to improve our predictive potency. More successful prediction would indeed be a powerful component in the prevention and control effort.

At the broadest level of conclusion, this book's content most clearly summates to the view that aggression is a complex, multidetermined set of phenomena requiring for its prevention and control complex, multifaceted solutions. Much of this final, future-oriented chapter is devoted to the operationalization in a research context of this belief in and quest for appropriate complex, multifaceted and, especially, effective solutions. Toward this end, the authors examine optimal strategies for the *multidimensional* measurement of aggression. We defend our strongly held belief that powerful interventions must be *multitargeted,* that is, designed to impact simultaneously at diverse levels of causality. Effective prevention and control interventions, we believe, must also be *multichannel* in their impact, that is, at each level of intervention several modes of aggression expression may be operative and thus require broad spectrum and diverse intervention efforts. Our proposed focus is also *multiprocess* and, thus, seeks to emphasize that when devising, studying, and implementing multitargeted interventions with multichannel procedures at each level of intervention, one must target for not only the prevention and control of pro-aggression influences, but also the enhancement and facilitation of anti-aggression, prosocial potentialities. Finally, as the very contents of this book makes clear, and as we feel the very existence of the Syracuse University Center for Research on Aggression confirms, our final chapter also stresses our belief that the optimal grand strategy for seeking fuller prevention and control of aggression is a *multidisciplinary* strategy. Perhaps an appropriate means for concluding this prefatory statement, and underscoring our belief in the special value of multidisciplinary efforts, is to quote here this book's concluding few lines:

> we believe aggression will yield most readily when the artificial borders of academic disciplines are breached, ideas permitted to more fully intermingle, and new concepts at the interface of disciplines encouraged to emerge and be scrutinized. It is in this spirit, and toward the goal of identifying, examining, and disseminating increasingly more effective interventions for the prevention and control of aggression that this book has been offered.

Arnold P. Goldstein
Syracuse University

Acknowledgments

Jerry Frank of Pergamon Press has been a wise and patient editor throughout the planning, writing, and production of this book. His sound advice and recommendations are most thoroughly appreciated by all of us.

A special acknowledgment of thanks and appreciation is also extended to our parent organization, Syracuse University. Our Center was welcomed as a concept by the University's administration, encouraged as it became a concrete plan, and warmly supported into reality. We thank you heartily, Syracuse University.

1

Child Abuse: Toward a Comprehensive Model

Harold R. Keller
and
Diane Erne

Child abuse, while of growing concern to large numbers of professionals and the public, is not a unique product of our time and place (Kellum, 1974; Langer, 1974; Redbill, 1968; Ross, 1980). To some extent, the growing concern is illustrated in the great flux of popular and professional books on the topic in recent years (e.g., Bahar, Hyman, Jones, Jones, Kerr, & Mitchell, 1976; Bakan, 1971; Billingsley & Giovannoni, 1972; Chase, 1975; Costa & Nelson, 1978; Decourcy & Decourcy, 1973; Fontana, 1971; Franklin, 1975; Garbarino & Stocking, 1980; Gerbner, Ross, & Zigler, 1980; Gil, 1970; Helfer & Kempe, 1974, 1976; Justice & Justice, 1976; Kalmar, 1977; Kempe & Helfer, 1972; Steinmetz & Straus, 1974; Straus, Gelles, & Steinmetz, 1980; Volpe, Breton, & Mitten, 1980; Walters, 1975; Young, 1964). Since 1976, the American Humane Association (AHA, 1981) indicates there has been a steady increase from year to year in the number of reports of child abuse.

This chapter initially will discuss briefly the scope of the problem of child abuse in terms of definitional issues, incidence, and sequalae. Then we will examine various theoretical models (psychiatric, sociological, social-situational, and integrative) and their related treatment approaches. Child abuse is a complex multidimensional phenomenon, for which no one theoretical explanation is adequate. We propose that a comprehensive model of child abuse requires a rigorous examination of families at multiple levels, including the abusing parent, the child victim, parent-child interactional patterns, and the setting in which abuse takes place considering both the immediate family context and the community and broader social context. A schematic of this comprehensive model might be the following:

$$\text{Child Abuse} = \boxed{\begin{array}{c}\text{Abusing} \\ \text{Parent}\end{array}} + \boxed{\begin{array}{c}\text{Child} \\ \text{Victim}\end{array}} + \boxed{\begin{array}{c}\text{Family} \\ \text{Interaction}\end{array}} + \boxed{\begin{array}{c}\text{Family} \\ \text{(Partner)}\end{array}} + \boxed{\begin{array}{c}\text{Community} \\ \text{(and Social Context)}\end{array}}$$

This chapter will develop and discuss the model in terms of its treatment and prevention implications. In so doing, characteristics of change agents and the need for coordination of interventive and preventive efforts will be emphasized. Finally, research and program evaluation needs will be discussed.

This review is restricted to a consideration of child abuse (or the use of excessive physical force) by caregivers primarily in the home setting. Review of related child abuse in other settings (such as residential institutions or our public schools) will be limited to its relevance as a

1

broader social context supporting and allowing family (parent to child) violence. Sexual abuse of children by adults will not be considered.

DEFINITION, INCIDENCE, AND SEQUALAE OF CHILD ABUSE

Issues in the Definition of Child Abuse

The definitional problem in the area of child abuse is a major one. There is no agreed upon definition of child abuse. This lack of consistency of definition reflects the inadequate theoretical development in the area and results in misleading and contradictory research results and in imprecise incidence reports.

There are three basic approaches to defining physical abuse, with many variations and each with its own set of limitations. First, abuse can be defined in terms of actions or outcomes. Straus (1979a) defined child abuse as "an attack by a parent involving punching, kicking, biting, hitting with an object, using knife or gun" (p. 213). A focus upon action or outcome has the advantage of quantifying the abuse with a minimum of inferences about the abuser's intent. It has the disadvantage of not differentiating between accidental injuries and intentionally inflicted physical injuries.

The second approach to defining physical abuse specifically uses the concept of intentionality (Burgess, 1979; Gelles, 1980a, b; Helfer, 1978). Parke and Collmer (1975) offer a third definitional approach emphasizing abuse as a culturally determined label. Because it incorporates more of the variables of concern in this multidetermined phenomenon, Parke and Collmer's definition of child abuse will be used in this review: "any child who receives nonaccidental physical injury (or injuries) as a result of acts (or omissions) on the part of his parents or guardians that violate the community standards concerning the treatment of children" (p. 513).

Incidence and Sequalae of Child Abuse

As already indicated, it is very difficult to determine the incidence of child abuse because of the varying definitions in the literature and across states. Cohen and Sussman (1975) pointed out that many states fail to distinguish between reports of abuse and neglect. Of those states that do, neglect reports far outnumber abuse reports. Most states do not distinguish between number of reports of suspected abuse/neglect and number of confirmed cases. National estimates of abuse range from Light's (1973) estimate of around 500,000 to Gil's (1970) estimate of 2.5 to 4.0 million cases per year. The most recent report of the AHA (1981) shows that almost three-quarters of a million children were reported as abused or neglected in this country during 1979.

Gelles' (1980a, b) national survey with the Conflict Tactics Scale (Straus, 1979b) found that 3.6 percent of children between 3 and 17 years of age were at-risk for serious injury through parental use of at least one dangerous form of violence (kicking, biting, hitting—beyond spanking—beating up, using a gun or knife) during 1975. This figure translates into 1.4 to 1.9 million children vulnerable to physical abuse in a year. It must be noted that, while this survey was one of the most careful and thorough, the figures are probably underestimates. A number of factors produced these probable underestimates including: parental self-reports provided the data; only intact families were surveyed; the violent acts of only one of the two parents were recorded; only children between the ages of 3 and 17 were included. The AHA (1981) reports that "major physical injuries" occur most frequently from birth to three years, decreases with age, then again increases during ages 12 through 16 forming a U-shaped relationship between age and physical abuse.

While estimates of the proportion of abused children who suffer from recurrent maltreatment vary (e.g., Johnson & Morse, 1968; Morse, Sahler, & Friedman, 1970; Whiting, 1977), the recurrence rate appears to be substantial. In Gelles' (1980a) national survey, a single incident occurred in only 6 percent of the abuse cases. The mean number of assaults on a child per year was 10.5 with a median of 4.5.

What happens to children who are abused? The harmful effects of child abuse range from superficial wounds to permanent physical, cognitive, and emotional impairment, and even death. Numerous investigators have found high rates of deviant neurological, mental, and emotional development among abused children (e.g., Elmer & Gregg, 1967; Gregg & Elmer, 1969; MacKeith, 1975; Martin, 1972; Martin & Beezley, 1974, 1977; McRae, Ferguson & Lederman, 1973; Morse, Sahler, & Friedman, 1970; Smith & Hanson, 1974; Soeffing, 1975; Till, 1975). Other indirect sequalae of child abuse are reported. MacKeith (1975) cited studies in Germany where a large proportion of criminals and murderers had been maltreated in childhood. Similarly, a large majority of delinquent and socially deviant adolescents in the United States indicate they were abused as children (Alfaro, 1978; Helfer & Kempe, 1976; Steele, 1976b). Baer and Wathey (1977) report a high incidence of abuse in the history of young adult drug abusers.

Attempts to learn what happens to children who are the victims of abuse are fraught with numerous methodological problems. Until recently, there were no studies that incorporated control groups to determine whether the frequency or magnitude of identified problems was any different from that found in samples of nonabused children of comparable characteristics. The Martin and Beezley (1977) study, for example, is laudable in that it used multidimensional assessment and psychometrically sound measures of physical, neurological, and intellectual functioning; but there was no assessment of comparable nonabused children. Kinard (1980a) pointed out in a methodological review that, additionally, early studies on sequalae employed small and select samples of abused children and, particularly in studies of emotional development, poor measurement instruments. Even when studying the same phenomena, there is considerable cross-study inconsistency in measurement instruments. Further, it is not clear, except in prospective studies, whether problems observed in an abused sample (even if different from those of a control group) are due to the abuse or whether the problems existed prior to the abuse.

The few studies that do employ control groups find significant differences between abused and control children. For example, Barahal, Waterman, and Martin (1981) compared social cognitive styles. They found that abused children had a more external locus of control (e.g., believed outcomes of events, especially negative events, were beyond their own personal control). Abused children understand less well increasingly complex social roles. While there were also differences in social sensitivity and perspective taking, those differences were attenuated by intellectual abilities. Abused and control children did not differ in moral judgments. Kinard (1980a) found differences in emotional development with abused children exhibiting lower emotional functioning than matched controls. The abused children misperceived trust tasks and had a more reality-oriented motivation, especially for unsuccessful outcomes. While controls did not manifest a strong relationship between aggressiveness and self-concept, the abused children showed a strong negative correlation between the two. Green (1978) compared physically abused children with two control groups, one neglected and the other normal. He found that physically abused children showed significantly more self-destructive behavior, including suicide attempts and self-mutilation. In a weaker retrospective study, Carroll, Schaffer, Spensley, and Abramowitz (1980) found a similar relationship between abuse and self-mutilation. They obtained retrospective reports about family experiences from self-mutilating young adult patients in a psychiatric institution and from a control sample of nonmutilating, nonsuicidal patients from the same setting.

Perhaps the most consistent and insidious finding in the child abuse literature is that abusing parents often were themselves physically or emotionally abused or neglected as children. The finding that abusive parents raise their children in the style in which they themselves were raised has been obtained in numerous studies by investigators of widely varying theoretical orientations (e.g., Fontana, 1968; Justice & Justice, 1976; Kempe & Helfer, 1972; Kempe, Silverman, Steele, Droegemueller, & Silver, 1962; Lukianowicz, 1971; Lystad, 1975; Melnick & Hurley, 1969; Oliver & Taylor, 1971; Ounsted, Oppenheimer, & Lindsey, 1975; Sameroff & Chandler, 1975; Silver, Dublin, & Lourie, 1969; Smith & Hanson, 1975; Spinetta & Rigler, 1972; Steele, 1976a, b; Steele & Pollock, 1968). This same result was obtained in Gelles' (1980a, b; Straus et al., 1980) national survey as well as the above studies with more select samples. Further, in a retrospective control group study, Conger, Burgess, and Barrett (1979) found a significantly greater history of punitive childrearing among abusive parents than among matched controls.

It is important to keep in mind that because many abusive parents report having been abused as children does not mean that children who are abused will *necessarily* grow up to be abusive parents. Such an overgeneralization, however, is frequently presented in the popular media and sometimes in professional literature as well. Hunter, Kilstrom, Kraybill, and Loda (1978) conducted a one year prospective study of 255 infants and their families. Twelve months later, they searched the state registry for confirmed reports of abuse and found ten (3.9 percent). That percentage is comparable to (slightly higher than) the percentage found in Gelles' (1980a, b) national survey. Nine of the ten abused children came from families with a parental history of an abusive and neglectful childhood. Hunter and Kilstrom (1979) made an intensive study of the files of those 9 families and compared them with 40 families from the Hunter et al. (1978) study who had a similar history of the parents having been abused as children. The infants in these 40 families were not reported as maltreated in that same twelve month period. This study will be reported in greater detail in later sections. The importance of this study here is that it describes a set of families who broke out of the apparent family pattern of transmitting a cycle of abusive parenting across generations. Such descriptions provide important leads for possible prevention and intervention strategies that might be effective. For example, the nonrepeating families had a broader network of available resources, and different family interactional patterns (supportive significant others) than the abuse repeating families. The assumption that abuse will result necessarily in the victim growing up to be an abuser is not only inaccurate, but also may limit our awareness of possible effective prevention and intervention strategies.

In spite of the discrepancies among reported incidence rates and the methodological problems with much of the research on sequalae of child abuse, there is general consensus that child abuse is a pervasive problem. Professional and public attention to this problem is needed. High priority should be given to the prevention, intervention, and treatment of abused and abusing families. One clear need is for uniform and standardized definitions of abuse and neglect to be used by states in their reporting as well as by practitioners and researchers.

THEORETICAL MODELS OF ABUSE AND ITS TREATMENT

As indicated earlier, a major deterrent to our understanding the magnitude of the problems (the personal, interpersonal, and social dynamics of abuse) and to our development of prescriptive interventive and preventive strategies has been the dearth of theoretical development in this area. Feshbach (1980) has argued that the area of child abuse needs to draw upon the extensive conceptual literature in the general area of violence and aggression. Similarly, Ainsworth (1980) has suggested the importance of developmental literature to the area of child abuse, particularly that concerned with the development of attachment.

Gelles and Straus (1979) and Burgess (1979) suggest that family violence is unique and, as such, requires unique theoretical formulations. They suggest there are a number of characteristics of families that make the family a unique setting for the likely occurrence of violence. While family members look to one another for protection, support, and fulfillment of love and intimacy needs, the family is also a unit set apart geographically from others outside the walls of the family dwelling. This latter characteristic can insulate the family from social constraints of others outside the family. In addition, the time together is much greater than in nonfamily relationships. Membership in families is nonvoluntary, and the range of activities and interests is greater in family interactions than in other situations where people choose to be with others having similar interests. Age and gender discrepancies within a family group are often greater than in other group settings. Activities are more likely to impinge upon the personal space and life-styles of others within the family setting. Family membership typically implies the right to influence others, and there is often inequality in ascribed roles within the family. Intrafamilial socialization practices allow and encourage violence through the general acceptance of punishment as a mode of discipline. Numerous writers (Burgess, 1979; Cicchetti, Taraldson, & Egeland, 1978; Justice & Justice, 1976; Parke & Collmer, 1975) have grouped these models into four general categories of theoretical frameworks—psychiatric or intraindividual, sociological, social-situational, and integrative models. As we examine each of these theoretical models, it should be apparent that each of these models relates to one or more components of our comprehensive model.

$$\text{Child Abuse} = \boxed{\begin{array}{c}\text{Abusing}\\\text{Parent}\end{array}} + \boxed{\begin{array}{c}\text{Child}\\\text{Victim}\end{array}} + \boxed{\begin{array}{c}\text{Family}\\\text{Interaction}\end{array}} + \boxed{\begin{array}{c}\text{Family}\\\text{(Partner)}\end{array}} + \boxed{\begin{array}{c}\text{Community}\\\text{(and Social Context)}\end{array}}$$

Psychiatric or Intraindividual Model

$$\boxed{\begin{array}{c}\text{Abusing}\\\text{Parent}\end{array}}$$

The intraindividual model—also referred to as psychiatric, psychopathic, psychodynamic, personality or character trait, and mental illness model—emphasizes the parent as the major cause of child abuse. It is assumed that abusive parents have certain personality characteristics that separate the abuser from other parents. This model implies that the abuser is mentally ill and, therefore, requires traditional psychodynamic psychotherapy for change. Certainly, a conceptual limitation of this model is the use of acts of violence as indices of mental illness.

Etiological studies of child abuse from a psychiatric perspective have focused primarily on the personality characteristics of the abuser. Initially, writers in the child abuse literature suggested the presence of psychoses as a major etiological factor in child abuse. However, Spinetta and Rigler (1972), in a review of personality characteristics of abusive parents, reported that more recent studies consistently suggest that less than 10 percent of abusing parents showed severe psychotic tendencies. Kempe and Kempe (1976) indicate they find only 10-15 percent of their abusive parents have extremely poor prognosis for change, and that group includes, in addition to individuals classified as psychotics, severe character disorders (e.g., extreme alcoholism and drug addiction), and "fanatics" (e.g., persons of fundamentalist religion, unusual philosophy of life, or extremely moralistic).

The major limitation of this perspective is the inadequate evidence in support of the position. A large number of studies suggest personality characteristics of abusive parents based upon case records or personal interviews with single cases or small, nonrandom, clinical samples (for reviews see Cicchetti et al., 1978; Isaacs, 1981; Lystad, 1975; Parke & Collmer, 1975; Sameroff & Chandler, 1975; Spinetta & Rigler, 1972). Table 1.1 lists references to a variety of personality traits, as well as clusters of personality traits, that have been suggested in the literature as characterizing abusive parents. It should be noted that studies with control groups of nonabusing parents are rare (an early exception being Melnick & Hurley, 1969). It is apparent that no consistent set of personality traits or trait clusters have been identified. Many of the suggested personality characteristics are considerably less dysfunctional than might be suggested from a psychiatric model. Traits, particularly in early studies, are identified by clinical judgments. Few studies use psychometrically sound measures, and the suggested traits have rarely been validated with actual nontest behavior. Even with control groups, measurement changes and sample differences make comparison across studies difficult. Better measures must be used, and there needs to be cross-study consistency in measures.

It should be noted that merely having matched controls does not eliminate the problems involved in this mental illness model, as illustrated by Wright's (1976) "sick but slick" syndrome. When abusing parents appeared as healthy as nonabusers on various measures, particularly those with more apparent social desirability, Wright suggested the abusing parents have psychological problems but present themselves as healthy (sick but slick). Within such a view, the abusing parent, no matter how he or she responds, is mentally ill. Merely relabeling something does not explain the phenomenon. Green et al. (1974) and Lystad (1975) indicated we need to move away from conceptualizing child abuse as a homogeneous, unitary entity. Personality attributes of abusive parents do not seem to be sufficient to cause child abuse in the absence of other potentiating factors within the family and larger social system. Descriptive characterization of abusive parents might be a useful starting point in understanding child abuse, but it does not provide an explanation. Data do not allow adequate prediction of actual abusive behavior on the basis of parent characteristics (wihout additional information on other important factors), but knowledge of parent characteristics might be helpful in two other ways. First, such knowledge might help prediction of parents at risk due to poor (unusual) child rearing practices (e.g., Gray, Cutler, Dean, & Kempe, 1976; Schneider et al., 1972, 1976; Schneider, Pollock, & Helfer, 1972). Second, through the use of more complex designs, person variables can be related to various situational or setting variables and to treatment variables in a prescriptive manner—the latter as suggested by Goldstein (1978; Goldstein & Stein, 1976).

The primary treatment objective of the psychiatric model is the modification of deviant parental personality. The most common form of treatment has been individual psychoanalytically oriented psychotherapy. Such therapy, when used by skilled experienced therapists, has been shown to be effective in some cases (Fontana, 1971; Steele, 1975), but long-term effectiveness has not been demonstrated. The Steele-Pollock treatment program, which is based on individual analytic therapy, is most successful when incorporated with unorthodox treatment modes, such as home observation and teaching child rearing (Steele, 1975). While indicating that resolution of conflict with some emotional insight and understanding is typically necessary for permanent gains and altering long-term emotional relationships, Beezley, Martin, and Alexander (1976) acknowledge that cognitive, intellectual understanding without experiential relearning results in a parent who can explain the dynamics but who has changed nothing in his or her behavioral interactions (see Bandura, 1969, for a succinct discussion of this issue). Several factors, including personality characteristics, life-style of abusive parents, therapist time, client time, and monetary issues, often render psychoanalytic treatment impractical and place severe limitations on the type of individuals for whom the technique can be used (Cicchetti et al., 1978; Kempe & Helfer, 1972; Parke & Collmer, 1975; Steele, 1975).

Table 1.1 Suggested Personality Characteristics of Abusive Parents

Self-esteem, self-concept, self-critical—Albee, 1980; Blumberg, 1979; Gaines et al., 1978(c,ns); Green et al., 1974; Kempe & Kempe, 1976; Melnick & Hurley, 1969; Milner & Wimberly, 1980(c); Pollock & Steele, 1972; Roth, 1975; Schneider et al., 1976(c); Shorkey, 1980(c,ns); Smith & Hanson, 1975(c); Steele & Pollock, 1968.

Impulsivity— Bennie & Sclare, 1969; Green et al., 1974; Holter & Friedman, 1968; Johnson & Morse, 1968; Paulson et al., 1976(c).

Hostility, upset and angry—Beer, 1975; Johnson & Morse, 1968; Paulson et al., 1974(c); Schneider et al., 1972(c,ns); Seaberg, 1977; Smith & Hanson, 1975; Spinetta, 1978(c).

Over-controlled hostility—Thurber, 1979.

Isolated, lonely—Milner & Wimberley, 1979, 1980(c); Ounsted et al., 1975; Paulson et al., 1974(c); Roth, 1975; Schneider et al., 1972(c), 1976(c,ns); Shorkey, 1980(c); Spinetta, 1978(c).

Anxiety—Johnson & Morse, 1968; Smith et al., 1973.

Depression—Johnson & Morse, 1968; Milner & Wimberly, 1980(c); Paulson et al., 1974(c); Smith et al., 1973.

Rigidity—Holter & Friedman, 1968; Milner & Wimberley, 1979, 1980(c).

Fear of rejection—Alexander, 1972; Pollock & Steele, 1972; Roth, 1975.

Rejecting—Holter & Friedman, 1968; Melnick & Hurley, 1969(c).

Low frustration tolerance—Blumberg, 1979; Ounsted et al., 1975; Roth, 1975.

Role reversal, need for nurturance—Ainsworth, 1980; Green et al., 1974; Johnson & Morse, 1968; Melnick & Hurley, 1969(c); Steele & Pollock, 1968.

Self-centered—Holter & Friedman, 1968; Johnson & Morse, 1968.

Fearful—Spinetta, 1978(c).

Immature, dependent—Beer, 1975; Holter & Friedman, 1968; Hunter et al., 1978(c); Melnick & Hurley, 1969(c); Ounsted et al., 1975; Paulson et al., 1976(c); Steele, 1975.

Distrustful—Beer, 1975; Blumberg, 1979; Kempe & Helfer, 1972; Melnick & Hurley, 1969(c); Paulson et al., 1975(c).

Less intelligent—Sameroff & Chandler, 1975; Smith, Honigsberger, & Smith, 1975.

Neuroticism—Smith & Hanson, 1975(c).

Abnormal—Smith et al., 1975(c).

Drug/alcohol abuse—Aber, 1980.

Criminal—Smith et al., 1975(c).

Personality Trait Clusters

Merrill (1962; Bryant, Billingsley, Kerry, Lenfman, Merrill, Senecal, & Walsh, 1963)
  1) pervasive hostility and aggressiveness;
  2) rigidity, compulsiveness, and lack of empathy or flexibility manifested in child rejection and a concern with their own pleasures above those of their children;
  3) passive, dependent, and unaggressive.

Delsordo (1963)
  1) acute parental mental illness;
  2) overflow from the parent's aimless life (i.e., misuse of income, alcoholism, etc.);
  3) nonspecific parental disturbance;
  4) parent's harshness in disciplining children;
  5) parent's misplaced conflicts.

Zalba (1966, 1967)
  Locus in parents' personality:
    1) psychotic parent;
    2) pervasively angry and abusive parent;
    3) depressive, passive-aggressive parent.
  Locus within family system:
    4) cold, impulsive disciplinarians;
    5) impulsive but adequate parents in marital conflict;
    6) parents with identity or role crisis.

See also Boisvert, 1972; Fleming, 1967; Gil, 1970; Lukianowicz, 1971; Roth, 1975.

Note: c = control group design;
      ns = nonsignificant results, through controlled study or national survey

In light of the apparent disproportionate number of lower class abusers, this method is of limited wide-scale utility. Further difficulties with this model arise because of the inability of abusive parents who have been experientially, socially and educationally deprived to articulate, analyze, or label their feelings. Given the limitations within the theoretical, empirical, and treatment literature within the framework of this model, numerous writers have suggested the need to move away from or beyond the intraindividual model of abuse to consider broader interpersonal and social contextual variables (e.g., Antler, 1978; Beezley et al., 1976; Gelles, 1975; Newberger & Bourne, 1978; Ross & Zigler, 1980). Thus, the psychiatric or intraindividual model which focuses on the abusing parent, while useful, may best be viewed as dealing with only a segment of the equation.

Sociological Model

Family (Partner)	Community & Social Context

The sociological model of abuse focuses on cumulative environmental stresses. Gil (1970), based upon his national survey, was perhaps the earliest major proponent of this model and of related social reforms derived from the approach. Emphasis is placed upon the role of cultural attitudes toward violence, social class and social stress factors, housing and living conditions, unemployment, family size, and family-community relationships in the form of social isolation. The focus is on macrolevel variables such as social structures or arrangements, including norms, values, institutional organization, or systems operations, as they relate to individual violence. Gelles and Straus (1979) delineate six sociological theories of violence: functional, culture of violence, structural, general systems, conflict, and resource theories. They suggest that general systems and resource theories, in particular, are useful to explain intrafamily violence. Within general systems theory, the family is viewed as a goal-seeking, purposive, adaptive system. Violence is seen as a system product maintained by positive feedback processes. Intrafamily resources theory suggests that violence is used as a resource when other resources are lacking. As part of a larger integrative theory, Gelles (1982) proposes a social control theory that emphasizes the role of isolation in abusive families. He suggests that certain social and family structures reduce social controls that negatively sanction family members for acts of violence. In the absence of such social controls, family violence can and does occur because there is no cost involved for engaging in violent acts.

With regards to intervention, Gil (1970) and others (e.g., Albee, 1980; Almond, 1980; Kahn & Kamerman, 1980; Newberger & Bourne, 1978) advocate a number of means for combatting child abuse incidence rates, including systematic educational efforts directed at changing our culture's acceptance of physical punishment as a child rearing technique, elimination of poverty, redistribution of social and economic power, reduction of job discrimination and unemployment, better housing, comprehensive family planning, family life education and premarital counseling, comprehensive neighborhood-based national health service, and a full range of neighborhood-based social services aimed at reducing environmental stresses on family life and at assisting families with relational problems. While these factors are important in the etiology of child abuse, they alone cannot account for actual child abusive behavior. The suggested interventions appear critical particularly at the level of prevention and, as such, are necessary components of an integrated attack involving both intervention and prevention strategies on the problem of child abuse. Until recently, the data supporting this model and its derived intervention have been limited. Much of the research has been descriptive and correlational with limited samples of abusing families (e.g., Hyman, 1978).

One issue that has received a considerable amount of attention in the literature concerns the relationship between socioeconomic status and child abuse. The argument frequently is made that child abuse is classless, that it occurs at all socioeconomic levels. While it is quite accurate that child abuse does occur at all levels (e.g., Gelles, 1980a, b; Straus, 1979a), that does not mean there is no relationship between socioeconomic status and child abuse. An egalitarian view is that associating child abuse with lower socioeconomic status further stigmatizes the lower class. The argument is made that the middle and upper classes are disproportionately represented in unreported cases. If they were more open to public scrutiny, they would be reported more often. Pelton (1978) suggests that "undiscovered evidence is no evidence" and that the public scrutiny argument does not explain the facts that increased public awareness has not changed socioeconomic patterns, that child abuse is related to degrees of poverty within the lower socioeconomic levels, and that the most severe injuries occur within the poorest families. It must be noted that to say abuse is related to poverty does *not* say that poor people in general abuse their children. Pelton argues persuasively that a classlessness notion diverts our attention away from the real stresses of poverty and serves to maintain an ineffective psychodynamic model of treatment. Addressing directly the relationship between social class and abuse will allow consideration of important sociological variables and treatment strategies. Numerous investigators (e.g., Giovannoni & Billingsley, 1970; Smith, Hanson, & Nobel, 1975) have shown the inverse relationship between socioeconomic status and abuse rate, including the recently cited national survey (Gelles, 1980a, b; Straus, 1979a). This relationship is found with a variety of indices of status, including income, education, and occupation.

Other conditions associated with socioeconomic status have been shown to be related to abuse. For example, cumulative life changes and stresses have been shown to be significantly and positively related to child abuse (Conger et al., 1979; Gaines et al., 1978; Gelles, 1980a; Giovannoni & Billingsley, 1970; Justice & Duncan, 1976). All these studies, with the exception of Gelles' national survey, used control group designs. Giovannoni and Billingsley used clinical judgments of stress, while all the other studies employed a paper-and-pencil measure of life change or life stress. Gaines et al. (1978), however, found life stresses to be a significantly differentiating condition only for neglecting mothers relative to abusing mothers and a control group (which did differ from each other). Further Gelles found that, as number of stressful life events increased, the probability of severe violence to children increased.

Number of children might be viewed as another stress condition within a family. The national survey (Gelles, 1980a; Straus, 1979a) found that parents with two children have a 50 percent higher abuse rate than parents with one child. Among the poorest families, each additional child increases the probability of abuse. Among middle income families, the risk of child abuse increases with each child up to seven; no severe violence was found in middle income families with eight or more children. There was no relationship between number of children and abuse rate for wealthy families. Inadequate child spacing was also an important differentiating factor in the prospective studies of Hunter and Kilstrom (1979; Hunter et al., 1978).

Some of the most exciting research in this area relates to the issue of isolation and available resources both inside and outside the family. Giovannoni and Billingsley (1970) found that their abusing mothers had less knowledge about community resources than their control group. Hunter et al. (1978) found that social isolation without adequate intra- and extrafamily support systems, poor use of medical services, and inadequate child care arrangements were all important factors in their prospective study of families with premature and ill newborns. These same factors (presence of friends and/or extended family, participation in church or other social groups, and use of services of community agencies) were most important in breaking the intergenerational cycle of abuse (Hunter & Kilstrom, 1979). This research would strongly support Gelles and Straus' (1979) intrafamily resource theory that violence is used as a resource when other resources are lacking. While not a control group study, Ayoub and Pfeifer (1977; Pfeifer & Ayoub, 1976) found that 85 percent of high risk families who refused help, which was designed to deal directly with social isolation by providing coordinated agency support, had their children removed from their homes on grounds of abuse or neglect within six to twelve months after initial identification. In comparison, none of the families who accepted the comprehensive programming had children reported or hospitalized for abuse or neglect over the same period. Straus (1979a) suggested that the lack of differences found among black and white families in their national survey, in spite of the generally lower socioeconomic status of the black families, might have been due to the greater support provided by the extended black families. Garbarino, Crouter, and Sherman (1977) describe an innovative and nonintrusive multivariate approach to assessing neighborhood economic and social resources. Using census tract data for specified neighborhoods as indices of available resources, they were able to predict with amazing accuracy the occurrence of child abuse and neglect (i.e., the indices accounted for 81 percent of the variance in abuse and neglect rates—74 percent for abuse and 84 percent for neglect). Few studies in the social sciences can account for that level of variance! Garbarino et al. (1977) demonstrated a strategy whereby multiple regression is used to generate a predicted abuse rate which is then compared with an actual abuse rate for a given neighborhood. Where there are large discrepancies between predicted and actual abuse rates, further research might help in our understanding of potential determinants of abuse, and interventions might be implemented on the basis of follow-up information. For example, they surveyed two neighborhoods with the same predicted abuse rate but vastly different actual rates. The survey data indicated a pattern of extensive negative feelings in the high actual abuse rate area reflecting an unsupportive neighborhood environment. A more direct experimental test of the importance of resources is provided by Gray, Cutler, Dean, and Kempe (1977, cited in Garbarino, 1977). One hundred "abuse-prone" families were identified through a questionnaire and direct observation. Fifty families were randomly assigned to supplementary services (an active visiting nurse who attempted to establish an enduring relationship with the family), and 50 families were randomly assigned to a control group receiving the typical community services. After two years, the control families had a significantly higher abuse rate, and no known abuse occurred in the experimental group. These studies provide strong support for the hypothesis that isolation from potent resources is a necessary condition for child abuse. Even if resources are available, however, families need the knowledge and skills to make use of those resources. This suggests the need to consider person *and* setting variables.

Social-Situational Model*

Abusing Parent	Child Victim	Family Interaction	Family (Partner)	Community (and Social Context)

A recent trend in the child abuse area is to move away from an after-the-fact disease/treatment model to a more preventive learning model (Helfer, 1976a; Helfer & Kempe, 1976; Helfer, McKinney, & Kempe, 1976). Justice and Justice (1976) and Parke and Collmer (1975) suggest that a social-situational approach may help considerably in our understanding of child abuse and in the development of effective prevention and intervention strategies. The

---

*While both the Social-situational and the Integrative models each focus attention on several of the components of our Comprehensive model, in no existing instances does a Social-situational or Integrative approach focus on all components.

social situation in which the child is reared may affect the extent to which he/she is abusive as an adult. Interactional patterns between child and parent or between husband and wife may determine the conditions under which abusive patterns develop, are elicited (or triggered), and/or are maintained. Research from this perspective examines particularly the effects of punitive child rearing, inconsistent discipline, and punishment. Many studies, reported earlier, suggest a relationship between abusive behaviors of parents and the fact that they themselves were abused as children. Within the context of this model this relationship can be explained in terms of the aggression modeling literature and social learning theory (Bandura, 1973, 1977). The data demonstrate the effects of exposure to aggressive models on subsequent aggressive action (Feshbach, 1980).

Gelles and Straus (1979) described a variety of more specific theoretical versions within this model, including frustration-aggression theory, social learning theory, self-attitude theory, symbolic interactionism, exchange theory, and attribution theory. A common thread throughout all these views is a concern with multiple determinants of aggressive actions—intrapersonal variables (including cognitive and attitudinal, as well as emotional and trait), situational variables, interpersonal interactions, and most importantly, person-setting interactions. Gelles (1982; Gelles & Straus, 1979) has presented this model as central to his attempts at theoretical integration of the literature.

There are, as with other models, a number of methodological issues in the research. Until recently, the application of this model to the area of child abuse has been through inference based upon the general literature on aggression and parenting. There is little evidence from control group designs to support the frequent statements that abusive parents are inadequate in parenting skills (Jayaratne, 1977). A common sense definition would lead us to believe that abusive parents by definition have inadequate parenting skills and suggests that the problem may be with the methodology rather than the statement. Demonstrating that a treatment strategy derived from a social situational model is effective in changing the behavior of abusive parents does not mean that the conditions that the treatment was designed to ameliorate are *necessary* determinants of the abusive behavior. Certainly, one of the advantageous hallmarks of this approach is the emphasis upon direct assessment of problem behaviors through observation in relevant settings and the incorporation of appropriate experimental designs for evaluating treatment efficacy with single cases. It should be noted that single subject methodology can be used with any intervention strategy, not just those derived from a social situational model. At the same time, even while this methodology is one hallmark of the model, until recently quality designs have not been typical when studying child abuse interventions. Typically, interventions are multilevel, and investigators have failed to conduct component analyses of complex intervention packages. One further problem is the emphasis upon low frequency behaviors (abusive actions). Burgess (1979) and Conger (1982) have made a major contribution to this concern by identifying and measuring high frequency correlates (e.g., positive and negative parent-child interactions) of abusive behavior.

Burgess and Conger (1978) directly observed daily interactions of abusive, neglectful, and control families to determine whether those groups could be differentiated on the basis of their interactional patterns. The abusive and neglectful parents demonstrated lower rates of interaction overall, lower rates of positive interaction, and higher rates of negative interactions. The abusive mothers were the most different from the controls. Similarly, Egeland and Brunnquell (1977, cited in Burgess, 1979) found that abusive mothers displayed fewer appropriate care-giving behaviors and less positive affect during observations than nonabusing mothers. Redlich, Giblin, Starr, and Agronow (1980) observed mother-child dyads in a control group design. On more molecular response categories (e.g., manipulation of self and objects, specific body movements and postures, muscle tone/coordination, verbalizations, and facial expressions), they did not find significant group differences. In post hoc analyses, when dividing groups on the basis of mother's use of restriction and punishment (based upon Caldwell's home observation schedule), some differences in motoric behaviors and affect were obtained. Within the context of attachment or bonding literature, other studies have demonstrated the importance of early parent-child interactions within the first days of life, particularly with premature and ill newborns. In their prospective studies, Hunter and Kilstrom (1979; Hunter et al., 1978) found that less family-infant contact during early hospitalization was more likely to lead to abuse. In their study comparing families who broke the intergenerational cycle of abuse with repeaters, they found that nonrepeating families visited their newborn soon after birth and much more often than abuse repeating families. Daly and Wilson (1980) cite a dramatic unpublished experimental study by O'Connor et al. in Nashville in which low income primiparous mothers were randomly assigned to a hospital routine condition or an experimental condition allowing an additional six hours of mother-infant contact on each of the first two postpartum days. In a two-year follow up, 9 of 143 hospital routine children were victims of abuse, neglect, abandonment, or nonorganic failure to thrive in comparison to none of 134 experimental children. This represents a highly significant reduction in risk based upon twelve extra hours of contact in the first two days of life. In a related finding, Lynch (1975) found that 40 percent of a sample of severely abused children had been separated from their mothers during the first 48 hours after birth as opposed to 6 percent of their nonabused siblings.

The importance of modeling is critical to a social-situational model. As indicated earlier, studies suggesting an intergenerational cycle of abuse can be interpreted through modeling principles. Gelles' (1980a, b) national survey found that parents who reported having been abused as children were much more likely to abuse their own children than previously nonabused parents. There was also a relationship between duration of abuse as a child and abusing rate as an adult. Conger et al. (1979) found similar results with a matched control group design. Consistent with the modeling literature, observing violence (as opposed to being the target of violence) was also a highly significant variable in the national survey (Gelles, 1980a, b). That is, people who reported observing their own parents hitting one another had a much higher rate of violence toward their own children than people who reported having never seen their parents hit each other. Further, households with marital violence had higher rates of violence to children than households without marital violence. Similarly, in a control group study (Giovannoni & Billingsley, 1970), abusing mothers were found to have more marital difficulties than nonabusing mothers. When one combines the above results with our knowledge of the amount of violence portrayed on TV (Gerbner, 1980), it is apparent that the potential impact of modeling is tremendous.

As suggested by Gelles and Straus (1979), cognitive attributions and expectancies are pertinent variables within a social-situational model. Feshbach (1980) has suggested that attributions of intent, of personal responsibility, and of justice are important antecedents to abusive actions. The assumption that abusing parents have inappropriate expectations concerning their children's behavior and that that is one determinant of abusive behavior is so prevalent (Kempe & Helfer, 1972) that many intervention programs include instruction on normative development of children as one component in a total package (e.g., Otto & Smith, 1980; Wolfe, Sandler, & Kaufman, 1981). Friedrich and Boriskin (1976) suggest that parents' perception of their child as different, even if the child is in fact not atypical, can be an important determinant of abuse. Consistent with this model's consideration of the role of the child in abuse, two recent control group studies have examined abused children's perceptions and attributions of their families (Halperin, 1981; Herzberger, Potts, & Dillon, 1981). Both studies reported that abused children (and their nonabused siblings in the Halperin study) had much more negative perceptions of their family members. At the same time, children from abusive families were much more ambivalent about their parents in that they had both positive and negative perceptions of them. Herzberger et al. (1981) suggested that studying children's perceptions more thoroughly might aid our understanding of abuse. In particular, the variation in consequences of abuse might be due in part to children's interpretations of abusive incidents as indices of parental rejection, as caused by a parent's externally imposed frustration, as a legitimate means of resolving conflicts, or as an illegitimate means. (Maffei's preliminary dissertation results suggest that victim perception is an important variable in the sequalae of sexual abuse.) Little research within this model has directly evaluated the importance of child or parental attributions and expectancies.

As indicated earlier, within an interactional model, the child plays a role in abuse as well. Theoretical presentation and reviews of literature (e.g., Belsky, 1978; Friedrich & Boriskin, 1976, 1978; Garbarino, 1977; Gil, 1970; Green et al., 1974; Rose & Hardman, 1981; Sameroff & Chandler, 1975) all suggest that disabled and handicapped children, difficult (e.g., colicky or hyperactive) children, children of the "wrong" gender and low birth weight, and premature children are more likely to be victims of abuse. In their prospective research, Hunter and Kilstrom (1979; Hunter et al., 1978) found that abusers had the most seriously impaired newborns, and nonrepeaters (i.e., those families who broke the intergenerational cycle of abuse) had relatively healthier infants who were larger at birth, had fewer defects of residual medical problems, were one month closer to term, and behaved more like normal newborns. Infant risk was not a significant discriminator among abuse, neglect, and control groups in Gaines et al.'s (1978) study.

Treatment derived from the social situational model of child abuse makes use of behavioral principles and techniques for changing inappropriate interactions within the family. One set of techniques involves the modification of parental disciplinary behavior which avoids the use of physically punitive tactics. Case studies have employed various strategies for reteaching parents to use nonassaultive control methods (e.g., Crozier & Katz, 1979; DeBortali-Tregerthan, 1979; Hughes, 1974; Jeffery, 1976; Patterson, 1974; Polakow & Peabody, 1975; Sandler & Seyden, 1976; Sandler, Van Dercar, & Milhoan, 1978; Savino & Sanders, 1973). Parents are given programmed texts on child management, then taught with modeling or role playing ways of increasing prosocial behavior through reinforcement or of decreasing deviant behavior through alternatives to punishment. While these reports emphasize positive outcomes, they do not employ sufficient controls nor do they determine the efficacy of specific components within the multilevel packages. Sandler et al. (1978) and Crozier and Katz (1979) demonstrated long-term maintenance of the behavior changes. Denicola and Sandler (1980) employed a single subject design and examined the effects of parent training and self-control techniques. Using direct observation in the home, they found a reduction in total parental aversive behavior and an increase in prosocial behaviors (e.g., attention and approval). The abused children also showed an increase in prosocial and less aversive behavior. All effects were maintained at follow-up. Wolfe et al. (1981) employed a control group design (with a waiting list control) and an intervention program consisting of parent training in child development and in child management techniques, problem solving skills, and impulse control. A home visitor (a psychology graduate student) helped parents apply procedures they learned in a group training format. The total program was effective through a ten-week follow-up based upon home observations, caseworker report, and parental self-report. Child management skills increased, and fewer child problems were reported. Conger, Lahey, and Smith (1981) also used a control group design and a comprehensive home intervention including instruction in child management, stress management techniques, relaxation, couple relationships, and a supportive relationship with the family. Again, using direct observation, they found less negative and more positive interactions, decreased maternal depression, and effective child compliance to parental requests.

Since the social-situational model emphasizes that many sources of frustration present in the environment may serve as potential elicitors of anger, a second set of intervention approaches is anger control techniques in the face of potentially anger eliciting stimuli. These techniques include the reinforcement of incompatible nonangry responses, modeling and role playing of nonangry reactions, relaxation, systematic desensitization in the presence of anger-evoking stimuli, and cognitive behavioral strategies including stress-inoculation, self-instruction, thought stopping, and self-control (see Bandura, 1969, 1973, for a thorough description and explanation of these methods). The techniques have been shown to be effective with other aggressive populations, such as children (Gittelman, 1965) and antisocial adult males (Novaco, 1975; Rimm & Masters, 1979). The three controlled studies cited above included one or more of these strategies along with training in parenting skills. Solomon (1977) used Structured Learning (SL)—a comprehensive behavioral approach involving modeling, role playing, social reinforcement, and transfer training (Goldstein, 1973, 1981; Goldstein, Sprafkin, & Gershaw, 1976)—to train abusive parents in self-control skills. Relative to various control groups, she found it to be effective on a number of outcome and generalization measures, including directly observed use of the skill at home with their abused chidren. The effectiveness of SL was enhanced by a self-esteem increasing mastery condition which involved a task manipulation designed to lead the parents to attribute improved performance on the task to their own efforts.

Since research indicates that abusive parents are isolated from other people in their community (e.g., Alexander, 1972; Beezley, Martin, & Alexander, 1976; Helfer, 1976a; Justice & Justice, 1976; Kempe & Helfer, 1972; Kempe & Kempe, 1976; Ounsted et al., 1975; Roth, 1975; Schneider et al., 1972; Whiting, 1977), Parke and Collmer (1975) proposed a third general approach within this model. This strategy involves the use of modeling to increase parental social skills in the interest of decreasing the impact of isolation and increasing support systems. Some investigators (e.g., Beezley et al., 1976; Justice & Justice, 1976; Ounsted et al., 1975) have suggested that group treatment might be more effective with child abusing parents because of the social contact within the group. Numerous intervention programs have been conducted within group formats, including the control group studies by Wolfe et al. (1980) and Solomon (1977).

Parke and Collmer (1975) suggested a fourth set of techniques derived from the social situational model. These approaches attempt to modify the child's behavior. These techniques are derived from the work of Patterson and his associates (Patterson & Cobb, 1971, 1973; Patterson & Reid, 1970), who taught parents nonpunitive ways for dealing with their children's behavior. The interaction patterns described as the coercion process—in which the child's aversive behavior serves to elicit parental punitive behavior in such a way that the aversive interchange continues and escalates in intensity—is the focus of attention. Specific methods employed to alter children's behavior and preclude subsequent incidents of physical abuse include extinction, reinforcement of incompatible responses, time-out, verbal reasoning, communication skills, and negotiating skills (Bandura, 1969, 1973; Jeffery, 1976).

While the suggested approaches for working with child abusers from the social situational perspective seem potentially beneficial, there has been little systematic research with these techniques. The control group studies cited earlier (Conger et al., 1981; Denicola & Sandler, 1980; Wolfe et al., 1981) all showed improvements in children's behavior and in interactional patterns, as well as in parental behavior. As indicated earlier, few controlled studies have been conducted to test theoretical assumptions about child abuse within this model. Until recently, few controlled studies have been conducted with intervention techniques derived from this model. No component analyses have been conducted to determine active ingredients of multilevel treatment packages. No studies have attempted to address the prescriptive question of which approach works with which client/problem under what set of conditions with which kind of therapist (Goldstein, 1978; Goldstein & Stein, 1976).

Integrative Models

| Abusing Parent | Child Victim | Family Interaction | Family (Partner) | Community (and Social Context) |

The integrative models are based on the idea that child abuse is a multidetermined phenomenon, with primary factors suggested by other models being possible but not necessary causal factors in the occurrence of child abuse. Gelles (1973; Gelles & Straus, 1979), Justice and Justice (1976), and Young (1976) propose system theory approaches wherein they suggest, with variations, that all parts of the system mutually interact. They assume that personality traits, cumulative environmental stresses, cultural norms, and family interactional processes all contribute to child abuse. While less formal, other writers have proposed the explicit consideration of the above multiple levels—i.e., child and parent characteristics, environmental stresses, cultural norms and context, and family interactional patterns (Belsky, 1978; Friedrich & Boriskin, 1976; Lystad, 1975; Parke, 1978; Zigler, 1980). Others have suggested somewhat more limited integrative models, incorporating parent characteristics, child characteristics, and immediate environmental stresses (such as marital and family relationships) as interacting causal factors (e.g., Berger, 1980a,b; Green et al., 1974; Kempe & Helfer, 1972; Rathbone-McCaun & Pierce, 1978; Walters & Walters, 1980).

Others (e.g., Conger, 1982; Garbarino, 1977; Gelles, 1982; Gelles & Straus, 1979) have attempted to provide integrative theories within the context of particular conceptual orientations. While reviewing fifteen theoretical positions and attempting an initial integration within a general systems theory orientation, Gelles and Straus (1979) indicate the basic dependence of all positions on the process of social learning (from the social-situational model) and on the role played by stressful structural arrangements in the family setting and broader social context. Conger (1982) examines child abuse from a behavioral perspective and explicitly mentions the following factors: social acceptance of physical punishment and issues of family isolation (both of which serve to reduce restraints on abuse), parent and child characteristics (in terms of skills, beliefs, and cognitive expectancies), family interactional patterns, community resources and skills for effective use of those resources. Gelles (1982) combines exchange theory and social control theory. A basic assumption of exchange theory is that human interaction is guided by the pursuit of rewards and the avoidance of punishment and costs. He proposes that people are more likely to be violent in the home when the expected cost of violence is less than the rewards. The absence of effective social controls, as occurs in certain social and family structures, decreases costs of violent behavior. Garbarino (1977) presents an ecological perspective, suggesting that child abuse is a problem of mismatch between parent and child and between family and neighborhood. A parent may develop inadequately into a caregiver role creating stress between parent and child. There is considerable cultural support for the use of physical force against children, and another potential contributing factor is inadequate, or inadequate use of, family support systems. Hunter and Kilstrom's (1979; Hunter et al., 1978) prospective studies of families of premature and ill newborns certainly implicates all the variables indicated above by the many variations of integrative approaches.

Interventions derived from integrative models are interdisciplinary in nature, as suggested by model proponents and others (e.g., Beezley et al., 1976; Blumberg, 1979; Holter & Friedman, 1968; Johnson & Morse, 1968; Justice & Justice, 1978; Savino & Sanders, 1973;

Wasserman, 1967; Whiting, 1977). Most of the intervention strategies derived from the other models are proposed by these authors. In addition, such treatment modalities as family therapy, residential care for milieu experiences, and hotline and crisis interventions are suggested. Most of the writing about interventions within this model involves descriptions of what kinds of treatment and intervention packages ought to be implemented with abusive families. Little research, including case studies, has been conducted. Component analyses have not been made. While marshaling all available community resources in the attack on the problem of child abuse is important, the integrative models, as with the other models, provide little direction for the development of specific prescriptive intervention strategies.

Summary

There are limits to the applicability of any given theoretical position or model to the problem of child abuse. Certainly, given our current state of knowledge, there are limits to the degree of support for any particular model. As Gelles and Straus (1979) indicate, it is perhaps fruitless to attempt to determine which theory or model is most accurate as an explanation of child abuse. Rather, within the total process of the child abuse phenomenon, we might better try to address what aspect each theoretical model explains best. Similarly, the question of which treatment derived from the models is most effective is equally wasteful of investigator energy. As Goldstein (1978; Goldstein & Stein, 1976) has argued forcefully in other contexts, we need to address a prescriptive question. That is, what kind of intervention works with what level of the problem (individual, family, community, national) with what kind of client (abusing parent, abused child) with what kind of change agent?

As stated previously, it is apparent that child abuse is a multidimensional problem. Comprehensive preventive and interventive strategies must take in to account the following: parent characteristics, child characteristics, parent-child interactional patterns, setting variables including the immediate family context as well as the broader social context, and change agent characteristics.

MULTIPLE LEVELS OF CHILD ABUSE AND INTERVENTION

Understanding child abuse requires a rigorous examination of families at multiple levels. Such a comprehensive model must include the abusing parent, the child victim, parent-child interactional patterns, and the setting in which abuse takes place considering both the immediate family context and the community and broader social context.

Child Abuse = | Abusing Parent | + | Child Victim | + | Parent-child Interactions | + | Family (Partner) | + | Community (and Social Context) |

Intervention within such a comprehensive model must address each of those levels. In addition, characteristics of change agents must be considered, and intensive coordination of services must be maintained (Berkley Planning Associates, 1977).

This comprehensive model can be illustrated through a brief description of ALLIANCE, a child abuse coordinating agency in Syracuse, New York, directed by the second author. ALLIANCE has developed out of Erne's extensive experience with several thousand child abuse cases and her training of practitioners throughout the United States and Canada. In working with potential and indentified child abuse cases, Erne coordinates the services of Child Protection, hospitals, prenatal clinics, public health nurses, law enforcement, mental health professionals, schools, and personnel from Syracuse University. Each case referred to ALLIANCE has an individualized treatment team selected from the public and private services available within the county. The individual family member's needs as well as the total family's needs are taken into account in the selection of this team. Teams meet on the average of once a month; and, in 1981, there were 700 families served by the program. Parents attend almost all team meetings and are considered an integral part of the treatment planning process. A major component of the coordinated services is ALLIANCE's Parent Aide Program. Careful screening done with prenatal clinics and hospitals allows identification of pregnant mothers who might have difficulty forming attachments (or bonding) with their new infants. Such at-risk individuals along with identified abusive parents are offered services of parent aides who work in the homes providing nurturance, support, and effective modeling. In addition, parent aides along with other ALLIANCE team members provide concrete, skill-based parent training congruent with the characteristics of abusive parents.

Parent training is based upon Goldstein's (1973, 1981; Goldstein et al., 1976) Structured Learning (SL) approach and addresses all the above levels of child abuse. The SL approach incorporates modeling, role playing and behavior rehearsal, specific reinforcement strategies, and transfer training to enhance the actual use of acquired skills in daily living. Skill deficits in the areas of self-control, parenting (especially nonpunitive discipline techniques), marital relations, and peer relations are addressed in the parent training. In this way, intervention has an impact upon the abusing parent and indirectly upon the child, parent-child interactions, family interactions, and upon interactions of the parent and family with the broader community (particularly the area of more effective use of available and enhanced community resources). Involvement of parent aides in treatment and in the homes enhances the likelihood of transfer of daily living skills.

This parent skill training is conducted within the context of parent groups, helping abusive parents become aware of the universal nature of the problem ("I'm not alone in this!"). The skill focus of the intervention also serves to diffuse attention away from the abusive parent as an individual who is "sick" or "terrible," thus increasing the likelihood of participation in treatment. At the same time, ALLIANCE does coordinate more traditional therapeutic modalities for those individuals needing such services, including the small percentage of families with character disorders. While research (e.g., Heiko, 1981; Solomon, 1977) and program evaluation has shown ALLIANCE's comprehensive model to be effective, more research on this and related programs addressing multiple levels of abuse is needed. General treatment implications pertinent to these levels will be discussed now.

Parent Characteristics

Case studies and conceptual and empirical literature within all models suggest numerous parental characteristics that might be considered within interventive and preventive programs (see tables 1.1 and 1.2). Considerable research is needed to delineate these variables further. Greater specificity in definition, higher quality measurement, and replication with control group designs are needed. As these characteristics are more fully delineated and found to be relevant to the phenomenon of child abuse, a major question to be addressed is which characteristics are amenable to change by which strategies.

While traditional verbal therapies have been effective in some child abuse cases (Fontana, 1971; Steele, 1975), long-term effectiveness has not been demonstrated. As valuable as insight might be for long-term change, insight by itself is not sufficient for changed interactions without acquisition of new skills. Further, characteristics of abusive parents, life-style, time,

Table 1.2. Suggested Abusive Parent Characteristics (See also Table 1.1)

Skills

Parenting skills—Garbarino, 1977; Johnson & Morse, 1968; Smith et al., 1973; Zigler, 1980.

Use of punishment—Johnson & Morse, 1968; Melnick & Hurley, 1969(c); Pollock & Steele, 1972; Smith & Hanson, 1975.

Inappropriate expectations, poor knowledge of child development—Alexander, 1972; Garbarino, 1977; Gelles, 1982; Helfer, 1973; Isaacs, 1981; Johnson & Morse, 1968; Kempe & Helfer, 1972; Richmond & Janis, 1980; Spinetta, 1978(c); Spinetta & Rigler, 1972; Zigler, 1980.

Coping skills—Albee, 1980.

Attributions about intent, responsibility, justice—Feshbach, 1980; Friedrich & Boriskin, 1976.

Self-control—Milner & Wimberley, 1979(c).

Child-rearing attitudes—Neufeld, 1979(c).

Inability to distinguish feelings of parent and child—Holter & Freidman, 1968; Johnson & Morse, 1968; Paulson et al., 1975(c); Spinetta, 1978(c).

Demographic

History of abuse—Conger et al., 1979(c); Fontana, 1968; Gelles, 1980a; Hunter & Kilstrom, 1979(c); Hunter et al., 1978(c); Justice & Justice, 1976; Kempe & Helfer, 1972; Kempe et al., 1962; Lukianowicz, 1971; Lystad, 1975; Melnick & Hurley, 1969(c); Oliver & Taylor, 1971; Ounsted et al., 1975; Pollock & Steele, 1972; Sameroff & Chandler, 1975; Schneider et al., 1976(c); Silver et al., 1969; Smith & Hanson, 1975; Spinetta & Rigler, 1972; Steele, 1976a; Steele & Pollock, 1968; Straus et al., 1980.

Early parenthood—Aber, 1980; Bolton et al., 1980(c,ns); Gelles, 1980a; Hyman, 1978; Kinard & Klerman, 1980(c,ns); Richmond & Janis, 1980; Smith et al., 1975(c).

Large family, close spacing—Hunter et al., 1978(c); Hyman, 1978; Maden & Wrench, 1977; Straus, 1979a.

Skin color—Gelles, 1980a(ns); Seaberg, 1977; Straus, 1979a(ns).

Low intelligence—Sameroff & Chandler, 1975; Smith et al., 1975(c).

Gender (female)—Gelles, 1980a,b; Gil, 1970; (male) Maden & Wrench, 1977; Seaberg, 1977; Straus, 1979a.

Single parent—Maden & Wrench, 1977; Zigler, 1980.

Lower education—Gelles, 1980a (inverted-U); Hunter et al., 1978(c).

Lower socioeconomic status—Gelles, 1980a,b; Giovannoni & Billingsley, 1970(c); Pelton, 1978; Smith et al., 1975(c); Straus, 1979a.

Note: c = control group design
ns = nonsignificant results, through controlled study or national survey

and monetary issues (given the frequent lower socioeconomic status) often render verbal therapies impractical (Cicchetti et al., 1978; Parke & Collmer, 1975).

Skill deficits (parenting, discipline, coping, and self-control) appear to be amenable to treatments derived from the social-situational model. Modeling, role playing and behavior rehearsal, specific reinforcement strategies, and transfer enhancement techniques (Goldstein & Kanfer, 1979) have all been shown to be effective with other problems, and as components within intervention programs for abusive parents. Anger control techniques (e.g., Goldstein & Rosenbaum, 1982) have been shown to be effective with other groups and to a limited extent with abusive parents. Skill acquisition and anger control techniques introduce some interesting questions. One could argue that the abusive behavior is due to skill deficits and therefore suggest skill enhancement training. At the same time, it might be argued that the abusive parent has the skills, but those skills are not manifested because of the individual's inability to inhibit and control anger. Therefore, anger control strategies might be recommended. It might also be that the parent has both skill deficits and minimal self-control in which case both sets of strategies might be employed, possibly in a sequential manner with anger control being acquired first. These and other questions need to be addressed through more assessment of the scope of the parent's problem and through research designs that allow determination of the relative efficacy of these strategies under specified problems and conditions.

Abusive parents' felt isolation might be aided through the development of communication skills (with people both in and out of the family). Conducting treatment within a group context might deal with the isolation as well. Such treatment (regardless of content) can communicate the "universal" nature of abuse ("I'm not the only one like this"). The group context can provide opportunities for practicing communication skills and for developing new acquaintances. The acquisition of communication skills should help abusive parents use available community resources more effectively. Cognitive behavioral strategies might address parental attributions that result in or justify abusive behavior.

Gelles (1982) has suggested that change agents not accept parents' rationalization that attribute their violent actions to drugs, alcohol, or the inability to control themselves. An important treatment implication of this suggestion is that the abuser must cognitively accept personal responsibility for his/her violent and abusive behavior, thus canceling their "hitting license." Teaching basic knowledge of child development appears important, given the frequently reported inappropriate expectations of abusive parents. Bavolek (1981) has described a conceptual framework from which parenting education programs can develop instructional strategies designed specifically for abusive parents. Based upon a review of the literature on parenting attitudes and practices of abusive parents, Bavolek specifically addresses the issues of inappropriate parental expectations, alternatives to punishment, parental awareness of children's needs, and role reversal.

Psychologists typically view interventions focused specifically upon the individual as necessary for change at the individual parent level. However, treatments addressing the broader social context might have specific interventive or preventive effects upon individual parents as well. Increasing the availability of medical and social services would impact upon the isolation of abusive parents. Addressing unemployment, job discrimination, housing, inequitable education, and family planning issues would do much to reduce the stresses with which abusive parents from lower socioeconomic backgrounds must cope. In other words, coping, parenting, and self-control skills may be intact, but the multiple stresses imposed by our current social system may so overwhelm the individual that those skills cannot be effectively used. The frequently obtained higher abuse rates among women than men is often attributed to the inequitable responsibility for care of children. Gelles (1980a,b) found that homes with shared child care responsibilities had lower abuse rates than those with responsibility designated for one parent. Parenting instruction for adolescents and prenatal identification programs would serve a preventive role in the acquisition of skills and family planning knowledge. Indeed, interventions addressing the broader social context will be useful as preventive measures.

Child Characteristics

As indicated earlier, a variety of child conditions (including the parent's perception of a child as different) appear to play a role in child abuse. Difficult to manage or disabled children may create additional stress for an already at-risk parent. One treatment strategy might be to teach children directly more appropriate behaviors, as in the case of hyperactive and socially dysfunctional children. At the same time, the child might be less important as an antecedent to abuse if parents were taught more appropriate child management skills. In addition, the child level of the abuse problem might be addressed by teaching parents more appropriate age-related expectancies concerning their children. Parents need to learn that their parenting role changes with age changes in their children. Provision of better services for disabled and handicapped children might also address this level of the abuse problem. Such services must include the families to a considerably greater extent. While PL 94-142 mandates the inclusion of parents in assessment and decision making for their handicapped children in the schools, too often such involvement is at a token level. Soeffing (1975) has outlined a set of strategies recommended by a task force of the Council for Exceptional Children that schools might use in addressing the needs of handicapped and abused children. Comprehensive health and support services for families with low birth-weight, premature, or ill infants is necessary at this level (Ayoub & Pfeifer, 1977; Hunter & Kilstrom, 1979; Hunter et al., 1978; Pfeifer & Ayoub, 1976).

In addition to consideration of the child as an antecedent to abuse, we need to consider treatment strategies for the child once abuse has occurred. Most of the attention in the abuse treatment literature has focused upon the parents. The victim of the abusive acts must also be helped, not only because of the possible deleterious sequalae of abuse but also as a preventive strategy to break the intergenerational cycle of abuse. Aber (1980) has called for more systematic research in this area. He suggests we need to examine the harmful effects upon the child of various post-disclosure events, including parental behaviors, family integrity, and the impact of court decisions and service strategies. Hunter and Kilstrom's (1979) study of parents of premature and ill infants who did and did not repeat the previous generation's abusive behavior is pertinent here. Nonrepeating parents had more resources available to them at the time of their being victims and later as parents. Abused children often are either highly aggressive or socially withdrawn (Martin, 1976). As such, social skills training and anger control techniques are important strategies for victims of abuse. In addition, given the data on abused children's attributions (Halperin, 1981; Herzberger et al., 1981), cognitive approaches might prove beneficial as well. These children accept personal responsibility for the parental punishment and often report the punishment as justified. These children need to distinguish between the acceptance of responsibility for one's own actions and the inappropriateness of excessive physical punishment.

Parent-Child Interactional Patterns

Burgess and Conger's (1978; Burgess, 1979; Conger, 1982) finding of a strong relationship between parent-child interactional patterns and abusive behavior was a major breakthrough. At the same time, measures of these patterns used in recent studies typically focus upon discrete categories of interactional participants' responses. More complex time sequential analyses of interactions are not used (see Sackett, 1978a,b). Such analyses would examine the bidirectional influences in such interactions (i.e., effects of child upon parent, parent upon child, and family members in general upon each other). Such reciprocity of influence is emphasized in the child development literature in general (see, e.g., Bell, 1968, 1974, 1977) as well as in the child abuse literature.

Because of behavioral interrelationships, treatment focusing upon either participant (parent or child) will have some indirect influence upon the interactional patterns. More direct approaches upon the participants and their interactional patterns should be more effective. Control group studies (Conger et al., 1981; Denicola & Sandler, 1980; Wolfe et al., 1981) with treatment packages derived from a social situational model have been shown to be effective in changing interactional patterns. These strategies have focused upon coercive interactional patterns, communication skills, and negotiation skills. Unfortunately, these studies (and other less controlled ones) have not made component analyses to determine effective treatment ingredients. Certainly, encouragement of immediate parental interaction with infants at birth is needed in order to enhance maternal, paternal, and child bonding or attachment and thus reduce the likelihood of abuse. The attributions of interactional participants need to be addressed, and cognitive behavioral strategies might be beneficial in dealing with inappropriate and irrational attributions. Gelles (1982) has suggested the importance of inequitable power within families as a possible determinant of abuse. The teaching of negotiation skills and joint decision-making congruent with the child's developmental level might be helpful. Finally, family therapy via systems theory approaches (Justice & Justice, 1976) can address parent-child interactional patterns as well. Grodner (1977) describes a highly individualized treatment approach focusing upon parent-child interactions. Parents engage in interactions with their children and observe effective teacher/trainer-child interactions. Thus, parents receive direct training, modeling, feedback, and considerable support.

Setting—Immediate Family and Broader Social Contexts

In a discussion of the influence of settings upon behavior, Bronfenbrenner (1977) distinguished among the following levels of settings: the setting in which the individual is currently interacting (e.g., the home or family), those settings in which the individual does interact though not at the particular point in time (e.g., child's school, playground, grocery store, etc.), those settings in which other social participants within the immediate home setting interact (e.g., the father's work place when the mother is the abuser), social institutions with which none of the participants directly interacts (e.g., school board, government offices, community mental health clinic, etc.), and pervasive national and cultural value orientations that are implicitly or explicitly carried out by social institutions and/or transmitted by media. Garbarino (1977) has articulated well the importance of these levels of settings on the abuse problem in his ecological theory.

At the level of the family, abusive families have been found to be characterized as having marital conflicts, unsatisfactory marriages, and general family violence including verbal abuse (Alexander, 1972; Helfer, 1973; Hunter et al., 1978; Hyman, 1978; Jensen et al., 1977; Lukianowicz, 1971; Milner & Wimberley, 1979, 1980; Ounsted et al., 1975; Straus, 1979a). Children living with one natural parent and one step-parent are more likely to become victims of abuse (Daly & Wilson, 1980; Hunter et al., 1978). Families where there is inequitable sharing of child care and of decision making also have higher abuse rates (Gelles, 1980a,b, 1982). As indicated earlier, greater amounts of family stress and life changes are also related to child abuse.

As one moves beyond the immediate family setting, the previously cited isolation of abusive families is manifested not only within the immediate family context but also in the form of isolation from extended family, neighbors, and the broader community. Abusive families participate less in community organizations. Availability of economic, health, and social resources is also related to abuse. At broader institutional and national levels, influences include the general acceptance of the use of physical punishment (N. Feshbach, 1980; S. Feshbach, 1980; Garbarino, 1977; Gelles, 1980a,b, 1982; Steinmetz & Straus, 1974; Zigler, 1980), TV and magazine coverage (Gerbner, 1980; Signorielli, 1980), institutional abuse of children and handicapped people (Blatt, 1980; N. Feshbach, 1980), national policies accepting the use of corporal punishment of children in our schools (N. Feshbach, 1980) or, in other countries, prohibiting the use of corporal punishment of children (Kahn & Kamerman, 1980), and an attitude of exploitation of the weak by the powerful (Albee, 1980).

Intervention at these broader levels of influence is difficult but no less necessary. At the level of the family, skill enhancement techniques again are useful. Specifically, marital and communication skills should help with conflict and with intra- and extrafamily isolation. Skills for coping with stress generally, and particularly with those stresses associated with lower socioeconomic status, are necessary treatment components. Negotiation skills and shared decision making will be important within many abusive families, as will the teaching of alternatives to verbal abuse and punishment (or the teaching of positive nonaversive styles of interaction).

Previously mentioned interventions derived from the sociological model are particularly appropriate at broader social context levels. Kahn and Kamerman's (1980) cross-cultural comparison of child abuse showed that those countries that explicitly prohibit the use of corporal punishment and/or that define child abuse more broadly as part of general health services for children tend to move toward more general improvement of all services for all children. The availability of child planning services, child care, and health and social services must be greatly increased. The acquisition of social and communication skills should increase the likelihood of parents' effective use of more available resources.

Parent training must emphasize the deleterious effects of the use of punishment and must teach discipline strategies that do not rely upon physical punishment. Parent training must be more readily available to more people and to individuals prior to their decision to conceive children. Such training can be done in a manner that takes into account differing values of various people. Media executives and personnel must become more aware of the impact of the media upon child abuse in particular and violence in general. Their lack of awareness of issues in the area of child abuse and of the impact of media upon those issues is demonstrated in a set of articles in the book by Gerbner et al. (1980; Keller, 1982). National policies prohibiting the use of corporal punishment of children and handicapped people in schools and residential institutions must be clearly and publicly stated.

Change Agent Characteristics

Little specificity is provided in the literature concerning characteristics of change agents that promote effective treatment of abusing parents. Such knowledge would be helpful in providing more effective helper-helpee matches. This issue of prescriptive matching is critical to the general area of helping relationships (Goldstein, 1978; Goldstein & Stein, 1976), as well as specifically to helping abusive parents (Cicchetti et al., 1978). When working with abusive parents, therapists are dealing with less motivated clients, in fact clients who are often resistant to help. Helpers must learn to cope with the frustrations of working with such resistant individuals. The helper and helping agency must assume a more active role in the change process than is typical for many traditional verbal therapies. For example, providing transportation and physically bringing clients to sessions or providing treatment in the home (the setting of concern) is often necessary for bringing about cooperation in the change process (Fontana, 1971). The therapist needs to be more available when working with abusive parents (Alexander, 1972). Fifty-minute sessions once or twice per week may not be sufficient for a given client. Because of the multiple levels of the abuse problem, more than one change agent is needed. Therefore, change agents must be knowledgeable of other disciplines and able and willing to communicate with professionals from other disciplines (Beezley et al., 1976). Clearly, such multidisciplinary treatment requires considerable coordination so that necessary services are provided without undue duplication of services (Berkeley Planning Associates, 1977).

Lay therapists in the form of parent aides are beneficial to the change process with abusive parents (Berkeley Planning Associates, 1977). It could be argued that parent aides are necessary for maintenance and transfer of treatment effects into the daily living settings of abusive parents. As with professional therapists, little empirical research has been conducted to determine selection criteria for those characteristics related to successful helping. Beezley et al. (1976) suggest that parent aides should have parenting experience, considerable life experience, generally good feeling about their own parenting, and demonstrate effective coping with their own problems. Kempe and Helfer (1972) suggest that parent aides be matched with clients according to socioeconomic status, race, and educational level. In addition, they suggest the importance of flexibility, nurturance, patience and compassion, willingness to listen and be noncritical, and empathy. At the same time, parent aide modeling needs to be concrete and direct.

Summary

It should be apparent that all levels of abuse may be attacked by strategies focusing on any one or more of the levels (i.e., parent, child, parent-child interactions, family, and broader social context). Further, strategies delivered at any one level might impact upon multiple levels. Much more sophistication is needed in the delineation of treatment programs and their evaluation through quality research. Such research or treatment evaluation requires greater clarity in the description of treatment strategies, treater characteristics, focus of treatment, and characteristics of target(s) of treatment. Variables within each of the above aspects need to be investigated systematically. Because of our still limited knowledge, multiple measures of treatment efficacy at all levels of potential impact are needed. Such multidimensional measurement might determine unanticipated beneficial and/or deleterious consequences of different treatment strategies. Similar delineation and evaluation is needed in the area of prevention of child abuse.

PREVENTION

Most strategies discussed to this point have focused upon some level of intervention after some form of abuse has occurred. Within a continuum of services, such intervention is referred to as tertiary prevention. That is, intervention is focused upon some part of the problem already manifest and may result in prevention of future occurrences of the problem. It must be noted, though, that little treatment research has addressed the long-term maintenance of treatment effects. Primary prevention, at the other end of the continuum, relates to intervention before child abuse occurs. With the exception of interventions derived from the sociological models, few interventive strategies appear to address directly the primary preventive needs in the area of child abuse.

Prevention of child abuse requires a major national commitment to the problem. Ross' (1980) historical review of child abuse has clearly demonstrated the need for such a long-standing commitment to prevention. Ross and Zigler (1980) have called for a greater valuing of children, in the form of a national commitment to the well-being of all children. Related to such a national child orientation are the needs to eliminate social norms that legitimize (and even glorify) violence in society and in the family (Gelles, 1982), to eliminate the use of corporal punishment in our social institutions (Blatt, 1980; N. Feshbach, 1980; Ross & Zigler, 1980), and to reconceptualize abuse as part of a continuum of behaviors that reflect the possible ways parents relate to their children (Zigler, 1980). Zigler contends that our current conceptualizations of abuse that appear to emphasize the deviance or difference of abusing parents interfere with the establishment of preventive programs. By placing abuse on a parenting continuum, similarities among parents are emphasized, and people are more likely to help those with similar features.

As the primary transmittors of our national and cultural value orientations, the media need to help create a more sophisticated awareness of child abuse and family life in general. Ross and Zigler (1980) argue that television in particular should provide more complex portrayals of family life, present specials aimed at parents and children which show greater appreciation of children and their needs, portray reduced violence and alternatives to the use of physical punishment. Kahn and Kamerman (1980), Carlsson (1981), and Davies (1975) describe other countries where child abuse is defined more broadly as part of general health services for children. Those countries appear to have a greater likelihood of reporting abuse, and seem to show a general improvement of all services for all children in need of help.

At a less philosophical level, those assuming a sociological model as well as others have proposed numerous primary prevention strategies. These include improved and more accessible family planning services (Zigler, 1980), homemaker services (Zigler, 1980), child care services (Zigler, 1980), comprehensive medical health services generally and specifically that result in reduced premature births (Zigler, 1980), enhanced opportunities for early parent-child bonding or attachment (Helfer, 1976b; Ross & Zigler, 1980), baseline standards of living through reduced unemployment and housing improvements (Hobbs, 1980; Ross & Zigler, 1980), increased capacity of criminal justice and social service systems (Gelles, 1982; Ross & Zigler, 1980; Solnit, 1980), private companies structured to accommodate family life (Ross & Zigler, 1980), and extensive parenting education (e.g., Helfer, 1976b; Richmond & Janis, 1980; Ross & Zigler, 1980; Zigler, 1980). Solnit (1980) has argued that not only must the capacity of social services be increased, but also services that parents can voluntarily participate in must be made available. He argues that such voluntary services must be made attractive and accessible. Voluntary community services would serve more readily the primary prevention needs and avoid the ethical issues involved in involuntary programs for already abusing parents or for parents at-risk for child abuse. Parenting education programs range from highly structured programs for abusive parents (such as Wolfe et al.'s, 1981 program) to less structured self-help groups for abusive or at-risk parents, such as Parents Anonymous (Berkeley Planning Associates, 1977). Valentine-Dunham and Gipson (1980) describe a preparenting program for high school students in which they are taught anger control strategies, alternative responses to stress, and appropriate responses to children's behaviors.

Formal socializing institutions such as schools must become involved in child abuse prevention as well. McCaffrey and Tewey (1978), through a task force of the Council for Exceptional Children, have described a set of guidelines and suggestions for the provision of a continuum of interrelated school services coordinated with community resources. The regular classroom teacher (Gifford & Morgavi, 1981; Griggs & Gale, 1977) and the special educator (Rose & Hardman, 1981) who works with handicapped and disabled children, frequent targets of abuse, can be "front-line" workers relating to families, thus needing to be informed about child abuse and its prevention. School support personnel such as school psychologists (Kline, Cole, & Fox, 1981) can also provide preventive services.

One aspect of prevention that has received a fair amount of empirical work is that area concerned with early identification and screening for parents at-risk for child abuse. Helfer (1976a) and Kempe (1976) have advocated comprehensive and massive early screening of child-rearing patterns. They propose administering surveys to high school students and to pregnant women and observing mothers with their babies in the delivery room and both parents at initial feedings. Solnit (1980) and Brody and Gaiss (1976) have discussed the ethical and legal issues on both sides of the screening issue. On the positive side of a mandatory screening program is the child's right to be free from physical harm, plus the likelihood that those parents most in need might not volunteer if the program were not mandatory. On the other hand, a mandatory program would infringe upon parental rights, increase the probability of false-positive predictions, result in unmotivated parents in parenting programs, and increase the likelihood that law enforcement agencies might subpoena screening test results. Clearly, the rights of all parties must be balanced, the potential emotional effects of labeling must be minimized, and participants must be informed that screening for a problem does *not* definitely diagnose it. This last point is particularly pertinent to available screening instruments for child abuse.

The Michigan Screening Profile of Parenting (Schneider, Helfer, & Pollock, 1972; Schneider, Hoffmeister, & Helfer, 1976; Schneider, Pollock, & Helfer, 1972), the Child Abuse Potential Inventory (Milner & Ayoub, 1980), and the Family Psychosocial Risk Inventory (Hunter et al., 1978) have shown some degree of success within the context of research programs, but considerable refinement and cross-validation is needed before they could be used clinically. Paulson et al. (1974, 1975, 1976) have used MMPI profile analysis to identify parents at-risk for child abuse. However, there has been considerable cross-study inconsistency in MMPI abuse indices, and Furlong and Leton (1977) found questionable validity of Paulson's MMPI scales in a cross-validation study. False-positive rates are not satisfactorily low with such measures. A number of investigators have proposed the use of direct observation of early parent-infant interactions, and particularly of attachment or bonding (Ainsworth, 1980; Floyd, 1981; Gray, et al., 1976; Hurd, 1975; Olson, 1976). However, these observational systems have not been validated, and observer reliability would need to be demonstrated and maintained for their routine use in hospital settings. Burgess and Conger's (1978; Burgess, 1979; Conger, 1982) observational system of parent-child interactions in the home with older children does have excellent data and possibly could be used for purposes of identification of at-risk parents with additional data.

Discriminant analyses of national survey data (Gelles, 1980a,b; Straus, 1979a) suggest a number of characteristics that are associated with child abuse and that might serve as indices of parents-at-risk. While the characteristics are congruent with those on the previously cited screening instruments (e.g., social isolation, verbal aggression toward child, husband to wife verbal and physical aggression, history of parents having been abused as children, dissatisfaction with standard of living, inequitable sharing of home and childrearing responsibilities, etc.), Gelles and Straus caution against use of their profiles for screening purposes.

Ayoub and Pfeifer (1977; Pfeifer & Ayoub, 1976) described a comprehensive interdisciplinary, hospital-based screening and voluntary prevention program. While they do not use controlled evaluative data, reported success rates are outstanding. It seems critical that helping agencies devise means of providing attractive and accessible voluntary services for parents in general, and particularly those who might be at-risk for abuse.

It should be apparent that prevention, as with direct intervention with abusing parents, requires programs that address multiple levels of the abuse problem. Multiple disciplines must be involved in service delivery. Interdisciplinary services often involve communication difficulties, and there is the potential for undue duplication of services as well as for people wanting and/or in need of services "falling between the cracks." Considerable coordination of preventive and interventive services must be explicitly planned and implemented within communities (Berkeley, 1977). Research and evaluation are necessary, though typically ignored and poorly financed, functions of coordinating agencies if we are to improve our preventive and interventive services to abusing parents.

RESEARCH AND EVALUATION NEEDS

Critical comments concerning child abuse research have been made throughout this chapter. This section will summarize research and evaluation needs in general. Ross and Zigler (1980) have recommended strongly that state and federal agencies concerned with child abuse should earmark 1-5 percent of child services monies for research. Such a minimal expenditure is necessary if we are to understand fully this complex phenomenon and if we are to develop effective interventive and preventive strategies.

In order to conduct meaningful research, definitional issues (Ross & Zigler, 1980) will have to be dealt with. Investigators need to be more explicit in the definition of abuse from which they are operating. Ideally agreed upon definitions of child abuse would make easier cross-study comparisons. While a number of writers (Burgess, 1979; Conger, 1982; Garbarino, 1977; Gelles, 1982; Gelles & Straus, 1979) have made recent and significant theoretical contributions, more needs to be done to explicate the unique aspects of intrafamily (parent to child) abuse as well as to integrate the area of child abuse with larger bodies of knowledge, such as research on aggression (S. Feshbach, 1980) and developmental psychology (Ainsworth, 1980). As Gelles and Straus (1979) have commented, the issue is not so much to determine which theoretical position is most accurate but, rather, to determine what aspect(s) of the abuse problem a given theory best explains.

Studies on the etiology and on sequalae of abuse need to make use of longitudinal designs and prospective (rather than retrospective) approaches. Our focus needs to reflect the complexity of the phenomenon, as well as the general trend in psychological literature. We can no longer limit the focus of study to just the abusing parent. Rather, we must place research on child abuse within the context of person-setting interactions. At the broadest levels of setting considerations, ecologically based research will add an important dimension to our knowledge. The work of Garbarino and his associates (1977; Garbarino et al., 1977; Garbarino & Stockings, 1980) is most helpful and explicit in terms of how to conduct abuse research from an ecological perspective. The use of control groups in child abuse research has been increasing (Plotkin, Azar, Twentyman, & Perri, 1982) and is imperative for our further understanding of etiology and sequalae. Inclusion of control groups is particularly important in studies of the sequalae of abuse. Given the importance of family dysfunction in general in child abuse, control groups of nonabused children and of children of dysfunctional though non-child-abusive families are critical. At present, it is not clear whether observed cognitive or emotional effects are due to the abuse, due to family disruptions independent of abuse, or represent typical developmental variations.

With respect to interventive or preventive research much more sophistication is needed in the delineation of treatment programs and their evaluation. Evaluation of treatment efficacy requires greater clarity in the description of treatment strategies, treater characteristics, focus of treatment, and characteristics of the target(s) of treatment. Variables within each of the above aspects (i.e., treatment strategy, level of focus, target of intervention, change agent) need to be investigated systematically. Again, complex designs that combine these variables in group designs are needed. It is not just a question of which treatment approach is most effective with abusive parents. Rather, our interventive and preventive research needs to address the prescriptive question (Goldstein, 1978; Goldstein & Stein, 1976) of which strategy works with what level of the abuse problem with what kind of client with what kind of change agent under what conditions.

It certainly is the case that many researchers and clinicians do not have access to sufficient numbers of abusive and nonabusive parents to conduct group research. In addition, for various reasons, it may not be practical in given situations to use group designs. There is a rapidly growing technology for conducting single-case research and its analysis (Hersen & Barlow, 1976; Kratochwill, 1978). The techniques are such that they can be used by the practicing clinician as well as the researcher. While they have been developed within a behavioral perspective, the strategies can be used within the context of any change orientation. The rapidly growing literature on program evaluation (e.g., Price & Polister, 1980) is a useful source. Justice and Justice (1976, 1978) have demonstrated the utility of Goal Attainment Scaling for measuring change in abuse research. Both group and single case treatment research must gather long-term follow-up data on maintenance and transfer of intervention effectiveness. As part of the concern with transfer of effects, it is important that multiple measures be used so that we might determine potential unanticipated treatment effects at other levels of the abuse problem. Examining any phenomenon within a systems or ecological perspective suggests that making a change at one level of an interacting system will have effects at other levels within in the system.

Both etiological and treatment studies require the use of multiple measures. Such a research tactic will enable us to understand more fully this complex multidimensional problem of abuse as well as help us identify multiple effects of interventive and preventive strategies. Cone's (1978) behavioral assessment grid serves as an effective guide for the range of measures to employ. Most pertinent to our concern here is his method dimension that presents methods of measurement arranged along a continuum of directness. That is, possible measures are arranged according to the extent to which the methods measure actual behaviors of concern and measure them at the time and place of their natural occurrence. These methods range from the most indirect measures such as interviews and self-report and ratings by others to direct observation by self and others in laboratory or clinic settings to direct observation in the settings of concern (home). The child abuse literature has been dominated by almost the exclusive use of indirect measures. The concern with use of direct measures is most crucial in treatment outcome research (Friedman, Sandler, Hernandez & Wolfe, 1981). Straus' (1979b) Conflict Tactics Scales appear to be an excellent indirect measure of intrafamily aggressive behavior. Those scales can be used in a time based format and become self-observation scales. Garbarino's (1977) nonintrusive ecological measures offer exciting possibilities for research on broader contextual issues. At the most direct end of the continuum, naturalistic observation procedures (e.g., Sackett, 1978a,b) must be used in more abuse research. Certainly, one problem is the cost in terms of time, though observational approaches can be implemented in a variety of cost-effective ways (e.g., Keller, 1980). While abusive acts are relatively low frequency and probably reactive to observational measurement, Burgess and Conger's (1978) finding of strong correlations among parent-child interactional patterns and abuse makes the use of direct observation more practical and fruitful. However, observational research that has been conducted has been primarily categorical in nature. We need to make use of observational procedures that allow sequential analyses of interactions. Finally, with the use of multiple measures, we must make greater use of multivariate statistical procedures for analyzing our data.

REFERENCES

Aber, J. L. The involuntary child placement decision: Solomon's dilemma revisted. In G. Gerbner, C. J. Ross, & E. Zigler (Eds.), *Child abuse: An agenda for action*. New York: Oxford University Press, 1980.

Ainsworth, M. D. S. Attachment and child abuse. In G. Gerbner, C. J. Ross, & E. Zigler (Eds.), *Child abuse: An agenda for action*. New York: Oxford University Press, 1980.

Albee, G. W. Primary prevention and social problems. In G. Gerbner, C. J. Ross, & E. Zigler (Eds.), *Child abuse: An agenda for action*. New York: Oxford University Press, 1980.

Alexander, H. The social worker and the family. In C. H Kempe & R. E. Helfer (Eds.), *Helping the battered child and his family*. Philadelphia: Lippincott, 1972.

Alfaro, J. D. Summary report on the relationship between child abuse and neglect and later socially deviant behavior. New York State Assembly Select Committee on Child Abuse, March 1978.

Almond, P. O. What we were up against: Media views of parents and children. In G. Gerbner, C. J. Ross, & E. Zigler (Eds.), *Child abuse: An agenda for action.* New York: Oxford University Press, 1980.

American Humane Association. *The national study of child neglect and abuse reporting.* Denver, CO: American Humane Association, 1981.

Antler, S. Child abuse: An emerging social priority. *Social Work,* 1978, *23,* 58-61.

Ayoub, C., & Pfeifer, D. R. An approach to primary prevention. The "At-Risk" program. *Children Today,* 1977, *6,* 14-17.

Baer, A. M., & Wathey, R. B. Covert forms of child abuse: A preliminary study. *Child Psychiatry and Human Development,* 1977, *8,* 115-128.

Bahar, E., Hyman, C., Jones, C., Jones, R., Kerr, A., & Mitchell, R. *At risk: An account of the work of the battered child research department.* NSPCC. London: Routledge & Kegan Paul, 1976.

Bakan, D. *Slaughter of the innocents: A study of the battered child phenomenon.* Boston: Beacon, 1971.

Bandura, A. *Principles of behavior modification.* New York: Holt, Rinehart & Winston, 1969.

Bandura, A. *Aggression: A social learning analysis.* New York: Prentice-Hall, 1973.

Bandura, A. *Social learning theory.* Englewood Cliffs, NJ: Prentice-Hall, 1977.

Barahal, R. M., Waterman, J., & Martin, H. P. The social cognitive development of abused children. *Journal of Consulting and Clinical Psychology,* 1981, *49,* 508-516.

Bavolek, S. J. Educational setting for the primary prevention of child abuse and neglect with school age children. In R. B. Rutherford, A. G. Prieto, & J. E. McGlothlin (Eds.), *Monograph in behavior disorders,* 1981.

Beer, S. A medical social worker's view. In A. W. Franklin (Ed.), *Concerning child abuse.* New York: Churchill & Livingstone, 1975.

Beezley, P., Martin, H., Alexander, H. Comprehensive family oriented therapy. In R. E. Helfer & C. H. Kempe (Eds.), *Child abuse and neglect: The family and the community.* Cambridge, Mass.: Ballinger, 1976.

Bell, R. Q. A reinterpretation of the direction of effects in studies of socialization. *Psychological Review,* 1968, *75,* 81-95.

Bell, R. Q. Contributions of human infants to caregiving and social interaction. In M. Lewis & L. A. Rosenblum (Eds.), *The effect of the infant on its caregiver.* New York: John Wiley, 1974.

Bell, R. Q. Socialization reexamined. In R. G. Bell & L. V. Harper (Eds.), *Child effects on adults.* Hillsdale, NJ: Lawrence Erlbaum, 1977.

Belsky, J. A theoretical analysis of child abuse remediation strategies. *Journal of Clinical Child Psychology,* 1978, *7,* 117-121.

Bem, D. J. *Beliefs, attitudes and human affairs.* Belmont, CA: Brooks/Cole, 1970.

Bennie, E. H., & Sclare, A. B. The battered child syndrome. *American Journal of Psychiatry,* 1969, *125,* 975-979.

Berger, A. M. The child abusing family: I. Methodological issues and parent-related characteristics of abusing families. *American Journal of Family Therapy,* 1980, *8,* (3), 53-66. (a)

Berger, A. M. The child abusing family: II. Child and child-rearing variables, environmental factors and typologies of abusing families. *American Journal of Family Therapy,* 1980, *8* (4), 52-68. (b)

Berkeley Planning Associates. Evaluation of child abuse and neglect demonstration projects 1974-1977. Vol. IV: A comparative description of the eleven projects; final report. U.S. Department of Commerce, National Technical Information Service (#PB-278 441), December 1977.

Billingsley, A., & Giovannoni, J. *Children of the storm.* New York: Harcourt, 1972.

Blatt, B. The pariah industry: A diary from purgatory and other places. In G. Gerbner, C. J. Ross, & E. Zigler (Eds.), *Child abuse: An agenda for action.* New York: Oxford University Press, 1980.

Blumberg, M. L. Collateral therapy for the abused child and the problem parent. *American Journal of Psychotherapy,* 1979, *33,* 339-353.

Boisvert, M. S. The battered child syndrome. *Social Casework,* 1972, *53,* 475-480.

Bolton, F. G., Langer, R. H., & Kane, S. P. Child maltreatment risk among adolescent mothers: A study of reported cases. *American Journal of Orthopsychiatry,* 1980, *50,* 489-504.

Brody, H., & Gaiss, B. Ethical issues in screening for unusual child-rearing practices. *Pediatrics Annuals,* 1976, *15,* 106-112.

Bronfenbrenner, U. Toward an experimental ecology of human development. *American Psychologist,* 1977, *32,* 513-531.

Bryant, H. D., Billingsley, A., Kerry, G. A., Leefman, W. V., Merrill, E. J., Senecal, G. R., & Walsh, B. G. Physical abuse of children: An agency study. *Child Welfare,* 1963, *42,* 125-130.

Burgess, R. L. Child abuse: A social interactional analysis. In B. B. Lahey & A. E. Kazdin (Eds.), *Advances in clinical child psychology* (Vol. 2). New York: Plenum, 1979.

Burgess, R. L. & Conger, R. D. Family interaction in abusive, neglectful, and normal families. *Child Development,* 1978, *49,* 1163-1173.

Carlsson, B. The children's ombudsman: A spokesman for children. Unpublished paper, Sweden (ERIC # ED205296), December 1981.

Carroll, J., Schaffer, C., Spensley, J., & Abramowitz, S. I. Family experiences of self-mutilating patients. *American Journal of Psychiatry,* 1980, *137,* 852-853.

Chase, N. F. *A child is being beaten: Violence against children, an American tragedy.* New York: Holt, Rinehart & Winston, 1975.

Cicchetti, D., Taraldson, B., & Egeland, B. Perspectives in the treatment and understanding of child abuse. In A. P. Goldstein (Ed.), *Prescriptions of child mental health and education.* New York: Pergamon Press, 1978.

Cohen, S. J., & Sussman, A. The incidence of child abuse in the United States. *Child Welfare,* 1975, *54,* 432-443.

Cone, J. D. The behavioral assessment grid (BAG): A conceptual framework and a taxonomy. *Behavior Therapy,* 1978, *9,* 882-888.

Conger, R. D. Behavioral intervention for child abuse. *The Behavior Therapist,* 1982, *5,* 49-53.

Conger, R. D., Burgess, R. L., & Barrett, C. Child abuse related to life change and perceptions of illness: Some preliminary findings. *Family Coordinator,* 1979, *28,* 73-78.

Conger, R. D., Lahey, B. B., & Smith, S. S. An intervention program for child abuse: Modifying maternal depression and behavior. Paper presented at Family Violence Research Conference, University of New Hampshire, Durham, 1981.

Costa, J. J., & Nelson, G. K. *Child abuse and neglect: Legislation, reporting, and prevention.* Lexington, MA: Lexington Books, 1978.

Crozier, J., & Katz, R. C. Social learning treatment of child abuse. *Journal of Behavior Therapy and Experimental Psychiatry,* 1979, *10,* 213-220.

Daly, M., & Wilson, M. Discriminative parental solicitude: A biological perspective. *Journal of Marriage and the Family,* 1980, *42,* 277-288.

Davies, J. M. The battered child syndrome—Detection and prevention. *Nursing Mirror,* 1975, *140,* 56-57.

DeBortali-Tregerthan, G. J. A behavioral treatment of child abuse: A case report. *Child Behavior Therapy,* 1979, *1,* 287-293.

Decourcy, P., & Decourcy, J. *A silent tragedy.* New York: Alfred, 1973.

Delsordo, J. D. Protective casework for abused children. *Children,* 1963, *10,* 213-218.

Denicola, J., & Sandler, J. Training abusive parents in child management and self-control skills. *Behavior Therapy,* 1980, *11,* 263-270.

Elmer, E., & Gregg, G. S. Developmental characteristics of abused children. *Journal of Pediatrics,* 1967, *40,* 596-602.

Feshbach, N. D. Corporal punishment in the schools: Some paradoxes, some facts, some possible directions. In G. Gerbner, C. J. Ross, & E. Zigler (Eds.), *Child abuse: An agenda for action.* New York: Oxford University Press, 1980.

Feshbach, S. Child abuse and the dynamics of human aggression and violence. In G. Gerbner, C. J. Ross, & E. Zigler (Eds.), *Child abuse: An agenda for action.* New York: Oxford University Press, 1980.

Fleming, G. M. Cruelty to children. *British Medical Journal,* 1967, *2,* 421-422.

Floyd, L. A model for assisting high-risk families in neonatal nurturing. *Child Welfare,* 1981, *60,* 637-643.

Fontana, V. *The maltreated child.* Springfield, Ill.: C. C. Thomas, 1971.

Fontana, V. J. Further reflections on maltreatment of children. *New York Journal of Medicine,* 1968, *68,* 2214-2215.

Franklin, A. W. (Ed.), *Concerning child abuse.* New York: Churchill Livingstone, 1975.

Friedman, R. M., Sandler, J., Hernandez, M., & Wolfe, D. A. Child abuse. In E. J. Mash & L. G. Terdal (Eds.), *Behavioral assessment of childhood disorders.* New York: Guilford, 1981.

Friedrich, W. M., & Boriskin, J. A. The role of the child in abuse: A review of the literature. *American Journal of Orthopsychiatry,* 1976, *46,* 580-590.

Friedrich, W. M., & Boriskin, J. A. Primary prevention of child abuse: Focus on the special child. *Hospital & Community Psychiatry,* 1978, *29,* 248-251.

Furlong, M. J., & Leton, D. A. The validity of MMPI scales to identify potential child abusers. *Journal of Clinical Psychology,* 1977, *6,* 55-57.

Gaines, R., Sandgrund, A., Green, A. H., & Power, E. Etiological factors in child maltreatment: A multivariate study of abusing, neglecting, and normal mothers. *Journal of Abnormal Psychology,* 1978, *87,* 531-540.

Garbarino, J. The human ecology of child maltreatment: A conceptual model for research. *Journal of Marriage and the Family,* 1977, *39,* 721-735.

Garbarino, J., Crouter, A. C., & Sherman, D. Screening neighborhoods for intervention: A research model for child protective services. *Journal of Social Service Research,* 1977, *1,* 135-145.

Garbarino, J., & Stocking, S. H. *Protecting children from abuse and neglect.* San Francisco: Jossey-Bass, 1980.

Gelles, R. J. Child abuse as psychopathology: A sociological critique and reformation. *American Journal of Orthopsychiatry,* 1973, *43,* 611-621.

Gelles, R. J. The social construction of child abuse. *American Journal of Orthopsychiatry,* 1975, *45,* 363-371.

Gelles, R. J. A profile of violence toward children in the United States. In G. Gerbner, C. J. Ross, & E. Zigler (Eds.), *Child abuse: An agenda for action.* New York: Oxford University Press, 1980.(a)

Gelles, R. J. Violence in the family: A review of research in the seventies. *Journal of Marriage and the Family,* 1980, *42,* 873-885. (b)

Gelles, R. J. An exchange/social control approach to understanding intrafamily violence. *The Behavior Therapist,* 1982, *5,* 5-8.

Gelles, R. J., & Straus, M. A. Determinants of violence in the family: Toward a theoretical integration. In W. R. Burr, R. Hill, F. I. Nye, & I. L. Reiss (Eds.), *Contemporary theories about the family.* New York: Free Press, 1979.

Gerbner, G. Children and power on television: The other side of the picture. In G. Gerbner, C. J. Ross, & E. Zigler (Eds.), *Child abuse: An agenda for action.* New York: Oxford University Press, 1980.

Gerbner, G., Ross, C. J., & Zigler, E. (Eds.) *Child abuse: An agenda for action.* New York: Oxford University Press, 1980.

Gifford, C. S., & Morgavi, G. F. Child abuse and neglect: The role of education. *Kappa Delta Pi Record,* 1981, *17,* 73-75.

Gil, D. G. *Violence against children: Physical child abuse in the United States.* Cambridge, Mass.: Harvard University, 1970.

Giovannoni, J. M., & Billingsley, A. Child neglect among the poor: A study of parental adequacy in families of three ethnic groups. *Child Welfare,* 1970, *49,* 196-204.

Gittelman, M. Behavior rehearsal as a technique of child treatment. *Journal of Child Psychology and Psychiatry,* 1965, *6,* 251-255.

Goldstein, A. P. *Structured learning therapy: Toward a psychotherapy for the poor.* New York: Academic Press, 1973.

Goldstein, A. P. (Ed.) *Prescriptions for child mental health and education.* New York: Pergamon Press, 1978.

Goldstein, A. P. *Psychological skill training: The Structured Learning technique.* New York: Pergamon Press, 1981.

Goldstein, A. P., & Kanfer, F. (Eds.) *Maximizing treatment gains.* New York: Academic Press, 1979.

Goldstein, A. P., & Rosenbaum, A. *Aggress-less.* Englewood Cliffs, NJ: Prentice-Hall, 1982.

Goldstein, A. P., Sprafkin, R. P., & Gershaw, N. J. *Skill training for community living: Applying structured learning therapy.* New York: Pergamon Press, 1976.

Goldstein, A. P., & Stein, N. *Prescriptive psychotherapies.* New York: Pergamon Press, 1976.

Gray, J., Cutler, C., Dean, J., & Kempe, C. H. Perinatal assessment of mother-baby interaction. In R. E. Helfer & C. J. Kempe (Eds.), *Child abuse and neglect: The family and the community.* Cambridge, Mass.: Ballinger, 1976.

Green, A., Gaines, R., & Sandgrund, A. Child abuse: Pathological syndrome of family interaction. *American Journal of Psychiatry,* 1974, *131,* 882-886.

Green, A. H. Self-destructrive behavior in battered children. *American Journal of Psychiatry,* 1978, *135,* 579-582.

Gregg, G., & Elmer, E. Infant injuries: Accident or abuse? *Pediatrics,* 1969, *44,* 434-439.

Griggs, S. A., & Gale, P. The abused child: Focus for counselors. *Elementary School Guidance & Counseling,* 1977, *11,* 187-194.

Grodner, B. A family systems approach to child abuse: Etiology and intervention. *Journal of Clinical Child Psychology,* 1977, *6,* 32-35.

Halperin, S. L. Abused and non-abused children's perceptions of their mothers, fathers and siblings: Implications for a comprehensive family treatment plan. *Family Relations,* 1981, *30,* 89-96.

Heiko, R. Consultee-centered and problem-solving consultation services to paraprofessionals working with child abusing parents in an SLT program. Unpublished doctoral dissertation, Syracuse University, 1981.

Helfer, R. E. The etiology of child abuse. *Pediatrics,* 1973, *51,* 777-779.

Helfer, R. E. Basic issues concerning prediction. In R. E. Helfer & C. H. Kempe (Eds.), *Child abuse and neglect: The family and the community.* Cambridge, Mass.: Ballinger, 1976.(a)

Helfer, R. E. Early identification and prevention of unusual child-rearing practices. *Pediatric Annals,* 1976, *5,* 91-105.(b)

Helfer, R. E. Introduction: Putting child abuse and neglect into perspective. In B. J. Kalisch, *Child abuse and neglect: An annotated bibliography.* Westport, Conn.: Greenwood, 1978.

Helfer, R. E., & Kempe, C. H. (Eds.), *The battered child.* Chicago: University of Chicago Press, 1974.

Helfer, R. E., & Kempe, C. H. (Eds.), *Child abuse and neglect: The family and the community.* Cambridge, Mass.: Ballinger, 1976.

Helfer, R. E., McKinney, J., & Kempe, R. Arresting or freezing the developmental process. In R. E. Helfer & C. H. Kempe (Eds.), *Child abuse and neglect: The family and the community.* Cambridge, Mass.: Ballinger, 1976.

Hersen, M., & Barlow, D. H. *Single case experimental designs: Strategies for studying behavior change in the individual.* New York: Pergamon Press, 1976.

Herzberger, S. D., Potts, D. A., & Dillon, M. Abusive and nonabusive parental treatment from the child's perspective. *Journal of Consulting and Clinical Psychology,* 1981, *49,* 81-90.

Hobbs, N. Knowledge transfer and the policy process. In G. Gerbner, C. J. Ross, & E. Zigler (Eds.), *Child abuse: An agenda for action.* New York: Oxford University Press, 1980.

Holter, J. C., & Friedman, S. B. Child abuse: Early case findings in the emergency department. *Journal of Pediatrics,* 1968, *42,* 128-132.

Hughes, R. C. A clinic's parent-performance training program for child abusers. *Hospital and Community Psychiatry,* 1974, *25,* 779-782.

Hunter, R. S., & Kilstrom, N. Breaking the cycle in abusive families. *American Journal of Psychiatry,* 1979, *136,* 1320-1322.

Hunter, R. S., Kilstrom, N., Kraybill, E., & Loda, F. Antecedents of child abuse and neglect in premature infants: A prospective study in a newborn intensive care unit. *Pediatrics,* 1978, *61,* 629-635.

Hurd, J. M. Assessing maternal attachment: First step toward the prevention of child abuse. *JOGN Nursing,* 1975, *4,* 25-30.

Hyman, C. Some characteristics of abusing families referred to the NSPCC. *British Journal of Social Work,* 1978, *8,* 171-179.

Isaacs, C. A brief review of the characteristics of abuse-prone parents. *The Behavior Therapist,* 1981, *4,* 5-8.

Jayaratne, S. Child abusers as parents and children: A review. *Social Work,* 1977, *22,* 5-9.

Jeffery M. Practical ways to change parent-child interaction in families of children at risk. In R. E. Helfer &

S. H. Kempe (Eds.), *Child abuse and neglect: The family and the community.* Cambridge, Mass.: Ballinger, 1976.

Jensen, D. E., Prandoni, J. R., Hagenau, H. R., Wisdom, P. A., & Riley, E. A. Child abuse in a court-referred, inner city population. *Journal of Clinical Child Psychology,* 1977, *6,* 59-62.

Johnson, B., & Morse, H. A. Injured children and their parents. *Children,* 1968, *15,* 147-152.

Justice, B., & Duncan, D. F. Life crisis as a precursor to child abuse. *Public Health Reports,* 1976, *91,* 110-115.

Justice, B., & Justice, R. *The abusing family.* New York: Human Sciences, 1976.

Justice, B., & Justice, R. Evaluating outcome of group therapy for abusing parents. *Corrective & Social Psychiatry & Journal of Behavior Technology, Methods & Therapy,* 1978, *24,* 45-49.

Kahn, A. J., & Kamerman, S. B. Child abuse: A comparative perspective. In G..Gerbner, C. J. Ross, & Zigler (Eds.), *Child abuse: An agenda for action.* New York: Oxford University Press, 1980.

Kalmar, R. *Child abuse: Perspectives on diagnosis, treatment and prevention.* Dubuque, Iowa: Kendall/Hunt, 1977.

Keller, H. R. Issues in the use of observational assessment. *School Psychology Review,* 1980, *9,* 21-30.

Keller, H. R. Review of child abuse: An agenda for action. In G. Gerbner, C. J. Ross, & E. Zigler (Eds.), New York: Oxford University Press, 1980. *Aggressive Behavior,* 1982, *8,* 298-301.

Kellum, B. Infanticide in England in the later Middle Ages. *History of Childhood Quarterly,* 1974, *1,* 367-389.

Kempe, C. H. Approaches to preventing child abuse: The health visitors concept. *American Journal of Diseases of Children,* 1976, *130,* 941-947.

Kempe, C. H., & Helfer, R. E. (Eds.), *Helping the battered child and his family.* Philadelphia: Lippincott, 1972.

Kempe, C. H., Silverman, F. N., Steele, B. F., Droegemueller, W., & Silver, H. K. The battered child syndrome. *Journal of the American Medical Association,* 1962, *181,* 17-24.

Kempe, R., & Kempe, C. H. Assessing family pathology. In R. E. Helfer & C. H. Kempe (Eds.), *Child abuse and neglect: The family and the community.* Cambridge, Mass.: Ballinger, 1976.

Kinard, E. M. Emotional development in physically abused children. *American Journal of Orthopsychiatry,* 1980, *50,* 686-696. (a)

Kinard, E. M. Mental health needs of abused children. *Child Welfare,* 1980, *59,* 451-462. (b)

Kinard, E. M., & Klerman, L. V. Teenage parenting and child abuse: Are they related? *American Journal of Orthopsychiatry,* 1980, *50,* 481-488.

Kline, D. F., Cole, P., & Fox, P. Child abuse and neglect: The school psychologist's role. *School Psychology Review,* 1981, *10,* 65-71.

Kratochwill, T. R. *Single subject research: Strategies for evaluating change.* New York: Academic Press, 1978.

Langer, W. Infanticide: A historical survey. *History of Childhood Quarterly,* 1974, *1,* 353-367.

Light, R. Abused and neglected children in America: A study of alternative policies. *Harvard Educational Review,* 1973, *43,* 556-598.

Lukianowicz, N. Battered children. *Psychiatrica Clinica,* 1971, *4,* 257-280.

Lynch, M. A. Ill-health and child abuse. *The Lancet,* 1975, 317-319.

Lystad, M. H. Violence at home: A review of the literature. *American Journal of Orthopsychiatry,* 1975, *45,* 328-345.

MacKeith, R. Speculations on some possible long-term effects. In A. W. Franklin (Ed.), *Concerning child abuse.* New York: Churchill Livingstone, 1975.

Maden, M. F., & Wrench, D. F. Significant findings in child abuse research. *Victimology,* 1977, *2,* 196-224.

Martin, H. P. The child and his development. In C. H. Kempe & R. E. Helfer (Eds.), *Helping the battered child and his family.* Philadelphia: Lippincott, 1972.

Martin, H. P. (Ed.) *The abused child: A multidisciplinary approach to developmental issues and treatment.* Cambridge, MA: Ballinger, 1976.

Martin, H. P., & Beezley, P. Prevention and the consequences of child abuse. *Journal of Operational Psychiatry,* 1974, *6,* 68-77.

Martin, H. P., Beezley, P. Behavioral observations of abused children. *Developmental Medicine and Clinical Neurology*, 1977, 19, 373-387.

McCaffrey, M., & Tewey, S. Preparing educators to participate in the community response to child abuse and neglect. *Exceptional Children*, 1978, 45, 114-122.

McRae, K., Ferguson, C., & Lederman, R. The battered child syndrome. *Canadian Medical Association Journal*, 1973, 108, 859-866.

Melnick, B. & Hurley, J. R. Distinctive personality attributes of child-abusing mothers. *Journal of Consulting and Clinical Psychology*, 1969, 33, 746-749.

Merrill, E. J. Physical abuse of children: An agency study. In *Protecting the battered child*. Denver: Children's Division, The American Humane Association, 1962.

Milner, J. S., & Ayoub, C. Evaluation of "at risk" parents using the Child Abuse Potential Inventory. *Journal of Clinical Psychology*, 1980, 36, 945-948.

Milner, J. S., & Wimberley, R. C. An inventory for the identification of child abusers. *Journal of Clinical Psychology*, 1979, 35, 95-100.

Milner, J. S., & Wimberley, R. C. Prediction and explanation of child abuse. *Journal of Clinical Psychology*, 1980, 36, 875-884.

Morse, C. W., Sahler, O., & Friedman, S. A three-year follow-up study of abused and neglected children. *American Journal of Diseases of Children*, 1970, 120, 439-446.

Neufeld, K. Child-rearing, religion and abusive parents. *Religious Education*, 1979, 74, 234-244.

Newberger, E. H., & Bourne, R. The medicalization and legalization of child abuse. *American Journal of Orthopsychiatry*, 1978, 48, 593-607.

Novaco, R. W. *Anger control*. Lexington, Mass.: Lexington Books, 1975.

Oliver, J. E., & Taylor, A. Five generations of ill-treated children in one family pedigree. *British Journal of Psychiatry*, 1971, 119, 473-480.

Olson, R. J. Index of suspicion: Screening for child abusers. *American Journal of Nursing*, 1976, 76, 108-110.

Otto, M. L., & Smith, D. G. Child abuse: A cognitive behavioral intervention model. *Journal of Marital and Family Therapy*, 1980, 6, 425-429.

Ounsted, C., Oppenheimer, R., & Lindsey, J. The psychopathology and psychotherapy of the families: Aspects of bonding failure. In A. W. Franklin (Ed.), *Concerning child abuse*. New York: Churchill Livingstone, 1975.

Parke, R. D. Child abuse: An overview of alternative models. *Journals of Pediatric Psychology*, 1978, 3, 9-13.

Parke, R. D., & Collmer, C. W. Child abuse: An interdisciplinary analysis. In E. M. Hetherington (Ed.), *Review of child development research*, Vol. V. Chicago: University of Chicago Press, 1975.

Patterson, G. R. Intervention for boys with conduct problems: Multiple settings, treatment, and criteria. *Journal of Consulting and Clinical Psychology*, 1974, 42, 471-481.

Patterson, G. R., & Cobb, J. A. A dyadic analysis of "aggressive" behavior. In J. P. Hill (Ed.), *Minnesota symposia on child psychology*, Vol. 5. Minneapolis: University of Minnesota Press, 1971.

Patterson, G. R., & Cobb, J. A. Stimulus control for classes of noxious behavior. In J. S. Knutson (Ed.), *The control of aggression: Implications from basic research*. Chicago: Aldine, 1973.

Patterson, G. R., & Reid, J. B. Reciprocity and coercion: Two facets of social systems. In C. Newunger & J. Michael (Eds.), *Behavior modification in clinical psychology*. New York: Appleton-Century-Crofts, 1970.

Paulson, M. J., Afifi, A. A., Chaleff, A., Liu, V., & Thomason, M. A discriminant function procedure for identifying abusing parents. *Suicide*, 1975, 5, 104-113.

Paulson, M. J., Afifi, A. A., Chaleff, A., & Thomason, M. L. The MMPI: A descriptive measure of psychopathology in abusive parents. *Journal of Clinical Psychology*, 1974, 30, 387-390.

Paulson, M. J., Schwamer, G. T., & Bendel, R. B. Clinical application the Pd, Ma and (OH) experimental MMPI scales to further understanding of abusive parents. *Journal of Clinical Psychology*, 1976, 32, 558-564.

Pelton, L. H. Child abuse and neglect: The myth of classlessness. *American Journal of Orthopsychiatry*, 1978, 48, 608-617.

Pfeifer, D. R., & Ayoub, C. An approach to the prophylaxis of child abuse and neglect. *Journal of Oklahoma State Medical Association,* 1976, *69,* 162-167.

Plotkin, R. C., Azar, S., Twentyman, C. T., & Perri, M. G. A criticial evaluation of the reserach methodology employed in the investigation of causative factors of child abuse and neglect. *Child Abuse and Neglect,* 1982, *5,* 449-455.

Polakow, R. L., & Peabody, D. B. Behavioral treatment of child abuse. *International Journal of Offender Therapy and Comparative Criminology,* 1975, *19,* 100-103.

Pollock, C. B., & Steele, B. G. A therapeutic approach to the parents. In C. H. Kempe & R. E. Helfer (Eds.), *Helping the battered child and his family.* Philadelphia: Lippincott, 1972.

Price, R. H., & Polister, P. E. (Eds.) *Evaluation and action in the social environment.* New York: Academic Press, 1980.

Rathbone-McCaun, E., & Pierce, R. Intergenerational treatment approach: An alternative model of working with abusive/neglectful and delinquent prone families. *Family Therapy,* 1978, *5,* 121-141.

Redbill, S. A history of child abuse and infanticide. In R. E. Helfer & C. H. Kempe (Eds.), *The battered child.* Chicago: University of Chicago Press, 1968.

Redlich, R., Giblin, P. T., Starr, R. H., & Agronow, S. J. Motor and social behavior in abused and control children: Observations of parent-child interactions. *Journal of Psychology,* 1980, *106,* 193-204.

Richmond, J. B., & Janis, J. Child health policy and child abuse. In G. Gerbner, C. J. Ross, & E. Zigler (Eds.), *Child abuse: An agenda for action.* New York: Oxford University Press, 1980.

Rimm, D. C., & Masters, J. C. *Behavior therapy: Techniques and empirical findings.* New York: Academic Press, 1979.

Rose, E., & Hardman, M. L. The abused mentally retarded child. *Education & Training of the Mentally Retarded,* 1981, *16,* 114-118.

Ross, C. J. The lessons of the past: Defining and controlling child abuse in the United States. In G. Gerbner, C. J. Ross, & E. Zigler (Eds.), *Child abuse: An agenda for action.* New York: Oxford University Press, 1980.

Ross, C. J., & Zigler, E. An agenda for action. In G. Gerbner, C. J. Ross, & E. Zigler (Eds.), *Child abuse: An agenda for action.* New York: Oxford University Press, 1980.

Roth, F. A practice regimen for diagnosis and treatment of child abuse. *Child Welfare,* 1975, *54,* 268-273.

Sackett, G. P. (Ed.) *Observing behavior.* Vol I. *Theory and applications in mental retardation.* Baltimore: University Park Press, 1978. (a)

Sackett, G. P. (Ed.) *Observing behavior.* Vol II. *Data collection and analysis methods.* Baltimore: University Park Press, 1978. (b)

Sameroff, A. J., & Chandler, M. J. Reproductive risk and the continuum of caretaking casualty. In F. D. Horowitz (Ed.), *Review of child development research,* Vol. IV. Chicago: University of Chicago Press, 1975.

Sandler, J., Van Dercar, C., & Milhoan, M. Training child abusers in the use of positive reinforcement practices. *Behavior Research and Therapy,* 1978, *16,* 169-175.

Sandler, O., & Seyden, T. Groups for parents: A guide for teaching child management to parents. *Journal of Community Psychology,* 1976, *4,* 3-63.

Savino, A. B., & Sanders, R. W. Working with abusive parents: Group therapy and home visits. *American Journal of Nursing,* 1973, *73,* 482-484.

Schneider, C., Helfer, R. E., & Pollock, C. The predictive questionnaire: A preliminary report. In C. H. Kempe & R. E. Helfer (Eds.), *Helping the battered child and his family.* Philadelphia: Lippincott, 1972.

Schneider, C., Hoffmeister, J. K., & Helfer, R. E. A predictive screening questionnaire for potential problems in mother-child interaction. In R. E. Helfer & C. H. Kempe (Eds.), *Child abuse and neglect: The family and the community.* Cambridge, Mass.: Ballinger, 1976.

Schneider, C., Pollock, C., & Helfer, R. E. Interviewing the parents. In C. H. Kempe & R. E. Helfer (Eds.), *Helping the battered child and his family.* Philadelphia: Lippincott, 1972.

Seaberg, J. R. Predictors of injury severity in physical child abuse. *Journal of Social Service Research,* 1977, *1,* 63-76.

Shorkey, C. T. Sense of personal worth, self-esteem, and anomia of child abusing mothers and controls. *Journal of Clinical Psychology*, 1980, *36*, 817-820.

Signorielli, N. Covering abuse: Content and policy—magazine coverage. In G. Gerbner, C. J. Ross, & E. Zigler (Eds.), *Child abuse: An agenda for action*. New York: Oxford University Press, 1980.

Silver, L. B., Dublin, C., & Lourie, R. Does violence breed violence? Contributions from a study of the child abuse syndrome. *American Journal of Psychiatry*, 1969, *126*, 404-407.

Smith, S. M., & Hanson, R. 134 battered children: A medical and psychological study. *British Medical Journal*, 1974, *3*, 666-670.

Smith, S. M., & Hanson, R. Interpersonal relationships and child-rearing practices in 214 parents of battered children. *British Journal of Psychiatry*, 1975, *127*, 513-525.

Smith, S. W., Hanson, R., & Noble, S. Parents of battered babies: A controlled study. *British Medical Journal*, 1973, *4*, 388-391.

Smith, S. M., Hanson, R., & Noble, S. Parents of battered children: A controlled study. In A. W. Franklin (Ed.), *Concerning child abuse*. New York: Churchill Livingstone, 1975.

Smith, S. M., Honigsberger, L., & Smith, C. A. EEG and personality factors in child batterers. In A. W. Franklin (Ed.), *Concerning child abuse*. New York: Churchill Livingstone, 1975.

Soeffing, M. Abused children are exceptional children. *Exceptional Children*, 1975, *42*, 126-133.

Solnit, A. J. Too much reporting, too little service: Roots and prevention of child abuse. In G. Gerbner, C. J. Ross, & E. Zigler (Eds.), *Child abuse: An agenda for action*. New York: Oxford University Press, 1980.

Solomon, E. J. Structured learning therapy with abusive parents: Training in self-control. Unpublished doctoral dissertation, Syracuse University, 1977.

Spinetta, J. J. Parental personality factors in child abuse. *Journal of Consulting and Clinical Psychology*, 1978, *46*, 1409-1414.

Spinetta, J. J., & Rigler, D. The child-abusing parent: A psychological review. *Psychological Bulletin*, 1972, *77*, 296-304.

Steele, B. F. Working with abusive parents from a psychiatric point of view. *Children Today*, 1975, *4*, 3-5.

Steele, B. F. Experience with an inter-disciplinary concept. In R. E. Helfer & C. H. Kempe (Eds.), *Child abuse and neglect: The family and the community*. Cambridge, Mass.: Ballinger, 1976. (a)

Steele, B. F. Violence within the family. In R. E. Helfer & C. H. Kempe (Eds.), *Child abuse and neglect: The family and the community*. Cambridge, Mass.: Ballinger, 1976. (b)

Steele, B. F., & Pollock, C. B. A psychiatric study of parents who abuse infants and small children. In R. E. Helfer & C. H. Kempe (Eds.), *The battered child*. Chicago: University of Chicago Press, 1968.

Steinmetz, S., & Straus, M. *Violence in the family*. New York: Dodd Mead, 1974.

Straus, M. A. Family patterns and child abuse in a nationally representative American sample. *Child Abuse and Neglect*, 1979, *3*, 213-225. (a)

Straus, M. A. Measuring intrafamily conflict and violence: The Conflict Tactics (CT) scales. *Journal of Marriage and the Family*, 1979, *41*, 75-88. (b)

Straus, M. A., Gelles, R. J., & Steinmetz, S. K. *Behind closed doors: Violence in American family*. Garden City, NY: Doubleday, 1980.

Thurber, S. Child abuse and the excessive control of aggression. *Psychological Reports*, 1979, *44*, 994.

Till, K. A neurosurgeon's viewpoint. In A. W. Franklin (Ed.), *Concerning child abuse*. New York: Churchill Livingstone, 1975.

Valentine-Dunham, K., & Gipson, M. T. A brief, preventative approach to child abuse. Paper presented at meetings of Western Psychological Association, Honolulu, May 1980.

Volpe, R., Breton, M., & Mitton, J. *The maltreatment of the school-aged child*. Lexington, MA: Lexington Books, 1980.

Walters, D. R. *Physical and sexual abuse of chidren: Causes and treatment*. Bloomington, IN: Indiana University Press, 1975.

Walters, J., & Walters, L. H. Parent-child relationships: A review, 1970-1979. *Journal of Marriage and the Family*, 1980, *42*, 807-822.

Wasserman, S. The abused parent of the abused child. *Children*, 1967, *14*, 175-179.

Whiting, L. The central registry for child abuse cases: Rethinking basic assumptions. *Child welfare,* 1977, *56,* 761-767.

Wolfe, D. A., Sandler, J., & Kaufman, K. A competency-based parent training program for child abusers. *Journal of Consulting and Clinical Psychology,* 1981, *49,* 633-640.

Wright, L. The "sick but slick" syndrome as a personality component of parents of battered children. *Journal of Clinical Psychology,* 1976, *32,* 41-45.

Young, L. *Wednesday's children: A study of child neglect and abuse.* New York: McGraw-Hill, 1964.

Young, M. Multiple correlates of abuse: A systems approach to the etiology of child abuse. *Journal of Pediatric Psychology,* 1976, *1,* 57-61.

Zalba, S. R. the abused child: I. A survey of the problem. *Social Work,* 1966, *11,* 3-16.

Zalba, S. R. The abused child: II. A typology for classification and treatment. *Social Work,* 1967, *12,* 70-79.

Zigler, E. Controlling child abuse: Do we have the knowledge and/or the will? In G. Gerbner, C. J. Ross, & E. Zigler (Eds.), *Child abuse: An agenda for action.* New York: Oxford University Press, 1980.

2
Spouse Abuse
Diane Goldstein

In 1971, Erin Pizzey opened the doors to the Chiswick Women's Aid in Chiswick, England. Originally, it was designed to be a meeting place where women could come and talk about their problems with other women. Shortly after it opened, Women's Aid became the first refuge for abused wives who came looking for shelter from marital violence as well as to share their tales of horror and victimization. By 1979, there were 100 shelters in England and 60 in the United States, and the number of women seeking safety from battering relationships reached well into the thousands. As the subject of spouse abuse more fully entered public awareness through the growth of the women's movement, social scientists began formally investigating marital violence. The first question they had to answer was whether or not spouse abuse existed. Although they were certain that marital violence occurred, its extent was not clear. Recent estimates have suggested that marital violence occurs in at least one out of six American households on a yearly basis, and affects more than one out of four American couples at some time during their marriage (Straus, Gelles, & Steinmetz, 1980). Over the past decade, services available to the victims and perpetrators of marital violence have expanded and spouse abuse has been recognized as a frequent domestic problem. Despite these changes, effective control and prevention programs have just begun to be instituted. Few have been studied to determine their efficacy.

The purpose of this chapter is to review research on marital violence, and to examine both current and recommended control and prevention programs. The chapter will begin with a brief review of the history and scope of spouse abuse, and theories used to explain marital violence. This will be followed by a section on factors associated with marital violence. Next, a discussion of control and prevention techniques will be presented. The chapter will conclude with a section on future directions for research and intervention. Now that researchers have shown that marital violence is a serious social and psychological problem in the United States and abroad, the next step should be to implement effective control and prevention programs to treat and ultimately eliminate spouse abuse.

HISTORICAL OVERVIEW

Although the subject of marital violence has experienced a recent upsurge in public and professional attention during the past 10 years, the occurrence of marital violence is hardly a new phenomenon. As early as Biblical times, men were given the social and legal right to physically abuse their wives. One of the earliest rationalizations for the mistreatment of wives was popularized in the Biblical creation story of Adam and Eve. Not only was Eve blamed for Adam's fall, but as punishment God put her in Adam's charge, commanding "and thy desire shall be to thy husband and he shall have rule over thee." Discussing the implications of the creation story, Steinmetz and Straus (1974) noted:

> The curse placed by God on all women when Eve sinned is only the earliest example in our culture of the sex restrictive ethic, the placing of the "blame for sex" on women, and the resulting negative definition of women—all of which tend to make women legitimate objects of antagonism.

Invoking Biblical sanctions, early Christian and Roman societies practiced wife servitude and beating. By 753 BC, Roman women were defined as "necessary and inseparable possessions" of their husbands. Constantine, the first Christian emperor of Rome, had his young wife executed when she reached adulthood after gaining the empire by marrying her.

Centuries later, the rights of husbands to use physical force on their wives became legally sanctioned in church and common law doctrine. The first official church law, the Decretum, stated that women should be subject to their men in order to prevent them from leading mankind further astray. Similarly, in the *Rules of Marriage,* Friar Cherubino (1450) wrote that men should beat their wives when verbal reprimands failed because it was better to "punish the body and correct the soul, than to damage the soul and spare the body." The practice of wife-beating was incorporated into English common law in 1763 under the auspices of Sir William Blackstone who commented that, since husbands were legally responsible for their wives, they should be able to chastise them as they would apprentices or children. In 1824, wife-beating was written into U.S. law when a Mississippi judge ruled that moderate chastisement would be allowed in order to enforce the salutary restraint of domestic discipline, but that husbands could not use a switch bigger than their thumbs. This decision became known as the "rule of thumb" practice, and was later contested in several states which tried to outlaw wife-beating. Unfortunately, the same state courts which overturned the "rule of thumb" qualified their decisions by adding that grounds for abuse applied only to cases in which permanent damage had been inflicted. Likewise, they advocated the popular solution that spouse abuse was a personal problem which should be dealt with behind closed doors.

Although wife-beating is no longer legally sanctioned by current practices, it is implicitly legitimized through the sex-role attitudes which characterize the U.S. criminal justice system, and American society in general. Among these implicit sanctions are the failure of legal authorities to recognize spouse abuse as a criminal offense and thereby punishable by incarceration, the attitudes of family court judges and other "helping" agencies who often blame the wives for provoking their husbands while failing to appreciate the life-threatening situation that they are in, and finally, the pervasive pattern of male domination within the American family. In attempting to understand why the occurrence of marital violence has even begun to be questioned, several writers have suggested (Hilberman, 1980; Straus, 1974) that the shift in public attention toward spouse abuse has been influenced by the emergence of the women's rights movement and the increased sensitivity of social scientists to the severity of violence which characterizes American life. Increased public awareness and small changes in the legal response to spouse abuse during the 1970s have been a start in the right direction, but the legal and social legitimization of violence against women has a cultural heritage several thousand years old.

INCIDENCE, SCOPE, AND DEFINITION

Most researchers have defined spouse abuse as the deliberate action on the part of one spouse to inflict serious and/or repeated physical injury on the other spouse. In most cases, the partner receiving the battering is the wife and the husband is her assailant. Couples who are cohabiting, but not legally married, may still be included in this definition. Variations in the definition of spouse abuse have included the consideration of "psychological" battering as abusive behavior and the degree of physical injury which must be inflicted to qualify as abuse. Walker (1979) suggested that a battered woman is a woman who has been repeatedly subjected to any forceful physical or psychological behavior by a man in order to coerce her to do something he wants her to do without any conception of her rights. She said that it is a mistake to regard battering as confined to physical injury, because this definition neglects the "slow emotional torture" which may be equally as damaging as the "sharp, quick, physical blows." Straus, Gelles & Steinmetz, (1980) have differentiated between "normal" violence, i.e., any action carried out with the intention of causing physical pain or injury, such as spanking a child for misbehaving; and "abusive" violence, which has a high potential of injuring the person being hit, such as punching, kicking, biting, hitting with an object, shooting, or stabbing. Scott (1974) used the following continuum to categorize the severity of marital violence: (1) not requiring medical attention, (2) requiring outpatient attention, and (3) requiring hospitalization.

Operationalizing spouse abuse as deliberate physical injury, recent studies have shown that marital violence occurs yearly in at least one out of six American families (Straus, Gelles, & Steinmetz, 1980) and may occur in as many as half of all American couples during their married life (Gelles, 1974). For about 1,700 women each year, this violence results in their death (Steinmetz, 1980). In a study using a nationally representative sample, Straus, Gelles, & Steinmetz (1980) found that 16 percent of the families they interviewed reported a violent incident during the past year, while 28 percent reported a violent incident over the course of their marriage. An even more alarming finding was that the incidence of "abusive" violence (e.g., guns, knives, beatings) was almost as high as the occurrence of "normal" violence (e.g., pushing, slapping). Translating these percentages into the total number of marriages affected by spouse abuse, they reported that of the 47 million couples in the United States in 1975, 1.7 million Americans were faced with a knife or a gun by a spouse, and over 2 million had been "beaten up." With regard to the frequency of "abusive" violence between husbands and wives during a one-year period, they found that 47 percent of the husbands beat their wives three or more times a year, and 53 percent of the wives beat their husbands three or more times a year. However, their data did not show what percent of the women were violent in self-defense, which has frequently been cited as the cause of their abusive behavior (Wolfgang, 1957).

In an investigation of violence among friends and relatives, the National Crime Survey Study (U.S. Justice Dept., 1980) indicated that, of the 1 million single-offender incidents of violence reported, 58 percent occurred between spouses and ex-spouses. Of these single offender incidents, 80.9 percent of the spousal victims reported injuries, the most common being bruises, black eyes, cuts and scratches, or swellings.

Estimates of spouse abuse were derived from semiannual interviews between 1973 and 1976 with approximately 136,000 occupants of a representative sample of some 60,000 housing units in the United States. They included all violent incidents between intimates, whether or not they were reported to the police. From in-depth interviews with 80 families, Gelles (1974) found that 54 percent of the spouses studied had used physical force on each other at some time during their marriage. Employing a probability sample of couples in New

Castle, Delaware, Steinmetz (1977) reported that 60 percent of these couples had engaged in at least one violent incident in their marriage. Research has also shown that intrafamilial homicide accounts for 20-40 percent of all homicides (Curtis, 1974).

While such investigations may alert social scientists to the severity of marital violence which characterizes American violence, it is likely that some of these figures may be an underestimate of the actual occurrence of spouse abuse. Several reasons have been cited as the source of underreporting. First, most studies have only surveyed intact couples and confined their questions to interactions with the current mate. Levinger (1966) found that one-third of the women in his sample cited physical abuse as the reason for their seeking a divorce. Therefore, studies which have ignored marital interactions with a previous spouse may be greatly underestimating the actual extent of marital violence (Steinmetz, 1980; Straus, Gelles, & Steinmetz, 1980). Another problem has been that people may be reluctant to report extreme physical violence because they feel ashamed or guilty about these incidents. As the occurrence of spouse abuse has become publicly recognized in the past 10 years, more battered wives have stepped forward, but the social stigmatization and personal guilt associated with being battered have continued to keep many silent. Finally, because many violent acts are perceived as socially normal behavior (e.g., slapping, pushing), they may simply fail to be reported. Results from the 1968 interview survey conducted for the National Commission on the Causes and Prevention of Violence indicated that 20 percent of the nationally represented sample approved of husband and wife hitting.

One of the more consistent findings which has emerged from the research on marital violence has been that abuse is not associated with geographic area, racial, ethnic or religious background, or income level. It is a widespread problem present in all segments of American society. Based on a volunteer sample of 400 battered women, Walker (1979) found that about one-third of the women were professional women. In his study of 600 couples who were in the process of getting divorced, Levinger (1966) found that 40 percent of lower-class women, and 23 percent of middle-class women reported physical abuse by their spouses. Similarly, a 1979 survey of wife abuse in Kentucky (Steinmetz, 1980) found that income levels were not good predictors of family violence. Although wife-beating has traditionally been associated with low income and certain ethnic groups, it is probable that this myth has survived because these groups are more likely to rely on public agencies such as the police and social services to intervene in crisis situations. For a middle or upper-class woman, such problems are usually dealt with privately, by soliciting the aid of their personal physicians or attorneys (Hilberman, 1980).

THEORIES OF MARITAL VIOLENCE

In the following sections, theories of marital violence and empirical evidence supporting the different theoretical positions will be reviewed. Theoretical models will be presented first, with research evidence presented next in the corresponding sections. The three theoretical orientations which will be discussed are: (1) the individual model, (2) the structural or social-psychological mode, and (3) the societal or sociocultural model. Empirical studies which address factors associated with the individual model will be presented in the sections on characteristics of abusive men and abused women. Research evidence on variables related to the structural or social-psychological model will be reviewed in the section on family and cultural variables, and will include a discussion of violence and victimization as learned behavior patterns from one's family of origin, stress and coping responses in the current marital relationship, and sex-role socialization. Finally, societal or sociocultural factors will be presented in the section on family and cultural variables, and will include a discussion of sex-role socialization, and the cultural legitimization of violence against women.

While research on the incidence and factors associated with marital violence has grown in the past 10 years, the development of a comprehensive theory which explains the acquisition and maintenance of marital violence has received relatively less attention. Most models have been based on post-hoc examination of the data with few researchers proposing a theoretical model first, and then testing its propositions. Another factor which has delayed the development of a comprehensive model of marital violence was the initial emphasis on individual psychopathology as the cause of this phenomenon. Because traditional theories of spouse abuse focused on the "masochistic" needs of female victims and "psychopathic/sadistic" personalities of their male assailants, numerous family and societal factors, which have recently been suggested as important contributors to the occurrence of spouse abuse, were neglected. Likewise, the clinical implications of viewing spouse abuse as limited to "sick" individuals kept effective control and prevention techniques from evolving, and also reinforced the view of marital violence as a private rather than public problem.

The Individual Model

In terms of current theoretical models, three general ways of understanding marital violence have been proposed. The first is the psychiatric or *individual* model. Although intraindividual factors are emphasized in the *individual* model, they are no longer assumed to be the exclusive cause of spouse abuse. Furthermore, traditional characterizations of "masochistic" wives and "sadistic" husbands have been replaced by other personality characteristics as causes of marital violence. Many researchers have suggested that batterers are not psychopaths or "sick" individuals, but ordinary men who have low self-esteem and resort to violence, a learned pattern of behavior, when life stresses become intolerable (Davidson, 1978; Freize, 1976; Moore, 1980). Similarly, abused wives are not seen as "sick" or "masochistic," but normal women who become locked in a cycle of marital violence because they are emotionally and often financially dependent on their battering husbands (Hilberman, 1980; Walker, 1979). Moore (1980) commented that the profile of the battered woman looks almost identical to that of the batterer. "She is all ages, all ethnicities, from all socioeconomic groups, has a low level of self-esteem, and for the most part has very traditional notions of male and female behavior" [p. 20]. Reviewing the psychodynamics of abused wives, Walker (1979) has proposed a modification of Seligman's (1977) "learned helplessness" model to account for this phenomenon. Originally, Seligman suggested that when an animal or person learns that the responses made are independent of the outcome of events, a cluster of depressed symptomatology may emerge which includes decreased motivation to respond, cognitive perceptions of an inability to effect desired outcomes, and feelings of depression and anxiety. In her adaptation of this paradigm, Walker remarked that the experience of repeated batterings produces a "learned helplessness" response in abused wives who become convinced that nothing they can do will stop the abuse. Feelings of depression and anxiety are also common (Hilberman & Munson, 1978; Rounsaville, 1978).

The Structural Model

The second, and currently most popular model of explaining marital violence, has been the *structural* or *social-psychological* model (Gelles, 1982; Straus & Hotaling, 1980) which emphasizes the contribution of family factors in the development of wife-beating. Several aspects of family life have been implicated as causal elements from a *structural* perspective. One of the primary explanations for the origins of marital violence has been that violence is the product of witnessing and/or experiencing physical abuse during childhood. In this learning model, it is assumed that violent behavior is acquired in one's family of origin, and will be elicited and maintained in one's family of procreation by situational factors (e.g., stress). Another important structural approach which examines family interactions in the maintenance of violent behavior is the cycle theory of marital violence. While slightly different variations of this explanation have been proposed (Feldman, 1979; Straus, 1973; Walker, 1979), the main idea has been that spouse abuse is maintained through repetitive cycles of battering and conciliatory behaviors. Several studies have shown that (after a beating,) husbands act remorseful and try to make-up with their wives which frequently persuades the woman to remain in the battering relationship (Hilberman, 1980; Walker, 1979). Not only does she feel relieved that the violence has temporarily ended, but she also experiences renewed faith that the violence will truly end this time. As Walker (1979) comments:

> In this phase the batterer behaves in a charming and loving manner. . . . He begs her forgiveness and promises her that he will never do it again. His behavior is described as typical of a little boy who has done something wrong, the child caught with his hand in the cookie jar. . . . He manages to convince everyone concerned that this time he really means it. [p. 65]

A third group of structural theorists have discussed the balance of power, status, and resources within the family system as the foundation for spouse abuse. This model is exemplified by Goode's introduction of the concepts of power and status as determining factors in marital violence. In the first theory of family violence, Goode (1971) proposed that force or its threat was the "ultimate" resource which was used to maintain the family power structure. Identifying three other types of family resources (e.g., money, respect, likability), he hypothesized that husbands with sufficient amounts of these resources would not need to use violence to preserve their position. However, men who were lacking or insufficient in these other resources would need to rely on violence, the "ultimate" resource, in order to guarantee their continued power. Research has supported the contribution of power and status factors in the occurrence of spouse abuse (Hornung, McCullough & Sugimoto, 1981; O'Brien, 1971). A fourth structural model has emphasized the contribution of stress to the production of marital violence. The basic assumption of this model was that, when external pressures (e.g., unemployment) pushed the family stress threshold past its optimum level, failure to resolve the problem situation and reduce the level of family stress could lead to frustration and possibly marital violence. Farrington (1980) added that, because families encounter a high amount of stress regularly and tend to be poorly equipped to handle these stresses, they are particularly vulnerable to encountering problem situations which lead to increased frustration, and potentially, marital violence. Research has similarly supported this model (Gelles, 1974; Straus, Gelles, & Steinmetz, 1980).

The Societal Model

A third approach to understanding marital violence has been the *societal* or *sociocultural* model. The main factors implicated in this model were sex-role attitudes and sexual inequality, and the cultural legitimization of violence through societal practices and values popularized by the mass media. Several researchers have suggested that patterns of female victimization and male aggression are acquired through sex-role socialization (Straus, 1980; Walker, 1981). Once developed, these behaviors are maintained by cultural norms and values which support female subordination and male dominance. Dobash and Dobash (1979) argued that the patriarchal structure of Western society, maintained by economic and social processes, has led to the subordination of women, and a historical pattern of systematic violence directed toward wives. While laws regarding spouse abuse are changing, the failure to recognize spouse abuse as a criminal offense has implicitly sanctioned the use of violence against women. Finally, the mass media has played a powerful role in culturally legitimizing the use of violence in general. In reviewing the amount of violence on television, Gerbner and Gross (1976) reported that the typical citizen who watches prime time TV will be exposed to shows in which more than half of all characters are involved in some violence, and one of ten in killing. The amount of gratuitous violence in current motion pictures is also extremely high (Straus, 1980). Several researchers have reported a relationship between the amount of media violence and the acquisition of norms, values, and attitudes which favor violence (Beaulieu, 1978; Straus, 1980).

FACTORS ASSOCIATED WITH MARITAL VIOLENCE

Although a search for factors associated with marital violence have comprised the bulk of clinical and empirical research in this area, several methodological problems have arisen which need to be considered before reviewing these studies. One concern in assessing the results of these studies has been the issue of sampling bias. Sample populations have been drawn from police records and social service agency files (Gelles, 1974), public advertisement in a national magazine (Prescott & Letko, 1977), hospital emergency rooms (Rounsaville, 1978; Rounsaville, Lifton & Bieber, 1979), and abuse treatment centers (Rosenbaum & O'Leary, 1981). In addition to not knowing the comparability of these sample populations to each other, the extent of generalizability between these select groups and the larger population of men and women engaged in an abusive marital relationship has frequently been questioned (Gelles, 1979; Rosenbaum & O'Leary, 1981). As Gelles has noted (1979), individuals who present themselves for treatment at some agency are likely to differ from those who remain unidentified.

A second methodological problem has been the failure to employ appropriate comparison and control groups in studies of marital violence (Coleman, 1980; Rosenbaum & O'Leary, 1981). Because most studies have failed to include a comparison group of maritally discordant, nonabusive husbands or wives, it has not been possible to separate the effects of marital discord inherent in an abusive relationship from the occurrence of physical violence. In a recent investigation which compared the responses of abusive husbands and wives to maritally discordant, nonabusive partners and satisfactorily married partners, Rosenbaum and O'Leary (1981) found that abused wives were not psychologically different than their nonabused, maritally discordant counterparts. However, their results also indicated that abusive husbands were psychologically different than either of the two comparison groups, suggesting that the occurrence of physical violence, and not marital discord per se, contributed to these differences. Without appropriate comparison groups such as those employed in their investigation, valuable information might have been lost.

A third methodological issue has been the use of self-report as the primary, and often only, source of data (Gelles, 1979). Although people have been more open in discussing marital violence than social scientists initially expected, there is the possibility that they may be reluctant to disclose certain aspects of their personal lives during structured and semi-structured interviews and may distort facts about the occurrence of marital violence even on self-report measures because it is such a "sensitive" subject. Furthermore, because many individuals have been studied during crisis periods, researchers may have obtained an exaggerated picture of the negative qualities associated with abusive relationships. Another problem has been that descriptions of battering men are often based on their wives' reports only, which could similarly lead to distorted conclusions. Finally, the failure to include standardized measures to obtain information from couples involved in marital violence has limited both the validity and generalizability of the data which has been gathered.

A fourth methodological issue has been the diversity in developing an operational definition of spouse abuse. For example, as noted earlier, while most researchers have defined spouse abuse as intentional physical injury by one spouse toward the other, some investigators (e.g., Walker) have argued that any comprehensive definition of spouse abuse must include psychological injury as well.

Despite these methodological problems, the concurrence between clinical accounts and newer empirical investigations on the causes of marital violence has been strong and lends support to the credibility of clinical and empirical findings. In two recent investigations which employed apropriate comparison groups and standardized measures (Rosenbaum & O'Leary, 1981; Goldstein, 1982), investigators found that several factors (e.g., witnessing parental-spouse abuse and/or experiencing physical punishment as a child, having low self-esteem) which had been identified in clinical accounts as important contributors to the occurrence of marital violence were supported by empirical findings. Similarly, other recent studies of spouse abuse which have utilized more rigorous scientific procedures have supported the relationship between clinically identified variables associated with marital violence and its occurrence (Carroll, 1977; Hornung, McCullough, & Sugimoto, 1981; Ulbrich & Huber, 1981).

The remainder of this section will review some of the main factors associated with marital violence. This review is not intended to be exhaustive, but to highlight some of the key variables which will need to be considered in designing and implementing effective control and prevention programs.

Characteristics of Abusive Men

In the past five years, low self-esteem, dependency, alcohol use, lack of responsibility, and traditional attitudes about the roles of men and women have each been identified as important psychological characteristics of abusive husbands. With regard to low self-esteem, marital abuse has been viewed as the husband's attempt to overcome his feelings of powerlessness and inadequacy, and to defend his self-esteem. Both clinical and empirical accounts have supported an association between marital violence and low self-esteem (Ball, 1977; Coleman, 1980; Moore, 1980; Symonds, 1978; Walker, 1979). In a recent empirical study employing appropriate comparison groups and standardized measures, Goldstein (1982) found that maritally violent men obtained lower self-esteem scores on an adjective checklist and the Rosenberg Self-Esteem Scale than maritally discordant, nonabusive husbands, or satisfactorily married men. A related factor, dependency, has been posited to lead to the occurrence of marital violence as either the husband's attempt to defend against needing his wife, or his frustration at her for failing to serve his dinner on time, discipline the kids the right way, and in short, not living up to his expectations of the "ideal"wife (Coleman, 1980; Elbow, 1977; Feldman, 1979; Gullattee, 1979; Hilberman & Munson, 1977). Wife-beaters have often been described as childlike, remorseful and yearning for nurturance when they are not beating their wives, particularly during the "make-up"phase of the marital violence cycle (Coleman, 1980; Hilberman & Munson, 1978; Walker, 1979). Similarly, several investigations have shown that abusive men often become suicidal, psychotic, or thrown into an emotional panic when their wives leave or threaten to leave (Coleman, 1980; Hilberman & Munson, 1978).

Alcoholism is a third factor which has frequently been noted as an attribute of battering men (Gayford, 1979; Gelles, 1974; Gerson, 1978; Hilberman & Munson, 1978). Drinking accompanied the violence in 60 percent of Gelles' (1974) sample and 93 percent of Hilberman & Munson's (1978) sample. Gayford (1975) described drunkenness as occurring regularly in 52 percent of the men, and occasionally in an additional 22 percent. Most researchers currently agree that alcohol in battering homes gives both the battering man and his battered wife an excuse for the violence (Moore, 1980). As Moore remarked, alcohol consumption relieves the man of the responsibility for his behavior, and gives the wife justification for remaining in the relationship in the hope that he will control his drinking which will end his aggressiveness.

Two final psychological qualities which have been used to describe wife beaters are their failure to take responsibility for their actions, and their endorsement of traditionalist attitudes toward men and women. One of the main problems in identifying and treating abusive husbands has been that they do not seek outside help because they do not view their behavior as their problem. Denying that anything is wrong with them, their excuses have ranged from blaming their wives for provoking them by any slight frustration to claiming that they couldn't help themselves because they were out of control. Related to their inability to admit to their wrongdoing, many battering men hold very traditional attitudes about the roles of men and women, and believe that it is acceptable to hit their wives because society has given them this right. Furthermore, since most of these men are low in self-esteem, they may be particularly vulnerable to situations which threaten their male authority or feelings of adequacy (e.g., being told by a wife what to do, being fired from a job), and may resort to physical aggression as the "ultimate resource" in preserving their control within the family. Clinical accounts have supported this conclusion (Ball, 1977; Coleman, 1980; Moore, 1980).

Characteristics of Abused Women

Among the characteristics attributed to abused women, low self-esteem, dependency problems, depressed symptomatology, over-assuming responsibility for being battered, and traditional values about men and women have received considerable attention as primary factors in becoming and remaining a battered woman. In many ways, the clinical picture of abused wives is similar to that of their battering husbands except that the women seem to respond to this situation by becoming depressed and paralyzed whereas the men seem to react by externalizing their anger and beating their wives. The differences in these behavior patterns may be explained as the product of socialization practices which teach women to cope with stress by taking it out on themselves, and men to deal with their frustrations by taking it out on others. Furthermore, situational constraints, such as the men being physically stronger, may prevent the women from becoming outwardly aggressive.

Like the men, many studies have shown that battered women have low self-esteem (Ball, 1977; Carlson, 1977; Moore, 1980; Rounsaville, 1979; Walker, 1979). Carlson (1977) observed devastatingly low self-regard among her sample of 101 battered women. In a survey of 109 family case studies, Ball (1977) found that abused wives repeatedly had problems of low self-esteem. Because abused wives tend to perceive themselves as worthless and incompetent, such feelings have been associated with their inability to leave the battering relationship (Rounsaville, et al., 1979), beliefs that they deserve to be beaten (Davidson, 1978; Straus, 1977), and high dependency needs (Gayford, 1975). In addition to feelings of low self-esteem, battered women have been characterized as being psychologically dependent on their abusive husbands (Davidson, 1979; Hilberman & Munson, 1978; Walker, 1979). Some investigators have suggested that the woman's dependency needs have developed from early sex-role training (Moore, 1980) or childhood deprivation (Ball, 1977; Gayford, 1979), while others have hypothesized that these dependency needs are the product of repeated physical beatings (Hilberman & Munson, 1977; Walker, 1979). Many of these women have grown up believing that they need a man to take care of them, and their inability to stop the beatings reinforces the attitude that they lack the resources to control their own lives. Convinced that they cannot survive on their own, battered women may cling to their assailant husbands even at the cost of repeated physical abuse.

Characterized by feelings of low self-esteem and high dependency needs, battered women frequently display depressed symptomatology. Of Gayford's sample of 100 women, 71 had symptoms that were treated with antidepressants and tranquilizers, 42 had attempted suicide, 46 at some time had been referred to a psychiatrist, and 21 had a diagnosis of depression. From his survey of 31 battered women, Rounsaville (1978) reported that over half his sample had significant symptoms of depression. Other clinical studies have also shown high incidents of depressed symptomatology among abused wives (Hilberman & Munson, 1978; Walker, 1979). While investigators have disputed whether low self-esteem and dependency precede or are the product of repeated physical abuse, they agree that depressed symptomatology is situationally determined by the battered woman's repeated victimization. Rounsaville (1978) suggested that abuse is a difficult life problem, and that depression is the result of the woman's continued exposure to a frustrating, dangerous situation at home rather than a reflection of her masochistic tendencies, or a sign of mental illness. Similarly, Hilberman and Munson (1977) have described the battered woman syndrome as a study in paralyzing terror in which the stress was unending and the threat of assault ever present.

> They were drained, fatigued, and numb, without the energy to do more than minimal household chores and child care. They had a pervasive sense of hopelessness and despair about themselves and their lives. They saw themselves as incompetent, unworthy and unlovable, and were ridden with guilt and shame. They thought they deserved the abuse, saw no options and felt powerless to make changes. [Hilberman, 1980, p. 1341]

Two other factors which have been cited as important psychological attributes of abused wives have been their traditionalist attitudes about men and women, and their over-assuming responsibility for the battering episodes. While many women grow up believing women are subordinate to men, particularly in a marital relationship, battered wives have overly endorsed this stereotyped assumption. They are most likely to believe they need a man to take care of them, and have often selected their battering husbands because they initially presented themselves as good caretakers as well as being strong and controlling (Walker, 1979). Furthermore, they have learned that the role of women is to be good wives and mothers, and if something goes wrong in their marriage, it is their fault, and their responsibility to correct it. In her investigation of 109 family case studies, Ball (1977) noted that battered wives identified strongly with the marital role, and sought help in preserving their marriages to "salvage their ideal against the reality of the situation." Seventy-five percent of the women Walker (1979) surveyed reported a "Dresden doll" upbringing in which they learned very early in their lives that their competence in areas other than the social arena would not be useful to them during their adulthood. This orientation has been associated with the abused wife's desperate attempt to make her marriage work by being a better housekeeper, keeping herself socially isolated to assuage her husband's jealousy, and, in general, placing her husband's needs before her own. Likewise, her traditionalist values have contributed to the battered woman's readiness to assume the responsibility for her beatings. Aside from the battered woman's traditionalist values, Walker (1979) suggested that battered women may perceive themselves as responsible for their partner's violence in order to feel that they have some control over the situation. If these women remain convinced that it is something they have done which produces the batterer's aggression, they may continue to hope that, by changing their behavior and creating a stress-free environment for their batterers, they can prevent future beatings.

Family and Cultural Variables

While a number of family and cultural factors have been identified as relevant to spouse abuse, the following four variables seem especially important, and thus will be discussed in this section: (1) violence and victimization as learned behavior patterns from one's family or origin, (2) stress and coping responses within the current marital relationship, (3) sex-role socialization, and (4) the cultural legitimitization of violence against women. To the extent that societal norms influence family child-rearing practices, these factors may be interdependent and reinforce each other in contributing to the occurrence of spouse abuse.

Violence and Victimization As Learned Behavior Patterns. In terms of acquiring the predisposition to becoming an abusive husband or an abused wife, learned behavior patterns from one's family of origin have been noted as the most significant influence. Studies have consistently shown that maritally violent men either witnessed their fathers beating their mothers or were themselves abused as children (Ball, 1977; Carlson, 1977; Carroll, 1977; Gayford, 1979; Rosenbaum & O'Leary, 1981; Straus, Gelles, & Steinmetz, 1980). Rosenbaum and O'Leary (1981) found that abusive husbands were significantly more likely to have been abused as children and to have witnessed parental spouse abuse than maritally discordant, nonabusive husbands or satisfactorily married men. From their nationally representative sample, Straus, Gelles, & Steinmetz (1980) reported that husbands who were reared in the most violent homes (i.e., both observing marital violence and experiencing physical punishment) had a rate of wife abuse 600 times greater than husbands from nonviolent homes. The effects of either witnessing parental abuse, or experiencing physical punishment, also led to significantly greater incidents of spouse abuse.

Unlike studies of battering men, investigations with abused wives have produced mixed results regarding the association between observed marital violence and later abuse. Although several investigations have found that battered women were more likely to witness abuse and be abused as children (Ball, 1977; Carlson, 1977; Carroll, 1977; Gayford, 1979; Hilberman and Munson, 1977; Straus, Gelles, & Steinmetz, 1980), others have failed to report this finding (Rosenbaum & O'Leary, 1981; Star, 1980; Walker, 1979). Despite these differences, such findings have not negated the importance of identifying patterns in the woman's family of origin which predispose her to becoming an abused wife. Other experiences in the woman's family of origin which have been cited as contributing to her predisposition to become an abused wife range from exposure to sex-role stereotyping by traditionalist fathers who "treated their daughters like fragile dolls" (Davidson, 1978; Walker, 1979) to low familial warmth and disruptive family relations during childhood and adolescence (Carroll, 1977; Rounsaville, 1978). In a recent study of women who had repeatedly experienced violence in relationships with alcoholic husbands, Hanks and Rosenbaum (1978) identified three distinct types of families of origin. The most illuminating finding of this investigation was the striking similarity between the woman's current marital relationship and her parent's marital relationship.

Stress and Coping Responses. Stress has been an important factor associated with the occurrence of marital violence in current marital relationships. According to the proposed vulnerability model presented in the next section, children who have grown up in violent homes and learned to use violence as a problem solving strategy, and other "high risk" individuals (e.g., those with low self-esteem, high dependency needs) will engage in an episode of marital violence when situational pressures become too great. Once the violent episode has occurred, it will be followed by an initial period of tension reduction which will reinforce its repeated occurrence. Unfortunately, since the violence will not ultimately resolve the problem situation, stress will reaccumulate in the marital relationship until it deteriorates into another violent episode. With regard to abusive men, Frieze (1976) remarked that battering occurs when there is some form of stress in a man's life coupled with violence because the person knows no other form of response.

In a survey of 57 families, Steinmetz (1977) found that the major sources of marital conflict were disciplining the children, disagreements over in-laws, changes due to pregnancy, and changes in sex-roles which were not mutually shared. Gelles (1976) reported that one-fourth of the women in his sample of 80 families were battered during pregnancy. From their survey of 2,143 families, Straus, Gelles, & Steinmetz (1980) found that the greater the number of stressful life events a family encountered in the past year, the greater were the chances that the spouses had engaged in marital violence. Included in their 18 stressful life events were pregnancy, financial pressures (low income), problems outside the home (unemployment, problems at work), sexual problems, in-law troubles, and problems with children (being suspended from school, doing something illegal). Another group of marital stressors related to marital violence have been situations in which the husband's power position is threatened. Based on college students' reports of parental violence, Allen and Straus (1980) found that the more the wife's fund of legitimate resources exceeded her husband's, the greater the likelihood of spouse abuse. Likewise, their results revealed that the more legitimate resources the husband had, the lower the incidence of marital violence. Comparing violent and nonviolent couples, O'Brien (1971) and Hornung, McCullough, and Sugimoto (1981) reported that violent men were frequently lower in achieved status (e.g., unemployment, education) than their wives. O'Brien hypothesized that the frustration resulting from the discrepancy between the husband's ascribed and achieved status leads to marital violence as a means of reaffirming the husband's power position.

Sex-role Socialization. Sex-role socialization has been a third factor associated with the acquisition and maintenance of spouse abuse. This process is influenced by both family and cultural norms, and includes both learned behavior patterns and the development of attitudes about the roles of men and women. Through direct reinforcement and vicarious learning (parental modeling), children are trained to behave in different ways based on whether they are male or female. In homes where parental values and practices endorse equal roles for men and women, these differences may be small. On the other hand, in families which have strong "traditionalist" attitudes regarding the roles of men and women, these differences may be quite large. As noted in the preceding sections on individual characteristics related to spouse abuse, both clinical and empirical investigations have shown that "traditionalist" values and stereotypic learned behavior patterns frequently contribute to a person becoming a battering man or a battered woman. Using data from a national probability sample, Ulbrich and Huber (1981) reported that men who saw their fathers hit their mothers were more likely to approve of violence against women. From a survey of clinical and nonclinical control families, Carroll (1977) found the transmission of family violence occurred most often in same-sex linkages. Men who received a high amount of punishment from their fathers were more likely to report marital violence as an adult than women who received a high amount of physical punishment from their fathers. Similarly, women were more likely to report marital violence if they had been subjected to a high amount of physical punishment by their mothers. In addition to the effects of family sex-role training, societal norms have also endorsed unequal sex-role practices which have supported the occurrence of marital violence. Because men are still seen as dominant and women as subordinate in American society, the attitude that men have a right to control their wives, even by physical force, has often been maintained. Likewise, this influence may explain how men and women who do not grow up in violent homes have become wife-beaters and battered women.

The Cultural Legitimization of Violence Against Women. A final societal variable which has influenced the maintenance of spouse abuse in the United States has been the cultural legitimization of violence against women. Straus (1974, 1980) has frequently described the marriage license as a "hitting license," asserting that the myth of family nonviolence coexists with social norms that imply the right of family members to strike each other. Furthermore, as noted in the introduction to this chapter, cultural values which condone wife-beating have been implicitly sanctioned through police and court intervention procedures. Empirical studies have similarly indicated that violence against women has been legitimized through societal standards (Churchill & Straus, 1980; Pogrebin, 1974; Stark & McEvoy 1970). In a survey conducted for the U.S. National Commission of the Causes and Prevention of Violence, Stark and McEvoy (1970) found that one-quarter of the persons interviewed said they could approve of a husband or wife hitting each other under certain circumstances. Studying the reactions of male bystanders to violence against women, Pogrebin (1974) reported that men aided women when they were assaulted by other women, but not when they were assaulted by men. Combined with individual and family factors, cultural norms which legitimize violence against women have produced a significant barrier in controlling and preventing spouse abuse.

Integrating Theory and Research on Marital Violence: A "Vulnerability" Model

While each theoretical perspective has contributed to explaining the occurrence of marital violence and been supported by some empirical evidence, no model has attempted to provide a comprehensive understanding of the occurrence of spouse abuse by integrating the contributions of these three sets of factors. Because marital violence represents a complex social and psychological problem which is multiply determined by individual, social-psychological, and sociocultural factors, the following "vulnerability" model is proposed as a way of conceptualizing marital violence which integrates the contributions of these three sets of factors (Goldstein, 1982).

In examining the etiology of schizophrenia, Zubin and Spring, (1975) developed a "vulnerability" model to account for this phenomenon. They hypothesized that all individuals had a certain "vulnerability" to becoming schizophrenic based on early childhood experiences and their psychological organization. However, this "vulnerability" would not express itself in a schizophrenic episode until the individual's optimum stress threshold was exceeded, which again varies between individuals. Applying this model to the occurrence of marital violence, it is assumed that all individuals have a certain "vulnerability" to engage in spouse abuse as either the assailant or victim, when their optimum stress level is exceeded. Predisposing factors which may contribute to the development of an individual's "vulnerability" to spouse abuse include the aforementioned individual, family, and cultural influences (e.g., low self-esteem, witnessing parental spouse abuse and/or experiencing physical punishment as a child, sex-role socialization). Frequently discussed external pressures which may lead to above optimum stress levels include unemployment, pregnancy, and other stressors which have been identified (Straus, Gelles, & Steinmetz, 1980). Once certain predisposing factors and external pressures which contribute to the occurrence of spouse abuse are empirically verified, the proposed "vulnerability" model may be helpful in the early identification and treatment of couples who are at "high risk" for experiencing marital violence.

THE CONTROL AND PREVENTION OF SPOUSE ABUSE

Over the past decade, social scientists have devoted considerable energy to investigating the incidence and scope of spouse abuse, factors associated with spouse abuse, and its multiple causes. Investigations have generated a useful if beginning working knowledge of the phenomenon of spouse abuse. However, the design and implementation of effective intervention strategies to control and prevent marital violence has barely begun. Without the development of such programs, this serious social and psychological problem cannot be stopped, and ultimately eliminated.

The remainder of this chapter will review extant intervention techniques, and the research which has examined their effectiveness. Strategies which have been recommended, but not necessarily investigated or implemented, will also be introduced. Techniques will be classified according to the level of prevention at which they intervene: (1) primary prevention, (2) secondary prevention, and (3) tertiary prevention. Primary prevention has been defined as those techniques which attempt to prevent the problem before it starts. Included in this category have been various methods aimed at eliminating sexist attitudes in society, reducing the cultural legitimization of violence, and changing family child-rearing practices (e.g., physical discipline, sex-role stereotyping) which lay the foundation for the next generation of battering men and battered women. Secondary prevention has been defined as those techniques aimed at early identification of battering men and women. This category has included home visits, telephone hotlines, out-patient visits, crisis intervention counseling, and other related methods. Tertiary prevention has been defined as those techniques which have been employed after the repeated occurrence of marital violence, when the problem has usually become deeply enmeshed in the family system. It has also been the level at which the majority of current intervention techniques have impacted. Included in this group of strategies have been safe houses for battered women, most legal and police interventions, and a variety of psychological treatments.

In her comments on the need for primary, secondary, and tertiary prevention programs, Walker (1979) stated that all three levels of intervention must go on simultaneously. Other investigators have also noted the need for more effective prevention programs at all three levels (Gelles, 1979; Hilberman & Munson, 1977; Straus, Gelles, & Steinmetz, 1980). Although changing the sexist and violent nature of American society may seem farreaching, only radical solutions can lead to the ultimate prevention of spouse abuse in the United States. As Walker (1979) remarked:

> If a woman remains in a safe house long enough to remove herself permanently from a battering situation, she must be able to shift to a less controlled environment where she can rebuild her life. But only a change in popular attitudes will enable society to be ready to receive her. [p. 190]

Recent changes in the public awareness of spouse abuse and popular attitudes toward women have been a start in the right direction, but much more is needed.

Tertiary Prevention Programs

Because tertiary prevention programs have comprised the bulk of intervention techniques for controlling spouse abuse, they will be reviewed first. In addition, they will be divided into five categories: (1) safe houses, (2) police intervention, (3) legal solutions, (4) psychological treatments, and (5) other helping services (community support groups, social service agencies, medical treatment). At the tertiary level, most prevention programs have been designed for treating battered women. Despite the contribution of both spouses to the cycle of marital violence, researchers have suggested that battered women need to be recognized as the "primary" victims of marital violence because, in comparison to their husbands, they are more likely to be seriously injured (Straus, 1980; Walker, 1979) and they are locked into the marriage more due to economic and social constraints (Gelles, 1976; Martin, 1976). Furthermore, battering men have been more reluctant than their wives to identify themselves and seek treatment for this problem.

The first step in the control of marital violence must be to provide battered wives with shelter and safety. The development of women's shelters in the United States and abroad has been designed to meet these needs (Hilberman, 1980; Pizzey, 1974; Walker, 1979). Women's shelters or safe houses have provided abused wives with immediate protection from the battering situation as well as the opportunity to regain control over their lives within a safe and supportive milieu. The first women's shelter, Chiswick Women's Aid, was opened by Erin Pizzey in 1971, and was founded on a total therapeutic community model. Divided into three phases, the main goal of this program was to help the battered woman regain a sense of control over her life within a supportive environment. During each of the three phases, women were expected to assume greater amounts of responsibility for their own welfare and the welfare of others in the house in order to help them recognize that they were competent individuals who had the ability to take care of themselves. Once they had learned to perceive themselves as non-"helpless," capable adults, they could decide either to leave the battering relationship, or at least to recognize that they had this option. Walker (1979) reported that about 50 percent of the women who stay in women's shelters for longer than one week will not return to live with their batterers. She also noted that this percentage rises dramatically if the safe house remains open to those women who return home and then want to come back to the refuge.

In the initial phase of Pizzey's program, women are housed in a crisis receiving center where responsibilities are assigned according to each one's abilities at the time. However, each is expected to have some share of the responsibility for decision making and house management. Supportive services such as child care are available at this stage. After a brief stay at the crisis center, women are encouraged to move to one of the second-stage houses. Although responsibilities and house management continue to be shared communally, each woman is expected to have an equal part in this process. Following this phase, women have the option of either providing their own housing or moving to a third-stage house if there is room for them. Like second-stage houses, women at third-stage houses are expected to have an equal share in decision making and house management. Walker (1979) described the women and children in third-stage houses as having developed a remarkably close sense of community which provided them with a beneficial alternative to the nuclear family setting.

While few programs have copied Pizzey's model exactly, safe houses in the United States have adopted a similar strategy. The first step at American shelters has been to give the battered woman time to adjust to the fact she is not going home, if this is what she has decided to do. Following this three to four week period, staff and other house residents help the battered woman take an inventory of her skills and decide what she will need to survive on her own. From the fourth to sixth week, efforts are aimed at helping the women take concrete steps toward reaching these short-term goals. Again, the primary goal has been to aid battered women in recognizing that they are competent individuals who can take care of themselves, and do not need to stay in an abusive relationship. Despite the drawbacks of women's shelters, such as crowding and a limited potential for educational or vocational training, the biggest problem has been that there are not enough safe houses in the United States and abroad to accommodate the thousands of battered women who have come forward.

Police Intervention

Intervening in domestic disputes is one of the most common and dangerous services that police officers are expected to provide (Bard, 1977; Stephens, 1977). The FBI uniform Crime Report (1974) indicated that 27.5 percent of the nation's police officers were assaulted while answering domestic complaints. Similarly, Straus, Gelles, and Steinmetz (1980) reported that as many police are killed answering domestic violence calls as are killed pursuing armed robbers. Paterson (1979) stated that more officers are killed and injured answering domestic complaints than any other type of call. Despite these hazards, techniques for dealing with domestic violence calls are rarely included in police recruit and in-service training programs (Bard, 1977).

Several reasons have been given to explain the failure of police departments to implement effective training programs and intervention procedures for dealing with marital violence. One problem has been overcoming the cultural bias of the criminal justice system which has traditionally viewed marital violence as a "personal" problem which should be settled privately between husbands and wives. Because wife-beating is classified as a "civil offense" in most states, officers cannot arrest abusive husbands on criminal charges unless they have done something like violate an order of protection. Another obstacle has been broadening the traditional role ascribed to police officers from that of "law enforcer" to one of "skillful mediator." While intervening in domestic disputes using verbal mediation has traditionally been left to social workers and other service providers, police officers are usually the ones who are called to manage domestic conflicts (Bard, 1971).

Although training procedures have often not prepared officers to handle marital disputes, studies in which officers have been trained in negotiation skills, (Bard, 1969; Bard, Zacker, & Rutter, 1972) have shown that applying such techniques to handling domestic violence calls reduces the amount of physical injury to the officers, reduces the likelihood of these problems recurring, and is received favorably by the couples who are helped. The main emphasis of these training programs has been to teach officers the interpersonal skills used in managing conflict situations (Bard, 1969; Goldstein, Monti, Sardino, & Green, 1979). Components of the training procedure have included didactic and experiential learning exercises which involve family crisis interactions. Officers role-play their responses to hypothetical intrafamilial disputes, and then receive feedback from other group members about how they have done. Some training programs have also included self-understanding workshops in order to sensitize the patrolmen to their own values, attitudes, and automatic responses. Utilizing these techniques in training a select group of officers from the New York City Police Department, Bard (1970) reported that there were no injuries to the officers who participated in the program during its 22 month operational phase. In addition, no homicides occurred among any of the 962 families seen by this specially trained unit. Similar findings were reported in another study conducted by Bard (1970) in which training was provided to a class of recruit officers. Such studies suggest that training police officers in the skills required to manage domestic conflicts could provide a valuable resource in controlling spouse abuse.

Legal Solutions

In recent years, the legal system's response to spouse abuse has gradually been improving. Several states have criminalized spouse abuse, and community dispute centers have developed as specialized agencies to handle domestic disagreements. Despite these changes, overcoming the cultural biases which have traditionally characterized the American criminal justice system has often been an obstacle in the development and implementation of effective legal policies which could control marital violence (Blair, 1979; Paterson, 1979). Although Wolfgang (1958) reported that 35-50 percent of all homicides are intrafamilial, marital violence is the only type of assault that is not considered a criminal offense.

Historically, the American legal system has viewed spouse abuse as a "personal" problem which should be handled privately between husbands and wives. One of the main problems of adopting this attitude has been the failure to criminalize wife-beating, which has created additional difficulties. Since spouse abuse is considered a civil offense, the wife cannot have her husband arrested unless he has violated an order of protection, or committed some felony or misdemeanor. Furthermore, unless the police officers enforce the order, the man will not be arrested. The reluctance of police officers to act in domestic disputes has been discussed in the previous section. Another problem which has developed from viewing marital violence as a "personal" problem and categorizing it as a civil offense has been the trial procedures for handling spouse abuse cases. Because marital violence is considered a civil offense, cases are usually brought before family court judges whose orientation has been to try to keep the family together by helping them obtain psychological aid to handle their "personal" differences. Instead of enforcing legal restraints, they have preferred utilizing tactics such as a "cooling off" period, psychiatric visits, and social counseling to repair the situation. In his review of the law's response to marital violence, Maidment (1977) stated that the courts are still hesitant to legislate criminal proceedings which they view only as a last resort.

While the legal system's historical orientation to spouse abuse has sometimes hindered the development and implementation of effective legal intervention in controlling spouse abuse, newly created policies and practices are beginning to change this situation.

One of the more innovative and successful techniques designed toward the goal of controlling marital violence has been the development of community dispute centers which help the district attorney's office in handling spouse abuse cases. The Miami Citizen Dispute Settlement Center (Miami, Dade County, Florida) has been a model for this type of program. Upon arrival at the state attorney's office, the complainant is preliminarily interviewed by a paralegal who immediately refers him/her to one of the intake counselors at the center. The complainant is then informed of all his/her legal remedies, and explained the mediation process by which the center operates. If he/she accepts, a mediation hearing will be arranged at which the position of the complainant and her/his assailant will be heard by a non-lawyer—a psychologist, sociologist, or other counseling specialist. After giving each party the opportunity to tell his/her version of the incident, the mediator helps the couple find a solution to their problem which is formalized in a written agreement. If this agreement is violated, the Center has the option to return it whole to the prosecutor, rehear it, or refer it to another court or social agency. In most cases in Dade County, only a rehearing has been required. Dellapa (1977) reported that, during its first year of operation, the Center had 94.9 percent successful resolution with a 4.1 percent recidivism rate. Other cities (New York; Columbus, Ohio; Kansas City, Mo.) have successfully implemented similar programs. Furthermore, these findings suggest that the development of community dispute centers in other cities could provide an effective legal intervention for controlling marital violence.

Psychological Treatments

Three main strategies have been employed in psychological interventions: (1) treating the battered woman, (2) treating the batterer, and (3) conjoint treatment. Methods for treating battered women have included individual and group psychotherapy. The primary goals of psychotherapy with abused wives have been to help the woman build or restore her self-esteem and sense of competency, recognize her feelings of anger and rage at being abused, and help her plan new life alternatives whether she decides to leave or remain in the battering relationship.

Because battered women tend to endorse many commonly held myths about wife-beating (e.g., the violence is "normal"; she deserves it for being bad or provocative), one of the techniques psychotherapists have used is to educate the women about the occurrence of spouse abuse. In addition to letting abused women know that they are not alone in their suffering as many of these women have been socially isolated, clinicians have helped battered women to improve their self-esteem by challenging their beliefs about the violent situation (e.g., violence is "not" normal; she is "not" the cause).

As battered wives begin to accept that they are not responsible for their husband's behavior and their self-esteem improves, feelings of anger and rage which have been denied often appear. These feelings should be discussed in therapy as well as used to reinforce the battered woman's developing belief that she is a worthwhile person who does not deserve to be abused. Lieberkneckt (1978) hypothesized that when a woman is beaten she goes through a grieving process in which she mourns the loss of her self-respect, hoped for love, etc. During the first stage, when she is unaware of her feelings of rage and remorse, he suggested that psychotherapists give the woman unconditional support without forcing her awareness of the situation. However, he remarked that, once the woman enters the second phase when she recognizes these feelings, the therapist should reinforce these feelings and help her to perceive new alternatives. In the final stage of treatment, therapists have helped women identify new life alternatives and plan concrete steps for approaching these goals (Lieberkneckt, 1978; Hilberman, 1980). Even for women for decide to remain with their partners, Walker (1979) noted that it is important for them to increase their self-esteem and overcome feelings of "helplessness" so that they can be appropriately independent or dependent within the relationship. Other therapeutic issues which have been identified as important in treating abused wives have been letting the battered woman progress at her own speed, avoiding sexist attitudes which would reinforce her feelings of victimization, accepting the patient's ambivalence about the battering relationship, and helping her to overcome her mistrust of the therapist and her own feelings.

In an article reviewing the effects of group psychotherapy on a select group of abused wives, Rounsaville, et al. (1979) reported that, of the six women who attended his 20-week treatment program regularly, none was abused by the end of the treatment. Despite the limited generalizability of Rounsaville's sample, his study was a step in the right direction, and suggests that group psychotherapy may be an effective treatment strategy for some abused women. The main elements of his therapeutic intervention involved utilizing a group format, and focusing group discussions on concrete aspects of the battering situation rather than individual psychodynamics. A group format was used to help the women overcome feelings of social stigmatization and to provide an alternate means of support while they were separated, at least psychologically, from their battering relationships. Discussions focused on concrete aspects of spouse abuse rather than individual psychodynamics and stressed the sociological aspects of spouse abuse (e.g., the social pressures on the women to stay married) in order to minimize the negative feelings the women might have about themselves, help them stop blaming themselves for the violence, and strengthen their feelings of competency. In general, the goals of the group were to help the women take charge of their lives and stop being abused in addition to giving up their psychological dependence on their abusive partners. For the women who remained in Rounsaville's group for its duration, these goals appear to have been reached.

With regard to abusive husbands, few psychological treatments have been developed and implemented to help battering men. One recent alternative which appears promising has been the development of a strategy for treating spouse-abusive men which involves their participation in a psychoeducational treatment program, (Rockland County, 1981; Rosenbaum, 1982). Employing a group format, workshops have been divided into two phases. During the first half, men are introduced to the basic skills which comprise this intervention. These skills have emphasized the illegitimate and damaging aspects of violent behavior in addition to stressing the attitude that marital violence is controllable behavior which can be changed. Initially, men are given the opportunity to ventilate their feelings and share their stories without the group leaders challenging them. As the workshop progresses, the group leaders use examples from the men's stories to illustrate the skills, and become increasingly more confrontive about challenging the men's attitudes about their behavior, such as continuing to insist that they are "out of control" or "she deserved it."

In the second half of the program, men are taught different ways of responding to potential violence-provoking situations. Initially, the men are taught to identify the cues that inform them that they are becoming angry, and to plan an alternate course of action they can take before they become violent, such as leaving the situation or calling another group member to help "talk them down" and defuse the tension. Other strategies that the men are taught to cope with potential violence-provoking situations have included relaxation-training or similar alternative forms of tension reduction (e.g., exercise), and improving communication with their wives so that mounting frustration may be addressed before it escalates into an episode of spouse abuse. Results from a preliminary study of participants in the Spouse Abuse Educational Workshop (Rockland County, N.Y.) indicated that, of the 29 men who were assessed at follow-up, 21 had stopped beating their wives. In addition, 24 of the 29 men sought ongoing psychological aid after the workshop ended. While these findings are limited by the generalizability of this sample to other groups of abusive men, the small number of participants, and the failure of 15 additional participants to respond to follow-up inquiries, they suggest that the men's psychoeducational workshop program may be successful in treating some maritally violent men.

Couples therapy has been a third approach used to control the occurrence of spouse abuse. Like programs employed with the men, interventions with violent couples have utilized behavioral techniques to help the couples control and change their behavior. Methods have included helping the couple identify cues that contribute to angry exchanges, having them develop an alternative plan of action (e.g., having one leave the situation) to prevent the conflict from developing into an episode of marital violence once the cues are identified, and helping them acquire and practice new problem solving strategies such as constructive communication and negotiation skills (Jacobson & Margolin, 1979; Margolin, 1979; Walker, 1979). Another element of most of these programs has been to have the couple increase the frequency of positive interactions between them by using contingent reinforcement plans, or arranging situations which will be mutually rewarding for both partners (e.g., love days). To overcome the initial resistance of abusive couples to accept responsibility for their problem, additional techniques have been designed. Walker (1979) starts her program by explicitly stating to the couple that the reason they need treatment is because he is a battering man and she is a battered woman. To communicate the same message, Margolin (1979) suggested that therapists emphasize that abusiveness is learned behavior by helping the couple to identify cues that elicit and maintain violent interactions, that abusiveness is a mutual problem by exploring the couple's history, and that abusiveness is related to poor problem solving skills. Once this initial barrier is eliminated, effective intervention can begin.

Other Services

Other service providers who have regular contact with victims and perpetrators of marital violence have included medical personnel, social workers, and various social service workers. Like other institutions, attitudes and policies endorsed by medical and social service agencies are starting to change to provide more effective intervention to control marital violence. As with other institutions, these agencies have frequently encountered resistance to the development and implementation of more effective intervention programs from the cultural biases associated with treating spouse abuse. One problem has been adopting a policy of noninvolvement because workers are reluctant to get involved in a situation which has traditionally been regarded as a "private" family matter. In discussing barriers to identifying and treating abused wives, Rounsaville (1978) commented that the failure of ordinary helping agencies such as social workers and medical personnel to provide adequate assistance to battered women has perpetuated the occurrence of wife-beating in the United States.

A second problem has been the influence of culturally stereotyped ideas about marital violence which have sometimes shaped the attitudes of medical personnel and social service workers. In a study of attitudes of service providers toward victims and perpetrators of spouse abuse, Davis and Carlson (1981) reported that traditional family service and medical personnel resort to characterological blame the most, hold both the victim and abuser most responsible, think that prevention is most difficult, and yet are most sympathetic. Their total sample was comprised of 499 respondents, and included workers from public welfare agencies (n = 88), police departments (n = 119), hospitals (n = 95), probation departments (n = 34), family service agencies (n = 122), domestic violence shelters and hotlines (n = 21), and family court judges (n = 20). Each participant received a brief scenario which depicted a woman presenting herself at an emergency room for treatment of injuries resulting from a beating inflicted by her husband. After reading the scenario, respondents were asked to assess how likely they thought each of the following factors played a role in what happened: the characters of the husband and the wife; behaviors of the husband and the wife occurring prior to the incident; and stressful events that occurred to the husband and wife prior to the incident. While traditional family service and medical personnel attributed responsibility for abuse to the characters of the husband and the wife, the factor which is probably most difficult to change, they were also the most sympathetic.

One way to help change this situation might be to educate medical personnel and social service workers about the causes of marital violence. In their investigation, Davis and Carlson (1981) also reported that service providers who had closer contact with victims and perpetrators of marital violence (e.g., shelter workers) were more likely to attribute the occurrence of marital violence to some action on the part of the husband and the wife, or stress. Without specialized training or direct contact with abusive partners, it appears less surprising that medical personnel and social service workers may endorse cultural myths about marital violence, such as attributing responsibility for the violent episode to personality problems on the part of the husband or wife (Davidson, 1978; Walker, 1979). Furthermore, in situations where personnel have been specifically trained to handle spouse abuse, they have reacted differently. Walker (1979) noted that emergency room staff who had been trained to identify battered women responded more efficiently. At the Denver General Hospital, a badly injured woman is immediately escorted into a private waiting room where a trained social worker assists her as soon as possible, and the nurse on duty assesses the severity of her injuries. If a nurse suspects battering, this is recorded on the patient's chart to alert other emergency room staff. She is directly asked if her injuries are due to physical abuse; and, whether or not she admits to being abused, she is given the telephone number of the nearest helping agency. If the injured woman says she was beaten, all reported details of the incident and the full descriptions of her injuries are reported on the chart, and may be used in future legal proceedings. With specialized training and instruction, medical personnel and social service workers could contribute to the effective control of spouse abuse.

Prescriptive Interventions

While battered women may share certain psychological attributes and situational conditions, recent studies have revealed significant differences in personality styles (Hanks & Rosenbaum, 1977; Snyder & Fruchtman, 1981) and coping responses (Gelles, 1976; Pfouts, 1978) between battered women. Similarly, investigations have shown that battered men have different personality styles despite some shared psychological characteristics (Elbow, 1977; Symonds, 1978), and accept varying degrees of responsibility for their violent behavior (Davidson, 1978). To the extent that abused wives and abusive husbands are psychologically different from their respective group members and deal with the battering situation in different ways, intervention methods should be chosen prescriptively to be responsive to these differences. Other factors which should also be considered in choosing an intervention program include the chronicity of the battering relationship, and the degree to which the situation is immediately life-threatening to the woman.

Regardless of personality differences or coping responses, the first prescriptiveness-relevant factor which should be addressed with any battered woman is her need for safety and shelter. If her life is in immediate danger, workers should help her find a safe refuge where she and her children can stay. Once this need is met, other tertiary prevention methods (e.g., psychological help, legal assistance) may be employed. For the woman who is not in immediate danger and is not requesting a place to stay, other prevention strategies may be recommended. With regard to differences in personality attributes, Steinmetz (1980) delineated two subtypes of battered wives: The "Saturday-Night Brawler" who is an active provocateur and participant in marital violence, and the "chronic-battered woman" who is a passive recipient of her husband's abuse. Based on this distinction, she suggested that different services should be provided to these two groups, with immediate safety and protection as the first goals in treatment with chronic-battered women since they are more likely to be fatally injured during these episodes.

Dividing battered women into five subtypes based on characteristics such as frequency and severity of abuse, usual precipitants, relationship stability, etc., Snyder and Fruchtman (1981) recommended prescriptive interventions according to subtype assignment. For Type I women for whom abuse was infrequent and occurred within a stable relationship, conjoint marital therapy in which a behavioral approach (e.g., Margolin, 1979) was utilized to control marital violence was recommended. For Type II and III women who experienced the most severe abuse, the investigators suggested educating these women about community resources and appropriate actions which they could take upon threat or occurrence of violence. For women who were unlikely to return to a battering relationship once violence had occurred, primarily Types III and IV women, interventions aimed more directly at helping these women establish their independence, such as finding independent domiciles, and obtaining vocational, educational, and legal counseling were recommended. In addition, it would seem important for Type IV women to get psychological aid and find shelter for their children, as they are the ones who are most likely to be abused by their mother's partners. Since Type V women are distinguished by an extensive history of violence in their family of origin and are most likely to accept it as a normal part of their lives, like other women who choose to remain with abusive partners, they may need to be informed about where to go to seek shelter from being beaten when violence apears imminent or has already occurred.

Davidson (1978) outlined three groups of intervention programs based on how the woman wanted to deal with the battering situation at the current time. Three types of battered wives were identified: (1) the woman who is resigned to her fate, (2) the woman who is anxious to change the wife-beater, but wants to remain in the marriage, (3) the woman who wants to get out, and change her own life. For women who were resigned to their fate, Davidson recommended several ways to help them cope with their situation. Suggestions ranged from having the women consider how they could respond differently to potential battering situations to prevent future abuse (e.g., remaining neutral, having someone over) to ways in which the women could improve themselves and increase their self-esteem such as building up their health, learning independence skills like handling their own finances, and becoming less dependent on material possessions for their security. Relaxation training or practicing meditation was recommended for tension reduction. With regard to the woman who was anxious to change the wife-beater, but wanted to stay in the marriage, Davidson suggested that these women speak to a trained counselor or someone like a good friend to help decide what they want to do about this situation. However, he cautioned these women that they must realize that, without some cooperation from their husbands, nothing they can do will significantly change their husbands' behavior. Other guidelines noted for these women included having them identify patterns in the violence so that they could try to avoid these situations, and having them talk with their husbands about the problems they are having to work on to change the situation. For women who want to change their lives and leave the battering relationship, Davidson recommended that they start by finding immediate help in a crisis shelter. In addition to obtaining temporary support while separating from their abusive partners, services provided by crisis shelters include helping abused women find independent living quarters, getting temporary income assistance, and receiving job training.

From a study of 35 violent families, Pfouts (1978) divided the coping responses of abused wives into four categories: (1) self-punishers, (2) aggressors, (3) early disengagers, and (4) reluctant late disengagers. He posited that the woman's decision to stay or leave the abusive situation was determined by whether or not the pay-off for remaining in the relationship was greater than the pay-off for leaving. For women who left (i.e., early disengagers, reluctant late), the benefits of leaving outweighed the benefits of staying. Although Pfouts did not suggest different intervention techniques according to this typology, such differences should be considered. Likewise, women who stay and resort to self-punishment as a coping mechanism will require a different type of intervention than those who stay and become aggressive.

Aside from her immediate decision about what to do, other factors which may influence her decision to remain or leave the battering relationship should also be addressed in selecting an intervention plan. Several studies have shown that one of the main reasons women stay in abusive relationships is because they lack the financial resources to leave their husbands (Gelles, 1976; Pfouts, 1978). Therefore, vocational training, higher education, or help in obtaining a job might be needed before the wife can be able to decide whether she wants to stay or leave. Gelles (1976) found that holding a job best differentiated between those wives who sought help and those who did not. The duration of the battering relationship may similarly affect the battered woman's decision making, and subsequent help-seeking behavior. Peretti and Buchanan (1978) reported that chronic and acute battered women gave different reasons for remaining with their abusive husbands. Chronic women said they stayed because they were concerned about their children, and felt dependent on the total marriage rather than their abusive husbands. On the other hand, acute battered women reported that they remained with their violent partners because they felt financially dependent on them, questioned their abilty to attract another man, and feared their husbands' retaliation if they tried to seek help from the police or others. Like other differences, these characteristics should be incorporated into the development and implementation of prescriptive treatment programs.

While investigators have found differences between battered men in psychological attributes and responses to the battering situation, prescriptive treatment programs have not been proposed. One important difference might be to separate those men for whom violence represents a skill deficit in problem solving capabilities from those who have alternative problem solving skills but have resorted to aggression as a response to increased situational stresses. For the first group of men, skill training in alternative problem solving skills such as constructive communication and negotiation might be most appropriate. For the second group of men, relaxation training or other stress management techniques in addition to helping them alter stressful life situations might be most therapeutic. Chronicity may be another significant factor, as over time men who use abuse as a coping mechanism although they have other problem solving skills may tend to lose these skills because they have not practiced them, and have replaced them with aggression as their primary coping technique. For these men, reeducation in nonaggressive problem solving strategies should also be included in their treatment. Although these differences may be used prescriptively, the primary goal of treatment programs with abusive husbands must be to stop their violent behavior. Once this objective is obtained, different methods for helping the men successfully maintain their nonviolent behavior may be implemented according to their individual needs.

Secondary Prevention

The main goal of secondary prevention programs has been to identify the occurrence of marital violence early in its development when it may be easier to successfully intervene. Although several methods exist which could be utilized to identify the occurrence of marital violence early in its development, they have frequently not been effectively employed. One method which might prove useful as a secondary prevention technique would be to routinely examine police records for families in which either of the spouses had been charged with domestic disturbance or assault. Results from a study by the Kansas City Police (1973) indicated that incidents of interpersonal assault and homicide were somewhat predictable, and might have been prevented if police and other service providers had intervened sooner. In 26.5 percent of the homicides and 37.3 percent of the assaults, police records showed that one of the participants had been arrested for disturbance or assault in the preceding two years. Records also indicated that in the two years prior to the domestic assault or homicide, police had been at the address of the disturbance at least once in 85.4 percent of the cases; and five or more times in 53.9 percent of the cases.

Another potential secondary prevention strategy would be rountine screenings by hospital and medical personnel when badly battered women present themselves for treatment. As Walker (1979) noted, hospital staffs can be trained to identify battered women, and this can facilitate earlier intervention in the development of this problem.

A third method which could be used to identify marital violence early in its development would be to routinely screen all families who come in contact with any of the service providing agencies (e.g., hospitals, mental health clinics, family protective services, courts and police, etc.) for individual and family characteristics which would predispose them to having these problems. These "high risk" families could be periodically monitored by service providers through telephone contacts, letters, or home visits so that when tension starts to build in these families, service providers could intervene prior to the onset of spouse abuse. Additionally, if they would screen for these families during their initial contacts with them, they could offer them services as soon as they were identified. The earlier the problem is treated, the more likely it is to be controlled. While this suggestion may seem overly idealistic, it is unfortunately true that the sooner intervention programs are implemented, the more likely they are to succeed. In Dade County at the community dispute center where marital violence cases receive immediate attention and prompt intervention, the recidivism rate is only 4.1 percent.

Primary Prevention

Primary prevention involves those set of methods which could potentially eliminate the occurrence of spouse abuse before it starts. These solutions are aimed at changing family and cultural values and practices which have perpetuated wife-beating. While impacting at this level may encounter the greatest resistance, it is unlikely that marital violence will be more frequently prevented unless family and cultural attitudes and practices which shape the development and maintenance of this problem are changed.

One step which should be taken immediately is to make spouse abuse a "criminal" offense (Gelles, 1982; Straus, 1980). Because most states regard spouse abuse as a "civil" offense, police and legal interventions have often been ineffective. Likewise, attitudes which promulgate the occurrence of wife-beating have been reinforced. If spouse abuse were criminalized, police officers, district attorneys, and judges would be required to respond differently. Similarly, changes in legal policies might facilitate changes in cultural values which would strengthen the position that spouse abuse is an "illegitimate" act.

Another focus of primary prevention involves changing the sexist structure of American society. Although this may be the hardest goal to achieve, it is a critical step in eliminating marital violence in the United States. Because American society has traditionally regarded women as second-class citizens and legitimized this attitude through policies endorsed by societal institutions, man's governing role in the family, and society at large, has been upheld. For men and women to have more equal roles at home so that women are not regarded as subservient and subject to their husbands' control, cultural practices outside the home must change. Men and women must receive more equal treatment under the law. They must have more equal opportunity within the employment sphere. Sex-role practices within the education system must also be altered. Socialization techniques which promote equal treatment between boys and girls must be culturally endorsed. Likewise, attitudes and policies which support eqalitarian roles in marital relationships must be implemented. Between making concrete policy changes and adopting values which regard men and women as equal, society can be a powerful agent in preventing spouse abuse.

If changes in cultural policies and attitudes seem radical and farreaching, primary prevention techniques which involve changes at the family level will be equally challenging. However, without these changes, the possibility of preventing marital violence in future generations may be impeded. As noted in an earlier section on violence and victimization as learned patterns of behavior from one's family of origin, the family has a critical role in shaping a child's predisposition to become involved in marital violence as an adult. Because children are malleable and are shaped by early direct and vicarious learning experiences (e.g., being physically punished, witnessing interparental abuse), family interactions which legitimize the use of violence and train children to hit the ones they love must gradually be eliminated. Sex-role stereotyping has often been identified as a factor in perpetuating learned patterns of violence and victimization. While this goal will also be difficult to achieve, children may have greater difficulty acquiring egalitarian sex-role behaviors and values if these behaviors and values are not practiced in their parental homes. On the other hand, if children can develop egalitarian sex-role attitudes and practices from direct and vicarious learning experiences within their families, perhaps they will have a better chance of not becoming the next generation of adults involved in marital violence.

In addition to gradually changing family practices and values which may have an important role in shaping the development of marital violence, cultural attitudes and values which legitimize the use of violence must similarly be revised. Again, these solutions may appear overly idealistic and extremely resistant to change, but if societal policies and attitudes could possibly begin to approximate these reforms such changes might facilitate the prevention of marital violence. At the government level, policies which legitimize the use of violence could be replaced with practices which promote the use of nonviolent alternatives. More specifically, these reforms could include supporting nuclear arms limitations, advocating domestic disarmament by passing stricter gun control legislation, and supporting laws which would prohibit the use of corporal punishment in schools. Aside from governmental reforms, changes in policies endorsed by the mass media could provide another technique for reducing the cultural legitimization of employing violence to obtain desired goals. Although restrictions on the portrayal of violence would be left to media personnel, any reduction in their depiction of violence as a legitimate problem-solving strategy would be facilitative.

Other primary prevention methods have included public awareness campaigns, women's advocacy groups, and techniques aimed at modifying the situational pressures which contribute to spouse abuse. To facilitate attitudinal and policy changes which could lead to the ultimate prevention of marital violence, public awareness campaigns have been employed by women's advocacy groups, social scientists, and media personnel (Gelles, 1982). In the past 10 years, these groups have brought the subject of spouse abuse out in the open. Without these national information campaigns, it is unlikely that current changes in values and policies regarding marital violence would have occurred. While women's advocacy groups have contributed to primary prevention efforts by helping disseminate information on spouse abuse, they have similarly promoted the elimination of marital violence by advocating equal rights for women.

A final primary prevention technique which has been recommended is to try to directly modify the situational stressors which facilitate the development of marital violence. This approach has been incorporated into intervention programs which have involved reducing unemployment, helping with family planning, and other techniques aimed at directly changing situational stressors.

FUTURE PERSPECTIVES

In the past decade, social scientists have developed a fairly good understanding of the dynamics of marital violence. However, intervention programs aimed at preventing and controlling this significant psychological and social problem have been less in evidence. While controlled research on the etiological factors associated with spouse abuse is still needed, other research areas should be investigated to facilitate the development and implementation of effective control and prevention techniques.

One approach could be longitudinal research to monitor children who are at "high risk" for becoming maritally violent as adults, and observe which factors contribute most to the development of this problem. Similarly, "high risk" families could be observed across time in order to identify the variables most strongly related to the onset of episodes of spouse abuse. If some of the factors related to the occurrence of spouse abuse can be identified, then it may be possible to design treatment approaches which incorporate techniques for changing these factors. However, it may not be easy to isolate these variables due to the previously mentioned problems associated with investigating marital violence.

An alternative strategy could be to examine the individual and family characteristics of people who are at "high risk" for becoming maritally violent, but do not become abusive husbands or abused wives. By studying these individuals, service providers might also learn what elements to use in planning intervention programs. In addition to investigating "high risk" populations, research on extant control and prevention techniques should be conducted. Studies on the efficacy of different intervention methods as well as studies isolating active treatment components should be employed. Likewise, investigations which identify "prescriptive" methods for treating different clients should be implemented.

Initially, improved intervention should be focused on providing shelter and safety for the battered women, and addressing their immediate financial, emotional, and legal needs. Similarly, immediate attention should be aimed at changing the attitudes of service providers who work with abused wives and abusive husbands, and developing and implementing programs for abusive men. Furthermore, programs need to be developed for treating children of maritally violent partners. By modifying current deficits in controlling marital violence, the foundation will be laid for implementing more long-term, farreaching prevention techniques. Although such methods will require changes in cultural values, revisions in the organization of the American family, and modifications in institutional practices, they are critical if greater prevention and control of marital violence is to be obtained.

Despite the radical nature of these solutions, the ethical considerations of not implementing effective control and prevention programs are equally extreme. Effective intervention in controlling and preventing marital violence must begin now, so that marital violence can be eliminated in future generations.

REFERENCES

Allen, C. & Straus, M. Resources, power, and husband-wife violence. In M. Straus and G. Hotaling (Eds.), *The social causes of husband-wife violence.* Minneapolis, Minn.: University of Minnesota Press, 1980, 94-114.

Ball, M. Issues of violence in family case work. *Social Casework,* 1977, *58,* 3-12.

Bard, M. Family intervention police teams as a community mental health resource. *The Journal of Criminal Law, Criminology and Police Science,* 1969, *60,* 247-250.

Bard, M. Training police as specialists in family crisis intervention. Washington, D.C.: U.S. Government Printing Office, 1970.

Bard, M. Family crisis intervention: From conceptualization to implementation. In M. Roy (Ed.), *Battered women: A psychosociological study of domestic violence.* New York: Van Nostrand Reinhold Co., 1977.

Bard, M., Zacker, J., & Rutter, E. Police family crisis intervention and conflict management: An action research analysis. Final report to National Institute of Law Enforcement and Criminal Justice, LEAA, U.S. Department of Justice, 1972.

Bass, D., & Rice, J. Agency responses to the abused wife. *Social Casework,* 1979, *60,* 338-342.

Beaulieu, L. Media, violence, and the family: A Canadian view. In Eekelaar, J. and Katz, S. (Eds.), *Family violence: An interdisciplinary study.* Toronto, Canada: Butterworth & Co., LTD., 1978, p. 58-68.

Blair, S. Making the legal system work for battered women. In D. Moore (Ed.), *Battered women*. Beverly Hills, Calif.: Sage Publications, 1979, 101-118.

Carlson, B. E. Battered women and their assailants. *Social Work*, 1977, *2*, 455-460.

Carroll, J. C. The intergenerational transmission of family violence: The long-term effects of aggressive behavior. *Aggressive Behavior*, 1977, *3*, 289-299.

Churchill, L., & Straus, M. Unpublished report. In M. Straus & G. Hotaling (Eds.), *The social causes of husband-wife violence*. Minneapolis, Minn.: University of Minnesota Press, 1980, Chapter 3.

Coleman, K. Conjugal violence: What 33 men report. *Journal of Marital and Family Therapy*, 1980, *6*, 207-213.

Coleman, K., Weinman, M. C., & Hsi, B. P. Factors affecting conjugal violence. *The Journal of Psychology*, 1980, *105*, 197-202.

Curtis, L. *Criminal violence: National patterns and behavior*. Lexington, Mass.: Lexington Books, 1974.

Davidson, T. *Conjugal crime*. New York: Hawthorne Books, 1978.

Davis, D. V., & Carlson, B. E. Domestic violence: Where does the fault lie? An attributional study of helping professionals' attitudes. Unpublished report, 1981.

Dellapa, F. Mediation and the community dispute center. In M. Roy (Ed.), *Battered Women: A psychosociological study of domestic violence*. New York: Van Nostrand Reinhold, 1977.

Dobash, R. E., & Dobash, R. *Violence against wives*. New York: Free Press, 1979.

Elbow, M. Theoretical considerations of violent marriages. *Social Casework*, 1977, *58*, 35-44.

Farrington, K. M. Stress and family violence. In M. Straus & G. Hotaling (Eds.), *The social causes of husband-wife violence*. Minneapolis, Minn.: University of Minnesota Press, 1980, 94-114.

Feldman, L. Marital conflict and marital intimacy: An integrative psychodynamic-behavioral-systemic model. *Family Process*, 1979, *18*, 69-78.

Frieze, I. Research on psychological factors in battered women. Portions from a National Institute of Mental Health grant proposal, November 1, 1976.

Gayford, J. J. Wife-battering: A preliminary survey of 100 cases. *British Medical Journal*, 1975, *1*, 94-97.

Gayford, J. J. Ten types of battered wives. *The Welfare Officer*, 1976, *25*, 5-9.

Gayford, J. J. The aetiology of repeated serious physical assaults by husbands on wives. *Medical Science and the Law*, 1979, *19*, 19-24.

Gelles, R. J. *The violent home*. Beverly Hills, California: Sage, 1974.

Gelles, R. Violence and pregnancy: A note on the extent of the problem and needed services. *Family Co-ordinator*, 1975, *24*, 81-86.

Gelles, R. J. Abused wives: Why do they stay? *Journal of Marriage and the Family*, 1976, *38*, 659-668.

Gelles, R. *Family violence*. Beverly Hills, Calif.: Sage Publications, 1979.

Gelles, R. J. Doestic criminal violence. In M. E. Wolfgang & N. A. Weiner (Eds.), *Criminal Violence*. Beverly Hills, Calif.: Sage, 1982.

Gerbner, G. & Gross, L. Violence profiles numbers 1-7: Trends in network television drama and viewer conceptions of social reality, 1967-1975. Philadelphia, Penn.: University of Penn., Annenberg School of Communications, 1976.

Gerson, L. W. Alcohol-related acts of violence: Who was drinking and where the acts occurred. *Journal of Studies on Alcohol*, 1978, *39*, 1294-1296.

Goldstein, A. P., Monti, P. J., Sardino, T. J., & Green, D. J. *Police crisis intervention*. New York: Pergamon Press, 1979.

Goldstein, A. P., & Rosenbaum, A. *Aggress-Less*. Englewood Cliffs, N. J.: Prentice Hall, 1982.

Goldstein, D. The relationship between self-esteem and marital violence: A study of spouse-abusive men. Masters thesis, 1982, submitted for publication.

Goode, W. J. Force and violence in the family. *Journal of Marriage and the Family*, 1971, *33*, 624-636.

Gullattee, A. C. Spousal abuse. *Journal of the National Medical Association*, 1979, *71*, 335-344.

Hanks, S. E., & Rosenbaum, C. P. Battered women: A study of women who live with violent alcohol-abusing men. *American Journal of Orthopsychiatry*, 1977, *47*, 291-306.

Hilberman, E. Overview: The "wife-beater's wife" reconsidered. *American Journal of Psychiatry,* 1980, *137,* 1336-1347.

Hilberman, E., & Munson, K. Sixty battered women: A preliminary report. Paper presented at the meeting of the American Psychiatric Association, Toronto, 1977.

Hilberman, E., & Munson, K. Sixty battered women. *Victomology: An International Journal,* 1978, *2,* 460-470.

Hornung, C. A., McCullough, C., & Sugimoto, T. Status relationship in marriage: Risk factors in spouse abuse. *Journal of Marriage and the Family,* 1981, 675-692.

Jacobson, N. S., & Margolin, G. *Marital therapy: Strategies based on social learning and behavior exchange theory.* New York: Brunner/Mazel, 1979.

The Kansas City, Missouri Police Department. Domestic violence and the police. Unpublished report, 1973.

Kelley, C. M. Federal Bureau of Investigation, 1974, *Uniform Crime Reports.* Washington: Government Printing Office, 1974.

Levinger, G. Sources of marital dissatisfaction among applicants for divorce. *American Journal of Orthopsychiatry,* 1966, *26,* 803-897.

Lieberkneckt, K. Helping the battered wife. *American Journal of Nursing,* 1978, *4,* 654-656.

Maidment, S. The laws' response to marital violence in England and the USA. *International and Comparative Law Quarterly,* 1977, *26,* 403-444.

Margolin, G. Conjoint marital therapy to enhance anger management and reduce spouse abuse. *American Journal of Family Therapy,* 1979, *4,* 3-24.

Markovitch, A. Refuges for battered women. *Social Work Today,* 1976, *7,* 34-35.

Martin, D. *Battered wives.* San Francisco: Glide, 1976.

Moore, D. M. (Ed.) *Battered women.* Beverly Hills, Calif.: Sage, 1980.

Nichols, B. B. The abused wife problem. *Social Casework,* 1976, *57,* 27-32.

O'Brien, J. E. Violence in divorce prone families. *Journal of Marriage and the Family,* 1971, *33,* 692-698.

Paterson, E. J. How the legal system responds to battered women. In D. Moore (Ed.), *Battered women.* Beverly Hills, Calif.: Sage, 1979, 79-100.

Peretti, P. O., & Buchanan, M. Psycho-socio-behavioral variables of encuring chronic and acute battered wife roles. *Psychologia: An International Journal of Psychology in the Orient,* 1978, *21,* 63-69.

Pfouts, J. H. Violent families: Coping responses of abused wives. *Child Welfare,* 1978, *57,* 101-111.

Pizzey, E. *Scream quietly or the neighbors will hear.* London: Penguin Books, 1974.

Pogrebin, L. C. Do women make men violent? *Ms,* 1974, *3,* 49-55.

Prescott, S., & Letko, C. Battered women: A social-psychological perspective. In R. Roy (Ed.), *Battered women.* New York: Van Nostrand Reinhold, 1977, 72-96.

Rockland County. The men's psychoeducational workshops training program. Rockland County, New York, 1981, unpublished manuscript.

Rosenbaum, A., & O'Leary, K. D. Marital violence: Characteristics of abusive couples. *Journal of Consulting and Clinical Psychology,* 1981, *49,* 63-71.

Rosenbaum, A. The men's educational workshops training manual. Syracuse University: Syracuse, New York, 1982, unpublished manuscript.

Rounsaville, B. J. Battered wives: Barriers to identification and treatment. *American Journal of Orthopsychiatry,* 1978, *48,* 487-494.

Rounsaville, B., Lifton, N., & Bieber, M. The natural history of a psychotherapy group for battered women. *Psychiatry,* 1979, *42,* 63-77.

Scott, P. Battered wives. *British Journal of Psychiatry,* 1974, *120,* 433-441.

Seligman, M. Chapter in Maser, J. and Seligman, M. (Eds.), *Psychopathology.* San Francisco: W. H. Freeman & Co., 1977.

Snyder, D. K., & Fruchtman, L. A. Differential patterns of wife abuse: A data-based typology. *Journal of Consulting and Clinical Psychology,* 1981, *49,* 878-885.

Star, B. Patterns of family violence. *Social Casework,* 1980, *61,* 339-346.

Stark, R., & McEvoy, J. Middle class violence. *Psychology Today,* 1970, *4,* 52-65.

Stein, A. & Frederich, L. *The impact of TV on children and youth.* Chicago: University of Chicago Press, 1975.

Steinmetz, S. K. *The cycle of violence: Assertive, aggressive and abusive family interaction.* New York: Praeger, 1977.

Steinmetz, S. K. Women and violence: Victims and perpetrators. *American Journal of Psychotherapy,* 1980, *3,* 334-349.

Steinmetz, S. K., & Straus, M. A. *Violence in the family.* New York: Harper & Row, 1974.

Stephens, D. Domestic assault: The police response. In M. Roy (Ed.), *Battered women: A psychosociological study of domestic violence.* New York: Van Nostrand Reinhold Co., 1977.

Straus, M. A. A general systems theory approach to a theory of violence between family members. *Social Science Information,* 1973, *12,* 105-125.

Straus, M. Leveling, civility, and violence in the family. *Journal of Marriage and the Family,* 1974, *36,* 13-29.

Straus, M. A. Normative and behavioral aspects of violence between spouses: Preliminary data on a nationally representative USA sample. Unpublished manuscript, University of New Hampshire, 1977, 1978.

Straus, M. A. The marriage license as a hitting license: Evidence from popular culture, law and social science. In M. Straus and G. Hotaling (Eds.), *The social causes of husband-wife violence.* Minneapolis, Minn.: University of Minnesota, 1980.

Straus, M. A., Gelles, R. J., & Steinmetz, S. K. *Behind closed doors: Violence in the American family.* Garden City, New York: Anchor Press, 1980.

Straus, M. A., & Hotaling, G. T. (Eds.), *The social causes of husband-wife violence.* Minneapolis, Minn.: University of Minnesota Press, 1980.

Symonds, M. The psycho-dynamics of violent-prone marriages. *American Journal of Psychoanalysis,* 1978, *38,* 213-222.

Ulbrich, P., & Huber, J. Observing parental violence: Distribution and effects. *Journal of Marriage and the Family,* 1981, *43,* 623-631.

U.S. Department of Justice. Intimate victims: A study of violence among friends and relatives. Washington, D. C.: Government Printing Office, 1980.

Walker, L. E. *The battered woman.* New York: Harper & Row, 1979.

Walker, L. E. Battered women: Sex-roles and clinical issues. *Professional Psychology,* 1981, *12,* 81-91.

Wolfgang, M. E. Victim-precipitated criminal homicide. *Journal of Criminal Law, Criminology and Police Science,* 1957, *48,* 1-11.

Wolfgang, M. E. *Patterns in criminal homicide.* New York: John Wiley, 1958.

Zubin, J. & Spring, B. Vulnerability—A new view of schizophrenia. *Journal of Abnormal Psychology,* 1975, *86,* 103-126.

3

Violence in School

Berj Harootunian
and
Steven J. Apter

The focus of this chapter is aggression in schools, directed toward either people or property. While student misbehavior has been part of the folklore of the American school, it should be clear that we are not concerned with the usual types of student pranks and mischief but, rather, on the escalation of school violence that has taken place both quantitatively and qualitatively since 1960. As Rubel (1977) has noted, the fights between students have changed from words and fists to aggravated assault with lethal weapons. The rapid escalation of violence in school, particularly between the years 1960 and 1975, mirrors the rise in crime in the larger community.

The Safe School Report issued in 1975 by the Senate Subcommittee chaired by Senator Bayh presented survey data from 750 school districts. The results showed that between 1970 and 1973 homicides increased by 18 percent, rapes and attempted rapes increased by 40 percent, robberies increased by 37 percent, assaults on students increased by 85 percent, assaults on teachers increased by 77 percent, burglaries in school increased by 12 percent, and the number of weapons confiscated by school personnel increased by 54 percent. The dramatic increase in violence is evidenced by the number of assaults on teachers over time; there were 15,000 in 1955; 41,000 in 1971; 63,000 in 1975; and 110,000 in 1979. This sharp increase vis-à-vis teachers has added the term the "battered teacher syndrome"—a combination of stress reactions including anxiety, depression, disturbed sleep, eating disorders, elevated blood pressure, and headaches—to the lexicon of aggression.

Although attacks on teachers are illustrative of the violence problem in schools, it should be stressed that the vast majority of aggressive incidents are directed toward other students. McDermott (1979) found that 78 percent of personal victimizations in schools (assaults, larcenies, rapes, and robberies) were against students. Ianni (1978), in his study of the correlates of aggression, reports that students at about age 13 run the greatest risk of physical attack, with seventh graders most likely to be subject to attack and twelfth graders least likely. The majority (58 percent) of attacks involve victims and attackers of the same race; 42 percent are interracial.

Other correlates of school violence include such variables as style of leadership and governance of the school—firm, fair, and consistent style is linked to lower aggression while arbitrary, severe leadership tends to be associated with high levels of aggression; school size—the larger the school or unit of instruction, the higher the incidence of aggression; size of community—large cities have a higher proportion of schools reporting violence, while suburban and rural schools follow with fewer.

Aggression toward school property has revealed an increase similar to the increase in violence toward persons. School vandalism increased tremendously throughout each year of the 1970s through the middle of the decade and then leveled off at a very high plateau (Casserly, Bass & Garrett, 1980; Inciardi, 1978; Rubel, 1977). The price of vandalism for the schools went from $100 million in 1969 to $600 million in 1977. While school enrollments increased 86 percent between 1950 and 1975, school arson increased 859 percent, or ten times as much (Rubel, 1977). Even when the effect of inflation is discounted, the school arson costs increased by 179 percent.

Over the years, school vandalism has become a more egalitarian act. Today, the school vandal is just as likely to be middle class as lower class (Howard, 1978), white as non-white (Goldmeir, 1974), and (for some acts like graffiti) female as male (Richards, 1976). School vandals tend to be between 11 and 16 years old (Ellison, 1974); are frequently truant (Greenberg, 1974); have been held back a grade or more (Nowakowski, 1966); often have been suspended from school (Yankelovich, 1975); but on formal psychological evaluations demonstrate no more disturbance than students who do not vandalize (Richards, 1976).

Vandalism tends to be higher in older schools or schools with obsolete facilities and low staff morale (Greenberg, 1969) as well as schools with higher teacher turnover rates (Leftwich, 1977). A number of other characteristics are also related to the incidence of vandalism—community crime level such as geographic density of students, number of nonstudent intruders present in the school, and the nature of family discipline.

We have presented the above outline of school violence to emphasize that it is a real, ongoing problem confronting America's schools. Actually, the problem may even be more severe than the data indicate. Inconsistent or unclear definitions of violence and vandalism, poor or nonexistent records, unwillingness to report acts of aggression, variations in reporting procedures, and school administrator concern with appearing inadequate all contribute to lower estimates and reports of aggressive incidents. In fact, Ban and Ciminello (1977) have estimated that actual levels of school aggression may be 50 percent higher than reported.

In the rest of this chapter, we briefly note some of the theoretical explanations of crime by school-age youngsters. We follow that by reviewing various perspectives of the school's role vis-à-vis aggression and violence. In turn, we then consider a number of aggression-reduction approaches the school might employ; specific strategies which teachers and school personnel might apply in dealing with disruptive individuals; the context of violence beyond the school; and, finally, what currently can be gleaned from the many experiences, programs, and writings that have as their goal the reduction, if not the elimination, of violent behavior in schools.

HYPOTHESES FOR YOUTH CRIME

In their review of research on crime in schools, McPartland and McDill (1977) identified five major themes in theories of youth crime:

1. The theme of *restricted opportunity* emphasizes the barriers many young people must hurdle to achieve the good jobs, material possessions, and status that symbolize the American dream. In this view, criminal acts represent youngsters' frustrations with the system which holds them back, and schools are easily identifiable targets.
2. The theme of *subcultural differences in values and attitudes* is based on the notion that sub-

cultures exist in which middle-class values and aspirations are rejected and crime and violence are a fact of life. In such neighborhoods and communities, residents are continually
exposed to violent behaviors, and the supports needed to combat such actions can deter-
iorate rapidly.

3. A third theme, *prolonged adolescent dependence,* is based on the contradictory experience of most teenagers in America today. While most adolescents have the ability to take
on adult responsibilities and the desire to be autonomous, society seems to provide no
place for their contributions. The resulting frustration may be expressed in delinquent behaviors designed to demonstrate independence.

4. The fourth theme states that *seriously damaged personalities,* more than environmental
and societal conditions, are the basis for the most serious criminal behaviors among youth.
Delinquency, in this view, is the expression of the individual's inability to control his own
aggressive and antisocial impulses. Youngsters who commit violent criminal acts are probably seriously emotionally disturbed.

5. Finally, according to the theme of *labeling and stereotyping,* youngsters may come to view
themselves as criminal or delinquent or "bad" because others in authority continually communicate that image to them. Such a process may be viewed as an example of a self-fulfilling prophecy where the imposition of a label sets in motion a chain of events that validate
the label or stereotype.

While McPartland and McDill note that the first three themes above (restricted opportunity,
subcultural differences, and prolonged adolescent dependence) are primarily sociological in
nature and the last two themes (seriously damaged personalities, and labeling and stereotyping) more psychologically-based, each of the five themes rasies a range of potential intervention strategies. While interventions may occur at the community or school or program level,
the predominant tendency has been to intervene with problematic individuals. Over the
years, schools have developed a variety of formats for dealing with those children and youth
who have been involved in school episodes of violent behavior.

Such individual-centered interventions range from the provision of academic support services and the development of diagnostic-prescriptive learning centers to disciplinary policies of
full or partial exclusion. For the most part, however, interventions aimed at individuals consist
of assignment to special education programs and teachers, and implementation of a variety of
counseling and behavior modification strategies. We consider these in somewhat more detail
below, but let us first examine the relationship between the school and violent behavior.

THE ROLE OF THE SCHOOL

There is considerable controversy about whether the school provokes or ameliorates aggressive behavior. Gold (1978) believes that the school controls the major social and psychological forces that create delinquency and, consequently, is a "significant provoker of delinquent
behavior [p. 307]." The findings of Elliott and Voss (1974) are in agreement with Gold. They
carried out a longitudinal study of school behavior and its relationship to delinquency and
dropout, and maintain that "the school is the critical generating milieu for delinquency [p.
203]." According to Elliott and Voss, the school fosters in one setting all of the necessary conditions for aggressive or disruptive behavior. The school categorizes students as failures or
successes soon after their arrival and makes their failure obvious to themselves and others.
Delinquency and aggression in school is a way for these youngsters to save face and defend
themselves from such humiliations.

Polk and Schafer (1972) also attribute the bases for delinquent and violent behavior to the schools. They argue that the organizational structure of most American schools ensures students who will fail and who will be discipline problems, especially students from low-income families. Polk and Schafer conclude that commitment to violent behavior by youth results from negative school experiences.

Elliott and Voss (1974) found that dropouts had a higher rate of police contacts while in school than graduates, but their police contacts declined to a lower rate than graduates after dropping out of school. This finding is crucial to the argument of those who regard the school as a contributor to the violence problem. Additional evidence by Frease (1973) and Kelly (1975) on tracking systems used in secondary schools suggests that organizational structures used by educational institutions such as tracking may be at the root of disruptive and delinquent behavior. Frease (1973) indicates that students in low academic tracks become more and more unhappy with and less committed to school and develop more associations with peers who are predelinquent or delinquent. Kelly (1975) reported that school pretracking position was the best predictor of delinquent behavior when the effects of such variables as achievement in school, sex, and socioeonomic status were controlled. In summary, individuals who maintain that the school is the principal cause of aggression argue that children almost from the start of their schooling become labeled as "losers" by teachers, administrators, and other youngsters and end up fulfilling that expectation.

Hyman (1979) has noted that the public response to children's misbehavior in America seems to be growing increasingly more punitive. Whether this attitude is a cause or an effect of the often noted finding that *discipline* seems to be the most frequent public response to the question, "What is the major problem in schools today?" is unclear. What is clear is that youngsters run a great risk of being hurt in school and the hurt is not always administered by other children.

One unfortunate result of the American public's punitiveness may be the institutional acceptability of the hitting of children. The Supreme Court's refusal to provide children with constitutional protection from paddling is, in Hyman's view and in ours, another contributing factor to increased levels of school violence. Thus, despite the fact that considerable evidence refuting the use of corporal punishment exists in the psychological literature, we have now legitimized such actions by school personnel. The end result of such a policy may very well turn out to be *increased* levels of school violence by youngsters.

The literature on child abuse is expanding rapidly, and elsewhere in this volume an extended discussion of that topic is available. Our interest in school violence, however, demands closer inspection of the relationship between the physical mistreatment of children and their eventual involvement in aggression against persons or property.

What are the effects of the use of "corporal punishment" on misbehaving youngsters in schools? *The Last Resort* is a newsletter devoted to discussion of just such questions. In one recent issue (May/June 1981), articles reprinted from U.S. newspapers described the following incidents:

- A Florida teacher accused of pulling children's teeth and taking crutches away from an injured youngster.
- Two Virginia junior high students who required emergency room treatment after being beaten on the heads with a stick by an angry teacher.
- A Colorado teacher who was finally dismissed after 29 incidents of violence against students that occurred over a 10-year period.
- An Alaska father who filed a criminal complaint against a teacher who paddled and severely bruised his son.

- The (unsuccessful) fight against corporal punishment by parents of youngsters in a Delaware school district.
- An Ohio first-grader who spent parts of four consecutive days isolated in a 5' by 5' closet as punishment for misbehavior. The boy's father consented to the punishment which the principal described as an effort to avoid further corporal punishment (the child had already been paddled several times).
- Reviews of corporal punishment policies in a number of school districts.
- Parents who decided to leave an Arkansas community after a school paddling left a 4 by 6 inch welt on their son's backside.
- Successful attempts to replace corporal punishment by discipline based on the work ethic in a Florida junior high school and by a written policy of assertive discipline in an Ohio middle school.

If corporal punishment by a parent in the home can result in aggressive acts by youngsters in school and community, can we believe that the same punishment inflicted by school authorities won't have similar results? Schools have some responsibility for providing appropriate and effective models of intervention for their communities. Many parents "go along" with school policies of corporal punishment even when they approach physical and psychological child abuse, because teachers and administrators are professionals and "must know what's right for children."

Further, often physical punishment is used on those children who are least likely to benefit and most likely to learn the wrong lesson; that if you're bigger, force is an appropriate intervention to get what you want. The public perception of the need for "old fashioned discipline" may be the major factor in the continual acceptance of a situation that frequently leads to the abuse of children and an increase in school violence. The line between corporal punishment and physical abuse is very easily transgressed. Children do not have the same protections against transgressions as incarcerated criminals do in prisons. In an editorial titled "Regents Buckle on Spanking," the *New York Times* (March 15, 1980) decried the New York State Board of Regents decision (by a 7 to 6 vote) to favor corporal punishment in schools. The decision was a reversal of an earlier vote that would have urged repeal of corporal punishment legislation, came after increased evidence of the dangers of school-paddling policies, and would have no impact on teacher's rights to self-defense, according to the *Times*. Further, the editorial noted that

> The victims, as studies show, are almost never muscular, undisciplined adolescents; they are young children. Are children, then, not now safeguarded against abuse? Some insist they are protected. But as Regent Kenneth Clark, the distinguished psychologist, says, "There is no lobby for the children. They are subject to the degree of stability or instability of the particular individual responsible for them at that moment."

Others who have examined the problem of school violence take a different perspective. They maintain that the school, while an important factor, is not the main source of disruption and delinquency. McPartland and McDill (1977) concluded that the school contributes to student aggression but is not the source of the problem. Feldhusen and his colleagues concur with this viewpoint (Feldhusen, Aversano, & Thurston, 1976; Feldhusen, Roeser, & Thurston, 1977; Feldhusen, Thurston, & Benning, 1973). For eleven years through testing, interviews, and behavioral measures, they collected and analyzed data on over 1,500 children who could be categorized as showing persistent prosocial or disruptive behavior in Grades 3, 6, or 9. Feldhusen and his associates reported that school related factors were not as important as family variables in differentiating the prosocial and aggressive children. They also note that delinquency can be predicted over the long term with considerable accuracy by such variables as the teachers' original assessments of behavior, sex, and IQ.

The Bayh Subcommittee Report (Bayh, 1977) provides still another view of the role of schools. Gangs use schools as their base of operations and recruiting, drug sales, extortion, robberies, and meetings all take place within the school, especialy in big-city schools. Some of the aggressive behavior by these gangs is not necessarily for material gain (McPartland & McDill, 1977) and may be an extension of street-corner norms and behavior into the school (Foster, 1974). Neill (1978) believes that gangs currently are at the root of fear among teachers and students; and Latin gangs, in particular, are the most serious problem confronting big-city schools.

In sum, the school provides gangs an accessible target of opportunity to carry out all of their activities with relatively little risk. But this role obviously makes the school a victim rather than the source of violence as noted earlier. More importantly, violence and aggression are not the sole province of low-income, inner-city, or minority students. As we noted at the beginning of this chapter, the increase in school-related aggressive behavior has occurred in urban, suburban, and rural schools—schools in which gangs are difficult to find.

Wenk (1975) provides yet another perspective on school violence. He believes the increase in disruptive behavior in schools is a reflection of the disparity between society's greater complexity and instability and the maintenance of school programs intended for and geared to a simpler, more predictable world.

Any examination of violence in school would be incomplete without explicit consideration of learning disabilities and learning problems. Zimmerman and his colleagues (1978) have posed the question succinctly by asking, "Is it possible that children are sentenced in court not because of what they did on the streets, but because of what they could not do in the classroom? [p. 20]." Among deliⁿquent youth, estimates of the extent of learning disabilities range as high as 73 percent (Zimmerman et al., 1978). Rector, Barth and Ingram (1980) describe the school's response to such youth as follows:

> An acting-out child can be seen as disruptive by a teacher who then treats the child accordingly. While this may be an indication of learning disability or of a learning problem, the child may be labeled as disruptive. This affects the child's self-esteem, which can already be affected by his inability to understand or control his behavior. Not only does he feel incompetent, but he is perceived as incompetent by others. The result can be rejection, alienation, and hostility. The end product can be delinquency. [p. 129]

Regardless of the many sources and explanations of disruptive behavior, it is still the school in the end that must cope with aggression, work with violent youth, and provide alternatives to detention and institutionalization. There is reason for some optimism in even the most difficult situations. The New York City public schools recently reported reading and mathematics scores above national norms for the first time in years. School crime such as assaults, narcotics, and arson also declined between 1977 and 1982; but weapon possession, robbery, larceny, and sex offenses increased over the same time period (Maeroff, 1982).

In the next section of this chapter, we want to look specifically at some strategies or changes which the school might employ to reduce crime. Since most of these suggestions are based on intuitive or theoretical positions rather than on accumulation of evidence, they should be thought of as guides for decisions by schools and should not necessarily be construed as hard and fast rules with wide-ranging generalizability. Their applicability will depend on the particular type and level of problem confronting the school, the human and material resources available to the school, and perhaps, most crucially, on the willingness of the school to be open to alternatives which involve change to some degree.

PROGRAMS FOR PREVENTION AND REMEDIATION

Every school desires to prevent and remediate violent and disruptive student behavior. In a sense, there are at least as many programs to counter violence in the schools as there are schools. Indeed, in some communities there are probably more programs than school systems, since some have several different efforts underway. Los Angeles, for example, has more than forty programs to combat violence in the schools (Marvin, McCann, Connolly, Temkin & Henning, 1977).

Probably the majority of programs to curb aggression in schools is based on intuitive insights rather than research evidence and has undergone no systematic evaluation (Feldhusen, 1979). These programs, as a rule, all report some degree of success and may vary considerably. One type is exemplified by Van Avery (1975) who implemented a "humanitarian"program at the high school level in Sarasota, Florida. The program revolved around the collaboration of students, teachers and staff, administration, parents, school board, and community in the enforcement of school rules. According to Van Avery, no violence occurred and complaints about student behavior were minimal.

But approaches to the treatment of violence from a very different perspective also yield positive results. For example, a "law and order" approach (Wint, 1975) in Wyandach, New York, emphasized strict discipline, rules, quiet classrooms, and the learning of basic skills. The principal was in charge and supported teachers; on the first day of school rules were made clear and explicit; and misbehaving students were punished quickly and consistently. Once full of violence and disorder, the school after three years was described as "peaceful and well-organized."

In their survey of school programs designed to combat violence, Marvin and his colleagues (Marvin et al., 1977) found that: 1) each of these programs is tailored to the individual needs of the particular school; 2) many different approaches have been attempted; 3) many of these programs seem to reduce violence and disruption in the schools; and 4) one of the major factors in the successful reduction of school violence appears to be close cooperation among school personnel, outside community agencies, parents, students, and the community at large.

A factor that might be a crucial antecedent to any successful program to counter school violence and one not specified by Marvin et al. (1977) may be the explicit recognition that there is an aggression problem in the school. It may be that schools which initiate special programs to reduce disruption and violence have acknowledged and defined a problem that needs attention. The reason why most programs designed to reduce school violence are reported as successes may be less a matter of what they do and more a result of the fact that they do *something*.

Support for this thesis can be found in Duke's (1978) survey of 100 randomly selected high schools in New York and 100 in California. Urban and nonurban high school administrators responded by identifying their three most severe discipline problems as skipping class, truancy, and lateness to class. Data on teachers, on the other hand, suggest classroom disruption, fighting, and disrespect for teacher authority as the most pressing problems. It is noteworthy that administrators ranked fighting, disruption, drug use, and profanity among the least important discipline problems in school. Duke believes that students would rate theft and fighting as their most serious problems. In his words:

> If my speculations concerning teacher and student perceptions of the most pressing discipline problems are accurate, it becomes somewhat more understandable why a "crisis" in school discipline seems to exist. *Each of the three major role groups involved in high schools is concerned primarily about a different set of discipline problems. Self-interest dictates priorities. [p. 326]*

Thus, the different perceptions of school violence may contribute to the difficulty of the problem. Resolving the differences and clearly defining the problem may be the most important step in reducing school disruptions.

In their survey of 137 programs to combat school violence, Marvin and his associates (1977) were able to classify and summarize the findings into four major categories: security systems, counseling services, curricular/instructional programs, or organizational changes. Security systems concentrate on the protection of staff and students from outsiders and from violence, vandalism, and other aggressive and criminal acts within the school. Counseling services provide intensive services for students in trouble or attempt to coordinate these services for such youth and their families between the school and other agencies. Curricular/instructional programs focus on helping disruptive students attain or develop skills through various specific curricula or instructional programs such as reading, mathematics, personal management, and conflict resolution. Organizational modifications have as their goal a change in the structure of the schools by making them more responsive to the problems and situations brought on by disruptive youngsters.

While most programs can be classified under these four headings, we have used another set of categories for differentiating attempted solutions to school violence and vandalism (Goldstein, Apter, & Harootunian, 1983). These nine categories together with specific examples of activities depicting each follow:

1. *Student oriented*—Diagnostic learning centers, regional occupational centers, part-time programs, academic support services, group counseling, student advisory committee; student patrols (interracial), behavior modification—contingency management, behavior modification—time out, behavior modification—response cost, bahavior modification—contracting, financial accountability, school transfer, interpersonal skill training, problem solving training, moral education, value clarification, individual counseling, more achievable reward criteria, identification cards, peer counseling, participation in grievance resolution, security advisory council, school safety committee.

2. *Teacher oriented*—Aggression management training for teachers; increased teacher-student nonclass contact; increased teacher-student-administration group discussions; low teacher-pupil relationship; firm, fair, consistent teacher discipline; self-defense training; carrying of weapons by teachers; legalization of teacher's use of force; compensation for aggression-related expenses; individualized teaching strategies; enhanced teacher knowledge of student ethnic milieu; increased teacher-parent interaction.

3. *Curriculum*—Art and music courses, law courses, police courses, courses dealing with practical aspects of adult life, prescriptively tailored course sequences, work study programs, equivalency diplomas, schools without walls, schools within schools, learning centers (magnet schools, educational parks), continuation centers (street academies, evening high schools), minischools, self-paced instruction, idiographic grading.

4. *Administrative*—Use of skilled conflict negotiators, twenty-four hour custodial service, clear lines of responsibility and authority among administrators, school safety committee,

school administration-police coordination, legal rights handbook, school procedures manual, written codes of rights and responsibilities, aggression management training for administrators, democratized school governance, human relations courses, effective intelligence network, principal visibility and availability, relaxation of arbitrary rules (regarding smoking, dressing, absences, etc.).

5. *Physical school alterations* — Extensive lighting program; blackout of all lighting; reduction of school size; reduction of class size; closed off isolated areas; increase staff supervision; implement rapid repair of vandalism targets; electronic monitoring for weapons detection; safety corridors (school to street); removal of tempting vandalism targets; recess fixtures where possible; install graffiti boards; encourage student-drawn murals; paint lockers bright colors; use ceramic-type, hard surface paints; sponsor clean-up, pick-up, fix-up days; pave or asphalt graveled parking areas; use plexiglass or polycarbon windows; install decorative grillwork over windows; mark all school property for identification; use intruder detectors (microwave, ultrasonic, infrared, audio, video, mechanical); employ personal alarm systems; alter isolated areas to attract people traffic.

6. *Parent oriented* — Telephone campaigns to encourage PTA attendance, antitruancy committee (parent, counselor, student), parenting skills training, parents as guest speakers, parents as apprenticeship resources, parents as work-study contacts, increased parent legal responsibility for their children's behavior, family education centers.

7. *Security personnel* — Police K-9 patrol units, police helicopter surveillance, use of security personnel for patrol, use of security personnel for crowd control, use of security personnel for intelligence gathering, use of security personnel for record keeping, use of security personnel for teaching (e.g., law), use of security personnel for counseling, use of security personnel for home visits, development of school security manuals.

8. *Community oriented* — Helping hand programs, restitution programs, adopt-a-school programs, vandalism prevention education, mass media publication of cost of vandalism, open school to community use after hours, improved school-juvenile court liaison, family-back-to-school week, neighborhood day, vandalism watch on or near school grounds via mobile homes, encourage reporting by CB users of observed vandalism, community education programs, more and better programs for disruptive/disturbed youngsters.

9. *State and federal oriented* — Establish uniform violence and vandalism reporting system; establish state antiviolence advisory committee; stronger gun control legislation; enhanced national moral leadership; better coordination of relevant federal, state, community agencies; stronger antitrespass legislation; more prosocial television programs; less restrictive child labor laws.

The problem of violence and delinquency is much greater than the school can manage alone in their current state. All of the attempts listed above are indicators that schools can begin to solve the problem of disruptive behavior in a variety of ways. The decision about which approach is most appropriate for a particular school will be a function not only of the nature of the violence in that school, but as well on how and by whom the problem is defined. What may be viewed as a problem of violence in one setting may in another setting be seen as "normal" or "acceptable" behavior. Parents' perspectives of misbehavior and disruption may vary considerably from the teachers' and, in turn, from the students' perspectives. Moreover, community characteristics will to a considerable degree reflect how disruptive behavior is labeled and consequently handled. Aggressive behavior in one setting may be viewed as a learning problem to be overcome, while in another it may lead to expulsion from school and more severe consequences. Clearly, aggression takes place in schools, but the problems and its solutions are not defined by the school alone or its boundaries.

BEYOND THE SCHOOL: AN ECOLOGICAL ANALYSIS

The problem of school violence may be "bigger" than the school context in which it occurs. In fact, the long-standing belief that outside-of-school interventions may have a very substantial impact upon in-school problems points to the critical need for schools to tie their programs to community needs and concerns if they are to effectively serve their students.

This broader view looks beyond the walls of the school for examples of strategies and techniques with potential positive impact on school violence. For instance, the community education movement represents one comprehensive attempt to forge formal and long-lasting school-community linkages. Other community programs that touch on the school violence issue include cooperative school/social agency efforts and a variety of models for developing home-school linkages.

The basis for this broader view of school violence may be found in the ecological perspective, developed in psychology by Kurt Lewin, Roger Barker, and others and utilized more increasingly in special education (see Apter, 1982; Hobbs, 1966, 1975, 1982). Instead of focusing only on individuals, ecologists are more interested in examining ecosystems: interaction systems comprised of living things and the nonliving habitat. Ecologists typically do not view inappropriate behavior as based in physical illness or located solely within a disruptive individual, but prefer to look at a disturbed ecosystem, in which disturbance can more profitably be viewed as a "failure to match."

The ecological orientation to troubled youngsters is based on the assumption that each child must be viewed as a complete entity surrounded by a unique minisocial system or ecosystem. When the various aspects of a child's system are working together harmoniously, ecologists say that the ecosystem is congruent or balanced, and the child appears to be "normal." On the other hand, when such congruence does not exist, the child is likely to be considered deviant (out of harmony with social norms) or incompetent (unable to perform purposefully in the unchanged setting). When this is the case, ecologists say that the system is not balanced; that particular elements are in conflict with one another. Such conflicts are termed "points of discordance"; specific places where there is a "failure to match" between the child and his/her ecosystem. According to ecologists, the search for solutions to the problem of inappropriate behavior, including the problem of school violence, must focus on these points of discordance and the resulting failure to match. Such a perspective raises a number of important implications, some of which are listed below.

1. Behavior must be viewed, at least in part, as culturally relative. Behavior that is "normal" in one environment may be viewed as deviant in a different behavior setting.
2. Interventions must focus on all elements of a given ecosystem—not only on the identified child.
3. Interventions must focus on the realities existent in a given ecosystem. While it is obviously difficult to change the environmental conditions which surround many of the youngsters involved in school violence, ignoring those conditions is not likely to reduce the level of aggression in schools.
4. Especially in schools where the focus for so long has been on changing the child to fit the system, this perspective advocates considerable change in program planning. For example, interventions can focus on changing adult behavior, creating new staff roles, developing new program formats, and working cooperatively with community agencies. Clearly, targeting intervention on the identified child is just one of many strategies.

The ecological view emphasizes the importance of *interactions*; which individuals at what particular points in time in which physical and psychological environments are prone to violence? Consequently, the ecological perspective can also emphasize a variety of targets for intervention; setting-focused as well as individual-focused.

There is some evidence for this interactionist point of view. Chess, Thomas, Rutter, and Birch (1963), for example, have studied the interaction of youngsters' temperament and environment in the production of behavioral disturbances. They concluded that temperament alone could not account for behavioral disturbances.

> Rather, it appears that behavioral disturbance as well as behavioral normality is the result of the interaction between the child with a given patterning of temperament and significant features of his developmental environment. Among these environmental features, intrafamilial as well as extrafamilial circumstances such as school and peer-group, are influential. [p. 147]

Parke (1979) points out that social-emotional development must be seen as having multiple causes and multiple sources of influence.

> The child is embedded in a variety of social systems and settings in which various agents shape the child's social-emotional development. These range from smaller immediate settings and systems such as the family or peer group, in which the child has considerable influence, to larger or more remote systems such as the school, the community, or the wider culture, over which the child has less control. [pp. 930-31]

The interaction (or lack thereof) between home and school may be an especially significant factor in school violence. For example, Walberg (1972) has noted that "a general propensity to be a delinquent and to be apprehended" is negatively associated with frequency of school talks with parents, frequency of family outings, and the amount of scheduled study time [p. 295]. Similarly, Goldstein, Cary, Chorost, and Dalack (1970) studied the relationship between family patterns and school performance of youngsters labeled emotionally disturbed and concluded "that any comprehensive attempt to predict school success should include family background variables . . . [p. 17]."

Finally, with regard to the relationship between school violence and broader societal conditions, McPartland and McDill (1977) have noted that there "appears to be a significant negative association between the health of the economy or the availability of jobs and the level of youth crime . . . [pp. 7-8]." Hyman (1979) points out that it is unrealistic for us to believe that youngsters who perceive little hope for justice in society at large will expect to be treated fairly by schools. Instead, the school's emphasis on competition and grades and categorization may only serve to increase the alienation of already alienated youth.

What follows are brief descriptions of some of the ways in which educators can use local community resources to help combat violence in their schools.

Community Education

Community education may be described as follows:

1. The community school building also serves as a community center. While "school" may be the major program offered from 9 a.m. to 3 p.m., other educational programs for children and adults are available before and after regular school hours.
2. The school staff includes at least one person (community school director) who is responsi-

ble for the development and implementation of appropriate "nonschool" program offerings.

3. The school is governed by a community advisory council whose membership represents the school's community.

4. Community schools support cooperative efforts with other community agencies and resources and frequently conduct neighborhood needs assessments to determine local educational needs.

It has been estimated that approximately 40 percent of the nation's schools may be at least somewhat involved in community education programs. Many participating schools are found in small rural districts while most community education programs in urban areas are concentrated in central city areas where drop-out rates are high, attendance is low, and violence is frequent.

All community education programs are aimed at reducing student alienation and isolation, a probable major cause of school violence. A strongly-held belief of community educators is that the provision of meaningful opportunities for the involvement of neighborhood citizens in school program development can lead to increased citizen participation in the educational process and ultimately to increased community support for the schools. Similarly, increased opportunities for student involvement can lead to increases in youth support for school programs, to decreased student alienation, and ultimately to a reduction in school violence. In order for this to occur, however, youth programs and real opportunities for involvement must exist. Further, such programs must be viewed as relevant and meaningful by the youngsters for whom they are intended.

A number of studies focus on the impact of community education on school violence. Ellison (1974) analyzed the impact of community schools in a problem-filled district near San Francisco. Ellison's community schools were not randomly chosen, and there were clear differences between the community schools and the "control" schools on a number of dimensions (community schools had a higher percentage of student turnover and students from broken homes; a lower percentage of students achieving at or above grade level). Not surprisingly, Ellison found that conversion to community schools had little or no impact on rates of school vandalism. Unexpectedly, however, Ellison did find a community-wide decrease in vandalism during the time of the study.

Palmer (1975) found a positive correlation between citizen participation in community education programs and decreased levels of school vandalism. Palmer also noted a significant decrease in four (of the sixteen) crime categories used for the study; but, since increases were noted in other categories and no differences found in a third group, results pertaining to community crime were obviously inconclusive.

Perhaps the most complete documentation of the impact on school violence and vandalism by programs of community education may be found in school districts with the strongest commitment to principles of the community education movement. Flint, Michigan, can serve as the primary example, since community education was born in Flint nearly 50 years ago when Charles Stewart Mott contributed funds to provide school-based recreational programs for neighborhood children.

By comparison to national statistics, Flint schools appear to be escaping the frequently-reported increases in school violence and vandalism. Steele (1978) reports that for the 1973-76 period, the frequency of "homicides, robberies, assaults on students and teachers, burglaries of school buildings, and drug and alcohol offenses on school property were lower than national statistics [p. 90]." While these figures appear quite promising, it is difficult to know to what extent they are attributable to the program of community education or if they are tied more directly to other features of the Flint system such as the written statement of "student rights and responsibilities," the employment of neighborhood adults as security aides in secondary schools, and/or the use of electronic security devices.

Despite these mitigating factors, the potential of community education programs to reduce incidents of school violence and vandalism seems clear. At a vocational skills center operated by the Flint School District, usage is constant, security guards and devices are not utilized, and vandalism is almost nonexistent. In "community schools" in Washington, D.C., few serious crimes have been reported. Vandalism is minimal at the John F. Kennedy School and Community Center in Atlanta, Georgia, home of an Atlanta middle school and twelve community agencies. The same can be said for the Dana P. Whitmer Human Resources Center, a combination elementary school and community facility in the heart of the downtown business district in Pontiac, Michigan.

Howard (1978) has hypothesized that community education programs may be effective in reducing school violence to the extent that they meet the perceived needs of the area residents. That is, residents must have opportunities to offer input *and* their views must be incorporated into the developing community education programs.

Similarly, Rubel (1977) has noted that school violence may actually be elicited when school decisions are made in a seemingly arbitrary manner without soliciting or incorporating student involvement. Finally, Steele (1978) has concluded that community schools that do not incorporate students concerns and interests into developing programs will continue to reflect the increasing levels of violence seen in so many public schools today. On the other hand, Steele notes that:

> Schools that make a difference in the lives of young people are relevant because they "involve" the students at critical decision points in the educational process: in equitable and continuing planning, development, and evaluation of school-related programs. That is the substance of Community Education. [p. 93]

School Violence and Parents

The Parents' Network of the National Committee for Citizens in Education has produced a handbook (*Violence In Our Schools: What To Know About It — What To Do About It*) for parents and others concerned with the problem of school violence. This 52-page pamphlet is full of useful information including recent survey results of school violence rates; guidelines to help recognize warning signs of increasing violence in your local school; ideas for involving teachers, students, community residents and others in plans to decrease school violence; names and addresses of organizations that might provide even more information or assistance; a summary of recent relevant state legislation. One of the most useful sections may be Appendix B, " Some Do's and Don'ts For Your Child's Safety," which includes tips such as:

> DON'T
> Send you child to school early without being sure another adult on the school end knows about it and approves.
> Ignore your children if they complain or say they are worried about being in certain places in the school or on the school grounds.
>
> DO
> Caution your children about talking with adults they don't recognize while in school in the halls, bathrooms or other places.
> Talk with school personnel about using children to run errands. This usually means they would be alone and increases danger to their safety.

The Parents Network suggested that pamphlet readers might want to duplicate their list and distribute it to interested persons. Clearly, the publication of materials such as these must be viewed as oe very important kind of community intervention into the problem of school violence.

Another example of a community intervention based on parent efforts is the "Helping Hand" program. Recognizing that school violence often spills out of the school buildling into local neighborhoods, especially in the hours immediately surrounding the school day, Helping Hand programs were initiated in the mid-1960s in an effort to increase the safety of youngsters traveling to and from school. Since then, such programs have been adopted by a number of schools across the country. According to the National School Resource Network (1980):

> The key to the Helping Hand Program is the identification of places where children can go for assistance. This identification is generally a placard in the window with a symbol that all children are taught to recognize—most often a large, red handprint. Children being teased, attacked, or intimidated are taught that they can go to any place with a red hand in the window and that someone will be there who will "let them in" and assist them in obtaining whatever help may be necessary. [p. 2-2]

While formal evaluations of the impact of helping hand programs on school violence are not yet available, the National School Resource Network notes that a number of schools and parent groups perceive the programs to be effective. For example, schools in Washington, D.C., are expanding their helping hand programs to all the elementary schools because there is a belief that the model program resulted in a decrease in the number of to-and-from-school incidents and the conviction that the existence of helping hand locations lowers anxiety levels of many students.

TOWARD THE REDUCTION OF SCHOOL VIOLENCE

Schools in America have assumed or had imposed upon them a wide range of tasks that were formerly the province of other social institutions. The assumption of these tasks by the school, according to some (Sennet, 1980), has resulted in "purposive disorder." But when the "purposive disorder" has been accompanied by more violence, vandalism, arson, theft, etc., the school must consider more than everyday responses to solve the dilemma of aggression. We have presented in brief a listing of an array of soutions which schools have attempted, but no single approach will likely be sufficient.

Over the short term, solutions such as giving or allowing the principal more authority might result in reductions in violence. But more important is the nature of the person who would wield this authority. There is evidence that the principal is crucial in establishing the social-psychological climate in a school. The climate, in turn, influences not only the academic accomplishments of the students but the incidence of delinquent behavior as well (Rutter, 1979; Wynne, 1980). Calls for strong principal leadership as the way of curing the ills of school violence are probably too simplistic and are more a reflection of the more conservative ideologies in vogue currently. Wynne (1980) has explicitly recommended a return to more conservative principles in which the authority of the teacher and the school is restored. On the basis of 40 case studies, including elementary, secondary, public, private, church-related, and inner-city schools, he recommends establishing discipline by writing, publishing, and circulating a clear set of rules for student behavior, enforcing the rules firmly and fairly, and providing swift and appropriate punishment for rule violators.

In contrast, Wenk (1975) focuses on the individual student, and to reduce violent he would completely change the public school system. He believes that schools, as currently structured, fail to provide students sufficient opportunity to develop into responsible citizens. To make the school more responsive to all of its students, Wenk has proposed a continuum of five levels of strategies for school programs as follows:

> *Primary Action.* An *a priori* education and human services model to improve the lives of students.
> *Primary Prevention.* A strategy that is aimed at children in need who are not necessarily "delinquency prone." The focus is on providing help to the student who requires it.
> *Prevention.* A program that focuses on individual children who are likely to become deviant. These children are "targeted" as delinquency prone.
> *Treatment or Sanctions.* This strategy is aimed at youngsters manifesting inappropriate or maladaptive behaviors that have become unacceptable and have elicited responses from school or community authorities and, in all likelihood, will involve the criminal justice system.
> *Rehabilitation and Correction.* This strategy addresses delinquents who have returned to the school on probation or parole.

Wenk's approach is important to note because it provides the school with a comprehensive and integrated set of programs. Unfortunately, it has not been implemented in its totality and is not likely to be, but it does provide schools a long-range blueprint of what is possible.

Another broad-scale approach has been developed by Duke (1980) through his Systematic Management Plan for School Discipline. Duke maintains that schools can deal with behavior problems in school by acknowledging that a school is made up of interdependent units and by making sure that each of these organizational units is functioning properly and is related to the others. Of particular importance in his model are school rules and sanctions, school records and information processing, conflict-resolution methods, trouble-shooting mechanisms, community involvement, environmental design, and staff development. To implement Duke's model, a three-phase process is required: 1) preliminary assessment, 2) planning and enactment of the plan, and 3) review and revision. The strategy involves much deliberation and participation in order to effect changes that would reduce disruptive behavior. Duke's approach also is comprehensive and at the same time very practical. Its implementation will require considerable change in the way schools are operated.

The respective recommendations of Wynne, Wenk, and Duke, of course, do not exhaust the ways that have been proposed for curbing school violence. Short of eliminating public education, the three approaches reflect a good portion of the available spectrum. While the evidence as to which approach works best to counter aggression in schools is moot, there is general agreement that what is currently occurring is insufficient. Consequently, if a school intends to alleviate some of the problems of violence confronting it, change of some sort is necessary.

If we view the school as an ecological system or part of a system, any change in one aspect of the system implies changes or adjustments in other aspects. Schools, like most institutions, resist change for any number of reasons. Change may threaten the insecure, may involve risk-taking by teachers and administrators, may require leadership that is not available, may run counter to union priorities, or may involve a complex set of reactions. There are many other reasons why schools will not do something about the problem of school crime, but both the public and school personnel themselves increasingly find inertia on the school's part an unacceptable response to school violence and vandalism.

What we have tried to say in this chapter is, while there is no simple panacea to violence, it has been and can be confronted successfully by schools and school personnel who are imaginative and willing to take risks. The school uniquely is the institution where the forces bearing upon the behavior of youth all come together. School violence, thus, involves a complex set of variables. Consequently, its reduction will require a renewed spirit of cooperation and effort on the part of all the constituencies encompassing the school. The many ways schools have attempted to reduce aggressive behavior give evidence that creative alternatives for solving the problem of violence will continue to be realized if the school will admit its seriousness. No other institution in American society has either the challenge or the opportunity vis-à-vis the reduction of violence.

REFERENCES

Apter, S. J. *Troubled children/troubled systems.* New York: Pergamon Press, 1982.

Ban, J. R., & Ciminello, L. M. *Violence and vandalism in public education.* Danville, Ill.: The Interstate Printers & Publishers, Inc., 1977.

Bayh, B. Our nation's schools—A report card: "A" in school violence and vandalism. Washington, D. C.: Preliminary report of the subcommittee to investigate juvenile delinquency, U.S. Senate, April 1975.

Bayh, B. (Chairman). *Challenge for the third century: Education in a safe environment—Final report on vandalism.* Washington: D.C.: U.S. Government Printing Office, 1977.

Casserly, M. D., Bass, S. A., & Garrett, J. R. *School vandalism: Strategies for prevention.* Lexington, Mass.: Lexington Books, 1980.

Chess, S., Thomas, A., Rutter, M., & Birch, H. Interaction of temperament and environment in the production of behavioral disturbances in children. *American Journal of Psychiatry,* 1963, pp. 142-47.

Duke, D. L. *Managing student behavior problems.* New York: Teachers College, Columbia University, 1980.

Elliott, D. S., & Voss, H. L. *Delinquency and dropout.* Lexington, Mass.: Lexington Books, 1974.

Ellison, W. S. An analysis of the impact of community schools on the reduction of school vandalism in a selected district. Ph.D. dissertation, University of Michigan, 1974.

Feldhusen, J. Problems of student behavior in secondary schools. In D. L. Duke (Ed.), *Classroom management.* (The seventy-eighth yearbook of the National Society for the Study of Education, Part II.) Chicago: The Society, 1979, pp. 217-44.

Feldhusen, J. F., Aversano, F. M., & Thurston, J. R. Prediction of youth contacts with law enforcement agencies. *Criminal Justice and Behavior,* 1976, *3,* 235-53.

Feldhusen, J. R., Roeser, T. D., & Thurston, J. R. Prediction of social adjustment over a period of six or nine years. *Journal of Special Education,* 1977, *11,* 29-36.

Feldhusen, J. R., Thurston, J. R., & Benning, J. J. A longitudinal study of delinquency and other aspects of children's behavior. *International Journal of Criminology and Penology,* 1973, *1,* 341-51.

Foster, H. L. *Ribbin', jivin', and playin' the dozens.* Cambridge, Mass.: Ballinger, 1974.

Frease, D. E. Schools and delinquency: Some intervening processes. *Pacific Sociological Review,* 1973, *16,* 426-48.

Gold, M. Scholastic experiences, self-esteem, and delinquent behavior: A theory for alternative schools. *Crime and Delinquency,* 1978, *24,* 290-309.

Goldmeier, H. Vandalism: The effects of unmanageable confrontations. *Adolescence,* 1974, *9,* 49-56.

Goldstein, A. P., Apter, S. J., & Harootunian, B. *School violence.* Englewood Cliffs, N.J.: Prentice-Hall, 1983.

Goldstein, K. M., Cary, G. L., Chorost, S. B., & Dalack, J. D. Family patterns and the school performance of emotionally disturbed boys. *Journal of Learning Disabilities,* 1970, *3,* 10-17.

Greenberg, B. *School vandalism: A national dilemma.* Menlo Park, Calif.: Stanford Research Institute, 1969.

Greenberg, B. School vandalism: Its effects and paradoxical solutions. *Crime Prevention Review,* 1974, *1,* 11-18.

Hobbs, N. Helping disturbed children: Psychological and ecological strategies. *American Psychologist,* 1966, *21,* 1105-15.

Hobbs, N. *The futures of children*. San Francisco: Jossey-Bass, 1975.

Hobbs, N. *The troubled and troubling child*. San Francisco: Jossey-Bass, 1982.

Howard, J. L. Factors in school vandalism. *Journal of Research and Development in Education*, 1978, *11*, 13-18.

Hyman, I. A. Psychology, education and schooling: Social policy implications in the lives of children and youth. *American Psychologist*, 1979, *34*, 1024-29.

Ianni, F. A. J. The social organization of the high school: School-specific aspects of school crime. In E. Wenk & N. Harlow (Eds.), *School crime and disruption*. Davis, Calif.. Responsible Action, 1978.

Inciardi, J. A., & Pottieger, A. E. (Eds.) *Violent crime: Historical and contemporary issues*. Beverly Hills, Calif.: Sage Publications, 1978.

Kelly, D. H. Status origins, track positions, and delinquent involvement. *Sociological Quarterly*, 1975, *12*, 65-85.

Leftwich, D. A study of vandalism in selected public schools in Alabama. Doctoral dissertation, University of Alabama, 1977.

Maeroff, G. I. The state of the city's schools. *The New York Times*, September 12, 1982, p. 6E.

Marvin, M., McCann, R., Connolly, J., Temkin, S., & Henning, P. Current activities in schools. In J. M. McPartland & E. L. McDill (Eds.), *Violence in schools*. Lexington, Mass.: Lexington Books, 1977, pp. 53-70.

McDermott, M. J. *Criminal victimization in urban schools*. Albany, N.Y.: Criminal Justice Research Center, 1979.

McPartland, J. M., & McDill, E. L. *Violence in schools: Perspectives, programs and positions*. Lexington, Mass.: Lexington Books, 1977.

National Committee for Citizens in Education. *Violence in our schools: What to know about it, what to do about it*. Columbia, Md.: National Committee for Citizens in Education, 1975.

National Education Association. Danger—School ahead: Violence in the public schools. Washington, D.C.: National Education Association, 1977.

National School Resource Network. *School violence prevention manual*. Cambridge, Mass.: Oelgeschlager, Gunn & Hain, Inc., 1980.

Neill, S. B. Violence and vandalism: Dimensions and correctives. *Phi Delta Kappan*, 1978, *59*, 302-07.

Nowakowski, R. Vandals and vandalism in the schools: An analysis of vandalism in large school systems and a description of 93 vandals in Dade County schools. Doctoral dissertation, University of Miami, 1966.

Palmer, J. L. A study of community education program as a deterrent of violence and vandalism in a small rural Michigan community. Ph.D. dissertation, University of Michigan, 1975.

Parke, R. D. Emerging themes of social-emotional development. *American Psychologist*, 1979, *34*, 930-31.

Polk, K., & Schafer, W. E. *Schools and delinquency*. Englewood Cliffs, N. J.: Prentice-Hall, 1972.

Rector, M. G., Barth, S. M., & Ingram, G. The juvenile justice system. In M. Johnson (Ed.), *Toward adolescence: The middle school years*. (Seventy-ninth yearbook of the National Society for the Study of Education, Part I.) Chicago: The Society, 1980, 114-134.

Richards, P. Patterns of middle class vandalism: A case study of suburban adolescence. Doctoral dissertation, Northwestern University, 1976.

Rubel, R. J. *Unruly school: Disorders, disruptions, and crimes*. Lexington, Mass.: D. C. Heath, 1977.

Rutter, M., Maughan, B., Mortimore, P., & Ouston, J. *Fifteen thousand hours: Secondary schools and their effects on children*. Cambridge, Mass.: Harvard University Press, 1979.

Sennett, R. *Authority*. New York: Knopf, 1980.

Steele, M. Enrolling community support. *Journal of Research and Development in Education*, 1978, *11*, 84-93.

Van Avery, D. The humanitarian approach. *Phi Delta Kappan*, 1975, *57*, 177-78.

Walberg, H. J. Urban schooling and delinquency: Toward an integrative theory. *American Educational Research Journal*, 1972, *9*, 285-300.

Wenk, E. A. Juvenile justice and the public schools; mutual benefit through educational reform. *Juvenile Justice*, 1975 (August), pp. 7-14.

Wint, J. The crackdown. *Phi Delta Kappan,* 1975, *57,* 175-76.

Wynne, E. A. *Looking at schools: Good, bad, and indifferent.* Lexington, Mass.: Lexington Books, 1980.

Yankelovich, D. How students control their drug crisis. *Psychology Today,* 1975, *9,* 39-42.

Zimmerman, J., Rich, W. D., Keilitz, S., & Broder, P. K. *Some observations on the link between learning disabilities and juvenile delinquency.* Williamsburg, Va.: National Center for State Courts, 1978.

4

Juvenile Delinquency

Barry Glick

If a man have a stubborn and rebellious son, that will not hearken to the voice of his father, or the voice of his mother, and though they chasten him, will not hearken unto them; then shall his father and his mother lay hold on him, and bring him out unto the elders of his city, and unto the gate of his place; and they shall say unto the elders of his city: "This our son is stubborn and rebellious, he doth not hearken to our voice; he is a glutton, and a drunkard." And all the men of his city shall stone him with stones, that he die; so shalt thou put away the evil from the midst of thee; and all Israel shall hear and fear. [Deuteronomy 21:18-21]

HISTORY AND DEVELOPMENT

The problem of juvenile delinquency has plagued human social order for thousands of years. How to prevent delinquency or control youth once they have performed delinquent acts has been the concern of parents, school officials, and community leaders. The complexity of the juvenile justice system in the United States is so vast that a total dollar amount spent to control or prevent juvenile delinquency is unavailable. However, approximately 1.3 million cases were heard in juvenile courts throughout the United States during 1980.

Both in the United States and Canada, the juvenile justice system is organized at the state or provincial levels of government. Most states have a governmental agency that sets standards and policies for youth development and delinquency prevention services as well as youth rehabilitation programs. Historically, the juvenile justice system evolved from the child-caring institutions of the late nineteenth and early twentieth centuries. As early as 1825, there was a growing concern with the undisciplined behavior of boys, especially those who were neglected by their families. The Society for the Prevention of Pauperism established a house of refuge for these types of youth, an intervention approach subsequently replicated in several large urban areas. By 1877, the Charity Organization Society, the Associations for Improving the Condition of the Poor, as well as other church affiliated groups began to support larger refuge houses and institutions to care for those children without family support, or in trouble within their communities. Until the establishment of the first juvenile court in Chicago, in

1899, however, no formal system of rehabilitation or control for delinquency was empowered to send children to institutions.

Voluntary child care agencies grew throughout the United States in order to deal with the delinquent incapable of living at home. By 1925, the training school, a large institution that was self-sufficient and housed delinquent youth from age 7 to 21 was prominent throughout the northeast and south. Unfortunately, many such institutions became repositories for youth and relied on regimentation and corporal punishment to rehabilitate them. The American Law Institute was so concerned with the failures of institutional placements of juveniles that in 1940 it strongly recommended that Youth Correction Authorities be established throughout the United States. The states of California, Massachusetts, Minnesota, Texas, and Wisconsin heeded the recommendation and formed some sort of youth authority. The purpose of these youth authorities was to establish a board responsible for considering the special needs of youth and ordering the commitment of those youth for whom it appeared necessary to the most appropriate insitution. By 1945, states like New York formalized their youth commissions into state agencies responsible for youth programs and services.

Presently, the juveline justice system is a combination of public and private programs and services. These programs represent an array of community and noncommunity-based residential facilities that are available to local family courts, as they dispose of juvenile cases. While standards for each program are usually maintained and monitored by state agencies, there is broad discretion at the local level as to which juveniles are placed and where.

THEORIES OF DELINQUENCY

A variety of delinquency theories have been posited, especially since World War II. The need for communities to better understand why their youth increasingly became involved with anti-social behaviors, why juvenile crime increased, and what interventions were possible to curb juvenile delinquency served as the impetus for theory development.

Most theories fall within two broad perspectives: those that deal with control issues; and those that deal with cultural deviance isssues. Both perspectives have contributed to a better understanding of delinquency, formed the basis upon which delinquency intervention programs were created, provided the theoretical base upon which empirical data could be collected, and served to generate a synthesis of information so that new principles could be extrapolated.

Control Theories

Control theories assume that the proclivity to the antisocial lies within the individual, that society is essentially blameless, that morality is self-evident, and that the focus for intervention purposes must be upon the individual—who is considered deviant and thus in need of assistance in controlling internal, antisocial tendencies. Nettler (1974) explained in his social control theory that "social behavior requires socialization." Individuals become social or acquire morals through social interaction processes. According to Nettler, successful socialization of the individual leads to conformity of societal norms, while improper socialization leads to nonconformity. In this definition, juvenile delinquency is a consequence of unsuccessful and improper socialization. It may be suggested that the core of the social control theories posit that there is a breakdown or absence of effective social controls. Indeed, Hirschi (1969) stated that juvenile delinquency occurs when the youth's relationship to society is weak or broken. He suggests that the elements of the bond to society include attachment, commitment, involvement, belief; and the significant units of control in society are the family, school, and law. Juvenile delinquency is probable when there is inadequate social attachment on the part of the youth to parents and school; an inadequate or nonexistent commitment to occupational success or educational processes; and a lack of development in the moral right of the law and the belief to uphold it. Juvenile delinquency programs that subscribe to this theory would attempt to strengthen the youth's moral bonds with the community by encouraging (1) attachment to others, (2) conventional behaviors and actions, and (3) opportunities to generate the youth's belief in the moral law of society and order of community.

The basic thrust of the social control theoretical perspective is moral and social development. It relies on social influences that surround the youth and assumes that, with adequate community and social intervention, children will develop a commitment to those educational and occupational aspirations that are taught by schools and will develop a belief that the rules of society are to be obeyed.

Control Theory Programs

There have been some promising intervention programs developed based upon the social control theory perspective. The first group attempt to deal with the youth's commitment toward others, as exemplified in those programs growing from a volunteer big brother-big sister model. One such program is operated in Sussex County, Delaware, in which volunteers were matched with fatherless boys in order to reduce or prevent delinquency (Robinson & Webb, 1976). Self-reports by volunteers, professional staff, parents, and other sources indicated that, of the 69 youth involved with the program, 98 percent had exhibited at least some improvement in specific problem areas. However, while such anecdotal evidence suggests that the program basically accomplished what was proposed, there were problems in recruiting volunteers to match with the youngsters involved, and the relationship directly with the juvenile justice system of Sussex County was minimal. Another program operated in Ohio in which unruly girls, 13-17 years of age, were matched with trained women volunteers whose goal it was to develop a close, personal, and task-oriented relationship (Price & Toomey, 1980). Referrals were made by county departments of social services. A cross-sectional survey of participants indicated that 80 percent of the clients wanted to be volunteers in the future, but did not feel that the program actually solved their problems. Volunteers said they would recommend the program to friends, thought the program did help build a close relationship, but agreed that it was least effective in solving clients' problems. A third program, a variation of the big brother concept, was operated by the California State Department of Health in Sacramento (Teal, 1978). This peer project paired high school problem youth with younger youth who also exhibited problem behaviors. An evaluation design was implemented in which an experimental group of eight high school problem youth functioning as counselors were paired with younger youth and a control group that had six such counselors paired with youth younger than they were given the Gough Adjective Checklist, other relevant psychological testing, and structured interviews. The counselors in the experimental group were trained for two weeks, two hours per day, four days per week. The training program concentrated on group support and trust formation. Four of the eight counselors in the experimental group stayed for the entire 2.5 years of the project. All four remaining in the project graduated from high school and attended college. Tests indicated that the primary change in these peer counselors was their confidence about their ability to determine their own destinies. At the conclusion of the project, of the six control peer counselors who did not receive training nor have continuous interactions with younger problem youth, two were in prison, and one had just been released. Results for the younger clients were not definitive, although those in the experimental group indicated a slightly more positive change in their behaviors then the control group.

The second group of control theory programs attempts to deal with the youth's commitment toward and involvement in educational processes and occupational successes. Most of these programs may be categorized as alternative school experiences. The New Jersey State Law Enforcement Planning Agency, in its annual projects report (1979), described four alternative school projects designed to prevent delinquency. Students who exhibited multiple truancies and suspensions, absenteeism, school vandalism, as well as low academic achievement were referred to these alternative school sites. The projects provided low student to teacher ratios, separate educational facilities and academic equipment, and special community support services. Data were collected by informal interviews, formal questionnaires, and observation. Indirect criteria such as attendance records, referrals to family courts, and reading and mathematics achievement scores were also evaluated. All four projects reported substantial success in retaining students at school.

A related program is described by Bratter (1979). The author, along with two teachers, a probation officer, and community workers, dealt with 24 violent and uneducable juvenile delinquents who were told to attend their alternative school system and be successful, or face incarceration. With this structuring as context, and as a result of a process of relationship building and goal setting, all youth successfully completed the program and were not institutionalized. However, the success of the program goals seemed to result from individualized learning experiences, clear and strict delineation of rules to control behavior, and personalized attention toward the youth. Hawkins (1980) summarized many of the school-related factors that appear to promote juvenile delinquency, e.g., academic failure, weak commitment to school and academic education, and attachments to classmates who were also delinquent. Specific elements which needed to be developed as part of alternative educational programs were small program size; low student-teacher ratios; caring, competent teachers supported by a committed administration; individualized instruction with curricula tailored to the individualized needs of the youth; and a system of rewards directed toward goal-oriented academic achievements.

Cultural Deviance Theories

The cluster of theories which propose that juvenile delinquency results from the youth's desire to conform to cultural values which are directly in conflict with those of the conventional, accepted moral and social order are known as cultural deviance theories. Miller (1957) stated that certain lower class cultural values are in conflict with, and antithetical to, dominant middle class values. While directing much of his theory toward juvenile delinquent lower class boys, Miller, in the purest sense, believes individuals who conform to lower class culture and undergo normal socialization processes "almost automatically become deviant, particularly in relation to legal standards." If indeed delinquents are a normal outcome of lower class culture, then implied in Miller's theory is the notion that these youngsters are so encapsulated within their social culture that conventional values and law have different meaning and are irrelevant to their daily existence.

Wolfgang and Ferracuti (1967) focused on yet another aspect of cultural deviance, that of the violent subculture. They define juvenile delinquency as a "set of values, attitudes, beliefs, and behavior patterns which are shared in high population density urban areas and support the use of physical aggression and violence as an interaction form and way to solve problems." Moreover, they elaborate that this violent behavior is learned and is both tolerated and prescribed within the lower class structure.

Two cultural deviance theories have been particularly influential. In contrast to the control theories described earlier, both reject the notion that criminal deviance is, on one basis or another, an innate characteristic of the individual. Instead, they propose such behavior is learned as an adaptation to real-world societal and cultural forces. The *Differential Association Theory* (Sutherland, 1970) holds that criminal behavior is learned behavior, and derives from interactions the individual has with small groups of intimates or peers who are engaged in such behaviors. Both general criminalistic attitudes and motivations, as well as specific antisocial behaviors are learned, according to Sutherland. Such learning, he proposes, involves precisely the same mechanisms involved in learning any other type of behavior. The American practice of prohibiting individuals on probation or on parole from penal institutions from associating with known felons is one practical outgrowth of the Differential Association Theory. Community-based treatment programs, in which incarceration in penal institutions for certain convicted felons is avoided altogether, are a second differential association effort to minimize contact with sources of criminal learning. These are but two examples of the manner in which the impact of the Differential Association Theory remains significant in the United States at the present time.

Differential Opportunity Theory (Cloward & Ohlin, 1960) takes us one more step away from an individual locus of responsibility for so-called deviance, toward societal sources of criminal behavior. Cloward and Ohlin propose that criminal behavior grows from differential access to legitimate and illegitimate opportunities to reach both personal and social goals. When culturally approved means are blocked, illegitimate opportunities are sought and used. In their words:

> the disparity between what lower class youth are led to want and what is actually available to them is the source of the major problem. . . . Adolescents who form delinquent subcultures . . . have internalized an emphasis upon conventional goals, and unable to revise their aspirations downward, they experience immense frustration; the exploration of nonconformist alternatives may be the result. [p. 17]

The core of the cultural deviance theories attempts to integrate and address three related issues: (1) the problem of the apparent concentration of juvenile delinquency within certain social strata of society or neighborhoods; (2) the process by which youths perform high delinquency actions in groups, and the problems that ensue when these groups menace existing cultural structures; and (3) the process by which an individual within a specific geographic area comes in contact with or engages in delinquent behaviors.

Cultural Deviance Theory Programs

There are a plethora of juvenile delinquency programs that grow from the cultural deviance theoretical perspective. Many of these have gained popularity and are known to the general public because they have attempted to actually change community structures and their organization. One such program, called Scared Straight, was developed by prisoners sentenced to life terms in the Rahway Correctional Facility in New Jersey (U.S. Congress, 1979). The inmates, who refer to themselves as the "Lifers' Group," designed the program themselves and support it almost entirely by their own funds. They invite groups of juveniles, 9-12 years of age, to visit the prison. The youngsters, who are usually first offenders, are given a tour of the prison including the cell block and solitary confinement areas, and then brought to an amphitheater in which the inmates spend up to one and a half hours with the youth providing a brutal portrayal of prison life. In a rather caustic manner, the youth are subjected to prisoners humiliating them for their stupidity and making wrong decisions. The prisoners' graphic descriptions of prison culture and the realities of a life of crime culminates in the prisoners urging the juveniles to return to their communities, attend school, complete their education, and become trained to enter the job market. The initial, enthusiastic reports on the effectiveness of this program state that only 100 youth of the 3,500 juveniles who have visited the Rahway program have committed further offenses. Many have been reported to have changed their relationship with their parents, joined new peer groups, and returned to school. Although the program seems to be successful, there are opponents to it who have expressed that the program is too harsh for youngsters, and gives a false message to those prisoners who participate. Enough of a concern was expressed that the House Subcommittee on Human Resources convened hearings on the "Scared Straight" program on June 4, 1975. The program still continues in either replicated or modified form elsewhere.

One prison that replicated the Rahway program was in Orleans Parish (New Orleans), Louisiana (Ashcroft, 1979). Funded through an LEAA grant during the fall of 1978, Angola State Prison brought youths from New Orleans into the institution for a "Scared Straight" presentation. Even though records of juveniles indicated that the program seemed to be having a desired impact because in all but seven cases arrests decreased, nevertheless, the program was shut down because of the negative community opinions and evaluations of the Rahway program. Yet another scared straight type program was operated at the Menard Correctional Center in Illinois (Zandt, 1979). Similar to the other programs, its intent was juvenile delinquency prevention. This program involved an experimental group of 94 youth who toured the prison and sat through the presentation by inmates, and a control group that comprised 67 youth who did not tour the prison nor receive any group discussion. Both groups were given the Jesness Behavior Inventory and Piers Harris Children's Self-Concept Scale. The tests generally indicated no significant differences between the two groups in self-concept or propensity toward antisocial behaviors.

Another set of programs developed to curb juvenile delinquency based upon cultural deviance theory has to do with leisure time. In an attempt to involve the community, and thereby impact cultural values within the community organization, these programs are usually directed toward peer groups of youth with an activity reorientation. One of the more successful programs of recent years is the National Youth Projects Using Minibikes (NYPUM) (National Youth Project, 1976). The NYPUM program involves youth who have been arrested in their communities. The youth are involved in a program which allows them to learn how to drive and maintain minibikes on dirt trails in their local communities. During this process, the youth are also required to attend groups twice a week during which time they share problems and learn problem solving methods. Additionally, each youth is required to develop an individual contract which is evaluated periodically at the youth group meetings. The average cost per participant for the NYPUM program is $257. Results indicate that 76 percent of the youth who participated in the program were not rearrested during their participation with NYPUM; while those who were rearrested during their participation demonstrated a net shift of 25.8 percent toward less serious offenses.

Another subset of leisure programs have been developed for rural delinquent youth who pose a different challenge for those who work with delinquents. The Tuskegee Institute Human Resource Development Center operated a multifaceted rural youth services program in a six country area of Alabama (Wall & Hawkins, 1979). The recreational programs that were developed resulted in 1,200-1,600 youths joining clubs in their local communities. These youths participated in arts and crafts activities, field trips, and other small group interactions. Many of the topics discussed with peers were then explored with parents or other persons significant to the youth. All of the youth who participated volunteered for the program as an alternative to stricter disciplinary measures for actions they had performed. The program participants, however, were selected primarily because they lived in high risk juvenile crime communities and not because of the severity of an offense they committed. As was true for most of the other programs described above, early anecdotal reports on the efficacy of the Tuskagee effort are clearly promising.

Other Theories

In addition to the social control and cultural deviance theories of delinquency, two "sociopolitical" theoretical positions have had at least a modest impact on programming of interventions to deal with juvenile delinquency. Both formulations place emphasis upon forces lying outside the individual as responsible for, in their terms, "so-called" criminal behavior. The social labeling theory (Becker, 1963; Lemert, 1967; Schur, 1971) is one major example. The differential association and differential opportunity views both concerned themselves with the person's reaction to social forces; the social labeling perspective focuses instead on society's reaction to the person. Stress is placed not upon the transgressive or aggressive behavior of the individual which brings him to the attention of legal authorities but, instead, upon society's reaction to this behavior. Deviance is seen not as a property inherent in any given behavior, but as a property conferred on behavior by societal representatives. The assignment of a label, e.g., "juvenile delinquent," is held by social labeling theorists to create an expectation in both others and the person himself regarding probable future deviance. Over time, this self-fulfilling prophecy quality of the label or stereotype functions to increase the actual occurrence of such behavior. The created role of "delinquent" or "criminal" enforces a progressive commitment to rule violation and deviation. While not seeking to explain the original infractionary or criminal behavior, social labeling theorists, therefore, believe that America's criminal justice system creates much of the very deviance it is mandated to correct, and that the further into this system an individual gets, the fuller and more tenacious are the effects of being labeled.

The recent movement in America to decriminalize certain activities, e.g., status offenses by juveniles; the increased use of diversion strategies which keep persons out of the criminal justice system altogether; or probationary tactics which move them out of the system after adjudication but prior to incarceration are positive attempts to thwart the deviance-enhancing effects of social labeling.

A more extreme sociopolitical theory of criminal behavior is radical theory (Abadinsky, 1979), sometimes called by its proponents the "new criminology" (Meir, 1976). Going well beyond social labeling theory, this orientation focuses on the political meanings and motivations underlying society's definitions of crime and crime control. Crime, in their view, is a phenomenon largely created by those who possess wealth and power (by definition and as a function of America's social structure). America's laws are the laws of the ruling elite and are used to subjugate the poor, minorities, and the powerless. The specific propositions which constitute Radical Theory (Quinney, 1974) further define its essence:

1. American society is based on an advanced capitalist economy.
2. The state is organized to serve the interests of the dominant economic class—the capitalist ruling class.
3. Criminal law is an instrument of the state and ruling class to maintain and perpetuate the existing social and economic order.
4. Crime control in capitalist society is accomplished through a variety of institutions and

agencies established and administered by a governmental elite, representing ruling class interests, for the purpose of establishing domestic order.

5. The contradictions of advance capitalism—the disjunction between existence and essence—require that the subordinate classes remain oppressed by whatever means necessary, especially through the coercion and violence of the legal system.

6. Only with the collapse of capitalist society and the creation of a new society, based on socialist principles, will there be a solution to the crime problem.

The radical theory of criminal behavior has to date rendered a limited, but no unimportant "consciousness-raising" service to American society. While the likelihood of implementation of the preferred solutions of radical theory does not seem to have increased appreciably, America (especially its social and behavioral scientists) does appear to be more aware of social conflict, instances of misuse of America's criminal justice system, racism, exploitation, and related social ills relevant to criminal behavior.

PREVENTION AND CONTROL

No matter what theoretical perspective is adopted, no matter what geographical location or even target population, the issues of what is prevention and what is control when dealing with the juvenile delinquent are paramount. Lejins (1967) defined prevention and control as follows: "If societal action is motivated by an offense that has already taken place, we are dealing with control; if the offense is only anticipated, we are dealing with prevention." When reviewing the variety of programs in the juvenile justice system, historically what have been described as preventive programs for juvenile delinquents have really been programs for the control of delinquency. Indeed, by definition, any juvenile who is already involved with the courts, or identified by the schools as incorrigible or truant, or has posed problems to families such that juvenile justice intervention is required may already be within the realm of control programming.

Prevention Programs

There are two types of preventive programs: primary and secondary. Primary prevention is the purest kind of prevention intervention because there is no attempt to correct juvenile delinquent activities, nor is there any effort to deal with groups of youth who are characterized as delinquent or vulnerable to becoming involved with delinquency. Indeed, these types of programs may best be described as youth development programs and may be designed for the general population within a given community. Boys Clubs of America, Inc., Boy and Girl Scouts, recreational programs such as Little League and Pop Warner Leagues are but a few examples of these programs. Unfortunately, many of these primary prevention programs are based upon middle class ethics and standards, which are not generalizable to poor, lower class communities. In fact, those who are proponents of the cultural deviance theory perspective would argue that these programs are not prevention programs at all since they do not address the issues and conditions of life within the culture that must be ameliorated.

Secondary prevention programs are those that focus upon youngsters on the periphery of delinquency who may be labeled predelinquent; or youth who are not involved with the juvenile justice system but may be considered high risk youth on other bases.

There are a multitude of secondary prevention programs throughout the United States. One of the earliest programs to be developed and implemented resulted from the work of Shaw (1929). Based upon a study of the distribution of crime and delinquency by geographical areas within the city of Chicago, Shaw concluded that delinquency seemed to be pervasive and indigenous to those parts of the city where policies created slums, and where "traditions of criminal behaviors were generated by immigrants, the unemployed, and the dispossessed." As a result of Shaw's initiative, the Chicago Area Project was created to deal with juvenile delinquency within the community. Within the local committee involved, groups were formed to foster a spirit of cooperation, to engender consensus among the community decision makers, and to provide programs for individual growth. As an outgrowth of that initial effort, the project continued and was revitalized, once in 1942, and then again in 1979. Most recently, a Chicago city-wide coalition was formed, comprised of special interest groups, in order to focus on broad social, economic, and political issues. With the aid of facilitators, and using a power conflict model strategy, prevention programs in Chicago poverty areas are now directed by local priority.

Another example of a secondary prevention program is that of the Prevention Specialist Program, which is an intensive program to prevent juvenile delinquency in the White Bear Lake area of Minnesota (Sullivan, 1979). The program is directed to potentially delinquent youth prior to the onset of adolescence. Prevention specialists provide therapy to the families of elementary and preschool youth identified by school officials, church ministers, or community leaders as being potential delinquents. In addition, the program offers parent education classes as well as volunteer resources to those youths who need extra attention. While preliminary interviews seem to indicate that the program seems to be of value, there is no data to formally determine the program's success.

A review of a variety of secondary prevention programs suggests that there may be a core of services necessary for the intervention to succeed. These include individual counseling, group counseling, parent training, and crisis intervention. Further, it seems necessary that these services be well coordinated by administrators and integrated appropriately within the community. The St. Elizabeth's Community Services Center in Philadelphia is a case in point. Their program was designed to provide short-term services to the community in order to prevent delinquency. In its final report (1975), the program was evaluated as providing adequate and satisfactory services; however, because of poor administrative coordination, those services appear not to have impacted the community as effectively as they could have.

Finally, there are a set of secondary prevention programs which impact the juvenile justice system in order to reduce the costs of operations within the system and reduce the number of youth who enter the system. This class of programs is commonly referred to as diversion programs or alternatives to incarceration programs. The diversion programs are usually operated through the county departments of probation. The goal of these programs is to divert youths from ever becoming official cases in family courts. The alternatives to incarceration programs are usually community-based programs and may be operated by government agencies or private services. The alternatives programs, however, usually deal with youth who have already been to family court and adjudicated a delinquent. Rather than send the youth out of the community to an institution, if an alternative program is available, the court may order the youth placed in such an alternative program.

The federal government through the Department of Justice has funded a number of studies in this domain, one of which was the National Assessment of Diversion and Alternatives to Incarceration (1977). The major objective of this project was to conduct a nationwide survey and assessment of diversion and alternatives to incarceration programs. Generally, it was found that community-based programs provided a supplementary service to the juvenile justice systems already in place, rather than an actual alternative to detention and correctional institutions for youth. Thus, youth who were intended to be incarcerated were; while these programs provided services to youth who ordinarily would have been put on probation by juvenile courts.

Control Programs

In the most traditional interpretation, control of juvenile delinquency has meant the youth's removal from his family unit and regular environment. Once a youngster's actions have been so offensive to the community as to require court action to adjudicate and label the youth a juvenile delinquent, or a person in need of supervision, the youth is removed from his parent's supervision and home; then control of those delinquent behaviors is indicated. Programs that deal with the control of juvenile delinquency must take into consideration the health and safety of the youth, as well as the safety and security of the community. While a major portion of programs that deal with juvenile delinquents may be characterized as occurring in large institutions, attempts have been made to reduce the size of the institution so as to prevent warehousing these youth; or create innovative alternatives to reach the goals of the control issue. Even though there are some control programs that are operated by the private sector, the major burden falls upon the public sector, and usually the state government.

One of the larger state systems is operated by the New York State Division for Youth which provides programs and services for approximately 5,000 youths, 2,000 of whom are placed directly in Division for Youth facilities. There are over 60 such institutions and programs throughout New York state that have been organized into a program-level system according to the level of security the facility provides and the amount of financial and staff resources appended to it. There are seven levels of programming in this system. Level I are the Secure Centers that restrict the youth's mobility and structure the youth's activities. The youth placed in these facilities have been adjudicated Juvenile Delinquents by family courts and have committed felonies such as burglary and assault. Youths are also placed in these facilities if they have been convicted by adult criminal courts as Juvenile Offenders. The Level II programs are Limited Secure Centers. Although they do not lock youths in, they do restrict the youths' access to communities and youth movement by staff supervised activities. Youth placed in these facilities are also adjudicated Juvenile Delinquent. Level III facilities are special residential centers to deal with delinquent youth with special needs, usually those who are emotionally disturbed or in need of special education. Level IV programs are residential centers located in rural areas of the state. These programs may be work camps, or small institutions, or short-term treatment facilities that accept either adjudicated Juvenile Delinquents or Persons In Need of Supervision. Level V programs are Youth Development Centers that are located in the larger urban centers of the state (Brooklyn, Manhattan, Syracuse, and Buffalo). These facilities are self-contained programs that offer the full range of services to youth and their families, from intake to aftercare. These reflect the Division for Youth's attempt to respond to the deinstitutionalization movement of the early 1970s. These centers have the capacity for multiple programming as well as specialized services for a targeted population identified by the local community in which the center is located. Level VI programs are community-based facilities and are either urban homes which house up to 25 youngsters, or the traditional group home that houses approximately seven youngsters and attempt to provide a homelike atmosphere using a live-in house-parent staff to provide supervision and nurturance. The division also provides foster home care and independent living to help expedite the transition of youth back into community living.

MODEL CONTROL PROGRAMS

Project New Pride: Denver, Colorado

The National Institute of Law Enforcement and Criminal Justice has designated Project New Pride as "Exemplary" (Blew & Bryant, 1977). This is one of 23 programs throughout the nation so designated because of its overall effectiveness in reducing crime and improving the criminal justice system, its adapatability to other jurisdictions, its objective evidence of achievement, and its demonstrated cost effectiveness. The initial funding for the project came from the Denver Mile High Chapter of the American Red Cross. The Denver Anti-Crime Council continued the funding, and currently the project is funded by the Colorado Division of Youth Services. Youngsters range in age from 14 to 17; have an active arrest or conviction for burglary, robbery, or assault; have had two prior convictions for similar offenses; are Denver residents; and are referred through the court's probation placement division. The New Pride Project accepts 20 youths at four month intervals, and has provided services to more than 220 individuals.

The primary goals of the project are to reduce recidivism for client offenses, job placement of clients, to reintegrate youth into schools, to remediate academic and learning disabilities, to provice counseling services, and to provide cultural education programming. It is reported that during a 12 month period, Project New Pride placed 70 percent of its clients in either full or part-time jobs following their vocational training program. Many of its participants also seemed to have more positive attitudes toward school as indicated by a return to school rate of over 40 percent. Additionally, 32 percent of a control group were arrested at least once for their referral offenses, compared with 27 percent of New Pride clients. Of particular interest is the fact that Project New Pride spends approximately $4,000 per year per client to keep a youth from being institutionalized. When compared with the average cost to house a youth in a Colorado facility ($12,000), the potential savings to that state's taxpayer is over $1 million.

The services offered by Project New Pride are community based and integrated for the youth by a small client-to-staff ratio. The first three months of a youth's placement in the program are intensive services followed by a nine month treatment program geared to the individual's interests and needs. Follow-up services may require anywhere from daily to weekly contact with project staff. Services provided include education, counseling, employment, and cultural education. The education program provides one-to-one tutoring at the Project's Alternative School; or intensive work with specialists at the Project's Learning Disabilities Center. In the first two years of operation, the education program determined that 78 percent of the participants were found to have at least two learning disabilities. The counseling program attempts to match clients with counselors who can serve as models for the participants and best respond to the youngsters' individual needs. The counselor is expected to be involved with all parts of the participants' life and must have frequent contacts with the youth's family, school personnel, and significant others such as welfare workers, probation workers, or ministers. During the follow-up period, the counselor sees the participant weekly. The employment program offers participants an intensive job preparation component that introduces clients to the world of work, employer expectations, as well as practical experience. A job placement specialist provides the youth with realistic options as well as on-the-job training and support. The cultural education program is designed to afford the participant an opportunity to broaden horizons beyond their immediate neighborhood. Field trips, community exploration trips, camping weekends, restaurant dinners, and recreational excursions afford the youth these opportunities on a regular basis.

Achievement Place: Lawrence, Kansas

Achievement Place is a community-based group home treatment program for adjudicated Juvenile Delinquents who are remanded there as an alternative to incarceration in an institution (Fixsen, Phillips, & Wolf, 1973). The program is operated under a teaching family model which was developed at the University of Kansas. The program components, which may be described as a behavior modification program, include: a multilevel token economy system, a social reinforcement system, and a self-government system. Achievement Place is designed to correct behavioral deficiencies in youngsters by teaching youth behaviors that are socially appropriate. Thus, the treatment intervention assumes that the delinquent youth has not learned how to interact with others in a prosocial manner.

The initial population admitted to Achievement Place included 61 percent White, 29 percent Black, 7 percent American Indian, and 2 percent Mexican-American. Achievement tests given to this group indicated that they were on average two grade levels behind in school, and 57 percent of the group had already failed at least one grade in school prior to placement. All of the youth had been adjudicated in family court, 52 percent of whom were involved in felonies. After some years of operating experience and some research effort, it was found that intake selection criteria should include youths between the ages of 12 and 16, an I.Q. of at least 70, who have a problem with the court or the school that places the youngster in jeopardy of institutionalization, probable adjudication by the court, and failing experience in a less restrictive environment such as probation. It is suggested that youngsters who exhibit violent offenses such as murder, rape, or armed robbery; youths who show physiological dependence on drugs; or youths who suffer from serious physical disabilities be excluded from the program.

At the core of the program are the "teaching parents," who are the only professionals employed at Achievement Place. The teaching parents are the overall coordinators of the program and are responsible for implementing the point system as well as the counseling interventions with each youth. They meet with the youth and the youth's parents regularly, and interact with the juvenile court personnel, school officials, and other community representatives. The teaching parents also have the responsibility to plan and implement the social reinforcement system and regulate the self-government system within the home. Each of the teaching parents is provided an intensive training program that culminates in certification after one year. Recertification is required annually.

Data available in 1981 priced the annual cost per bed at Achievement Place at $6,000. Compared to $30,000 for institutional placement, this seems to indicate that the program is cost effective.

Higher Horizons: Highland, New York

Higher Horizons is a program developed in 1971 within the New York State Division for Youth to serve as a release and diversion program for youth placed with the Division by Family Courts. Based on the philosophy and educational principles of the Outward Bound Schools, Higher Horizons offers intensive wilderness experiences for youth and staff for 3 to 28 days. The program was initially funded by Title I ESEA grants, but is now entirely state funded. The expressed purpose of the program is to either provide early release to youth institutionalized in Division facilities after their completion of a 28 day Higher Horizon wilderness effort; or divert youths from institutional placement who have been placed with the Division and are still in their communities, by their completing a 27 day program.

The Higher Horizons program begins with an initial three-day orientation to wilderness challenges (Bowne, 1982). Although each course is individually tailored to the group, the general curricula includes basic outdoor skills training, training expeditions, rock climbing and rapell, rescue training, community services project, a three-day solo, a marathon, and an expedition. The entire thrust of the experience is to demonstrate to the youth, through planned, incremental steps, the kinds of innate talent and potential they each possess. Each environment barrier and challenging situation provides the youth with experiences that have the potential to lead to individual growth and the group's increased cohesion and trust in one another. Although daily group counseling sessions are held throughout the entire program, the important components of the program are viewed as the intense interaction among participants, mastery of skills, and goal attainment.

The second aspect of the Higher Horizon program is the Project Center. The Center is the physical plant to which facilities send groups in order to experience intense intervention, direction of goals, or remediation. Facility groups may spend from one to fourteen days at the Center in activities which meet specific facility objectives or treatment goals. Thus, Higher Horizons serves as a resource center to which facility staff and youth may go in order to begin a new counseling group on its way to therapeutic interactions, or free an established group that experiences limited interaction.

ISSUES

There are a number of issues and problems which impact the juvenile justice system's direction, and influence the way programs are planned and services implemented. While these factors may be described separately with their own unique characteristics, they are not mutually exclusive, and may have an interactive if not cumulative effect upon the juvenile justice system. Their implications are substantial since many of these issues impact upon the system's service delivery, program operations, resource training, and fiscal planning.

Public Opinion

One important issue is public opinion. Indeed, there has been a great change in the tenor and patience of the public with the juvenile delinquent. The evolution from the first refuge house for youth who were undisciplined a little more than a century ago, to the child prison for the juvenile offender of today clearly indicates how attitudes of the public have changed. The get-tough-on-crime mandate of the 1968 presidential election has snowballed into a nation-wide movement which now requires that we get the young felons off the street, treat them as adults, and lock them away for long periods of time. Indeed, the average citizen has little tolerance for the delinquent youth, and is less motivated to provide liberal, nonpunitive alternatives for them.

The Law

The law and legal issues present additional challenges for the future. At the very least, juvenile laws have been changed to reflect the will of the people. More than 60 percent of the states have strict laws to deal with the juvenile delinquent who is violent. The severest of these is the Juvenile Offender Act of 1978 passed by the state of New York. It stipulates that youth as young as 13 years of age may be tried, convicted, and sentenced as adults for certain crimes—

murder, rape, arson, and armed robbery. Unlike any other state, New York's law treats the youth as an adult from the beginning of the adjudication process in that the county district attorney prosecutes the case in criminal court and *initiates* the proceedings there. Stipulations in the law allow either the district attorney or the criminal court judge to transfer the case to family court. All other states reverse the procedure in that the action is initiated in the juvenile court in which the judge then has the right to defer the action to an adult criminal court. One result of this law is an increase in the amount of time a juvenile spends in the criminal justice system. Since the Juvenile Offender Law allows for criminal sentencing, youth may spend life sentences in jail. In New York state for example, there are currently about 30 youth 13-17 years of age sentenced for murder and serving life sentences in jail. While they usually spend time until their 21st birthday in a juvenile secure center, they may be transferred to an adult correctional facility at the age of 16, or 18.

However, it is not only the Juvenile Offender Laws themselves that impact the legal aspects of the juvenile justice system. There have been court cases and precedents which further complicate matters. For example, there is the movement within the legal profession to change the nature of the family court from one which has wide latitude in matters before it to respond in "the best interest of the child," to that of the more traditional adversary procedure. In addition, there are organizations that wish to protect the child's civil liberties and rights. These groups often monitor court proceedings, bring litigation against state agencies in matters of law, and advocate for youth as individuals or groups. Such matters as the right to treatment, lengthy and unjustified detention, as well as quality of programs both residential and educational have been impacted upon as a result of litigation brought by civil action groups on behalf of the child. Finally, there is the court procedure and the court bureaucracy itself that so often creates havoc within the juvenile justice system. The variance from one family court to another, the broad discretion on the part of the judge in matters before the court to determine the adjudication and placement of the youth are but examples.

Research and Development

Yet another issue involves research and development within the juvenile justice system and all that implies. With all the anecdotal descriptions available in the field of programs and services for youth, there are limited empirical studies as to what works with the juvenile delinquent. In the absence of sound classification and diagnostic systems, with the debate still raging as to how to define prevention of delinquency or what to do to control it, little conclusive data can be collected in order to refine the system. Additionally, program evaluation is still at a primitive stage of development. Unfortunately, most programs provide data and base their evaluations in the absence of theoretical orientation and models, with weak research designs, and without adequate information collection procedures.

Fiscal Resources

The human services are in deep trouble because of the scarce fiscal resources now allocated to them. During a period of time when more money is needed to deliver the same level of services, budgets at the national, state, and municipal levels are shrinking. The economic chaos of the 1980s that has impacted on individuals within our society has also burdened the juvenile justice system. Programs are fraught with problems of inflation, limited financial resources from traditional governmental agencies, and an increased mandate either legally or because of increased numbers of youths who enter the system. The reality is that the total amount of money available to the juvenile justice system will not increase; indeed, it will dwindle. The challenge that now faces the program and service providers is not merely the reallocation of funds or the reordering of priorities. The impact of the budget crunch requires that administrators of programs begin to coalesce, eliminate duplication of services, and create innovative alternatives to current practices. Simultaneously, policymakers need to plan and encourage the practitioner to become effective and efficient service providers. There need to be mechanisms developed where program administrators and state or county executives are rewarded by saving money within the juvenile justice system. Simply as money is saved, it ought not be withdrawn and allocated elsewhere, but reinvested, perhaps on a shared basis so that both partners save some without destroying the original dollar amount provided.

SUMMARY

The purpose of this chapter was to present an overview of important aspects of the prevention and control of juvenile delinquency. These included theories of prevention and control as they relate to the area of juvenile delinquency. Also presented was a brief history of the development of the juvenile justice system, followed by an in-depth review of various theories of juvenile delinquency. Interfaced with the theories are illustrations of promising intervenion programs and services within the juvenile justice field. Three model programs were described, followed by a discussion of critical issues demanding our continuing attention.

APPENDIX

For more information regarding juvenile delinquency prevention and control programs, one may write to:

The American Correctional Association
4321 Hartwick Road, Suite L-208
College Park, Maryland 20740

The New York Corrections and Youth Services Asociation
P.O. Box 1733
Albany, New York 12201

National Center for Juvenile Justice
701 Forbes Avenue
Pittsburgh, PA 15219

National Institute for Juvenile Justice and Delinquency Prevention
633 Indiana Avenue NW
Washington, D.C. 20531

National Institute of Law Enforcement and Criminal Justice
U.S. Department of Justice
Washington, D.C. 20531

REFERENCES

Abadinsky, H. *Social service in criminal justice*. Englewood Cliffs, N.J.: Prentice-Hall, 1979.

Akers, R. L. Socio-economic status and delinquent behavior: A retest. *Journal of Research in Crime and Delinquency*, 1964, *1*, 38-46.

Akers, R. L. *Deviant behavior: A social learning approach*. Belmont, CA.: Wadsworth, 1977.

Akers, R. L. Social learning and deviant behavior: A specific test of a general theory. *American Sociological Review*, 1979, *44:4*, 636-55.

Ashcroft, J. L. Closeout report on the Orleans Parish (LA) Juvenile Awareness Program. U.S. Department of Justice, Washington, D.C., 1979.

Becker, H. S. *Outsiders: Studies in the sociology of deviance*. Glencoe, Ill.: Free Press, 1963.

Blew, M., & Bryant, P. Project "New Pride"—An exemplary project. National Institute of Law Enforcement and Criminal Justice, U.S. Government Printing Office, Washington, D.C., July 1977.

Bowne, C. E. Higher Horizons: Adventure and Challenge. In B. Glick (Ed.) *The Forum;* Vol. 8, No. 1, Spring 1982; pp. 18, 29.

Bratter, T. E. Educating the uneducable—The little ole' red school house with bars in the concrete jungle. *Journal of Offender Counseling, Services and Rehabilitation*, 1979,*4*, 95-108.

Clark, P., & Wenninger, E. P. Socio-economic class and area as correlates of illegal behavior among juveniles. *American Sociological Review*, 1962, *27*, 826-34.

Clark, W. A. Approaches to rural juvenile delinquency prevention. U.S. Department of Justice, Washington, D.C., June 1968.

Cloward, R. A., & Ohlin, L. E. *Delinquency and opportunity*. New York: The Free Press, 1960.

Cressey, D. R., & Ward, D. *Delinquency, crime and social process*. New York: Harper & Row, 1969.

Fixsen, D. L., Phillips, E. L., & Wolf, M. M. Achievement place: Experiments in self-government with predelinquents. *Journal of Applied Behavior Analysis*, 1973, *6*, 31-49.

Glaser, D. Criminality theories and behavioral images. *American Journal of Sociology*, 1955, *61*, 433-44.

Haskell, M. R., & Yablonsky, L. *Juvenile delinquency*. Chicago: Rand McNally, 1978.

Hawkins, J. D. *Alternative education—Exploring the delinquency prevention potential*. U.S. Department of Justice, Washington, D.C., 1980.

Hirschi, T. *Causes of delinquency*. Berkeley, Calif.: University of California Press, 1969.

Hughes, R. *I am my brothers keeper*. New York: W.P.I.X., 1977.

Jensen, G. F. Parents, peer and delinquent action: A test of the differential association perspective. *American Journal of Sociology*, 1972, *78*, 562-75.

Johnson, R. E. *Juvenile delinquency and its origins: An integrated theoretical approach*. New York: Cambridge University Press, 1979.

Klein, M. Gang cohesiveness, delinquency and a street-work program. *Journal of Research in Crime and Delinquency*, 1969, *6:2*, 135-66.

Klein, M. *Street gangs and street workers*. Englewood Cliffs, N.J.: Prentice-Hall, 1971.

Kobrin, S. The Chicago area project—A 25 year assessment. *The Annals*, March 19-29, 1959.

Kvaraceus, W. C. *Prevention and control of delinquency—The school counselor's role*. Boston, MA: Houghton Mifflin, 1971.

Landis, P. H. *Social control*. New York: J. B. Lippincott, 1939.

Lejins, P. The field of prevention. In W. E. Amos & A. T. Wellford (Eds.), *Delinquency prevention: Theory and practice*. Englewood Cliffs, N.J.: Prentice-Hall, 1967.

Lemert, E. M. *Human deviance, social problems, and social control*. Englewood Cliffs, N.J.: Prentice-Hall, 1967.

Meier, R. The new criminology: Continuity in criminological theory. *Journal of Criminal Law and Criminology*, 1976, *67*, 461-69.

Miller, W. B. The impact of a community group work program on delinquent corner groups. *Social Services Review*, 1957, *31:4*, 390-406.

Miller, W. B. Inter-institutional conflict as a major impediment to delinquent prevention. *Human Organization*, 1958, *17*, 20-23. (a)

Miller, W. B. Lower class culture as a generation milieu of gang delinquency. *Journal of Social Issues*, 1958, *41*(3), 5-19. (b)

Miller, W. B. Preventative work with secret corner groups: Boston delinquency project. *Annals of American Academy of Political and Social Services*, 1959, *322*, 98-106.

National Youth Project. National youth project using mini-bikes annual. Los Angeles, CA, 1976.

Nettler, G. *Explaining crime.* New York: McGraw-Hill, 1974.

New Jersey State Law Enforcement. *Supportive services for students in local public schools.* U.S. Department of Justice, Washington, D.C., 1979.

Nye, F. I. *Family relationships and delinquent behaviors.* New York: Wiley and Sons, 1958.

Ohlin, L., & Cloward, R. The prevention of delinquent subcultures. In Martin S. Swinburg and Earl Rubington (Eds.), *The Solution of Social Problems.* New York: Oxford University Press, 1963.

Patterson, G. R., & Reid, J. B. Intervention for families of aggressive boys: A replication study. *Behavior Research and Therapy*, 1973, *11*, 383-94.

President's Commission on Law Enforcement and Administration of Justice. *The Challenge of Crime in a Free Society.* Washington, D.C.: U.S. Government Printing Office, 1967.

Price, C., & Toomey, G. Pre-delinquent girl—Does a volunteer friend program help. *Adolescence*, 1980 (Spring), *15:57*, 55-64.

Quinney, R. *Critique of legal order: Crime control in capitalist society.* Boston: Little, Brown, 1974.

Robinson, P., & Webb, W. Big brothers of Sussex County—Big brothers of Delaware. *A Project Evaluation*, 1976, pg. 28.

Schur, E. *Labeling deviant behavior: Its sociological implications.* New York: Random House, 1971.

Shaw, C. R. *Delinquency areas.* Chicago: University of Chicago Press, 1929.

Shaw, C. R., & McKay, H. D. *Juvenile delinquency in urban areas.* Chicago: University fo Chicago Press, 1942.

Sullivan, M. A. White Bear Lake prevention specialists program. Minnesota Crime Control Planning Board Research and Evaluation Unit, St. Paul, MN. 55101, 1979.

Sutherland, E. H., & Cressey, D. R. *Principles of criminology.* (8th ed.) New York: J. B. Lippincott, 1970.

Teal, S. E. Companionship approach to delinquency prevention. *Crime Prevention Review*, 1978 (July) *5:4*, 35-45.

U.S. Congress. Oversight on scared straight—Hearings before the House subcommittee on human resources. *Congressional Report—96th Congress*, 1979.

U.S. Federal Bureau of Investigation. *Uniform Crime Reports.* Preliminary annual release. Washington, D.C.: U.S. Government Printing Office, 1980.

U.S. Federal Bureau of Investigation. *Uniform Crime Reports.* Preliminary annual release. Washington, D.C.: U.S. Government Printing Office, 1981.

Voss, H. Differential association and containment theory: A theoretical convergence. *Social Forces*, 1969, *47:4*, 381-91.

Wall, J. S., & Hawkins, J. D. *Delinquency prevention through alternative education.* National Institute for Juvenile Justice and Delinquency Prevention; Office of Juvenile Justice and Delinquency Prevention; Law Enforcement Assistance Administration; U.S. Department of Justice, 1979.

Wall, J. S., Hawkins, D., Lishner, D., & Fraser, M. *Juvenile delinquency prevention: A compendium of 36 program models.* National Institute for Juvenile Justice and Delinquency Prevention; Office of Juvenile Justice and Delinquency Prevention; U.S. Department of Justice. Washington, D.C.: U.S. Government Printing Office, 1981.

Wolfgang, M. E., & Ferrecerti, F. *The subculture of violence.* London: Tavistock Publications, 1967.

Wolfgang, M. E., Figlio, R. M., & Sellin, T. *The subculture of violence: Toward an integrated theory in criminology.* London: Tavistock, 1967.

Zandt, J. V. *Menard correctional center juvenile tours impact study.* Illinois Law Enforcement Commission. Chicago, IL, 1979.

5
Toward the Elimination of Rape:
A Conceptualization of Sexual Aggression Against Women

Patricia J. Morokoff

It is the objective of this chapter to provide a comprehensive description of rape and to suggest theoretical conceptualizations which will both elucidate the meaning of rape and suggest strategies toward its prevention. Rape can be described in many ways. Those attempted here are legal, experiential, criminal, and attitudinal approaches. Theoretical conceptualizations incorporate descriptive statistical data, cross-cultural findings, and laboratory research on sexuality and aggression. These data strongly suggest that rape is a pervasive problem that must be addressed at many levels. The approach toward prevention emphasized here involves dissipation of rape myths through public education, psychological and social research to determine the means by which sexual aggression is taught, and political development of greater power and prestige for women in our society.

THE MEANING OF RAPE

A concept such as rape is one for which many definitions may apply. Of greatest significance are the statutory definitions and judicial decisions that determine criminal guilt (legal), the impact on the life of the victim and offender (experiential), the statistical characteristics of the offense (criminal), and the societal expectations of what behaviors constitute rape (attitudinal). Clearly, each interacts with the others in cyclic redefinition.

The Legal Definition of Rape

The definition of forcible rape utilized by the FBI (1982) in gathering statistics from crime reporting areas across the country is "the carnal knowledge of a female forcibly and against her will." This is a definition that has its origins in common law, that body of law that relies on "custom and usage" as interpreted by courts and is distinct from statutory law which consists of laws enacted by legislatures. Richmond (1980) specifies how each word in this definition developed specific meaning. Carnal knowledge implies penetration of the vagina by the penis.

Degree of penetration does not determine carnal knowledge, so even the slightest vulvar penetration has typically qualified. Only a male is defined as a rapist, and only a female may be raped. For a rape to be accomplished, force or threat of force must be used. (The FBI definition goes on to say that in tabulations of cases of forcible rape, "assaults or attempts to commit rape by force or threat of force are also included.") Finally, the assault must be against the will of the victim, signifying that it occurs without her consent.

Proof of each of these components of the definition has traditionally been required to obtain a conviction of rape. Thus, proof that penetration occurred, proof that force or threat of force was used, and proof that consent was not given by the female to the male have all been necessary to prove in court. The nature of evidence necessary to constitute proof has varied considerably from jurisdiction to jurisdiction. In some states, the victim's testimony is sufficient; in others, corroboration of her testimony is required. In an analysis of corroboration, consent, and character in the trial of rape cases, Hibey (1975) defines corroboration as "support of a fact by evidence independent of the mere assertion of the fact." Also cited by Hibey are wordings from decisions reached in various states. For example, a 1970 Indiana decision (*Grimm v. State*) asserted that "uncorroborated testimony of the victim is sufficient to sustain the judgment of conviction"; a 1970 Kentucky decision (*Robinson v. Commonwealth*) specified "unsupported testimony of prosecutrix if not contradictory or incredible, or inherently improbable, may be sufficient to sustain a conviction of rape." However, in the District of Columbia as of 1970 (*United States v. Jenkins*) "testimony of the victim must be corroborated both as to the corpus delecti and the identity of the accused"; and in Nebraska, according to *Texter v. State*, "testimony of prosecutrix alone is not sufficient to warrant a conviction but must be corroborated by other evidence on material points." Brodyaga and his colleagues (1975) report that corroboration is still required in five jurisdictions: Georgia, Idaho, Nebraska, D.C., and the Virgin Islands.

One possible legal defense to the charge of rape rests on identification. Its logic says that a rape did occur, but that the defendant is not the one who committed the rape. Identification of the defendant rests on the victim's ability to describe the appearance of the defendant, the specifics of the incident, and her opportunity to observe. These may depend on the lighting available, how much time was spent together, and how long she waited before reporting to the police. Identification procedures include a police lineup and police photographs from which the victim picks the accused. Corroboration from a witness and particularly from a police witness (as when the police arrive during the execution of the crime) will be the most convincing type of evidence.

The type of corroboration which will support the claim of the victim that penetration occurred includes medical evidence. In recent years, many hospital emergency rooms have established procedures which will facilitate the victim's ability to prosecute her case, in addition to providing improved care. Medical evidence includes description of general appearance such as bruises, cuts, and torn or bloody clothing; collection of laboratory specimens of vaginal secretions observed for presence of live sperm; fingernail scrapings; alien pubic hair; and photographs of genital and breast injuries (Brodyaga et al., 1975; Hilberman, 1976). Other types of evidence may enter into corroborating penetration, however, such as whether the accused had opportunity to commit the crime, the emotional state of the victim in reporting the crime, and whether she has motive to falsely accuse the defendant. Thus, it is evident that implicit in the corroboration requirement is the assumption that the victim may have an ulterior motive for making her charge. It has been pointed out that no other area of criminal law requires corroboration by the victim (Borgida, 1980).

The requirement that the penetration be accomplished "forcibly and against the victim's will" leads to two significant consequences. One is that a victim who is physically bruised or otherwise visibly injured will be more likely to impress the police, who are typically the first or second institutional agents she meets (depending on whether she first calls the police or goes to the hospital), and the jury that she was legitimately raped. In a study of experiences encountered by rape victims as they progress through the medical-legal system following rape, Holstrom and Burgess (1978) recorded the number of convictions versus acquittals of defendants as a function of severity of injury of the victim. Seventeen cases were observed to come to trial. Of the nine acquittals, only one victim had moderate to severe injuries. For the eight convictions, the pattern was reversed: over half included moderate to severe injury. Emotionally convincing case reports of such jury-bias have also been reported. For example, Wood (1975) cites a rape case in the *Washington Post:*

> A dramatic illustration of this phenomenon is a recent case in the District of Columbia in which seventeen-year-old Santionta C. Butler was accused of raping a George Washington University student and forcing her and another female student to commit sodomy. Although Butler conceded that he committed the crimes his confession was not admitted at trial due to technical reasons. The jury, composed of four men and eight women, acquitted, according to one juror because the women neither resisted enough nor tried to escape. According to testimony at trial, both victims were hysterical after the crime, and one was found by a physician to have at least ten sizeable bruises on her body. One woman, who had been beaten repeatedly on the head, said that she was afraid that Butler had a gun. . . .

McCahill, Meyer, and Fischman (1981) also provide data relevant to this issue. They followed all cases of rape reporting to the emergency room of Philadelphia General Hospital between April 1973 and June 1974. A sample of 171 cases were referred for trial. For those victims on whom scratches could be observed, 80 percent of the defendants were convicted, compared to 56 percent where no scratches were observed. (The overall conviction rate was 59.1 percent.) Additionally, in those cases where there was some victim precipitation (defined as such when the victim's naivete or lack of judgment led to the situation where the rape occurred), and where no roughness and no weapon was used, the conviction rate was zero.

The second (and related) consequence of requirements of force and resistance is that the outcome of the trial frequently depends on the issue of consent, which has been described (Loh, 1981) as the "basic definitional element of rape." Thus, if it can be established that the victim gave her consent for the penetration to occur, the charge of rape is not justified. This defense is the most difficult for the victim because it is her word against the defendant's, who admits penetration occurred but claims the victim gave her consent. Her task is made more difficult by the admissibility of evidence related to her prior sexual history. It is true, of course, that all testimony given by all witnesses (the victim is a witness in the government's prosecution) must be relevant to the case being tried. The logic behind which the victim's previous sexual history has been considered relevant is as follows: because the jury must make a decision as to whether the current act of sexual intercourse was consensual, it is relevant for jurors to know whether the victim had previously engaged in consensual intercourse, and how frequently (Hibey, 1975). An additional reason for admitting evidence of the victim's promiscuity is to discredit her credibility as a prosecution witness (Borgida, 1980). Thus, if she is promiscuous she is not to be believed. As pointed out by Borgida, this is another case in which rape laws differ from the rest of criminal law, for in no other area of law is a woman discredited as a witness based on her sexual history. While evidence related to specific prior consensual sexual acts has been a controversial issue, admission of such evidence has generally been agreed upon as relevant when the past sexual experiences are with the defendant or when they were very recent and so might account for presence of semen in her vagina (Berger, 1977; Borgida, 1980; Richmond, 1980).

As may be inferred from these evidence admission rules, the issue of prior relationship between the victim and offender is of great importance in determining whether a case may be successfully prosecuted. Holstrom and Burgess (1978) studied the outcome of all cases brought to the emergency room of Boston City Hospital during a one year period. They found that of 39 cases of women who knew their assailants, only one culminated in a conviction of the rapist, and this was a case in which a five-year-old girl was "brutally raped by an acquaintance in the neighborhood [p. 246]." They further report police officers' reactions to hearing of a relationship between victim and offender. "It is a strong case if the assailant is a stranger. One officer told a victim,"You didn't know the guy, right? We've got a strong case [p. 43]." For the victim not only to know her assailant but be married to him places the act outside of the definition of rape in common law, which typically requires that rape be illicit carnal knowledge (Richmond, 1980).

A number of factors converge to make many victims feel that it is they who are on trial and not the defendant. The victim must testify in court whereas the defendant need not testify, by virtue of the sixth and fifth amendments to the Constitution respectively. These aspects of the courtroom experience are thus fundamental to our system of criminal justice. As a result, the victim must relive the rape experience in front of the defendant who has a right to be present during the trial, in front of members of the press, and before the general public. Furthermore, under common law, if a defense of consent is employed, the victim's sexual history may be explored in court whereas the defendant's may not unless he wishes it. McCahill, Meyer, and Fischman (1981), studying reactions of rape victims, found that victims who went to trial versus those who did not experienced more nightmares, described the quality of their heterosexual relationships as worse, and had a decreased level of social activity one year after the rape. In fact, fear of trial procedures was cited as a reason by one-third of victims who chose not to report the crime to the police (Battelle Law and Justice Study Center, 1978).

An awareness of the need for reform has resulted in much discussion in law journals (Berger, 1977; LeGrand, 1973; Wood, 1973) as well as the media (e.g., the TV movie, "A Case of Rape"). In the last decade, at least forty states have modified laws relating to rape (Loh, 1981). According to Loh, rape law reform has occurred as a result of the convergence of three national movements: the codification of criminal laws in many states modeled after the American Law Institute's Model Penal Code (1962), the women's rights movement, and the national concern for law and order.

An important area of reform has related to admission of prior sexual history evidence. It has cogently been argued that a number of unjust acquittals have resulted from admission of sexual history testimony and that this prospect is a deterrent against the decision of a victim to prosecute (Borgida, 1980). Borgida has divided states into three categories based on evidentiary rules pertaining to use of prior sexual history with persons other than the defendant. Eleven states including the District of Columbia currently fall into the category of no exclusionary rules, in other words, common law. Twenty-one states have passed laws which Borgida classifies as moderate reform laws. This means that prior sexual history evidence is excluded unless a consent defense is raised, subject to a statutory standard of relevance. This typically means that a hearing is held outside the hearing of the jury where the defense counsel presents arguments for the admission of sexual history testimony to the judge, who has considerable discretion in determining whether such evidence would unduly bias the jury. Nineteen states have passed moderate evidentiary rule reforms. In these states, a blanket exclusion of all evidence pertaining to prior sexual history of the victim is made. The assumption underlying this reform is that prior sexual history evidence will bias a jury to such an extent that it cannot be properly evaluated.

Borgida empirically investigated how the three levels of evidentiary rules would affect juror verdicts. Actual jurors, on the last day of their jury duty, read the facts of a hypothetical rape trial utilizing a consent defense. They were asked to make a judgment about degree of victim consent and to determine a verdict. Degree of prior sexual history testimony was manipulated within the trial facts to correspond to amount typically available under common law (unlimited), moderate reform (some), and radical reform (none). When no prior sexual history information was provided, 53 percent of the jurors gave a guilty verdict, whereas the percent of guilty verdicts was significantly lower for common law and moderate reform (both 33 percent). It was concluded that only radical reform (no prior sexual history testimony permitted) will increase the rate of convictions. Jurors were also asked to indicate via an open-ended question whether there was any other information they would have liked in making their decisions. Jurors in both the moderate and radical reform conditions requested information about the victims' previous sexual history five times more often than jurors in the common law condition.

Other legislative reform with respect to rape laws relates to the statutes themselves. The common law definition presented at the beginning of this section has been modified in many states. The first comprehensive reform rape legislation was passed in Michigan in 1974. Instead of the old common law definition of rape, four degrees of sexual assault have been defined depending on presence of a deadly weapon, whether serious injury to the victim occurs, and whether there is sexual penetration. Sentencing depends on the degree of sexual assault, thus helping to create a situation where the crime does not seem unequal to the punishment. Many states have very harsh punishments for rape, e.g., death or life imprisonment. As a consequence, district attorneys would often lower the charge to assault to better obtain a conviction. The Michigan reform eradicated corroboration requirements and necessity that force had been used, and erected a radical evidentiary rule for prior sexual history (Ben Dor, 1976).

A similar reform law was passed in Washington in 1976, dividing rape into three degrees with corresponding degrees of punishment. Loh (1981) conducted a pre-post investigation of the impact of this reform on charging and disposition of rape complaints. Under the common law, 37 percent of cases charged with rape resulted in convictions, 23 percent were dismissed, and 35 percent resulted in convictions of lower charges. Under the reform law, 56 percent resulted in conviction of one of the three degrees of rape, 28 percent were dismissed, and 13 percent resulted in conviction of other charges. Loh indicates that, while conviction for rape has indeed increased, if the conviction of rape and other crimes are combined, the figures remain the same pre and post reform (72 percent and 71 percent respectively). Furthermore, punishment for rape, depending on degree, may be less than for another charge. Thus, the results of the reform are to make it easier to specifically convict a defendant on a charge labeled rape, which is an important step according to Loh who describes the reform law as a "truth-in-criminal-labeling statute." Loh also found that prosecutors used the same standards in estimating how convictible a particular defendant would be (and thus whether to charge him with rape) before and after the reform.

Besides statutory charges, other aspects of reform have included increasing the privacy afforded the victim and legislating jury instruction. In the past, judges have typically given cautionary instructions to the jury that a rape charge can easily be made and that the woman's testimony must be examined with caution (Borgida, 1980). California legislation has prohibited certain instructions including such phrases as "unchaste character" from use in jury instruction (Brodyaga et al., 1975).

The Meaning of Rape to the Victim

In order to understand the experience of rape from the victim's perspective, three examples of rape reported in the literature are presented. McCombie and Arons (1980) describe the following:

Barbara D. is a 19-year-old college freshman at a large urban university. She grew up in a small town in Vermont with her mother, father, and older sister. Barbara had moved to the city to attend college only two months before the rape. Her assailant was a young man she had met at school a few weeks earlier. Barbara explained that on her first date, he asked if they could stop by his room to pick up his wallet. Once there, they had a drink and began to talk. They kissed a few times, but Barbara rebuffed his attempts to touch her breasts. At this point, they resumed their conversation, and the young man began to discuss his childhood and how angry he was at his father. Barbara reported that her date then "became wild" and began to slap her face. He threw her down on the floor, took off her clothes, and forced her to have oral sex and vaginal intercourse. During the assault he said he "loved her" and wanted to "make a woman" of her. Barbara described feeling unable to move or to make a sound. She felt that if she didn't cooperate, she might be killed. The episode lasted about an hour, after which he apologized to her and sent her home in a cab. Barbara had been a virgin until this time. [p. 153]

Two other cases are described by McCahill, Meyer, and Fischman (1981).

The victim, a 38-year-old black woman, had been separated for many years and was living with her father, sister, and two nieces. She had been employed for approximately 4 years and had no current or recent sexual involvements with men.

One day, while her family was away, an intruder entered through the unlocked front door. The victim awoke when she felt someone on top of her, but she was able to see only a knife. When she began to scream, her attacker covered her face with a pillow. She was ordered to wrap her legs around the offender and "act like you're enjoying it." When she tried to push the pillow away from her face because of difficulty in breathing, the rapist shouted "I'll kill you."

The victim was raped twice, and her purse was taken. She is convinced that she recognized the rapist's voice and believes that she knows him. She is terrified of being home alone, and under no circumstances does she allow men to enter her home when she is alone: "I don't want any male friends visiting. How will I know it wasn't him?" Soon she began to believe that the rapist was a soldier whom she had previously known and who was home on leave at the time of the rape. Still, her fear of being home alone did not diminish. [p. 28]

The victim, a 16-year-old white female, lived with her parents. She had had some difficulties in her family relationships. She had been cited at least ten times for truancy and had been arrested once as a runaway when she had gone away for a weekend without telling her parents.

One night, while her parents were away, the victim went outside when she heard an ice cream truck. On her way back to the house, a man held a knife to her throat and forced her into a car where another man was waiting. While the men drove to an abandoned house, the victim was forced to remain on the floor of the car. She was punched in the mouth when she tried to scream and was choked to prevent her from making a sound while passing a police car. She was raped by both offenders and then released. She found herself in an unfamiliar neighborhood and telephoned a neighbor for assistance on returning home. [p. 29]

These cases illustrate several characteristics which will be seen to be statistically common in rape incidents, but contrary to popular conceptions of rape. In the first case, the rape occurs on a date, in the room of the assailant, following a certain amount of sexual interaction. It may be very difficult for the general public, police, or jurors to believe that after going back to her date's room and engaging in preliminary sexual interaction, the woman has not given her consent for further sex. The second case illustrates a woman who may or may not have known her assailant, and who was attacked in her own home. The third case illustrates a victim with a bad reputation (truancy, arrest as a runaway). In this instance, she is subject to a pair rape. Pair rapes and gang rapes are not uncommon as subsequent data will attest. It is also of relevance to note that in each of these cases the victim would, under common law, have some difficulty in proving that her experience was rape.

While the rapist as a clinical entity (a committer of sex offenses) has frequently been studied (Abramson, 1944, 1960; Cohen, Seghorn, & Calmas, 1969; Gebhard, Gagnon, Pomeroy, & Christenson, 1965; Guttmacher, 1951; Karpman, 1954; Rada, 1978), the victim of sexual assault received little attention until the past decade. In understanding the reaction of the victim to rape, the initial impact is before the rape, when the victim first becomes aware she is in danger. Burgess and Holstrom (1976, 1980) studied all the women in a one year period who were admitted to the emergency wards at Boston City Hospital. Structured interviews were conducted with these women. Counseling was provided, and the authors personally attended all court dates if the victim prosecuted. These victims were thus followed over a several year period. In order to understand the coping strategies of rape victims during the attack, Burgess and Holstrom divided the experience into three phases: prior to the attack, during the period when the victim first becomes aware that she was in danger; during the attack; and escaping from the assailant after the attack. Coping strategies of 92 women were analyzed. In response to the threat of attack, over one-third of the women interviewed were either physically or psychologically paralyzed and so unable to carry out a strategy for avoiding or escaping danger. For the majority, however, one or more strategies was employed. These included verbal attempts such as trying to talk her way out of the situation, stalling for time, reasoning with the assailant to try to get him to change his mind, bargaining by offering to pay him or give something, threatening, joking, and attempts to gain sympathy. The authors report that victims made such statements as "I'm a married woman," "I'm a virgin," "Don't touch me," "My husband is due home soon." Some victims also employed physical strategies such as pushing the assailant away or utilizing an available weapon such as broken glass. Victims often made a cognitive assessment of possible alternatives for escape including assessment of the risk involved.

The second phase of the rape experience begins when the assailant physically attacks the victim. Coping strategies at this point focus on surviving the experience. Most of the victims in this study perceived the experience as life threatening. All viewed it as acutely stressful. Thus, survival of the experience first entailed not being killed. The authors tabulated frequency of victims utilizing cognitive, affective, and verbal strategies, as well as those employing physical action, psychological defense, and physiological reaction. Cognitive strategies, employed by 31 percent, included mentally focusing on a thought, such as "keep cool, you can do it" to keep their mind off the event that was occurring. Some victims memorized details such as identifying characteristics of the assailants, license plates, etc., a distancing strategy which is also adaptive in later being able to provide information which may lead to conviction. Verbal strategies employed by 26 percent included screaming (which sometimes alerted police) and talking, including playing along with the rapist. A number of reported cases involved the rapist asking the victim if she is enjoying the experience. Many victims report responding affirmatively in order not to anger her assailant. Such responses or other ways in which the victim helps to hurry the rape along may be used against her, however, by defense counsel in trial proceedings. For example, Hibey (1975) illustrates the approach counsel may take on cross-examination:

Q: Isn't it a fact that upon the occasion of at least the third intercourse, you assisted the third man in the completion of the sexual act to the extent of assisting him in penetrating you?
A: No, that's not true, sir.
Q: Is it not a fact that on the occasion of the third intercourse, you said to the man "come on, come on"? (Short pause) Did you hear my question?
A: Yes, I heard your question, sir.
Q: Do you have an answer?
A: No, no. If I used the words "come on," it meant please leave me alone; "come on, don't do this to me. . . ."

Seventeen percent of the victims cried during the attack. Physical resistance such as struggling was employed by 26 percent of the victims. Involuntary use of psychological defenses such as denial, dissociative reactions, and rationalization—"I felt sorry for him if this was the only way he knew how to get sex [Holstrom & Burgess, 1978, p. 3]"—were observed in 19 percent of the sample. Involuntary physical reaction such as "choking, gagging, nausea, vomiting, pain, urinating, hyperventilating, and losing consciousness" were observed for 11 percent of the sample.

In the third phase of the attack, escaping, victims used strategies such as bargaining for freedom, making assurances she would not report the rapist, accepting his apologies for his behavior, or physically freeing herself if she had been tied. Holstrom and Burgess emphasize that all of these strategies are coping mechanisms which aid the victim in surviving a life threatening experience. With respect to implications for counseling, these coping responses are positive behaviors which can be used to demonstrate to the victim her ability to survive and master even the most difficult life-threatening crisis.

Research investigation has been made of the potential deterrence value of various victim reactions. Brodsky (1976) made video tapes of a variety of potential rapist-victim interactions based on nine victim response categories including self-punitiveness ("I'll kill myself if you do this"), admission of illness or pregnancy, verbal attacks, and an effort to communicate on a personal level. Thirty-nine convicted rapists watched the tapes and judged them with respect to how effective that approach would have been as a personal deterrent. Twenty-three percent of the rapists indicated that talking to them calmly in a human way would have deterred them and 30 percent said a flat, unequivocal refusal would have been successful. A number indicated that their victims had resisted by verbal attack and that that was ineffective.

The rape victim's need to cope with stress does not end with the termination of the attack. One of the earliest investigations of the victim's adjustment following rape was conducted by Sutherland and Scherl (1970), who followed 13 rape victims aged 18 to 24 over a one year period. These authors identified three post-rape phases. The first is an acute reaction characterized by shock and anxiety occurring within days following the rape. Anxiety, they noted, was particularly generated by issues related to necessity to make others aware of the rape and to decide whether to press charges. As the nonspecific anxiety associated with acute trauma subsides over a period of a few days to a few weeks, the second phase, "outward adjustment," begins. The authors characterize this as a period of "pseudo-adjustment" during which the victim returns to her normal life tasks and during which denial or suppression of the rape occurs. During this period, the victim typically does not wish to "gain insight through treatment." The third phase (not assigned a time frame) is labeled integration and resolution. The authors observed that at this point the women in the sample became depressed and felt a need (not present at Stage 2) to talk. They emphasize that this depression is a normal aspect of resolution.

The model was modified by Burgess and Holstrom (1974a, b) who proposed a two-phase rape trauma syndrome based again on their sample of 92 adult women who were victims of forcible rape. In analysis of their socioeconomically and racially heterogeneous sample, Burgess and Holstrom adapted the goals and methods of crisis intervention to treatment of the rape victim. Thus, the two-phase syndrome comprised of an acute phase characterized by disorganization, lasting four-five weeks, and a long-term process of reorganization is consistent with other analyses of crisis reaction such as Lindemann's (1977) description of survivors of the Coconut Grove fire. Burgess and Holstrom describe physical symptoms common in the first two weeks following rape (acute phase): physical trauma such as soreness and bruising, muscle tension associated with headaches, nightmares, and sleeping disorders, stomach pains and nausea, gynecologic symptoms, and rectal bleeding. Emotional reactions occur also, focused on fear of being killed by the assailant, anger over disruption of her life, humiliation, and self-blame. The phenomena of victim self-blame and particularly rape victim self-blame is an important one because of its wide societal implications. A case is cited by Burgess and Holstrom (1974a) in which a young woman was assaulted in her hallway by a man with a knife while unlocking her apartment door. He pushed her inside and she was able to take his knife away but was beaten and raped. The woman stated afterward, "I keep wondering maybe if I had done something different when I first saw him, that it wouldn't have happened; neither he nor I would be in trouble. Maybe it was my fault. See, that's where I get stuck when I think about it. My father always said whatever a man did to a woman, she provoked it [p. 983]." The second phase of reorganization often involves alterations of the physical environment, e.g., moving to a safer location, or changing her phone number; and also involves development of nightmares, sexual fears and phobic reactions to being alone, being indoors, being outdoors, crowds, etc. The counseling strategy advocated is again based on a crisis intervention model following the assumptions that the victim was a normally functioning woman before the crisis and that treatment should focus on effects of the rape.

Holstrom and Burgess' research largely relies on the careful recordings of the participant observers. Many of their observations were tested in a more structured empirical manner in a study conducted by McCahill, Meyer, and Fischman (1981) who were able to confirm and amplify many of the observational findings. They obtained their sample from all women examined at the emergency room of Philadelphia General Hospital during a one year period. Each woman was assigned to a social worker who attempted to make a home visit in order to conduct an interview. Of the total sample of 1,401 women, a home visit was completed for 790. Follow-up interviews were also conducted after three (N = 307), seven (N = 217), and eleven months (N = 213). The researchers assessed victim adjustment with respect to factors previously reported as affecting rape victims, including disturbances in sleeping, heterosexual relations, social activities, and fears. Results showed that the emergence of specific symptoms were related to characteristics of the victim and characteristics of the rape incident. For example, if the rape occurred indoors, the victim tended to be phobic of staying indoors, if it occurred out of doors, she was more likely to be phobic outside. With respect to extent of violence in the rape incident, a nonlinear relationship was found. A low level of rape violence and a high level of rape violence seemed to lead to the greatest adjustment difficulties. It is intuitively easy to understand difficulties associated with a life-threatening experience and these were born out: e.g., three-quarters of all victims who were choked during the rape were still afraid of being alone on the street one year later. However, the victim who does not encounter violence during the rape may have different problems of an equally severe nature. Women in this category had a higher incidence of impaired sexual relations with their partners both immediately following the rape and one year later. Guilt and blame from others over not doing more to resist may mediate such effects.

The same U-shape relationship was found between adjustment and type of sexual acts demanded. It seems that mock affection, fondling, and caressing from the rapist may make these experiences difficult to subsequently accept from the partner. The effect on adjustment of the victim-offender relationship was also unexpected. Previous acquaintance with the attacker, even if the acquaintance was so slight that he was a relative stranger, led to worse adjustment reactions than if he were a total stranger. The authors interpret this finding in the following way. To the extent that a woman has control over the circumstances related to the rape, she will feel more secure. If she were raped by a total stranger, she can avoid strangers by not going out alone, by not admitting strangers into her home, etc. If the rapist is a casual acquaintance, however, interaction may be much more difficult to curtail, since one must relate to persons such as neighbors and delivery men in order to function. Of the thirteen symptoms studied here, ten were still being experienced by 25 percent or more of the victims one year after the rape. Increased fear of the streets, negative feelings toward unknown men, and decreased social activities were experienced by over half of the victims after a year. These findings led the authors to conclude "Rape is a devastating phenomenon. It dramatically changes the way in which the victim perceives the interacts with other people, and it often changes the way in which she perceives herself. Its effects are not always short-lived."

Feldman-Summers, Gordon, and Meagher (1979) report similar findings with respect to the impact of rape on sexual satisfaction. They asked rape victims to report pre-rape levels of satisfaction with a variety of sexual activities. Satisfaction of autoerotic and affectionate activities remained constant pre- and post-rape. However, significantly less satisfaction was derived from all other activities such as intercourse and genital touching. Retrospective ratings were made of satisfaction with these activities one week following the rape and two months following the rape. While improvement occurred over the two months for many activities, including intercourse, it was still significantly less than pre-rape. To control for the possibility that pre-rape levels of satisfaction were idealized, a nonvictim sample was also obtained. Pre-rape levels of satisfaction for the victim group did not differ from those reported by the nonvictim group.

Crisis intervention implemented by a rape crisis center has been the treatment model of choice in helping to restore victims to pre-crisis functioning (Abarbanel, 1976; McCombie, 1976; McCombie & Arons, 1980; McCombie & Stern, 1976). It has been argued (McCombie & Stern, 1976) that the rape crisis center is best associated with a hospital. This is due to the necessity for emergency gynecological services for the victim and the availability of other medical and psychiatric services on a 24-hour basis at the emergency room. In fact, in recent years, the medical management of the rape victim has received attention in the medical literature (Enos & Beyer, 1978; Halbert & Jones, 1978; Hunt, 1977; Seltzer, 1977). The focus of such discussions is on sensitivity to the emotional as well as physical trauma of the rape victim, significance of the physician-patient relationship, importance of taking a careful history including description of the assault, careful physical examination including collection of evidence, prevention of pregnancy and venereal disease, and referral for crisis intervention.

Rape crisis intervention, while typically conceptualized as short-term (15 sessions or less), is not superficial. Notman and Nadelson (1980) stress the necessity of understanding the impact of rape on the victims' emotions, unconscious fantasies, and defense mechanisms. They and others have observed a striking lack of anger in the victims' initial reaction to the rape, with victims often rationalizing why the rapist committed the act. Guilt and shame have been observed to be predominant affective reactions. Impact of the rape may depend largely on what stage of life the victim is at when attacked because of impact on completion of psychosexual and psychosocial tasks (Burgess & Holstrom, 1976; Notman & Nadelson, 1980). Because of the observed long-term reactions suffered by a sizeable proportion of rape victims, it has been argued that the crisis model based on grief invoked in mourning a loss is not the best model for approaching rape treatment (Williams & Holmes, 1981). This argument seems convincing, particularly in light of striking differences in the level of social support likely to be encountered by a rape victim versus a survivor of the loss of a family member.

The Meaning of Rape to the Offender

Convicted rapists have been intensively studied through psychological testing, physiological evaluation, and interview (Groth & Birnbaum, 1979; Rada, 1978). In a study of forcible rape conducted for the Law Enforcement Assistance Administration (Battelle Law and Justice Study Center, 1978), convicted rapists were interviewed at Atascadero State Hospital, a maximum security mental institution in California. One rapist provided the following account:

I went to work. There were two girls at work who planned to go the park—the lake the next day which we did. One girl we dropped off home; the other girl I went to a bar with and she said, "I want to be with you tonight." So I figured I'd have a piece of ass but I got too drunk and threw up and she went off with somebody else that she picked up at the bar. I went home and woke up angry in the morning and I was determined to get a piece of ass—if I couldn't I would rape. I drove around this area that I knew there were some girls living in these apartments and this one girl that I particularly wanted to rape—I rang her doorbell, this guy answered the door and I made up some excuse about my car being broken down and I wanted some assistance and to use the telephone. I saw this girl walk into her apartment carrying her laundry and I asked her if she had a telephone and she said "yes." And that I could use it and I made up a couple of phony phone calls working my courage up and she offered to give me a dime and I grabbed her and pulled her down and I told her I wouldn't hurt her if she cooperated. I was in her apartment and I made sure the door was locked when I went in. I tied her up and took her clothes off and went to the bedroom and raped her. I was feeling angry. Afterwards I had a cigarette and talked to her about 45 minutes and I split. She walked back to her car and invited me over for a date—she conned me—and I thought everything was okay. I was fooling myself. [p. 12]

What are the motives for behavior such as this convict described? In their clinical evaluation of over 500 offenders, Groth and Birnbaum (1979) and Groth and Burgess (1977) have identi-fied two motives for rape which they believe permit a dichotomous categorization of rapists. The motive they believe is by far the most common is power. These rapists wish to control and dominate their female victims. They wish to demonstrate their masculinity through rape. In thinking back over his past experiences, one such rapist said, "I thought I'd like to be like an animal, to take her body without her say-so. I thought by having the power, I'd enjoy it a whole lot more." Such a rapist also perceives the victim as enjoying the experience, as verbal-ized by one offender, "She wanted it, she was asking for it. She just said 'no' so I wouldn't think she was easy. The only reason she yelled rape was she got home late and her husband knew she hadn't been out with her girlfriend." Of their convicted rapist sample, they cate-gorized 55 percent as predominantly displaying this motive.

The other motivator is anger. In this case, the sexual act is used not for sexual gratification or domination, but as a way of degrading and getting back at women who are perceived to be base and untrustworthy. One such rapist said, "I wanted to knock the woman off her pedestal, and I felt rape was the worst thing I could do to her." Forty-five percent of the rapists fell into this category. According to the authors, rape of this type is typically accompanied by more physical abuse (such as beating) and, therefore, is overrepresented in the population of con-victed rapists who formed most of their sample.

In the convicted sample, another very small subcategory (5 percent) was comprised of sadistic rapists who derive sexual pleasure from their aggressive acts and engage in sadism, dismemberment, or sexual homicide. Such cases often receive much media attention but clearly represent a very small proportion of actual rapes occurring.

Other theorists have conceptualized the issue of motive somewhat differently from Groth and his colleagues. Rada (1978), who investigated histories of over 300 sex offenders, hy-pothesizes that the basic motive is always power or domination, but that this may take different forms. For some, the expression of control is primarily sexual; for some, primarily aggressive; and, for others, a combination resulting in sexual humiliation. If one equates sexual domina-tion with Groth's power rape category and aggressive domination with his anger rape, the two categorization schemes appear very close.

Motivation for rape may also be conceptualized developmentally as a result of negative ex-periences during maturation. In Groth and Birnbaum's sample, they found that one third of the offenders (including attackers of both adult women and children) reported a sexually traumatic experience while growing up. In the case of the rapist sample (only offenders against adult women), these traumatic episodes often took the form of the child witnessing a disturbing sexual activity involving one or both parents. In those cases where the rapist had himself been victim of a sexual attack, it was most often incestuous, that is, committed by a family member, and usually a female family member. According to Groth and Birnbaum (1979), "The offender's adult crimes may be in part a repetition and an acting out of sexual offense he was subjected to as a child, a maladaptive effort to solve an unresolved early sexual trauma."

Rada (1978) found that about one quarter of his sample had been subject to parental cruelty or beatings as children. He also indicates that a clinical observation of rapists has frequently produced the picture of the family constellation in which the mother is dominant, punitive, controlling, and seductive, while the father is weak or absent. The etiological significance of such experience is that "when the mother is cruel and sadistic the future hostility of the son is more likely to be directed toward women specifically because of the actual pain, suffering or humiliation that the rapist feels he has suffered [p. 33]." While such clinical impressions have persisted, they have been difficult to document in rigorous research.

In order to understand the rapist from the psychiatric perspective, numerous variables have been studied for their potential in discriminating the rapist from the nonrapist. These have included response to personality inventories, projective tests, and tests of cognitive functioning. Such efforts have been largely unsuccessful (Rada, 1978). However, use of alcohol has been related to rape. Rada (1975) found that of 77 rapists committed to Atascadero State Hospital, 35 percent were classified as alcoholic and 50 percent were drinking at the time of the offense. All of the alcoholic rapists were drinking heavily at the time of the offense.

Rada, Kellner & Laws (1976) have also examined the hypothesis that men who aggress sexually have higher levels of testosterone than their nonaggressive counterparts. A comparison was made of plasma testosterone levels in 52 rapists and 12 child molesters, utilized as an institutional control because of the lack of violence in their assaults. The plasma testosterone levels of rapists on the average were in the normal range and showed no difference from either child molesters or normals. However, rapists who were categorized as using the greatest amount of violence in the commission of their crime had a significantly higher level of plasma testosterone than the other rapists. The one rapist who had committed murder had the highest testosterone level. Rada concludes that plasma testosterone level does not predict rape but that increased testosterone level may facilitate more intense aggression under certain circumstances.

Criminal Statistics

Tabulation of the incidence of rape known to the police is published yearly by the FBI in the Uniform Crime Reports (FBI, 1982). This is a publication designed to combine data on certain crimes from reporting areas across the country. In order to accomplish this massive task, the International Association of Chiefs of Police was formed in 1927 and standardized definitions for various criminal offenses were created, such as the one for forcible rape cited at the beginning of this chapter. Detailed tabulation is made of eight crimes making up the Crime Index. These include murder, forcible rape, robbery, aggravated assault, burglary, larceny-theft, motor vehicle theft; arson was added to the list in 1978. Murder, forcible rape, robbery, and aggravated assault are categorized as violent crimes. As of the 1982 report, 15,000 reporting areas contributed statistics, representing nearly 230 million people. In 1981, there were 81,536 offenses of forcible rape known to the police. "Known to the police" indicates that a complaint was made, was determined by the police to be founded, and a rape or attempted rape charge was filed. The rate of rape per 100,000 inhabitants for 1981 was 35.6. To the average reader, this statistic will probably have little meaning. It can be put into context by comparison (1) to the rate of other crimes and (2) to the rate in previous years. Table 5.1 compares the rate of violent crimes as well as the total making up the Crime Index in 1972 and 1981.

In examining this table, it is apparent that the overall rate of crime has increased dramatically in the past ten years (32 percent), and that the rate of rape has increased more than any other violent crime. The difference is particularly astounding when compared to the rate of increase for murder (less than 10 percent). A frequently raised issue is whether the rate of rape has increased, or whether there has been an increase in the reporting of rape. Such an increase in reporting is reasonable to expect due to the institution in many police departments of special rape investigation units, in many cases utilizing women officers and training programs. Reporting increase might also be expected as a function of increased awareness among the public resulting from the women's rights movement, TV programs about rape, and visible rape crises centers in the community. It is probable that there has been an increase in the report of rape. However, a number of factors enter into determining the true increase in rape.

First, it can be seen from table 5.1 that the rate of all violent crime has increased in recent years. Thus, it seems highly probably that the actual rate of rape has also increased. Second, increased reporting does not necessarily mean an increase in rapes reported in the UCR. In order to be reported as rape, the police must determine whether the complaint is founded. At the discretion of the police, a lesser charge, either a lesser sexual offense or a nonsexual charge such as assault or aggravated assault, may be lodged. This typically depends on police estimation of how successful it would be to obtain a conviction for a given charge (Holstrom & Burgess, 1978). In Philadelphia, a number of variables are significantly associated with lodging a lesser sexual offense charge. These include cases where the assault episode lasted less than 15 minutes, where the victim had been attacked by the offender before, where the offender is a family member, where no physical force is used, where no weapon is used, where the victim is unemployed, and where the offender is not a stranger (McCahill, Meyer, & Fischman, 1981). Of the 1,401 women who went to the Philadelphia General Hospital emergency room with an alleged sexual assault, 53.8 percent were reported to the FBI by the police as rape. It is evident that the police use a particular standard for assessing what crimes can bring a conviction for rape and so charge accordingly. It seems likely that those crimes most clearly defined societally as rape (attack by a stranger who uses force or a weapon) are not the subset among which reporting increases may be expected. In other words, there has always been a social awareness that perpetrators of such crimes should be prosecuted. It is precisely the subset of rapes that do not fit this mold (acquaintance rape in which the victim

Table 5.1.   Change in Rate of Crimes between 1972 and 1981

CRIME	Rate per 100,000 inhabitants		
	1972	1981	PERCENT CHANGE
Murder	9.0	9.8	8.2
Rape	22.5	35.6	36.8
Robbery	180.7	250.6	27.9
Aggravated assault	188.8	280.9	32.8
Total crime index	3961.4	5799.9	31.7

Source: Uniform Crime Reports-1981 (FBI, 1982).

submits) for which social awareness has increased, and for which reporting increases might be expected. However, the data collected by McCahill and his colleagues (1981) suggest such cases have a likelihood of not being charged as rape.

Over the past two years, the rate of rape appears to have leveled off and actually decreased by 2.2 percent from 1980 to 1981. This decrease is consistent with that of other violent crimes: rate of murder decreased 3.9 percent and the rate of aggravated assault decreased 3.3 percent. Examining the ten-year trend from 1972 to 1981, the FBI (1982) says, "the high increasing rate that characterized forcible rape over the years has either slowed or come to a halt." Again, this does not seem to be due to any changes specific to detection or prosecution of rape, but seems to represent a general trend with respect to violent crime.

The Uniform Crime Reports also indicates the number of crimes cleared by arrest and information on persons arrested. A crime is considered cleared when the offender is actually taken into custody. In 1981, 48 percent of forcible rape offenses were cleared by arrest. While rape is an infrequent crime relative to other crime index crimes, like murder, it tends to have a higher rate of clearance than the more frequent crimes against property. The rate of clearance for murder in 1981 was 72 percent, for aggravated assault 58 percent, and for burglary 14 percent. The clearance rate for rape, despite national attention, has not increased over recent years. The national clearance rate in 1977 was 51 percent, in 1980 it was 49 percent. If one looks at rate of conviction, the prospect of deterring the crime through punishment becomes even gloomier. According to Rabkin (1979), for every 100 reported offenses, 16 are convicted of forcible rape and an additional four of lesser offenses.

It is known that a large percent of actual rapes are not reported to the police. Major reasons for not reporting rape include fear of police treatment, fear of trial procedures, fear of publicity, not wishing family and friends to know, lack of interest in the case shown by police, and fear of revenge by the offender (Battelle Law and Justice Study Center, 1978). The subjective experience motivating not reporting is described in the Study Center's report:

> Rape can be the most terrifying event in a woman's life. The sexual act or acts performed are often intended to humiliate and degrade her; bottles, gun barrels and sticks may be thrust into her vagina or anus; she may be compelled to swallow urine or perform fellatio with such force that she thinks she may strangle or suffocate; her breasts may be bitten or burned with cigarettes. In many instances her hope is to save her life—not her chastity. Her terror may be so overwhelming that she urinates, defecates or vomits. If she escapes without serious outward signs of injury, she may suffer vaginal tears or infections, contract venereal disease, or become impregnated. For months or even years afterward, she may distrust others, change residences frequently and sleep poorly. Her friends and family may blame or reject her. [p. 15]

Studies of victimization are able to shed light on the issue of how many rapes go unreported. Such research involves random selection of participants with whom interviews are conducted in their homes. Questions related to crimes for which they have been the victim are asked. An approximate ratio of one crime reported for every four actually experienced has emerged across studies (Battelle Law and Justice Study Center, 1978; Curtis, 1976). It is highly likely, however, that when individuals are asked whether they have experienced rape, the same prejudices as to what constitutes rape will bias their answers as the biases held by jurors in determining guilt.

Before addressing the issue of attitudes toward rape, empirical findings related to the occurrence of rape will be presented. Quite a bit is known about the characteristics of rapists, victims, the typical modus operandi, and other aspects of the crime. These facts frequently differ dramatically from popular conceptions.

A major source of information about both offenders and victims is a study conducted by Amir (1971) in Philadelphia. He obtained access to police records and conducted a sociological analysis of all recorded rapes during the years 1958 and 1960. There were 358 rapes recorded in 1958 and 298 recorded in 1960, for a total of 646 cases of rape. The number of offenders involved was much larger (1,292) as a result of group rapes. A second source of information about characteristics of rape is a study conducted for the Law Enforcement Assistance Administration (Battelle Law and Justice Study Center, 1978) in which rape complaints in five cities (Seattle, Detroit, Kansas City, New Orleans, and Phoenix) were analyzed.

Analysis of race of both victims and offenders finds that blacks are highly overrepresented. Amir (1971) found that 82.5 percent of offenders were black, and 80.5 percent of victims were also black. According to Amir, the potential for a black woman to become a rape victim was twelve times greater than that of a white woman, and the rate of black offenders was twelve times the rate of white offenders (calculated on the basis of population in each racial group). In the LEAA study, black offenders were also overrepresented, exceeding whites in percentage of the total in each city except Phoenix. Similarly, according to the Uniform Crime Reports (FBI, 1982) for the nation as a whole, 50.2 percent of arrested offenders were white, 48.2 percent were black. This ratio is not specific to rape. For violent crimes in the Crime Index, 45.7 percent of arrests were of blacks. Substantiation that black women are more often victims can be found in McCahill et al.'s (1981) study in Philadelphia where 73.4 percent of the women were black.

A second important finding with respect to race is that most rapes are intraracial. According to Amir (1971), 77 percent of the rapes were committed by black males against black females, while 16 percent were committed by white males against white females. Black men raped white women in only 3 percent of the cases, while white men were reported to have raped black women in 4 percent. Of these four categories, the one which would seem most susceptible to underreporting is rapes of blacks by whites. The white person's conception that blacks tend to rape whites appears statistically unfounded, although Curtis (1976) indicates this category may be increasing.

The issue of bias in these data is a significant one. Examination of data relating occupation to race of offender would lead one to believe that essentially no white males with occupation higher than unskilled laborer commit rapes. (Amir, 1971, reports only 25 such men out of his sample of 1,292.) A variety of data confirm that this picture is inaccurate. According to Dietz (1978), social status and race of the offender are variables which will mitigate against report of the offender by the victim, report by the police in their records, probability of an arrest being made, probability that the jury will convict, and harshness of the sentence employed by the judge. For example, Dietz documents the extreme disproportion of blacks who have been given the death sentence as punishment for rape in comparison to whites. This might lead one to conclude that there are a large number of black men raping black women. However, lack of statistical evidence of rape in the white community does not mean it does not occur but, rather, that it tends to fall into a category of crime that cannot easily be prosecuted as rape.

Another characteristic of offender and victim that has been studied is age. Amir (1971) found that the age range of 15 to 19 encompassed the greatest percent of rapists (40 percent), with the 20 to 24 range second (25 percent). The Uniform Crime Reports (FBI, 1982) substantiates this youthful proclivity, as the highest frequency of arrests were made of 20 year olds. With respect to victims, the LEAA report states that over 50 percent were under 21. In Philadelphia, McCahill et al. (1981) found that 64.2 percent of victims were under 21. Also in Philadelphia, Amir found that the age range of 15 to 19 encompassed the highest percent of victims (like offenders), but that the 10 to 14 age group was second highest. Amir also reports that offenders tend to pick victims in their own age range. The difference in age was five years or less 63.8 percent of the time.

The most likely marital status of offenders, according to Amir, was single or below the age of marriage (83 percent) as it was also for victims (70 percent). In this sample, single status was clearly a result of youthful age rather than an inability to find a marital partner or a decision not to marry. For convicted adult offenders, Groth and Burgess (1977) found that one third of the sample of 133 offenders were currently married, and Gebhard et al. (1965) report that for 140 heterosexual aggressors against adults, 59 percent were currently or previously married.

The number of offenders participating in the assault was studied with particular care by Amir (1971). Of the 646 cases of rape he studied, 57 percent were single offender rapes, while 43 percent were termed group rapes (two or more offenders). In the LEAA study, percent of group rape was much lower, however, ranging from 16 percent of rapes in Seattle to 31 percent in Detroit. In studying available data, Dietz (1978) found a number of factors related to group rape. The offenders in group rape (1) are more frequently younger, (2) are more frequently from lower status ethnic groups in those cities with pronounced ethnic hierarchies, (3) more often live in the vicinity of the scene of the rape and the victim's residence, (4) have more often been drinking alcohol, (5) are more often neighbors or acquaintances of the victim, (6) less often previously intimate with the victim, and (7) less often have a previous arrest record for offenses against persons or sex offenses than the offenders in single rape. In addition, these rapes tend to involve greater employment of force, are more often committed in an automobile than the residence of one of the participants, more frequently begin in the street and occur more during recreation times (summer, weekend, evening). Statistics and information related to group rape thus create a picture of a group of teenagers who have been drinking, who forcibly rape a female in their neighborhood, often in one of their cars. For the victim, group rape is particularly disturbing because of the helplessness felt in confrontation with more than one assailant. Any coping strategies that may have been developed appear particularly futile. McCahill et al. (1981) found that one of the variables associated with a nonoffense charge (rather than rape of a lower offense) in Philadelphia is the presence of more than one offender. Thus, despite its occasion for personal trauma to the victim, group rape does not facilitate legal recourse.

The stereotype of the sex-craved rapist jumping out of the bushes to attack an unsuspecting woman is further invalidated by data addressing victim-offender relationship and place of rape. In Amir's (1971) data, less than half of the offenders (42.3 percent) were total strangers to the victim; 33 percent fell into an intermediate category of relationships composed of general acquaintances and close neighbors. Furthermore, for 82 percent of those cases for which information on residence was available, the offender and victim lived in the same neighborhood (defined as five city blocks). In most of these, not only did the offender and victim live in the same neighborhood, but the rape occurred there as well (68 percent). Very few of the rapes in Amir's sample involved close friends or boyfriends, but Dietz (1978) observes that it is highly likely that the extent to which the offender is known to the victim will influence whether she reports the rape. McCahill et al. (1981) found a significant statistical relationship between lodging of a lesser sexual offense charge by police and the existence of some prior acquaintance between offender and victim. Thus, it seems highly likely that more intimate level of acquaintance is underrepresented in Amir's data.

Several studies concur that about half of rapes take place in either the victim or offender's home (Amir, 1970; Battalle Law and Justice Study Center, 1978; McCahill et al., 1981). According to Amir, the most frequent starting point of the rape, however, is on the street (42 percent) with the victim's home being the second most likely location. In almost half the cases, the starting point was different from the place where the rape actually occurred. The high proportion of rapes starting on the street and moving to one of the participant's homes support Burgess and Holstrom's (1974b) concept of a confidence rape, in which there is interaction between assailant and victim prior to the attack, during which time the assailant attempts to gain the victim's trust. He may in fact be previously known to the victim and trick her into thinking he has intentions other than rape. Furthermore, according to Amir, most rapes are planned (82 percent). The figure rises to 90 percent for group rapes. Weapons were threatened or used in almost half the cases (Battelle Law and Justice Study Center, 1978). About one fifth of victims experience brutal beatings (Amir, 1971; McCahill et al., 1981).

To summarize, a composite picture of a "typical" police record rape would show a teenage boy (or group of boys) of lower socioeconomic status planning to attack a young girl known casually from the neighborhood. The attack would be likely to take place during recreational hours, would employ force, and possibly a weapon would be involved.

In 55 percent of his cases, Amir found that victim response to the rape could be characterized as submissive. Submission, however, was correlated with the type of intimidation or threat applied. According to Amir, "It seems that when confronted with a threat to her life or physical well-being, the victim was not willing to resist or fight." Such a characterization is not inconsistent with use of coping strategies previously outlined, with the exception of physical resistance.

Attitudes Toward Rape

The statistical picture of rape is quite inconsistent with popular conceptions. Feild (1978) devised a Rape Knowledge Test to measure factual knowledge about rape. It contained 14 items of the following form:

Among which racial combination do most rapes occur?
1. black males and black females
2. black males and white females
3. white males and white females
4. white males and black females

Administration of this test to a sample of 1,448 men and women produced a mean score of 4.59, or just slightly better than chance given a possible range of 0 to 14.

Development of the Rape Knowledge Test was part of a larger study to assess attitudes toward rape. Feild (1978) developed a 32-item scale composed of statements such as, "A woman can be raped against her will," and "Most women secretly desire to be raped," to which respondents indicated agreement on a six point scale. The instrument was administered to 528 women and 528 men from the general public, 254 police officers, 20 convicted rapists, and 118 rape crisis counselors. Factor analysis allowed eight factors to be extracted, thus indicating, according to Feild, that rape attitudes are best understood as multidimensional. Most of the factors are areas for which a body of literature is available, and pertinent here.

Victim Precipitation. Two of Feild's factors relate to the degree to which a woman is held responsible for her own rape, or is perceived as engaging in behaviors which are precipitative. Stereotypic attitudes say that a woman cannot be raped against her will and that a rape victim is either a woman who changed her mind afterwards, or a woman who behaved provocatively and so got what she deserved. A number of studies have demonstrated sex differences in attributing responsibility for rape to the victim. Feild's (1978) data show that men believe to a greater extent than women both that it is a woman's responsibility to prevent rape and that victims precipitate rape through their appearance and behavior. Rumsey and Rumsey (1977) asked subjects to indicate both defendant's and victim's responsibility when given information about a rape case as it would be presented to a jury. They found that when the evidence "weighed heavily against the defendant," males and females equally held the defendant responsible. When the evidence was less conclusive, the male subjects attribution of responsibility to the defendant was significantly lower and attribution of responsibility to the victim higher. Female subjects' attribution of responsibility remained unchanged when evidence was less conclusive. Calhoun, Selby, Cann, and Keller (1978) found that, after reading a rape description, males were more likely than females to perceive the victim as playing a role in her rape.

A second variable that has been shown relevant to the belief that women are responsible for precipitating rape is attractiveness. Calhoun et al. (1978) found that a physically attractive victim is perceived by subjects as playing a somewhat greater role in her rape, although she received a higher degree of social acceptance than a physically less attractive victim. On the other hand, Seligman, Brickman, and Koulack (1977) found that a physically unattractive victim was seen as provoking her rape more than the physically attractive victim. Such a difference was not seen for victims of robbery or assault, and the difference was greater for male than female subjects. The authors explain this finding through additional data which indicate that subjects believed it less probable that the unattractive victim would actually have been raped. Therefore, they reason, the unattractive victim must have done something to precipitate the rape. This assertion is supported by analysis of instances where the Philadelphia police marked a victim's complaint as "unfounded." In 53.3 percent of the cases marked unfounded, the victim was obese, compared to only 14.2 percent of founded cases (McCahill et al., 1981).

With respect to social status, Jones and Aronson (1973) found that greater fault was attributed to a married woman or virgin than to a divorced woman who was raped. Again, the interpretation of the findings rests on the concept that if the victim is socially acceptable, she must have done something to have precipitated her misfortune. While lacking consistency, results within the area of attractiveness and social status do indicate that such factors are not irrelevant in determining blame.

Attitudes toward sex, family, and women are another set of variables which may determine ones view of the victim as being responsible. Klemmack and Klemmack (1976) randomly surveyed women over the age of 18 in Tuscaloosa, Alabama. Each respondent was presented with seven situations and asked to indicate whether she believed it was rape or not. A five-level scale of certainty was employed. The incidents ranged from the stereotype description of a man jumping out of the shadows as the woman walks to her car late at night to a situation where the woman is raped in her own home by her boyfriend. All fit the common law definition of rape, although the situations varied in degree to which force and resistance were described. Results indicated that women with a more nontraditional outlook on the family and sex roles were more likely to perceive a situation as rape. Similarly, tolerance of sex before marriage was positively related to perception of the situations as rape. Among these women, it was also true that the likelihood that a given situation would be defined as rape was inversely related to the degree of personal relationship between participants. "If any relationship is known to exist between the victim and the accused, no matter how casual, the proportion of those who consider the event rape drops to less than 50 percent [p. 144]." Feild (1978) found that a high score on Spence and Helmreich's Attitudes Toward Women Scale (more liberal) was associated with a belief that women are not primarily responsible for preventing rape.

Feild also assessed relationship of race to a belief in women's responsibility in preventing rape and found adherence to this belief associated with black racial status. Interestingly, black racial status was also correlated with the belief that the victim's appearance and behavior are *not* precipitants of rape.

Motivation for Rape. A belief that sex is the motivation for rape is part of the prototypic image of the sex-starved male who cannot find a woman and so is forced to rape in order to satiate his needs. As previously discussed, this perception is rejected by Groth and Birnbaum (1979) who state:

> we find that either anger or power is the dominant component and that rape, rather than being primarily an expression of sexual desire, is, in fact, the use of sexuality to express these issues of power and anger. Rape, thus, is a pseudosexual act, a pattern of sexual behavior that is concerned much more with status, hostility, control, and dominance than with sensual pleasure or sexual satisfaction. [p. 13]

The assertion that the offender must rape in order to have a sexual outlet is refuted by Groth and Burgess' (1977) data on 133 offenders of adult victims. Of this sample, one third were engaging in regular sexual intercourse with a spouse, and the majority had active sexual relationships with one or more women. Nevertheless, the stereotype of rape focuses on sexual desire as a motivator, rather than on anger or power.

Feild (1978) found that men believed to a greater extent than women that need for power over women is *not* a motivation for rape. He also found a correlation between liberal attitudes toward women and a belief that sex is not the primary motivation for rape.

Other factors identified by Feild as components of attitudes toward rape include beliefs about the normality of the rapist, severity of punishment due him, and the desirability of a woman after being raped. He found that men and particularly black men are likely to believe that a rapist is normal. Males also believed that punishment for a rapist should be harsher than women did, a finding corroborated by Rumsey and Rumsey (1977). Liberal attitudes toward women were also associated with a belief that punishment should be more severe. Stereotypic attitudes ascribe a stigma to the woman who has been raped, viewing her as having been shamed and disgraced or damaged in the case of a virgin. Feild's data indicate that men were more likely to believe that a women is less desirable after being raped, as were blacks, while liberal attitudes toward women were inversely related to this belief. Overall, Feild's data suggest that the general public does attach a negative stigma to the rape victim. His data also showed that training programs such as those utilized by police could reverse such attitudes.

In order to assess factors contributing to belief in inaccurate stereotypes about rape, Burt (1980) devised and assessed a rape myth acceptance scale (RMA). This scale and a variety of other instruments were administered in an interview to 598 randomly sampled Minnesota residents. Over half the sampled individuals endorsed the statements, "A woman who goes to the home or apartment of a man on the first date implies she is willing to have sex," and "In the majority of rapes the victim was promiscuous or had a bad reputation." Over half estimated that more than 50 percent "of reported rapes are reported because the woman was trying to get back at a man she was angry with or was trying to cover up an illegitimate pregnancy." The goal of the research was to determine attitudinal, personality, and experience variables that predict acceptance of rape myths. Using a multiple regression analysis, it was determined that three attitudinal variables relate to RMA total score. The strongest predictor was score on an acceptance of interpersonal violence scale, developed for the study, containing items such as "Being roughed up is sexually stimulating to many women," and "A man is never justified in hitting his wife." Other significant predictors were scored on a sex role stereotyping scale and an adversarial sexual beliefs scale. An interesting finding of the study was the similarity in predictors of rape myths between males and females. Burt concludes that rape attitudes are "strongly connected" to other deeply held and pervasive attitudes such as sex role stereotyping, distrust of the opposite sex, and acceptance of interpersonal violence in resolving conflicts. She further concludes that "the world is indeed not a safe place for the rape victim."

Attitudes of Special Groups. Attitudes discussed to this point represent beliefs held by the general population. Attitudes of specific groups within the population are also of interest, particularly those who interact with the rape victim: the rapist, the police officer, physicians, and rape counselors (note that juries, who certainly affect the rape victim, are selected from the general public). Feild (1978) compared attitudes held by rapists, the police, citizens, and rape crisis counselors. The police officers and rapists were most similar in attitude. The citizens' attitudes, while not as similar to rapists as police officers', were aligned more closely with the rapist than with rape crisis counselors' beliefs. Significant differences on each factor extracted from the attitudes toward rape scale were found between rapists and rape crisis counselors, with rapists emerging as pro-rape and counselors emerging as anti-rape.

In their study of rape victims' experiences with the criminal justice system, Holstrom and Burgess (1978) made observations about police attitudes. They were able to identify what the police officers in Boston felt to be a good case (one that could be prosecuted). A good case was one in which the victim's story was consistent, she had no previous psychiatric or legal trouble, she was forced to accompany the assailant, did not know the assailant, was emotionally upset afterwards, and had injuries and other corroborating evidence. They report that police find rape to be a heinous crime, but are suspicious of claimants whose story does not meet the standards of a "good case." McCahill et al. (1981), in their study of victims in Philadelphia, report similar police criteria for reporting rapes. They calculate that the police report only half of the rapes reported to them. A number of variables (some previously indicated) are significantly correlated with the tendency for police to mark a case as unfounded, to use a nonoffense charge, or to use a less serious charge than rape. Twenty-seven percent of rape complaints were not believed, and so marked as unfounded or given a nonoffense charge. For the remaining complaints, 14 percent were given a lesser offense charge. The presence of a policewoman was found to dramatically increase the credibility of the victim. According to the authors, "Where a policewoman is present, even if only in the capacity of a secretary, cases disappear or receive nonoffense labels less often, and are marked as founded more often. . . ." Characteristics of the victim which lead her not to be believed by police include obesity, a psychiatric history, and welfare status. The Law Enforcement Assistance Administration identified 51 police departments nationwide employing innovative methods in the treatment of rape cases. The departments were studied and their innovations as well as guidelines for police were put together in a prescriptive package (Brodyaga et al., 1975). This report indicates that many police departments have formed specialized sex crime squads, many employing female officers. Factors recommended in organizing such units were training of police investigators, utilization of civilian aides, and innovations in investigating the crime.

The attitudes of medical personnel were studied by Holstrom and Burgess (1978), including physicians and nurses in the emergency room. The staff concern often focused on determining whether a case was "legitimate" or not, in other words, whether the woman was really raped. The staff sympathy for a victim related to such factors as whether she was a child, whether she was beaten, and/or whether she was intoxicated. Holstrom and Burgess' procedure required an emergency room nurse to call them whenever a rape victim came in. One of the nurses told them on one occasion that the offender was someone known to the victim and added, "I didn't know if you wanted to come in for that [p. 73]." McGuire and Stern (1976) assessed attitudes of physicians as well as male and female students toward rape. They found that the (male) physicians' responses were similar to those of the male students. The males reported believing that rape occurs less often and involves less trauma than females believed. King, Rotter, Calhoun, and Selby (1978) surveyed physicians' and rape crisis counselors' responses to statements concerning rape causality and the severity of consequences for the victim. Results showed that the physicians believed to a greater extent than the counselors that the rape incident was precipitated by the personality traits of the victim and had been triggered by the victim's behavior. Rape crisis counselors assessed a longer time necessary for recovery, a greater need for psychological treatment, and greater consequences for the children of rape victims than did physicians.

The rather substantial aggregate of data now available tends to point in one direction. It appears that the general population ascribes to many misconceptions about rape, focusing on the woman's role in provoking rape, men's motives for rape, and why women initiate rape complaints with the police. Such beliefs are held by women themselves and probably account for the finding that rape victims suffer greater guilt reactions and have more difficulty recovering when little physical force is used in the rape. The beliefs are also held by the woman's family and husband, contributing to the lack of support sometimes reported by victims. Numerous instances are cited in the literature of rejection by husband or boyfriend following rape. But these beliefs are equally held by nurses and physicians in emergency room facilities. One of the more striking findings to emerge is the fact that police, citizens, and rapists tend to hold similar attitudes toward rape. In fact, in comparing citizens, police, and rape crisis counselors, the factorial dimensions underlying their belief systems are quite similar, though not necessarily the content of the beliefs. Thus, the conclusion begins to emerge that these beliefs, as discrepant from fact as they are, are part of a cultural belief system about women and men. It is hardly surprising then that rape common law, formulated by persons socialized within our culture, should institutionalize such misconceptions in the form of requirements for corroboration, resistance, and admissibility of sexual history testimony about the victim. In fact, the total institutional response to the rape victim is completely consistent with the prevalent popular (mis)conceptions about rape.

THEORY APPLIED TO RAPE

What then can explain the occurrence of rape? An explanation would need to account for the statistical observations that rape is often committed by young black men of low socioeconomic status and that rape is often committed in groups. Because of the homogeneity of offenders who account for such a high proportion of rapes, Amir (1971) proposes the application of Wolfgang and Ferracuti's (1967) concept of a subculture of violence. In such a subculture, group norms condone aggressive behavior including sexual violence toward women. Amir feels that several aspects of his data specifically support this interpretation. First are what he refers to as the ecological boundaries of the crime, that is, the tendency for the offender and victim to live in the same neighborhood and to be of the same race and approximate age. The assumption is that violent behavior and criminality are learned socioculturally, and that learning and continued maintenance of the criminal behavior occurs within a peer group. During group rape, the individual has an opportunity to define his role within the peer group. The prevalence of group rape is thus supportive of the subculture of violence hypothesis. Amir emphasizes that he is not proposing a subculture of rape; that the subcultural norms condone many types of violence, including rape.

Curtis (1976) refines this conceptualization, elaborating on characteristics of the poor black subculture. Curtis distinguishes between a subculture and a contraculture, hypothesizing the existence of both a black poverty subculture and a violent contraculture. A subculture differs from a dominant culture in values but is not in conflict with the dominant culture. In a counterculture, however, there is a shared system of values which both differ from and are in conflict with the dominant culture. These values are learned from experiences such as economic constraints, as well as from members of the counterculture peer group. According to Curtis, generation of the violent counterculture occurs primarily in the context of the poor black males' definition of his masculinity. The argument is as follows. Masculine success in the dominant (white male) culture is predominantly defined as economic success. However, there are other characteristics of successful masculinity not related to economics, which include such qualities as being tough, being able to hold liquor, and having sexual success with many women. Because economic opportunities are blocked to the poor black male, he focuses on the noneconomic aspects of masculinity. In fact, observations of sexual values in the ghetto have shown that the sexual success of the young male is of great significance in determining his status, which may depend on the number of females he can attract. However, not only is attractiveness to women encouraged by the peer group but also sexual exploitation of women. Curtis argues that, again, exploitation of women is a characteristic of the dominant culture, and that as this is an opportunity for success not blocked to the poor black male, its significance is exaggerated in the counterculture. An important difference between Amir and Curtis' explanations are the extent to which women are seen as playing a precipitant role in sexual aggression. Amir perceives poor black women as part of the subculture of violence, engaging provocatively in order to be a part of the boys' groups. Curtis places these women outside the violent counterculture (that is, not adopting values in conflict with the dominant culture) but within the black poverty subculture. It is also relevant to note that not all poor black males may adopt the values of the counterculture, although peer group pressure to behave criminally would be a strong incentive.

A particularly provocative element of Curtis' construction is the focus on exploitation of women in the white male culture, a focus then mirrored in the counterculture but without restraints on overt violence. Curtis documents the supposition of exploitation of women in the dominant culture by reference to the popularity of media expositions of rape: ". . . from 1971 to 1973 at least twenty major films shown in the United States—like *A Clockwork Orange*, *Straw Dogs*, *Blume in Love*, and *Save the Tiger*—served rape to their audiences."

In an insightful analysis of social factors related to rape, Dietz (1978) extends this notion, contending that both sexual exploitation and violence are normative in the dominant American culture. He points to prevalent depersonalized portrayals of women: "Whatever the psychological underpinnings of a man's depersonalization of women, he can find support for this attitude in the portrayal of women in the mass media." Prevalence of violence in the culture can be observed from emerging statistics on wife abuse (Rosenbaum & O'Leary, 1981; Straus, 1980). Thus, each of the elements making up rape are commonly accepted: sexual intercourse, coercion, and male domination of females.

How do these elements express themselves in the sexual interactions of youths in white America? An important series of studies has been conducted (Kanin, 1957, 1969, 1970; Kanin & Parcell, 1977; Kirkpatrick & Kanin, 1957), evaluating sexual aggression by college males. One of the most important findings here is the prevalence of aggression utilized by males toward the goal of gaining sexual access to women. Over 50 percent of college women surveyed reported being offended at some level of erotic intimacy over the academic year studied. The level of aggression respondents were asked to report on were, according to Kanin (1969, 1970) "usually not sufficiently violent to be considered rape attempts [but] involved forceful attempts at removing clothing and forceful attempts to maneuver the female into a physically advantageous position for sexual access," often resulting in screaming, crying, fighting and pleading. Over one fifth of the women reported that a forceful attempt at intercourse had been made during the year. While this figure is astoundingly high, other evidence suggests it is generalizable to other populations. In Burt's (1980) random sample of Minnesota adults, 27 percent of the women said they had ever had someone attempt to force sex on them. It is also of interest that none of the college women had reported the offense to the authorities, despite the fact for 6 percent the offense was characterized as "aggressively forceful attempts at sex intercourse in the course of which menacing threats or coercive infliction of physical pain were employed." Of the offended women, on the average, each had had six experiences with sexual aggression. Consistent with women's reactions to forcible rape, less than half reported feeling angry after the offense; guilt and fear were the most prevalent reactions.

Kanin (1969) also obtained questionnaire data from college males. Twenty-five percent reported engaging in at least one sexually aggressive episode since entering college. Interviews were conducted with a portion of these males in order to evaluate the type of pair relationship within which such aggression occurs. It was determined that, while aggression can occur within any stage of the dating relationship, most of such episodes occur on a first date or a pickup. Women's behavioral reactions to the episode seemed to depend not on the degree of violence used, but the intimacy of the relationship: women aggressed against on a first date were likely to scream or fight back while the woman aggressed against by her steady date would cry and express disillusionment. Aggression was most likely to occur in a relationship where the pair were dissimilar with respect to religion, age, social status, and intelligence. Of those men subscribing to a double standard (premarital sex is okay for men, not for women), aggressive sexual exploitation occurred most against women perceived as less attractive and less intelligent (hence, a less likely marriage prospect). It is interesting that in studying the offended versus nonoffended women (Kanin 1957), few differences were identified which would differentiate the two groups of women.

Case history data from offenders suggested some strong motivational patterns. The majority (70 percent) of aggressive episodes were preceded by genital petting. The remainder occurred following some sexual interaction. Thus, all acts of aggression occurred in the context of the woman's refusal to carry sexual activity further. Kanin suggests the utility of viewing males and females as representing separate subcultures, each adhering to separate systems of values and shared beliefs. The advancement of sexual intimacy to the level of genital petting is perceived differently within the two subcultures: men see it as signifying potential intercourse while women see it as an end point permitting partial gratification of desires. Thus, miscommunication may occur as a result of mutual misunderstanding. This misunderstanding becomes an aggressive episode when the female's "no" is further misunderstood as coyness and a signal to proceed. Other misassumptions made by the male subculture include beliefs that wearing of provocative clothing means the woman desires intercourse. However, misunderstanding is not the only reason males engage in aggression. Kanin (1969) discusses the use of sexual aggression as an instrument of social control. A common male subcultural belief is that teasing or exploiting the dating relationship (golddigging) is "norm violative" behavior for a female. For women perceived as engaging in such behavior, sexual aggression may be used as a punishment to teach her a lesson. The attitude is, "If she acts like a good girl, she will be reciprocated, but if she acts like a bad girl, she will have to perform like one (Kanin, 1969)." Kanin also reports this attitude to be more prevalent among working class males, which he attributes to a greater adherence to a sexual double standard, sharper separation of male and female worlds, and greater sanction of physical aggression.

Another male perception which may lead to the view that aggression is justified is the belief that a woman is promiscuous. If the man has the perception that a woman is "easy," he may expect her to behave in this manner and be angered or frustrated if she does not. As stated by one study subject, "When a male doesn't respect a girl and he knows she is nothing but a whore anyway, I feel he is entitled to use force because he knows it isn't her first time." Hearing from his friends that the girl "puts out" or gaining that impression from something about her dress or behavior, and then finding her unwilling to go past genital foreplay, may be a source of extreme aggravation and frustration.

Like the ecological boundaries of the rapist of crime statistics, college sexual aggressors share certain characteristics, according to Kanin, which distinguish them from nonaggressive college males. Most males (60 percent) who are sexually aggressive in college report having been sexually aggressive in high school as well, although the incidence of such episodes is greater in high school (an average of 5) than in college (an average of 2). Kanin (1970) details strategies used by 80 percent of these males to get sex: planned intoxication, telling his date he loves her, threatening to leave or end the relationship if she does not comply. Apparently such maneuvers work: the aggressive male is much less likely to be a virgin than the nonaggressive male. Nevertheless, he is more dissatisfied with his sex life, a fact Kanin attributes to his "inability to achieve high erotic aspirations." This higher dissatisfaction is mirrored by higher expectations of what would be required for sexual satisfaction. When asked how many ejaculations per week would be required for sexual satisfaction, the aggressives reported significantly more (3.7) than the nonaggressives (2.7).

Like the violent counterculture, this male subculture offers highest status to those males who obtain the greatest sexual success. This is no deviant subculture, however. "Males who are affiliated with groups that are strongholds of the male subculture, social fraternities for example, are under greater pressure to succeed sexually and therefore they experience a greater sense of deprivation." As opposed to the violent counterculture, it is not sex obtained through violent means that is rewarded here. However, in the face of strong peer pressure for sexual success, rejection by a woman, particularly one designated as an easy target, may lead to aggression. Exceptions to the pattern of avoiding overt rape may be cited, however. For example, an incident at Duke University resulting in the dissolution of the Beta Phi Zeta fraternity can be cited. Apparently, group rape was committed against an intoxicated freshwoman who had been secured by pledges assigned the task of "finding a drunk woman for a gang bang (Barrett, 1982)."

Kanin also has found psychological characteristics consistent with Groth and Birnbaum's (1979) and Rada's (1978) description of the family backgrounds of incarcerated rapists. With respect to relationship with mother, Kanin found that only 53 percent of the aggressives compared to 71 percent of nonaggressives indicated some degree of love for their mothers. It was also true that more of the aggressive males (72 percent) reported "having been deeply hurt or disappointed by a girl they cared for" than the nonaggressive males (50 percent). The convergence of these two sources of hostility toward women showed 90 percent of aggressive males either not loving their mothers of having been hurt by a previous girlfriend. Also like rape in the counterculture, sexual aggression among certain college male peer groups is not an isolated aggressive response. The aggressive males displayed a higher level of general aggression than the nonaggressive males. According to Kanin, the combination of a high level of aggression and a hostility toward women supported by a peer group demanding sexual exploitation is a strong configuration predictive of sexual aggression.

Kanin's evidence in combination with the theories of Amir and Curtis provides much support for the supposition that sexual aggression is normative among a sizeable proportion of the population in the United States. The dominant white youth's tendency toward exploitation, stopping (in most cases) just short of physical coercion, is reflected and exaggerated in the more extreme aggression that is normative within a violent counterculture. This view of rape as the extreme of a behavioral continuum for sexual aggression and sexual exploitation is supported by Koss and Oros (1982). They devised a Sexual Experiences Survey designed to detect unreported instances of rape and sexual aggression of varying degrees. The result of utilizing this instrument in survey fashion supported the dimensional view of rape. Increasing numbers of female students reported having had an experience, as type of coercion became more moderate, from 6.4 percent who had been raped (almost the identical figure found by Kanin) to 32 percent who reported feeling unable to stop a man because he was so aroused, even though intercourse was not desired. While clearly the majority of males are not sexually aggressive, institutionalized supports for sexual aggression are available, supporting males who select vulnerable or maritally undesirable women as targets of sexual exploitation.

Malamuth has investigated propensity to rape among college males (Malamuth, 1981a; Malamuth & Check, 1980; Malamuth, Haber, & Feshbach, 1980) by asking subjects to indicate the likelihood that they would rape "if they could be assured of not being caught and punished ((Malamuth, 1981b)." Across studies, likelihood was typically reported on a five-point scale, with higher ratings corresponding to higher likelihood. An average of about 20 percent indicated a likelihood of '3' or higher, a figure which matches Kanin's 25 percent who acknowledged committing a sexually aggressive act. From these studies of sexual aggression on the college campus, it appears that about 6 percent of women are raped. Given our knowledge that sexual aggression is more normative in the working class than among college students, there is no reason to suspect that the figure would be less among other same aged groups in the population. For this age range, then, the rate of four times the reported 70 per 100,000 women produced by victimization studies (.28 percent) is clearly a gross underestimate of the magnitude of the problem.

Rape as Victimization of Women

Women as Legitimate Victims. Rape is not just an act where violence is inflicted, it can also be seen as an act in which exploitation and victimization occurs. But it is a victimization in which both offender and victim rarely perceive the legitimacy of the victim's complaint, where the victim is often seen as precipitating her abuse, and where the stigma attached to public awareness of the offense may be greater for the victim than the offender. It is for such reasons that Weis and Borges (1975) view the woman raped as a case of a legitimate victim, i.e., someone societally perceived as deserving of (and thus not compensatable for) victimization.

> Victimization refers to societal processes that before, during, and after the event simultaneously render the victim defenseless and partly responsible for it. Victimization includes the preparation of the victim for the crime, his or her experience during the crime and the treatment he or she will encounter as part of the aftermath of the crime.

It is contended that social conditions structure those situations which will produce rape, ensure that women will do little to interfere with their assailants, create negative sanctions for reporting rape, and render ineffective the attempts to blame the rapist. For example, the dating situation juxtaposes women who are socialized to be passive and dependent on men for economic as well as emotional well being with men who are socialized to be dominant, aggressive, and in competition with other males for sexual status. That women not only are frequent victims, but by popular consensus deserve to be (except in the case of stranger rape or extreme brutality), can be observed in society's reaction to a charge of rape. If it is not denied (because opinion says she probably consented), it is justified (popular opinion says she got what she deserved). Comparative consideration of the victimology of rape and assault may help to elucidate the point.

In recent years, the field of victimology (study of victims) has addressed the issue of compensation for victims of violent crimes. A superficial consideration of the issue would suggest the need for corroboration that the crime of assault occurred. If a fund were simply available to pay victims of crime, what would stop anyone from crying victim in order to earn the compensation? Such logic is disturbingly reminiscent of issues raised with respect to need for corroboration of rape. But there is a difference. In rape, no monetary compensation is being sought, merely the conviction of the offender; an event which would hardly be considered compensation to the victim of assault. But is it not, perhaps, perceived as compensation to the rape victim? For many (all?) women are perceived as having adequate motivation to cry "rape," just for the satisfaction of having a particular male convicted, while only the assault victim who stands to gain monetary compensation is thought to have motive for false accusation. It is thus that the social realities of rape are elucidated by the perception of all women as victims.

As a person who deserves victimization, then, the woman (again except in unusual circumstances) is blamed for being raped. Blaming the victim can be explained in several ways. On a general level, it is true that in our competitive, success-oriented society, all victims are blamed. The victim of a misfortune such as an auto accident has been judged to be at fault if the accident had severe consequences, but less so when the consequences were not as severe (Chaiken & Darley, 1973; Walster, 1966). These findings have been explained by the "just world" hypothesis, that victims of severe misfortune cannot have been singled out by chance alone because we live in a just world where people who are good experience positive consequences and people who are bad are punished. Belief in such a theory helps to convince the individual that he or she is not vulnerable to similar misfortunes. Attribution of blame to an innocent victim has been observed for misfortunes ranging from an auto accident to death by murder (Weis & Borges, 1975). Blaming oneself for a misfortune has similarly been observed in cases of auto accidents, criminal victimization (including rape), and disease such as cancer (Janoff-Bulman & Lang-Gunn, 1982). In fact it is Janoff-Bulman and Lang-Gunn's hypothesis that behavioral self-blame (e.g., self-statements such as "I should not have left the house unlocked") is an adaptive response associated with quickened recovery from the misfortune and a decreased perception of future vulnerability. This conceptualization has been specifically applied to rape victims of whom 74 percent, according to rape crisis counselors, engaged in self-blame following the assault (Janoff-Bulman, 1979). However, an important distinction needs to be drawn between attribution of blame and attribution of moral responsibility. The robbery victim who did not lock the doors may blame him or herself, but is not likely to feel morally responsible for the theft. The victim of "date-rape", on the other hand, is likely to feel guilt over her own moral responsibility in creating the conditions of her adversity, and society is likely to be quick to concur.

Thus, while the rape victim, like any victim, is held responsible by society for the mistakes which led to the misfortune, the rape victim has additional burdens to bear. She was not merely naive or careless, she was provocative and is now blaming the man for the consequences. It seems that one of the responsibilities of women in the dating situation is to determine how far to go sexually. Men are assumed to be "creatures" of strong and perhaps uncontrollable sexual desire who will understandably always strive for full gratification (intercourse). And, indeed, there is no stigma attached or negative consequence for realizing this goal; in fact, as previously discussed, there is great potential reward in terms of status in the peer group. For women, there is both stigma (bad reputation) and negative consequences (possible pregnancy), and so it is her responsibility to stop the petting when she feels it has gone far enough. It is, thus, the female responsibility to control the male sexual urge. When rape is claimed, one reason it may be disbelieved is that it is the woman's own responsibility to make sure sex does not go further than she wished. If she arouses her partner to the point where no one can control his sexual desire, she has only herself to blame. Thus, the aggressor is given free reign to exercise his desires and it is the victim's job to control them or else be held accountable.

Another rationale sometimes expressed for blaming the rape victim is a masochistic nature attributed to women. "When women say 'no' it is because they prefer being taken by force" is the logic. Psychiatric documentation of the female's masochistic character can readily be found (Deutsch, 1944). Sexual submission has been touted as the key to female sexual satisfaction in psychoanalytically oriented sex manuals such as *The Power of Sexual Surrender* (Robinson, 1959). According to Robinson, ". . . the excitement comes from the act of surrender. There is a tremendous surging physical ecstasy in the yielding itself, in the feeling of being the passive instrument of another person, of being stretched out supinely beneath him, taken up will-lessly by his passion as leaves are swept up before a wind [p. 158]." It has further been touted in popular erotica such as the pornographic classic, *Story of O* (Reage, 1965), which depicts the pleasure for a women of sexual pain and humiliation. The fact that women themselves often are aroused by fantasies of rape (Hariton & Singer, 1974) is often cited as further evidence for the validity of the belief that women desire to be handled roughly. Presence of masochism means blame of the rape victim because it nullifies her resistance as proof of lack of consent. Women are so masochistic, the explanation goes, that they will often promote physical roughing up because "it's more exciting" that way. Likewise, the degradation involved in many rapes does not stand as proof that the woman failed to provide consent, because she may have sought it.

A brief discussion of the dynamics of the dominant/submissive dichotomy in sexual relationships seems relevant here. While clearly no woman experiences pleasure in being forced to have sex against her will, there may be sexual pleasure for women, as there may be for men, in playing a submissive role. In fact, it can be contended that much of what is considered erotic in our culture involves portrayal of women in submissive/masochistic poses. It has also been pointed out in recent writings that, if persons find themselves subjected to sexual abuse without possibility of escape and over an extended time period, masochism may be adaptive (Brownmiller, 1975; Gates, 1978).

An illustrative example, also revealing of motivation for rape, is the case of rape in the prison setting. The frequent occurrence of male rape of other males in prison has been documented (Davis, 1970). Within the prison, as in society at large, rape does not occur as a sporadic or isolated event. According to Brownmiller (1975), "Prison rape is generally seen today for what it is: an acting out of power roles within an all-male, authoritarian environment in which the younger, weaker inmate, usually a first offender, is forced to play the role that in the outside world would be assigned to women." In accord with the generally high level of violence condoned as normative within a prison society, this rape frequently involves brutal beatings and particularly abusive and sadistic components. But it is the association of sexual success with status that marks the similarity between the prison rape and rape in the outside world. Those who do the raping are considered "men," those who submit are viewed as playing the female role. And perhaps even more often than in the outside world, rape is used as a means of punishment or social control.

From time to time such situations are brought to the public attention. A recent series of articles in the *Washington Post* (Tofani, 1982) reported interviews with convicts who raped and who had been raped. One inmate named Welcher who reported raping several men a week over a two year period, expressed his views: "In jail you're not a homosexual if you're the aggressor. You're more of a man if anything. It goes back to the mentality of the street, the definition of a man. On the street, a man is producing babies, having women, having sex. Sex is one of the things you identify with manhood. In jail manhood is everything because you have nothing else." Welcher himself rejected the use of beating to gain sexual compliance. Instead, he would offer a victim protection from other prisoners in exchange for regular sex for himself and a few friends. With regard to motives for rape, Welcher said, "Everyone likes to dominate so you make sure there are two groups, the dominant and the not. You have to maintain that separation." He further explained why he and the others felt a need to dominate: "Because they've been dominated. They been stepped on. They're poor, from the streets, from broken families. That's the way of life on the streets. But nobody wants to be at the bottom. Everyone wants to be the pimp, the stick-up man. That's the only thing they relate to. They bring the same thing to jail." According to Tofani, the inmates expressed no guilt over their actions. "They believe that a 'real man'—their words—would kill rather than get raped. In their view a man who is raped must be homosexual and therefore should not mind it." If he were not he would fight to the death rather than be raped. It is consequently not surprising that it is difficult for some members of the male subculture to understand how a woman who has no marks on her could have been raped. Clearly, these views substantiate the view of rape or sexual aggression as an expression of masculinity and dominance.

But they also coincide with the idea that the rape victim wanted it or was asking for it if he did not prevent it. Men in prison are beaten and raped into adopting the role of women. In some instances, they are bought and sold among prisoners, or set themselves up as prostitutes (Brownmiller, 1975). The most articulate spokesperson of this group is the French novelist Jean Genet who glorifies the role of recipient of brutal sexual abuse. By accepting the status of slave and perceiving the receipt of brutality as an expression of love, Genet elevates masochism to the martyrdom of sainthood. Feminist writers have pointed out the parallels with the much praised female role of sufferer (Millet, 1970). Rape in prison thus illustrates how the dominant/submissive, sadistic/masochistic nature of rape does not rely on the presence of males and females, but rather a permissive attitude toward aggression and a desire for a dominant class and a submissive class, with the latter perceived as masochistic. In some exceptional cases, individuals in such circumstances may even become masochistic as an adaptation.

To complete the role of women as societally legitimized victims of rape, the reporting of rape to authorities is made difficult through stigmatization. To reveal that rape occurred is to acknowledge a sexually illicit experience. In spite of new sexual mores, a young woman may not wish her parents or school officials to know she had illicit sex, or was in a position where it was demanded. Kirkpatrick and Kanin (1957) describe the insidious development of a stigmatized situation in this way: "In abstract ideal-typical terms, member B of an AB pair is urged by member A to participate in behavior desired by A but prohibited by primary group and institutional controls. B may develop ambivalent resistance but yield to a point where stigma would be involved with disclosure." Aggression at this point (which is the point according to Kanin at which it usually occurs) is almost certain not to be reported. It has already been identified how capacity to gain compensation, even in the form of societal acknowledgement of guilt of the offender, is limited.

Social History of Victimization Through Rape. In her magnus opus on the social history of rape, Brownmiller (1975) develops a thesis of rape as the means by which men control women. "From prehistoric times to the present, I believe, rape has played a critical function. It is nothing more or less than a conscious process of intimidation by which *all* men keep *all* women in a state of fear [p. 15]" (original italics). Brownmiller develops her thesis as follows. Within the context of Judeo-Christian law, the relationship of development of laws against rape to development of laws for protection of property rights is put forward. Women did not have rights under laws such as the Code of Hammurabi of ancient Babylonia and were thus property of either father or husband. One way to acquire this property was capture by force, a practice existing in England until the fifteenth century according to Brownmiller. However, capture of a woman within your own community violated the rights of the original owner. Thus, the payment of a brideprice, an amount paid to the father for his daughter, was written into law. Because the bride must be a virgin, the rape of a virgin (which destroyed her value and ability to marry) became a severely punished act. Under some circumstances, the transgressor could make amends by paying the specified amount and marrying his victim. This option persisted under English common law. Rape of a married woman did not carry such penalties and tended to be considered under the rubric of adultery, focusing blame on both parties. Thus, the true meaning of rape under ancient law as well as early English common law was the theft of virginity, and thus a crime against property.

Early precedents for the modern wariness of a false rape charge are pointed out by Brownmiller. She cites the Biblical parable of Joseph and Potiphar's wife. Potiphar's wife accuses the innocent Joseph of rape, for which he is put in jail, much later to be released when he correctly interprets the Pharoah's dreams. Thus, the message of a woman's capacity to injure an innocent man was taught.

Legal reforms gradually appeared in English law. As the nationalization movement progressed, the Crown took an interest in the prosecution of rape, extending this protection to women other than virgins. With the Statutes of Westminster at the end of the thirteenth century, the assailant of a married woman was subject to prosecution by the Crown, even if the woman did not pursue the case herself, and was subject to punishment equal that of the rapist of a virgin.

The bulk of Brownmiller's treatise deals with documenting instances of rape in war and other periods of subjugation of one group of men by another. Records are existent, and in testimonial after testimonial from antiquity to World War I, World War II, and Viet Nam, it becomes clear that rape is an act that members of an army perform on the women of a conquered area. Domination of one group of men by another means sexual access to their women, and often in a way that humiliates the conquered man (e.g., he is forced to watch). Other examples are given: Belgian women including nuns were raped in the Congo in 1960 during the Congolese drive for independence; white women were raped by American Indians; Indian women were raped by white men; the rape of black women by white men was institutionalized during American slavery, some women even being designated as breeders. A recent example at the time of this writing was the repeated rape of a Palestinian nurse during the Christian Lebanese massacre in Beirut.

This view of rape as an act of domination clearly coincides with Groth and Birnbaum's (1979) conceptualization of power as an intrapsychic motive for rape. It also provides perspective on punishment for rape as an issue in race relations in the United States. For a white man to have sex with a black woman might be considered by him his due, but for a black man to have sex with a white woman was considered a rebellion against the social structure, and all too frequently punished by death. The phony rape charge framed against a black man has been the arena for elucidation of political injustice from the Scottsboro trial to the novel *To Kill a Mockingbird*. However, exclusive focus on the rape charge as a vehicle for racial oppression may have obscured issues relevant to sexual oppression.

But beyond the documenting of the use of rape by men to dominate other men, Brownmiller focuses on male domination of females through rape. Like Kanin's undergraduates who would teach a lesson to the tease, rape as a means of punishment is not uncommon in tribal societies. In our own culture, punishment by gang rape has been sanctioned by the Hells Angels (Thompson, 1967) to punish women who violate subgroup norms. Besides its use as punishment, rape can be a method by which women are encouraged to remain dependent on men (Gates, 1978). Without a male protector, the possibility of rape is much greater, they argue. That men take the role of protector extremely seriously is evident in case reports of guilt experienced by men whose mother, sister, wife, or daughter was raped. This seriousness is also culturally evident in such films as *Death Wish* in which the character played by Charles Bronson goes out to seek revenge for rape on his own.

One function of the law is to equalize the physically weak and physically strong. Thus, each individual does not need to physically protect himself and his property, because society will use its collective brawn to punish the violator of his rights. This protection has not been extended to women, who are only beginning to enjoy equal status under the law. Instead, a woman has been forced to rely on her individual protector (husband or father) and the state has been extremely reluctant to intervene within that family unit, even when abuses of power within the family have been well documented.

Cross-cultural Factors in Rape. In response to this picture of male domination, the question emerges—Why? Is it simply human nature, the fact that men are the physically stronger of the sexes, or as Brownmiller hypothesizes, the biological accident that the genitals of one sex can function as a weapon? The context of rape has been studied cross-culturally in an attempt to identify cultural correlates of sexual aggression (Sanday, 1981). Characteristics of 156 standard sample societies were coded as rape prone, rape free, or intermediate. A rape prone society was defined as one having a high incidence of rape, using rape as a ceremonial act, using rape as punishment, and sexually assaulting enemy women during warfare. Eighteen percent of the societies were classified as rape prone (a designation which would clearly include our own society) while 47 percent were classified as rape free. Descriptions of a number of rape prone societies show elements very much in common with our own. According to Sanday, "In general, the profile presented by Amir is reminiscent of the pattern of rape found among the Kikuyu, where a band of boys belonging to a guild roamed the countryside in search of a woman to gang rape as a means of proving their manhood and as a prelude to marriage [p. 20]." Sanday asserts that rape appears to occur in "cultures of violence" in which women are regarded as property. This concept generated two hypotheses. One was that rape would occur in societies characterized by violence internal to itself and toward neighboring groups: societies disposed to war, male toughness, interpersonal violence, and raiding of other groups for wives. The second half of the concept was formulated into the hypothesis that rape would occur in societies characterized by male dominance, that is, those in which women do not have power and authority, political decision making opportunity, rights as citizens, and in which special places were designated for the congregation of each sex separately. Highly significant correlations between rape prone status and existence of aggression and male domination were found. The rape free societies were characterized by sexual equality. According to Sanday:

> The key to understanding the relative absence of rape in rape free as opposed to rape prone societies is the importance, which in some cases is sacred, attached to the contribution women make to social continuity. . . . In tribal societies women are often equated with fertility and growth, men with agression and destruction. More often than not, the characteristics associated with maleness and femaleness are equally valued.

Sanday also tested the psychological hypothesis that a family configuration involving a close, dependent, and possibly seductive relationship between mother and son but aloof relationship between father and son or daughter predisposes toward rape. This was tested by coding societal characteristics including the nature of mother-son and father-daughter relationships and proximity of father in care of infants. These characteristics were not as strongly related to rape as the variables previously discussed, but did show some predictive ability, particularly the role of the father. Finally, the notion that sexual repression produces rape was tested by relating variables such as age at marriage, and attitude toward premarital sex with rape proclivity. No significant relationships were found and this hypothesis was not upheld. Sanday thus emphasizes that violence, including sexual violence, is socially learned and that rape appears to be learned in the cultural context of interpersonal violence and male dominance. She further states that, where there is not an imbalance between environmental resources and population needs, where harmony with the environment exists, rape is rare. Where competition for resources prevails, the "male role is accorded greater prestige." Our society would seem to fit well into Sanday's conceptualization. We are engaged in global conflict for diminishing resources. Male characteristics are valued, female devalued, and aggressive means of conflict resolution are glorified.

In order to address the topic of prevention of rape, the focus must shift to the sources of sexual aggression in our culture. Recent research certainly confirms Sanday's assumption that aggression can be taught (Bandura, 1969). The assumption is logical also that violence toward women will occur, whether in wife abuse or rape, as long as women are subordinate and aggression is condoned. However, the intersection of the two major ideologies (violence and domination of women) is worthy of special note and may have special relevance to the control of rape. This intersection includes sexual aggression, and the issue arises of whether we do in fact teach sexual aggression specifically in our culture. Do we go beyond teaching that men are dominant and that aggression is a way to solve problems? Do we also teach (not in youth peer groups but in the culture at large) that sexual aggression is rewarding?

Aggression and Arousal in the Laboratory

One manner in which sexual aggression might be rewarding would be if it were sexually arousing. Evidence suggests that, in fact, rape is not sexually arousing to the attacker. Groth and Burgess (1977) found that one third of a group of convicted rapists had difficulty in achieving an erection or ejaculating during the rape, with an even larger group failing to achieve sexual gratification for reasons such as successful victim resistance. Nevertheless, if the rapist believes that it will be sexually gratifying, this perception may influence his decision to rape. This does not mean that desire for a sexually gratifying experience is the primary motivational force. It makes sense that the sexual act would not be chosen as a vehicle for expression of power or anger, however, if the rapist believed he would not find it sexually arousing.

Abel, Barlow, Blanchard, and Guild (1977) directly measured the sexual arousal of convicted rapists in reaction to different stimuli. The goal of the research was to differentiate rapists and nonrapists on the basis of erection measures. The comparison group of nonrapists in this case was patients described as presenting sexual deviations including pedophilia, exhibitionism, and homosexuality. The results showed that the rapists were equally aroused to both rape and mutually desired intercourse depictions, while the nonrapists had significantly less arousal to scenes of rape than the mutually desired sex. On the basis of this, a rape index was defined as erection to rape cues divided by erection to mutually enjoyable intercourse cues. A rape index of .5 (arousal to rape half as much as arousal to mutual sex) separated most rapists from most nonrapists. The index was further found to have utility in predicting those individuals who had the highest frequency of rape and who had most engaged in use of force during the rape.

Abel et al. (1977) also measured responses of rapists to purely aggressive cues: audio scenes of the physical assault of a woman with no sexual content. Erection to pure aggressive cues was 40 percent less overall than that to rape cues, but was almost perfectly correlated (r = .98). Combining data from the rape index and arousal to pure aggression was felt to have potential clinical utility in predicting the dangerousness of a rapist. This data also seems to support the hypothesis that an expectation of arousal may be a contributor to the decision to rape.

However, a growing literature suggests that the normal population finds rape equally as arousing as depictions of mutually desired sex, as long as arousal to such stimuli is in any way disinhibited. Malamuth (1981a) utilized an audiotape description of rape that was "virtually identical to that used by Abel et al. (1977)." For male subjects, arousal elicited by the audio rape description was relatively high, and was of the same magnitude as that elicited by a description of consenting sex (subjective mean rating of 42 percent of maximum arousal). Two differences between the studies by Malamuth and Abel were identified. One was that Malamuth's audio rape description was read by a female voice; and, second, the experimental setting was a university laboratory rather than a jail or treatment institution. Both factors might be expected to give permission for greater arousal to rape: a woman's voice might indicate that she approved of the action; the institutional setting suggests lack of tolerance for deviate arousal patterns.

The portrayed reaction of the victim has also been shown to influence sexual arousal to rape cues. Malamuth and Check (1980) found that, while arousal was less to a depiction of rape in which the victim was portrayed as abhorring the experience than to a depiction of mutually desired sex, no difference was found (using penile tumescence as a dependent measure) when the rape victim was portrayed as becoming aroused. Thus, the victim's arousal was facilitative of subject arousal, regardless of the fact that force was employed in the narrative. In Abel et al.'s stimulus materials, the victim was not portrayed as experiencing any pleasure. In a related study, Malamuth, Haber, and Feshbach (1980) presented a written description of rape to both male and female subjects. They found that males' self-reported arousal to a rape description in which no arousal on the part of the victim was portrayed averaged around 3.5 on a 5 point scale, and was equivalent or greater than arousal to either a violent or nonviolent portrayal of mutually desired sex to which the subject had been previously exposed. It was found that males' rated arousal was significantly higher than females'; however, females did report substantial arousal to the rape depiction (around an average of 3 on a 5 point scale).

An additional study (Malamuth, Heim, & Feshbach, 1980) sought to tease out relative contributions to arousal of whether the rape was planned, whether the victim experienced pain, and whether the victim experienced an involuntary orgasm or nausea. Eight versions of the same rape story were thus read by male and female subjects. Results indicated low to moderate levels of arousal, depending on condition. For male subjects, the most arousing story involved the victim's experience of both orgasm and pain, which received a mean arousal rating of 3 on an 8 point scale. For female subjects, the most arousing story portrayed orgasm and no pain (also 3 on an 8 point scale).

These studies indicate that, under various conditions (e.g., victim arousal portrayed, rape story read by female voice), the description of rape is equally arousing to the average person as a description of mutually desired sex. Furthermore, indication of pain on the part of the victim (if she is also involuntarily aroused) can add to male arousal. Given that it is not an uncommon perception that women do enjoy and would be aroused by victimization (Malamuth, Haber, & Feshbach, 1980), these findings suggest that a sizeable portion of the male population may believe that it would be sexually arousing to force sex on a woman.

Malamuth (1981b) has specifically studied the relationship of arousal to rape cues, perception of victim's arousal, and other factors to self-reported likelihood to rape among college males. Across a number of studies, Malamuth and his colleagues asked males to indicate whether they would rape if they could be assured of not being caught and punished. As previously discussed, 35 percent of all males studied reported some likelihood of raping under these conditions. Likelihood of raping (LR) has been found to be highly correlated with a belief that the victim in an audio rape description enjoyed being raped and that women in general would enjoy victimization (Malamuth & Check, 1980; Malamuth, Haber, & Feshbach, 1980). Furthermore, high LR was correlated with the perception that the victim did not experience pain, identification with the rapist, and a belief that rape victims are responsible for their rape.

Malamuth and colleagues have further demonstrated convincingly that self-reported likelihood to rape is associated with sexual arousal to depictions of rape (but not consenting sex) (Malamuth, Haber, & Feshbach, 1980; Malamuth & Check, 1980). Malamuth and Check (1981b) formed high and low LR groups, then exposed both to portrayals of mutually desired sex, rape in which the victim is portrayed as abhorring the experience, and rape in which the victim is portrayed as being aroused. High likelihood of rape subjects displayed lowest penile arousal to mutually desired sex, intermediate arousal to the abhorred rape, and greatest arousal to the victim-aroused rape. The low likelihood of rape subjects showed more arousal to the mutually desired sex than the abhorred rape (consistent with other findings). These findings are highly similar to Abel et al.'s (1977) findings and suggest that there are commonalities in the population of convicted rapists and male college students who claim a likelihood of rape.

The question of whether these males believe that rape would be arousing has been directly examined (Malamuth, 1981a). A positive correlation was found between likelihood of rape and endorsement of the belief that rape would be arousing. Malamuth (1981b) has made a convincing argument that this one-item self-report measure has validity as an index of actual propensity to rape. He argues that rapists have been demonstrated to differ from normals with respect to acceptance of rape myths and with respect to arousal (at least under inhibited conditions) to rape depictions. Validity of the LR rating is supported by its correlation with acceptance of rape myths (e.g., the woman enjoys victimization) and arousal to rape depictions. Further validational evidence is provided by findings that LR rating is correlated with self-report of having used force against women in sexual situations. Finally, using a paradigm in which subjects believed they were delivering shocks to another student, high LR males were shown to deliver more shocks, express more anger, and express more desire to hurt a woman who had previously angered them than low LR males (Malamuth, 1981b).

Thus, a considerable amount of evidence supports the contention that a person who would rape (or who thinks he would rape) believes the experience would be arousing. It might be inferred that a source of this belief is his own arousal to pornographic depictions of rape and his own fantasies.

Here it is appropriate to remember that both low LR and high LR men are aroused by rape descriptions. It is only the rape descriptions in which no overt description of victim pleasure is included that differentiate these groups. It seems that the high LR men infer victim pleasure, even when it is clearly stated that the victim abhors the experience, and in which no allusion is made to her pleasure. But given that the average response (both male and female) is arousal to "positive" rape descriptions, it becomes very easy to understand the difficulties inherent for the victim in reporting a rape case, much less having it successfully prosecuted, especially, but not exclusively, when it is acquaintance rape. In fact, there is very good intuitive reason why rape would be arousing to imagine. We live in a society where themes of dominance and submission characterize the essence of maleness and femaleness. The image of a strong, powerful man dominating a woman, forcing her to submit sexually, is a powerful erotic image that is probably arousing to most men and women. Rape is perceived as a logical extension of this culturally ingrained theme. Examination of pornography reveals that most of what is perceived as erotic embodies themes of dominance and submission. It is for these reasons that beliefs and attitudes about rape are part of our most fundamental nature. Rape, however, is the act of being forced to have sex with someone with whom the individual does not wish to have sex. This is why it is not perceived as a sexual experience by the victim, and although it may in a small percent of cases turn out to be sexually arousing to the rapist, by definition it never is to the victim.

However, our cultural belief is that forced sex (domination) is arousing and our erotica depicts it as such. A question of great social significance is whether actual violence toward women is increased by exposure to such violent erotic portrayals. Evidence suggests it is. Malamuth and Check (1981a) had subjects complete three inventories after viewing films shown on campus. The inventories were Acceptance of Interpersonal Violence, Rape Myth Acceptance, and Adversarial Sexual Beliefs (Burt, 1980). Subjects saw either two films portraying sexual violence (*Swept Away* and *The Getaway*) or two non-sexually-violent control films (*A Man and a Woman*, and *Hooper*). Observation of the sexually violent films led to a significant increase for males' scores on the Acceptance of Interpersonal Violence inventory and a nonsignificant increase on the Rape Myth Acceptance scale. Female scores decreased on both scales after viewing the sexually violent films and were lower overall than males scores.

Perhaps more to the point, however, evidence of increased aggression toward women has been observed to follow exposure to sexually violent films. In order to assess these findings, a brief description of the research paradigm will be presented. Interpersonal aggression has a long history of measurement in the laboratory utilizing a Buss (1961) aggression machine. This is a device by which a subject can ostensibly deliver varying degrees of electric shock to another person, typically perceived to be another subject but in reality a confederate of the experimenter. In this manner, the capacity of intervening variables to mediate aggression of an angered subject may be measured. A standard paradigm has involved two "subjects" arriving for an experiment at the same time (one the real subject, the other a confederate). A manipulation in which the confederate angers the subject follows. Often blood pressure or other autonomic nervous system measures are taken to test the effectiveness of the anger manipulation. Next, a stimulus such as a film is shown which might be expected to interact with the subject's anger. Finally, the subject is given an opportunity to shock the confederate. Results of studies conducted in this manner indicate that a mild erotic stimulus (e.g., pictures of nudes) will decrease intensity of shock delivered compared to a neutral stimulus (Baron, 1974; Baron & Bell, 1977), but that highly erotic stimuli (pictures of sexual acts) will produce equal or increased shock levels over neutral stimuli (Baron & Bell, 1977; Donnerstein & Barrett, 1978; Donnerstein, Donnerstein, & Evans, 1975). Such research did not suggest that the sex of the target of aggression differentially affected intensity of shock used. Donnerstein and Barrett (1978) varied the sex of the target and found that lower intensity of shock was administered to female than male targets after angered subjects viewed an erotic film. However, blood pressure of the subjects who had been angered by women remained higher than that of subjects angered by men, suggesting that they were actually angrier, but just not acting upon it due to societal injunctions against aggression toward women.

Donnerstein and Hallam (1978) devised a methodology for disinhibiting societal prohibitions for aggression against women. They simply gave the male subjects a second chance to deliver shocks after the first set was complete, reasoning that the first set would serve to lower aggressive inhibitions. Subjects viewed a highly erotic film, a purely aggressive film (clips from *The Wild Bunch*), or no film, followed by the opportunity to aggress against either a male or female target. All subjects initially underwent an anger manipulation. In the first set of aggression trials, results supported previous findings: aggression toward males and females for both film types was comparable (although greater than following no film). For the second set of trials, exposure to the erotic film produced more aggression toward the female target than the male target. This study constituted the first demonstration that exposure to erotica can increase aggression toward a woman.

Donnerstein (1980a, 1980b) examined the effect of a film depicting rape on aggression toward women, reasoning that this film content, like the double aggression opportunity, might lower inhibitions against aggression toward women. The aggressive erotic (rape) film was compared to an erotic and neutral film for subjects who had either been previously angered or not. Target of aggression (male or female) was also varied. As in previous studies, shock intensity delivered to males and females did not differ following exposure to the erotic film. However, shock delivered to females following the rape film was significantly higher than that delivered to males, and in fact, this was the stimulus condition under which the greatest intensity of shock was delivered. Increased shock was delivered after the rape film even if the subject had not been previously angered. These findings could not be explained in terms of greater physiological arousal produced by sexual aggression, as blood pressure was not found to be greater following the aggressive erotic than the erotic film. Thus, this study clearly demonstrates aggression toward women following exposure to rape stimuli.

Donnerstein and Berkowitz (1981) tested effects of a "positive" outcome rape film versus a "negative" outcome rape film on aggression toward men and women following anger induction. Both of the rape films portrayed a woman who goes to study with two men. She is "tied up, stripped, slapped, and sexually attacked." For the positive outcome, the film is preceded by an introduction stating that the woman becomes a willing participant by the end of the film, and is shown smiling at the end. For the negative outcome film, the introduction states "she finds the experience humiliating and disgusting" and is shown suffering at the end. Results were simlar to Donnerstein (1980a, 1980b). Aggression toward men was no different for either rape film than the erotic film. For women targets, both versions of the rape film produced increased aggression. In a second experiment using the same stimulus films, subjects were either angered or not by a female confederate. Results here showed different reactions to the two versions of the rape film. For the "positive" ending, increased aggression was displayed toward the female confederate whether the subject had previously been angered or not. For the "negative" ending, no increased aggression was displayed by non-angered subjects. It was only the angered subjects who showed increased aggression. The authors hypothesize that different processes took place for the two versions of the rape story. For the "positive" outcome story they speculate that a messge of "aggression is justified" was communicated. Permission for aggression against women presumably also extended to the experimental setting. Subjects exposed to the "negative" outcome film were hypothesized to take away the same "aggression is justified" message *if* they were angry at a woman and thus desirous of seeing a woman hurt. In the angered case, then, the victim's pain cues would be reinforcing. On the other hand, if the subject did not at the time wish to see a woman hurt, he would not find this observation of pain rewarding or stimulating. These subjects would thus not aggress against the female confederate.

Why do men aggress more against women than men after seeing a film of rape? Donnerstein and Berkowitz speculate it is because of a stimulus-response association between the woman on the screen who was a target for aggression and the woman in the experiment. This type of explanation, in effect saying that generalization occurs exclusively because both are female, seems simplistic. A more convincing explanation might be the disinhibition hypothesis that a film portraying aggression against women communicates that aggression against women is permissable in the experimental setting. Indeed, Donnerstein and Hallam (1978) found a high level of aggression against men following a film portraying aggression against males (clips from *The Wild Bunch*). Such possibilities could be readily tested by varying the sex of the film target of aggression.

The disinhibition explanation takes on social significance when one considers that women are often seen as legitimate targets of sexual aggression, and that it is exactly under the conditions of anger (for not permitting intercourse) that most sexual aggression against women occurs. Thus, these data draw a strong connection between exposure to sexually violent films and actual aggression against women. It seems that this may occur regardless of an individual's affective state but is even more likely when he is angry. Only observing an explicit message indicating that the rape was upsetting to the victim seemed to inhibit this level of aggression. This research, like that of Malamuth and his colleagues, shows that sexual violence portrayed as a positive experience for the female victim has particularly negative implications, as aggression is made to seem justified and desirable. Additionally, Malamuth and Check (1980) found that subjects who had been pre-exposed to depiction of rape as arousing to the victim felt the victim of a subsequent rape portrayal experienced less trauma than subjects who had been pre-exposed to either a portrayal of rape as abhorred or a portrayal of mutually desired sex. It additionally increased the male subjects' estimations of the percent of men who are likely to rape. In other words, portraying a victim as experiencing arousal leads to beliefs that rape can be arousing and may be a desirable behavior. Furthermore, Malamuth, Haber, and Feshbach (1980) found that pre-exposure to a sexually violent story led to an increased correlation for males between arousal to a rape story and perception of pain experienced by the victim. This was not found for females. One interpretation of this correlation is that, as a male is exposed to more sexual violence, he begins to be aroused by infliction of pain on a female victim. This interpretation is supported by the finding that the combination of victim pain and orgasm was more arousing to male college students than victim arousal but no pain (Malamuth, Heim, & Feshbach, 1980). It has been demonstrated that pre-exposure to a portrayal of rape in which the victim is sexually aroused leads to increased sexual arousal to a depiction of rape where no victim arousal is described. On the other hand (like Donnerstein and Berkowitz's (1981) findings for aggression) explicit description of the victim's abhorrence of rape led to less arousal to a subsequent rape description.

Ethical issue has been raised over the use of "positive" descriptions of rape in psychology experiments, particularly because exposure seems to produce a variety of negative attitudinal effects and potentially dangerous behavioral ones. Sherif (1980) addressed this issue, citing possible deleterious effects created by presenting students with "totally false" depictions of rape outcomes. Adequacy of debriefing procedures was also addressed. Partially as a result of her concerns, there is currently an ethical standard in place for use of portrayals of rape, particularly those suggesting victim arousal. Subjects are given information to the effect that the depictions are false and do not represent reality. Effectiveness of this debriefing has been assessed (Donnerstein & Berkowitz, 1981) and found to produce significant decrease in adherence to rape myths over nondebriefed subjects.

These laboratory findings have serious social implications. Malamuth and Check's (1981a) field study suggests negative effects of mainstream films not designated as X-rated. The potential for explicit sexually violent films to increase rape and sexual aggression against women seems clear. Concern is further generated as these materials appear to be increasing in the popular media. Malamuth and Spinner (1980) surveyed issues of *Playboy* and *Penthouse* from 1973 to 1977. They found a significant increase in sexually violent pictures in the magazines during this five-year span. In *Penthouse* magazine, the number of sexually violent pictures increased from essentially zero in 1973 to close to three per issue in 1977.

Despite the consistency of laboratory data in underlining potential negative effects of violent pornography, the actual relationship between rape and pornography is not clear. The data show that exposure to such stimuli produces increased laboratory aggression. However, this aggression (shock delivery) is quite different from rape, and generalization to sexual aggression against an interacting victim cannot necessarily be made. One method that has been used to study the relationship between pornography and rape is the exploration of the histories of convicted rapists. Goldstein (1973) compared rapists and persons convicted of other sex crimes to normals selected from the Los Angeles community. Results showed that rapists had no greater exposure to pornography, including sado-madochistic pornography than controls. However, the rapists were the highest group (90 percent) reporting that, as adolescents, pornography stimulated them to desire sexual activity. As adults, they were still the highest group (80 percent) compared to only 37 percent of normal controls. Furthermore, as adolescents, 80 percent of the rapists reported that they had wished to try an act seen in an especially arousing (peak) experience with erotica, compared to only 48 percent of normal controls as adolescents.

Davis and Braucht (1973) studied the effect of exposure to pornography on development of sexual deviance, including rape. Subjects were drawn from a variety of backgrounds including jail inmates. The authors conclude that, "The pattern of obtained results leaves open the possibility that early exposure to pornography plays some causal role in the development of sexually deviant life-styles," but note that increased exposure could also be a product of the deviant life-style.

Clinical interviews with rapists have produced more evidence that rapists are aroused by fantasizing about rape and may utilize sado-madochistic pornography toward such an end. Groth and Birnbaum (1979) observed that rapists motivated by desire for power would fantasize about sexual conquest and rape. One such individual reported, "I would fantasize about confronting a girl with a weapon, a knife or a gun, and that she would tell me that I didn't need it and that she wanted me, and that she wanted me sexually [p. 26]." Another power rapist would fantasize "having a girl tied up, spread-eagle, to the bed. She was helpless and I was the master. I'd satisfy myself, get what I wanted, and she would enjoy it—even though I had her tied up, she would enjoy it and have an orgasm. She wouldn't try to fight me or break loose from the ropes [p. 37]." Of the sadistic rapist, Groth and Birnbaum say, ". . . sadistic themes are the focus of his masturbatory fantasies. He is interested in sadomasochistic pornography. . . . " One such rapist said, "I found myself having sexual fantasies that would put women in precarious positions. I was thinking about this more and more, like devising a rack, perhaps, that would spread her legs as wide open as they could possibly be spread. . . ."

The extent to which media portrayals influence or reinforce such images is open to debate. Clearly, pornography is not responsible for rape, it is the individual in both a moral and clinical sense who is responsible for his own acts. Yet, attitudes and arousal patterns clearly are taught. Masturbatory conditioning is a behavioral procedure that has been shown effective in changing the stimulus that produces sexual arousal (Davidson, 1968; Marquis, 1970). This procedure involves having the subject imagine a previously neutral or unarousing image prior to ejaculating. In repeated trials, as the subject pairs an image with the reinforcement of ejaculation, he begins to find that image arousing. In fact, training in arousal to mutually enjoyable intercourse cues has been shown to be effective in treating sadistic rapists and is a major component of the general treatment for rapists (Abel, Blanchard, & Becker, 1976, 1978). Since even neutral objects have been conditioned to be arousing through this procedure (Rachman & Hodgson, 1968), it seems highly likely that arousal to antisocial acts (violence to women) may be conditioned through repeated masturbation to such stimuli. If pornography combining violence and sex is becoming more common, as suggested by recent research (Malamuth & Spinner, 1980), this may constitute a social policy issue of importance.

However, policy issues related to pornography are highly complex and controversial. In the late 1960s, public concern reached a high level, and the President's Commission on Obscenity and Pornography (1970) was formed. The general conclusions of the commission were that pornography does not produce undesirable effects on its users and is not an issue of social concern. The studies conducted under this commission have been criticized, however, for not examining effects of materials portraying violence and exploitation (Donnerstein, 1981b), and more recent research has certainly challenged its conclusion. Regardless of laboratory outcome, the control of such materials is in direct conflict with the tenet of freedom of speech.

While general societal agreement exists over the necessity of controlling many products viewed as dangerous to the consumer, very little agreement exists about control of printed materials and film. Many have argued that pornography depicts women in a dehumanized, degrading manner and teaches that women are essentially masochistic (Gager & Schurr, 1976). Furthermore, Brownmiller (1975) asserts that the concern of liberals for freedom of speech would not be heard if pictorials portrayed other groups besides women as the subject of abuse. She says:

> I wonder if the ACLU's position might change if, come tomorrow morning, the bookstores and movie theaters lining Forty-second Street in New York City were devoted not to the humiliation of women by rape and torture, as they currently are, but to a systematized, commercially successful propaganda machine depicting the sadistic pleasure of gassing Jews or lynching blacks? [p. 395]

Groth and Birnbaum (1979), while firmly stating that banning pornography will not stop rape, assert that "pornography is a media equivalent to the crime of rape. It is the sexual expression of power and anger [p. 9]."

In order for our society to address this issue in a responsible manner, there must be a clear separation between appropriate concern over antisocial effects of pornography and the restrictive desire to enforce a moral code on consenting adults. Those who wish to suppress nonviolent sexual expression have in the past typically been the ones advocating against pornographic material. These goals need not coincide. However, restriction of violent pornography is not in itself a solution. Pornography is a reflection of societal values which cannot be changed by legal fiat. The source of such values which leads us to view women in submission as arousing must be understood.

PREVENTION OF SEXUAL AGGRESSION

The conclusions found to be supported in this literature review are as follows. Rape represents one extreme of several dimensions of sexually violent and exploitative behaviors. First, a continuum of sexual goals may be posited, including kissing and hugging at one extreme and oral, anal, and vaginal intercourse at the other. Any of these goals may be obtained through use of force. Second, a continuum of force may be conceptualized which may be used to obtain any of these sexual goals, ranging from mild pressure to brutal beating. Finally, a continuum of exploitation may be conceived in which physical force represents one extreme of coercive tactics which would also include strategies such as threat of loss of love. From this perspective, it has been seen that, while convicted rapists are typically drawn from an "ecologically bound" subsample of the population, sexual aggression is common to all societal levels.

Thus, far from being the product of a mentally deviate personality, sexual aggression (although not typically at its most extreme) is itself the norm. This fact appears to derive from several societal conditions. One is the existence of a male-dominant culture. This phrase is not meant to suggest that men necessarily dominate interpersonal relationships but, rather, that men have most political decision making opportunities and control most of the resources. Another is the fact that aggression is condoned, albeit more within some subgroups than others, e.g., the counterculture of violence. Finally, male status is determined in part (again, more so among some subgroups than others) by sexual prowess with women.

A potential consequence of a gender polarized society is unequal involvement in child care, and this is characteistic of our own society. This would seem to produce the type of close mother-son, distant father relationships often seen as etiologically relevant to development of rape, homosexuality, and some sexual deviations.

Even the convergence of these tendencies would not predict rape, however, without a reciprocal societal belief that sexual aggression against women is legitimate. This legitimacy is partially determined by the belief that a male's sexual urges cannot be controlled and that if a woman arouses them she must face the consequences. It is further determined by the cultural belief that women are essentially masochistic. In our competitive and aggressive society, submission is equated with masochism. Thus, the sources of rape as normative are societally structured. Reinforcement of the message is available (to those who choose to observe it) in the form of increasing media focus on sexual violence.

Many avenues, all extremely important, are available to facilitate control of sexual aggression. Learning of self-defense tactics by women, study of successful strategies for deterring the rapist, and exploration of programs to treat the convicted rapist so he will not repeat the offense are examples. In addition to focus on the individual level, societal focus is also necessary. Three factors seem important for impacting at this level.

Public Education about Rape

Education about the meaning of rape is essential. It appears not to be difficult to change misconceptions about rape (Donnerstein & Berkowitz, 1981). The specific information that rape is not a potentially pleasurable form of sexual expression can be taught as well as information about the serious and longlasting effects of rape on the victim. While rape prevention and crisis centers have been performing this function for some time, a very large segment of the population has not yet been educated. Changes in public attitude can have a far reaching impact. Such "consciousness raising" may influence the male who chooses which tactics to use to get his date into bed; the police officer who makes a decision whether to lodge a charge; the jury member who determines guilt. Clearly, a part of this education must be simple communication between male and female subcultures in order to expose erroneous beliefs. Additionally, however, this information could be formally taught in introductory psychology and sociology courses, medical school lectures, sex crime unit police training, and health education in high school.

Evaluation of Societal Mechanisms by which Aggression Toward Women is Taught

Portrayals of rape and sexual violence in the mass media may be one mechanism by which aggression toward women is taught and studies to date indicate negative consequences of exposure to them. Other mechanisms include permissive societal attitudes toward violence within the family. While spouse and child abuse have been revealed to be frequent events, societal attempts to deal with this violence are often ineffective. Thus, the child is taught that violent means of resolving interpersonal conflict is permissible.

Sexual violence on television may merit special examination because of its high frequency of exposure to children and adolescents. Certainly, television programs do portray men using force to obtain sex from women. While the effects of televised violence have been well documented, effects of sexual violence need careful additional evaluation.

Increase in Power of Women

As women gain more power (i.e., political decision making opportunities and access to resources), women will be more valued members of society and less the cultural image for martyr and deserving victim. It is entirely possible that part of the increase in violent pornography observed in the past decade is a backlash phenomenon precipitated by actual gains in women's rights. This is an optimistic view, for if this were the case, this backlash may be expected to subside as continued gains are made. Many legitimate avenues of retribution for sexual victimization have in the past been closed, e.g., communal support and criminal prosecution of the offender. Development and utilization of such societal support mechanisms has occurred within the context of the women's rights movement and can be expected to increase as women gain more power.

CONCLUSIONS

Rape has been shown to be one end of a societally condoned continuum of sexual aggression against women. The strategies suggested above are offered toward the goal of changing this pattern. But what form would the relationship between men and women take if these changes were implemented? In tribal societies where men and women share equal power and prestige, the power relationship between the sexes can be characterized as separate but equal. Women are valued for feminine characteristics, men for masculine ones. However, in our own society, men and women are increasingly sharing the same attributes and privileges. Contraception enables women to enjoy the sexual freedom previously available only to men. Mechanization in the workplace allows women to hold many jobs which previously required the greater physical strength of men. Women are entering traditionally "male fields," while men are entering the domain of homemaking and childrearing. It is unlikely that equal power and prestige for men and women in our society will be characterized by polarized sex roles. Thus, elimination of sexual aggression against women cannot be achieved here (as it is in tribal, rape-free societies) because of the great value attached to uniquely feminine qualities. Rape will be eliminated if and when women are seen as inappropriate targets of exploitation.

REFERENCES

Abarbanel, G. Helping victims of rape. *Social Work,* 1976, *21,* 478-82.
Abel, G. G., Barlow, R. H., Blanchard, E. B., & Guild, D. The components of rapists' sexual arousal. *Archives of General Psychiatry,* 1977, *34,* 895-903.
Abel, G. G., Blanchard, E. B., & Becker, J. V. Psychological treatment of rapists. In M. J. Walker and S. L. Brodsky (Eds.), *Sexual assault.* Lexington, Mass.: Lexington Books, 1976.
Abel, G. G., Blanchard, E. B., & Becker, J. V. An integrated treatment program for rapists. In R. Rada (Ed.), *Clinical aspects of the rapist.* New York: Grune and Stratton, 1978.
Abrahamsen, D. *Crime and the human mind.* New York: Columbia University Press, 1944.
Abrahamsen, D. *The psychology of crime.* Columbia University Press, 1960.
American Law Institute, *Model penal code* (Proposed Official Draft 1962). Philadelphia, PA: American Law Institute, 1962.
Amir, Menachem. *Patterns in forcible rape.* Chicago: The University of Chicago Press, 1971.
Bandura, A. *Principles of behavior modification.* N.Y.: Holt, Rinehart & Winston, 1969.

Baron, R. A. The aggression-inhibiting influence of heightened sexual arousal. *Journal of Personality and Social Psychology*, 1974, *30*, 318-22.

Baron, R. A., & Bell, P. A. Sexual arousal and aggression by males: Effects of type of erotic stimuli and prior provocation. *Journal of Personality and Social Psychology*, 1977, *35*, 79-87.

Barrett, K. Date Rape: A campus epidemic? *Ms.*, September 1982.

Battelle Law and Justice Study Center. Forcible rape: Final project. Law Enforcement Center Assistance Administration. U.S. Government Printing Office. 1978.

Ben Dor, J. Justice after rape: Legal reform in Michigan. In M. J. Walker and S. L. Brodsky (Eds.),. *Sexual assault*. Lexington, Mass.: Lexington Books, 1976.

Berger, V. Man's trial, woman's tribulation: Rape cases in the courtroom. *Columbia Law Review*, 1977, *77*, 1-101.

Borgida, E. Evidentiary reform of rape laws: A psychological approach. In P. D. Lipsitt and B. S. Sales (Eds.), *New directions in psychological research*. New York: Van Nostrand Reinhold, 1980.

Brodsky, S. L. Prevention of rape: Deterrence by the potential victim. In M. J. Walker and S. L. Brodsky (Eds.), *Sexual assault*. Lexington, Mass.: Lexington Books, 1976.

Brodyaga, L., Gates, M., Singer, S., Tucker, M., & White, R. *Rape and its victims: A report for citizens, health facilities, and criminal justice agencies*. Law Enforcement Assistance Administration. U.S. Government Printing Office, Washington, D.C., 1975.

Brownmiller, S. *Against our will: Men, women and rape*. N.Y.: Simon and Schuster, 1975.

Burgess, A. W., & Holstrom, L. L. Rape trauma syndrome. *American Journal of Psychiatry*, 1974, *131*, 981-85. (a)

Burgess, A. W., & Holstrom, L. L. *Rape: Victims of crisis*. Bowie, Md.: Robert J. Brady, 1974. (b)

Burgess, A. W., & Holstrom, L. L. Coping behavior of the rape victim. *American Journal of Psychiatry*, 1976, *133*, 413-17.

Burgess, A. W., & Holstrom, L. L. Rape typology and the coping behavior of rape victims. In S. L. McCombie (Ed.), *The rape crisis intervention handbook: A guide for victim care*. New York: Plenum Press, 1980.

Burt, M. R. Cultural myths and supports for rape. *Journal of Personality and Social Psychology*, 1980 *38*, 217-30.

Buss, A. H. *The psychology of aggression*. New York: Wiley, 1961.

Calhoun, L. G., Selby, J. W., Cann, A., & Keller, G. T. The effects of victim physical attractiveness and sex of respondent on social reactions to victims of rape. *British Journal of Social and Clinical Psychology*, 1978, *17*, 191-92.

Chaiken, A., & Darley, J. M. Victim or perpetrator? Defensive attribution of responsibility and the need for order and justice. *Journal of Personality and Social Psychology*, 1973, *25*, 268-75.

Cohen, M., Seghorn, T., & Calmas, W. Sociometric study of the sex offender. *Journal of Abnormal Psychology*, 1969, *74*, 249-55.

Curtis, L. A. Rape, race, and culture: Some speculations in search of a theory. In M. J. Walker and S. L. Brodsky (Eds.), *Sexual assault*. Lexington, Mass.: Lexington Books, 1976.

Davis, A. J. Sexual assaults in the Philadelphia prison system. In J. H. Gagnan and W. Simon (Eds.), *The sexual scene*. Chicago: Transaction/Aldine, 1970.

Davis, K. E., & Braucht, G. N. Exposure to pornography, character, and sexual deviance: A retrospective survey. *Journal of Social Issues*, 1973, *29*, 183-96.

Davison, G. Elimination of a sadistic fantasy by a client-controlled counterconditioning technique: A case study. *Journal of Abnormal Psychology*, 1968, *73*, 84-90.

Deutsch, H. *The psychology of women*, Vol. I. New York: Grune and Stratton, 1944.

Dietz, P. E. Social factors in rapist behavior. In R. Rada (Ed.), *Clinical aspects of the rapist*. New York: Grune and Stratton, 1978.

Donnerstein, E. Aggressive erotica and violence against women. *Journal of Personality and Social Psychology*, 1980, *39*, 269-77. (a)

Donnerstein, E. Pornography and violence against women: Experimental studies. *Annals of the New York Academy of Sciences*, 1980, *347*, 277-88. (b)

Donnerstein, E., & Barrett, G. Effects of erotic stimuli on male aggression toward females. *Journal of*

Personality and Social Psychology, 1978, *36*, 180-88.

Donnerstein, E., & Berkowitz, L. Victim reactions in aggressive erotic films as a factor in violence against women. *Journal of Personality and Social Psychology*, 1981, *41*, 710-24.

Donnerstein, E., Donnerstein, M., & Evans, R. Erotic stimuli and aggression: Facilitation or inhibition. *Journal of Personality and Social Psychology*, 1975, *32*, 237-44.

Donnerstein, E., & Hallam, J. Facilitating effects of erotica on aggression against women. *Journal of Personality and Social Psychology*, 1978, *36*, 1270-77.

Enos, W. F., & Beyer, J. C. Management of the rape victim. *American Family Physician*, 1978, *18*, 97-102.

Federal Bureau of Investigation. *Uniform crime reports for the United States — 1981*. U.S. Government Printing Office, Washington, D.C., 1982.

Feild, H. S. Attitudes toward rape: A comparative analysis of police, rapists, crisis counsellors and citizens. *Journal of Personality and Social Psychology*, 1978, *36*, 156-79.

Feldman-Summers, S., Gordon, P. E., & Meagher, J. R. The impact of rape on sexual satisfaction. *Journal of Abnormal Psychology*, 1979, *88*, 101-05.

Gager, N., & Schurr, C. *Sexual assault: Confronting rape in America*. New York: Grosset and Dunlop, 1976.

Gates, M. Introduction. In J. R. Chapman and M. Gates (Eds.), *The victimization of women*. Beverly Hills, Calif.: Sage Publications, 1978.

Gebhard, P. H., Gagnon, J. H., Pomeroy, W. B., & Christenson, C. V. *Sex offenders: An analysis of types*. New York: Harper and Row, 1965.

Goldstein, M. J. Exposure to erotic stimuli and sexual deviance. *Journal of Social Issues*, 1973, *29*, 197-219.

Groth, A. N., & Birnbaum, H. J. *Men who rape: The psychology of the offender*. New York: Plenum Press, 1979.

Groth, A. N., & Burgess, A. W. Rape: A sexual deviation. *American Journal of Orthopsychiatry*, 1977, *47*, 400-06.

Guttmacher, M. S. *Sex offenses*. New York: Norton, 1951.

Halbert, S. R., & Jones, D. E. D. Medical management of the sexually assaulted woman. *The Journal of Reproductive Medicine*, 1978, *20*, 265-74.

Hariton, E. B., & Singer, J. L. Women's fantasies during sexual intercourse. *Journal of Consulting and Clinical Psychology*, 1974, *42*, 313-22.

Hibey, R. A. The trial of a rape case: An advocate's analysis of corroboration, consent, and character. In L. G. Schultz (Ed.), *Rape victimology*. Springfield, Ill.: Charles C. Thomas, 1975.

Hilberman, E. *The rape victim*. Washington, D.C.: American Psychiatric Association, 1976.

Holstrom, L. L., & Burgess, A. W. *The victim of rape: Institutional reactions*. New York: John Wiley, 1978.

Hunt, G. R. Rape: An organized approach to evaluation and treatment. *American Family Physician*, 1977, *15*, 154-58.

Janoff-Bulman, R. Characterological versus behavioral self-blame: Inquiries into depression and rape. *Journal of Personality and Social Psychology*, 1979, *37*, 1798-1809.

Janoff-Bulman, R., & Lang-Gunn, L. Coping with disease and accidents: The role of self-blame attributions. In L. Y. Abramson (Ed.), *Social-personal inference in clinical psychology*. New York: The Guildford Press, 1982.

Jones, C., & Aronson, E. Attribution of fault to a rape victim as a function of respectability of the victim. *Journal of Personality and Social Psychology*, 1973, *26*, 415-19.

Kanin, E. Male aggression in dating-courtship relations. *American Journal of Sociology*, 1957, *63*, 197-204.

Kanin, E. J. Selected dyadic aspects of male sex aggression. *Journal of Sex Research*, 1969, *5*, 12-28.

Kanin, E. Sex aggression by college men. *Medical Aspects of Human Sexuality*, 1970, *4*, 25-40.

Kanin, E., & Parcell, S. Sexual aggression: A second look at the offended female. *Archives of Sexual Behavior*, 1977, *6*, 67-76.

Karpman, B. *The sexual offender and his offenses*. New York: Julian Press, 1954.

King, H. E., Rotter, M. J., Calhoun, L. G., & Selby, J. W. Perceptions of the rape incident: Physician's and volunteer counselors. *Journal of Community Psychology*, 1978, *6*, 74-77.

Kirkpatrick, C., & Kanin, E. Male sex aggression on a university campus. *American Sociological Review*, 1957, *22*, 52-58.

Klemmack, S. H., & Klemmack, D. L. The social definition of rape. In M. J. Walker and S. L. Brodsky (Eds.), *Sexual assault*, Lexington, Mass.: Lexington Books, 1976.

Koss, M. P., & Oros, C. J. Sexual experiences survey: A research instrument investigating sexual aggression and victimization. *Journal of Consulting and Clinical Psychology*, 1982, *50*, 455-57.

LeGrand, C. E. Rape and rape laws: Sexism in society and law. *California Law Review*, 1973, *61*, 919-41.

Lindemann, E. Symptomatology and management of acute grief. In A. Monat and R. S. Lazarus (Eds.), *Stress and coping*. New York: Columbia University Press, 1977.

Loh, W. D. Q: What has reform of rape legislation wrought? A. Truth in criminal labelling. *Journal of Social Issues*, 1981, *37*, 28-52.

Malamuth, N. M. Rape fantasies as a function of exposure to violent sexual stimuli. *Archives of Sexual Behavior*, 1981, *10*, 33-47. (a)

Malamuth, N. M. Rape proclivity among males. *Journal of Social Issues*, 1981, *37*, 138-57. (b)

Malamuth, N. M. Factors associated with rape as predictors of laboratory aggression against women. Paper presented at the Annual Meetings of the Canadian Psychological Association, Toronto, Ontario, June 1981. (c)

Malamuth, N. M. & Check, J. V. P. Penile tumescence and perceptual responses to rape as a function of victim's perceived reactions. *Journal of Applied Social Psychology*, 1980, *10*, 528-47.

Malamuth, N. M., & Check, J. V. P. The effects of mass media exposure on acceptance of violence against women: A field experiment. *Journal of Research in Personality*, 1981, *15*, 436-46. (a)

Malamuth, N., & Check, J. The effects of exposure to aggressive pornography: Rape proclivity, sexual arousal and beliefs in rape myths. Paper presented at the Annual Convention of the American Psychological Association, Los Angeles, California, August 1981. (b)

Malamuth, N. M., Haber, S., & Feshbach, S. Exposure to sexual violence, sex differences, and the "normality" of rapists. *Journal of Research in Personality*, 1980, *14*, 121-37.

Malamuth, N. M., Heim, M., & Feshbach, S. Sexual responsiveness of college students to rape depictions: Inhibitory and disinhibitory effects. *Journal of Personality and Social Psychology*, 1980, *38*, 399-408.

Malamuth, N. M., & Spinner, B. A longitudinal content analysis of sexual violence in the best-selling erotic magazines. *The Journal of Sex Research*, 1980, *16*, 226-37.

Marquis, J. N. Orgasmic reconditioning: Changing sexual choice through controlling masturbatory fantasies. *The Journal of Behavior Therapy and Experimental Psychiatry*, 1970, *1*, 234-71.

Mathiasen, S. E. The rape victim: A victim of society and the laws. *Williamette Law Journal*, 1974, *11*, 36-55.

McCahill, T. W., Meyer, L. C., & Fischman, A. M. *The aftermath of rape*. Lexington, Mass.: Lexington Books, 1981.

McCombie, S. L. Characteristics of rape victims seen in crisis intervention. *Smith College Studies in Social Work*, 1976, *46*, 137-58.

McCombie, S. L. & Arons, J. H. Counseling rape victims. In S. L. McCombie (Ed.), *The rape crisis intervention handbook: A guide for victim care*. N.Y.: Plenum Press, 1980.

McGuire, L. S., & Stern, M. Survey of incidence of and physician's attitudes toward sexual assault. *Public Health Reports*, 1976, *91*, 103-09.

Millet, K. *Sexual politics*. Garden City, N.Y.: Doubleday, 1970.

Notman, M. T., & Nadelson, C. C. Psychodynamic and life-stage considerations in the response to rape. In S. L. McCombie (Ed.), *The rape crisis intervention handbook: A guide to victim care*. New York: Plenum Press, 1980.

Presidential Commission on Obscenity and Pornography. U.S. Government Printing Office, Washington, D.C., 1971.

Rabkin, J. G. The epidemiology of forcible rape. *American Journal of Orthopsychiatry*, 1979, *49*, 634-47.

Rachman, S. J., & Hodgson, R. J. Experimentally induced fetishism: Replication and development.

Psychological Record, 1968, *18,* 25-27.

Rada, R. T. Alcoholism and forcible rape. *American Journal of Psychiatry,* 1975, *132,* 444-46.

Rada, R. Psychological factors in rapist behavior. In R. Rada (Ed.), *Clinical aspects of the rapist.* New York: Grune and Stratton, 1978.

Rada, R. T., Kellner, R., & Laws, D. R. Plasma testosterone levels in the rapist. *Psychosomatic Medicine,* 1976, *38,* 257-68.

Rada, R. T., Kellner, R., & Winslow, W. W. Plasma testosterone and aggressive behavior. *Psychosomatics,* 1976, *17,* 138-42.

Reage, P. *Story of O.* New York: Grove Press, 1965.

Richmond, A. E. Rape law and the judicial process. In S. L. McCombie (Ed.), *The rape crisis intervention handbook: A guide for victim care.* New York: Plenum Press, 1980.

Robinson, M. N. *The power of sexual surrender.* New York: Signet Books, 1959.

Rosenbaum, A., & O'Leary, K. D. Marital violence: Characteristics of abusive couples. *Journal of Consulting and Clinical Psychology,* 1981, *49,* 63-71.

Rumsey, M. G., & Rumsey, J. M. A case of rape: Sentencing judgments of males and females. *Psychological Reports,* 1977, *41,* 459-65.

Sanday, P. R. The socio-cultural context of rape: A cross-cultural study. *Journal of Social Issues,* 1981, *37,* 5-27.

Seligman, C., Brickman, J., & Koulack, D. Rape and physical attractiveness: Assigning responsibility to victims. *Journal of Personality,* 1977, *45,* 554-63.

Seltzer, V., Medical management of the rape victim. *Journal of the American Medical Women's Association,* 1977, *32,* 141-44.

Sherif, C. W. Comment on ethical issues in Malamuth, Heim and Feshbach's "Sexual responsiveness of college students to rape depictions: Inhibitory and disinhibitory effects." *Journal of Personality and Social Psychology,* 1980, *38,* 409-12.

Straus, M. Victims and aggressors in marital violence. *American Behavioral Scientist,* 1980, *23,* 681-704.

Sutherland, S., & Scherl, D. J. Patterns of response among rape victims. *American Journal of Orthopsychiatry,* 1970, *40,* 503-11.

Thompson, H. S. *Hell's angels.* New York: Random House, 1967.

Tofani, L. Rape in the county jail: Prince George's hidden terror. *The Washington Post,* September 27-28, 1982.

Walster, E. Assignment of responsibility for an accident. *Journal of Personality and Social Psychology,* 1966, *3,* 73-79.

Weis, K., & Borges, S. S. Victimology and rape: The case of the legitimate victim. In L. G. Schultz (Ed.), *Rape victimology,* Springfield, Ill.: Charles C. Thomas, 1975.

Williams, J. E., & Holmes, K. A. *The second assault: Rape and public attitudes.* Westport, Conn.: Greenwood Press, 1981.

Wolfgang, M., & Ferracuti, F. *The subculture of violence.* London: Tavistock, 1967.

Wood, P. L. The victim in a forcible rape case: A feminist view. In L. G. Schultz (Ed.), *Rape victimology.* Springfield, Ill.: Charles C. Thomas, 1975.

6

Physiology, Dominance, and Aggression in Humans*

Allan Mazur

I will depart from this volume's central themes of prevention and control, for to speak of these along with physiology would invite suggestions for castration, lobotomy, and the screening (and subsequent monitoring) of chromosomally unusual newborns. Such "control" measures would be morally dubious even if their scientific basis were well established, but the science itself is uncertain and controversial. For the present at least, the physiology of aggression is fit only as a topic of academic study and not as a basis for policy.

Ethical and practical problems make physiological research on humans a difficult task which has not proceeded too far. The number of review articles on this topic nearly equals the number of original research reports (e.g., Bell, 1978; Dixson, 1980; Leshner, 1978; Mazur, 1976, 1982; Moyer, 1974; Rada, Kellner, & Winslow, 1976), reflecting intense interest in an exciting area of study, but there is an over-reliance on animal studies, with questionable extensions to human behavior.

A particular problem in extending animal results to humans comes from the common failure to distinguish aggressive behavior from dominance behavior. An individual will be said to act *aggressively* if its apparent intent is to inflict physical injury on another member of its species. This refers to face-to-face actions such as punching, biting, shoving, or clubbing, but does not include verbal abuse or distal or symbolic actions such as aerial bombing or voting for capital punishment. An individual will be said to act *dominantly* if its apparent intent is to achieve or maintain a status advantage—gaining power, prestige, or valued prerogatives—over another member of its species. Dominance behavior may be aggressive or intimidating, but it need not be; and among adults of the higher primates, particularly man and the apes, it usually takes nonaggressive forms including vocalization and physical gesturing (Mazur, 1973).

Most relevant animal research has looked at intermale aggression among species that achieve and maintain status aggressively, such as rodents. Most of these results may be regarded as linking hormones with dominance behavior as well as with aggressive behavior, since the two are intertwined. In apes and man, where dominating and aggressive behaviors are often sepa-

*This chapter quotes extensively from my chapter "Hormones, aggression, and dominance in humans," in B. Svare (Ed.), *Hormones and aggressive behavior.* New York: Plenum, 1983.

145

rated, hormones may be related to one but not the other. Some clarity emerges out of the apparently inconsistent research findings if we keep this distinction in mind.

There would be little gained from an exhaustive overview of physiological research on aggression, since the work is fragmented. Instead, I will concentrate on three questions which are the major foci of recent work. First, is there any physiological basis to the common observation that males are more aggressive than females? Second, is aggressiveness among men related to their levels of circulating testosterone? It is important to clearly distinguish these two questions. The first asks if physiological processes, which include the production of testosterone, produce males who behave more aggressively than females, apart from the influences of culturally prescribed sex-role learning. The second question asks if, among physically mature men, the amount of testosterone circulating in the blood is related to (and perhaps a cause of) their degree of aggressive behavior. An affirmative answer to the first question does not necessarily imply an affirmative answer to the second. The third question to be taken up is whether or not aggressiveness among women is related to the menstrual cycle?

SEX DIFFERENCES IN AGGRESSION

Among humans, males are more aggressive than females (Maccoby & Jacklin, 1974). Boys also engage in more rough-and-tumble play, and perhaps boys are no more aggressive than girls of comparable activity level, a possibility which has not been tested. Nonetheless, an overall sex difference in aggressiveness is found across most cultures where relevant measurements have been taken (Omark, Omark, & Edelman, 1975; Whiting & Edwards, 1973). There appears to be consensus on this point and also on the fact that most cultures contain stereotypes of males as the more aggressive sex, thus providing a learning environment which perpetuates this difference. Controversy arises as to whether, *in addition* to sex role learning, there are physiological factors which predispose males toward greater aggressiveness (Tieger, 1980).

Maccoby and Jacklin point out that boys and girls differ in aggressiveness even before the age of six, which seems too young to be fully explained by sex role learning. Males are also more aggressive than females in most nonhuman primate species, including our nearest relatives, the chimpanzees (Maccoby & Jacklin, 1980). Male rhesus monkeys are more aggressive than females even when raised in isolation from adults, with no opportunity for intergenerational learning (Harlow, 1965). Thus, a sex difference in aggression appears to be a feature of the general primate pattern.

A hormonal explanation for the development of sex differences in aggression, which is well supported by studies of rodents and monkeys, seems attractive for humans as well. Genetically male fetuses develop testes which produce androgens, the male sex hormones, including testosterone. These influence the development of secondary sexual characteristics. A genetically male fetus which is somehow deprived of androgen will have female-appearing genitals, whereas a genetically female fetus exposed to androgen will develop male-appearing genitals. The principle of differentiation, somewhat simplified, appears to be: add androgen and obtain a male; add nothing and obtain a female (Money & Ehrhardt, 1972). This principle appears applicable to sexual patterns of behavior as well as to physical characteristics. If pregnant rhesus monkeys are given testosterone, their female infant offspring, presumably exposed to the testosterone as fetuses, show threat behavior and rough-and-tumble play which greatly exceed those shown by normal females but are more typical of infant males (Goy, 1970). As adults they are more aggressive than normal females (Eaton, Goy, & Phoenix, 1973).

Obviously, humans cannot be experimentally manipulated in this way, but there have been unfortunate instances in which human fetuses have received abnormal amounts of various sex hormones with effects on subsequent development. Genetically female fetuses may receive excess androgen from their own abnormally functioning adrenocortical glands, being born with varying degrees of masculinized genitals, from a slightly enlarged clitoris to a normal looking penis and empty scrotum. Also, some normal fetuses have been subjected to androgen and other sex hormones which were given to their mothers to prevent miscarriage. A number of studies have attempted to assess these children, though the data are messy, and the research usually lacks controls and is based on small samples. In their recent review of this work, Meyer-Bahlburg and Ehrhardt (1982) note the lack of clear-cut results but conclude that general trends are consistent with the hypothesis that fetal exposure to androgen increases subsequent aggressiveness; a conclusion which ought to be regarded cautiously.

The androgen hypothesis of sex differences in human aggression is promising but certainly not well tested. Future research might profitably focus on androgen effects during adolescence, which seem more accessible to study in human subjects than do in utero effects. Boys experience rapidly rising testosterone levels from about the age of 12 to 20 (Brotherton 1976:301; Frasier, Gafford, & Horton 1969). The beginning of this period is a time of increased dominating behavior, fighting and intermale competition, similar to the increased aggression and dominance behavior of male apes during puberty (Hamburg, 1971). If the timing of a boy's rise in testosterone and the development of his secondary sexual characteristics allow good predictions of subsequent aggressive or dominating behaviors, then a causal role for androgen in producing these behaviors would be increasingly plausible.

In one study of 58 normal 16-year-old boys, testosterone level correlated with degree of physical maturity (as measured by development of pubic hair), and also with two among several pencil-and-paper measures of aggressiveness. While the relationship of these questionnaire responses to actual behavior is unknown, it is noteworthy that the items which most strongly correlated with testosterone are those reflecting aggressive responses to *provocation* and *threat*, as opposed to unprovoked or impulsive aggressiveness (Olweus, Mattsson, Schalling, & Low, 1980). Provocation and threat commonly occur during the dominance challenges which are common among adolescent boys, suggesting that testosterone is more closely related to dominating behavior than to aggression per se. The same researchers studied 40 delinquent boys (ages 14 to 19) and found testosterone only slightly associated with the degree of aggressiveness or dominance (Mattsson, Schalling, Olweus, Low, & Svensson, 1980). Thus, results to date are not wholly consistent, but they do suggest that the rise in testosterone which boys experience during puberty encourages increased dominance behavior, some of which may take aggressive forms.

Before concluding this discussion of sex differences in aggression, it is worthwhile commenting on the reputed hyperaggressivity of XYY males, which has received so much popular attention. It is well known that a normal person has two sex chromosomes: XY if male, XX if female. There are, however, abnormal individuals who have more than two, or only one sex chromosome. Thus, some males have an "extra" Y chromosome, and it has been conjectured that if the presence of one Y chromosome in normal males is associated with high aggressiveness (relative to females), then an abnormal male with two Y's might be extra aggressive, perhaps because of a heightened testosterone level. Reports that relatively large numbers of XYY males are found in maximum security mental institutions, compared to their incidence in the general population, support this hypothesis. It is well documented by now that XYY men are more likely than XY men to have criminal arrests, but when the crimes are examined in detail, they are not particularly violent ones, nor do fragmentary endocrine studies indicate abnormally high testosterone levels (Borgaonkar & Shah, 1974; Witkin, Mednick,

Schulsinger, Bakkestrom, Christiansen, Goodenough, Hirschhorn, Lundsteen, Owen, Philip, Rubin, & Stocking, 1976). XYY men are tall and tend to have low measured intelligence, suggesting that the propensity for criminal acts, or more particularly, for being arrested and sentenced for such acts, may be explained by these factors rather than by increased aggressiveness. Furthermore, it appears that men with abnormal XXY genotypes are also overrepresented in the same kinds of mental-penal institutions as XYY men, and this outcome cannot be explained as the result of an "extra Y" chromosome (Mazur & Robertson, 1972; Witkin, et al., 1976). At present, there seems little reason to believe that XYY males are hyperaggressive because of an androgen effect produced by the double Y; however, the issue has not been settled definitively.

CIRCULATING TESTOSTERONE AND AGGRESSION IN MEN

Castration is a traditional method for gentling a bull, perhaps because it removes the animal's major source of testosterone. In America and Europe during this century, hundreds of deviate men, usually sex offenders of low intelligence, have been castrated. The "success" of this treatment has been cited in support of the claim that the level of testosterone circulating in an adult male is related to his degree of aggressiveness. However, these data are of questionable value, usually being anecdotal, lacking both proper control groups and direct measures of aggression, and sometimes showing distinct biases. For example, Hawke (1951) reports on his castrates:

> Many of these individuals so treated were vicious homesexuals (sic) and very brutal in attacks on small children. They were very unstable and would create a disturbance at every opportunity. After castration, they become stabilized, and those who cannot be paroled are good useful citizens in the institution.
>
> In our experimental work, we have administered Testosterone, the male hormone . . . , [to some castrates]. In a number of cases, after we had treated them for a period of two or three weeks, the floor supervisor would call up and ask if I would not be willing to stop administering Testosterone to certain individuals who had reverted to all of their anti-social tendencies, were attacking small children, starting fights, breaking windows and destroying furniture. We would stop the administration of Testosterone in these individuals, and within a few days they would be restabilized and cause no further ward disturbances. We have felt that this proves the male hormone is the exciting factor in these cases. [p. 222]

Castrated sex criminals, often with records of violent crime, appear to have low recidivism rates (LeMaire, 1956). This may be due to a hormone effect or, alternatively, to the effectiveness of castration as a symbolic deterrent, the parolee wondering what more would be cut off should he be caught again. Bremer (1959) reports that castration does not reduce aggressiveness per se but does reduce libido and might thereby remove the motivation for repeated sex offenses. While these castration studies suggest a causal link between testosterone and aggression, they are surely not compelling.

With the development of radioimmunoassays for testosterone, several investigators attempted to correlate naturally occurring variation in circulating testosterone with aggressiveness. While this is a relatively simple matter with laboratory animals, it is difficult and unethical to encourage or even allow high aggression in humans. Thus, when Persky, Smith, and Basu (1971) tried this approach with men as subjects, they measured aggression by administering paper-and-pencil tests, which are not reliably related to actual aggressive acts (Buss, Fischer,

& Simmons, 1968; Ehrenkranz, Bliss, & Sheard, 1974; Kreuz & Rose, 1972). Their report of a high correlation between testosterone production rate and "aggression" has been widely cited, so it is worth examining this result in some detail. Their basic data display is a matrix of correlations between seven personality scales and three testosterone measures (plasma testosterone level, testosterone production rate, and metabolic clearance rate), producing 21 correlations. The correlations are calculated for two separate subject groups, one consisting of young men (n = 18) and the other of older men (n = 15), so there is a total of 42 testosterone-personality correlations. Three of these 42 correlations are significant at the .05 level or better, which is about what one would expect by chance, given the null hypothesis. Two of the significant correlations relate score on the Buss-Durkee Hostility Inventory to plasma testosterone level and to testosterone production rate, but only for the younger men; for the older men, one of these correlations is negative (but nonsignificant) and the other is near zero. (The third significant correlation relates testosterone production rate to an anxiety scale, among the younger subjects, and is not relevant here.)

The authors of this study consider these results to be evidence of a testosterone-aggression link in men, which is a reasonable interpretation and one that has been widely accepted. However, one can equally well consider the few significant correlations to be chance outcomes, particularly since they are not repeated among the older subject group or with other personality scales which purport to measure aggression and hostility. Note, too, that, since plasma testosterone level and testosterone production rate were highly correlated to each other, their respective correlations with the Buss-Durkee scale are redundant.

Several subsequent attempts at other laboratories to relate testosterone levels to pencil-and-paper measures of aggression or hostility, including the Buss-Durkee Inventory and other scales, have usually failed to replicate significant correlations (Brown & Davis, 1975; Doering, Brodie, Kraemer, Moos, Becker, & Mechanic, 1975; Dotson, Robertson, & Tuchfeld, 1974; Ehrenkranz, Bliss, & Sheard, 1974; Kreuz & Rose, 1972; Meyer-Bahlburg, Boon, Sharma & Edwards, 1973; Monti, Brown, & Corriveau, 1977; Rada, Kellner, & Winslow, 1976). Even counting the two significant correlations among 16-year-old boys (Olweus et al., 1980), discussed above in the context of adolescent development, as a successful replication, the failures to replicate are far more numerous. It now seems unlikely that plasma testosterone level is correlated in any substantial way with aggression as measured on common personality scales.

Kreuz and Rose (1972) tried to relate testosterone to observable aggressive behavior rather than limiting themselves to pencil-and-paper scales of aggressiveness. Among their subjects, 21 young male prisoners with records of violent crime, plasma testosterone was not related to frequency of fighting while in prison, to frequency of verbal aggression while in prison, or to scores on the Buss-Durkee Hostility Inventory. However, the ten men with histories of more violent and aggressive offences *during adolescence* had significantly higher testosterone levels than the other men without such adolescent histories.

Kreuz and Rose suggest that the men who are presently high in testosterone were also relatively high as adolescents, or entered maturity earlier than the others. Their high testosterone back in the teenage years may have made these men relatively violent at that time. Unfortunately, there is little information on the stability of testosterone levels over years-long periods, but Doering et al. (1975) report large fluctuations in individuals' testosterone levels over a period of two months, so longer-term stability seems doubtful. In view of the tenuous causal linkage between present testosterone concentration and violent activity years earlier, one would like to see a replication of this result before accepting it as valid.

Ehrenkranz et al. (1974) measured testosterone levels in three groups of prison convicts (n = 12/group). One group was made up of "socially dominant" *but unaggressive* men who were in prison for nonviolent crimes. "They were recognized by prison staff and other inmates as socially dominant and had asserted themselves into prestigious jobs and positions in inmate hierarchies [p. 470]." A second group was composed of men who were "chronically aggressive"; all were in prison for violent crimes, and they continued to show aggressive and threatening behavior while in prison. The third group consisted of convicts who were neither dominant nor aggressive. The socially dominant (but unaggressive) group and the chronically aggressive group did not have significantly different mean testosterone levels, but both had significantly higher levels than the nondominant unaggressive group. Unfortunately, the interpretation of these results is clouded because the relative dominance of the aggressive men is not reported. It seems unlikely that they were a submissive lot, and perhaps they were more dominant than the "socially dominant" group. Thus, the aggressive group may have had high testosterone because of their aggressiveness or because of their dominance. In any case, it is clear that the "socially dominant" group had high testosterone without aggression.

In sum, the available data on testosterone and aggression in men provide a weak and inconsistent picture. The weight of evidence is against a relationship between testosterone and pencil-and-paper measures of aggression. Of two attempts to relate testosterone to presently-occurring observable aggressive behavior in men, one gave a negative and one a positive result. One reported relationship between present testosterone level and long-past violent behavior is problematic and must be regarded as dubious unless a successful replication is reported. Taken together, there is not much evidence from human subjects favoring the hypothesized link between circulating testosterone level and aggression in adult males.

CIRCULATING TESTOSTERONE AND DOMINANCE IN MEN

The distinction between aggressive behavior and dominating behavior is particularly important for humans, who often assert their dominance without any intent to cause injury. It may be the case that circulating testosterone is related *primarily* to dominance behavior among men and not to aggression except in situations where dominance happens to be asserted aggressively. Ehrenkranz et al. (1974) showed that socially dominant but *unaggressive* prisoners had relatively high plasma testosterone, not significantly different from the testosterone levels of aggressive prisoners (who may have been dominant too). Nearly all primate studies which have been interpreted as linking testosterone to aggression (Dixson, 1980) may as easily be interpreted as linking testosterone with dominating behavior (Mazur, 1976).

If there is a link between testosterone and dominance, the primate studies suggest that it works in two directions. First, changes in testosterone may influence changes in dominating behavior, with heightened testosterone facilitating attempts to achieve or maintain high status, and decreased testosterone inhibiting such attempts. Various manipulations of testosterone in monkeys and apes (via castration or hormone injection) have had mixed results but with some support for a causal link from hormones to behavior. At present there are no firm data on the effect of testosterone on dominance in humans.

Causation may work in the opposite direction with changes in dominating behavior causing changes in testosterone level, as has been demonstrated in monkeys. Successful attempts to achieve or maintain status seem to increase plasma testosterone while unsuccessful attempts or defeats seem to produce a decline in testosterone (Rose, Bernstein, & Gordon, 1975). In order to test for this effect among humans, one might place men in a competitive situation where some will win status and others lose it; testosterone in the winners should rise and in the losers should fall. In a small study of this sort, young male subjects competed in doubles tennis matches where each winner received a prize of $100. In two matches with decisive triumphs, the four losers showed drops in testosterone one hour after the matches while three of the four winners showed rises in testosterone. In a third match, where the victory was by the slimmest of margins and the players did not feel that there had been a clear triumph, winners and losers all showed testosterone drops (Mazur & Lamb, 1980). Elias (1981) has recently reported a similar finding among college wrestlers, winners of competitive matches showing greater increases in testosterone than losers.

Testosterone has been measured in a few other situations where men have undergone status changes. Five male seniors in medical school showed relative rises in testosterone the day after they received their M.D. degrees (Mazur & Lamb, 1980). Twenty-seven army recruits during basic training (Rose, Bourne, Poe, Mougey, Collins, & Mason, 1969), and 18 young men in Officer Candidate School (Kreuz, Rose, & Jennings, 1972), showed very low testosterone levels compared to control populations, perhaps because of their degraded status in these training situations, though other stress factors might also account for their low levels. (Unfortunately, testosterone was not measured in their instructors, who would be expected to show high levels.) Perhaps these results will encourage more empirical work in this promising but barely explored area.

THE MENSTRUAL CYCLE

According to folklore and common experience, women's moods are often correlated with their menstrual cycles. In particular, the days before menstruation and the first days of blood flow are regarded as negative mood days marked by irritability, depression, and lethargy. Correlations between mood and menstrual cycle have been reported in a number of studies, some methodologically poor and with sexist biases (Sherif, 1980), but also in others without these weaknesses. Rossi and Rossi's (1980) study of 82 college women over a 40-day period, which is methodologically strong and without apparent sexist bias, found relatively positive moods at the middle (ovulatory) phase of the menstrual cycle, and relatively negative moods in the week preceding menstruation and the first day or two of bleeding. Women taking birth control pills, who therefore do not experience the normal monthly fluctuations in estrogen and progesterone, did not report these mood fluctuations, a fact which the Rossis regard as indirect evidence that the mood cycle is caused by hormone changes.

One might expect that mood cycles would be reflected in corresponding monthly cycles of misbehavior, mishap, or morbidity; and a number of studies, particularly by Dalton (1964, 1968), document such effects. Of particular concern here is the claim that women, in their irritable phase, are prone to angry outbursts of aggression (Dalton, 1964; Moyer, 1974). Cooke (1945) reported that 84 percent of violent crime committed by Parisian women occurred on menstrual or premenstrual days, but this often cited number is based on hearsay evidence of doubtful veracity. A first-hand report of women on a prison farm claimed that, of 42 inmates guilty of violent crimes and whose menstrual dates could be recalled, 62 percent committed their crimes during the premenstrual week and 17 percent while menstruating, giving a total figure very close to Cooke's 84 percent (Morton, Additon, Addison, Hunt, & Sullivan, 1953). However, the method of fixing the date of the crime relative to the date of menstruation, apparently based solely on the inmates' memory of these events months earlier, seems inadequate to the task, and the result may not be credible.

Dalton (1964) studied a girls' school in which older students, age 16-18, served as prefects who were permitted to punish the younger girls for misbehavior. The 11 prefects punished significantly more than would be expected by chance during the first four days of their own periods, but they punished less than expected during four days of the premenstruum. The form of punishment is not reported, but presumably it was not an infliction of physical injury and thus was not really aggression as it is defined in this review.

Hands, Herbert, and Tennent (1974) studied 23 women who had been housed at least six months in a secure hospital ward for patients with dangerous, violent, or criminal propensities. If patients became particularly disturbed, and especially if they started "acting out," then it was the practice to confine them to their rooms. Records were kept of these confinements and also of menstrual dates, and a comparison of these data showed significantly more confinements in the week before menstruation than would be expected by chance (also see statistical corrections by James, 1974). Some caution is obviously required in interpreting this result since confinement may not be an adequate proxy measure for aggressive behavior.

In the best study to date on aggression and menstruation, Ellis and Austin (1971) followed 45 prison inmates through three complete menstrual cycles. During this time period, prison officials recorded for the study 174 aggressive acts, about one-third being physical attacks and the rest verbal abuse. Both physical and verbal attacks were concentrated at greater-than-expected levels in the premenstrual and menstrual days, and these were also the days of highest feelings of irritability, according to inmates' self-reports.

A number of criticisms have been raised against the whole body of menstrual studies (Laws & Schwartz, 1977; Parlee, 1973), the most interesting being these.

First, the particular phase of the cycle that is associated with mishaps and morbidity shifts from study to study and from behavior to behavior, sometimes being the premenstruum, sometimes menstruation itself, and occasionally ovulation. Timing is confounded by the wide variation in cycle length from woman to woman, and for some women from one cycle to the next. However, if one assumes that the "negative phase" of the cycle is the week prior to menstruation and the first day or two of bleeding—consistent with Rossi and Rossi's (1980) careful mood study, then most reported periods of high mishap misbehavior and morbidity fall within this phase (making allowances for small sample fluctuations).

Second, most menstrual studies have focused on unusual populations such as prisoners or patients in psychiatric wards, and it is not clear that effects observed in such settings are generalizable to the larger population.

Third, since it is known that stressors can alter the timing of menstruation, causing it to be early, late, or missed altogether (Dalton, 1968), the possibility remains that mishaps are the cause of menstrual onset rather than its effect. For example, a woman in midcycle, involved in an auto accident, might start to menstruate because of the stress experience. An investigator, timing the accident from the woman's first subsequent period, would falsely conclude that the accident had occurred during the premenstruum. One should note, however, that such effects could obscure a real premenstrual effect as easily as exaggerate it. If the accident had occurred in the premenstruum, and the resulting stress had delayed or eliminated the imminent onset of bleeding, then the investigator would erroneously place this mishap outside of the premenstruum.

Finally, it must be emphasized that even if behaviors and moods are firmly correlated with particular phases of the menstrual cycle, it is still not obvious that hormonal changes are the causes of these behaviors and moods. The strong social expectations which girls learn about the menstrual period and its dysfunctions, even before they reach menarche (Clarke & Ruble, 1978), may serve as self-fulfilling prophecies.

In sum, there is a substantial body of evidence indicating that women experience relatively negative moods during the week preceding and the first days of menstruation. There does appear to be an increase in morbidity and misbehavior at that time, including aggression against others. It is plausible that this aggression is the result of hormone induced irritability. But valid objections can be raised against the data obtained so far, and even accepting the cyclicity of aggression, its causal link to hormonal change has not been demonstrated.

CONCLUSIONS

Physiological influences on human aggression have not been firmly established and must be regarded as speculative at this time. However, there are promising leads which may eventually show hormonal effects. Boys are physically more aggressive than girls in diverse cultures, and since this difference is often present among very young children, it seems unlikely to be wholly due to sex-specific training. Androgens are known to be important in sex differentiation at the fetal and adolescent states, so it seems plausible that similar hormonal effects will be implicated in the sex difference in aggression.

Among adult males, level of plasma testosterone may be related to aggressiveness, but studies of humans to date are weak and inconsistent. It seems as plausible to link testosterone to dominance behavior (which is often unaggressive in humans) as to aggression per se. Furthermore, if such links exist, they may be reciprocal ones, with dominance or aggressive behavior affecting hormone levels as well as hormones affecting dominance or aggression.

Irritable individuals of either sex may be particularly prone to outbursts of angry aggression. In females, however, the menstrual cycle is correlated to mood with irritability being relatively high in the premenstrual and early menstrual phases. It appears that some women are more likely to be aggressive during these high-irritability phases, though it is not clear that this is an explicitly hormonal effect since other explanations are feasible.

REFERENCES

Bell, R. Hormone influences on human aggression. *Irish Journal of Medical Science*, 1978, *174*, 5-9.

Borgaonkar, D., & Shah, S. The XYY chromosome male—Or syndrome? In A. Steinberg and A. Bearn (Eds.), *Progress in medical genetics*. Vol. 10. New York: Grune and Stratton, 1974.

Bourne, P., Coli, W., & Dahl, W. Affect levels of special forces soldiers under threat of attack. *Psychological Reports*, 1968, *22*, 363-66.

Bremer, J. *Asexualization*. New York: Macmillan, 1959.

Brotherton, J. *Sex hormone pharmacology*. London: Academic Press, 1976.

Brown, W., & Davis, G. Serum testosterone and irritability in man. *Psychosomatic Medicine*, 1975, *37*, 87.

Buss, A., Fischer, H., & Simmons, A. Aggression and hostility in psychiatric patients. *Journal of Consulting and Clinical Psychology*, 1968, *32*, 21.

Clarke, A., & Ruble, D. Young adolescents' beliefs concerning menstruation. *Child Development*, 1978, *49*, 231-34.

Cooke, W. Presidential address: Differential psychology of American women. *American Journal of Obstetrics and Gynecology*, 1945, *65*, 457.

Dalton, K. *The premenstrual syndrome*. Springfield, IL: Charles C Thomas, 1964.

Dalton, K. Menstruation and examinations. *Lancet*, Dec. 28, 1968, *2*, 1386-88.

Dixson, A. Androgens and aggressive behavior in primates: A review. *Aggressive Behavior*, 1980, *6*, 37-67.

Doering, C., Brodie, J., Kraemer, H., Moos, R., Becker, H., & Mechanic, D. Negative affect and plasma testosterone: A longitudinal human study. *Psychosomatic Medicine*, 1975, *37*, 484-91.

Dotson, L., Robertson, L., & Tuchfeld, B. Some correlations among alcohol, cigarettes, hormones, and hostility. Mimeo. Washington Insurance Institute for Highway Safety, 1974.

Eaton, G., Goy, R., & Phoenix, C. Effects of testosterone treatment in adulthood on sexual behavior of female pseudohermaphrodite rhesus monkeys. *Nature*, 1973, *242*, 119-20.

Ehrenkranz, J., Bliss, E., & Sheard, M. Plasma testosterone: Correlation with aggressive behavior and social dominance in man. *Psychosomatic Medicine*, 1974, *36*, 469-75.

Elias, M. Serum cortisol, testosterone and testosterone binding globulin responses to competitive fighting in human males. *Aggressive Behavior*, 1981, *7*, 215-24.

Ellis, D., & Austin, P. Menstruation and aggressive behavior in a correctional center for women. *The Journal of Criminal Law and Police Science*, 1971, *62*, 388-95.

Frasier, J., Gafford, F., & Horton, R. Plasma androgens in childhood and adolescence. *Journal of Clinical Endocrinology and Metabolism*, 1969, *29*, 1404-08.

Goy, R. Early hormonal influences on the development of sexual and sex-related behavior. In F. Schmitt, G. Quarton, T. Melnechuck, and G. Adelman (Eds.), *The neurosciences: Second study program*. New York: Rockefeller University Press, 1970.

Hamburg, D. Psychobiological studies of aggressive behavior. *Nature*, March 5, 1971, *230*, 19-23.

Hands, J., Herbert, V., & Tennent, G. Menstruation and behavior in a special hospital. *Medicine, Science, and the Law*, 1974, *14*, 32-35.

Harlow, H. Sexual behavior in the rhesus monkey. In F. Beach (Ed.), *Sex and behavior*. New York: John Wiley, 1965.

Hawke, C. Castration and sex crimes. *American Journal of Mental Deficiency*, 1951, *55*, 220-26.

James, W. Letter. *Medicine, Science, and the Law*, 1974, *14*, 290.

Kreuz, L., & Rose, R. Assessment of aggressive behavior and plasma testosterone in a young criminal population. *Psychosomatic Medicine*, 1972, *34*, 321-32.

Kreuz, L., Rose, R., & Jennings, J. Suppression of plasma testosterone levels and psychological stress. *Archives of General Psychiatry*, 1972, *26*, 479-82.

Laws, J., & Schwartz, P. *Sexual Scripts*. Hinsdale, IL: Dryden Press, 1977.

LeMaire, E. Danish experiences regarding the castration of sexual offenders. *Journal of Criminal Law, Criminology, and Police Science*, 1956, *47*, 294-310.

Leshner, A. *An introduction to behavioral endocrinology*. New York: Oxford University Press, 1978.

Maccoby, E., & Jacklin, C. *The psychology of sex differences*. Stanford: Stanford University Press, 1974.

Maccoby, E., & Jacklin, C. Sex differences in aggression: A rejoinder and reprise. *Child Development*, 1980, *51*, 964-80.

Mattsson, A., Schalling, D., Olweus, D., Low, H., & Svensson, J. Plasma testosterone, aggressive behavior, and personality dimensions in young male delinquents. *Journal of the Academy of Child Psychiatry*, 1980, *19*, 476-90.

Mazur, A. Cross-species comparison of status in established small groups. *American Sociological Review*, 1973, *38*, 513-30.

Mazur, A. Effects of testosterone on status in primate groups. *Folia Primatologica*, 1976, *26*, 214-26.

Mazur, A. Hormones, aggression, and dominance in humans. In B. Svare (Ed.), *Hormones and aggressive behavior*. New York: Plenum, 1983.

Mazur, A., & Lamb, T. Testosterone, status, and mood in human males. *Hormones and Behavior*, 1980, *14*, 236-46.

Mazur, A., & Robertson, L. *Biology and social behavior*. New York: Free Press, 1972.

Meyer-Bahlburg, H., Boon, D., Sharma, M., & Edwards, J. Aggressiveness and testosterone measures in man. *Psychosomatic Medicine*, 1973, *35*, 453.

Meyer-Bahlburg, H., & Ehrhardt, A. Prenatal sex hormones and human aggression: A review, and new data on progestogen effects. *Aggressive Behavior*, 1982, *8*, 39-62.

Money, J., & Ehrhardt, A. *Man and woman, boy and girl*. Baltimore: Johns Hopkins University Press, 1972.

Monti, P., Brown, W., & Corriveau, D. Testosterone and components of aggressive and sexual behavior in man. *American Journal of Psychiatry*, 1977, *134*, 692-94.

Morton, J., Additon, H., Addison, R., Hunt, C., & Sullivan, J. A clinical study of premenstrual tension. *American Journal of Obstetrics and Gynecology*, 1953, *65*, 1182-91.

Moyer, K. Sex differences in aggression. In R. Friedman, R. Richart, and R. Vande Wiele (Eds.), *Sex differences in behavior*. New York: John Wiley and Sons, 1974.

Olweus, D., Mattsson, A., Schalling, D., & Low, H. Testosterone, aggression, physical, and personality dimensions in normal adolescent males. *Psychosomatic Medicine*, 1980, *42*, 263-69.

Omark, D., Omark, M., & Edelman, M. Formation of dominance hierarchies in young children. In T. Williams (Ed.), *Psychological Anthropology*. The Hague: Mouton, 1975.

Parlee, M. The premenstrual syndrome. *Psychological Bulletin*, 1973, *80*, 454-65.

Persky, H., Smith, K., & Basu, G. Relation of psychologic measures of aggression and hostility to testosterone production in man. *Psychosomatic Medicine*, 1971, *33*, 265-77.

Rada, R., Kellner, R., & Winslow, W. Plasma testosterone and aggressive behavior. *Psychosomatics*, 1976, *17*, 138-42.

Rose, R., Bernstein, I., & Gordon, T. Consequences of social conflict on plasma testosterone levels in rhesus monkeys. *Psychosomatic Medicine*, 1975, *37*, 50-61.

Rose, R., Bourne, P., Poe, R., Mougey, E., Collins, D., & Mason, J. Androgen response to stress. II. Excretion of testosterone, epitestosterone, androsterone, and etiocholanolone during basic combat training and under threat of attack. *Psychosomatic Medicine*, 1969, *31*, 418-36.

Rossi, A., & Rossi, P. Body time and social time: Mood patterns by menstrual cycle phase and day of week. In J. Parsons (Ed.), *The psychobiology of sex differences and sex roles*. New York: McGraw-Hill, 1980.

Ruble, D., Brooks-Gunn, J., & Clarke, A. Research on menstrual-related psychological changes: Alternative perspectives. In J. Parsons (Ed.), *The psychobiology of sex differences and sex roles*. New York: McGraw-Hill, 1980.

Sherif, C. A social psychological perspective on the menstrual cycle. In J. Parsons (Ed.), *The psychobiology of sex differences and sex roles*. New York: McGraw-Hill, 1980.

Tieger, T. On the biological basis of sex differences in aggression. *Child Development*, 1980, *51*, 943-63.

Whiting, B., & Edwards, C. A cross-cultural analysis of sex differences in the behavior of children aged three through eleven. *Journal of Social Psychology*, 1973, *91*, 171-88.

Witkin, H., Mednick, S., Schulsinger, F., Bakkestrom, E., Christiansen, K., Goodenough, D., Hirschhorn, K., Lundsteen, C., Owen, D., Philip, J., Rubin, D., & Stocking, M. Criminality in XYY and XXY men. *Science*, 13 August 1976, *193*, 547-55.

7

Behavior Modification Approaches to Aggression Prevention and Control

Arnold P. Goldstein

If an act of overt aggression is conceptualized as the end product of a sequence of observable and covert events or steps, the potential exists for intervening—for seeking aggression control—at any one or more of these steps. Concretely, a frequent sequence of overt aggression precursors, and the aggression control interventions appropriate for each, are depicted in table 7.1. The present chapter provides an in-depth consideration and evaluation of each of these behavior modification approaches to aggression control. Their constituent procedures, research support, relation to other interventions, and place in the larger aggression control sequence will be examined.

SELF-INSTRUCTION TRAINING

A great deal of interest has emerged in recent years in the clinical application of long-established research findings concerning the influence of thought and language processes upon an individual's emotional state and overt behavior. Ellis' (1962) rational-emotive therapy, Goldfried and Davison's (1976) cognitive restructuring therapy, and Meichenbaum's (1977) stress innoculation intervention are three primary examples of the considerable contemporary interest in language mediated cognitive therapy procedures. Each of these approaches relies heavily upon instructing the client to alter his self-statements, his internal dialogue in more rational, constructive, positive ways. Novaco (1975) comments:

> Self-instruction techniques aim to obtain changes in problem behavior by modifying what clients say to themselves—that is, rather than simply attend to environmental contingencies, the self-instruction format broadens the focus of treatment to include the client's self-statements which precede, accompany, and follow environmental events. Changing a person's self-statements is also an integral part of Ellis' rational-emotive therapy, which is predicated on a concept of maladjustment stipulating that it is not events themselves that cause distress but rather a person's interpretations and internal sentences about those events. Ellis' therapeutic approach involves bringing the client's internal sentences to an explicit level and forcefully demonstrating to him that they derive from an irrational belief system. The task for the client in rational-emotive therapy is to unlearn his

Table 7.1. Behavior Modification Interventions in the Pre-Aggression—Overt Aggression Sequence

STEP	INTERVENTION
1. Arousal-Enhancing Interpretation of External Stimulus	Self-Statement Disputation
2. Heightened Affective Arousal	Relaxation Training
3. Arousal of the Other Person	Calming Training
4. Malcommunication	Communication Training
	Negotiation Training
	Contracting
5. Mismanagement of Contingencies (Reinforcement of Undesirable Behaviors)	Correct Contingency Management
6. Prosocial Skill Deficiencies (Inability to Perform Desirable Behaviors)	Prosocial Skill Training

irrational beliefs by checking his self-statements, seeing their source in irrational premises, and using a new set of beliefs and self-statements provided by the therapist. [p. 7]

While Ellis' (1962) approach to self-statement alteration relies heavily upon confrontation and persuasion, Meichenbaum's (1977) self-instruction training proceeds via a combination of modeling, guided practice, and shaping. In work with hospitalized schizophrenics (Meichenbaum & Cameron, 1973), impulsive children (Meichenbaum & Goodman, 1971), and test-anxious college students (Meichenbaum, 1972), Meichenbaum and his co-workers sought to train self-control skills via:

1. Therapist modeling in the presence of the client of constructive self-instructions by talking to himself aloud while engaging in the relevant task.
2. Having the client perform the task with the guidance of the same instructions, verbalized again by the therapist but, in this instance, as guidance for the client rather than self-instructing by the therapist.
3. Having the client perform the task while instructing himself aloud.
4. Having the client perform the task while self-instructing in a whisper.
5. Having the client perform the task while covertly self-instructing.

Thus, in the Meichenbaum approach, a process of progressive internalization is encouraged as a means of gradually substituting constructive for maladaptive self-instructions.

The most relevant and extensive application of the self-instructional change strategy to the domain of anger and toward the goal of anger control was conducted by Novaco (1975). Novaco's basic premise was that anger is fomented, maintained, and inflamed by the self-statements made by the individual in provocation situations. What self-instructions should optimally be used to counter these effects and maximize anger reduction? Novaco (1975) argued that effective self-instruction ideally would derive from a series of postulates which proposed that anger management would be enhanced by:

1. A task orientation towards provocation, rather than an ego orientation
2. High rather than low self-esteem
3. Nonantagonistic response skills
4. Awareness of one's own arousal
5. Ability to use one's own arousal as a cue for use of nonantagonistic skills

6. Perception of being in control of provocation situations
7. Ability to dissect provocation sequences into stages and use stage-appropriate self-instructions
8. Use of self-congratulatory self-statements for positive anger management
9. Use of relaxation training to reduce tension and arousal.

These several self-instruction generating postulates led Novaco (1975) to propose to clients seeking anger management assistance that the following self-statements be utilized. Note that, in response to postulate seven above, the self-statement examples below are sequenced in accordance with the stage of the provocation for which they are designed as an appropriate response.

Preparing for a provocation:
    1. I can work out a plan to handle this.
    2. If I find myself getting upset, I'll know what to do.
    3. Time for a few deep breaths of relaxation. Feel comfortable, relaxed, and at ease.
    4. This could be a testy situation, but I believe in myself.
Confronting the provocation:
    1. Stay calm. Just continue to relax.
    2. You don't need to prove yourself.
    3. It's really a shame that this person is acting the way she is.
    4. There's no need to doubt myself. What he says doesn't matter.
Coping with arousal and agitation:
    1. My muscles are starting to feel tight. Time to relax and slow things down.
    2. Getting upset won't help.
    3. It's reasonable to get annoyed, but let's keep the lid on.
    4. My anger is a signal of what I need to do. Time to talk to myself.
Self-reward:
    1. It worked!
    2. I'm doing better at this all the time.
    3. I actually got through that without getting angry.
    4. That wasn't as hard as I thought.

In what remains the most significant study of self-instruction procedures on anger control conducted thus far, Novaco (1975) examined the utility of use of self-statements such as the foregoing by a sample of individuals actually experiencing anger control problems in their daily lives. The 34 participating individuals were assigned to four treatment conditions. The first, *combined treatment*, consisted of self-instruction training using Meichenbaum's (1974) procedures, and self-statements like those procedures and statements noted above plus relaxation training following Jacobson's (1964) procedures. The second group of individuals received self-instruction training only. The third underwent only relaxation training, and the final experimental group was constituted as an attention control condition.

On a series of behavioral, self-report, and physiological measures, results of this investigation were unambiguous. The combined treatment condition resulted in highly significant improvement in participants' ability to manage anger in comparison to the attention control condition. Less effective, but still clearly superior to attention control participants, was the self-instructions only condition. Participation in relaxation training only also yielded differences significantly favoring such participants in comparison to attention controls, but to a less powerful degree than for self-instruction only participants. The combined treatment tended to yield more substantial anger management change on several measures than did self-instructions only, a trend even more pronounced for the combined versus relaxation only treatments. Novaco (1975) comments:

> The results of the project demonstrate that cognitive control procedures can be effectively used to regulate anger arousal. . . . Through the making of self-statements, clients were able to influence their perception of provocations ("Maybe he's having a rough day" or "There's no need to take it personally") and to guide their response to the problem situation ("Don't act like a jerk just because he is," or "What do I want to accomplish here"). The use of such covert procedures imparts to the person an explicit sense of personal control, which has the effect of diminishing the threat value of the provocation as well as increasing one's response options. Discovering that there are alternative ways of perceiving and responding to provocations plays a major role in the development of competence for anger management. [p. 48]

This important investigation, it should be stressed, yielded evidence not only substantiating the value for anger control of self-instructions training, but also of relaxation training. Novaco (1975) observes in this regard:

> The relaxation procedures enabled subjects to be more aware of the tension and agitated states that can lead to anger, as well as result from it. The training in relaxation techniques provided them with a means of modifying the tension states that predispose them to anger and importantly gave them a sense of mastery over troublesome internal states. As a person learns that he can induce self-relaxation, he develops the cognition that he is able to control arousal states. [p. 48]

A small number of additional investigators have examined the anger management potential of self-instruction training. Snyder and White (1979) report positive effects for such training in a study involving aggressive delinquents. Hamberger and Lohr (1980) report similar success with a spouse-abusing client in a case study report. Such results are clearly encouraging. Equally clear, however, is the need for further empirical scrutiny.

CONTROL METHODS

Relaxation Training

Relaxation training is the systematic application of tension-sensitizing and tension-release procedures in order to achieve a state of deep muscular relaxation. Rooted historically in decades' old techniques originated by Jacobson (1929, 1964), popular in contemporary usage especially as a component of systematic desensitization procedures (Wolpe, 1969), and empirically demonstrated to be effective in an extended series of investigations (Grimm, 1980; King, 1980; Luiselli, Marholin, Steinman, & Steinman, 1979; Rimm, DeGroot, Boord, Heiman, & Dillow, 1971), relaxation training and its deep muscular relaxation consequence is an important technique for reducing the tension and arousal levels which so often function as immediate precursors to overt aggression.

Phase One. Tension-Relaxation Cycles. The first component of relaxation training is responsive to the just noted observation regarding the heightened tension levels which frequently precede aggressive behavior. In order to both enable the individual to interrupt the tension build up process as early as possible, as well as to maximize his or her awareness of the "feel" of relaxation by introducing procedures which actively contrast it with its opposite (tension), relaxation training begins with having the individual engage, in cyclical sequence, in tension-enhancing and relaxation-enhancing behaviors. To do so in the most effective manner, a series of steps are usually employed.

Step 1. The client is asked first to select an appropriate time and place, one in which he or she wil be undisturbed in a quiet atmosphere for approximately a half hour. Instructions to get comfortable then follow, i.e., loosening clothing, dimming lights, finding a comfortable chair and position in it, and so forth.

Step 2. The essence of relaxation training, largely reflected in this step, is perhaps best communicated by quoting our exact instructions to clients when implementing this step (Goldstein & Rosenbaum, 1982):

> Let your eyes close gently, do not shut them tight. You are now ready to begin. Start with the hands. Tense them by making tight fists with both hands and hold the tensed position as you slowly recite T-E-N-S-E. Say one letter about every two seconds so that you are tensing the muscles for about ten seconds. After approximately ten seconds of tension, relax the hands quickly and let them continue to relax while you slowly recite R-E-L-A-X-R-E-L-A-X. Again, say one letter every two seconds so that you are relaxing for about twenty seconds. This is one tension-relaxation cycle. Repeat the cycle again, still with your hands. For each muscle group do two cycles (i.e., Tense-Relax, Tense-Relax) and then move on to the next muscle group. [p. 17]

Step 3. The client is then instructed in conducting two tension-relaxation cycles for the musculature in his or her arms, shoulders, neck, forehead, eyes and nose, mouth, chest and back, abdomen, and legs and feet. Phase one in its entirety, therefore, consists of twenty tension-relaxation cycles, i.e., two each for ten muscle groups. Further instructions to clients during this step are:

> As you do each of these exercises, let your mind relax as well as your body. Focus your attention within your body. As you tense and relax each muscle group, focus on the bad feelings of tension within that part of your body and then on the good feelings of relaxation in that part. Notice what it feels like when those muscles are tense, so that you will recognize tension when it occurs naturally. [p. 17]

Phase Two. Relaxation Only. The goal of phase two is to move the individual toward deeper levels of relaxation. The tension-sensitizing aspects of the training are deleted and the individual is instructed to concentrate on getting each muscle group more and more deeply relaxed. This phase seeks to establish a level of concentration on relaxation which will enable the final phase, deep relaxation, to occur.

Phase Three. Deep Relaxation. As above, an exact quotation here of our instructions to actual clients provides the essence of this phase:

> Just let your entire body relax as you focus on a pleasant scene. It sometimes helps to imagine yourself lying on the beach on a warm sunny day, or drifting peacefully on a raft in a pool, or lying under a shady tree in the cool grass on a warm day. Find and imagine a scene that makes you feel good and imagine it as you relax. Let the rubber bands unwind all the way. Sink deeply into your chair or bed. Breathe deeply, slowly, evenly. Tune out the outside world completely. Continue this final phase for about three minutes or so, then gradually open your eyes. You should feel refreshed and very relaxed.

Most clients, after approximately two weeks of daily practice of this three-phase process, are able to drop the first phase and commence with the Relaxation Only phase. In turn, a week or two of practice at this level typically enables the individual to commence directly with phase three, perhaps in response to the self-command, "Relax." For those readers interested in actually utilizing deep muscular relaxation, further detail regarding its constituant procedures and their implementation is provided by Benson (1975), Bernstein and Borkovec (1973), Goldstein and Rosenbaum (1982), and Walker (1975).

A great deal of research has sought to examine the effectiveness of relaxation training. While conclusions safely drawn from this body of literature must be tentative, cumulative findings are decidedly encouraging. Relaxation training has been studied as an intervention with both adults and children experiencing a wide array of tension-associated problems. Its effectiveness has been demonstrated in applications to insomnia (Borkovec, Grayson, O'Brien, & Weerts, 1979; Pendleton & Tasto, 1976), essential hypertension (Taylor, Farquhar, Nelson, & Agras, 1977), tension headache and migraine (Luther, 1971; Warner & Lance, 1975), test taking anxiety (Delprato & Dekraker, 1976; Russell & Sipich, 1974), public speaking anxiety (Goldfried & Trier, 1974; Weissberg, 1975), self-injurious behavior (Steen & Zuriff, 1977), and general tension and anxiety (Borkovec, Grayson, & Cooper, 1978; Sherman & Plummer, 1973).

Mechanisms underlying such tension-reduction effects are not fully clear. Some investigators have been able to demonstrate a relationship of tension reduction to concurrent physiological changes (Jacobson, 1964; Paul, 1969). Others report the absence of such relationships (Parker, Gilbert, & Thoresen, 1978), and still others report mixed findings (Connor, 1974; Fee & Girdano, 1978). Thus, while the psychophysiological bases for the tension-reducing effects of relaxation training remain in need of further clarification, the effects themselves appear to be both substantial and relatively reliable across tension-associated disorders.

Rimm, DeGroot, Boord, Heiman, & Dillow (1971) were able to demonstrate directly the value of relaxation training for persons who experience anger in automobile-driving situations. Herrell (1971) reported similar success in a case study of a soldier who became excessively angry when given orders. Evans (1971) and Sanders (1978) have also presented case study descriptions of the successful application of relaxation procedures with aggressive individuals. Somewhat more ambiguous, but still encouraging outcomes have emerged in a further series of systematic applications of relaxation in yet other anger or aggression contexts (Evans, Hearn, & Saklofake, 1973; O'Donnell & Worell, 1973; Von Benken, 1977) and, as discussed earlier, Novaco's (1975) work yields further support for anger-control effects of relaxation in the context of a self-instruction format.

CALMING OTHERS

Relaxation training and self-instruction training, it will be recalled, represent attempts to intervene during the anger phase of the Instigation→Anger→Aggression sequence. The several additional interventions we will consider in the remainder of this chapter, including procedures for calming others, address more directly the goal of aggression control. Unlike the other aggression control procedures to be examined shortly, those designed to calm aggressive others do not for the most part rest on a strong empirical base. Modeling calmness, encouraging talking, listening openly, showing understanding, reassuring the other person, and helping them save face—the six procedures for calming others to be described—grow primarily from the clinical lore of the existential psychotherapies and the clinical experience of the crisis intervention movement. Our own two extended applications of these procedures are also more clinical-experiential than empirical in nature. The first, *Police Crisis Intervention* (Goldstein, Monti, Sardino, & Green, 1978) sought to train on-line police officers in the effective use of these procedures when faced with highly aggressive individuals involved in marital or family disputes. The second, *Aggress-Less* (Goldstein & Rosenbaum, 1982) attempted to develop calming-others expertise in lay individuals confronted with aggressive spouses, children, or others. While both of these applications yielded effects which appeared quite promising, the need for systematic and careful empirical examination of these procedures remains clear.

Modeling Calmness

Modeling has an especially long and substantial history in psychology. Vicarious or observational learning effects have been demonstrated in connection with a particularly broad array of behaviors of diverse types, including several demonstrations that aggression is often learned via imitative or modeling processes. The opposite, modeling of aggression control behaviors, is much les ommon, especially in research contexts. Nevertheless, as noted above, we feel there is a great deal of reason (by extension of existing findings, and by clinical experience) to believe that such modeling-instigated aggression control effects do obtain.

An individual, we suggest, can serve as a model of calmness—and thus contribute to reducing the aggression of an observing other—by means of facial expression; posture; gestures; what is said; and the tone, speed, and loudness of how things are said. Specifically, the calm person's face shows an unwrinkled forehead; eyebrows not drawn down or together; eyes open normally, with neither the staring or squinting of anger or the wide openness of surprise; nose not wrinkled or with flared nostrils; lips parted normally, neither pressed together nor pulled back as in snarling. The calm person is more likely sitting than standing; arms at sides, not crossed; hands open, not in fists; movements are slow and fluid, not fast or jerky; head, neck, and shoulders are relaxed, not tense or rigid. The calm person's voice is even rather than jumpy; soft or moderate rather than loud; slow or moderately paced rather than rapid; contains pauses; and avoids shouting, sharpness, or considerable unevenness. These are the several overt signs of calmness which may be displayed by a model seeking to calm an aggressive other.

Encouraging Talking

In the view of many clinicians, especially those subscribing to an hydraulic model of aggression, the opportunity to talk it out, get it off one's chest, or ventilate one's feelings is a primary approach to controlling aggressive behavior. While the present writer, holding a nonhydraulic, social learning perspective on aggression and its control, is less optimistic about the supposed singular potency for aggression-control purposes of such ventilation; it is, we believe, appropriate to include this approach as but one of several contributing procedures to a multiple-determined calming others effect. A useful and perhaps noninstigating strategy in doing so is often to help the aggressive person to explain what he hopes you and he might constructively do about it—rather than having him explain why he became aggressive in the first place, which in fact is likely to reinstigate high levels of arousal and consequent aggressive behavior. Effective tactics for encouraging others to talk include asking open-ended questions (questions beginning with "what," "why," or "how"), responding to the person with encouragement to talk ("Tell me more." "Mm-hmm"), and other methods we will describe below (listening openly, showing understanding, giving reassurance).

These steps all encourage the other person to talk *more*. If the content of the talking thus elicited is primarily an angry recapitulation of why the person became aggressive in the first place, then all we will have accomplished is a reinstigation of aggression, rather than calming. Thus, talking more will be especially useful as a calmative if, as the talk-elicitation procedures are used, other steps are taken to make this increased talk calm talk. This can be done in a number of ways. Disputants in an aggressive argument can be physically separated and spoken with individually. When asking open-ended or other questions, one should ask only one question at a time, and be as specific as possible. The aggressive person(s) should also be told that to make sure you understand them, you would like them to talk lower, slower, and more simply. One should also richly reward calmness as it is displayed, by telling the other person that their frankness, openness, and, especially, their calmness is appreciated.

Listening Openly

As the aggressive individual begins to respond to the other person's modeled calmness and encouragement to talk, a further increment toward calming him or her which may be implemented is the other person's open listening. Open listening in this context means trying hard to pay attention to what the aggressive person is saying, and overtly showing this effort in one's behavior. Such attentional behaviors include looking squarely at the aggressive person when he/she speaks, nodding one's head when appropriate, avoiding interrupting, leaning toward the other person, and listening as carefully as one can to what is being said.

Showing Understanding

Calming of aggressive behavior is also a frequent consequence of believing that one's feelings and actions are understood. Sometimes, showing understanding is best operationalized very simply, for example by saying "I see what you mean," "I can understand that," or by making similar statements. Other times, showing understanding is optimally implemented by use of restatement of content. This oft-employed feature of nondirective psychotherapy involves, in our instance, the person seeking to calm the other by saying back to him, in different words than he used, the essence of what he has said to you.

Often even more effective than such paraphrasing is to concentrate more on what the aggressive person is feeling than on the content of what he is saying, and then letting him know his feelings are accurately understood. Such reflection of feeling or use of empathy can be a major aid toward calming aggressive individuals. Being skilled in the use of empathy means first trying very hard to put oneself in the aggressive other's place. One should ask oneself what the other person is feeling and how strongly he is feeling it. One must seek to go beyond the content of the aggressive person's words and focus rather more on *how* he says something—the tone, speed, and loudness of his words; his breathing rate; stammering; gestures; posture; facial expressions; and other clues to the nature and strength of his affect.

Here are a few examples of restatement of content—which seek to paraphase content, and reflection of feeling—which seek to communicate an understanding of affect.

Aggressive person to you: "You shouldn't have left!"
Restatement: "You think I was wrong to have left."
Reflection: "You're really upset that I left."

Aggressive person to you: "Why the hell did they stop before the end!"
Restatement: "You believe they gave up too easily."

Reflection: "You feel let down that they didn't try hard enough."

Aggressive person to you: "Damn it, they took it and it was mine!"
Restatement: "You think you've been cheated."
Reflection: "You're really steamed, and feel cheated."

Reassuring the Other Person

People who are behaving aggressively often have either not attempted less forceful solutions to the problems upsetting them or, if they have, such attempts haven't succeeded. It will frequently be helpful in calming such persons to reassure them that nonaggressive alternatives do exist; and, further, that one is willing to help the other individual attempt such alternative problem solutions.

Reassurance may be expressed in a number of ways. Statements can be offered such as, "It will be OK, we've worked this out before." "I think we'll be able to handle this a step at a time." "I'm really interested in solving this with you." In addition, the aggressive person can be reminded of times in the past when he or others in fact successfully found and used nonaggressive solutions to this or similar problems. The reassurance offered should be aimed at reducing threat, arousing optimism for problem resolution, clarifying ambiguities, and expressing a willingness to help solve the given problem. Reassurance is best offered warmly and sincerely and, when appropriate, with a physical gesture of support, such as a hand on the other's shoulder. If not overused, and if one avoids minimizing the seriousness of real problems, reassurance can clearly be an effective component of efforts to calm aggressive others.

Helping Save Face

At times, calming others is especially problematic because the source of the other individual's aggression and the person seeking to calm the other are one and the same. If person A is, therefore, trying to calm person B—whose aggression is being directed toward A—A will be more successful to the degree he can aid B in listening openly, thinking objectively, and become more willing to consider compromise or other nonaggressive problem solutions. One means for meeting these ends involves helping person B save face, i.e., making it easier for him to retreat, back off, or back down gracefully. One can do so in several ways. A should avoid audiences in talking with B and, if necessary, provide him with face-saving rationalizations. A should also control the pace of his own concession-seeking and B's concession-giving by not asking for too much too soon. Perhaps most important to this face-saving effort, person A should also contribute to a compromise outcome, and offer B at least some substantial part of what B is aggressively demanding.

These several calming others procedures appear from the perspective of clinical application to be useful and effective means for reducing overt aggression. Their apparent utility is sufficient to warrant our strong encouragement of their rigorous and systematic investigation.

COMMUNICATION TRAINING

It often will be appropriate that the major procedures described in this chapter be viewed as optimally utilized in combination and in essentially the sequence in which we have presented them here. Thus, self-directed relaxation and self-instructions efforts are logically followed in dyadic conflict situations by other-directed calming efforts which, if successful, permit the parties in conflict to engage in problem-solving, constructive communication attempts. In the present section, therefore, we turn to an in-depth consideration of such communication procedures. Open and constructive communication, in turn, has the positive potential for leading to *negotiated* conflict resolutions whose terms are *contractually* secured. In keeping with our goal of sequencing chapter topics to parallel the likely flow of an entire aggression control event, negotiation and contracting are the respective topics of the sections of this chapter which follow the present one.

Interest in conflict-laden communication, and a companion focus upon training in problem-solving, constructive communication has been a central concern in recent years among professionals interested in marriage and marital therapy. The systems theory views of Lederer & Jackson (1968) and Watzlawick, Beavin, & Jackson (1967) placed early emphasis in their descriptions of marital disharmony on the high levels of ambiguous and vague communication between spouses in such marriages. Friedman (1972) similarly highlighted the role of inconsistent and often contradictory verbal and nonverbal communications as signposts of disordered marriages. Knox (1971) has described marital disharmony largely in terms of the lack of honest and direct communication, and both Eisler & Hersen (1973) and Fensterheim (1972) have stressed the couple's inability to express either positive or negative feelings. Related communication skills deficits have been central to the marital therapy and communications training work of most other investigators concerned with discord, conflict, and aggression in marital contexts (Bornstein, Anton, Harowski, Weltzein, McIntyre & Hocker-Wilmot, 1981; Carkhuff, 1971; Gottman, Notarius, Markman, Bank, Yoppi, & Rubin, 1976; Guerney, 1964; Jacobson & Martin, 1976; O'Leary & Turkewitz, 1978; Rose, 1977; Stuart, 1969; Weiss, Hops & Patterson, 1973). The communications training contents and constructive communication rules to which we now turn are a distillation from these several investigators of their major recommendations or curricula for discordant and conflicted communicators. *

Retargeting Communication Goals

An important first step in communication training is to aid the disputants in refocusing their efforts away from "winning" and toward more collaborative problem solution seeking behavior. As we state when instructing conflicted couples toward this end (Goldstein & Rosenbaum, 1982):

> Assume for a moment that you are about to have a serious argument with your spouse, your child or a co-worker. One of the most important factors determining the outcome of the argument is how you want it to come out. Is your goal to win, to beat the other person, to cut him down, to humiliate her? Remember, your intentions are crucial. If they are to defeat the other person, if it is you *versus* them, it is going to be quite difficult to either reduce the level of anger and aggression, or solve the aggression-causing problem constructively. If, however, your goal is to join with (not against) the other person to defeat the problem, and not the other person, your argument is off to a very positive start. [p. 42]

The win-win constructive communication strategy (Filley, 1975) to which these instructions point urges the disputants to consider both their own needs and the other person's, and to try

---

* As is true for most other types of skills training efforts, the communications skills which follow have typically been taught by means of such procedures as instructions, modeling, behavioral rehearsal, and performance feedback. These procedures are described in greater detail in the final section of this chapter.

to join with the other person to find a shared problem solution satisfying to both of them. This strategy contrasts sharply with the win-lose stance characteristically adopted by most dyadic disputants, a stance in which one (and usually both) party seeks to defeat the other.

Preparing for Communication

In addition to relaxation, self-instruction, calming others, and retargeting goals, there are other preparatory steps which disputants profitably may take for purposes of aggression control and constructive communication.

1. Plan on dealing with one problem at a time. Constructive communication in the context of aggression is complex and difficult enough to achieve when a single issue or problem is at focus. To attempt simultaneous solution of two or more such matters seriously increases the chances of failure. Thus, the rule we recommend is one problem at a time, sequencing them in order of significance if more than one exists.

2. Choose the right time and place. Disputants should be encouraged to take setting and time influences into consideration when planning communication attempts. Privacy is usually vital, as audiences typically hinder much more than assist. Potential interruptions should be minimized and, in general, a facilitative location and time should be selected.

3. Consider one's plan. A final preparatory step involves reviewing one's own views and feelings, as well as one's expectations about the other disputant's position. The communications trainee is thus urged to consider why he or she thinks and feels a particular way, what outcomes are desired, and how he or she can contribute concretely to a win-win solution—and also the likely thoughts, feelings, hoped-for outcomes, and possible constructive contributions of the other disputant.

Constructive Communication Rules

Once preparatory efforts are completed, constructive communication can commence. In communication training, specific rules for aggression-reducing, effective problem solving frequently include the following.

1. Acknowledge subjectivity. To help establish a facilitative climate for nondefensive communication, communication training often seeks to increase disputant's awareness of their own subjectivity. While disputants are often quick to perceive each other's beliefs and behavior as biased and highly subjective, they clearly tend to be disinclined to acknowledge reciprocal subjectivity in their own conflict-relevant behavior. In our approach to this step, we train disputants to be more aware of such lack of objectivity, but also to be explicitly open about it especially in the beginning stages of a potentially conflict-reducing confrontation. Phrases such as "I believe that. . . ." or "It seems to me that. . . ." are examples of such openness to possible subjectivity.

2. Be rational. Disputants are trained to present their position in a logical, step-wise, systematic manner. To maximize the clarity of their communications, they are urged to carefully explain the reasoning behind their views and the bases for their interpretation of events, as well as to define terms and ideas whenever there appears to be a possibility of misinterpretation.

3. Be direct. Communications training urges disputants to present what they have to say to the other person in a direct, straightforward, nonhostile manner. When offering what one believes, feels, and prefers, the effort must be made to avoid or minimize editing or half-truths. One's needs, feelings, intentions, and expectations should be presented as clearly as possible.

4. Make ongoing communication checks. Rather than assume one is being understood, disputants are taught to take overt steps in order to check out the adequacy of the ongoing communication. Disputants are urged to encourage the other person to ask questions, to be redundant on possibly hard to understand content, to explain their own ideas using as much as possible the other person's language and concepts, and to check out how successfully they are communicating in other ways.

5. Focus on behavior. Most approaches to communications training are decidedly behavioral in orientation, not only in how communication rules are taught, but also with regard to the rules themselves. In our procedures, for example, when describing to the other person one's own view of what happened and what one would like to happen, disputants are instructed to concentrate on actual actions the person has taken or might take—what was done, where, when, how often, how much. If the communication focus is on the other disputant's values, beliefs, personality, intentions, motivations, or other inner, unobservable qualities, we believe the likelihood of aggression-reducing constructive communication is substantially reduced. Simply stated we hold this view because character, personality, intentions, and other targets for potential change which can't be seen are considerably harder to alter and considerably more threatening as targets of change than are communication goals which are behavioral and observable—coming in on time, spending less money, picking up one's bicycle.

6. Reciprocate. Consistent with the spirit of preparing for problem-solving encounters whose goal is both aggression-reduction and the search for win-win problem solutions, we have found that willingness to reciprocate is an important lesson to learn in communication training. Disputants are taught to focus not only upon what they'd like the other person to do, but also their willingness to change their own behavior in specific and concrete ways. In addition to willingness to contribute to problem solutions, constructive communicators also acknowledge their contribution to problem causation, and thus disputants should be encouraged to do so.

7. Disclose yourself. Closely related to the theme of reciprocity is that of self-disclosure. Constructive communicators should be taught that they can encourage openness in others by being open about themselves. Such self-disclosure, when done gradually and offered appropriately in terms of its timing, depth, intimacy, and length, can contribute importantly toward fuller mutual understanding between communicating disputants.

8. Be empathic. In our earlier discussion of useful means for calming aggressive persons, we described the value for this purpose of showing understanding of the other person's feelings. Such empathic responding is also an especially valuable component of the type of constructive communication we are aiming for in this chapter between disputants, one or more of whom are overtly aggressive. As we have commented elsewhere in connection with this formulation (Goldstein & Rosenbaum, 1982):

> [y]our first step is to try to put yourself in the other person's place. Ask yourself what he or she is feeling, and how strongly. Communicating to the other person your understanding of his or her feelings is a crucial step in the problem-solving process. Your communication of empathy might be at the reflection level, in which you let the other person know your understanding of his or her feelings at the same level as they were shared with you. Or it might be at the implicit level, in which you go beyond what the person actually said to you, and beyond the person's own perception of his or her feelings, to share what you think may be the deeper, underlying feelings. . . . Your effort at being empathic . . . will help make the other person feel better understood. They . . . often will respond by becoming calmer, feeling closer, and trying to be empathic in return. [p. 46]

9. Check it out. Disputants should be trained to regularly take steps to make sure the message one thinks one is communicating is in fact the message heard by the other individual. By

either directly asking the other person, or by judging from their overt responses, one should periodically check to be sure accurate communication is occurring.

10. Pay attention to nonverbal behavior. For purposes just described, i.e., checking out messages received, as well as an aid to several of the other communication rules presented above, a skilled communicator regularly attends to the other person's nonverbal behavior. Gestures, posture, facial expression, skin color, breathing rate, and many other nonverbal behaviors signify—to the attentive observer—a great deal about the other person's feelings, acceptance of one's views, willingness to continue talking and listening, and overall progress toward problem solution.

11. Avoid communication blocks. In addition to the several "do's" represented by the ten communication rules just described, aggression-reducing and problem solving discourse is optimized when disputants avoid a number of aggression-enhancing, solution-avoiding communication errors. These include threats, commands, interruptions, sarcasm, put-downs, counterattacks, insults, teasing, and yelling. In addition, constructive communication will often be blocked by overgeneralizations ("You never . . . ," "You always . . ."), not responding (silence, sulking, ignoring), exaggeration (of the other's wrongness or one's own rightness), speaking for the other person, offering advice prematurely, lecturing, or shifting the topic inappropriately. Finally, and particularly to be avoided as they are especially potent instigators to renewed aggression, are kitchen-sinking, building straw men, and the use of guilt arousal.

In addition to our own utilization of this communications training curriculum (Goldstein & Rosenbaum, 1982; Goldstein, Sprafkin, & Gershaw, 1976), a number of other approaches to reducing aggression and enhancing communication in discordant and conflicted dyads using largely the same or analogous communications training contents have been both reported and systematically examined. Carkhuff's (1971) Systematic Facilitative Training is one such communications training approach, one in which special emphasis is placed on teaching empathy, warmth, and genuineness as a communicative base. Wells, et al. (1975) successfully demonstrated the utility of Systematic Facilitative Training in enhancing marital adjustment among high conflict married couples. Pierce (1973) worked with couples who acknowledged serious communication skills deficits, and showed the Carkhuff approach to be more useful vis à vis communication-enhancement than was more traditional insight therapy. Hickman & Baldwin (1971) reported an analogous positive demonstration of the effectiveness of this approach, in this instance as compared to both programmed text and no treatment conditions.

Guerney's (1964) Dyadic Relationship Enhancement method for communications training also rests on a reasonable foundation of empirical support. Ely and Guerney (1973) describe the impact of this approach as including diminishing hostile attitudes, increasing mutual understanding, and more effective communication patterns. Miller (1971), Nunally (1971), and Rappaport (1971) have each provided additional confirming evidence in support of the communication skill enhancement value of the Dyadic Relationship Enhancement method. Rose's (1977) Communications Skills Workshops, though more recently developed, also show beginning promise as a means of effectively teaching an array of communication skills similar to those we have described (Lubar, 1978; Rose, 1977). In addition, systematic communications training of the types portrayed above have been reported and empirically investigated with favorable results by Allred (1977); Argyle, Trower, & Bryant (1974); Brock (1978); Burka, Hubbell, Preble, Spinelli, & Winter (1971); Curran (1977); Gottman, Motarius, Gonso, & Markham (1976); Hanson (1971); Heiman (1973); Lieberman, King, DeRisi, & McCann (1975); McFall & Twentyman (1973); Rhode, Rasmussen, & Heaps (1971); Robin, Kent, O'Leary, Foster, & Prinz (1977); Terkelson (1976); Wyckoff (1978); and Zimmerman (1978).

NEGOTIATION TRAINING

In the preceding section, several types of facilitative communication, as well as the major programs used to teach them, were examined. The present section focuses on one further type of communication skill, singled out here for separate consideration to reflect its singular importance in the aggression-reduction and problem-solving arenas. We refer to negotiation skill.

It will be recalled that in our consideration of communication goals, the win-win outcome was described as the optimal communication target. In such conflict solutions, both parties get all or most of whatever they are seeking. While win-win goals should indeed remain first in one's communication strategy, it must be recognized that such outcomes are often hard to plan for or reach. It will very often be true, in interpersonal conflict situations, that one and usually both of the people involved will have to surrender at least part of their ideal outcome. By a process of bargaining, give and take, trading off, or negotiation, compromise can be mutually sought and successfully reached. Thus, while win-win solutions may be ideal, compromise outcomes—in which each party gains part of what he or she is seeking, and each also loses a part—may be the optimal solution that can realistically be expected in many instances. Clearly, such compromises in the face of conflict are preferable to a third and rather frequent type of interpersonal conflict outcome, the win-lose situation—in which one party obtains all that he or she sought and the other obtains nothing.

Preparation for Negotiation

A few preparatory steps exist whose use will aid potential negotiators in maximizing the chances that their subsequent negotiations will be effective and result in a mutually satisfactory compromise.

1. Remain calm. Perhaps this first step need not be reiterated again, but it is indeed a crucial determinant of the negotiations climate, and hence its eventual outcome. This step urges that the negotiators remain sensitive to their own and the other's arousal/anger level, and reuse relaxation and self-instructions (for self-calming) or the several techniques examined earlier for calming others whenever their respective anger levels warrant.

2. Choose negotiation goals. A second useful preparatory step involves negotiators getting their priorities and hoped-for conflict solutions clear in their own minds. Obviously, if compromise is their intent, the greater the range and number of goals which are acceptable, the greater the likelihood of a successful negotiated outcome. In our negotiation training (Goldstein et al., 1976; Goldstein & Rosenbaum, 1982), we urge negotiators to select goals based upon (a) what is fair; (b) what is manageable in terms of size or scope of the goals selected (when anger is high and trust low, smaller goals should be dealt with before larger ones); (c) their relationship with the other person, and what they would like it to be after the negotiation is completed; (d) the importance to the parties of whatever is being negotiated; (e) the level or risk each party is willing to run; and (f) each person's history as a negotiator, both in general and with the particular person involved in the present conflict.

3. Where and when to negotiate. As we suggested in connection with constructive communication, negotiation proceeds best when there is privacy and little chance of being interrupted. The presence of others during conflict negotiations has been shown to increase face-saving attempts, lengthen the negotiations, add outside pressures, and decrease openness and objectivity. Privacy, therefore, seems to be an especially desirable characteristic of effective negotiations. There are additional time and place considerations. Negotiations ideally should

be conducted at a neutral location—not her office, his den, or their apartment. Bargainers have been shown to be more assertive and less inclined to compromise when they are in their own surroundings, thus our recommendation of a neutral location.

4. When to negotiate. If possible, time limits should be avoided. Though time pressures can sometimes increase the likelihood of compromise, they more often lead to counterproductive consequences—a lowering of goals, an increase in demands, an increase in bluffing, and other nonconstructive communication. Finally, conflict negotiations ideally occur in person, on a face to face basis, and not by telephone. In negotiations conducted by phone, important matters are more likely to be omitted, time pressures become greater, the person called is often less prepared than the caller to negotiate, interruptions are more likely, facial expressions and gestures are not visible, misunderstandings may be more frequent, and it is easier for one of the parties to say "no" and thus end the negotiations in a noncompromising failure. These several reasons underscore the value of direct, in-person negotiations.

Negotiating Procedures

In our version of negotiation training (Goldstein & Rosenbaum, 1982), after appropriate attention to preparatory rules, trainees are instructed in the following, five-step negotiating sequence:

1. State your position. This is your opening statement. It is determined by the goals you are aiming for, the negotiating tactics you've decided to use, and how well you've prepared yourself to negotiate. Your opening position has a significant effect on how the negotiation eventually works out. It helps create the psychological climate between you and the other person—trust, level of toughness, cooperativeness, etc. We therefore urge a moderate opening position, in which you demand neither too much nor too little.

2. State your understanding of the other person's position. After presenting your viewpoint, this second negotiating step lets the other person know you are trying to understand his/hers. In a conflict situation, especially when anger levels are high, it is often difficult to be accurate about what the other person believes, wants, or is demanding. Yet, for a compromise to be reached, really understanding the other person's position is vital. So, when the other person is having trouble understanding your position, we recommend you make use of a technique called role reversal. You take his part and try to explain, argue for, and defend his position; and he should do the same for your position. Try to really be the other person. Go over and sit where he was sitting, and have him take your chair. Use his name as your own. Try to "get into his skin," and have him reciprocate. If you both do this energetically, your empathy for and understanding of each other's position will increase substantially.

3. Ask if the other person agrees with your statement of his/her position. This step is the "checking it out" we urged you to do in other attempts at constructive communication. This sequence of steps is building to the final one, in which you actually propose a specific compromise. Before doing so, you must be sure you accurately understand the other person's position, and this step is your way of doing it. So, check it out.

4. Listen openly to his or her response. The emphasis in this step is on "openly." One or both of you is angry. One or both of you is behaving aggressively. It may be easy to hear (especially if you both are shouting!), but hard to really listen. So, as you listen openly to the other person's response to your statement of his/her position, you should follow all the good listening rules we described in our discussion of calming others, and also (a) don't interrupt, (b) don't "tune out" information you don't like, (c) don't speak before thinking, (d) discourage distractions, do nothing but negotiate, and (e) try to listen as though you have to summarize to someone else what the other person is saying.

5. Propose a compromise. When you and the other person have gone through the first four negotiating steps enough times that you feel there has been a sufficient exchange of information and a sufficient increase in understanding each other's positions, it is time for a compromise solution to be proposed. Whether the compromise is some sort of 50-50, split-the-difference proposal, or some other arrangement, it is important that it meets some of the important needs and demands of *each* of you. Remember, in compromise solutions both of you win some of what you want, and both of you must lose a little also. It is often helpful if the compromise you propose is one that you would find acceptable if it were offered to you.

In proposing a compromise, you both demand and concede. You earlier chose your negotiating goals and set your priorities; and, now, through negotiation, you've gotten added information to help you adjust your goals or demands. When proposing to the other person what you want to get out of a compromise solution (these are your demands), and before you state what you are willing to give up or yield on (these are your concessions), try to (a) be direct, (b) be specific and behavioral (state exactly who you want to do what, where, when, and with whom), (c) explain the reasons for your demands, and (d) be sure you are reflecting your own priorities.

Tell the other person that if he or she will meet your demands, you will reciprocate with certain concessions. As with your demands, rank your possible concessions before proposing the compromise, and offer at first concessions which are of somewhat lesser importance to you, those that rank low. Your goal should be to give away enough to satisfy the other person, but not so much that the compromise is a bad deal for you. When trust is low, you may have to make somewhat larger concessions or more frequent concessions in order to stimulate the other person to do likewise. But when you do so, don't burn your bridges behind you. Make sure your concessions are tentative and reversible so that you can pull back if, after you've done a good bit of conceding, the other person doesn't reciprocate.

You have negotiated toward a compromise, made your demands, offered concessions. When the two of you agree, the conflict can, at least temporarily, be considered over. But what about those times when you have proposed what you feel is your best compromise offer, and it is not accepted, and you feel there are no more concessions you can make?

Breaking Deadlocks

There are a number of things you can do which have a reasonable chance of breaking even "dug in" negotiating deadlocks.

1. Increase bargaining room. This attempt to get things rolling again toward an acceptable compromise may mean lowering your goals a bit. The deadlock may end if you can add options or alternatives, change your terms or demands, concede a bit more, and increase your willingness to take risks.

2. Help the other person save face. The other person may be avoiding acceptance of your proposed compromise not because he or she actually *needs* further concessions from you, but because of fear that giving in or yielding means defeat or weakness. Often you can bring the negotiation to a successful conclusion if you can help the other person save face. This can be done by reminding the person about what *you* are conceding, by acknowledging the parts of his or her position you do agree with, and by showing you respect his/her right to those parts of the views you disagree with.

3. Take a break. Good negotiated solutions come from rested negotiators. Tired negotiators are usually less rational, more likely to make mistakes, and more likely to settle on outcomes they may later regret. So, if one or both of you is fatigued and negotiating poorly, call for time

out and take a break from the negotiation and from each other. Use the time to relax, to review your position and the other person's, to consult other people who may be helpful, to analyze the implications of both of your positions and the deadlock, or to simply distract yourself with another activity for a while.

4. Bring in a mediator. We all need help sometimes, and you should not be reluctant to seek it. If you and the other person seem firmly deadlocked, and can't break free on your own, the two of you may have to find a third person to mediate your conflict. It must be someone you *both* agree on, and someone who, hopefully, can help you both with at least some of the following deadlock breakers: reduce irrationality and think more objectively; clarify intentions, expected gains, and likely costs; explore the implications of your proposed compromise, the reasons for your deadlock, and possible new solutions; help in graceful retreats; referee; protect; encourage openness; help you both stay cool; and help you both continue engaging in constructive communication. The person can be a friend, a relative, a counselor, or someone else. Many such people exist, so don't hesitate to seek one out.

Obstacles to Negotiation

During your attempts to reach a good compromise with the other person by negotiating and breaking deadlocks, a number of obstacles may arise. Some may be the communication blocks we examined earlier. Others are especially likely to arise in and sabotage negotiations when the conflict is a heated one. One such obstacle is known as a self-fulfilling prophecy. This is an instance in which your expectation that the other person is likely to do something causes you to behave in ways that increase the chances the person actually does behave that way. So, check yourself. If you anticipate that the other person is going to demand more, or cheat, or become physically abusive, or whatever, try to figure out how realistic your expectation is and whether you are communicating it to the other person. If you are, you may be bringing on yourself the very things you don't want to occur.

Or you may be provoking the other person in other ways. Are you challenging him or her unnecessarily, cornering and leaving little room for the other person to maneuver? Do you have a chip on your shoulder, is the other's aggression due mostly to your provocation? Are you making extreme or nonnegotiable demands? Are you sending contradictory or conflicting messages that say "come close but stay away," or "that's a sufficient concession but I need still more," or "this is my final offer but I might have another one"? Are you both having trouble reaching a compromise because power, honor, self-esteem, reputation, saving face, or status have become more important than the issues you've been negotiating? Especially crucial here is when giving in or conceding becomes equal to weakness. Or are you laying down other smokescreens which are negotiation obstacles, such as focusing at length on minor details, stalling, coming up with new issues as the first one gets "close to home," getting hungry, or making a phone call, or going to the bathroom, or avoiding confrontation in other ways?

These several obstacles, smokescreens, avoiders, or end runs all serve as blocks to successful, compromise-reaching negotiation. When your negotiations are stalled or seem to be failing, these are the issues to explore. And have the other person do the same. If you both can honestly deal with self-fulfilling prophecies, unnecessary challenging, extreme demands, contradictory messages, symbolic issues, and the various smokescreens we have described, you are well on your way back to concluding a successful negotiation.

Negotiation training such as we have depicted here has received a moderate but accelerating degree of experimental examination. Kifer, Lewis, Green, and Phillips (1974) utilized instructions, behavioral rehearsal, and social reinforcement procedures to teach negotiation skills to predelinquent adolescents and their parents. Largely paralleling our own definition of the constituent steps in the negotiation process, the trainees were taught to conceptualize and verbalize:

1. Complete communication: Statements that indicate one's position regarding the situation being discussed and that are followed . . . by a request for the other person to state his position or respond to the position just expressed.
2. Identification of issues: Statements that explicitly identify the point of conflict in the situation. This statement may contrast the two opposing positions or try to clarify what the other's position is . . . or identify what one thinks the conflict is really about.
3. Suggestion of options: Statements that suggest a course of action to resolve the conflict. [p. 359]

In this investigation, both laboratory and home observation of conflict management behavior revealed significant increments in successful negotiations on the part of participating trainees.

Roberts (1974) reports similarly successful results, in this instance in the context of marital conflict, for what he terms "marital bargaining training." In fact, the bulk of the experimental literature on successful negotiation training has been reported in connection with marital conflict and attempts at its resolution. In much of this research, to be considered in depth in the section which follows, the negotiated compromise or other solution which emerges is concretized and potentially strengthened by being formalized in a written contract. It is this negotiation-contracting combination, therefore, to which we now wish to turn.

CONTRACTING

Solutions to volatile interpersonal conflicts, whether achieved through negotiation or by other means, are often fragile. They frequently are solutions which may be not only hard to reach, but also quick to crumble. The original conflict and its accompanying anger and aggression may re-escalate; one of the parties may have second thoughts; the agreement may not work the first time it is tried, and one of those involved may not wish to risk a second try; someone may need to save face; or brand new conflicts or complications may enter the situation. For these several reasons, new compromise or win-win solutions often may not be lasting solutions. Whatever can be done to make them more enduring, more binding, more likely to really be tried at some length before those involved decide to keep, change, or drop them, the better the outcomes are likely to be. One such "binder," designed to increase the chances that those making an agreement will actually try to carry it out, is the use of contracts.

A contract is basically an exchange agreement which spells out who is to do what, for whom, and under what circumstances. It makes expectations explicit, and enables the people involved to know the relative costs and benefits of doing something. A good, behavior-change contract consists of the following components.

Relevant dates. Every contract should specify the dates it begins, ends, or is renegotiated.

Behaviors Targeted for Change. This is the contract's goal, what the parties to the contract will do to meet the agreement. As much as possible, the goals or targets of a contract should be determined by the people who will have to meet the contract. When the parties involved actively participate in setting goals and related contract-building procedures, they are much more likely to have the commitment and motivation to see it through. It is for such reasons that negotiation and contracting have so frequently been utilized together in behavior modification interventions.

In our view, goals set should ideally be *behavioral* goals, avoiding general targets or ambiguous planned changes. The specification of goals should make explicit what behaviors will be changed, by whom, where, when, how much, how often, and any other considerations which lead to concrete and clear behavioral goals. General goals such as "behave better," "control myself," or "stay out of trouble" are harder to both define or keep track of than such concrete goals as "avoid yelling for three days" or "talk quietly and slowly to my spouse" or "respond by telling my boss what I honestly believe or disagree about when he tries to bulldoze me." In setting such goals, one should remember to aim low at first by contracting for easier-to-change behaviors initially, and gradually work up to goals which are harder to reach.

The behavior targeted for change can be aggression itself, with the goal of the contract being aggression reduction, control, or management. However, it is recommended strongly that, whenever possible, goals be stated in terms of what the parties of the contract *will* do, not what they will seek to *avoid* doing. Better to make one's goal "speak at a normal level" than "avoid yelling." "Dealing with others in a friendly manner" is a better way of stating one's goal than is "staying out of fights." "Listening openly to my wife" is preferable to "not tuning her out." So, we urge that contractual goals not only be concrete, but also stated in terms of acts which will actually be performed, not whose performance will be avoided.

Rewards. A crucial part of every contract are the rewards that are promised if the individual changes the behaviors targeted as goals. This is the person's incentive or motivation for agreeing to the contract. Several aspects of the reward or reinforcement delivered influence its behavior change potency.

Type of Reward. Rewards can be objects, events, or other behaviors performed by the parties to the contract. In setting up a contract, it is highly desirable to make sure that each person involved has a major say in choosing his or her own potential rewards. In this way, one increases his/her motivation to succeed in reaching the contract's goals. Sometimes reward selection can be done best by presenting the person with a list of rewards or a "reward menu" from which to choose. In contracts between spouses, rewards that have been used are gifts, displays of affection, quiet conversation time, going to a movie and a special dinner, or a way of dressing. Teenagers have been parties to contracts specifying such rewards as increased allowance, time watching TV, staying out longer, having a party, and number or length of phone calls. And reciprocally, their parents' contracts have called for such payoffs, if goals are reached, as the teenager doing certain chores, homework, introducing friends, or getting up each morning with no hassle. Almost any event or object can serve as a reward if desired by the individual.

Amount of Reward. The amount of reward to be specified in the contract should fit the difficulty of the contract's behavior-change goal. Easier goals should mean smaller rewards; difficult goals should result in promise of greater rewards. Ideally, the first time or two one uses contracting to help change one's own or someone else's behavior, modest goals should be set and small rewards for reaching them promised.

When to Reward. It should be made clear in formulating every contract that the reward is to be delivered *after* the person enacts the behavior contracted for, never before. Thus, it would be appropriate contractually to state: "If you do your English and Chemistry homework now [behavior change goal], you may get out for two hours later [reward]." The other way around, i.e., reward before behavior change, will almost always prove to be an ineffective contract (i.e., "You can go out for two hours now, if you promise to do your English and Chemistry homework later.")

Other Reward Rules. Reward should be given as soon as possible after the behavior change occurs. If the behavior change called for in the contract is difficult, reward should be contracted for and given for clear progress toward the overall goal. And, finally, contracts should be drawn up to reward accomplishment, not obedience. The contract should state, "If you do X, you'll be rewarded with Y", not "If you do what I tell you to do, I will reward you with Y." The first approach, rewarding accomplishment, leads to independence. The second, rewarding obedience, encourages dependence.

Penalties. Just as progress toward and accomplishment of a contract's goals should be rewarded, lack of progress or failure should be penalized. The penalty included in the contract, just like its rewards and goals, should be specific, concrete, behavioral, and, if possible, determined by the people involved in the contract. Penalties may take many forms. Losing routine pleasures (TV, dessert), doing unpleasant household chores, contributing money to political or other causes *opposite* to those one actually believes in, postponing or cancelling special events (trips, visits). Whatever the penalty chosen, the parties involved need to be sure it hurts enough that there will be motivation to avoid it. Some penalties are what psychologists call "linear," i.e., they even up the failure. For example, a contract may be written so that a child loses a minute of play time for every minute he fights with his brother. Ten minutes late yields a penalty of ten minutes less play time. In other contracts, a geometric penalty is used—there is a doubling or tripling in the penalty of the nature of the failure. Coming to dinner 10 minutes late brings a penalty of 20 or 30 minutes lost play time. Yet another type of penalty involves what has been called a performance deposit. At the beginning of the contract, the person puts up an amount of money or valuables and gets them back or gives them up permanently as he or she meets or fails to meet the behavior change goals of the contract. Regardless of the type of penalty used, the important thing is that, just as the reward given should fit the difficulty of the behavior changed, the penalty imposed should correspond to the nature of the failure which occurs.

Bonuses. It is often wise to include a bonus clause in behavior change contracts. These are special rewards to be given if the person exceeds the behavior change goal he agreed to try for, or reaches the agreed upon goal much more quickly than contracted for. Bonuses can be the same rewards contracted for already, but in greater quantity; or bonus rewards can be different and even more special things one does or gets following exceptional change.

Record-keeping. It will often be difficult to know whether or not the people involved in the contract have reached their behavior-change goal, and thus should be given a reward, penalty, or bonus, unless a clear record of their behavior is kept. One or both parties to the contract may have a general feeling of progress, but may not be sure. Keeping a record avoids this uncertainty. When a compromise or other conflict solution has been negotiated, and a contract drawn up to help make it work, it usually is a good idea to start keeping a record of the behavior involved a week or two *before* the contract starts. This base-line information can then be used as the standard or reference point to judge progress after the contract has gone into effect. Different ways, all of them simple, have been used to keep such records—a tally sheet put up on a closet door, an index card carried in one's purse or pocket, marks made on a calendar, a golf wrist counter, and so forth.

We have now described the clauses or components that make up a typical behavior-change contract—starting and ending dates, behavior change goals, rewards, penalties, bonuses, and record keeping. In addition to these components, there are a number of steps one can take to strengthen contracts still further.

Contracts Should be Written. Contracts should always be in writing. It makes them seem like legal documents, and increases the sense of commitment and involvement of the people whose contract it is. Putting things in writing also decreases the chances that there will be a misunderstanding later on.

Contracts Should be Signed. The parties involved in the contract should sign it, as should one or two witnesses, if they are available. If appropriate, the signing should be a bit of a ceremony with some fanfare. Getting signatures in this manner will also help increase commitment to the fulfillment of the contract.

Contracts Should be Fair. Rewards, penalties, and goals should be consistent. As in business contracts, one must be careful to avoid ambiguous words or ideas, hidden clauses, double meanings, and "fine print." All of the people who are involved in the contract should have an equal part in writing it. Force or coercion must be avoided, either in setting the terms of the contract or as the person tries to carry them out. Above all, one should not enter into a contract unless one fully intends to try to meet its terms.

Contracts Should be Public. Behavior-change contracts exist to help people in conflict situations change their behavior. Unlike business and other legal contracts, behavior-change contracts work best when they are not kept in a desk drawer, strong box, or bank vault. The more public they are, the more they can serve as a spur or reminder to the parties involved to meet their terms. So we recommend that contracts be posted where they can be regularly and easily seen—a door, a bedpost, a refrigerator, etc.

Contracts Should be Reviewed Regularly. Human behavior is never static. Especially in the volatile situation of conflict and the fragile circumstances of compromise, what was true yesterday may have changed by tomorrow. Those involved in the contract should use their record-keeping to judge whether progress is being made. If the answer is no after a reasonable time, adjustment in the terms of the contract may be necessary, or an entirely new contract may be appropriate. The behavioral goals may be too difficult, the rewards may be too miserly, the penalties may be too great. Thus, it is clearly important that contracts be reviewed regularly.

We have so far in this section explained what a contract consists of, and steps that can be taken to strengthen its effectiveness. Before presenting some examples of actual contracts, there remains one further topic to examine. The contractual terms we have described can be used in two different ways. Especially for people in conflict situations, which contractual arrangement is chosen may make a great deal of difference in whether or not the behavior-change goal is reached.

Good Faith Contracts

If a husband and wife, parent and child, or two office mates are in conflict, each member of the given pair may agree to a contract in which "If I do X, I'll get Y," whatever the other person in conflict does. Both people in conflict agree to their own contractual stipulations. The two contracts are *not* tied to each other. They are parallel, independent contracts. For each person, the reward possible is an outside event or object, not a change in the other person's behavior. The important point here is that if the two contracts are tied together (as we will see below), and one fails, they both fail. For example, if they both sign a contract which states "If I do X, the other will do Y" and one fails to meet the responsibility involved, then there is no contractual reward motivating the other person to change. It makes considerable sense to us to recommend that the use of contracts, in most conflict relationships, start with these good faith or parallel contracts. When trust may be low, and common fate a risky strategy, good faith contracts are the wisest choice.

Quid Pro Quo Contracts

A quid pro quo contract is a linked-together exchange, give-and-get contract in which both parties agree to a "You do X, I'll do Y" arrangement. Unlike the good faith contract, in which the rewards indicated were outside events or objects, the reward in a quid pro quo contract is always a reduction or change in someone else's problem behavior. A quid pro quo (something for something) contract is a common fate contract. If one party decides not to deliver, the contract is in trouble. All things considered, the risk of failure is greater for a quid pro quo contract than for a good faith contract. But a quid pro quo contract, when it works, results in the two people involved providing each other with reciprocal rewards. This is the opposite of what happens in an aggressive, interpersonal conflict situation, in which the parties engage in reciprocal punishment behavior. Thus, the quid pro quo arrangement is indeed one to aim for. It provides exactly the relationship one should ultimately seek in trying to build nonaggressive, mutually rewarding dyads.

It seems that the wisest overall strategy in the use of contracts, therefore, is to begin their use with good faith contracts. This is consistent with the plan we have recommended a number of times elsewhere in this chapter of aiming relatively low at first, and then graduating to larger possible risks and rewards. When one sees that this first type of contract is succeeding, moving on to the use of quid pro quo arrangements then becomes appropriate. Sample contracts are depicted in Figures 8.1 and 8.2.

Jane Smith was pleased that she and her husband reached a compromise regarding her parents' visit, but was concerned that John had carried on so—yelling, shouting, threatening—on the way to reaching the compromise. They decided to draw up the following contract, a good faith contract for John.

Behavior-Change Contract

Behavior-Change Goal: To speak to Jane at a normal, conversational level whenever I speak to her at home or outside.
Reward: Buy myself the tie I've been admiring in the window of the Men's Shop.
Penalty: Not watch the bowl game next Saturday.
Bonus: Get the tie and take in the movie I've been wanting to see if our conversations go especially well.
Record-Keeping: Mark tallies on the wall calendar every time I speak to her the right way.
Beginning Date: _7/19_ *Ending Date:* _7/26_

Signature: _____

Fig. 8.1. A sample good faith contract

Two assistant managers in an office, Fred White and Ron Jones, frequently and forcefully argued over who had access at given times to the services of their shared secretary. The negotiations which they held led to this quid pro quo contract.

Behavior-Change Contract

It is hereby agreed that:
    (A) Fred White will make use of his shared secretary's services only until 3:30 PM Mondays and Thursdays and all morning on Wednesdays if, in return, Ron Jones avoids seeking her services during these time periods.
    (B) Ron Jones will make use of his shared secretary's services only until 3:30 PM on Tuesdays and Fridays and Wednesday afternoons until 3:30 PM if, in return, Fred White avoids seeking her services during these time periods.
    (C) Every day at 3:30, the shared secretary will stop whatever task she is working on, check with Fred White and Ron Jones about rush work and, if any exists from either party, she will give that work priority.
    Date: 7/9/82

Signatures:_____   (Fred White)

          _____   (Ron Jones)

          _____   (Al Harrison, witness)

Fig. 8.2. A sample Quid Pro Quo Contract

Research on Contracting

A number of investigations have been conducted in an effort to evaluate the behavior change potency of contracting procedures. In some of these studies, contracting was examined as it operated alone; in others, a treatment package was constituted and studied, a package consisting of such components as communication training, negotiation training, and contracting. While these studies are modest in number and experimental control, their combined thrust is clearly in support of the efficacy of contracting for behavior change purposes.

The first such investigation was conducted by Stuart (1969) who utilized quid pro quo contracts with four husbands who received tokens under their contracts for accelerating their time spent engaged in conversation with their wives. The tokens were exchangeable for increased physical contact with their wives. Study results in all four cases were substantial increases in both conversational and physical contact behaviors, behavior changes maintained on follow-up measurement also. Rappaport and Harrell (1972) also report an early case study of successful use of contracting. Stuart (1971) conducted successful extension of contracting in a case study involving a delinquent girl and her family. Stuart's early work stimulated a series of subsequent investigations involving use of contracting which were conducted by Weiss, Patterson, and their associates at the Oregon Research Institute. In these studies, contracting was a component of a treatment package containing communications training, negotiation training, and contracting. These studies, essentially replicated case studies, did not seek to tease out the behavior change impact of the three separate components, but did indeed suggest the potency of the package as a whole. In terms of both effectiveness of communication for problem-solving purposes, and rewardingness, i.e., the extent to which spouses reward rather than punish one another, conflicted couples undergoing the treatment package reported substantial gains, most of which sustained on 3-6 month follow-up (Patterson & Hops, 1972; Weiss, Birchler & Vincent, 1974; Weiss, Hops & Patterson, 1973). The problem-solving and rewardingness findings noted above, as well as enhanced marital satisfaction, were also reported by Jacobson (1977) in a study evaluating the same treatment package, but this time against the concurrent behavior and satisfaction change reported by a minimal treatment control group not receiving the treatment package.

Azrin, Naster, and Jones (1973) evaluated a similar treatment package, one they termed "reciprocity counseling." Here, negotiation and contracting were utilized to teach couples to behave in more reciprocally rewarding ways to one another. All but one of the 12 participating couples reported significantly greater marital happiness after the reciprocity counseling as compared to behavior change as a result of their earlier participation in a placebo therapy procedure.

We concur with Jacobson (1978); Jacobson and Martin (1976); and Liberman, Levine, Wheeler, Sanders, and Wallace (1976) who view the studies briefly described above as providing suggestive positive evidence for the utility of contracting, and treatment packages of which it is a part. As they each remind us, definitive studies of its impact are yet to be conducted, and clearly well deserve to be, in response to the encouraging beginnings we have described.

CONTINGENCY MANAGEMENT

Contingency management is a set of behavior modification techniques which by one means or another contingently present or withdraw rewards or punishments (e.g., environmental consequences) to alter the behavior which precedes these consequences. Specifically, if one's goal is to increase the likelihood that a given (e.g., prosocial) behavior will occur, one follows instances of its occurrence with positive consequences, i.e., by means of one or another technique for presenting a reward or removing an aversive event. In a directly analogous management of contingencies, if one's goal is to decrease the likelihood that given (e.g., antisocial) behavior will occur, one follows instances of its occurrence with negative consequences, i.e., by means of one or another behavior modification technique for presenting an aversive event or removing a rewarding event. To decrease the disruptiveness, aggression, or acting-out behavior of a given youngster, for example, and simultaneously increase the chances that he or she will behave in a constructive, prosocial manner, the skilled contingency manager will often use a combination of aversive or reward-withdrawing (for the aggression) and aversiveness-reducing or reward-providing (for the constructive behaviors) techniques. A few formal definitions here will help clarify further the substance of the contingency management process.

A *reinforcer* is an event which increases the subsequent frequency of any behavior which it follows. When the presentation of an event following a behavior increases its frequency, the event is referred to as a *positive reinforcer*. Praise, attention, special privileges, and tokens or points exchangeable for toys or snacks are a few examples of positive reinforcers. When the removal of an event following a behavior increases the subsequent frequency of the behavior, the event is referred to as a *negative reinforcer*. When a youngster ceases to behave in a disruptive manner following his or her teacher's yelling at him to do so, we may say that the youngster has negatively reinforced, and thus increased the future likelihood of, teacher yelling. When the presentation of an event following a behavior decreases its subsequent frequency, the event is referred to as a *punisher*. In the above example, the teacher's yelling which was negatively reinforced by the student's decrease in disruptive behavior functions as a punishment to the student to the extent that it decreases the likelihood of subsequent student disruptiveness. A second way of decreasing the probability of a given behavior is by *removing positive reinforcers* each time that the behavior occurs. Ignoring the behavior or removing the reinforcer of attention (i.e., extinction), physically removing the person from important sources of reinforcement (i.e., time out), and removing the reinforcers from the person (i.e., response cost) are three means of contingently managing behavior by removing positive reinforcers. To repeat, these four groups of techniques—positive reinforcement, negative reinforcement, punishment, and the removal of positive reinforcers—constitute the core general methods of contingency management.

Though much of the basic thinking relevant to the contingency management approach to human behavior has been available for a number of years (Mowrer & Mowrer, 1938; Skinner, 1938; Watson & Rayner, 1920), it wasn't until the 1950s that it began to find substantial, overt implementation in hospitals, clinics, schools, and other institutions in which one found disturbed or disturbing adults and youngsters. Skinner's (1953) book *Science and Human Behavior* was a significant stimulus to this growth, as were a large number of investigations, conducted during the 1950s and 1960s in the several contexts noted above, all of which successfully demonstrated the behavior change effectiveness of contingency management. Much of this research sought to alter the highly aggressive or otherwise severely deviant behavior of institutionalized emotionally disturbed, autistic, or developmentally disabled children and adolescents, and did so with considerable levels of success (Ayllon & Michael, 1959; Ferster & DeMeyer, 1962; Lovaas, Schaeffer, & Simmons, 1965; Wolf, Risley, & Mees, 1964). In outpatient clinic and laboratory settings, successful use of contingency management was reported with such diverse behaviors as delinquency rates (Patterson, Ray, & Shaw, 1968; Schwitzgebel, 1964), social withdrawal (Allen, Hart, Buell, Harris, & Wolf, 1964; Lovaas, Koegel, Simmons, & Long, 1973), fearfulness (Lazarus & Rachman, 1967; Patterson, 1965), hyperactivity (Allen, Henke, Harris, Baer, & Reynolds, 1967; Hall, Lund, & Jackson, 1968); depression (Wahler & Pollio, 1968); anorexia (Bachrach, Erwin, & Mohr, 1965; Leitenberg, Agras, & Thomson, 1968), mutism (Sherman, 1965; Straughan, 1968), and dozens of other diverse deviant behaviors involving many hundreds of youngsters. As shall be made explicit throughout this section, the general success of this orientation to behavior change has flowered further in the 1970s and 1980s, finding still wider application across many, many behaviors and settings.

The application of contingency management procedures is typically preceded by a small number of preparatory steps—deciding on the desirable goal behaviors to be sought, observing and recording the undesirable target behaviors one will seek to change in order to accomplish the behavioral goals, identifying positive reinforcers for the target person, and selecting the optimal continency management procedure(s) to apply.

Selecting behavior change goals is usually the initial step, a step often requiring the behavior modifier to respond to several considerations in addition to the simple desirability of encouraging prosocial behavior and discouraging the antisocial. For example, in a discussion addressed to teachers regarding behavior change goal selection in classroom contexts, we observed (Goldstein, Apter, & Harootunian, 1983):

> What will be the behavioral climate of your classroom? What student behaviors will be defined by you as truly disruptive and as impediments to learning, and which will be tolerated and perhaps even welcomed as normative and maybe even facilitative of the learning process? Not only should behavior change goal selection concern itself with reducing those aggressive, disruptive, acting-out behaviors which interfere with the learning process but, simultaneously, such planning of behavior modification must be acutely responsive to normal student developmental stages, conducted to the extent possible in collaboration with the students who are involved themselves, and appropriately but not overly responsive to both teacher needs and the influence on decisions about classroom decorum of overall school climate and policy.

In general, selection of behavior change goals should be done carefully, in collaboration with the person whose behavior is to be altered, with full consideration of the range of alternative goals possible and desirable, and with recognition of the potential impact of the behavioral changes sought on both the individual's real world significant others and on the target person himself.

The second preparatory step for effective contingency management is the specification of the undesirable or inappropriate behaviors to be altered, a step which ideally proceeds by means of systematic *observation and recording*. There are a number of purposes that are served by this process. Systematic observation and recording seeks to identify not only which behaviors are undesirable, and thus possibly to be changed, but also the rate or frequency of such behaviors. This establishment of a *base rate* permits the behavior modifier to determine later (against the base rate) whether the behavior is remaining constant, increasing in rate or frequency or, as is hoped, actually decreasing. This *monitoring* of change in the behavior over time is, then, the second purpose of systematic observation and recording. Finally, since after the establishment of a base rate level it is suggested that the behavior modifier intervene with one or more contingency management procedures, the third purpose of observation and recording is to *evaluate* the success or failure of the completed intervention. At all three stages of this process—establishment of a base rate, monitoring, and evaluation of outcome—it is crucial that observation and recording be conducted in a *systematic* manner. Many authorities on classroom contingency management, for example, have commented that teacher guesses regarding the rate or frequency of a given student's aggressive, disruptive, or acting-out behavior are very often erroneously high. It is as if a small number of perhaps seriously disruptive behaviors by a student leads to a teacher global impression of the student as "a troublemaker" or as "chronically aggressive," an impression or label which often clouds the fact that by far most of the time that youngster is engaged in appropriate behaviors. Thus, for these several reasons, it is crucial to obtain an accurate accounting of how often or how long the target person engages in problematic behaviors.

The third prerequisite step necessary when preparing to apply contingency management procedures is the *identification of positive reinforcers* for the target person. What objects, activities or events will in fact serve as reinforcers for the particular target person involved? Four types of positive reinforcers have been identified—material, social, activity and token.

Material or tangible reinforcers are actual desirable goods or objects to be presented to the individual contingent upon his or her enactment of appropriate behaviors. One especially important subcategory of material reinforcement, primary reinforcement, occurs when the contingent event presented satisfies a basic biological need. Food is one such primary reinforcer.

Social reinforcers, most often expressed in the form of attention, praise, or approval, are a particularly powerful and frequent reinforcer. In classroom contexts, for example, both teacher lore and extensive experimental research testify to the potency of teacher-dispensed social reinforcement in influencing a broad array of personal, interpersonal, and academic student behaviors.

Activity reinforcers are those events which the individual freely chooses to engage in when he or she has an opportunity to engage in several different activities. Given freedom to choose, many youngsters will watch television rather than complete their homework. The parent wishing to use this activity reinforcer information will specify to the youngster that he or she may watch television for a given time period contingent upon the prior completion of the homework. Stated otherwise, the opportunity to perform a high probability behavior (given free choice) can be used as a reinforcer for a lower probability behavior.

Token reinforcers, usually employed when more easily implemented social reinforcers prove insufficient, are symbolic items or currency (chips, stars, points, etc.) provided to the target person contingent upon the performance of appropriate or desirable behaviors. Tokens thus obtained are exchangeable for a wide range of material or activity reinforcers. The system by which specific numbers of tokens are contingently gained (or lost), and the procedures by which they may be exchanged for the backup material or activity reinforcers, is called a token economy.

Given the wide array of potential reinforcers of these several types, and the fact that almost any event may serve as a reinforcer for one individual but not another, how may the contingency manager decide which reinforcer(s) may be optimally utilized with a particular youngster at a given point in time? Most simply, the target person can straightforwardly be asked which events he or she would like to earn. Often, however, this approach will not prove sufficient since people are frequently not fully aware of the range of reinforcers available to them or, when aware, may discount in advance the possibility that the given reinforcer will actually be forthcoming in a particular instance. When this is the case, other reinforcement-identification procedures must be employed. Carr (1981) and others have reported three procedures which typically have been used for this purpose.

1. Observing effects. The contingency manager can often make an accurate determination whether a given event is in fact functioning as a reinforcer by carefully observing its impact on the target person. It probably is if the person (1) asks that the event be repeated, (2) seems happy during its occurrence, (3) seems unhappy when the event ends, or (4) will work in order to earn the event. If one or more of these reactions is observed, the chances are good that the event is a positive reinforcer and that it can be contingently provided to strengthen appropriate, nonaggressive behaviors.

2. Observing choices. As we noted above in connection with activity reinforcers, when a target person is free to choose among several equally available activities, *which one* he or she chooses, and *how long* he or she engages in chosen activity are both readily observed, target person-identified positive reinforcers.

3. Questionnaires. A small number of questionnaires exist which have been utilized effectively in identifying positive reinforcers. Tharp and Wetzel's (1969) Mediation-Reinforcer Incomplete Blank and Homme's (1971) Reinforcing Event Menu are two prominent examples.

Once having chosen the desirable goal behaviors to seek, the reinforcers to provide following their occurrence, and the undesirable behaviors to be reduced or eliminated, the preparatory phase of contingency management is completed. The behavior modifier may then proceed to selecting and applying specific contingency management procedures.

Presenting Positive Reinforcers

A basic principle of contingency management is that the presentation of a reinforcing event contingent upon the occurrence of a given behavior will function to increase the likelihood of the recurrence of that behavior. Research has demonstrated a substantial number of considerations which influence the success of this reinforcement effort, and thus which optimally should be reflected in its presentation when seeking to increase appropriate behaviors.

Be Contingent. While this rule for reinforcer presentations may be largely obvious at this point, it is a crucial rule which is sometimes forgotten or implemented inadequately. The connection between the desirable behavior and the subsequent provision of reward should be made clear and explicit to the target person. This description, as is true for all aspects of a contingency management effort, should be behaviorally specific, i.e., it is the connection between particular behavioral acts and reinforcement which is made clear, not behaviorally ambiguous comments about "good behavior," "being a good person," "being well behaved," or the like.

Reinforce Immediately. Related to the communication of the behavior-reinforcement contingency, the more immediately the presentation of reinforcement occurs following the desirable behavior, the more likely is its effectiveness. Not only will rapid reinforcement augment the message that the immediately preceding behavior is desirable, but delayed reinforcer presentation runs the risk that a sequence will occur of (a) desirable behavior → (b) undesirable behavior → (c) reinforcement intended for (a) which in actuality reinforces (b).

Reinforce Consistently. The effects of positive reinforcement on altering behavior are usually gradual, not dramatic. It works to slowly strengthen behavior over a period of time. Thus, it is important that positive reinforcement be presented consistently. Consistency here means not only that the contingency manager must be consistent himself, but also that he make certain as best he can that his reinforcement delivery efforts are matched by similar efforts from as many other important persons in the target person's life as possible.

Frequency of Reinforcement. When first beginning to try to establish a new, appropriate behavior, the contingency manager should seek to reinforce all or almost all instances of that behavior. This high frequency of reinforcement is necessary initially to establish or firmly root the behavior in the individual's behavioral repertoire. Once it seems clear that the behavior has actually been acquired, it is appropriate for the contingency manager to thin the reinforcement schedule, decreasing his presentation of reinforcement so that only some of the target person's desirable behaviors are followed by reinforcement. This thinner reinforcement schedule or, as it is known, partial reinforcement strategy is an important contribution to the continued likelihood of the appropriate behavior because such a reinforcement schedule more closely parallels the sometimes-reinforced-sometimes-not reaction the target person's appropriate behavior will elicit in other settings from other people. The contingency manager's partial reinforcement of the target person's appropriate behaviors may be on a fixed time schedule (e.g., at the end of each meeting), a fixed number of responses schedule (e.g., every fifth instance of the appropriate behavior), or on variable time or number of response schedules. In any event, the basic strategy for reinforcement frequency remains—a rich level for initial learning; partial reinforcement to sustain performance.

Amount of Reinforcement. In our discussion above of frequency of reinforcement, we began to distinguish between learning, i.e., acquiring knowledge about how to perform new behaviors, and actual performance, i.e., overtly using these behaviors. The amount of reinforcement provided influences performance much more than learning. People will learn new, appropriate behaviors just about as fast for a large as a small reward, but they are more likely to perform the behaviors on a continuing basis when large rewards are involved. Yet, rewards can be too large, causing a satiation effect in which the target person loses interest in seeking the given reinforcement because it is "too much of a good thing." Or, they can be too small—too little time on the playground, too few tokens, too thin a social reinforcement schedule. The optimal amount can be determined empirically. If a person has in the past worked energetically to obtain a particular reinforcer but gradually slackens off and seems to lose interest in obtaining it, a satiation effect has probably occurred and the amount of reinforcement should be reduced. On the other hand, if he seems unwilling to work for a reinforcer you believe he desires, try giving it to him once or twice for free, i.e., not contingent on a specific desirable behavior. If he seems to enjoy it and even wishes more of the same, the amount you had been using may be too little. Increase the amount, make it contingent, and observe whether it is yielding the desired, behavior modification effect. If so, the amount of reinforcement you are offering is appropriate.

Variety of Reinforcement. In our discussion above, we mentioned a reinforcement satiation effect due to an excessive *amount* of reinforcement. There is a parallel type of satiation of reinforcement, occurring when the contingency manager uses the same approving phrase or other reward over and over again. The target person may perceive such reinforcement as taking on a mechanized quality, and thus lose interest in or responsiveness to it. By varying the content of the reinforcer presented, its potency can be maintained. Thus, instead of a "nice job" repeated four or five times, a mix of comments—"I'm really proud of you," "You're certainly doing fine," "Well done"—are more likely to yield a sustained effect.

Pair with Praise. Our earlier statements about types of reinforcers emphasized that social reinforcement is most germaine to enduring behavior change, though there were circumstances under which an emphasis upon material, activity, or token reinforcers was (at least initially) more appropriate. To aid in the desired movement toward social reinforcement, the contingency manager should seek to pair all presentations of material, activity, or token reward with some expression of social reinforcement—an approving comment, a pat on the back, a wink, a smile, and so forth.

Shaping New Behaviors. Reinforcement cannot be presented contingent upon new behaviors when such behaviors are not part of the youngster's behavioral repertoire. John cannot be rewarded at all for talking over his disputes with other students, no less at the proper frequency, amount, consistency, and so forth, if he never does so. Yet, the teacher is not doomed here to perpetual waiting, reinforcers at the ready, for nonemergent desirable behaviors. Approximations to such desirable negotiating behaviors, even remote approximations, can be positively reinforced. Looking at the other disputant, walking toward him, discussing an irrelevant (to the dispute) topic are all reinforceable steps in the direction of the ultimately desired behaviors. By a process of such reinforcement of successively closer behaviors (to the final target behavior), coupled with successive withdrawal of such reinforcement for ever less good approximations, the behavior change process can proceed in a stepwise fashion in which the target person's behaviors are systematically shaped into ever-better approximations to the final target behavior.

Contingency management operationalized by the presentation of positive reinforcers rests on a particularly substantial base of experimental support. Especially comprehensive reviews of this evidence include Bandura (1969), Gambrill (1977), Kazdin (1977), O'Leary and O'Leary (1976, 1977), and Walker (1979). Individual studies which seem to us to be particularly instructive of methods and results involving these procedures as applied to persons displaying aggressive or disruptive behavior are Adams (1973); Becker, Madsen, Arnold, and Thomas (1967); Bornstein, Rychtarik, McFall, Bridgewater, Guthrie, and Anton (1980); Buys (1972); Hall, Panyan, Rabon, and Broden (1968); Kirschner and Levine (1975); Pinkston, Reese, LeBlanc, and Baer (1973); Sewell, McCoy, and Sewell (1973); and Ward and Baker (1968).

Removing Positive Reinforcers

The contingency manager's behavior modification goal with persons displaying aggressive behaviors is, in a general sense, twofold. Both sides of the behavioral coin—appropriate and inappropriate, prosocial and antisocial, desirable and undesirable—must be attended to. In a proper behavior change effort, procedures are simultaneously or sequentially employed to reduce and eliminate the inappropriate, antisocial, or undesirable components of the target person's behavioral repertoire, and increase the quality and frequency of appropriate, prosocial, or desirable components. This latter task is served primarily by the contingent presentation of positive reinforcement. Conversely, the contingent removal of positive reinforcement in response to aggressive, disruptive, or similar behaviors is the major behavior modification strategy for reducing or eliminating such behaviors. Therefore, in conjunction with the procedures discussed above for presenting positive reinforcement, the contingency manager should also simultaneously or consecutively employ one or more of the three positive reinforcer removing techniques we now wish to examine.

Extinction

1. *Knowing when to use extinction.* Extinction is the withdrawal or removal of positive reinforcement for aggressive or other undesirable behaviors which have been either deliberately or inadvertently reinforced in the past. Its use can be thought of prescriptively. It is the procedure of choice with milder forms of aggression, such as threats, swearing, or other forms of verbal aggression, or low amplitude physical aggression. More generally, extinction should be used when other individuals are not in any serious physical danger from the aggression being displayed by the target person.

2. *Provide positive reinforcement for appropriate behaviors.* We mentioned this rule earlier, and wish to stress it here. Attempts to reduce inappropriate behavior by reinforcement withdrawal should always be accompanied by tandem efforts to increase appropriate behaviors by reinforcement provision. This combination of efforts will succeed especially well when the appropriate and inappropriate behaviors involved are opposites, or at least incompatible with one another. With aggressive youngsters in a classroom setting, for example, one can reward in-seat behavior, ignore out-of-seat behavior; reward talking at conversational level, ignore yelling.

3. *Identify the positive reinforcers maintaining inappropriate behaviors.* These are the reinforcers to be withheld. Using essentially the same observation and recording procedures described earlier in conjunction with the identification of positive reinforcers maintaining appropriate behaviors, the contingency manager should discern what the target person is working for, what are his or her payoffs, what are the reinforcers being sought or earned by aggression, disruptiveness, and similar behaviors. To stay with the example we are using in this section of aggression in a classroom context, very often the answer will be attention. Being looked at, stared at, yelled at, talked to, turned toward, or laughed at are common teacher and peer reactions to a youngster's aggression. The withdrawal of such positive social reinforcement by ignoring the behaviors, by turning away, by not yelling or talking or laughing at the perpetrator are the teacher and classmate behaviors which constitute extinction.

4. *Use extinction consistently.* As was true for the provision of reinforcement, its removal must be done consistently for its intended effects to be forthcoming. This rule of consistency means that both the contingency manager and others in the target person's environment must act in concert, and that the contingency manager must be consistent with herself or himself across time.

5. *Use extinction for a long enough period of time.* Aggressive behaviors often have a long history of positive reinforcement and, especially if much of that history is one of intermittent reinforcement, efforts to undo it will have to be sustained. Carr (1981) suggests that, within a week, clear reductions in aggressive behavior should be observable. There are, however, two types of events to keep in mind when judging the effectiveness of extinction efforts. The first is what is known as the "extinction burst." When extinction is first introduced, it is not uncommon for the rate or intensity of the aggressive behavior to first *increase* sharply before it begins its more gradual decline toward a zero level. It is important that the contingency manager not get discouraged during this short detour in direction. Its meaning, in fact, is that the extinction is beginning to work. On occasion, inappropriate behaviors which have been successfully extinguished will reappear, for reasons that are difficult to determine. Like the extinction burst, this spontaneous recovery phenomenon is transitory, and will disappear if the teacher persists in the extinction effort.

The effectiveness of extinction in modifying inappropriate or undesirable behaviors in a classroom context has been demonstrated by many investigators, including Brown and Elliott (1965); Jones and Miller, (1974); Madsen, Becker, and Thomas (1968); Martin and Foxx (1973); Wahler, Winkel, Peterson, and Morrison (1965); and Ward and Baker (1968).

Time Out. Time out is a procedure for removal from positive reinforcement in which a target person who engages in aggressive or other inappropriate behaviors is physically removed from all sources of reinforcement for a specified time period. As with extinction, its purpose is to reduce the (undesirable) behavior which immediately precedes it and on which its use is contingent. It differs from extinction in that extinction involves the removal of reinforcement from the person, while in time out the person is usually removed from the reinforcing situation. In classroom practice with aggressive youngsters, time out has typically taken three forms. Isolation time out, the most common form, requires that the youngster be physically removed from the classroom to a time out room following specific procedures described below. Exclusion time out is somewhat less restrictive, but also involves physically removing the youngster from sources of reinforcement. Here, the youngster is required to go to a corner of the classroom, perhaps sit in a "quiet chair" (Firestone, 1976), sometimes also behind a screen. There is no removal from the classroom, but there is exclusion from classroom activities for a specified time period. Nonexclusion time out (also called contingent observation), the least restrictive variant, requires youngsters to "sit and watch," on the periphery of classroom activities, observing the appropriate behaviors of other youngsters. It is a variant which, in a sense, combines time out with modeling opportunities. Its essence is to exclude youngsters from a participant role for a specified time period, while leaving intact their opportunity to function as an observer. The implementation of time out, in any of its forms, optimally employs the steps we wish to now describe.

1. *Knowing when to use time out.* Extinction, it will be recalled, was our recommended procedure for those aggressive or otherwise undesirable behaviors which could *safely* be ignored. Behaviors potentially injurious to other youngsters require a more active contingency management response, one possibility of which is time out. Yet, it is also often the case that, for many youngsters at the upper junior high school and senior high school levels, physical removal of the student by the teacher is neither wise, appropriate, or even possible. For such youngsters, procedures other than extinction or time out to be discussed later in this section will have to be employed. Thus, to reflect both the potential injuriousness of the youngster's behavior and the youngster's age and associated physical status, time out is recommended as the technique of choice for youngsters aged 2 to 12 who are displaying high rates of severely aggressive behavior of potential danger to other individuals. It is also the procedure to utilize

for less severe forms of aggression when the combination of extinction and positive reinforcement for milder levels of aggression has been attempted and has failed.

2. *Providing positive reinforcement for appropriate behaviors.* All we have said in our earlier discussion of the implementation of this step as part of the extinction process applies with regard to time out. These procedures, providing positive reinforcement and time out, should be used in tandem. When possible, the behaviors positively reinforced should be opposite to, or at least incompatible with, those for which the time out procedure is instituted.

3. *Arranging an effective time out setting.* We will focus our description of the characteristics of an effective time out setting on an *isolation* time out arrangement, though its general principles readily carry over to both exclusion and nonexclusion time out environments. Essentially, two general principles are involved. The first concerns the youngster's health and safety. The physical characteristics of the time out setting should be a small, well-lit, and well-ventilated room which provides a place for the youngster to sit. The second principle reflects the fact that the central quality of this procedure is time out from positive reinforcement. It must be a boring environment, with all reinforcers removed. There should be no attractive or distracting objects or opportunities. No toys, television, radio, books, posters, people, windows to look out, sound sources to overhear, or other obvious or not-so-obvious potential reinforcers. A barren, isolation area is the optimal time out environment.

4. *Placing a youngster in time out.* A number of actions may be taken by the contingency manager when initiating time out for a given youngster that serve to increase the likelihood of its effectiveness. As with the rapid presentation of positive reinforcement contingent upon appropriate behaviors, time out is optimally instituted immediately following the aggressive or other behaviors one is seeking to modify. Having earlier explained to the target person the nature of time out, as well as when and why it would be used, its initiation should be implemented in a more or less "automatic" manner following undesirable behavior, i.e., in a manner which minimizes the social reinforcement of the aggression. Concretely, this means placing the youngster in time out without a lengthy explanation, but with a brief, matter-of-fact description of his or her precipitating behaviors. This placement process is best conducted without anger by the contingency manager, and without (when possible) having to use physical means for moving the youngster to the time out room. In addition to these considerations, the effectiveness of time out is further enhanced by its consistent application when appropriate, by the same contingency manager on other occasions as well as by other contingency managers (teachers, parents, peers, etc.). Immediacy, consistency, and the several actions aimed at minimizing contingency manager presentation of reinforcement following inappropriate behavior will each function to augment the behavior change effectiveness of time out.

5. *Maintaining a youngster in time out.* The skilled contingency manager must deal with two questions during a youngster's period in time out: "What is he or she doing?" and "For how long should time out last?" The first question, dealt with by monitoring by the contingency manager, seeks to make certain that the time out experience is not in fact functioning as a pleasant, positively reinforcing one for a given youngster. For example, rather than serve as a removal from positive reinforcement, time out may in reality be a removal from an aversive situation (negative reinforcement) if it is instituted at a time when a youngster is in an unpleasant situation from which he would prefer to escape, or if it (time out) helps him avoid such a situation. Similarly, if monitoring reveals that the youngster is singing or playing enjoyable games, the effectiveness of time out will be lessened. Unless the situation can be made essentially nonreinforcing, a different behavioral intervention may have to be used.

With regard to the duration of time out, most of its successful implementations have been from 5 to 20 minutes long, with some clear preference for the shorter levels of this range. When experimenting to find the optimal duration for any given youngster it is best, as White,

Nielsen, and Johnson (1972) have shown, to begin with a short duration (e.g., 3 to 5 minutes) and lengthen the time until an effective span is identified, rather than successively shortening an initially lengthier span. This latter approach would, again, risk the danger of introducing an event experienced as positive reinforcement by the youngster when your intention was quite the opposite.

6. *Releasing a youngster from time out.* We noted earlier in connection with extinction that the implementation of a withdrawal *of* positive reinforcement not infrequently leads to initial instances of an "extinction burst" in which more intense or more frequent aggressiveness appears before it begins to subside. Similarly, with withdrawal *from* positive reinforcement, i.e., time out. The first few times a youngster is placed in time out, there may occur what might be termed a "time out burst" of heightened aggressiveness. These outbursts will usually subside, especially if the contingency manager adds to the duration of the time out span the same number of minutes that the outburst lasted.

Whether the release of the youngster was on schedule or delayed for reasons just specified, the release should be conducted in a matter of fact manner and the youngster should be quickly returned to regular classroom activities. Lengthy explanations or apologies by the contingency manager at this point in time are, once again, tactically erroneous provisions of positive reinforcement which communicate to the youngster that acting-out will bring him a short period of removal from reinforcement and then a (probably lengthier) period of undivided attention from the contingency manager.

The effectiveness of time out in substantially reducing or eliminating aggressive or disruptive behaviors has been demonstrated by Allison and Allison (1971); Bostow and Bailey (1969); Calhoun and Matherne (1975); Drabman and Spitalnik (1973); Patterson, Cobb, and Ray (1973); Vukelich and Hake (1971); and White, Nielsen, and Johnson (1972).

Response Cost. Response cost refers to the removal of previously acquired reinforcers contingent upon, and in order to reduce future instances of, the occurrence of inappropriate behaviors. The reinforcers previously acquired and herein contingently removed may have been earned, as when the use of response cost procedures is a component of a token reinforcement system, or they may have been simply provided, as is the case for a "free-standing," no token economy response cost system. In either instance, reinforcers are removed (the cost) whenever previously targeted undesirable behaviors occur (the response). The two other means we have examined for the systematic removal of positive reinforcement, extinction and time out, have not infrequently proven insufficient for delinquent or severely aggressive mid- and late adolescents, even when combined with contingency manager praise or other reinforcement for appropriate behaviors. In a number of these instances, response cost procedures—especially when combined with the provision of positive reinforcement (via a token economy system) for desirable behaviors—have proven effective. Thus, not only must our selection of approach be a prescriptive function of target youngster characteristics, we must also continue in implementing this approach to combine its usage with tandem procedures for providing positive reinforcement of appropriate behaviors.

We will not detail here the several rules for the effective implementation of a token economy system, as they overlap considerably with rules delineated earlier for the provision of non-token positive reinforcers, and may be found in Ayllon and Azrin, 1968; Christopherson, Arnold, Hill, and Quilitch, 1972; Kazdin, 1975; Morris, 1976; and Walker, Hops and Fiegenbaum, 1976. What we do wish to specify, however, are those rules for token or nontoken reinforcement removal which constitute the essence of the response cost procedure.

1. *Define inappropriate behaviors in specific terms.* As with every other contingency management procedure, it is requisite that the contingency manager think, plan, and act *behavior-*

ally. When specifying the inappropriate target behaviors whose occurrence will cost tokens, points, privileges, or other commodities or events, specific overt acts must be delineated, not broader behavioral characterological categories. Thus, "is aggressive" (a characterological observation) or "acts aggressively" (a broad behavioral observation) is too vague, but "swears, makes threats, raises voice, raises hands, pushes classmate" are all useful specifications.

2. *Determine the cost of specific inappropriate responses.* Just as is the case for the amount, level, or rate of positive reinforcement to be provided contingent upon desirable behaviors, the specific cost to be lost contingent upon undesirable behaviors must be determined—whether such cost is a finite number of tokens or points, a finite amount of time the television will be kept off, or otherwise. Cost setting is a crucial determinant of the success or failure of the implementations of this approach. Yet, other aspects of response cost implementation will make demands on the contingency manager's skills as a creative economist. The relation of points or other reinforcers available to earn to those which can be lost, the relationship of cost to the severity of the inappropriate behavior for which that cost is levied, and a host of similar marketing, pricing, and, ultimately, motivational considerations may come into play and thus require a substantial level of contingency management expertise.

3. *Communicate contingencies.* Once the contingency manager has decided upon the specific token, point, or privilege value of the appropriate and inappropriate behaviors, it is necessary that these values be communicated to the target persons. In a classroom context, for example, a reinforcer value list indicating earnings and losses should be drawn up and posted in a readily visible manner.

4. *Remove reinforcement.* Target persons must be able to not only know in advance what earnings and losses are contingent upon what desirable and undesirable behaviors, but each must have ongoing access to his or her own earnings status. Walker (1979) has developed a simple, easily used delivery/feed-back system which gives each youngster ongoing cumulative information indicating (a) when response cost (or earnings) has been applied, (b) which specific behaviors it was applied to, and (c) how many points have been lost (or earned) as a result.

As was true for the other major procedures in use for the removal of positive reinforcement, extinction, and time out, optimal implementation of response cost requires that the contingency manager be (a) *consistent* in his or her application of it across target persons and across time for each target person; (b) *immediate* in delivering contingent costs as soon as possible after the occurrence of inappropriate behavior; and (c) *impartial* and *inevitable*, in that an instance of such behavior leads to an instance of response cost near automatically, with an absolute minimum of special circumstances, special target persons, or special exceptions.

A number of investigations have independently demonstrated the behavior modification effectiveness of response cost procedures, e.g., Burchard and Barrera (1972), Christopherson et al., (1972), Kaufman and O'Leary (1972), O'Leary and Becker (1967), and O'Leary, Becker, Evans, and Saudargas (1969).

AVERSIVE STIMULI—PRESENTATION AND REMOVAL

The two contingency management approaches examined below, namely, the presentation of aversive stimuli (i.e., punishment) and the removal of aversive stimuli (i.e., negative reinforcement) are in our view generally less to be recommended than the positive reinforcement presentation and removal procedures discussed in earlier sections. Our several bases for this disinclination to recommend and utilize these procedures will be made explicit as we proceed below.

Punishment

Punishment is the presentation of an aversive stimulus contingent upon the performance of a given behavior, and is usually intended to decrease the likelihood of future occurrences of that behavior. Two of the major forms that punishment has taken in American classrooms are verbal punishment (i.e., reprimands) and physical punishment (i.e., paddling, spanking, slapping, or other forms of corporal punishment). The effectiveness of these and other forms of punishment in altering targeted inappropriate behaviors such as aggression has been shown to be a function of several factors:

1. Likelihood of punishment
2. Consistency of punishment
3. Immediacy of punishment
4. Duration of punishment
5. Severity of punishment
6. Possibility for escape or avoidance of punishment
7. Availability of alternative routes to goal
8. Level of instigation to aggression
9. Level of reward for aggression
10. Characteristics of the prohibiting agents

Punishment is more likely to lead to behavior change consequences the more certain its application, the more consistently and rapidly it is applied, the longer and more intense its quality, the less likely it can be avoided, the less available are alternative means to goal satisfaction, the greater the level of instigation to aggression or reward for aggression, and the less potent as a contingency manager is the prohibiting agent. Thus, there are clearly several determinants of the impact of an aversive stimulus on a target person's behavior. But let us assume an instance of these several determinants combining to yield a substantial impact. What, ideally, may we hope the effect of punishment on aggression or other undesirable behavior will be? A reprimand or a paddling will not teach new behaviors. If an aggressive youngster literally is deficient in the ability to ask rather than take, request rather than command, negotiate rather than strike out, all the contingency manager scolding, scowling, spanking, and the like possible will not teach the youngster the desirable alternative behaviors. Thus, punishment, if used at all, must be combined with teacher efforts which instruct the youngster in those behaviors he knows not at all. When the youngster does possess alternative desirable behaviors, but in only approximate form, punishment may best be combined with shaping procedures. And, when high quality appropriate behaviors are possessed by the youngster, but he is not displaying them, teacher use of punishment is optimally combined with any of the other procedures described earlier for the systematic presentation of positive reinforcement. In short, application of punishment techniques should always be combined with a companion procedure for strengthening appropriate alternative behaviors—whether these behaviors are absent, weak, or merely unused in the youngster's behavioral repertoire.

Our urging this tandem focus on teaching desirable alternative behaviors grows in particular from the fact that most investigators report the main effect of punishment to be a *temporary* suppression of inappropriate behaviors. While we are appreciative of the potential value of such a temporary suppression to the harried parent or classroom teacher seeking a more manageable home or classroom environment, it is not uncommon—because of this temporariness

—for such contingency managers to have to institute and reinstitute punishment over and over again to the same youngsters for the same inappropriate behaviors. To recapitulate, we have urged thus far in this section that, if punishment is used, its use be combined with one or another means for simultaneously teaching desirable behaviors—a recommendation underscored by the common finding that when punishment does succeed in altering behavior, such effects are often temporary.

In part because of this temporariness of effect, but more so for a series of even more consequential reasons, a number of contingency management researchers have assumed essentially an antipunishment stance, seeing rather little place for it, especially in the contemporary home or classroom. Their view responds to punishment research demonstrating such undesirable side effects of punishment as withdrawal from social contact, counteraggression toward the punisher, modeling of punishing behavior, disruption of social relationships, failure of effects to generalize, selective avoidance (refraining from inappropriate behaviors only when under surveillance), and stigmatizing labeling effects (Azrin & Holz, 1966; Bandura, 1973).

An alternative, propunishment view does exist. It is less widespread and more controversial but, as with the investigators cited above, seeks to make its case based upon empirical evidence. Thus, it is held, there are numerous favorable effects of punishment—rapid and dependable reduction of inappropriate behaviors, the consequent opening up of new sources of positive reinforcement, the possibility of complete suppression of inappropriate behaviors, increased social and emotional behavior, imitation and discrimination learning, and other potential positive side effects (Axelrod & Apache, 1982; Newsom, Favell, & Rincover, 1982; Van Houten, 1982).

The evidence is clearly not all in. Data regarding which punishers should appropriately be used with which youngsters under which circumstances is only partially available. At the present time, decisions regarding the home or the classroom utilization of aversive stimuli to alter inappropriate behaviors must derive from partial data, and each parent's and teacher's carefully considered ethical beliefs regarding the relative costs and benefits of employing punishment procedures. Our own weighing of relevant data and ethical considerations leads to our differential stance favoring the selective utilization at home or in classrooms of verbal punishment techniques, and our rejecting under all circumstances the use of corporal punishment or similar physical punishment techniques.

Verbal Reprimands. Though results are not wholly unmixed; the preponderance of research demonstrates that punishment in the form of verbal reprimands is an effective means for reducing disruptive behavior (Jones & Miller, 1974), littering (Risley, 1977), object throwing (Sajwaj, Culver, Hall, & Lehr, 1972), physical aggression (Hall, Axelrod, Foundopoulos, Shellman, Campbell, & Cranston, 1971) and other acting-out behaviors (O'Leary, Kaufman, Kass, & Drabman, 1970). These and other relevant studies also indicate, beyond overall effectiveness, that reprimands are most potent when the contingency manager is physically close to the target youngster, clearly specifies in behavioral terms the inappropriate behavior being reprimanded, maintains eye contact with the youngster, uses a firm voice, and firmly grasps the youngster while delivering the reprimand. Finally, White, Nielsen, and Johnson (1972) compared reprimands to other commonly employed forms of punishment and found reprimands to be superior in effectiveness. Our position favoring the selective use of reprimands to be superior in effectiveness. Our position favoring the selective use of reprimands rests jointly on our understanding of the foregoing research findings combined with our cost/benefit belief that such procedures not only have a high likelihood of being effective, but a low likelihood of being injurious—especially when combined, as we and others have repeatedly urged, with one or another means for presenting positive reinforcement for appropriate behaviors.

Corporal Punishment. Though we do not know of empirical evidence bearing upon New-som et al.'s (1982) speculation that physically painful punishment that succeeds in altering inappropriate behaviors may be less injurious and more helpful in toto to the target youngster than nonphysically painful but perhaps less effective alternatives, and are given pause by their speculation, we nevertheless herein take a stance opposed to corporal punishment in school (or any other) settings. As Axelrod and Apache (1982) urge, our guiding ethical principle is to urge "the implementation of the last drastic alternative which has a reasonable probability of success." Given the very substantial number of demonstrations of effectiveness of procedures involving the presentation of positive reinforcers, the similarly strong results bearing on techniques for removing such reinforcement, the just cited evidence vis à vis verbal punishment, and the major paucity of research evaluating the effectiveness of corporal punishment, we see no place for it in the domain of effective contingency management.

Yet 47 of America's 50 states permit corporal punishment; and its schoolhouse and community advocates seem to be loud, numerous, and growing. Is it, as Hagebak (1979) darkly suggests, that physically punitive teachers should ask themselves "whether they tend to interpret classroom problems as a personal threat, whether they inflict punishment to protect their self-esteem, whether they retaliate rather than consider the causes of disruptive behavior objectively, and whether they derive sexual satisfaction from inflicting physical punishment [47]"? Or, more parsimoniously, recalling our earlier definition of negative reinforcement, is parent or teacher use and reuse of corporal punishment a simple function of the fact that it intermittently succeeds in reducing or eliminating the youngster's disruptiveness, aggression, or other behavior experienced as aversive by the parent or teacher?

Whatever are the motivations and reinforcements which have sustained its use, corporal punishment—as with all means of punishment—fails to yield sustained suppression of inappropriate behaviors, *increases* the likelihood that the youngster will behave aggressively himself in other settings (Hyman, 1978; Maurer, 1974; Welsh, 1978), and makes no contribution at all to the development of new, appropriate behaviors. We feel quite strongly that one's behavior as a contingency manager must ethically be responsive to such accumulated empirical evidence. Ample research exists to firmly conclude that the science of behavior modification must replace the folklore of procorporal punishment beliefs.

Negative Reinforcement

Negative reinforcement is the final contingency management procedure we wish to consider, and our consideration of it will be brief. It will be recalled that negative reinforcement is the removal of aversive stimuli contingent upon the occurrence of desirable behaviors. Negative reinforcement has seldom been utilized as a behavior modification approach in a home or classroom context. The major exception to this observation is the manner in which youngsters may be contingently released from time out (an aversive environment) depending upon such desirable behaviors as quietness and calmness—such release serving as negative reinforcement for these behaviors. Unfortunately, negative reinforcement often proves important in a classroom context in a less constructive way. Consider a teacher-student interaction in which the student behaves disruptively (shouts, swears, fights), the teacher responds with anger and physical punishment toward the youngster, and the punishment brings about a (temporary) suppression of the youngster's disruptiveness. The decrease in student disruptiveness may also be viewed as a decrease in aversive stimulation experienced by the teacher, which functions to negatively reinforce the immediately preceding teacher behavior, e.g., corporal punishment. The net effect of this sequence is to increase the future likelihood of teacher use of corporal punishment. Analogous sequences may occur and function to increase the likelihood of other ineffective, inappropriate, or intemperate teacher behaviors.

This brief perspective on negative reinforcement concludes our consideration of aggression control by means of contingency management procedures. As we hope our presentation makes clear, these procedures rest on a particularly broad base of empirical support, and thus should typically assume a place of substantial importance in the planning and execution of behavior modification programs designed to prevent or control aggressive behavior.

PSYCHOLOGICAL SKILL TRAINING

Earlier in this chapter we examined research and practice bearing upon a number of interpersonal and related psychological skills (e.g., communication, negotiation) which, when learned to an adequate level of competence, arm the individual to deal more effectively with his or her own or another person's aggressive behavior. There are many more such conflict management skills. Their nature, how they are optimally taught, and a sense of the research evaluating these training methods constitute this final section of the present chapter. However, to place psychological skills training in its proper perspective vis à vis more traditional approaches to disturbed behavior, we wish first to briefly sketch its background and recent emergence as an important intervention strategy.

Until the early 1970s, there existed three major psychological approaches designed to alter the behavior of aggressive, unhappy, ineffective, or disturbed individuals—psychodynamic/psychoanalytic, humanistic/nondirective, and behavior modification. Though each differs from the others in several major respects, one of their significant commonalities is the shared assumption that the patient had somewhere within himself, as yet unexpressed, the effective, satisfying, nonaggressive, or healthy behaviors whose expression was among the goals of the therapy. Such latent potentials, in all three approaches, would be realized by the patient if the therapist were sufficiently skilled in reducing or removing obstacles to such realization. The psychoanalyst sought to do so by calling forth and interpreting unconscious material blocking progress-relevant awareness. The nondirectivist, who believes that the potential for change resides within the patient, sought to free this potential by providing a warm, empathic, maximally accepting therapeutic environment. And the behavior modifier, as illustrated in the previous section of this chapter, by means of one or more contingency management procedures, attempted to see to it that when the latent desirable behaviors or approximations thereto did occur, the patient received contingent reinforcement, thus increasing the probability that these behaviors would recur. Therefore, whether sought by means of interpretation, therapeutic climate, or by dint of offering contingent reward, all three approaches assumed that somewhere within the individual's repertoire resided the desired, effective, sought-after goal behaviors.

In the early 1970s, an important new intervention approach began to emerge—psychological skill training, an approach resting upon rather different assumptions. Viewing the helpee more in educational, pedagogic terms rather than as a patient in need of therapy, the psychological skills trainer assumed he was dealing with an individual lacking, deficient, or at best weak in the skills necessary for effective and satisfying interpersonal functioning. The task of the skills trainer became, therefore, not interpretation, reflection, or reinforcement but the active and deliberate teaching of desirable behaviors. Rather than an intervention called psychotherapy, between a patient and psychotherapist, what emerged was training, between a trainee and a psychological skills trainer.

The roots of the psychological skills training movement lay within both education and psychology. The notion of literally seeking to teach desirable behaviors has often, if sporadically, been a significant goal of the American educational establishment. The Character Education

Movement of the 1920s and more contemporary Moral Education and Values Clarification programs are but a few of several possible examples. Add to this institutionalized educational interest in skills training, the hundreds of interpersonal and planning skills courses taught in America's over 2,000 community colleges, and the hundreds of self-help books oriented toward similar skill-enhancement goals which are available to the American public, and it becomes clear that the formal and informal educational establishment in America proved fertile soil and explicit stimulation within which the psychological skills training movement could grow.

Much the same can be said for American psychology, as it too laid the groundwork in its prevailing philosophy and concrete interests for the development of this new movement. The learning process has above all else been the central theoretical and investigative concern of American psychology since the late nineteenth century. This focal interest also assumed major therapeutic form in the 1950s, as psychotherapy practitioners and researchers alike came to view psychotherapeutic treatment more and more in learning terms. The very healthy and still expanding field of behavior modification grew from this joint learning-clinical focus, and may be appropriately viewed as the immediately preceding context in which psychological skills training came to be developed. In companion with the growth of behavior modification, psychological thinking increasingly shifted from a strict emphasis on remediation to one that was equally concerned with prevention, and the bases for this shift included movement away from a medical model concept toward what may most aptly be called a psychoeducational theoretical stance. Both of these thrusts—heightened concern with prevention and a psychoeducational perspective—gave strong added impetus to the viability of the psychological skill training movement.

Perhaps psychology's most direct contribution to psychological skills training came from social learning theory, and in particular from the work conducted by and stimulated by Albert Bandura. Based upon the same broad array of modeling, behavioral rehearsal, and social reinforcement investigations which helped stimulate and direct the development of our own approach to skill training, Bandura (1973) comments:

> The method that has yielded the most impressive results with diverse problems contains three major components. First, alternative modes of response are repeatedly modeled, preferably by several people who demonstrate how the new style of behavior can be used in dealing with a variety of . . . situations. Second, learners are provided with necessary guidance and ample opportunities to practice the modeled behavior under favorable conditions until they perform it skillfully and spontaneously. The latter procedures are ideally suited for developing new social skills, but they are unlikely to be adopted unless they produce rewarding consequences. Arrangement of success experiences particularly for initial efforts at behaving differently, constitute the third component in this powerful composite method. . . . Given adequate demonstration, guided practice, and success experiences, this method is almost certain to produce favorable results. [p. 253]

Other events of the 1970s provided still further fertile ground for the growth of the skills training movement. The inadequacy of prompting, shaping, and related operant procedures for adding *new* behaviors to individuals' behavioral repertoires was increasingly apparent. The widespread reliance upon deinstitutionalization which lay at the heart of the community mental health movement resulted in the discharge from America's public mental hospitals of approximately 400,000 persons, the majority of whom were substantially deficient in important daily functioning skills. And, especially to this investigator, it had grown particularly clear that what the American mental health movement had available to offer lower social class clients was grossly inadequate in meeting their psychotherapeutic needs. These factors, i.e., relevant supportive research, the incompleteness of operant approaches, large populations of grossly skill deficient individuals, and the paucity of useful interventions for a large segment of American society—all in the context of historically supportive roots in both education and psychology—came together in the thinking of the present writer and others as demanding a new intervention, something prescriptively responsive to these several needs. Psychological skill training was the answer, and a movement was launched.

Our involvement in this movement, a psychological skill training approach we have termed Structured Learning, began in the early 1970s. At that time, and for several years thereafter, our studies were conducted in public mental hospitals with long-term, highly skill-deficient, chronic patients. As our research program progressed, and demonstrated with regularity successful skill enhancement effects (Goldstein, 1982), we shifted in our focus from teaching a broad array of interpersonal and daily living skills to adult, psychiatric inpatients to a more explicit concern with skill training for aggressive individuals. Our trainee groups included spouses engaged in family disputes violent enough to warrant police intervention (Goldstein, Monti, Sardino, & Green, 1978), child abusing parents (Solomon, 1978; Sturm, 1979), and overtly aggressive adolescents (Goldstein, Sprafkin, Gershaw, & Klein, 1980). For all of these trainee populations, the Structured Learning approach consists of the didactic procedures recommended by Bandura (1973) based upon empirical, social learning research. These procedures, which we now wish to describe, are (1) modeling, (2) role playing, (3) performance feedback, and (4) transfer training.

Structured Learning Procedures

Modeling. Structured Learning requires first that trainees be exposed to expert examples of the behaviors we wish them to learn. The 6 to 12 trainees constituting the Structured Learning group are selected based upon their shared skill deficiencies. Each potentially problematic behavior is referred to as a skill. Each skill is broken down into 4 to 6 different behavioral steps. The steps constitute the operational definition of the given skill. Using either live acting by the group's trainers or audiovisual modeling displays, actors portray the steps of that skill being used expertly in a variety of settings relevant to the trainee's daily life. Trainees are told to watch and listen closely to the way the actors in each vignette follow the skill's behavioral steps.

Role Playing. A brief spontaneous discussion almost invariably follows the presentation of a modeling display. Trainees comment on the steps, the actors, and, very often, on how the situation or skill problem portrayed occurs in their own lives. Since our primary goal in role playing is to encourage realistic behavioral rehearsal, a trainee's statements about his or her individual difficulties using the skill being taught can often develop into material for the first role play. To enhance the realism of the portrayal, the main actor is asked to choose a second trainee (co-actor) to play the role of the significant other person in his or her life who is relevant to the skill problem. It is of crucial importance that the main actor seek to enact the steps he or she has just heard modeled.

The main actor is asked to briefly describe the real skill problem situation and the real person(s) involved in it, with whom he or she could try these behavioral steps in real life. The co-actor is called by the name of the main actor's significant other during the role play. The trainer then instructs the role players to begin. It is the trainers' main responsibility, at this point, to be sure that the main actor keeps role playing and that he or she attempts to follow the behavioral steps while doing so.

The role playing is continued until all trainees in the group have had an opportunity to participate—even if all the same steps must be carried over to a second or third session. It should be noted that while the framework (behavioral steps) of each role play in the series remains the same, the actual content can and should change from role play to role play. It is the skill-deficiency problem as it actually occurs, or could occur, in each trainee's real-life environment that should be the content of the given role play. When completed, each trainee should be better armed to act appropriately in the given reality situation.

Performance Feedback. Upon completion of each role play, a brief feedback period ensues. The goals of this activity are to let the main actor know how well he or she followed the skill's steps or in what ways he or she departed from them, to explore the psychological impact of his enactment on the co-actor, and to provide the main actor with encouragement to try out his or her role play behaviors in real life. In these critiques, the behavioral focus of Structured Learning is maintained. Comments must point to the presence or absence of specific, concrete behaviors, and not take the form of general evaluative comments or broad generalities.

Transfer of Training. Several aspects of the Structured Learning sessions described above have, as their primary purpose, augmentation of the likelihood that learning in the training setting will transfer to the trainee's actual real-life environment.

Provisions of General Principles. Transfer of training has been demonstrated to be facilitated by providing trainees with general mediating principles governing successful or competent performance on the training and criterion tasks. This procedure has typically been operationalized in laboratory contexts by providing subjects with the organizing concepts, principles, strategies, or rationales that explain or account for the stimulus-response relationships operative in both the training and application settings. The provision of general principles to Structured Learning trainees is operationalized in our training by the presentation in verbal, pictorial, and written form of appropriate information governing skill instigation, selection, and implementation principles.

Overlearning. Overlearning is a procedure whereby learning is extended over more trials than are necessary merely to produce initial changes in the trainee's behavior. The overlearning, or repetition of successful skill enactment in the typical Structured Learning session is quite substantial, with the given skill taught and its behavioral steps (1) modeled several times, (2) role played one or more times by the trainee, (3) observed live by the trainee as every other group member role plays it, (4) read by the trainee from a blackboard and on the Skill Card, (5) written by the trainee in his or her Trainee's Notebook, (6) practiced in vivo one or more times by the trainee as part of the formal homework assignment, (7) practiced in vivo one or more times by the trainee in response to adult and/or peer leader coaching, and (8) practiced in vivo one or more times by the trainee in response to skill-oriented, intrinsically interesting stimuli introduced into his or her real-life environment.

Identical Elements. In perhaps the earliest experimental concern with transfer enhancement, Thorndike and Woodworth (1901) concluded that, when there was a facilitative effect of one habit on another, it was to the extent that, and because, they shared identical elements. Ellis (1965) and Osgood (1953) have more recently emphasized the importance on transfer of similarity between stimulus and response aspects of the training and application tasks. The greater the similarity of physical and interpersonal stimuli in the Structured Learning setting and the home, school, or other setting in which the skill is to be applied, the greater the likely transfer.

The "real-lifeness" of Structured Learning is operationalized in a number of ways. These operational expressions of identical elements include (1) the representative, relevant, and realistic content and portrayal of the models, protagonists, and situations in the live modeling or modeling tapes, all designed to be highly similar to what trainees are likely to face in their daily lives; (2) the physical props used in, and the arrangement of, the role-playing setting to be similar to real-life settings; (3) the choice, coaching, and enactment of the co-actors of protagonists to be similar to real-life figures; (4) the manner in which the role plays themselves are conducted to be as responsive as possible to the real-life interpersonal stimuli to which the trainee will actually respond with the given skill; (5) the in vivo homework; (6) the training of living units (e.g., all the members of a given ward or group home) as a unit.

Stimulus Variability. Callentine and Warren (1955), Duncan (1958), and Shore and Sechrest (1961) have each demonstrated that positive transfer is greater when a variety of relevant training stimuli are employed. Stimulus variability is implemented in our Structured Learning studies by use of (1) rotation of group leaders across groups, (2) rotation of trainees across groups, (3) having trainees re-role play a given skill with several co-actors, (4) having trainees re-role play a given skill across several relevant settings, and (5) use of multiple homework assignments for each given skill.

Real-Life Reinforcement. Given successful implementation of both appropriate Structured Learning procedures and the transfer enhancement procedures examined above, positive transfer may still fail to occur. As Agras (1967), Gruber (1971), Tharp and Wetzel (1969), and literally dozens of other investigators have shown, stable and enduring performance in application settings of newly learned skills is very much at the mercy of real-life reinforcement contingencies.

We have found it useful to implement several supplemental programs outside of the Structured Learning setting which can help to provide the rewards or reinforcements trainees need so that their new behaviors are maintained. These programs include provision for both external social reward (provided by people in the trainee's real-life environment) and self-reward (provided by the trainee himself or herself).

Aggression-Relevant Psychological Skills

By means of the four procedures just described, we have in a number of investigations taught several aggression-relevant skills to disputant spouses, abusive parents, delinquent adolescents, and other highly aggressive individuals. The skills, and their component behavioral steps, are as follows:

Asking for Help
1. Decide what the problem is.
2. Decide if you want help with the problem.
3. Identify the people who might help you.
4. Make a choice of helper.
5. Tell the helper about your problem.

Giving Instructions
1. Define what needs to be done and who should do it.
2. Tell the other person what you want him or her to do, and why.
3. Tell the other person exactly how to do what you want done.
4. Ask for his or her reaction.
5. Consider his or her reactions and change your direction if appropriate.

Expressing Affection
1. Decide if you have warm, caring feelings about the other person.
2. Decide whether the other person would like to know about your feelings.
3. Decide how you might best express your feelings.
4. Choose the right time and place to express your feelings.
5. Express affection in a warm and caring manner.

Expressing a Complaint
1. Define what the problem is, and who's responsible.
2. Decide how the problem might be solved.
3. Tell that person what the problem is and how it might be solved.
4. Ask for a response.
5. Show that you understand his or her feelings.
6. Come to agreement on the steps to be taken by each of you.

Persuading Others
1. Decide on your position and what the other person's is likely to be.
2. State your position clearly, completely, and in a way that is acceptable to the other person.
3. State what you think the other person's position is.
4. Restate your position, emphasizing why it is the better of the two.
5. Suggest that the other person consider your position for a while before making a decision.

Responding to the Feelings of Others (Empathy)
1. Observe the other person's words and actions.
2. Decide what the other person might be feeling, and how strong the feelings are.
3. Decide whether it would be helpful to let the other person know you understand his or her feelings.
4. Tell the other person, in a warm and sincere manner, how you think he or she is feeling.

Following Instructions
1. Listen carefully while the instructions are being given.
2. Give your reactions to the instructions.
3. Repeat the instructions to yourself.
4. Imagine yourself following the instructions and then do it.

Responding to Persuasion
1. Listen openly to the other person's position.
2. Consider the other person's possible reasons for that position.
3. Ask the other person to explain anything you don't understand about what was said.
4. Compare the other person's position with your own, identifying the pros and cons of each.
5. Decide what to do, based on what will benefit you most in the long run.

Responding to Failure
1. Decide if you have failed.
2. Think about both the personal reasons and the circumstances that have caused you to fail.
3. Decide how you might do things differently if you tried again.
4. Decide if you want to try again.
5. If it is appropriate, try again, using your revised approach.

Responding to Contradictory Messages
1. Pay attention to those body signals that help you know you are feeling trapped or confused.
2. Observe the other person's words and actions that may have caused you to have these feelings.
3. Decide whether that person's words and actions are contradictory.
4. Decide whether it would be useful to point out the contradiction.
5. Ask the other person to explain the contradiction.

Responding to a Complaint
1. Listen openly to the complaint.
2. Ask the person to explain anything you don't understand.
3. Show that you understand the other person's thoughts and feelings.
4. Tell the other person your thoughts and feelings, accepting responsibility if appropriate.
5. Summarize the steps to be taken by each of you.

Preparing for a Stressful Conversation
1. Imagine yourself in the stressful situation.
2. Think about how you will feel and why you will feel that way.
3. Imagine that other person in the stressful situation. Think about how that person will feel and why he or she will feel that way.
4. Imagine yourself telling the other person what you want to say.
5. Imagine the response that that will elicit.
6. Repeat the above steps using as many approaches as you can think of.
7. Choose the best approach.

Determining Responsibility
1. Decide what the problem is.
2. Consider possible causes of the problem.
3. Decide which are the most likely causes of the problem.
4. Take actions to test out which are the actual causes of the problem.

Responding to Anger
1. Listen openly to the other person's angry statement.
2. Show that you understand what the other person is feeling.
3. Ask the other person to explain anything you don't understand about what was said.
4. Show that you understand why the other person feels angry.
5. If it is appropriate, express your thoughts and feelings about the situation.

Setting Problem Priorities
1. List all the problems that are currently pressuring you.
2. Arrange this list in order, from most to least urgent problems.
3. Take steps (delegate, postpone, avoid) to temporarily decrease the urgency of all but the most pressing problem.
4. Concentrate on the most pressing problem.

Dealing with Being Left Out
1. Decide if you're being left out (ignored, rejected).
2. Think about why the other people might be leaving you out of something.
3. Decide how you could deal with the problem (wait, leave, tell the other people how their behavior affects you, talk with a friend about problem).
4. Choose the best way and do it.

Dealing with an Accusation
1. Think about what the other person has accused you of (if it is accurate, inaccurate, if it was said in a mean way or in a constructive way).
2. Think about why the person might have accused you (have you infringed on his or her rights or property?).
3. Think about ways to answer the person's accusations (deny, explain your behavior, correct other person's perceptions, assert, apologize, offer to make up for what happened).
4. Choose the best way and do it.

Dealing with Group Pressure
1. Think about what the other people want you to do and why (listen to other people, decide what the real meaning is, try to understand what is being said).

2. Decide what you want to do (yield, resist, delay, negotiate).
3. Decide how to tell the other people what you want to do (give reasons, talk to one person only, delay, assert).
4. Tell the group what you have decided.

Research Evaluation

Our Structured Learning research consists of a lengthy series of investigations, summarized in the book *Psychological Skill Training* (Goldstein, 1982). The major conclusions of this research include:

1. *Skill Acquisition*. Across diverse trainee populations and target skills, skill acquisition is a reliable training outcome—occurring in well over 90 percent of Structured Learning trainees. While pleased with this outcome, we are acutely aware of the manner in which therapeutic gains demonstrable *in the training context* are rather easily accomplished—given the potency, support, encouragement, and low threat value of trainers and therapists in that context—but that the more consequential outcome question by far pertains to trainee skill performance *in real-world contexts*, i.e., skill transfer.

2. *Skill Transfer*. Across diverse trainee populations, target skills and applied (real-world) settings, skill transfer occurs with approximately 50 percent of Structured Learning trainees. Goldstein & Kanfer (1979) and Karoly & Steffens (1980) have indicated that across several dozen types of psychotherapy involving many different types of psychopathology, the average transfer rate on follow-up is between 15 and 20 percent of patients seen. The 50 percent rate consequent to Structured Learning is a significant improvement upon this collective base rate, though it must immediately be underscored that this cumulative average transfer finding also means that the gains shown by half of our trainees were limited to in-session performance. Of special consequence, however, is the consistently clear manner in which skill transfer in our studies was a function of the explicit implementation of laboratory derived transfer-enhancing techniques such as those described earlier in this chapter.

3. *Prescriptiveness*. A prescriptive research strategy is, at heart, an effort to conceptualize, operationalize, and evaluate potentially optimal trainer x trainee x method matches. Prior to constituting such combinations, trainer, trainee, and training characteristics which may be active contributors to such matches must be examined singly and in combination. Stated otherwise, active and inert ingredients must be identified. A small and continuing series of multiple regression investigations conducted by us have begun to point to state, trait, cognitive, demographic, and sociometric predictors of high levels of skill acquisition and transfer (Anderson, 1981; Hoyer, Lopez and Goldstein, 1981). More such prescriptive ingredients research seems worthy of pursuit.

These brief, summary statements regarding the empirical evaluation of Structured Learning completes our consideration of it as a major example of a psychological skills training approach for aggressive individuals. We are certainly not alone in this effort. Perhaps 25 separate programs now exist in which social learning techniques are systematically utilized to teach an array of constructive, interpersonal behaviors. Several of these programs, as ours, incorporate an explicit focus—in whole or in part—on teaching prosocial behavior as a counterweight to aggression. These programs include Social Skill Training (Argyle, Trower, & Bryant, 1974; Frederiksen, Jenkins, Foy, & Eisler, 1976; Matson & Stephens, 1978), Assertion Training (Galassi & Galassi, 1977), Relationship Enhancement (Gureney, 1977), Basic Social Communication Skills (Hanson, 1971a, 1971b), Teaching Conflict Resolution (Hare, 1976),

Personal Effectiveness (Liberman, King, DeRisi, & McCann, 1975) and Alive and Aware (Miller, Nunally, & Wackman, 1975). Clearly, psychological skills training is well established as a substantial component in our array of procedures aimed at preventing and controlling aggression.

CONCLUSION

Behavior modification theory, application, and research have contributed substantially to our potential ability to prevent and control aggressive behavior. The several behavior modification methods described in this chapter combine to justify this conclusion, and to suggest that yet further development of them, combined with continued systematic evaluation of their efficacy, will yield even greater preventive and control success.

REFERENCES

Adams, G. R. Classroom aggression: Determinants, controlling mechanisms, and guidelines for the implementation of a behavior modification program. *Psychology in the Schools*, 1973, *10*, 155-68.

Agras, W. S. Behavior therapy in the management of chronic schizophrenia. *American Journal of Psychiatry*, 1967, *124*, 240-43.

Allen, K. E., Hart, B., Buell, J. S., Harris, F. R., & Wolf, M. M. Effects of social reinforcement on isolated behaviors of a nursery school child. *Child Development*, 1964, *35*, 511-18.

Allen, K. E., Henke, L. B., Harris, F. R., Baer, D. M., & Reynolds, N. J. Control of hyperactivity by social reinforcement of attending behavior. *Journal of Educational Psychology*, 1967, *58*, 231-37.

Allison, T. S., & Allison, S. L. Time out from reinforcement: Effect on sibling aggression. *Psychological Record*, 1971, *21*, 81-85.

Allred, G. Husband and wife communication training: An experimental study. Unpublished doctoral dissertation, Florida State University, 1977.

Anderson, L. Role playing ability and young children: The prescriptive question. Unpublished masters thesis, Syracuse University, 1981.

Argyle, M., Trower, P., & Bryant, B. Explorations in the treatment of personality disorders and neuroses by social skill training. *British Journal of Medical Psychology*, 1974, *47*, 63-72.

Axelrod, S., & Apache, J. (Eds.) *The effects and side effects of punishment on human behavior.* New York: Academic Press, 1982.

Ayllon, T., & Azrin, N. H. *The token economy: A motivational system for therapy and rehabilitation.* New York: Appleton-Century-Crofts, 1968.

Ayllon, T., & Michael, J. The psychiatric nurse as a behavioral engineer. *Journal of the Experimental Analysis of Behavior*, 1959, *2*, 323-34.

Azrin, N. H., & Holz, W. C. Punishment. In W. K. Honig (Ed.), *Operant behavior: Areas of research and application.* New York: Appleton-Century-Crofts, 1966.

Azrin, N. H., Naster, B. J., & Jones, R. Reciprocity counseling: A rapid learning-based procedure for marital counseling. *Behavior Research and Therapy*, 1973, *11*, 365-82.

Bachrach, A. J., Erwin, W. J., & Mohr, J. P. The control of eating behavior in an anorexic by operant conditioning techniques. In L. P. Ullmann & L. Krasner (Eds.), *Case studies in behavior modification.* New York: Holt, Rinehart & Winston, 1965.

Bandura, A. *Principles of behavior modification.* New York: Holt, Rinehart & Winston, 1969.

Bandura, A. *Aggression: A social learning analysis.* Englewood Cliffs, N.J.: Prentice-Hall, 1973.

Becker, W. C., Madsen, C. H., Arnold, C. R., & Thomas, D. R. The contingent use of teacher attention and praise in reducing classroom behavior problems. *The Journal of Special Education*, 1967, *1*, 287-307.

Beiman, I., Israel, E., & Johnson, S. During training and post-training effects of live and taped extended progressive relaxation, self-relaxation, and electromyogram biofeedback. *Journal of Consulting and Clinical Psychology*, 1978, *46*, 314-21.

Benson, H. *The relaxation response*. New York: Morrow, 1975.

Bernstein, D. A., & Borkovec, T. D. *Progressive relaxation training*. Champaign, Ill.: Research Press, 1973.

Borkovec, T. D., Grayson, J. B., & Cooper, K. M. Treatment of general tension: Subjective and physiological effects of progressive relaxation. *Journal of Consulting and Clinical Psychology*, 1978, *46*, 518-28.

Borkovec, T. D., Grayson, J. B., O'Brien, G. T., & Weerts, T. C. Relaxation treatment of pseudoinsomnia and idiopathic insomnia: An electroencephalographic evaluation. *Journal of Applied Behavior Analysis*, 1979, *12*, 37-54.

Bornstein, P. H., Anton, B., Harowski, K. H., Weltzein, R. T., McIntyre, T. J., & Hocker-Wilmot, J. Behavioral-communications treatment of marital discord: Positive behaviors. *Behavioral Counseling Quarterly*, 1981, *1*, 189-99.

Bornstein, P. H., Rychtarik, R. G., McFall, M. E., Bridgewater, C. A., Guthrie, L., & Anton, B. Behaviorally-specific report cards and self-determined reinforcements. *Behavior Modification*, 1980, *4*, 71-81.

Bostow, D. E., & Bailey, J. B. Modification of severe disruptive and aggressive behavior using brief timeout and reinforcement procedures. *Journal of Applied Behavior Analysis*, 1969, *2*, 31-37.

Brock, G. W. Unilateral marital intervention. Training spouses to train their partners in communication skills. Unpublished doctoral dissertation, Pennsylvania State University, 1978.

Brown, P., & Elliott, R. Control of aggression in a nursery school class. *Journal of Experimental Child Psychology*, 1965, *2*, 103-07.

Burchard, J. D., & Barrera, F. An analysis of timeout and response cost in a programmed environment. *Journal of Applied Behavior Analysis*, 1972, *5*, 271-82.

Burka, J., Hubbell, R., Preble, M., Spinelli, R., & Winter, N. *Communication Skills Workshop Manual*. Fort Collins, Colorado: University of Colorado Counseling Center, 1972.

Buys, C. J. Effects of teacher reinforcement on elementary pupils' behavior and attitudes. *Psychology in the Schools*, 1972, *9*, 278-88.

Calhoun, K. S., & Matherne, P. The effects of varying schedules of timeout on aggressive behavior of a retarded girl. *Journal of Behavior Therapy & Experimental Psychiatry*, 1975, *6*, 139-43.

Callantine, M. F., & Warren, J. M. Learning sets in human concept formation. *Psychological Reports*, 1955, *1*, 363-67.

Carkhuff, R. R. Training as a preferred mode of treatment. *Journal of Consulting Psychology*, 1971, *18*, 121-31.

Carr, E. G. Contingency management. In A. P. Goldstein, E. G. Carr, W. Davidson, & P. Wehr. *In response to aggression*. New York: Pergamon Press, 1981.

Christopherson, E. R., Arnold, C. M., Hill, D. W., & Quilitch, H. R. The home point system: Token reinforcement procedures for application by parents of children with behavior problems. *Journal of Applied Analysis*, 1972, *5*, 485-97.

Cocozza, J., & Steadman, H. Some refinements in the measurement and prediction of dangerous behavior. *American Journal of Psychiatry*, 1974, *119*, 1012-20.

Connor, W. H. Effects of brief relaxation training on automatic response and electromyogram biofeedback treatments for muscle contraction headaches. *Psychophysiology*, 1974, *11*, 591-99.

Curran, J. P. Skills training as an approach to the treatment of heterosexual-social anxiety: A review. *Psychological Bulletin*, 1977, *84*, 140-57.

Delprato, D. J., & Dekraker, T. Metronome-conditioned hypnotic-relaxation in the treatment of test anxiety. *Behavior Therapy*, 1976, *7*, 379-81.

Drabman, R., & Spitalnik, R. Social isolation as a punishment procedure: A controlled study. *Journal of Experimental Child Psychology*, 1973, *16*, 236-49.

Duncan, C. P. Recent research on human problem solving. *Psychological Bulletin*, 1958, *56*, 397-429.

Edelman, R. I. Effects of progress relaxation on autonomic processes. *Journal of Clinical Psychology*, 1970, *26*, 421-25.

Eisler, R. M., & Hersen, M. Behavior techniques in family-oriented crisis intervention. *Archives of General Psychiatry*, 1973, *28*, 111-16.

Ellis, A. *Reason and emotion in psychotherapy*. New York: Lyle Stuart, 1962.

Ellis, H. *The transfer of learning*. New York: Macmillan, 1965.

Ely, A. L., & Guerney, B. C. Efficacy of the training phase of conjugal therapy. *Psychotherapy: Theory, Research & Practice*, 1973, *10*, 201-07.

Evans, D. R. Specific aggression, arousal, and reciprocal inhibition therapy. *Western Psychologist*, 1971, *1*, 125-30.

Evans, D. R., Hearn, M. T., & Saklofake, D. Anger, arousal and systematic desensitization. *Psychological Reports*, 1973, *32*, 625-26.

Fee, R. A., & Girdano, D. A. The relative effectiveness of three techniques to induce the trophotropic response. *Biofeedback and Self-regulation*, 1978, *3*, 145-57.

Fensterheim, H. Assertive methods and marital problems. In R. D. Rubin, J. Henderson, & L. P. Ullman (Eds.), *Advances in behavior therapy*. New York: Academic Press, 1972.

Ferster, C. B., & DeMeyer, M. K. A method for the experimental analysis of the behavior of autistic children. *American Journal of Orthopsychiatry*, 1962, *32*, 89-98.

Ferster, C. B., & Skinner, B. F. *Schedules of reinforcement*. New York: Appleton-Century-Crofts, 1957.

Filley, A. C. *Interpersonal conflict resolution*. Glenview, Ill.: Scott, Foresman, 1974.

Firestone, P. The effects of side effects of timeout on an aggressive nursery school child. *Journal of Behavior Therapy & Experimental Psychiatry*, 1976, *6*, 79-81.

Frederiksen, L. W., Jenkins, J. O., Foy, D. W., & Eisler, R. M. Social skills training to modify abusive verbal outbursts in adults. *Journal of Applied Behavior Analysis*, 1976, *9*, 117-25.

Friedman, P. M. Personalistic family and marital therapy. In A. A. Lazarus (Ed.), *Clinical behavior therapy*, New York: Brunner/Mazel, 1972.

Galassi, M. D., & Galassi, J. P. *Assert yourself!* New York: Human Sciences Press, 1977.

Gambrill, E. D. *Behavior modification*. San Francisco: Jossey-Bass, 1977.

Goldfried, M., & Davison, G. *Clinical behavior therapy*. New York: Holt, Rinehart & Winston, 1976.

Goldfried, M. R. & Trier, C. S. Effectiveness of relaxation as an active coping skill. *Journal of Abnormal Psychology*, 1974, *83*, 348-55.

Goldstein, A. P. *Psychological skills training*. New York: Pergamon Press, 1982.

Goldstein, A. P., Apter, S., & Harootunian, B. *School violence*. Englewood Cliffs, N.J.: Prentice-Hall, 1983.

Goldstein, A. P., & Kanfer, F. (Eds.) *Maximizing treatment gains*. New York: Academic Press, 1979.

Goldstein, A. P., Monti, P. J., Sardino, T. J., & Green, D. J. *Police crisis intervention*. New York: Pergamon Press, 1978.

Goldstein, A. P., & Rosenbaum, A. *Aggress-less*. Englewood Cliffs, N.J.: Prentice-Hall, 1982.

Goldstein, A. P., Sprafkin, R. P., & Gershaw, N. J. *Skill training for community living*. New York: Pergamon Press, 1976.

Goldstein, A. P., Sprafkin, R. P., Gershaw, N. J., & Klein, P. *Skillstreaming the adolescent*. Champaign, Ill.: Research Press, 1980.

Goldstein, R. Brain research and violent behavior. *Archives of Neurology*, 1974, *30*, 1-18.

Gottman, J., Notarius, C., Markman, H., Bank, S., Yoppi, B., & Rubin, M. E. Behavior exchange theory and marital decision making. *Journal of Personality and Social Psychology*, 1976, *34*, 14-23.

Grimm, L. G. The evidence for cue-controlled relaxation. *Behavior Therapy*, 1980, *11*, 283-93.

Gruber, R. P. Behavior therapy: Problems in generalization. *Behavior Therapy*, 1971, *2*, 361-68.

Guerney, B. G. Filial therapy: Description and rationale. *Journal of Consulting Psychology*, 1964, *28*, 304-10.

Guerney, B. G., Jr. *Relationship enhancement*. San Francisco: Jossey-Bass, 1977.

Hagebak, R. Disciplinary practices in Dallas. In D. G. Gil (Ed.), *Child abuse and violence*. New York: AMS Press, 1979.

Hall, R. V., Axelrod, S., Foundopoulos, M., Shellman, J., Campbell, R. A., & Cranston, S. S. The effective use of punishment to modify behavior in the classroom. *Educational Technology*, 1971, *11*, 24-26.

Hall, R. V., Lund, D., & Jackson, D. Effects of teacher attention on study behavior. *Journal of Applied Behavior Analysis*, 1968, *1*, 1-12.

Hall, R. V., Panyan, M., Rabon, D., & Broden, M. Instructing beginning teachers in reinforcement procedures which improve classroom control. *Journal of Applied Behavior Analysis*, 1968, *1*, 315-22.

Hamberger, K., & Lohr, J. M. Rational restructuring for anger control: A quasiexperimental case study. *Cognitive Therapy and Research*, 1980, *4*, 99-102.

Hanson, R. W. Assertion training program. Unpublished manuscript, Palo Alto, Calif.: Veterans Administration Hospital, 1971. (a)

Hanson, R. W. Training program in basic communication skills. Unpublished manuscript, Palo Alto, Calif.: Veterans Administration Hospital, 1971. (b)

Hare, M. A. Teaching conflict resolution simulations. Presented at Eastern Community Association, Philadelphia, March 1976.

Heiman, H. Teaching interpersonal communications. *N. Dakota Speech & Theatre Association Bulletin*, 1973, *2*, 7-29.

Hellman, D. & Blackman, N. Enuresis, fire-setting, and cruelty to animals: A triad predictive of adult crime. *American Journal of Psychiatry*, 1966, *122*, 1431-35.

Herrell, J. M. Use of systematic desensitization to eliminate inappropriate anger. Presented at American Psychological Association, Washington, D.C., 1971.

Hickman, M. E., & Baldwin, B. A. The use of programmed instruction to improve communication in marriage. *Family Coordinator*, 1971, *20*, 121-25.

Homme, L. *How to use contingency contracting in the classroom*. Champaign, Ill.: Research Press, 1971.

Hoyer, W. J., Lopez, M. A., & Goldstein, A. P. Correlates of social skill acquisition and transfer by elderly patients. Unpublished manuscript, Syracuse University, 1981.

Hyman, I. A. Is the hickory stick out of tune? *Today's Education*, 1978, *2*, 30-32.

Jacobson, E. *Progressive relaxation*. Chicago: University of Chicago Press, 1929.

Jacobson, E. Variation in blood pressure with skeletal muscle tension and relaxation. *Annals of Internal Medicine*, 1939, *12*, 1194-1212.

Jacobson, E. *Anxiety and tension control*. Philadelphia, Pennsylvania: Lippincott, 1964.

Jacobson, N. S. Problem solving and contingency contracting in the treatment of marital discord. *Journal of Consulting and Clinical Psychology*, 1977, *45*, 92-100.

Jacobson, N. S., & Martin, B. Behavioral marriage therapy: Current status. *Psychological Bulletin*, 1976, *83*, 540-56.

Jones, F. H., & Miller, W. H. The effective use of negative attention for reducing group disruption in special elementary school classrooms. *The Psychological Record*, 1974, *24*, 435-48.

Karoly, P., & Steffens, J. J. (Eds.) *Improving the long-term effects of psychotherapy*. New York: Gardner Press, 1980.

Kaufman, K. F., & O'Leary, K. D. Reward, cost and self-evaluation procedures for disruptive adolescents in a psychiatric hospital school. *Journal of Applied Behavior Analysis*, 1972, *5*, 293-310.

Kazdin, A. E. *Behavior modification in applied settings*. Homewood, Ill.: Dorsey Press, 1975.

Kazdin, A. E. *The token economy*. New York: Plenum, 1977.

Kifer, R. E., Lewis, M. A., Green, D. R., & Phillips, E. L. Training predelinquent youths and their parents to negotiate conflict situations. *Journal of Applied Behavior Analysis*, 1974, *7*, 357-64.

King, N. J. The therapeutic utility of abbreviated progressive relaxation: A critical review with implications for clinical progress. In M. Hersen & A. Bellack (Eds.), *Progress in behavior modification*. New York: Academic Press, 1980.

Kirschner, N. M., & Levine, L. A direct school intervention program for the modification of aggressive behavior. *Psychology in the Schools*, 1975, *12*, 202-08.

Knox, D. *Marriage happiness*. Champaign, Ill.: Research Press, 1971.

Kozol, H., Boucher, R., & Garofalo, R. The diagnosis and treatment of dangerousness. *Crime and Delinquency*, 1972, *18*, 371-92.

Lazarus, A. A., & Rachman, S. The use of systematic desensitization in psychotherapy. *South African Medical Journal*, 1967, *31*, 934-37.

Lederer, W., & Jackson, D. D. *The mirage of marriage.* N.Y.: Norton, 1968.

Lefkowitz, M., Eron, L., Walder, L., & Heusmann, L. *Growing up to be violent.* New York: Pergamon Press, 1977.

Leitenberg, H., Agras, W. S., & Thomson, L. E. A sequential analysis of the effect of selective positive reinforcement in modifying anorexia nervosa. *Behaviour Research and Therapy*, 1968, *6*, 211-18.

Liberman, R. P., King, L. W., DeRisi, W. J., & McCann, M. *Personal effectiveness.* Champaign, Ill.: Research Press, 1975.

Liberman, R. P., Levine, J., Wheeler, E., Sanders, N., & Wallace, C. Experimental evaluation of marital group therapy, Behavioral vs. interaction-insight formation. *Acta Psychiatrica Scandinavia*, 1976, *17*, 10-16.

Lovaas, O. I., Koegel, R., Simmons, J. Q., & Long, J. S. Some generalization and follow-up measures on autistic children in behavior therapy. *Journal of Applied Behavior Analysis*, 1973, *6*, 131-66.

Lovaas, O. I., Schaeffer, B., & Simmons, J. Building social behavior in autistic children by use of electric shock. *Journal of Experimental Research in Personality*, 1965, *1*, 99-109.

Luber, R. F. Teaching models in marital therapy. *Behavior Modification*, 1978, *2*, 77-91.

Luiselli, J. K., Marholin, D., Steinman, D. L., & Steinman, W. M. Assessing the effects of relaxation training. *Behavior Therapy*, 1979, *10*, 663-68.

Luther, E. R. Treatment of migraine headache by conditioned relaxation: A case study. *Behavior Therapy*, 1971, *2*, 592-93.

Madsen, C. J., Becker, W. C., & Thomas, D. R. Rules, praise, and ignoring: Elements of elementary classrooms control. *Journal of Applied Behavior Analysis*, 1968, *1*, 139-50.

Martin, P. L., & Foxx, R. M. Victim control of the aggression of an institutionalized retardate. *Journal of Behavior Therapy and Experimental Psychiatry*, 1973, *4*, 161-65.

Matson, J. L., & Stephens, R. M. Increasing appropriate behavior of explosive chronic psychiatric patients with a social skills training package. *Behavior Modification*, 1978, *2*, 61-76.

Maurer, A. Corporal punishment. *American Psychologist*, 1974, *29*, 614-26.

McCord, J. Some child rearing antecedents to criminal behavior in adult men. *Journal of Personality and Social Psychology*, 1979, *37*, 1477-86.

McFall, R. M., & Twentyman, C. T. Four experiments on the relative contributions of rehearsal, modeling and coaching to assertion training. *Journal of Abnormal Psychology*, 1973, *81*, 199-218.

Meichenbaum, D. Cognitive modification of test anxious college students. *Journal of Consulting and Clinical Psychology*, 1972, *39*, 370-80.

Meichenbaum, D. Self-instructional training: A cognitive prosthesis for the aged. *Human Development*, 1974, *17*, 273-80.

Meichenbaum, D. *Cognitive behavior modification.* New York: Plenum, 1977.

Meichenbaum, D., & Cameron R. Training schizophrenics to talk to themselves: A means of developing attentional controls. *Behavior Therapy*, 1973, *4*, 515-34.

Meichenbaum, D., & Goodman, J. Training impulsive children to talk to themselves: A means of developing self-control. *Journal of Abnormal Psychology*, 1971, *77*, 115-26.

Miller, S. L. The effects of communication training in small groups upon self-disclosure and openness in engaged couples' systems of interaction: A field experiment. Unpublished dissertation, University of Minnesota, 1971.

Miller, S., Nunnally, E. W., & Wackman, D. B. *Alive and aware: Improving communication in relationships.* Minneapolis: Interpersonal Communication Programs, 1975.

Monahan, J. *The clinical prediction of violent behavior.* Rockville, Md.: National Institute of Mental Health, 1981.

Morris, R. J. *Behavior modification with children.* Cambridge, Mass.: Winthrop, 1976.

Mowrer, O. H., & Mowrer, W. A. Enuresis: A method for its study and treatment. *American Journal of*

Orthopsychiatry, 1938, *8,* 436-47.

Newsom, C., Favell, J. E., & Rincover, A. The side effects of punishment. In S. Axelrod & J. Apsche (Eds.), *The effects and side effects of punishment on human behavior.* New York: Academic Press, 1982.

Novaco, R. W. *Anger control.* Lexington, Mass.: Lexington Books, 1975.

Novaco, R. W. Stress inoculation: A cognitive therapy for anger and its application to a case of depression. *Journal of Consulting and Clinical Psychology,* 1977, *45,* 600-08.

Nunnally, E. W. Effects of communication training upon interaction awareness and empathic accuracy of engaged couples: A field experiment. Unpublished doctoral dissertation, University of Minnesota, 1971.

O'Donnell, C. R., & Worell, L. Motor and cognitive relaxation in the desensitization of anger. *Behavior Research and Therapy,* 1973, *11,* 473-81.

O'Leary, K. D., & Becker, W. C. Behavior modification of an adjustment class: A token reinforcement program. *Exceptional Children,* 1967, *33,* 637-42.

O'Leary, K. D., Becker, W. C., Evans, M. B., & Saudargas, R. A. A token reinforcement program in a public school: A replication and systematic analysis. *Journal of Applied Behavior Analysis,* 1969, *2,* 3-13.

O'Leary, K. D., Kaufman, K. F., Kass, R. E., & Drabman, R. S. The effects of loud and soft reprimands on the behavior of disruptive students. *Exceptional Children,* 1970, *37,* 145-55.

O'Leary, K. D., & O'Leary, S. G. *Classroom management.* New York: Pergamon Press, 1977.

O'Leary, K. D., & Turkewitz, H. The treatment of marital disorders from a behavioral perspective. In T. J. Paolino & S. McCrady (Eds.), *Marriage and the treatment of marital disorders from three perspectives: Psychoanalytic, behavioral, and systems theory.* New York: Brunner/Mazel, 1978.

O'Leary, S. G., & O'Leary, K. D. Behavior modification in the school. In H. Leitenberg (Ed.), *Handbook of behavior modification and behavior therapy.* Englewood Cliffs, N.J.: Prentice-Hall, 1976.

Osgood, C. E. *Method and theory in experimental psychology.* New York: Oxford University Press, 1953.

Parker, J. C., Gilbert, G. S., & Thoresen, R. W. Reduction of autonomic arousal in alcoholics: A comparison of relaxation and meditation techniques. *Journal of Consulting and Clinical Psychology,* 1978, *46,* 879-86.

Patterson, G. R. A learning theory approach to the treatment of the school phobic child. In L. P. Ullman & L. Krasner (Eds)., *Case studies in behavior modification.* New York: Holt, Rinehart & Winston, 1965.

Patterson, G. R., Cobb, J. A., & Ray, R. S. A social engineering technology for retraining the families of aggressive boys. In H. E. Adams & I. P. Unikel (Eds.), *Issues and trends in behavior therapy.* Springfield, Ill.: C. C. Thomas, 1973.

Patterson, G. R., & Hops, H. Coercion, a game for two: Intervention techniques for mental conflict. In R. E. Ulrich & P. Mountjoy (Eds.), *The experimental analysis of social behavior.* New York: Appleton-Century-Crofts, 1972.

Patterson, G. R., Ray, R., & Shaw, D. Direct intervention in families of deviant children. Unpublished manuscript, University of Oregon, 1968.

Patterson, G. R., & Reid, J. B. Reciprocity and coercion: Two facets of social systems. In C. Neuringer & J. Meichael (Eds.), *Behavior modification in clinical psychology.* New York: Appleton-Century-Crofts, 1970.

Paul, G. L. Chronic mental patients: Current status—future directions. *Psychological Bulletin,* 1969, *71,* 81-94.

Pendleton, L. R., & Tasto, D. L. Effects of metronome-conditioned relaxation, metronome-induced relaxation, and progressive muscle relaxation on insomnia. *Behavior Research and Therapy,* 1976, *14,* 165-66.

Pierce, R. M. Training in interpersonal communication skills with partners of deteriorating marriages. *Family Coordinator,* 1973, *22,* 223-27.

Pinkston, E. M., Reese, N. M., LeBlanc, J. M., & Baer, D. M. Independent control of a preschool child's aggression and peer interaction by contingent teacher attention. *Journal of Applied Behavior Analysis*, 1973, *6*, 115-24.

Rappaport, A. F. The effects of an intensive conjugal relationship modification program. Unpublished doctoral dissertation, Pennsylvania State University, 1971.

Rappaport, A. F., & Harrell, J. A behavior exchange model for marital counseling. *Family Coordinator*, 1972, *21*, 203-12.

Rhode, N., Rasmussen, D., & Heaps, R. A. *Let's communicate: A program designed for effective communication*. Presented at American Personnel and Guidance Association, April 1971.

Rimm, D. C., DeGroot, J. D., Boord, P., Heiman, J., & Dillow, P. V. Systematic desensitization of an anger response. *Behavior Research & Therapy*, 1971, *9*, 273-80.

Risley, T. R. The social context of self-control. In R. Stuart (Ed.), *Behavioral self management*. New York: Brunner/Mazel, 1977.

Roberts, P. V. The effects on marital satisfaction of brief training in behavioral exchange negotiation mediated by differentially experienced trainers. Unpublished doctoral dissertation, Fuller Theological Seminary, 1974.

Robin, A. L., Kent, R., O'Leary, K. D., Foster, S., & Prinz, R. An approach to teaching parents and adolescents problem-solving communication skills: A preliminary report. *Behavior Therapy*, 1977, *8*, 639-43.

Rose, S. D. *Group therapy: A behavioral approach*. Englewood Cliffs, N.J.: Prentice-Hall, 1977.

Russell, R. K., & Sipich, J. F. Treatment of test anxiety by cue-controlled relaxation. *Behavior Therapy*, 1974, *5*, 673-76.

Sajwaj, T., Culver, P., Hall, C., & Lehr, L. Three simple punishment techniques for the control of classroom disruptions. In G. Semb (Ed.), *Behavior analysis and education*. Lawrence, Kansas: University of Kansas Press, 1972.

Sanders, R. W. Systematic desensitization in the treatment of child abuse. *American Journal of Psychiatry*, 1978, *135*, 483-84.

Schwitzgebel, R. *Street corner research: An experimental approach to the juvenile delinquent*. Cambridge, Mass.: Harvard University Press, 1964.

Sewell, E., McCoy, J. F., & Sewell, W. R. Modification of an antagonistic social behavior using positive reinforcement for other behavior. *The Psychological Record*, 1973, *23*, 499-504.

Sherman, A. R., & Plummer, I. L. Training in relaxation as a behavioral self-management skill: An exploratory investigation. *Behavior Therapy*, 1973, *4*, 543-50.

Sherman, J. A. Use of reinforcement and imitation to reinstate verbal behavior in mute psychotics. *Journal of Abnormal Psychology*, 1965, *70*, 155-64.

Shore, E., & Sechrest, L. Concept attainment as a function of number of positive instances presented. *Journal of Educational Psychology*, 1961, *52*, 303-07.

Skinner, B. F. *The behavior of organisms: An experimental analysis*. New York: Appleton-Century-Crofts, 1938.

Skinner, B. F. *Science and human behavior*. New York: Macmillan, 1953.

Snyder, J. J., & White, M. J. The use of cognitive self-instructions in the treatment of behaviorally disturbed adolescents. *Behavior Therapy*, 1979, *10*, 227-35.

Solomon, E. J. Structured learning therapy with abusive parents: Training in self-control. Unpublished doctoral dissertation, Syracuse University, 1978.

Steadman, H. A new look at recidivism among Patuxent inmates. *The Bulletin of the American Academy of Psychiatry and the Law*, 1977, *5*, 200-09.

Steadman, H., & Cocozza, J. *Careers of the criminally insane*. Lexington, Mass.: Lexington Books, 1974.

Steen, P. L., & Zuriff, G. E. The use of relaxation in the treatment of self-injurious behavior. *Journal of Behavior Therapy and Experimental Psychiatry*, 1977, *8*, 447-48.

Straughan, J. The applications of operant conditioning to the treatment of elective mutism. In H. N. Sloane, Jr., & B. A. MacAulay (Eds.), *Operant procedures in remedial speech and language training*. Boston: Houghton Mifflin, 1968.

Stuart, R. B. Behavioral contracting within the families of delinquents. *Journal of Behavior Therapy and Experimental Psychiatry*, 1971, *2*, 1-11.

Stuart, R. B. Operant-interpersonal treatment for marital discord. *Journal of Consulting and Clinical Psychology*, 1969, *33*, 675-80.

Sturn, D. Therapist aggression tolerance and dependency tolerance under standardized client conditions of hostility and dependency. Unpublished masters thesis, Syracuse University, 1979.

Taylor, C. B., Farquhar, J. W., Nelson, E., & Agras, S. Relaxation therapy and high blood pressure. *Archives of General Psychiatry*, 1977, *34*, 339-42.

Terkelson, C. Making contact: Parent-child communication skill program. *Elementary School Guidance and Counseling*, 1976, *11*, 89-99.

Tharp, R. G., & Wetzel, R. J. *Behavior modification in the natural environment.* New York: Academic Press, 1969.

Thornberry, R., & Jacoby, J. *The criminally insane: A community follow-up of mentally ill offenders.* Chicago: University of Chicago Press, 1979.

Thorndike, E. L., & Woodworth, R. S. The influence of improvement in one mental function upon the efficiency of other functions. *Psychological Review*, 1901, *8*, 247-61.

Van Houton, R. Punishment: From the animal laboratory to the applied setting. In S. Axelrod & J. Apsche (Eds.), *The effects and side effects of punishment on human behavior.* New York: Academic Press, 1982.

Von Benken, E. A. Clinical reduction of anger and agression by systematic desensitization. Unpublished doctoral dissertation, University of Cincinnati, 1977.

Vukelich, R., & Hake, D. F. Reduction of dangerously aggressive behavior in a severely retarded resident through a combination of positive reinforcement procedures. *Journal of Applied Behavior Analysis*, 1971, *4*, 215-25.

Wahler, R. G., & Pollio, H. R. Behavior and insight: A case study in behavior therapy. *Journal of Experimental Research in Personality*, 1968, *3*, 45-56.

Wahler, R. G., Winkel, G. H., Peterson, R. F., & Morrison, D. C. Mothers as behavior therapists for their own children. *Behavior Research and Therapy*, 1965, *3*, 113-24.

Walker, C. E. *Learn to relax.* Englewood Cliffs, N.J.: Prentice-Hall, 1975.

Walker, H. M. *The acting-out child: Coping with classroom disruption.* Boston: Allyn & Bacon, 1979.

Walker, H. M., Hops, H., & Fiegenbaum, E. Deviant classroom behavior as a function of combinations of social and token reinforcement and cost contingency. *Behavior Therapy*, 1976, *7*, 76-88.

Ward, M. H., & Baker, B. L. Reinforcement therapy in the classroom. *Journal of Applied Behavior Analysis*, 1968, *1*, 323-28.

Warner, G., & Lance, J. W. Relaxation therapy in migraine and chronic tension headache. *Medical Journal of Australia*, 1975, *1*, 298-301.

Watson, J. B., & Rayner, R. Conditioned emotional reactions. *Journal of Experimental Psychology*, 1920, *3*, 1-114.

Watzlawick, P., Beavin, J. H., & Jackson, D. D. *Pragmatics of human communication — A study of interactional patterns, pathologies, and paradox.* New York: Norton, 1967.

Webster, R. E. A timeout procedure in a public school setting. *Psychology in the Schools*, 1973, *13*, 72-76.

Weiss, R. L., Birchler, G. R., & Vincent, J. P. Contractual models for negotiation training in marital dyads. *Journal of Marriage and the Family*, 1974 (May), 321-30.

Weiss, R. L., Hops, H., & Patterson, G. R. A framework for conceptualizing marital conflict. In F. W. Clark & L. A. Hamerlynch (Eds.), *Critical issues in research and practice.* Champaign, Ill.: Research Press, 1973.

Weissberg, M. Anxiety-inhibiting statements and relaxation combined in two cases of speech anxiety. *Journal of Behavior Therapy and Experimental Psychiatry*, 1975, *6*, 163-64.

Wells, R. A., Figurel, J. A., & McNamee, P. Group facilitative training with conflicted marital couples. In A. G. Gurman & D. G. Rice (Eds.), *Couples in conflict.* New York: Jason Aronson, 1975.

Welsh, R. S. Delinquency, corporal punishment and the schools. *Crime & Delinquency*, 1978 (July), 336-54.

White, G. D., Nielson, G., & Johnson, S. M. Timeout duration and the suppression of deviant behavior in children. *Journal of Applied Behavior Analysis,* 1972, *5,* 111-20.

Williams, C. D. The elimination of tantrum behavior by extinction procedures. *Journal of Abnormal and Social Psychology,* 1959, *59,* 269.

Wolf, M., Risley, T., & Mees, H. Application of operant conditioning procedures to the behavior problems of an autistic child. *Behavior Research & Therapy,* 1964, *1,* 305-12.

Wolfgang, M., Figlio, R., & Sellin, T. *Delinquency in a birth cohort.* Chicago: University of Chicago Press, 1972.

Wolpe, J. *The practice of behavior therapy.* New York: Pergamon Press, 1969.

Wyckoff, P. J. Communication skills training: A treatment of marital discord. Unpublished doctoral dissertation, Brigham Young University, 1978.

Zimmerman, A. R. The effects and effectiveness of a communication-oriented workshop in marital conflict resolution. Unpublished doctoral dissertation, University of Minnesota, 1978.

8

Moral Education

Deborah Zimmerman

One cannot follow moral principles if one does not understand (or believe in) moral principles. However, one can reason in terms of principles and not live up to these principles. . . . [F]actors additional to moral judgment are necessary for principled moral reasoning to be translated into "moral action."

—Kohlberg, 1973, p. 672

Those interested in the relationship between moral development and the prevention and control of aggression are continually confronted with a dilemma. While research indicates that the majority of American adolescents and young adults attain a conventional, "law and order" morality, which involves obedience of laws and the humane treatment of people, crime statistics show substantial and frequently increasing rates of overt aggressive behavior—juvenile delinquency, child abuse, and spouse abuse, to name a few. Why is it that many of the same persons who believe in being lawful and humane can also vandalize property, physically harm people, steal, lie, or cheat? This question clearly implies that a discrepancy may often exist between what one says one will do in a particular situation and what one actually does in that or a similar situation. An understanding of the roots of this discrepancy may provide the means by which effective prevention and intervention techniques can be implemented to alleviate the moral crisis in this country and the increasing rate of interpersonal aggression and other forms of criminal behavior.

The discussion will begin with a critical examination of Kohlberg's cognitive developmental theory of moral development. While other approaches to moral development have been generated, particularly within a social learning and psychoanalytic framework, Kohlberg's view is by far the most highly articulated and widely researched theory presently in existence. In addition, it's propositions have served as the foundation from which various interventions, specific to moral reasoning enhancement, have evolved. Although it is not within the scope of this discussion to critically evaluate and compare other approaches to moral development, the interested reader is referred to Sieber (1980) and Tice (1980) for an introduction to a social learning and psychoanalytic perspective of morality, respectively.

The second part of this chapter will address issues concerning the enhancement of moral reasoning through several intervention strategies, the distinction between moral and immoral behavior, and the relationship between moral reasoning and aggressive behavior. It will become apparent throughout the discussion that present theories of moral development are unable to explain the discrepancy between word and deed in real-life situations. Additional, and perhaps different, variables appear to be involved. Future research efforts must be directed toward the identification of these factors. The conclusion of the discussion will entail proposals for these research endeavors.

Kohlberg's Theory of Moral Reasoning

Over the last two decades Kohlberg's work has encompassed the systematic development, investigation, and refinement of a theory of moral reasoning. Using Piaget's cognitive developmental approach to moral development (Lickona, 1976; Piaget, 1932) and moral philosophy as the foundation for his theory, Kohlberg postulated that investigations of moral reasoning should encompass only those situations "in which conflicting interests and values lie and that morality involves reasoning and problem solving abilities which can be used to resolve these conflicts [Edelman & Goldstein, 1981, p. 286]." Specifying precisely what these reasoning and problem solving abilities involve has been a major focus of Kohlberg's work for many years. From this research, Kohlberg (1971a) was able to delineate three criteria which could be used to determine if an act or decision involved a moral component—prescriptivity, meaning that the decision originates from an internal sense of duty; universality, meaning that the ethical demands of the decision can be recognized by everyone; and primacy, describing the notion that nonmoral considerations are evaluated after moral ones have been examined. While Kohlberg maintains that these criteria provide some insight into the meaning of morality, it is not until the concept of justice is incorporated that its essence unfolds.

In fact, Kohlberg argues that morality can be conceptualized as the "principle of justice," which he describes as the basic understanding and acceptance of the value and equality of all human beings and as a reciprocity in all human interactions (Edelman & Goldstein, 1981). Specifically, Kohlberg (1979) states that:

> Justice is not a rule or a set of rules; it is a moral principle. By a moral principle we mean a mode of choosing which is universal, a rule of choosing which we want all people to adopt in all situations. . . . There are exceptions to rules, then, but no exception to principles. . . . There is only one principled basis for resolving claims: justice or equality. . . . A moral principle is not only a rule of action but a reason for action. As a reason for action, justice is called respect for persons. [pp. 69-70]

The importance of "justice" in Kohlberg's theory is further reflected in his description of the six stages of moral reasoning (see table 8.1), where it becomes apparent that a "sense of justice" becomes highly integrated and increasingly complex for individuals functioning at the most advanced level of moral reasoning.

It is important to note that Kohlberg does not believe that an individual reasons at only one stage in all situations. Rather, he sees people as reasoning primarily at one stage and secondarily at adjacent stages, either one stage below or above the predominate stage (Kohlberg, 1969). It is within this formulation that Kohlberg explains an individual's variability of responses to the Moral Judgment Interview (a method he developed to assess levels of moral development). This interview involves the presentation of a series of stories, all of which incorporate a moral dilemma which can be resolved by a number of alternative actions. Generally, the dilemma involves a conflict between behaving by conforming to authority figures or legal-

Table 8.1. Kohlberg's Six Stages of Moral Reasoning

I. PRECONVENTIONAL LEVEL

At this level, the child is responsive to cultural rules and labels of good and bad, right or wrong, but interprets these labels in terms of either the physical or the hedonistic consequences of action (punishment, reward, exchange of favors) or in terms of the physical power of those who enunciate the rules and labels. The level comprises the following two stages:

STAGE 1: PUNISHMENT AND OBEDIENCE ORIENTATION

The physical consequences of action determine its goodness or badness regardless of the human meaning or value of the consequences. Avoidance of punishment and unquestioning deference to power are valued in their own right, not in terms of respect for an underlying moral order supported by punishment and authority (the latter being stage 4).

STAGE 2: INSTRUMENTAL RELATIVIST ORIENTATION

Right action consists of that which instrumentally satisfies one's own needs and, occasionally the needs of others. Human relations are viewed in terms similar to those of the market place. Elements of fairness, or reciprocity, and equal sharing are present; but they are always interpreted in a physical pragmatic way. Reciprocity is a matter of "you scratch my back and I'll scratch yours," not of loyalty, gratitude, or justice.

II. CONVENTIONAL LEVEL

At this level, maintaining the expectations of the individual's family, group, or nation is perceived as valuable in its own right, regardless of immediate and obvious consequences. The attitude is one not only of *conformity* to personal expectations and social order, but of loyalty to it, of actively *maintaining,* supporting, and justifying the order and of identifying with the persons or groups involved in it. This level comprises the following two stages:

STAGE 3: INTERPERSONAL CONCORDANCE OR "GOOD BOY-NICE GIRL" ORIENTATION

Good behavior is that which pleases or helps others and is approved by them. There is much conformity to stereotypical images of what is majority or "natural" behavior. Behavior is frequently judged by intention: "he means well" becomes important for the first time. One earns approval by being "nice."

STAGE 4: "LAW AND ORDER" ORIENTATION

There is orientation toward authority, fixed rules, and the maintenance of the social order. Right behavior consists of doing one's duty, showing respect for authority, and maintaining the given social order for its own sake.

III. POST-CONVENTIONAL, AUTONOMOUS, OR PRINCIPLED LEVEL

At this level, there is a clear effort to define moral values and principles that have validity and application apart from the authority of the groups or persons holding these principles and apart from the individual's own identification with these groups. This level again has two stages:

STAGE 5: SOCIAL-CONTRACT LEGALISTIC ORIENTATION

Generally, this stage has utilitarian overtones. Right action tends to be defined in terms of general individual rights and in terms of standards that have been critically examined and agreed upon by the whole society. There is a clear awareness of the relativism of personal values and opinions and a corresponding emphasis on procedural rules for reaching consensus. Aside from what is constitutionally and democratically agreed upon, the right is a matter of personal "values" and "opinion." The result is an emphasis upon the "legal point of view," but with an emphasis upon the possibility of changing law in terms of rational considerations of social utility (rather than freezing it in terms of stage 4 "law and order"). Outside the legal realm, free agreement, and contract is the binding element of obligation. This is the "official" morality of the United States government and constitution.

STAGE 6: UNIVERSAL ETHICAL-PRINCIPLE ORIENTATION

Right is defined by the decision of conscience in accord with self-chosen *ethical principles* appealing to logical comprehensiveness, universality, and consistency. These principles are abstract and ethical (the Golden Rule, the categorical imperative); they are not concrete moral rules like the Ten Commandments. At heart, these are universal principles of justice, of the reciprocity and equality of human rights, and of respect for the dignity of human beings as individual persons.

Source: L. Kohlberg, "Stages of Moral Development as a Basis for Moral Education." In C. M. Beck, B. S. Crittendon, & E. V. Sullivan (Eds.), *Moral Education: Interdisciplinary Approaches.* New York: Newman Press, 1971, pp. 86-88.

social rules versus responding in accordance with the welfare or needs of others (Arbuthnot & Faust, 1981). The participant is asked to determine which action the character in the story should take and why. Through a series of probe questions, it is believed that the participant's decision-making processes concerning the resolution of these dilemmas as they relate to specific moral issues (i.e., value of human life, laws and rules, punishment and justice, truth and contract, property rights) could be ascertained. In addition, Kohlberg maintains that this technique can be used to investigate the major hypotheses underlying his theory.

In order to more fully understand Kohlberg's basic theoretical postulates, it is important to address the use of the cognitive-developmental approach in the specific area of moral development. First, unlike social learning or psychoanalytical approaches to moral development in which learned associations or emotions are emphasized respectively, the cognitive-developmental framework stresses cognition or thinking about rules, laws, and principles (Arbuthnot & Faust, 1981). Second, this approach clearly differentiates between the content and structure of moral reasoning, with the former reflecting "what" one is thinking (i.e., opinions, what one actually states in the reasoning process) and the latter referring to "how" one thinks (i.e., the thinking process which determines what one says) (Arbuthnot & Faust, 1981). This suggests that, although the content of an individual's response to a moral dilemma may vary, the structure or the reasoning process generally remains constant at a particular point in time. Furthermore, this idea implies that, while similarities may exist in the content of responses of, for example, a stage 1 and stage 2 person, the reasoning processes underlying the responses will be different.

Also basic to the cognitive-developmental approach is the notion of "stages." Kohlberg's hypothesis of distinct stages of moral development implies that, over the life span, there are qualitatively different ways of thinking and reasoning about moral issues (i.e., truth, justice, value of life). These qualitative changes are believed to emerge from transformations in the child's thought structure (Arbuthnot & Faust, 1981). Thus, at each successive stage of moral development, qualitative differences can be observed in the reasoning process. Implicit within this theory is the belief that these stages form an invariant sequence, with later stages representing more complex and abstract ways of reasoning (Kohlberg, 1973).

Evolving from the invariant sequence notion is the idea of hierarchical integrations, which has been described as a process in which the structures of an earlier stage serve as the building blocks for the structures of the next stage (Arbuthnot & Faust, 1981). While each successive stage represents a transformation of the preceding stage, the notion of hierarchical integrations also implies that each successive stage is more differentiated (i.e., more complex and more specialized) and more integrated (i.e., structured parts are better organized) than the prior stage.

Similar to the concept of hierarchical integrations, each stage is also believed to represent a structured whole, meaning that every stage reflects an organized system of thought (Kohlberg, 1973). Kohlberg's theory also posits that the "highest stage" represents the theoretically "ideal" endpoint of development, which may or may not be attained by all individuals depending upon a number of situational and personal factors (Edelman & Goldstein, 1981). And finally, the theory postulates that progression to more advanced stages is induced by cognitive conflict (Kohlberg, 1969).

It is the latter assumption which is particularly relevant to any clinical or research endeavor designed to enhance an individual's level of moral reasoning. Kohlberg (1969), Turiel (1974), and Piaget (1932) maintain that, through the child's interpersonal interactions with adults and peers, he/she is increasingly exposed to value conflictual situations which ultimately leads to cognitive conflict. Resolution of this conflict requires the child to experiment with alternative ways of reasoning which are typically representative of the next higher stage of moral judgment. This suggests that environmental stimulation may promote, within certain limits, the development of moral reasoning (Arbuthnot & Faust, 1981).

In addition, the literature suggests that critical periods exist in which the child must actively explore other means of dealing with his/her environment in order to prevent fixation at more developmentally immature levels (Kohlberg, 1969; Piaget, 1932; Turiel, 1974). For example, Kohlberg and Kramer's (1969) research indicates that, for Americans, one such critical or transitional period occurs between the ages of 10 and 13. It is during this period that a child typically moves from a preconventional to a conventional level of moral reasoning. Furthermore, they suggest that it is important for children to exhibit at least some conventional moral reasoning during this period in order to prevent fixation at a preconventional level. These ideas—that environmental stimulation can enhance moral reasoning and that critical transitional periods exist in the developmental sequence—suggest that the success of an intervention designed to promote moral reasoning may lie, in part, on the "readiness" of the individual to progress to higher stages of moral judgment. However, before a discussion of the literature concerning moral reasoning interventions is addressed, a critical evaluation of the empirical investigation of Kohlberg's basic theoretical postulations will be presented.

THE INVESTIGATION OF KOHLBERG'S BASIC PROPOSITIONS

A number of studies have provided empirical support for the basic hypotheses proposed by Kohlberg. Over the course of a longitudinal investigation of lower and middle-class American boys, between the ages of 10 and 16, Kramer (1968) and Kohlberg and Kramer (1969) found that moral reasoning did progress sequentially through six stages. In fact, the longitudinal data suggest that, although the time period between testings was four years, allowing the participants to move through more than one stage during that interval, only 10 percent of the people evidenced changes beyond one stage. The results also indicated that relatively few participants reached the highest stage of moral development and that the rate of development varied for different individuals. Similar results have also been found by Turiel (1966) in an investigation of individual's reasoning at Kohlberg's stages 2, 3, or 4, and by Lee (1971). Using 5 to 8 year old children, Kuhn (1976) also found progression to the subsequent stage at a one year follow-up.

Kohlberg's (Kohlberg & Kramer, 1969; Kohlberg & Turiel, 1971; Turiel, Edwards, & Kohlberg, 1977) cross-cultural research, which included the countries of Mexico, Turkey, India, Taiwan, Israel, and Canada, also provided support for the invariant sequence hypothesis. For instance, the results of studies involving 10, 13, and 16-year-old urban, middle-class boys of the United States, Mexico, and Taiwan and a comparable age group of boys in villages in Turkey and the Yucatan indicated that the predicted age-related changes occurred (when the changes occurred at all) in all of the boys regardless of country. Based on these studies, Kohlberg and his collaborators concluded that the invariant sequence hypothesis was culturally universal, even though rates of development and highest stage attained remained variable (lower for comparable groups in Turkey and the Yucatan). They also maintain that these results support the notion that all individuals reason about similar moral values (i.e., life, love, laws, contract, and punishment), regardless of culture or subculture. These conclusions have aroused extensive and diverse criticism in the literature. While each of these objections will be addressed in detail later in the discussion, at this time it is important to note that some of the criticisms are based upon methodological flaws, particularly in the scoring techniques developed and utilized by the Kohlberg group in these studies. Since that time, scoring methods have been revised and used in at least one reported replication study (Nisan & Kohlberg, 1978). In this study, the predicted sequence was found for both longitudinal and cross-sectional data.

Further support for the invariant sequence hypothesis is provided by studies which have suggested that moral judgment is significantly correlated with age (Grinder, 1964; Stuart, 1967; Whiteman & Kosier, 1964). Specifically, Colby, Kohlberg, and Gibbs (1979) found that while at age 10 approximately 63 percent of the child's statements reflect stage 2 reasoning, by age 24-26 only 5 percent of the statements reflect this stage. The results also indicated that there is an increase of stage 3 reasoning with age, but that it decreases by the end of adolescence, and that stage 4 reasoning emerges at approximately age 13-14 and increases with age. Other researchers have found similar distributions of stage responses (Arbuthnot, 1973, 1975; Arbuthnot & Faust, 1981; Faust & Arbuthnot, 1978; Haan, Smith, & Block, 1968; Kohlberg & Kramer, 1969). In studying these percentages, it is important to recognize that individual differences exist, with some of this variation accounted for by such factors as SES, intelligence, and education. Thus, the percentages presented are most appropriately viewed as rough estimations of the relationship between age and moral reasoning stage.

Related to the invariant sequence hypothesis is the question of the possibility of regression in moral stages. It has been suggested that further support for the invariant sequence hypothesis can be advanced if this regression is not noted. At this time, there is considerable debate among researchers on this question. A number of investigators have observed a regression in moral reasoning (from stage 5 to stage 2), particularly among college students (Haan, Smith, & Block, 1968; Holstein, 1976; Kohlberg & Kramer, 1969; Kramer, 1968; Turiel, 1974). In studying this phenomenon, Kohlberg and Kramer (1969) noted that it generally appears among middle-class students, between late high school and the early years of college, and that their moral reasoning scores during high school are quite advanced (mixture of stage 4 and stage 5 reasoning) in comparison to their age-related peers. Theoretically, Turiel (1974) and Kohlberg and Kramer (1969) argue that what appears to be a regression really reflects a transitional period, during which the individual experiments with alternative ways of reasoning about moral issues, and which ultimately leads to the enhancement of the moral structure. They maintain that the structure does not regress, even though the content of the individual's response may resemble that of a stage 2 reasoner. In support of this contention, Kohlberg and Kramer (1969) report that all of their participants who had evidenced stage regression had returned to, at least, a mixture of stage 4 and stage 5 reasoning, and in some cases elicited dominant stage 5 reasoning. Although these results in conjunction with the study utilizing the revised scoring technique and those indicating positive correlations between age and moral reasoning suggest that the invariant sequence hypothesis is still tenable in spite of the observed regressions in college students, more updated research is needed to validate this postulate.

The results of studies in the area of stage regression strongly imply that individuals are capable of lower stage reasoning even after progressing to higher stages. It is important to note that this idea is clearly reflected in some of Kohlberg's other theoretical hypotheses, and in the empirical investigations evolving from them. For example, while the structural whole hypothesis has been supported to some extent, most of the research evidence indicates that individuals reason at more than one stage at specific points in time (Arbuthnot & Faust, 1981; Kohlberg, 1973). In fact, the results suggest that generally 50 percent of the individual's reasoning reflects the dominant stage, with the remaining statements representing reasoning at adjacent stages (either a lower or higher stage).

Concerning the hierarchical integration hypothesis, many studies have shown that individuals understand reasoning at or below their own stage, but not more than one stage above their own (Rest, 1979; Rest, Turiel, & Kohlberg, 1969; Turiel, 1966). Rest (1979), for instance, asked adolescents to rewrite a number of moral statements in their own words and then to rank order them in terms of preference. The results indicated that participants correctly rewrote statements up to and representative of their own stage of reasoning, but not beyond that stage. However, although they were capable of comprehending reasoning below their own stage, participants typically gave these responses low preference ratings and preferred statements which reflected reasoning one stage higher than their present reasoning skills. Statements two stages beyond present reasoning ability were also given low preference scores. The fact that lower stage reasoning continues to be understood but not preferred has important implications for the development of measures of moral reasoning, a point which will be addressed in the following evaluative section of Kohlberg's theory.

A CRITICAL ANALYSIS OF KOHLBERG'S THEORY AND RESEARCH

A number of investigators have criticized Kohlberg's work on methodological, theoretical, and philosophical grounds. Most of these objections have evolved from the universally invariant sequence hypothesis, which Kohlberg claims has received support from both his 17-year longitudinal study and his cross-cultural work. Throughout these investigations, however, Kohlberg and his colleagues utilized the "aspect scoring system" for determining the participant's modal reasoning stage. Kurtines and Grief (1974) have criticized this scoring system on the basis of a lack of standardization of administration and scoring methods which they claim has resulted in a lack of support for the validity and reliability of the Moral Judgment Interview. They also maintain that Kohlberg's failure to provide information concerning the interrater reliabilities emerging from his longitudinal research, his failure to specify the number of dilemmas used, and the lack of a published scoring manual has made it difficult to investigate the theory by researchers outside his immediate group.

As mentioned previously, when Kohlberg and other researchers found data dissonant to the invariant sequence hypothesis, they proceeded to modify the original scoring system. What emerged was a new scoring system, called "issue scoring." While the Kohlberg group maintains that these modifications are necessary to the process of validating a theory, others argue that Kohlberg cannot continually refine his scoring methods (Fraenkel, 1976). If Kohlberg is to continually change his scoring system, he must publicly make these changes available so that other researchers can discern the inconsistencies between his early and later research, whether this research is longitudinal or cross-cultural in nature (Edelman & Goldstein, 1981). Since these criticisms, the Kohlberg group has developed a scoring manual which is available to the public. They have also begun to report reliability scores, making it easier for researchers to examine the status of Kohlberg's work.

The scoring of the Kohlberg interview is a time consuming and complex procedure which encompasses consideration of both the norms (previously called issues) and elements of moral reasoning. Norms refer to the values the individual is reasoning about and "reflect the distinctions considered important by sociologists in representing the different central norms or values of any social system [Kohlberg, 1978, p. 11]." Twelve norms have been identified which are believed to encompass any type of moral statement a person may make. They include life, property, truth, affiliation, authority, law, contract, conscience, punishment, erotic love and sex, civil rights, and religion. The Kohlberg group maintains that it is necessary to consider the norms involved in moral reasoning in order to avoid misclassifying a response due to the confusion of content and structure. The importance of identifying the norm active in an individual's reasoning process is clearly reflected by the research which suggests that differential rates of development may occur for different norms (Arbuthnot & Faust, 1981). Thus, any analysis of moral reasoning stage must consider the norms presented in the dilemma.

Utilization of the elements of morality is believed to be important to help discern how an individual "construes the importance or meaning of a norm [Kohlberg, 1978, p. 11]." Seventeen elements have been identified, some of which are obeying (consulting) persons, blaming (approving), good (bad) reputation, seeking reward (avoiding punishment), upholding character, balancing perspectives, and maintaining equity and procedural fairness. By identifying the norms and elements of a moral response prior to classifying the specific moral stage used, the Kohlberg group believes reliability efforts will be enhanced.

In fact, when reliability coefficients have been reported, they have been quite high. For example, test-retest reliabilities have yielded correlations ranging from .96-.99 for Form A and .97 for Form B (three forms exist within the issue scoring procedure). Percent agreement figures within one-third stage have also been good, with scores ranging from 93 to 94 percent for Form A and Form B respectively, and 100 percent for the two forms combined. However, lower percent agreement figures were obtained when using nine categories (pure stage and mixed stage scores)—Form A = 70-77 percent; Form B = 75 percent; Forms A and B = 80 percent; or 13 categories (using minor/major stage differentiations)—Form A = 59-70 percent; Form B = 62 percent; Forms A and B = 70 percent. The interrater reliability correlation on both Form A and Form B test-retest interviews was approximately .98 (Colby, Kohlberg, & Gibbs, 1979).

Although the reliability coefficients just cited imply that the Kohlberg issue scoring procedure has some utility for assessing moral reasoning, it has been suggested that other measures may be more appropriate to use in short-term intervention research and for capturing the issues relevant to a specific developmental age range (Carroll & Nelson, 1979). Thus, while Kohlberg's measure may prove to be valuable for long-term developmental investigations, its value may not be as pronounced for evaluating the effectiveness of various intervention programs or for a specific age range. Some support for this contention has been provided by Carroll and Nelson (1979), Carroll and Rest (1981), Rest (1979), and Enright (1980). These researchers have proposed or developed measures of moral reasoning designed to incorporate these intervention and age range considerations. While it is not within the scope of this discussion to address these measures, the interested reader is referred to the aforementioned sources for a detailed discussion of their rationale and empirical bases. It is important, however, to reiterate that, even though reliabilities are adequate for the revised scoring system, the fact remains that many of Kohlberg's theoretical conclusions were based upon studies utilizing the old scoring method. This implies that any interpretation based upon these studies must be advanced with extreme caution, and that attention should be directed toward reanalyzing the original work using the new scoring method.

Thus far, the discussion has centered upon criticisms of Kohlberg's unstandardized administration protocol and scoring technique, and the utility of his assessment procedure for research other than longitudinal developmental studies (criticism 1). Many other objections have been noted in the literature. In relation to Kohlberg's cross-cultural studies, critics have commented on his failure to specify subject characteristics, sample sizes, or the methods used to establish the moral stages in different cultures (Kurtines & Grief, 1974); his failure to adequately sample diverse cultures to support his claim of universality (Fraenkel, 1976; Simpson, 1974); his failure to determine if the values captured by the Moral Judgment Interview are deemed important within the particular culture investigated (criticism 2—this criticism is basic to the universal moral values assumption) (Simpson, 1974). He has been criticized for his failure to provide sufficient empirical support that a stage 6 (postconventional reasoning level) even exists within the cultures studied (criticism 3) (Simpson, 1974). Finally, although not related solely to the cross-cultural research, are philosophical objections to Kohlberg's description of the stage 6 "ideal" moral individual (criticism 4) (Peters, 1978; Simpson, 1974). Additional criticisms to Kohlberg's theory have emerged from the moral relativists (Raths, Harmin, & Simon, 1966), who maintain that moral principles are subjective, that values are not universal, and that Kohlberg's position of the "moral superiority" of the stage 6 reasoner is an elitist point of view.

It is apparent that many of these criticisms call into question a number of Kohlberg's basic theoretical premises. Recently, supporters of the Kohlberg approach have made concerted efforts to respond to these criticisms. Concerning objections involving methodological and assessment issues (criticisms 1 and 2), efforts have been made to more rigorously specify subject characteristics, sample sizes, and administration and scoring protocols, and, as previously mentioned, to develop new measures which tap broader aspects of moral reasoning. Specification of these procedures has enhanced opportunities for replication efforts.

The moderation of the criticisms concerning the existence of stage 6 reasoning (criticism 3) and of descriptions of the stage 6 reasoner as the "ideal" moral individual (criticism 4) cannot be so briefly summarized because, in contrast to the former objections which represent methodological problems, the latter two involve theoretical considerations. In fact, attempts to resolve them have emerged primarily from philosophical sources. Edelman and Goldstein (1981) describe the stage 6 individual as:

> [s]omeone who, in a totally rational and impartial way, considers and reasons through the conflicting interests and values of different individuals on the basis of an abstract respect for the universal equal rights of all people . . . this definition of the highest stage of moral development neglects or minimizes the importance of concrete moral habits . . . regulation in the way people behave or respond to certain social situations (Alston, 1971) and basic moral feelings . . . compassion, caring, guilt (Peters, 1978)—two aspects of morality which, along with moral reasoning, are necessary for actual moral *behavior*. [p. 308]

Thus, not only is there little empirical support for the existence of the stage 6 individual (Edelman & Goldstein, 1981), but even if reasoning of this form does occur, it does not necessarily represent an "ideal" way to think. Although objections to Kohlberg's lack of consideration of "moral habits and moral feelings" have primarily revolved around the stage 6 individual, it is suggested that it is a valid criticism for all six of the moral reasoning stages. Consequently, in line with Wilson's (1973) and Edelman & Goldstein's (1981) suggestion, an adequate definition of morality must incorporate its cognitive, affective, and behavioral components.

Wilson (1973), unlike Kohlberg, is one of the few investigators in the area of morality who has considered all three of these components. Briefly, he suggests that morality is comprised of the following aspects:

> 1. Concern and respect for other people as equals and consideration of the needs of others, as well as oneself. One attains these values by having the concept of a person which involves the recognition of the similarities and differences among human beings (cognitive component), claiming the concept as a moral principle by determining if the individual believes this is an important concept to use (cognitive component), by rule-supported feelings by determining if the person has any feelings of respect and consideration attached to human beings (affective component) and by helping others as a means of reflecting these feelings (behavioral component).

2. Awareness of feelings in oneself and others by determining if the individual has the concept of emotion (cognitive component) and the ability to identify and label emotions in oneself and others (affective and cognitive component).

3. Assessing the individual's knowledge of relevant hard facts (i.e., physical health, safety, laws) and the sources of these facts (does the person have the knowledge to make moral decisions?).

4. Determination of the individual's ability to use the above components to make decisions in various moral situations (cognitive component).

5. Assessment of the person's ability to translate the moral decision into overt behavior (behavioral component). [pp. 41-64]

It is apparent that, while Wilson's definition encompasses the three major aspects of morality, its complexity and vagueness make it difficult to utilize in investigations of moral reasoning. To fill this gap, Edelman and Goldstein (1981) have offered another definition of morality, using Wilson's component analysis as its foundation:

Morality involves those skills, values and abilities that comprise (1) thinking or reasoning (problem solving, decision making) in a rational way, while (2) showing an awareness of, and consideration for the needs, interests and feelings of others as well as oneself, and (3) behaving constructively, i.e., in ways that benefit both self and others, in the problematic or conflictual social-interpersonal situations which one encounters in one's daily interactions with other people. Morality, then, involves cognitive (thinking), affective (feeling), and behavioral (doing) aspects which are necessarily interrelated. . . . [p. 259]*

It must also be noted that this definition does not in any way negate Kohlberg's conception of morality. Rather, this definition serves to include, yet transcend, Kohlberg's original ideas. In addition, it attempts to moderate those criticisms emerging from Kohlberg's belief in the "ideal" stage 6 reasoning individual by incorporating the affective dimension of morality.

The discussion thus far has focused on Kohlberg's theoretical formulations, its associated research, and the criticisms emerging from both aspects. Many other studies conducted in the area of moral reasoning are based upon Kohlberg's theory but do not directly address his basic theoretical propositions. Their relevance to the present discussion lies in their ability to shed light on the crucial question, namely, the discrepancy between word and act. As this research is presented, it is important to recognize that the majority of these studies utilize Kohlberg's Moral Judgment Interview and older scoring technique. As such, it is suggested that they, too, may suffer from many of the same methodological flaws and objections that have been associated with Kohlberg's work. Thus, any conclusions emerging from the research to be presented must be viewed with the same caution as that exercised in examining Kohlberg's work.

RELATED RESEARCH IN MORAL REASONING

A number of investigators have explored the notion that, although "moral structures" are not synonymous with the "cognitive structures" proposed by Piaget, the process of moral development is related to and proceeds in a parallel fashion to cognitive development. The notion of parallel, yet distinct, processes of development is also implicit within Kohlberg's

---

*While the functional value of this definition for research purposes remains untested, it is clear that Edelman and Goldstein (1981) have succeeded in decreasing the ambiguity evident in Wilson's (1973) description of morality.

(1973) writings. In fact, significant correlations between cognitive levels, as measured by Piagetian tasks, and morality levels have been found by Arbuthnot (1973); Faust and Arbuthnot (1978); Harris, Mussen, and Rutherford (1976); Lee (1971); and Tomlinson-Keasy and Keasy (1974). Both Kohlberg (1973, 1976) and the latter authors even suggest that more advanced cognitive operations are a prerequisite to more complex moral judgment (i.e., cognitive stage delimits the moral stage attained), and that there is a discrepancy between the acquisition of logical operations and their application in moral situations. This discrepancy emerges because moral reasoning involves additional thinking processes above and beyond those required for a specific cognitive operation. Specifically, Kohlberg maintains that, while the concrete operational child is limited to reasoning at preconventional levels, the child who exhibits some formal operational thinking can reason at conventional levels. Table 8.2 depicts this hypothesized relationship between cognitive and moral stages.

Thus, cognitive abilities can be viewed as representing "necessary but not sufficient conditions for the development of moral reasoning skills [Arbuthnot & Faust, 1981, p. 49]." Further support for this idea has been provided by Faust and Arbuthnot (1978) and Sparling, Arbuthnot, Faust, and Key (1978). In these studies, greater advance in moral reasoning following a Moral Education program was found for those individual's functioning at higher cognitive levels. This suggests that the success of any program designed to enhance moral reasoning may, in part, be a function of the participant's level of cognitive operations.

Other factors which have been found to be significantly correlated with moral judgment are intelligence, with the coefficients ranging from .30 to .55 (Arbuthnot, 1973; Faust & Arbuthnot, 1978; Harris, Mussen, & Rutherford, 1976; Johnson, 1962; Kohlberg, 1964, 1969; Stuart, 1967; Whiteman & Kosier, 1964); parental attitudes (Johnson, 1962); self-confidence, security in social relationships with peers, and a reputation for being concerned with the welfare of others (Harris, Musson, & Rutherford, 1976); and egocentrism (Lee, 1971; Rubin & Schneider, 1973; Selman, 1971, 1980; Stuart, 1967; Ugurel-Semin, 1952).

It is the latter variable which is of particular relevance to this discussion. The association between egocentrism or perspective-taking and moral reasoning can be easily discerned from

Table 8.2.   Relationships Between Logical and Moral Stages

PIAGETIAN LOGICAL STAGE		MORAL STAGE
Preoperational; Concrete Operations (A) (physicalistic absolutism; categorical classification)	⟶	Stage 1 (punishment-obedience orientation)
Concrete Operations (B) (reciprocity, relativity)	⟶	Stage 2 (instrumental-relativist orientation)
Beginning Formal Operations (inverse of reciprocal)	⟶	Stage 3 (interpersonal concordance orientation)
Basic Formal Operations (A) * (total system perspective)	⟶	Stage 4 (legalistic-authority orientation)
Basic Formal Operations (B) * (consolidation of ability to separate variables; generalize; and formulate principles)	⟶	Stage 5 (social contract; higher law orientation)

*These relationships are speculative in the absence of data employing current scoring techniques for moral stages.
Source: J. B. Arbuthnot and A. Faust, *Teaching Moral Reasoning: Theory and Practice* New York: Harper & Row, 1981, p. 132.

Kohlberg's description of the moral stages (see Table 8.1). In fact, both Selman (1980) and Arbuthnot and Faust (1981) maintain that social perspective-taking represents one aspect of moral stage reasoning, so that, for example, at the preconventional level the perspective is restricted to one's own thoughts and expectations. Typically, this child will not recognize that others may have different thoughts, expectations, or intentions from their own. As Arbuthnot and Faust (1981) state, "there is you and there is I and there might be she, but we are not a group . . . in moral reasoning they think in individual rather than in group terms [p. 121]." Within the preconventional level, the major difference between the stage 1 and stage 2 reasoner in social perspective is that the latter and not the former understands the concept of mutuality or an awareness of the other's viewpoint. Nevertheless, the stage 2 social perspective remains hedonistic in nature, so that if a mutual agreement between two people does not exist, it is still morally acceptable to act in one's own self-interest. Thus, the welfare of others is only considered if one's own welfare is also preserved.

In contrast, at the conventional level, the child can understand the notion of interpersonal relationships and group membership. The reasoning of the conventional individual is such that sincere concern about the feelings of others and the welfare of society is kept in mind. One's needs are subordinated to the needs of others, and what is morally right is what supports or is determined by the society. The primary difference between the stage 3 and stage 4 reasoner is reflected in the former's conception of the "good group" and the latter's recognition of the "social good" (the entire society). As such, for the stage 3 reasoner, the viewpoint of all the group members is considered, behavior often reflects that which is acceptable to all group members, and relationships are viewed as something shared between people (Arbuthnot & Faust, 1981). The stage 4 reasoner transcends this conception of relationships by incorporating the notion of the impact the relationship has on the entire social group. Consequently, one behaves in ways that promote the society. For the individual reasoning at the postconventional level, the social perspective endorses the notion of universality because the principle of justice is applied to all individuals in all societies, regardless of whether society supports it or not. Table 8.3 summarizes the hypothesized relationship between stage of moral reasoning and social perspective.

A number of investigations have directly examined the relationship between moral reasoning and perspective-taking. Stuart (1967) extended the Piagetian notion of decentration into the area of moral judgment. Following Piaget's idea that decentration or "the ability to shift the given cognitive perspective" is one of the mechanisms needed for stage transition, Stuart hypothesized that the ability to shift perspective allows the child to move from objective to subjective moral judgments. Conversely, he hypothesized that all children capable of mature moral judgments would possess the ability to decentrate. The results of this study did, in fact, indicate that, among children in grades 2, 4, 6, and 8, the ability to decenter was significantly related to levels of moral reasoning. In addition, he suggests that "training in decentration may aid children in moving more swiftly toward cognitive maturity [p. 67]." Similarly, Selman (1971) found that the development of role-taking skills, which requires the ability to decenter or perspective-take, is significantly related to the development of conventional moral reasoning in children between the ages of 8 and 10. However, a follow-up report one year later on 10 participants whose role-taking and moral judgment level were originally low indicated that, while the ability to role-take is necessary for conventional moral thought, it is not a sufficient condition. Consequently, Selman suggests that perspective-taking in and of itself is not enough to promote transition to more advanced levels of moral judgment.

Thus, while the results of these studies indicate that the ability to perspective-take is positively related to levels of moral reasoning, one must also consider the potential relationship between these two variables and cognitive ability. Arbuthnot and Faust (1981) suggest that

Table 8.3. The Six Moral Judgment Stages

	CONTENT OF STAGE		
LEVEL AND STAGE	WHAT IS RIGHT	REASONS FOR DOING RIGHT	SOCIAL PERSPECTIVE
Level I — Preconventional Stage I — Heteronomous Morality	To avoid breaking rules backed by punishment, obedience for its own sake, and avoiding physical damage to persons and property.	Avoidance of punishment, and the superior power of authorities.	*Egocentric point of view.* Doesn't consider the interests of others or recognize that they differ from the actor's; doesn't relate two points of view. Actions are considered physically rather than in terms of psychological interests of others. Confusion of authority's perspective with one's own.
Stage 2 — Individualism, Instrumental Purpose, and Exchange	Following rules only when it is to someone's immediate interest; acting to meet one's own interests and needs and letting others do the same. Right is also what's fair, what's an equal exchange, a deal, an agreement	To serve one's own needs or interests in a world where you have to recognize that other people have their interests, too.	*Concrete individualistic perspective.* Aware that everybody has his own interest to pursue and these conflict, so that right is relative (in the concrete individualistic sense).
Level II — Conventional Stage 3 — Mutual Interpersonal Expectations, Relationships, and Interpersonal Conformity	Living up to what is expected by people close to you or what people generally expect of people in your role as son, brother, friend, etc. "Being good" is important and means having good motives and means having good motives, showing concern about others. It also means keeping mutual relationships, such as trust, loyalty, respect, and gratitude.	The need to be a good person in your own eyes and those of others. Your caring for others. Belief in the Golden Rule. Desire to maintain rules and authority which support stereotypical good behavior.	*Perspective of the individual in relationships with other individuals.* Aware of shared feelings, agreements, and expectations which take primacy over individual interests. Relates points of view through the concrete Golden Rule, putting yourself in the other guy's shoes. Does not yet consider generalized system perspective.

Stage 4 — Social System and Conscience	Fulfilling the actual duties to which you have agreed. Laws are to be upheld except in extreme cases where they conflict with other fixed social duties. Right is also contributing to society, the group, or institution.	To keep the institution going as a whole, to avoid the breakdown in the system "if everyone did it," or the imperative of conscience to meet one's defined obligations. (Easily confused with stage 3 belief in rules and authority).	*Differentiates societal point of view from interpersonal agreement or motives.* Takes the point of view of the system that defines roles and rules. Considers individual relations in terms of place in the system.
Level III — Post-Conventional, or Principled Stage 5 — Social Contract or Utility and Individual Rights	Being aware that people hold a variety of values and opinions, that most values and rules are relative to your group. These relative rules should usually be upheld, however, in the interest of impartiality and because they are the social contract. Some nonrelative values and rights like *life* and *liberty*, however, must be upheld in any society and regardless of majority opinion.	A sense of obligation to law because of one's social contract to make and abide by laws for the welfare of all and for the protection of all people's rights. A feeling of contractual commitment, freely enhanced upon, to family, friendship, trust, and work obligations. Concern that laws and duties be based on rational calculation of overall utility, "the greatest good for the greatest number."	*Prior-to-society perspective.* Perspective of a rational individual aware of values and rights prior to social attachments and contracts. Integrates perspectives by formal mechanisms of agreement, contract, objective impartiality, and due process. Considers moral and legal points of view; recognizes that they sometimes conflict and finds it difficult to integrate them.
Stage 6 — Universal Ethical Principles	Following self-chosen ethical principles. Particular laws or social agreements are usually valid because they rest on such principles. When laws violate these principles, one acts in accordance with the principle. Principles are universal principles of justice: the equality of human rights and respect for the dignity of human beings as individual persons.	The belief as a rational person in the validity of universal moral principles, and a sense of personal commitment to them.	*Perspective of a moral point of view* from which social arrangements derive. Perspective is that of any rational individual recognizing the nature of morality or the fact that persons are ends in themselves and must be treated as such.

Source: L. Kohlberg, "Moral Stages and Moralization: The Cognitive-Developmental Approach," in T. Lickona, ed., *Moral Development and Behavior* (New York: Holt, Rhinehart, & Winston, 1976), pp. 34–35.

223

each cognitive stage permits the development of more advanced role-taking stages and the latter, in turn, makes an enhancement in moral reasoning possible. In addition, they suggest that large differences can exist between a cognitive and role-taking stage, and between a role-taking and moral stage. However, they also maintain that these differences are generally much larger between cognitive and role-taking stages than between role-taking and moral stages. While the latter ideas remain speculative, the evidence clearly suggests that both cognitive and perspective-taking ability may have an impact on the efficacy of moral intervention programs. The following section involves a critical examination of a number of these interventions. By integrating the ideas developed in Kohlberg's theory, the research involving the relationship between cognitive, perspective-taking, and moral reasoning ability, and what will emerge in the subsequent discussion, clues concerning the roots of the word-act discrepancy will become apparent.

MORAL INTERVENTION PROGRAMS

Since the 1920s, researchers within the moral reasoning domain have extended their work into the intervention realm. This move was prompted by the belief that the traditional institutions—family, religion, and the schools—were no longer successful in preparing children for the moral conflicts they were confronted with (Arbuthnot & Faust, 1981; Edelman & Goldstein, 1981). Many researchers claim that these institutions promote rule-oriented reasoning (equating morality to conformity to conventions), rather than reasoning based on principles of justice (Arbuthnot & Faust, 1981; Edelman & Goldstein, 1981). Thus, when the rules of society change, the individual's rule-oriented reasoning no longer helps him/her to adequately resolve moral conflicts, and a "moral crisis" may ensue. A moral crisis is characterized by an increased frequency of anti-social behavior and value confusion, and a discrepancy between one's behavior and verbalized values. It emerges not only from questioning *what* values are worthwhile, but also from questioning *how* to apply values in specific situations or when values conflict with each other (Arbuthnot & Faust, 1981; Edelman & Goldstein, 1981). Consequently, techniques were developed with the primary goal of enhancing moral reasoning and the secondary goal of reducing anti-social behavior. Most of the procedures were designed so as to be utilized within school settings, and thus became movements in their own right (Character Education, Values Clarification, and Moral Education). In addition, some researchers have examined the efficacy of role-playing techniques for the enhancement of levels of moral reasoning.*

Role-Playing Techniques

One of the most utilized strategies for inducing change in moral reasoning has been through the implementation of role-playing procedures. Tracy and Cross (1973), using a population of 12-15 year old boys, first matched participants in pairs on morality scores, as measured by the Kohlberg interview technique. Subsequently, they randomly assigned these pairs to an experimental condition (exposure through role-playing to moral reasoning one stage above their dominant stage) or a no-treatment condition. The results indicated that treatment effectiveness was associated with initial levels of moral reasoning. Specifically, participants who ini-

---

*In the following discussion attention will be primarily directed toward Kohlberg's Moral Education procedure since his theory has been the focus of this chapter. The other three procedures will be addressed briefly so as to provide the reader with a sense of continuity within the moral intervention area.

tially scored at preconventional levels showed more improvement (more movement to higher levels of moral reasoning) than those originally responding at the conventional level. The authors suggest that a ceiling effect may exist for the treatments used in their study, implying that when the initial level of moral reasoning is relatively high (stage 3), the amount of change to be expected is diminished. This suggestion concurs with Blatt's (1970) finding of the inability to modify reasoning beyond conventional levels. It can also be suggested that movement beyond conventional reasoning, in both of these studies, did not occur as a result of a lack of participants thinking at a formal operational level. Nevertheless, the results of the former study indicate that moral reasoning can be enhanced, within limits, through role-playing.

Similar results were found by Arbuthnot (1975) in a study comparing the efficacy of a role-playing group (again this involved role-playing with someone reasoning at one or two stages above the participant's initially assessed level) with two control groups who either performed extraneous tasks or passively observed role-playing arguments. The results indicated that participants in the role-playing condition evidenced more immediate and delayed increases in moral reasoning as compared to participants in the two control groups, and that more change was observed for those who initially scored at lower levels of moral reasoning. However, in a study involving 11 and 12-year-old children, no differences were found between two role-playing groups and a passive listening group, although an overall change in moral concepts was found for all groups (Matefy & Acksen, 1976). In addition, exposure to moral positions two stages above the participant's initial level was more effective in producing change than exposure to positions one stage above initial levels.

It is important not to overlook the fact that the treatment conditions employed in these studies involved not only role-playing, but role-playing with people functioning at either one or two stages above the participant's initial level of moral reasoning. Thus, the evidence suggests that the role-playing process must provide examples of more advanced levels of moral reasoning. Just how much more advanced is a question which remains unanswered. Some researchers (Dubinsky, 1976; Keasey, 1973; Rest, Turiel, & Kohlberg, 1969; Turiel, 1966) suggest that one stage above the initial level is the most beneficial because it provides only moderately discrepant positions. For example, in the Rest, Turiel, and Kohlberg (1969) study, only those individuals asked to rephrase statements one stage beyond initial levels showed an increase in moral reasoning. Those receiving statements one stage below or two stages above initial reasoning levels did not show advancement in moral reasoning. In addition, while those participants who were exposed to one stage higher statements and who were asked to rephrase the statements advanced in moral reasoning, those who were passively exposed to one stage higher statements did not evidence this advance. Thus, these results suggest that active participation (similar to role-playing), in conjunction with exposure to one stage higher statements, is an effective method for enhancing moral reasoning. However, while these investigators tend to support Kohlberg's invariant sequence hypothesis, other research (Arbuthnot, 1975) suggests that it makes no difference if the reasoning is presented at one or two stages above the participant's initial level of reasoning. Clearly, this question remains an important area of inquiry.

Character Education

One of the earliest procedures developed to enhance moral qualities in school settings was Character Education,* with its primary goal being the development of the "moral character" of children. Moral character is typically described in terms of character traits (i.e., honesty,

---

*Character Education involves the teaching of specific values through such methods as class discussion, role playing, written exercises, and games.

altruism, responsibility), values, or standards of ethical conduct which are believed to be important to the welfare of the individual and society (Edelman & Goldstein, 1981). Those promoting the Character Education movement argue that the direct teaching of specific values in elementary schools will decrease the aggression prevalent in American society (Goble, 1973; Mayer, 1964; Trevitt, 1964). In fact, anecdotal evidence relevant to a number of programs—"The Good American Program" (Mayer, 1964); "As I Am, So Is My Nation" (Trevitt, 1964); "Character Education Curriculum" (American Institute for Character Education as cited in Edelman & Goldstein, 1981)—suggests that Character Education can be an effective technique for decreasing cheating behavior and increasing cooperative behavior. The rationale underlying the Character Education Curriculum, for example, is that, if children can learn to consider the consequences of their behavior, they will then choose to behave in ways beneficial to both themselves and society. Thus, the teaching of specific values within the Character Education Curriculum is achieved by helping students understand their utility as a framework from which moral decisions can be made. The interested reader is referred to the aforementioned sources, as well as to Bain and Clark (1966), Hill (1965), and Edelman and Goldstein (1981) for an excellent discussion of the history, rationale, curriculum, and methods of Character Education procedures.

This notion of "teaching specific values" has aroused considerable criticism from the public and the educational and psychological community. Many maintain that the teaching of particular values involves indoctrination, which Edelman and Goldstein (1981) described as "the teaching of certain values, attitudes or beliefs without due regard to thoughtful reflection and direct, open inquiry and discussion concerning their reasonableness and worth in light of other, alternative values or beliefs [p. 260]." Based on this definition, it seems that whether or not indoctrination occurs depends upon the procedures used to teach these values (Edelman & Goldstein, 1981). Thus, while procedures that do not permit reflection or inquiry are unwarrantable, those that teach values in ways which promote these aspects are believed to be desirable. In addition, critics have objected to the notion that a society could ever agree on what values are worthwhile or undesirable. While it seems that some values are often misconstrued as having a moral dimension and may be subject to considerable disagreement as to their moral worth, others may be subject to general societal agreement as to their worth (i.e., seeking alternatives, self-awareness, empathy) (Edelman & Goldstein, 1981). Thus, if Character Education programs can be taught in a nonindoctrinative manner, if values can be identified which the society (in general) agrees are desirable, and if sound empirical research (which is at present clearly lacking) supports its utility in enhancing moral reasoning and reducing aggressive behavior, then its implementation within the school setting would appear to be warranted.

It has also been suggested that Character Education programs lack explicit techniques for teaching children those cognitive processes involved in the moral reasoning process itself (Arbuthnot & Faust 1981; Edelman & Goldstein, 1981). For example, this approach does not assist the individual in deciding what to do when values are in conflict with each other. Consequently, it seems that procedures which emphasize the development of the cognitive skills required for effective problem solving in moral conflict situations will be more effective than Character Education procedures, particularly for older children, in promoting a morality based upon principles of justice.

Values Clarification

One program which emphasizes the development of problem-solving skills is Values Clarification. It was developed to help students acquire, clarify and apply their personal values to moral conflict situations through value clarifying exercises (i.e., public interview, alternate action search) in which particular values are not specifically emphasized. Strongly opposed to the rationale of the character educators (teaching specific values), Raths, Harmin, and Simon (1966, in Edelman & Goldstein, 1981, pp. 273-275) argued that:

> Values are relative to subgroups within societies and to individuals within subgroups . . . that values are relative to time, place and circumstances in a rapidly changing world . . . that values often conflict with one another . . . that values are a matter of personal discovery and choice . . . that the young need help in developing and clarifying their own values . . . that value confusion in the young leads to certain kinds of behavioral problems (i.e., apathy, uncertainty, overconformity, overdissention) . . . and that the schools have a responsibility to help the young clarify and develop their own values. [Edelman & Goldstein, 1981, pp. 273-275]

It is these assumptions which underlie the belief that Values Clarification programs should involve the teaching of the "process of valuing." The process of valuing incorporates the seven subprocesses of choosing freely, choosing from among alternatives, choosing after thoughtful consideration of the consequences of each alternative, prizing and cherishing, affirming, acting upon choices, and repeating (Raths, Harmin, & Simon, 1966). The authors maintain that the valuing process will permit students to examine, develop, choose, and revise values when necessary. In addition, it is apparent that the process of valuing focuses on the cognitive, affective, and behavioral dimensions of morality and thus clearly reflects the components of the definition of morality presented earlier. Those readers interested in a more extensive discussion of the history, rationale, curriculum, and methods of Values Clarification procedures are referred to Simon, Howe, and Kirschenbaum (1972), Simon and Olds (1976), and Kirschenbaum (1973, 1975).

Although some research provides tentative support for the efficacy of Values Clarification in reducing destructive behaviors and enhancing constructive behaviors (Edelman & Goldstein, 1981), much of it suffers from measurement difficulties and a lack of adequate control groups. Another problem with this multi-faceted approach involves the identification of its active ingredients (Edelman & Goldstein, 1981). Questions concerning the individual utility of the seven valuing processes and the value of a nonjudgmental classroom atmosphere have yet to be answered. As a result of these two problems, it is difficult to determine what attitudinal and behavioral changes each component promotes in students (Edelman & Goldstein, 1981).

Perhaps the most potent criticism, however, involves the fundamental assumption of value relativity. This implies that there are no "right" or "wrong" answers in the area of values, and that the role of the teacher is simply one of stimulating students to examine and clarify their own values. Thus, although values are not explicitly prescribed, neither are students confronted with the possible inadequacies of their values or asked to defend them in terms of their consistency with the principles of justice or equality (Arbuthnot & Faust, 1981). The point here is that, although supporters of Values Clarification maintain that it is a "value free" approach, the fact remains that they are imposing a value—that of value relativity—which is potentially subject to the same relativity constriction as any other value.

In addition, those supporting Values Clarification maintain that it will enhance "constructive" and decrease "destructive" behaviors, which implies that some behaviors are "good" while others are "bad." Once again, a value—that of good or bad—has been imposed. Thus, in the final analysis, it appears that a number of contradictions are inherent in the Values Clarification procedure. Many writers assert that all values are not relative, and that the values underlying nonaggressive behavior are more desirable than those underlying aggressive behavior (Edelman & Goldstein, 1981; Kohlberg, 1971a; Lickona, 1976). While the Values Clarification movement clearly does not support this nonrelativity viewpoint, it seems that

Kohlberg's Moral Education approach does incorporate the notion of nonindoctrination, as well as explicit techniques for facilitating the development of the cognitive skills necessary for effective problem solving in moral conflict situations.

Moral Education

Moral Education, as conceptualized by Kohlberg, should be based upon empirically supported and philosophically sound principles. He maintains that his cognitive-developmental theory of moral reasoning meets these stipulations, and that his theory provides the foundation from which explicit methods of Moral Education can be advanced. The goal of this approach, as described by Kohlberg, is that of enhancing an individual's ability to reason effectively about moral issues. While this goal captures the cognitive aspects of morality, the reformulation of morality proposed by Edelman and Goldstein (1981) necessitates that the goal of Moral Education transcend that described by Kohlberg. In light of this reformulation, Edelman and Goldstein (1981) propose that the goal of Moral Education is to

> facilitate the development of the cognitive, affective and behavioral aspects of morality through each of the stages. . . . [t]he aim is also to prevent developmental fixation or retardation at preconventional and conventional levels, especially during the critical transitional periods of pre- to early adolescence and adolescence to early adulthood, respectively. [pp. 293-294]

The practical application of Kohlberg's theory involves "classroom discussions of moral dilemmas" in which cognitively stimulating dilemmas are used to promote classroom discussions among the students. Since classrooms are likely to be comprised of students reasoning at diverse stages, Kohlberg maintained that the moral discussions engaged in would induce cognitive conflict in an individual's functioning at the lower stages and would provide role-taking opportunities which, over time, would result in a transition to the next higher stage of moral reasoning—at least for those students initially reasoning at the lower stages. While these teacher-led moral discussions are believed to prevent moral reasoning fixation in those students who lag behind their peers, supporters of Moral Education do not claim that it promotes the moral development of students who are progressing satisfactorily. Nevertheless, these higher stage reasoners are a crucial part of the Moral Education program, since during discussions they present statements which induce the cognitive conflict believed to be necessary for moral growth. While the presence of higher stage reasoners is an absolute necessity for the inducement of cognitive conflict, Edelman and Goldstein (1981) suggest that the potency of the cognitive conflict can be enhanced by considering such factors as the relevance the moral dilemma has for the individual, the extent to which the dilemma is presented in a context which promotes the mutual exchange of conflicting opinions, and the extent to which these opinions and underlying reasons reflect reasoning one stage higher than that of the lower reasoning individual.

Thus, it is apparent that Moral Education involves at least three conditions which are believed to enhance moral reasoning—role-taking opportunities through reciprocal social interaction, cognitive conflict over genuine moral dilemmas, and exposure to the next higher stage of reasoning (Edelman & Goldstein, 1981). It is these three basic principles, in conjunction with the notion that the teacher's role is that of promoting self-discovery of higher-stage reasoning, which form the basis for the specific procedures employed in Moral Education programs. After groups of from 8 to 15 individuals who reason at two or three consecutive stages are established, the teacher generally presents dilemmas which can induce cognitive conflict and which are relevant to the students. Subsequently, the teacher provides a rationale for Moral

Education, describes what the group will be like, what his/her role is, and what the format will be for group participation (Arbuthnot & Faust, 1981). A four-step process ensues in which group members are asked to confront a moral dilemma, state a tentative position, examine the reasoning, and reflect on an individual position (Edelman & Goldstein, 1981). Kohlberg and his collaborators maintain that these procedures, along with a teacher who is able to establish a nonjudgmental climate, are the conditions necessary to promote moral development.

In fact, the research evidence suggests that moral dilemma discussion groups can successfully enhance moral reasoning stages. The results of a study involving sixth (11-12 years) and tenth (15-16 years) graders, in which the experimenter led moral discussion groups (18, 45-minute sessions held weekly), indicated that students in the experimental classrooms showed significantly more upward change in moral reasoning (one-third stage increase) as compared to various control group classrooms (Blatt & Kohlberg, 1975). In addition, participants in the experimental condition maintained the change at a one year follow-up. The changes observed were generally in the direction of the next higher stage, implying that true learning, rather than rote learning of phrases, had occurred. Similarly, the results of a study by Colby, Kohlberg, Fenton, Speicher-Dubin, and Lieberman (1977) indicated that students in a moral discussion group led by teachers in the context of a social studies class, showed a significant upward change in moral reasoning as compared to students in control classrooms where no moral discussions were held. In addition, Colby et al. (1977) found that more change in moral reasoning occurred for students who were in the process of stage transition, who were in classrooms which consisted of students at diverse levels of moral reasoning, and who had teachers skilled in promoting reasoning at adjacent stages and who used a greater number of discussion periods.

In a series of studies reported by Sullivan (1980), Moral Education programs were again found to enhance moral reasoning. The results of a study using elementary school aged children indicated that while both the experimental group (twice weekly participation in a minicourse in ethics in which moral dilemma discussions were held for one academic year) and the control group (no participation in the ethics class) showed movement from primarily stage 1 to stage 3 reasoning on posttesting; only the experimental group evidenced some stage 4 reasoning and had completely abandoned the use of stage 1 reasoning. This developmental pattern was also evident at a one year follow-up (Sullivan, 1980).

In an earlier study using secondary school aged children, Beck, Sullivan, and Taylor (1972) found that there were no differences between the experimental and control groups in moral reasoning on posttests. However, a one year follow-up indicated that students in the experimental group evidenced more postconventional reasoning than did those in the control group. The authors maintain that the one year interval between posttesting and follow-up provided opportunities for students to use their newly learned reasoning skills and thus to consolidate stage 5 reasoning. In another study using high school students, the results were not so encouraging (Sullivan & Beck, 1975). No differences in moral reasoning enhancement were found for the experimental and control groups. The discrepancy between the results of the last two studies can be found in an examination of the teaching methods employed. In the latter study, an ethics textbook, reflecting the interests of the teachers and not the students was used. whereas in the former study a textbook was not employed. The authors argue that the use of a textbook created a more structured environment which restricted the type of moral discussions which could evolve. These results suggest that the relevance of the moral dilemmas used has significant effects on the success of a Moral Education program.

Other studies using direct moral discussion of real-life situations have yielded similar results. Rundle (1977), using a fifth grade classroom in which moral issues were taught by the experimenter and a teacher (29 hours) within the context of classroom democracy, found that the experimental classroom (discussed and modified classroom rules using democratic procedures) showed significantly more change (one-half stage) than students in either the classroom with no moral discussion or the one with moral discussion using hypothetical moral dilemmas. This again suggests that the efficacy of Moral Education programs is in part a function of the relevance of the dilemmas discussed. In addition, Rundle (1977) found that children in the experimental group performed significantly better on a cooperation task (brick-building) than those in the two control groups. It is important to recognize, however, that the group receiving moral discussion using hypothetical dilemmas was led by a teacher who had not received training in Moral Education procedures. Thus, the group differences may have resulted from differential levels of experience with Moral Education procedures rather than from exposure to real versus hypothetical dilemmas.

The work of Grimes (1974) indicated that moral discussion groups involving fifth and sixth grade children and their mothers can also lead to enhanced moral reasoning. Specifically, the results indicated that group discussions between mothers (the experimenter had trained them in this technique prior to the initiation of the study) and their children led to more change (between one-third and one whole stage) than groups in which children, without their mothers, discussed hypothetical moral dilemmas (one-third stage increase), as well as groups which did not discuss moral dilemmas at all (no change). The authors maintain that the presence of the mother increased the frequency of moral dilemma discussions in the home. Stanley (1976) found similar results in a study involving parents and their adolescent children. Not only did the parent/adolescent group (10 weeks) show moral growth (one-third stage increase), but at a one year follow-up they had also continued to hold weekly family meetings involving family fairness discussions. In contrast, the parent only group, as well as the control group, showed no significant pre-to-posttest gains.

A related series of studies has involved the deliberate combination of direct moral discussion with specific psychological education techniques. The latter technique encompasses such things as peer counseling, having adolescents conduct moral discussions with younger children, and learning listening and counseling skills, with the primary purpose being the enhancement of ego, not moral development. However, a number of studies in this area suggest that this combination results in moral as well as ego development (Alexander, 1977; Sullivan, 1975).

The utility of combining moral discussion groups and psychological education strategies is clearly revealed in a study by Harris (1976). High school juniors were randomly assigned to one of three groups—a values education course emphasizing moral discussion (18 weeks), a group in which psychological education (learning listening and counseling skills for 9 weeks) was followed by moral discussion (9 weeks), and a control group of students enrolled in an economics course. The results indicated that there were no significant differences between the two experimental groups in moral reasoning at posttesting. However, while participants who received the combined approach of psychological education and moral discussion evidenced moral reasoning gains in the moral discussion phase, no gains were observed in the psychological education phase. This suggests that psychological education can promote more rapid growth during the moral discussion phase (since the increase occurred in the second phase for this group, but throughout both phases for the moral discussion only group), and that the optimal placement of the psychological education technique is before the moral discussion phase. These results suggest that psychological education strategies may enhance the efficacy of Moral Education procedures.

In contrast, a study by Paolitto (1975), which focused on the development of social perspective-taking and moral reasoning in eighth graders, indicated that the experimental condition (moral discussion groups within the context of a health class, and which emphasized role-taking—one semester) did not significantly increase in either moral reasoning or perspective-taking. The treatment groups did, however, score significantly higher on adjusted posttest means as compared to the control group (regular health class). The author suggests that increases in perspective-taking did not occur because participants may have reached a ceiling on this skill. However, it can also be suggested that the lack of perspective-taking and moral reasoning advance may have resulted from the fact that perspective-taking skills were not explicitly taught within the context of the intervention.

Thus, although the Harris (1976) study suggests that a combined approach may enhance the effectiveness of Moral Education procedures, the Paolitto (1975) study does not. Resolution of these discrepant findings may lie in the fact that, in contrast to the Harris (1976) study, which used two separate procedures, the Paolitto (1975) study attempted to enhance moral reasoning and perspective-taking skills while using one approach. This suggests that if one's goal is to enhance perspective-taking and moral reasoning skills, it can be best achieved by employing those techniques specifically designed to enhance each ability separately. Furthermore, although the assumption that perspective-taking is a necessary but not sufficient condition for moral reasoning enhancement has only received tentative empirical support (Harris, 1976), it is suggested that the optimal placement of a technique designed to promote perspective-taking is prior to the program designed to enhance moral reasoning (Zimmerman, 1982).

While the hypothesis suggesting that perspective-taking ability is a prerequisite to moral reasoning enhancement remains unanswered, a number of conclusions can be made from the results of studies employing Moral Education procedures: (1) moral dilemma discussion groups can lead to significantly more moral growth (one-third to one whole stage increase over one academic semester) than in various control groups; (2) this change occurs when a range of reasoning stages are represented in the classroom; (3) the teacher must help the student probe his/her reasoning in an environment which promotes openness and trust; (4) the moral discussion must create divided opinions and controversy among the students; and (5) the most effective Moral Education interventions occur within discussions of real dilemmas in the context of a "real" group (e.g., the classroom, the family).

While these studies clearly indicate that Moral Education is an effective method for promoting "moral judgment," it is striking that the question of the enhancement of "moral behavior" has not been explicitly addressed in any of the investigations presented. It seems that in many studies of this kind there is the implicit assumption that enhancing moral reasoning will necessarily lead to increased elicitation of moral behavior. In view of Kohlberg's description of the six stages of moral development, this would appear to be a logical assumption. The research in this area, however, does not consistently confirm this assumption. The fact is that, while the Moral Education programs described have been found to successfully enhance moral reasoning, it still remains questionable whether they have any impact on moral behavior. Intervention studies have not directly addressed this question. How, then, is moral behavior studied? Is there any relationship between Kohlberg's reasoning stages and moral behavior? And, more basically, what is moral behavior?

MORAL BEHAVIOR

The Relationship Between Moral Reasoning and Unsocialized Behavior

While the study of moral behavior has primarily been undertaken in controlled laboratory settings and has usually involved the use of nondelinquent populations, there is some research evidence to suggest that a relationship exists between moral judgment and unsocialized behavior. These studies consistently yield positive correlations between aggressive behavior/delinquency and preconventional levels of moral reasoning. Specifically, Freudlich and Kohlberg (see Kohlberg, 1973) found that, while 23 percent of working class, nondelinquent adolescents reasoned at preconventional stages (usually characteristic of children under age 10), 83 percent of delinquent adolescents reasoned at stages 1 or 2. Similar results were found by Fodor (1972) in an investigation using 14-17 year old delinquent males (violations ranged from petty larceny to attempted homicide). Delinquents were found to score significantly lower on Kohlberg's Moral Judgment Interview as compared to nondelinquents.

A study by Campagna and Harter (1975) also indicated that sociopathic males evidenced significantly more preconventional reasoning than a matched sample of nonsociopathic males. Hudgins and Prentice (1973) similarly found that 14 to 16 year old nondelinquent males scored significantly higher (conventional level) on Kohlberg's moral dilemmas than a matched sample of delinquent males (preconventional level). Thus, all of these studies appear to provide support for Kohlberg's descriptions of the two preconventional stages. For both stage 1 and stage 2 individuals, behavior is either regulated by authority figures or some form of payoff, with little consideration of societal rules or norms. However, Hudgins and Prentice (1973) also note that "the relationship between moral judgment and moral action is not invariant . . . some nondeliquents used lower stages of moral reasoning than did delinquents, while some delinquents employed the higher moral stages used by nondelinquents [p. 151]." While this observation has important implications for the understanding of the discrepancy between moral reasoning and moral action, the authors do not address possible reasons for these individual differences. It is suggested that factors extraneous to the dependent variable under investigation may have been operative (i.e., situational variables). Before examining some of these variables, it is important to direct attention to studies examining another aspect of moral behavior, namely socialized behavior.

The Relationship Between Moral Reasoning and Socialized Behavior

The occurrence of prosocial behaviors has been found to be associated with levels of moral reasoning. In general, the literature suggests that a positive relationship exists between conventional (characteristic of preadolescents, adolescents, and adults) and postconventional (attained by only 10-15 percent of the adult population) stages and such prosocial behaviors as honesty, as measured by cheating behavior (Harris, Mussen, & Rutherford, 1976; Kohlberg & Turiel, 1971; Krebs, 1967; Schwartz, Feldman, Brown, & Heingartner, 1969), altruism, helping people in distress, and generosity (McNamee, 1977; Ugurel-Semin, 1952), nonviolence, as measured by refusal to inflict pain on other people (Kohlberg & Turiel, 1971) and conformity behavior (Fodor, 1972; Saltzstein, Diamond, & Belenky, 1972).

There is considerable debate in the literature concerning the validity of using these behaviors to draw conclusions about the relationship between moral reasoning and "moral behavior." In studies of honesty, for example, the evidence suggests that more conventional than postconventional reasoners cheated on tasks when there were no explicit authoritative or group sanctions preventing it. Kohlberg and Turiel (1971) maintain that, because the principled participants define the situation as one which involves mutual trust and equality of opportunity, they are less likely to cheat. In contrast, the conventional reasoners maintained that there was no reason to resist cheating since the authority figure (i.e., experimenter) did not disapprove of this behavior. Thus, it seems that one of the consequences of a rule-oriented morality is that behavior is in part controlled by the prevailing rules of the situation (Arbuthnot & Faust, 1981).

Postconventional reasoners are believed to behave according to principles, not rules. Therefore, when conventional rules for behavior are no longer present in a situation, the conventional reasoner's behavior is more likely to break down as compared to those reasoning at the principled level. These ideas were partially confirmed in a study by Harris, Mussen, and Rutherford (1976) in which fifth grade boys were administered a resistance to temptation task based on the duplicating technique (participants are asked to score their own tests after they have been scored by the experimenter) used by Hartshorne and May (1928). The results indicated that honesty was positively, although not significantly, correlated with moral reasoning scores. In contrast, the Krebs (1967) study yielded significant positive correlations between moral reasoning and resistance to temptation, as measured by a structured game in which it was easy to cheat. These somewhat discrepant findings may be related to the fact that, in the former as compared to the latter study, intelligence was partialled out, thus yielding somewhat lower correlations (intelligence accounted for a significant proportion of the variance). In general, then, the evidence suggests that a positive correlation exists between moral reasoning and honesty.

Concerning altruism, McNamee (1977) conducted an experiment in which the participant could help or not help a confederate drug user. Compliance with the experimenter's expectation was defined as the participant's unwillingness to help the confederate. The results indicated that, while all participants reasoning at stage 6 offered the confederate assistance, only 68 percent of stage 5 reasoners, 38 percent of stage 4 reasoners, and 28 percent of stage 3 reasoners offered some kind of assistance (either a referral or personal assistance). These results indicate that behavioral choice differs for higher and lower stage reasoners. The results of a study by Ugurel-Semin (1952) provide further support for the relationship between moral reasoning and altruistic behavior. Specifically, the results indicated that for 4 to 16 year old, Istanbul children, increases in moral judgment stage are associated with increasingly more mature justifications for their altruistic behavior.

The results of a study by Kohlberg and Turiel (1971), in the area of nonviolence, again provides support for a positive relationship between moral reasoning and moral behavior. The investigators administered the Moral Judgment Interview to participants in Milgram's study of obedience to authority and found that, while 75 percent of the stage 6 reasoners refused to continue shocking the confederate victim, stating that the researcher did not have a right to inflict pain on another person, only 13 percent of the lower stage reasoners (including stage 5) discontinued administering the shock. Although stage 5 reasoners often felt uncomfortable with the experiment, they continued to shock because both they and the victim had made a commitment to the researcher to participate in the study. In contrast, the stage 3 and stage 4 participants continued shocking the victim because of the experimenter's definition of the situation. Thus, it is apparent that, even though similar decisions may be elicited by people reasoning at different stages, the reasoning process underlying these behavioral choices differs for individual's functioning at different levels of moral development. And, finally, in a study examining the relationship between moral reasoning and conformity behavior, Saltzstein, Diamond, and Belenky (1972) found that significantly more stage 3 reasoners conformed to group opinion than those participants reasoning at stage 4 or stage 5.

In sum, the results of the studies presented in the last two sections consistently indicate that relationships exist between moral reasoning stage and aggressive and prosocial behavior. Throughout these investigations, moral or immoral behavior was conceptualized as either socialized or unsocialized behavior, respectively. As mentioned previously, a number of researchers have questioned the relevance of such behaviors for the study of moral behavior. It is in these criticisms that one finds explanations for the roots of the discrepancy between moral reasoning stage and moral behavior in real-life situations.

Explanations for the Discrepancy Between Word and Deed In Real-Life Situations

The primary criticisms emerging around the use of such behaviors as cheating, altruism, and conformity to study moral behavior have emerged within the Kohlberg group. Kohlberg (1969, 1973) and Turiel (1980) argue that these behaviors cannot always be viewed as representative of moral behavior because they do not take into consideration the individual's intentions and they do not reflect true moral dilemma situations. For example, Kohlberg (1969) argues that the invalidity of experiments utilizing honesty stems from the fact that they do not reflect true moral dilemmas. According to Kohlberg, a true moral dilemma involves a situation requiring the individual to choose between two courses of action in which "strong emotional reactions are activated." Kohlberg does not believe that cheating situations evoke these emotions. Damon (1980) supports a similar view. He maintains that tests of cheating and lying, for instance, are trivial and do not capture an individual's true moral concerns.

This implies that people may reason and behave differently when confronted with a hypothetical versus a real-life moral dilemma. Studies investigating this idea have yielded inconsistent findings. For example, in the McNamee (1977) study, discussed above, no discrepancy was found between reasoning in concrete versus hypothetical moral conflicts. However, in a study by Gerson and Damon (1975), using 4 to 10 year old children, there was considerable discrepancy between the stage of reasoning used in hypothetical versus concrete situations. The results indicated that lower levels of reasoning were employed in concrete situations of generosity (actual distribution of candy bars) as compared to hypothetical situations (hypothetical distribution of money). Similarly, Kohlberg, Kauffman, Scharf, and Hickey (1975) found that prisoners use lower stage reasoning when responding to concrete prison dilemmas as compared to standard hypothetical dilemmas.

The fact that individuals do not reason at only one stage, regardless of whether the issues (norms) are similar or dissimilar, makes these discrepant findings somewhat more interpretable. Nevertheless, these results also imply that extraneous variables may be operative in the reasoning process, having their effect on an individual's ultimate behavioral choice. This idea has received considerable support in the literature. For example, based upon a study which indicated that significantly more preconventional (70 percent) and conventional (55 percent) reasoners cheated than postconventional reasoners (15 percent), Kohlberg (1973) concluded that factors beyond moral judgment influence the translation of moral reasoning into moral action. This conclusion was based upon the fact that 15 percent of the principled reasoners still cheated, even though stage descriptions would suggest that they would not behave in this manner.

One factor which is believed to impact upon moral action is ego strength, defined as "attentional-will factors" (sense of will or purpose) (Grim, Kohlberg, & White, 1968). Kohlberg (1971b) suggests that ego-strength may lead to impulse control and the ability to delay gratification. Specifically, Kohlberg (1971b) maintains that the mediational effects of ego-strength factors may cause people "to differentially follow the moral judgments that they themselves make in the situation [p. 381]." Related to this factor is the question of the role of affect on moral behavior (Rothman, 1980). While little research has investigated the mediating role of affect, Ruma and Mosher (1967) found a positive relationship between the level of moral judgment of delinquents and the guilt they experienced around their behavior. Self-interest (Gerson & Damon, 1975) may be another variable which accounts for a considerable percentage of the variance in that it elicits different levels of personal investment in particular situations. The ability to role-take, perspective-take, or empathize may provide yet another link in the reasoning-behavior chain. Research in progress (Zimmerman, 1982) is examining the relationship between perspective-taking, moral reasoning, and aggressive behavior.

A host of situational factors have also been found to mediate moral behavior. These include such things as the use of hypothetical versus concrete, real dilemmas (Gerson & Damon, 1975; Haan, 1975; Keasey, 1977; Straughan, 1975), demand characteristics of the situation or experiment (Adair & Schachter, 1972; Orne, 1962), and the parameters (type and variety) of the moral conflict within a particular situation (Damon, 1980). It has been suggested that situational factors are particularly potent in concrete situations of moral decision making since the individual often has considerable personal investment in the outcome of the dilemma (Rothman, 1980). Other factors which have been proposed to account for the discrepancy between moral reasoning stage and moral behavior are age (increased consistency of moral behavior with increasing age) (Saltzstein, Diamond & Belenky, 1972; Turiel & Rothman, 1972) and the confusion between moral behavior and social conventional behavior (Turiel, 1980). Concerning the latter point, Turiel (1980) argues that a distinction must be made between moral issues, which involves consideration of justice, and conventional concerns, which involves issues relating to the expectations of others in society (i.e., mode of dress, forms of address). He maintains that it is unreasonable to assume that one's conception of social conventional issues should be related to one's conception of moral issues.

Thus, just as behavioral choices may vary for different individuals reasoning at the same stage, one person may behave differently across two situations even though the reasoning is the same. Nevertheless, although these factors are believed to influence the reasoning-behavior relationship, the degree of impact of each variable, alone or in combination, is as yet unknown. Furthermore, despite this impact, most researchers in the area of moral development continue to maintain that level of moral reasoning is the most influential factor, and, in fact, the only distinctively moral factor impacting upon moral behavior (Kohlberg, 1973). Support for this contention awaits future research.

From this discussion, three points can be made concerning the relationship between moral reasoning and moral behavior. First, it can be stated that advanced moral reasoning is a necessary but not sufficient condition for consistent moral behavior (Arbuthnot & Faust, 1981). In other words, while one can observe consistency between an individual's maturity of moral reasoning and maturity of behavior, one cannot always predict behavior from knowledge of the individual's reasoning stage in real-life situations. As Hoffman (1970) maintains, it seems reasonable to assume ". . . that both specificity and generality can be found in moral behavior as in any other trait. Individuals do vary between their general predispositions towards honesty and dishonesty but their actual behavior in moral conflict situations is not an all-or-none matter [p. 344]." Second, the discrepancy between moral reasoning and moral behavior in real-life situations can be accounted for by such mediating factors as situational variables, concrete versus hypothetical moral dilemmas, ego-strength, affect, role-taking ability, age, and the distinction between moral and social-conventional behavior. Important research endeavors must, therefore, continue to address the question of the role these mediating variables play in the moral reasoning-moral behavior chain. Third, the elicitation of prosocial or asocial behaviors cannot always serve to accurately reflect level of moral reasoning in experimental or real-life situations. Thus, it is clear that a complete understanding of moral behavior can be best achieved when the interaction between structural processes and mediating variables are considered.

CONCLUSIONS

It should be apparent from this discussion that the application of Moral Education procedures to the reduction of aggressive behavior involves the consideration of a myriad of factors. From an integration of the research evidence emerging from the moral intervention and moral behavior areas, questions concerning the utility of these procedures for the reduction of aggressive behavior emerge. While these techniques have proven to be effective for increasing moral reasoning stage, there is at present only a modest amount of evidence indicating that these effects are transferred to moral behavior in real-life situations. In light of the evidence suggesting that these factors may be at the root of the observed discrepancy between moral reasoning and moral behavior, one can also speculate that they may, in part, determine the efficacy of Moral Education programs for the reduction of aggression. It is suggested that the incorporation of these factors into moral intervention procedures will provide opportunities for the mutual enhancement of moral reasoning and constructive alternatives to interpersonal aggression. For instance, continued attention should be directed toward the substitution of concrete moral dilemmas for hypothetical ones. This may serve to increase the probability that enhanced moral reasoning is transferred to actual moral conflict situations where real behavioral decisions are made. Future research efforts might also attempt to incorporate methods designed to enhance ego-strength or empathy with traditional moral education procedures. As previously mentioned, research examining this idea is presently underway. However, regardless of the results of this research, it is important to recognize that in a "real-life" context, uncontrolled situational variables will undoubtedly continue to partly determine the behavioral choice elicited by the individual. Despite this, research to uncover some of these variables is still profitable.

The consideration of situational variables also provides the means by which one can begin to understand the placement of aggressive behavior within the moral-immoral domain. Aggressive behavior is commonly viewed as the intent to harm another person. It is suggested that it is this form of aggressive behavior which is associated with lower stages of moral reasoning. However, there are many other forms of aggressive behavior which do not necessarily involve the intent to harm another and, as such, do not fall within preconventional levels of moral judgment (i.e., accidently killing another to defend one's life; stealing to save the life of a loved one). While these behaviors are certainly aggressive, they, at the same time, reflect conventional and possibly postconventional levels of moral reasoning as presently defined by Kohlberg's theory. This implies that it is possible to differentiate between two types of aggressive behavior, with the first being reflective of preconventional reasoning and the second being representative of conventional or postconventional reasoning. Therefore, the question of whether a particular aggressive act is understood as "moral" or "immoral" depends upon the situational variables mediating the behavioral decision and, to a large extent, the way in which moral reasoning is presently described. In order to facilitate the placement of aggressive behavior within the moral-immoral domain, it may be necessary to modify our present conceptualization of morality. A reconceptualization may serve to bridge the gap between moral reasoning and aggression such that it will no longer be necessary to view aggressive behavior as an exemplar of the moral reasoning-moral behavior discrepancy.

REFERENCES

Adair, J. G., & Schachter, B. S. To cooperate or to look good?: The subjects' and experimenters' perceptions of each others' intentions. *Journal of Experimental Social Psychology*, 1972, *8*, 74–85.

Alexander, R. A moral education curriculum on prejudice. Unpublished doctoral dissertation, Boston University, 1977.

Alston, W. P. Comments on Kohlberg's "from is to ought." In T. Mischel (Ed.), *Cognitive development and epistemology*. New York: Academic Press, 1971.

Arbuthnot, J. Relationships between maturity of moral judgment and measure of cognitive abilities. *Psychological Reports,* 1973, *33,* 945-46.

Arbuthnot, J. Modification of moral judgment through role-playing. *Developmental Psychology,* 1975, *11,* 319-24.

Arbuthnot, J. B., & Faust, A. *Teaching moral reasoning: Theory and practice.* New York: Harper & Row, 1981.

Bain, O., & Clark, S. *Character education: A handbook of teaching suggestions based on freedom's code for elementary teachers.* San Antonio, Texas: The Children's Fund, 1966.

Beck, C., Sullivan, E. V., & Taylor, P. Stimulating transition to post-convention morality: The Pickering High School study. *Interchange,* 1972, *17,* 28-37.

Blatt, M. M. The effects of classroom discussion programs on children's level of moral judgment. Unpublished doctoral dissertation, University of Chicago, 1970.

Blatt, M., & Kohlberg, L. The effects of classroom moral discussion upon children's level of moral judgment. *Journal of Moral Education,* 1975, *4,* 129-61.

Campagna, A. F., & Harter, S. Moral judgment in sociopathic and normal children. *Journal of Personality and Social Psychology,* 1975, *31,* 199-205.

Carroll, J. L., & Nelson, E. A. Explorations in the evaluation of the moral development of pre-adolescents. Unpublished manuscript, November 1979.

Carroll, J. L., & Rest, J. R. Development in moral judgment as indicated by rejection of lower-stage statements. *Journal of Research in Personality,* 1981, *3,* 17-24.

Colby, A., Kohlberg, L., Fenton, E., Speicher-Dubin, B., & Lieberman, M. Secondary school moral discussion programmes led by social studies teachers. *Journal of Moral Education,* 1977, *6,* 90-111.

Colby, A., Kohlberg, L., & Gibbs, J. The longitudinal study of moral judgment. Paper presented at SRCD, San Francisco, March 1979.

Damon, W. Structural-developmental theory and the study of moral development. In M. Windmiller, H. Lambert, & E. Turiel (Eds.), *Moral development and socialization.* Boston: Allyn & Bacon, 1980.

Dubinsky, I. H. Induced change in moral judgment as a function of dominant stage, non-dominant stage exposure, and directional susceptibility. Paper presented at annual meeting of the Midwestern Psychology Association, Chicago, 1976.

Edelman, E. M., & Goldstein, A. P. Moral education. In A. P. Goldstein, E. G. Carr, W. S. Davidson, & P. Wehr (Eds.), *In response to aggression.* New York: Pergamon Press, 1981.

Enright, R. D. An integration of social cognitive development and cognitive processing: Educational applications. *American Educational Research Journal,* 1980, *17,* 21-41.

Faust, D., & Arbuthnot, J. Relationship between moral and Piagetian reasoning and the effectiveness of moral education. *Developmental Psychology,* 1978, *14,* 435-36.

Fodor, E. M. Delinquency and susceptibility to social influence among adolescents as a function of level of moral development. *Journal of Social Psychology,* 1972, *86,* 257-60.

Fraenkel, J. R. The Kohlberg bandwagon: Some reservations. *Social Education,* 1976, *40,* 216-22.

Gerson, R., & Damon, W. Relations between moral behavior in a hypothetical-verbal context and in a practical, "real-life" setting. Paper presented at Eastern Psychological Association, New York City, April 1975.

Goble, F. *The case for character education,* Pasadena, California: Thomas Jefferson Research Center, 1973.

Grim, P. F., Kohlberg, L., & White, S. H. Some relationships between conscience and attentional processes. *Journal of Personality and Social Psychology,* 1968, *8,* 239-52.

Grimes, P. Teaching moral reasoning to eleven year olds and their mothers: A means of promoting moral growth. Unpublished doctoral dissertation, Boston University, 1974.

Grinder, R. E. Relations between behavioral and cognitive dimensions of conscience in middle childhood. *Child Development,* 1964, *35,* 881-91.

Haan, N. Hypothetical and actual moral reasoning in a situation of civil disobedience. *Journal of Personality and Social Psychology,* 1975, *32,* 255-70.

Haan, N., Smith, M. B., & Block, T. The moral reasoning of young adults: Political-social behavior, family background, and personality correlates. *Journal of Personality and Social Psychology*, 1968, *10*, 183-201.

Harris, D. Psychological awareness and moral discourse: A curriculum sequence for moral development. Unpublished doctoral dissertation, University of Wisconsin, 1976.

Harris, S., Mussen, P., & Rutherford, E. Some cognitive, behavioral and personality correlates of maturity of moral development. *The Journal of Genetic Psychology*, 1976, *128*, 123-85.

Hartshorne, J., & May, M. A. *Studies in the nature of character.* Vol. I. *Studies in deceit.* New York: Macmillan, 1928.

Hill, R. C. *Freedom's code: The historic American standards of character, conduct and citizen responsibility.* San Antonio, Texas: The Children's Fund, 1965.

Hoffman, M. Moral development. In P. Mussen (Ed.), *Carmichael's manual of child psychology.* New York: John Wiley & Sons, 1970.

Holstein, C. B. Irreversible, stepwise sequence in the development of moral judgment: A longitudinal study of males and females. *Child Development*, 1976, *47*, 51-61.

Hudgins, W., & Prentice, N. M. Moral judgment in delinquent and non-delinquent adolescents and their mothers. *Journal of Abnormal Psychology*, 1973, *82*, 145-52.

Johnson, R. C. The study of children's moral judgments. *Child Development*, 1962, *33*, 327-54.

Keasey, C. B. Experimentally induced changes in moral opinions and reasoning. *Journal of Personality and Social Psychology*, 1973, *26*, 30-38.

Keasey, C. B. Young children's attribution of intentionality to themselves and others. *Child Development*, 1977, *48*, 261-64.

Kirschenbaum, H. Recent research in values education. In J. R. Meyer, B. Burnham, & J. Chotvat (Eds.), *Values education: Theory/practice/problems/prospects.* Waterloo, Ontario: Wilfrid Laurier University Press, 1975.

Kirschenbaum, H., & Simon, S. B. *Readings in values clarification.* Minneapolis, Minn.: Winston Press, 1973.

Kohlberg, L. Development of moral character and moral ideology. In M. L. Hoffman & L. W. Hoffman (Eds.), *Review of child development research.* Vol. 1. New York: Russell Sage Foundation, 1964.

Kohlberg, L. Stage and sequence: The cognitive-developmental approach to socialization. In D. A. Goslin (Ed.), *Handbook of socialization theory & research.* Chicago: Rand McNally, 1969.

Kohlberg, L. Education for justice: A modern statement of the platonic view. In T. Sizer (Ed.), *Moral education.* Cambridge: Harvard University Press, 1970.

Kohlberg, L. From is to ought: How to commit the naturalistic fallacy and get away with it in the study of moral development. In T. Mischel (Ed.), *Cognitive development and epistemology.* New York: Academic Press, 1971(a).

Kohlberg, L. Stages of moral development as a basis for moral education. In C. M. Beck, B. S. Crittendon, & E. V. Sullivan (Eds.), *Moral Education: Interdisciplinary approaches.* New York: Newman Press, 1971(b).

Kohlberg, L. The cognitive-developmental approach to moral education. *Journal of Philosophy*, 1973, *19*, 670-77.

Kohlberg, L. Moral stages and moralization: The cognitive-developmental approach. In T. Lickona (Ed.), *Moral development and behavior: Theory, research and social issues.* New York: Holt, Rinehart & Winston, 1976.

Kohlberg, L. Comprehensive progress report (July 1, 1975 through January 1, 1978). Center for Moral Education, Harvard University, 1978.

Kohlberg, L., Kauffman, K., Scharf, P., & Hickey, J. The just community approach to corrections: A theory. *Journal of Moral Education*, 1975, *4*, 243-60.

Kohlberg, L., & Kramer, R. G. Continuities and discontinuities in childhood and adult moral development. *Human Development*, 1969, *12*, 93-120.

Kohlberg, L., & Turiel, E. Moral development and moral education. In G. S. Lesser (Ed.), *Psychology and educational practice.* Chicago: Scott Foresman, 1971.

Kramer, R. Changes in moral judgment response pattern during late adolescence and young adulthood:

Retrogression in a developmental sequence. Unpublished doctoral dissertation, University of Chicago, 1968.

Krebs, R. L. Some relationships between attention and resistance to temptation. Unpublished doctoral dissertation, University of Chicago, 1967.

Kuhn, D. Short-term longitudinal evidence for the sequentiality of Kohlberg's early stages of moral judgment. *Developmental Psychology*, 1976, *12*, 162-66.

Kurtines, W., & Grief, E. B. The development of moral thought: Review and evaluation of Kohlberg's approach. *Psychological Bulletin*, 1974, *81*, 453-70.

Lee, L. C. The concomitant development of cognitive and moral modes of thought: A test of selected deductions from Piaget's theory. *Genetic Psychology Monographs*, 1971, *83*, 93-146.

Lickona, T. Critical issues in the study of moral development and behavior. In T. Lickona (Ed.), *Moral development and behavior: Theory, research, and social issues*. New York: Holt, Rinehart & Winston, 1976.

Matefy, R. E., & Acksen, B. A. The effect of role-playing discrepant positions on change in moral judgments and attitudes. *The Journal of Genetic Psychology*, 1976, *128*, 189-200.

Mayer, H. C. *The good American program: A teacher's guide to the direct teaching of citizenship values in the elementary grades*. New York: American Viewpoint, 1964.

McNamee, S. Moral behaviour, moral development and motivation. *Journal of Moral Education*, 1977, *7*, 27-31.

Nisan, M., & Kohlberg, L. University and cross-cultural variance in moral development: A longitudinal and cross-sectional study in Turkey. Unpublished paper, Cambridge, Mass.: Center for Moral Education, Harvard University, 1978.

Orne, M. T. On the social psychology of the psychological experiment: With particular reference to demand characteristics and their implications. *American Psychologist*, 1962, *17*, 776-83.

Paolitto, D. Role-taking opportunities for early adolescents: A program in moral education. Unpublished doctoral dissertation, Boston University, 1975.

Peters, R. S. The place of Kohlberg's theory in moral education. *Journal of Moral Education*, 1978, *7*, 147-57.

Piaget, J. *The moral judgment of the child*. London: Routledge & Kegan Paul, 1932.

Raths, L. E., Harmin, M., & Simon, S. B. *Values and teaching: Working with values in the classroom*. Columbus, Ohio: Charles Merrill, 1966.

Rest, J. R. The hierarchical nature of moral judgment: A study of patterns of comprehension and preference of moral stages. *Journal of Personality*, 1973, *41*, 86-109.

Rest, J. R. *Development in judging moral issues*. Minneapolis: University of Minnesota Press, 1979.

Rest, J. R., Turiel, E., & Kohlberg, L. Level of moral development as a determinant of preference and comprehension of moral judgments made by others. *Journal of Personality*, 1969, *37*, 225-52.

Rothman, G. R. The relationship between moral judgment and moral behavior. In M. Windmiller, N. Lambert, & E. Turiel (Eds.), *Moral development and socialization*. Boston: Allyn & Bacon, 1980.

Rubin, K. H., & Schneider, F. W. The relationship between moral judgment, egocentrism, and altruistic behavior. *Child Development*, 1973, *43*, 661-65.

Ruma, E. H., & Mosher, D. L. Relationship between moral judgment and guilt in delinquent boys. *Journal of Abnormal Psychology*, 1967, *72*, 122-27.

Rundle, L. The stimulation of moral development in the elementary school and the cognitive examination of social experience: A fifth grade study. Unpublished doctoral dissertation, Boston University, 1977.

Saltzstein, H. D., Diamond, R. M., & Belenky, M. Moral judgment level and conformity behavior. *Developmental Psychology*, 1972, *7*, 327-36.

Schwartz, S. H., Feldman, K. A., Brown, M. E., & Heingartner, A. Some personality correlates of conduct in two situations of moral conflict. *Journal of Personality*, 1969, *37*, 41-57.

Selman, R. L. Taking another's perspective: Role-taking development in early childhood. *Child Development*, 1971, *42*, 1721-34.

Selman, R. L. *The growth of interpersonal understanding: Developmental and clinical analyses*. New

York: Academic Press, 1980.

Sieber, J. E. A social learning theory approach to morality. In M. Windmiller, N. Lambert, & E. Turiel (Eds.), *Moral development and socialization*. Boston: Allyn & Bacon, 1980.

Simon, S. B., Howe, L. W., & Kirschenbaum, H. *Values clarification: A handbook of practical strategies for teachers and students*. New York: Hart, 1972.

Simon, S. B., & Olds, S. W. *Helping your child learn right from wrong: A guide to values clarification*. New York: McGraw-Hill, 1976.

Simpson, E. L. Moral development research: A case of scientific cultural bias. *Human Development*, 1974, *17*, 81-106.

Sparling, Y., Arbuthnot, J. B., Faust, D., & Key, W. The relationship between moral and Piagetian reasoning and the effectiveness of moral education in grade school children. Athens, Ohio: Ohio University, 1978.

Stanley, S. A curriculum to affect the moral atmosphere of the family and the moral development of adolescents. Unpublished doctoral dissertation, Boston University, 1976.

Straughan, R. R. Hypothetical moral situations. *Journal of Moral Education*, 1975, *4*, 183-89.

Stuart, R. B. Decentration in the development of children's concepts of moral and causal judgment. *The Journal of Genetic Psychology*, 1967, *111*, 59-68.

Sullivan, P. A curriculum for stimulating moral reasoning and ego development in adolescents. Unpublished doctoral dissertation, Boston University, 1975.

Sullivan, E. V. Can values be taught? In M. Windmiller, N. Lambert, & E. Turiel (Eds.), *Moral development and socialization*. Boston: Allyn & Bacon, 1980.

Sullivan, E. V., & Beck, C. Moral education in a Canadian setting. *Phi Delta Kappan*, 1975, *56*, 697-701.

Tice, T. N. A psychoanalytic perspective. In M. Windmiller, N. Lambert, & E. Turiel (Eds.), *Moral development and socialization*. Boston: Allyn & Bacon, 1980.

Tomlinson-Keasy, C., & Keasy, C. B. The mediating role of cognitive development in moral judgment. *Child Development*, 1974, *45*, 291-98.

Tracy, J. J., & Cross, H. J. Antecedents of shift in moral judgment. *Journal of Personality and Social Psychology*, 1973, *26*, 238-44.

Trevitt, V. *The American heritage: Design for national character*. Santa Barbara, California: McNally & Loftin, 1964.

Turiel, E. An experimental test of the sequentiality of developmental stages in the child's moral judgments. *Journal of Personality and Social Psychology*, 1966, *3*, 611-18.

Turiel, E. Conflict and transition in adolescent moral development. *Child development*, 1974, *45*, 14-29.

Turiel, E. The development of social-conventional and moral concepts. In M. Windmiller, N. Lambert, & E, Turiel (Eds.), *Moral development and socialization*. Boston: Allyn & Bacon, 1980.

Turiel, E., Edwards, C. P., & Kohlberg, L. Moral development in Turkish children, adolescents, and young adults. Cambridge, Mass.: Center for Moral Development, Harvard University, 1977.

Turiel, E., & Rothman, G. The influence of moral reasoning on behavioral choices at different stages of moral development. *Child Development*, 1972, *43*, 741-56,

Ugurel-Semin, R. Moral behavior and moral judgment of children. *Journal of Abnormal and Social Psychology*, 1952, *47*, 463-75.

Whiteman, P. H., & Kosier, K. P. Development of children's moralistic judgments: Age, sex, I.Q. and certain personal-experiential variables. *Child Development*, 1964, *35*, 843-50.

Wilson, J. *The assessment of morality*. Windsor, Berks: National Foundation of Educational Research, 1973.

Zimmerman, D. The enhancement of perspective-taking and moral reasoning via Structured Learning Therapy and Moral Education. Unpublished manuscript, 1982.

9

Media Influences on Aggression

George Comstock

Few questions about the mass media have been more persistent than those concerning their influence on interpersonal violence, antisocial behavior, and criminal acts. They have occupied several United States task forces and special commissions (Baker & Ball, 1969; Commission on Obscenity and Pronography, 1970; Pearl, Bouthilet, & Lazar, 1982a, 1982b; Surgeon General's Scientific Advisory Committee on Television and Social Behavior, 1972), numerous Congressional committees (Comstock, 1975; Murray, 1980), and many dozens of psychologists, sociologists, and other professional students of human behavior. Although certainly not the only issue receiving attention, and not at all one addressed in an invariant manner, the central issue has been whether or not the media, by their attention to violence, also contribute to it. The most popular focus, justly so if the popularity of the medium is taken as a measure of its influence, has been "television violence" (i.e., violent television entertainment). Theater movies, comic books, newspapers, magazines, and television all have made an appearance at one time or another in the unfolding inquiry. There is an extensive scientific literature, although not a definitive study. Yet, few answers have been widely accepted, and none of any consequence accepted universally. The hypotheses flee the hounds.

Nevertheless, the past three decades have seen not only public and political attention paid to questions concerning the effects of the media, but also significant scientific progress in addressing them. Answers have been forthcoming, although their interpretation often has been ambiguous and troublesome. As is perhaps more often the case than most recognize, the conclusion in this instance will not rest only on the data, "the evidence," but on the rules applied to those data—the assumptions and criteria introduced.

The focus here is on violence in television and film and whether it contributes to criminal acts or behavior seriously harmful to others. However, we will not confine ourselves to research in which such activity was unambiguously the target of inquiry. To do so would leave us with little to examine, and would deprive us of the guidance that social and behavioral science can provide.

MEDIA VIOLENCE AND THE PUBLIC

The controversy in the United States over media violence and its effects on the behavior of the public divides into four periods (Comstock, 1982):

Preparation of this paper was made possible by the support provided by the S. I. Newhouse Chair in Public Communications and the Dean of the S. I. Newhouse School of Public Communications, Edward C. Stephens.

Growing attention, from 1952 to 1967.
Intensive scrutiny, from 1968 to 1971.
Apathy and controversy, from 1972 to 1974.
Confrontation, from 1975 to the present.

It should be no surprise that television was at the center of contention. The period since World War II has been called, among other things, "the age of television." Television sets in use increased from 10,000 in 1946 to 10.5 million in 1950. By 1960, the figure was 54 million. By 1970, it was 93 million; accounting for over 96 percent of all American households.

Comic books never figured prominently after the ascendancy of television; a self-regulatory code quieted critics and sales fell from 600 million to half that as children increasingly turned to the new medium (Bogart, 1972). Movies consistently appeared as secondary to television for a handful of reasons: the self-regulatory labeling, the relative infrequency of exposure, the comparatively limited access of young children, and their exclusion from federal regulation and the injunction by the Communications Act of 1934 to perform in the "public interest, convenience, and necessity." There is also an understandable if not justifiable duality of perception, with violence on television often accepted as a characteristic of the medium while violence in theater films is taken as exclusive to particular movies.

Growing Attention (1952-1967)

In 1952, the first of subsequently many Congressional hearings devoted to one or another aspect of television programming was held. The site was the House Committee on Interstate and Foreign Commerce hearings, and the principal subject was violence and its possibly harmful effects. In 1954, 1961-62, and 1964-65, far more prominent hearings on the possible contribution of violent television entertainment to juvenile delinquency and crime were chaired by Thomas Dodd and Estes Kefauver before the Senate Judiciary Committee (United States Congress, 1955a, 1955b, 1956, 1963, 1965, 1966).

Each time, the pattern was much the same. The congressmen, supported by various "experts," expressed concern over the harmful influences of violent entertainment reaching young people in increased quantity because of television, and skepticism that broadcasters were making a sufficient effort to minimize or reduce it. Those representing the television industry promised to reduce violence while denying any evidence of harmful effects.

Empirical data, however, tell a somewhat different story. The medium, in fact, shifted pronouncedly toward action-and-adventure serials between the mid-1950s and mid-1960s, thereby making violence a staple of television entertainment. In addition, there was no sign that promises to reduce violence were ever followed by substantial or even discernible decreases (Baker, 1969; Baker & Ball, 1969).

In 1963, the first empirical evidence that television and film portrayals of violence might contribute to viewer aggressiveness appeared in a scientific journal known for its rigorous peer review and high standards, the *Journal of Abnormal and Social Psychology.* This evidence consisted of two separate experiments by different investigators.

In one, Bandura and his colleagues demonstrated that the physical and verbal aggressiveness of nursery school children could be heightened by exposure to a brief violent portrayal, and that such an effect occurred for the portrayal of a costumed "Cat Lady" intended to simulate the fantasy of children's programming as well as for portrayals of ordinarily attired adults (Bandura, Ross, & Ross, 1963). In the other, Berkowitz and Rawlings (1963) demonstrated that the aggressiveness of young adults could be heightened by exposure to a portrayal of a boxing match in which the physical abuse delivered by the victor is said to have been justified by the victim's own bad behavior. Thus, not only was there evidence that violent television and film portrayals might increase aggressiveness, but that such an effect might occur for both young children and young adults, and that certain factors sometimes advanced by those in the entertainment business as supposedly mitigating any harmful effects of violence—that it is fantasy or that it is justified retribution—might not be wholly effective.

The subject of these early experiments was aggressive behavior, a concept that embraces the socially tolerable (and, in some circumstances, the socially honored) as well as components of the criminal and harmful. The measure in the Bandura experiment was abuse of a Bobo doll, a large inflated rubber stand-up toy manufactured for playful attack. In the Berkowitz experiment, it was the evaluation given a lab assistant. Neither could be said to be criminal or seriously harmful. Nevertheless, these experiments are important not only because they initiated a now extensive scientific literature on violent portrayals and antisocial behavior, but because these and other studies of aggression provide valuable evidence in examining the possible contribution of media violence to criminal and antisocial behavior.

Intensive Scrutiny (1968-1971)

In the late 1960s, the question of the influence of the mass media on antisocial behavior became the subject of intensive and varied governmental examination. The Commission on Obscenity and Pornography (1970) concluded that exposure to pornography made no substantial contribution to antisocial behavior. The National Commission on the Causes and Prevention of Violence (1969) concluded that the evidence to date favored the view that television and film violence contributed to antisocial behavior on the part of the viewers. More central to its task of examining the causes of urban rioting by blacks, it chastised the news media for ignoring the inner cities and minority communities and thereby adding to feelings of isolation, helplessness, and deprivation. The Surgeon General's Scientific Advisory Committee on Television and Social Behavior (1972) concluded that the evidence from laboratory experiments, such as those by Bandura and Berkowitz, converged with that from surveys reflecting everyday events: for at least some young viewers, exposure to television and film violence stimulated subsequent aggressiveness.

The violence commission based its conclusion on a review of existing research (Baker & Ball, 1969). Both the pornography commission and the Surgeon General's committee drew on a substantial number of studies undertaken specifically for their use (Commission on Obscenity and Pornography, 1971a, 1971b; Comstock, Rubinstein, & Murray, 1972a, 1972b, 1972c, 1972d, 1972e). Thus, this brief period also saw a marked enlargement of the research on media and antisocial behavior.

Apathy and Controversy (1972-1974)

The declarations by the two federal task forces that violence in television and film entertainment was heightening antisocial behavior were followed by hearings before the Senate Commerce Committee in 1972 and 1974 that gave further currency to this view. Yet, there was no visible public response.

This apathy was the consequence of two commonplace phenomena. One is the lag that typically separates the experts' proclamations from their inclusion among the concerns and interests of individuals and organizations. The other is the understandable ineptness of the press in conveying scientific complexities to a naive public (Tankard & Showalter, 1977).

In contrast, the controversy was immediate among the scientific, media, and policy communities. The conclusion of the pornography commission was officially disavowed as simply unacceptable, although many in the scientific and media communities thought it fair and accurate. Many, particularly in the media and policy communities, thought the violence commission had exceeded the evidence in its conclusion about television and film violence. The cautious and arguably ambiguous phrasing of the report of the Surgeon General's committee was said to reflect a membership biased in favor of the television industry. Most knowledgeable social and behavioral scientists concurred with the committee's conclusion but thought the language was weak (Paisley, 1972). Nevertheless, a few thought the committee had erred, and certainly the media community as a whole thought, or at least wished, so. The notion of annually monitoring violence in television entertainment, introduced by the three years of data presented by Gerbner (1972) as part of the Surgeon General's inquiry, remains a subject of debate today, with the definition of violence and the implications of such monitoring for censorship and public misunderstanding at the center of the controversy (Comstock, 1982).

Confrontation (1975-   )

By the end of 1975, advocacy had replaced apathy, a circumstance that persists to the present. In response to renewed congressional objections to "sex and violence" on television, the Federal Communications Commission embarked on the ill-fated *ex officio* innovation of "family viewing"; whereby broadcasters outside of formal federal intervention agreed to avoid possibly offensive content between 7 and 9 p.m. Soon felled by judicial challenge (Cowan, 1979), its legacy includes the precept that 9 p.m. is a responsible arbitrary boundary dividing "family" from "mature" programming and the concept that the label "family" might apply to a block of hours instead of specific programs. It also merits some small credit for the frequency of situation comedies in early prime time, for they are equally attractive to children and adults and are free of criminal and seriously hurtful violence.

At the same time, "televised violence" became the target of a number of prominent organizations. The American Medical Association, spurred by a widely publicized article by Rothenberg (1975) in its journal, placed "television violence" on its agenda of public hazards. The national Parent-Teacher Association began a campaign against "television violence" that included open "hearings" in major cities.

These and other voices were added to that of Action for Children's Television, which had been raising a variety of questions about the adequacy of entertainment directed at or regularly viewed by children. The companies whose advertisements appeared frequently on violent programs were identified (Slaby, Quarforth, & McConnachie, 1976), and advocacy groups began to urge letter-writing campaigns and product boycotts to change the advertising policies of these firms. Behind all this agitation was a heightened belief that violence in the media contributes to antisocial behavior.

In 1976-77, an extensive series of hearings by the Subcommittee on Communications of the House Committee on Interstate and Foreign Commerce continued the tradition of Congressional inquiry. Lobbying by the broadcasters forestalled a report holding violent entertainment as harmful and self-regulation as ineffectual, but the vote was close (Albert, 1978). The confrontation between broadcasters and the Moral Majority and other fundamentalist groups with which this decade began is not new in its subject, although the rationale and aims of these advocates may differ from those of individuals and organizations previously raising questions about television and film violence. Perfectly in accord with those earlier voices, however, is the recently organized National Coalition On Television Violence (1980), a group that includes a number of psychologists and physicians. It blames violence in television and film entertainment for increasing behavior harmful to self and others.

EVOLUTION OF EVIDENCE

Since the publication of the Bandura and the Berkowitz experiments in 1963, literally dozens of empirical investigations have been added to the scientific literature. The progress that has occurred can be perceived by organizing these data into seven hypothetical steps, each contributing something unique to the state of knowledge about the possible contribution of television and film violence to criminal acts and behavior seriously harmful to others.

Step 1: The Decline of the Catharsis Hypothesis

At one time, many psychologists believed that vicariously experiencing violence through television and film portrayals would purge the viewer of aggressive impulses. Empirical evidence does not support this catharsis principle, although it does support the view that such vicarious experience may raise or lower the subsequent aggressiveness of a viewer. In 1961, Feshbach published an experiment in which angered subjects had displayed fewer signs of hostility after seeing a violent film episode. This outcome appeared to support the proposition that aggressive impulses could be purged by vicariously experiencing violence (Feshbach, 1961).

Berkowitz thought differently. He reasoned that in the Feshbach experiment the film had sensitized the subjects to their aggressive impulses, and that as a result they had curbed their expression of hostility. To test this interpretation, in his 1963 experiment, Berkowitz presented his angered subjects with the same violent film episode under two different conditions. In one, the violence was described as unjustified; in the other, as justified. His reasoning was that for angered subjects, a portrayal of justified violence would be less effective than a portrayal of unjustified violence in heightening inhibitions. He also substituted the expression of antagonism for expressed hostility in general through a questionnaire evaluating the performance of the person who purposely had angered the subjects, the lab assistant, making the results more pertinent to aggression against another person.

Thus, in this new formulation, we have angered subjects differing in only one respect—whether the violence in a film portrayal was described as justified or unjustified—with an opportunity to express hostility against their antagonist. The catharsis hypothesis would predict no noteworthy difference because of the identical experience of vicarious violence. If Berkowitz was correct about the role of disinhibition, we would expect greater aggression in the justified condition.

Catharsis failed this particular test. Berkowitz and Rawlings found that aggression was greater among those viewing the ostensibly justified violence. Two decades later, the empirical record tells us that the depiction of violence as justified or unjustified is only one of many ways in which a portrayal may raise or lower subsequent aggressiveness on the part of viewers, but that the purging of aggressive impulses by vicarious experience is not likely to be the explanation in those instances in which aggressiveness is reduced by exposure to a violent portrayal (Baron, 1977; Geen, Stonner, & Shope, 1975).

Step 2: The Development of Three Theoretical Explanations for the Effects of Violent Television and Film Portrayals on Aggressive Behavior

The ultimate goal of science is empirically validated explanation. Since those 1963 experiments, three theoretical formulations have been devised to explain such phenomena. *Social learning* theory (Bandura, 1971, 1978) holds that the capability of performing an act is enhanced by, and, if the act is wholly unfamiliar, may be attributed to observing its performance by another person. Observation of the setting and outcome of another's behavior are held to affect the appropriateness and efficacy attributed to a particular act. Thus, aggressive acts may be learned from television and film, and so too may their suitability and likely efficacy in a given set of circumstances.

Disinhibition and cue theory (Berkowitz, 1962, 1973) holds that television and film portrayals may alter either the restraint associated with an internal state, such as anger or the impulse to strike someone, or the response elicited by an external stimulus. In effect, television and film portrayals are said to alter the meaning attached to internal and external experience. Thus, aggressive acts may be inhibited or disinhibited by violent portrayals, and various environmental stimuli such as individuals and groups, objects and weapons, or physical settings can alter the likelihood of aggression.

Arousal theory (Tannenbaum & Zillmann, 1975) holds that the excitation created by exposure to violent or otherwise stimulating television portrayals may transfer to subsequent behavior, so that when subsequent behavior is aggressive such exposure may heighten its intensity. Thus, aggressive acts may be encouraged by the vicarious experience of television and film portrayals.

Each of these formulations construes vicarious experience as having effects analogous to those that might ensue from direct, real-life experience. None assumes that the identical event, when experienced vicariously, would have the same influence as when experienced directly; the context of what precedes and follows the experience, and the embedding of one in the mass media (often in entertainment) and the other in actuality would affect their interpretation and the verisimilitude extended to them. What they do assume is that the same body of variables or qualifications govern the influence of both vicarious and direct experience, variously heightening or modulating the influence of one or the other.

Step 3: The Introduction of Evidence from a Variety of Methods, Each with Its Own Advantages and Disadvantages

Both the Bandura and the Berkowitz experiments in 1963 were conducted in a laboratory setting; that is, in circumstances contrived especially for the purpose of the investigation. By the time of the Surgeon General's inquiry, about fifty such laboratory experiments in which exposure to violent television and film portrayals was manipulated and subsequent aggressiveness measured had been published. Almost all of them demonstrated a heightening of aggressiveness among subjects exposed to such portrayals.

The strength of laboratory experimentation as a mode of investigation is that it permits attribution of subsequent differences between subjects in control and treatment conditions to the manipulated experience. Except where the experimenter has grievously erred in design or execution, conditions are identical except for the manipulation. Its weakness is that there is much about laboratory experimentation ostensibly pertinent to television viewing that is artificial or distant from everyday life. Exposure typically is brief and not, as in the home, part of a continuing experience. Viewing in the laboratory is more likely to be attentive, rather than distracted and discontinuous as is common in the home (Comstock, Chaffee, Katzman, McCombs, & Roberts, 1978). The aggressiveness measured is a simulation conceivably different in character from that ordinarily displayed in real life.

The experimental setting cannot help but have an aura of unreality that conceivably would encourage behavior different from that which would follow exposure to the same stimuli in real life; that is, subjects may behave with greater abandon or as if they were playing a game.

In the laboratory, there is generally no chance of retaliation from a victim, a very real deterrent to aggressiveness in real life, with the result that behavior might be displayed in the experimental setting that in real life would be suppressed. Thus, the evidence from laboratory experiments in regard to television violence is not wholly credible as to its generalizability outside an experimental setting.

The Surgeon General's inquiry added support from data collected by very different means to the array of experimental findings—means largely immune to the challenges to which the experimental findings were susceptible (Comstock et al., 1978; Surgeon General's Scientific Advisory Committee, 1972). In several samples of children and adolescents from which data were collected on everyday television viewing and everyday aggressiveness, the two were found to be positively associated (Chaffee, 1972; Lefkowitz, Eron, Walder, & Huesmann, 1972, 1977; McIntyre & Teevan, 1972; McLeod, Atkin, & Chaffee, 1972a, 1972b). Young people who viewed a greater quantity of violent television in fact displayed a higher degree of aggressiveness in real life.

These data established what the experiments did not and could not—that in real life the viewing of violent television of the sort that is regularly broadcast in circumstances equally ordinary was positively associated with greater aggressiveness. They did *not* establish causality, the strengths and weaknesses of the survey being the mirror opposite of those of the laboratory experiment. The survey's strength is that it reports on actuality, not its simulation within the time and space confines of the laboratory. Its weakness is that cause-effect inferences are rarely justifiable.

These new data also supplied evidence beyond the documentation of a real life association between violence viewing and aggressiveness. While surveys are ill-suited for irrefutable causal inference, they do permit the exploration of various alternative hypotheses as to their plausibility. For example, the real life association between violence viewing and aggressiveness might be the result of the influence of that violent entertainment on viewers, but it also might be attributable to other sources. More aggressive youths might prefer entertainment that is more violent; aggressiveness and violence viewing would then be positively associated, but without any contribution by the latter to the former. Young people doing poorly in school might watch more television, either as a salve to their frustration or as a preferred activity that interferes with scholastic achievement, and might be more aggressive because of their academic frustration; again, association without any contribution to aggressiveness by television.

Socioeconomic status provides another alternative. Young people from families of lower socioeconomic status on the average spend more time watching television than do those from families higher in socioeconomic status, making it likely that they would be higher in the viewing of violent entertainment. Norms are more permissive and supportive in regard to aggressiveness among families lower in socioeconomic status, making an association between violence viewing and aggressiveness likely in a sample including such youth quite apart from any influence on aggressiveness of exposure to violent entertainment.

In these new data, none of these alternative explanations proved wholly to account for the observed association between the viewing of violence and aggressiveness, leaving the influence of television a plausible hypothesis. Thus, the Surgeon General's inquiry augmented the evidence from the laboratory with evidence from real life. The laboratory data demonstrated that exposure to violent portrayals could increase aggressiveness. The survey data documented that such exposure and such behavior were positively correlated in everyday life, and eliminated several competing hypotheses as explanations for that association. This is the "convergence" of evidence that the Surgeon General's advisory committee cited in concluding that there was empirical support for the hypothesis that the viewing of violent television entertainment increases the aggressiveness of young viewers.

Step 4: A Progressive Increase in the Ecological Validity of Manipulations and Measures

The 1963 Bandura experiment employed specially created television sequences featuring young adults, and as a principal measure of aggressiveness, attacks levied against a Bobo doll. The 1963 Berkowitz experiment employed a brief sequence from a commercial movie, *Champion,* and as a measure of aggressiveness, the opinion of the subjects regarding the competence of the lab assistant who conducted the experiment. Such manipulations and measures legitimately may be faulted as to their ecological validity. The manipulations do not match the ordinary television or film experience, and the measures, while undeniably reflecting shifts in behavior away from the placid or amiable, fall short of what many would label as aggressiveness.

The many dozens of laboratory experiments, field experiments, and surveys that followed, however, are not uniformly open to such criticism. The viewing of violence variously involved episodes from commercial television programs, including prime time and Saturday morning; entire programs and entire films; and consistently included behavior during play and social interaction, delivery of electric shock or noxious noise, peer reports of aggression and troublemaking, and self-reports of aggression and harmful and criminal behavior. Thus, the evidence currently available is not limited to data of questionable ecological validity, and makes it possible to address the question of whether the results of those 1963 experiments depended on peculiarities of the manipulations and measures.

Step 5: Sufficient Maturation of the Scientific Literature to Permit the Use of Meta-analyses

A meta-analysis is a quantitative assessment of a scientific literature in which the findings of the individual studies become the data (Glass, McGaw, & Smith, 1981). In a literature review, the results of studies are subjectively collated and assessed; in a meta-analysis, they are quantitatively aggregated as if each finding were a datum. Meta-analysis is a luxury of the growth of inquiry and is possible only after a particular issue has been investigated repeatedly. The literature on violence in the media and antisocial behavior has reached that point, and two such analyses are available.

Using correlation coefficients, statistical significance, or percentage differences between groups as the measure of degree of association, Andison (1977) tabulated the outcomes of 67 published laboratory experiments, field experiments, and surveys involving about 30,000 subjects and respondents as to whether the reported association between violence viewing and aggressiveness was null, modestly negative or positive, or strongly negative or positive. Hearold (1979), employing a measure of dispersion to convert all results to a comparable metric, aggregated the outcomes of 230 published and unpublished laboratory experiments, field experiments, and surveys involving about 100,000 subjects and respondents as to the degree or amount of association between exposure to antisocial, prosocial, or neutral portrayals and antisocial or prosocial behavior; a procedure that produced 1,043 comparisons, of which more than 650 involved antisocial behavior. Both Andison and Hearold then classified the quantified outcomes by such variables as methods, measures, and characteristics of the subjects and respondents.[1]

As a result, we can address the questions implicit in the last two steps by reference to something quite concrete—the pattern of tabulated outcomes. What has been the direction of results? By what circumstances has that direction varied? Have method, measure, or characteristics of those studied made a substantial difference? How substantial has been the difference in aggressiveness between those having experienced greater or lesser exposure to television and film violence? Andison and Hearold tell us that:

1. A very large majority of studies report a positive association between exposure to media violence and aggressiveness. The greater part by far of this majority is made up of modest rather than strong positive associations. There are very few instances of negative relationships. Most of those that are not positive are null.
2. A majority of outcomes remain positive regardless of the method, the measure, or the age of the population. Whether of nursery school, elementary school, or college age; whether laboratory experiment, field experiment, or survey; whether by imitation, delivery of noxious stimuli, response to a questionnaire, or ratings by others, positive outnumber the total of null and negative outcomes.
3. The size of the majority, however, is unambiguously affected by method and by measure. The majority of positive outcomes is greater for laboratory experiments than for field experiments and surveys. As a result, those measures common to the latter two methods also have majorities less substantial than measures common to the laboratory experiment. For example, the questionnaire, most frequently used in surveys, is associated with a less substantial majority of positive outcomes than the delivery of noxious stimuli, such as electric shock, a measure exclusively the province of the laboratory experiment. These frequencies come from Andison, who counted the number of relationships falling into various degrees of departure from null. Hearold, who calculates an average magnitude or degree of relationship, found that its departure in a positive direction from zero was not notable for field experiments but only for laboratory experiments and surveys, which together comprise about 90 percent of the comparisons involving antisocial portrayals and antisocial behavior.
4. The average degree of relationship, or difference in behavior between those who do and do not have the communication experience in question, falls between that for two popular educational interventions. Exposure to television and film violence has been associated with a markedly greater degree of aggressiveness than the halving of class size has been associated with pupil achievement, and with somewhat less aggressiveness than computer-based instruction has been associated with increased math skills. Neither of these educational interventions has had dramatic effects. Thus, television and film violence has been comparable in recorded association with antisocial behavior to the association of modestly successful educational interventions with heightened achievement.
5. The introduction of greater ecological validity in regard to the television and film experience does not reduce the relationship to null. When experiments using specially enacted television or film sequences are eliminated, the average degree of relationship is somewhat reduced but remains above that recorded for pupil achievement as a consequence of halving class size.
6. Violent and antisocial portrayals apparently heighten the likelihood of antisocial behavior and diminish that of prosocial behavior, while portrayals of prosocial behavior heighten the likelihood of similar behavior and diminish that of antisocial behavior. The first three of these associations occur when the ecological validity of the investigation is not considered, and remain when the analysis is confined to the more ecologically valid investigations; the fourth appears only among the more ecologically valid investigations.
7. The average degree of association between prosocial behavior and exposure to prosocial portrayals is substantially greater than that between antisocial behavior and exposure to

violent and antisocial portrayals, and this metric superiority persists when analysis is confined to the ecologically valid investigations. Undoubtedly, one reason is that the parallelism between the stimulus and the measured behavior typically has been greater in the prosocial than in the antisocial instances; another is that more frequently the television and film portrayals have been specially created for maximum behavioral influence. Nevertheless, the fact that the distinction remains after the introduction of increased ecological validity makes it cavalier to dismiss the possibility of substantial prosocial effects when television and film seek them.

8. Differences by sex and by age appear, but not those that would be expected from the first decade of experiments derived from social learning theory. Because of the consistency with which nursery school-age boys exhibited greater aggressiveness than girls (Bandura, 1973), these experiments led many to the supposition that violent portrayals were most likely to affect boys and young children. The totality of outcomes gives a different impression. On the average, boys and girls of nursery school age display equally heightened aggressiveness after exposure to a violent portrayal. Throughout elementary school, there is a modest decrease in degree of effect for both, and thereafter, the two diverge, with young women decreasing and young men increasing in degree of effect until the young women are markedly below and the young men are markedly above the average levels for those of nursery school age. Apparently the influence of the norms sanctioning greater male aggressiveness increases with age despite their reflection in those early social learning experiments, and effects are not only neither confined to nor more frequent in occurrence among young children, but among males they become more pronounced with age.

It is an axiom that the laboratory experiment is the most sensitive instrument for detecting communication effects, since it ensures precisely those conditions which may be absent in everyday life—exposure to the stimulus and measurement before intervening experience. Contrary and distracting communications, or time itself, may counter or dissipate any influence. The implication is that evidence from such experiments may be misleading. The meta-analyses document that this has not been the case in regard to television and film violence and aggressiveness. Regardless of method, the direction of results remains the same. The meta-analyses introduce a number of qualifications involving methods, measures, ecological validity, age, and sex; but they present nothing that would encourage a disavowal of the proposition that aggressiveness is increased by exposure to television and film violence.

Step 6: The Identification of Psychological Processes on Which Effects are Contingent

The laboratory experiment also permits the examination of the possible influence of factors that would be difficult or impossible to isolate in less contrived circumstances. Thus, it is from these experiments that we learn of the psychological processes responsible for any effects of television and film violence on aggressiveness. They record that among the factors likely to facilitate subsequent aggressiveness are:

1. Reward, or lack of punishment, for the perpetrator of violence (Bandura, 1965; Bandura et al., 1963; Rosekrans & Hartup, 1967).
2. Portrayal of the violence as justified by the behavior of the victim (Berkowitz & Rawlings, 1963; Meyer, 1972).
3. Association of cues in the portrayal that resemble those likely to be encountered in real life with violence, such as a victim in the portrayal with the same name as someone toward

whom the viewer holds animosity (Berkowitz & Geen, 1966, 1967; Geen & Berkowitz, 1967).

4. Portrayal of the perpetrator of violence as similar to the viewer (Rosekrans, 1967).
5. Portrayal of violent behavior ambiguous in intent as motivated by the desire to inflict harm or injury (Berkowitz & Alioto, 1973; Geen & Stonner, 1972).
6. Violence portrayed so that its consequences do not stir distaste or arouse inhibitions over such behavior (Berkowitz & Rawlings, 1963).
7. Violence portrayed as representing real events rather than events concocted for a fictional film (Feshbach, 1972).
8. Portrayed violence that is not the subject of critical commentary (Lefcourt, Barnes, Parke, & Schwartz, 1966).
9. Portrayals of violence whose commission particularly pleases the viewer (Ekman, Liebert, Friesen, Harnson, Zlatchin, Malstrom, & Baron, 1972; Slife & Rychiak, 1982).
10. Portrayals, violent or otherwise, that leave the viewer in a state of unresolved excitement (Zillman, 1971; Zillman, Johnson, & Hanrahan, 1973).
11. Viewers who are in a state of anger or provocation before seeing a violent portrayal (Berkowitz & Geen, 1966; Geen, 1968).
12. Viewers who are in a state of frustration after viewing a violent portrayal (Geen, 1968; Geen & Berkowitz. 1967; Worchel, Hardy, & Hurley, 1976).

This catalogue is readily construable as reflecting four basic dimensions. They are *efficacy* (reward or lack of punishment), *normativeness* (justified, consequenceless, intentionally hurtful violence), *pertinence* (commonality of cues, similarity to the viewer), and *susceptibility* (pleasure, anger, frustration, absence of criticism). Whatever in a portrayal or the circumstance of viewing that heightens belief in the efficacy, normativeness, or pertinence of violence will increase the likelihood that television and film violence will stimulate aggressiveness, and so too with whatever nurtures in the viewer a cognitive or emotional state conducive to aggressiveness. The findings, as is the case with all supposedly good science, record not only the past but are a basis for what is reasonable to expect in new circumstances.

Should we be surprised, then, that an occasional and perhaps banal theater movie is followed by juvenile rampages or gang fights? Or that a particularly striking act of violence in a movie or television drama is imitated by some viewers? Or that a particular characterization in a movie or television drama becomes the model for those viewers who liken themselves to such a person? Such events reflect nothing more than ordinary psychology, however bizarre they may appear initially.

Step 7: The Inclusion of Measures that Represent Criminal Acts or Harmful Antisocial Behavior

In the translation of the concept of aggression to specific measures, it is fair to say that the empirical literature has become progressively more valid. Bobo dolls and pen-and-pencil ratings have been replaced by the delivery of noxious stimuli and everyday behavior. Aggression, however, is not synonymous with criminal acts or harmful antisocial behavior. Certainly, those surveys of everyday television viewing and aggressiveness are not subject to the challenges addressed to the laboratory experiments on the basis of their ostensible artificiality, yet they do not necessarily bear directly on the question of media influence on serious antisocial behavior.

Three studies, however, meet such a criterion. They are the field experiments by Milgram and Shotland (1973), the British research by Belson (1978), and the quasi-experimental examination of archival data by Hennigan and colleagues (Hennigan, Heath, Wharton, Del-Rosario, Cook, & Calder, 1982).

In the principal experiment by Milgram and Shotland, the portrayal of a crime was followed about a week later by an opportunity for the viewers to commit a similar crime. Several versions of a *Medical Center* episode were shown to audiences at a New York preview house. While intoxicated, a featured character contemplates the theft of coins and bills from a hospital charity box. He is motivated by revenge and frustraton. In one version, he commits the theft and is arrested; in another, he commits the theft and flees successfully; in a third, he decides against the theft and instead makes a contribution. The control condition was a different *Medical Center* episode in which no comparable antisocial act occurred. Viewers were invited to pick up the premium of a radio at a mid-Manhattan office for their participation. Upon arrival, the premium-seeker was met by an unstaffed office and one of two signs. One stated that the distribution center had been moved to another office in the same building. The other announced curtly that no more radios remained and that the distribution center was closed. The visitor also found a hospital charity box, with one dollar within easy plucking.

Those informed that their trip had been in vain engaged in more thefts and attempted thefts from the charity box and the office than those directed to another distribution center, an apparent exemplification of the frustration-aggression hypothesis (Dollard, Doob, Miller, Mowrer, & Sears, 1939). However, Milgram and Shotland conclude that nowhere in several comparisons was exposure to any of the episodes involving hospital charity boxes associated with a greater rate of theft.

Quite apart from the fact that had these investigators chosen to investigate the hypothesis derivable from social learning and disinhibition and cue theories that portrayals of punished antisocial behavior will inhibit frustrated persons from displaying such behavior, they might have been led to a different conclusion about the influence of television [see their Table 3, p. 27],[2] there remains an inherent problem with such research unresolved by null results. It is simply that the several percentage points difference required for statistical significance implies an influence of immense magnitude. If such were the case, we might expect several million of the huge audiences for prime time television to be affected nightly, and each morning's television news to chronicle the crime waves following the violent portrayals of the night before. The decay in effect that would be expected over the lapse of several days, and the imposing threshold that one would expect even a minor crime to present for many people, strengthen skepticism. For Milgram and Shotland to have found criminal behavior directly traceable to exposure to one or another *Medical Center* a week earlier would represent awesome influence. The view that on the subject at issue this research is uninformative is enhanced by the fact that it is arguable that their data actually record an inhibiting of behavior as a consequence of television exposure (again their Table 3, p. 27), although they do not so interpret them.

This is why research involving behavior other than criminal acts and the seriously harmful is relevant to such acts and behavior. By the lower threshold of its measures, and in the case of laboratory experiments by the sensitivity of the mode of investigation, it registers realistic effects and associations. In the course of doing so, it identifies the aspects of television and film violence likely to figure in any contribution to antisocial behavior and eliminates alternative explanations for the apparent real-life association between such media violence and the varieties of antisocial behavior measured. That the influence apparently recorded would only infrequently register in the criminal and seriously harmful should not be a surprise, but accepted principle.

The Belson study examined 1,500 London male teenagers, collecting data on both their television viewing and a large number of other activities including those criminal in nature or seriously harmful to others. This serious antisocial behavior included thefts and physical brutality, such as burning a victim with a cigarette, rape, and attacking another with a motorcycle chain. He found engaging in serious antisocial behavior was associated independently of other variables with greater exposure to television and film violence. On the basis of a number of analyses, Belson concluded that it was more congruent with the evidence to believe that this media violence had contributed to the social violence than to believe that the socially violent person had sought out entertainment that was especially violent or that some factor other than the media was responsible for the higher exposure to television and film violence and the greater degree of serious antisocial behavior.

Whether Belson is justified in interpreting his survey data as identifying violent television and film entertainment as a cause of criminal acts and behavior seriously harmful to others is open to question, since *ex post facto* matching is not the equivalent of experimental manipulation. What is not open to question is his documentation of a positive association between the two. Thus, his data can be thought of as an advance in evidence from surveys analogous to that achieved by the increasing validity of the measures of aggression in laboratory experiments. The earlier surveys recorded associations between exposure to television violence and aggression, although it should be recognized that the scales included some behavior, such as fighting and stealing, that arguably falls within the range of the harmful and criminal. The Belson data extend that association to unambiguously criminal acts, and behavior that is unambiguously harmful to others. Thus, they give an ominous note to that convergence of experiments and surveys on which the Surgeon General's committee based its 1972 conclusion.

The study by Hennigan and colleagues takes advantage of a governmental edict to produce a natural experiment on a grand scale. In the early 1950s, the government halted television station licensing to assess certain technical problems. As a result, between 1951 and 1954, there were large numbers of communities with television and large numbers without. Hennigan and colleagues examined various indices of crime in rural and urban sites at two points in time at which the influence of television could be assessed—when the initial wave of communities obtained television, at which point the baseline or control condition was the communities without television; and when the remaining communities obtained television, at which time the baseline or control was the communities where television was already functioning. This paradigm not only experimentally reflects life in its natural disorder, but includes a replication or second test. When data were aggregated for cities and also by state, and at both points in time, the introduction of television was followed by an increase in larceny. The rates of other categories of crime—violent crime, burglary, and auto theft—were unchanged.

Hennigan and her colleagues (Hennigan et al., 1982) formally defined larceny as:

> The unlawful taking, carrying, leading, or riding away of property from the possession or constructive possession of another. Thefts of bicycles, automobile accessories, shoplifting, pocket-picking, or any stealing of property or article which is not taken by force and violence or by fraud. Excluded embezzlement, "con" games, forgery, worthless checks, etc. [p. 465]

Hennigan and colleagues observed that there was a great deal of violent crime in television entertainment during this period, as there has been since the introduction of the medium (Head, 1954; Remmers, 1954; Smythe, 1954), and concluded that social learning or emulation of portrayals was not responsible since violent categories of crime displayed no change. Instead, they suggest that the material goods and well-being so emphasized by television commercials and by the dramas themselves created a sense of relative deprivation or envy that could be redressed by theft. They are quite possibly correct, although it is certainly arguable that what took place was an emulation of the principle that antisocial and illegal means are effective in achieving goals—a principle frequently implicit in violent television drama (Larsen, Gray, &

Fortis, 1963). That is, the violent crime of television drama, in effect, was emulated, but on a scale at which gain was most likely and unpleasant consequences more readily evaded or less severe if suffered.

It is instructive to return to the Belson data on this question of the factors responsible for effects. Belson attempted to identify the attributes of the violent television and film drama associated with the severe antisocial behavior he recorded. He found violent sports, violent cartoons, violent science fiction, and slapstick not at all implicated, a result that gives considerable credibility to his analysis as a whole because it eliminates the possibility of some artifactual relationship of antisocial behavior with media exposure of any sort and implies an impressive degree of discriminability. What he did find as characteristic of violent entertainment most clearly associated with criminal acts and behavior seriously harmful to others are:

- Protagonists displaying great strength and power who defeat essentially weak villians.
- Violence with numerous victims, such as mass killings.
- Violence which erupts among friends, allies, or gang members.
- Violence which is extreme compared to the events leading up to it.
- Instances where "violence of a nasty kind appears to be sanctioned by showing it being done in a good cause or with seeming legality."
- Dramas that encourage identification with the aggressor.
- Violence of sufficient realism as to evade classification as fiction.

Obviously, the degree to which such attributes of entertainment are intercorrelated in the media reduces the claim that might be made from the data as to the independent influence of any single one, but it hardly requires imagination to construe these characteristics as collaborative of the findings of the earlier laboratory experiments. What is identified here as violent entertainment associated with criminal acts and behavior seriously harmful to others is violence that is effective or can be engaged in without risk or penalty, violence that is presented as a normative or ordinary means of settling conflicts even among friends and allies, violence likely to be particularly arousing, violence that is justified by events and the behavior of victim, violence that dehumanizes those who suffer from it by its application to groups instead of individuals, violence that involves the viewer in the perspective of the person responsible for it, and violence that is made life-like and thus pertinent to everyday affairs by its realism. Thus, we are returned by these data on criminal and severe antisocial behavior to those experiments which at first perhaps seemed curious but irrelevant to such activity.

At this point, the recent research on the effects of violent pornography becomes relevant (Donnerstein, 1980; Donnerstein & Barrett, 1978; Donnerstein & Berkowitz, 1981; Donnerstein & Hallam, 1978; Malamuth, Feshbach, & Jaffe, 1977). It appears that the Commission on Obscenity and Pornography may have been precipitous in its conclusion that exposure to pornography has no influence on antisocial behavior. More recent experiments indicate that pornography featuring violence against women stimulates subsequent aggression toward women, and especially so when the victim in the portrayal appears to gain some pleasure from the violence directed against her. The factor most clearly implicated as responsible is the portrayal of violence against a female in an erotic context. It is, as in the earlier experiments, the presence of aggressive behavior that results in the display of heightened aggressiveness; and, again, there is the link between the victim in the portrayal and the victim in the experimental setting, alike in these instances in their sex.

A recent comparison between television violence in Japan and in the United States also provides insight into the means by which violent television and film entertainment may contribute to antisocial behavior. Several years ago, TV Guide (Barnard, 1978) published an intriguing article describing Japanese television as among the most violent in the world, but pointing out that there was almost no concern on the part of anyone in Japan over the possibility that this violent entertainment contributed to greater aggressiveness or antisocial behavior. In effect, the article asked whether such concern and the associated research in the United States was culturally peculiar to this society or whether it was in fact misguided.

Iwao, deSola Pool, & Hagiwara (1981) tabulated the frequency of violent acts in Japanese evening television and found that it was almost precisely identical to the frequency of such acts in prime time television in the United States. However, they found that Japanese television violence was strikingly different in character from that in the United States.

In the United States, television violence is largely suffered by villains; is often minimal in terms of bloodletting, particularly in the case of wounds as contrasted with death; and is committed about as often by heroes or "good guys" as by villains. In Japanese-produced television, it is typically the hero who suffers violence. The hurtful effects of wounding are more frequently made clear by bleeding, and violence is much more frequently the act of a villain or "bad guy." As a result, Japanese-produced television is, in the words of the authors, "more often a morality story than is the American." It is entirely in accord with the American research that such television violence would not encourage aggressiveness or antisocial behavior, for it emphasizes the harm that it may bring, and identification with the victim rather than with the aggressor, and it associates violence not with socially sanctioned justice or retribution, but with the actions of villains.

SOME TESTS

There are questions that can be addressed to a body of studies that make no sense when there is but one or even a few. Meta-analysis is an example. There are also somewhat more qualitative tests that may be applied. These include the tests of consistency, method invariance, implied central tendency, substantiality, naturalism, seriousness, process and theory, and contiguity.

Consistency

The scientific literature on violent television and film portrayals and aggression is internally consistent in regard to a positive association between the two. As Andison's meta-analysis makes clear, a majority of laboratory experiments, field experiments, and surveys record such an association. The laboratory experiments establish a case for causation on the part of the portrayals by unambiguously demonstrating such cause-and-effect relationships within the experimental setting. The field experiments, although presenting a less sizable majority, do not encourage the rejection of that proposition by the more naturalistic, or ecologically valid, test they apply. The surveys, although again presenting a less substantial majority than the laboratory experiments, record an association in everyday life not readily explained by factors other than the influence of violent entertainment.

There are certainly laboratory experiments, field experiments, and surveys in which no association between exposure to violent television and film portrayals and aggression is apparent. The fact that a majority of empirical investigations record such an association places these contrary results not in the role of disconfirmation of the proposition that media violence increases aggressive behavior but in that of qualification. They simply demonstrate that in some circumstances such a relationship does not occur, either because of attributes of the subjects or respondents, the particular television and film portrayals involved, or the circumstances of exposure or subsequent behavior. The conclusion of the recent National Institute of Mental Health advisory committee (Pearl et al., 1982a) that "according to many researchers, the evidence accumulated in the 1970s seems overwhelming that televised violence and aggression are positively correlated in children" concurs with numerous earlier reviews based on the evidence accumulated by the time of their writing that aggressive behavior is increased by exposure to television and film violence (Bandura, 1973; Baron, 1977; Berkowitz, 1964; Bogart, 1972; Comstock et al., 1978; Eysenck & Nias, 1978; Goranson, 1970; Liebert, Neale, & Davidson, 1973; Murray, 1980) and with the conclusion of a convergence of evidence from experiments and surveys by the Surgeon General's advisory committee a decade earlier. The reviews that appear to reach a contrary conclusion (Feshbach & Singer, 1971; Hartley, 1964; Hoffman, 1981; Howitt & Cumberbatch, 1974; Kaplan & Singer, 1976; Klapper, 1960; Singer, 1971) either focus on the limitations of individual investigations or of a genre of investigation, and particularly the nonnaturalistic qualities of the laboratory experiment, beg the question by arguing that media depictions reinforce individuals' existing tendencies, or question whether the findings represent anything of social significance. They have not applied the test of consistency, which the accumulated evidence now appears to pass.

Method Invariance

Related to but distinct from the question of consistency is that of invariance in results when different manipulations and measures are employed. The question now becomes not whether results are consistent within and across genres of method, but whether they are markedly affected by the application of different techniques and procedures within such genres. Were that the case, one might conclude that the evidence from one of these sources reflects a phenomenon peculiar to the techniques involved and is thus narrow in generalizability to other circumstances.

This certainly does not seem to be the case with the laboratory experiments. Manipulations have varied from television portrayals enacted by young adults only a very few minutes in length to full-length commercial programs, with exposure to violent portrayals followed by increased aggressiveness for a varied collection of stimuli. The same may be said of the measures of aggression—choice of toys, play, ratings of another person, delivery of noxious stimuli—all have been demonstrated to increase as a consequence of exposure to a violent portrayal.

The field experiments typically involve exposure to complete programs or films and the observation of subsequent everyday behavior as the measure. Since these have a high claim to ecological validity, the similarity of techniques across field experiments does not on that ground subject them to skepticism. The surveys have involved recording exposure to commercial television programs, which in turn are scored as to violence to develop a violence viewing score for each individual. A variety of measures of aggressiveness have been employed, with the one most frequently associated with greater exposure to violent entertainment the ratings supplied by peers, although in the Belson data the principal measure was respondents' reports on their own past behavior.

The apparent validity of these measures rescues the survey as a genre from suspicion even though all measures of aggression have not been equally strongly, or in some instances, at all associated with the viewing of violent entertainment. The phenomenon of the association of exposure to television and film violence cannot fairly be said to be a product or artifact of particular techniques and procedures.

Implied Central Tendency

Every survey, whatever the topic and measures, will vary in the statistics produced as a consequence of the peculiarities of the sample. Since not all surveys of television viewing and aggressive behavior have recorded a positive association between such behavior and exposure to violent entertainment, it is reasonable to ask whether as a whole they imply a value for such an association that is positive, negative, or null. If it were the case that many surveys recorded an inverse association between the two, with greater exposure to television and film violence associated with lower levels of aggressive behavior, it could be taken to suggest that both the positive and negative associations simply represent deviation from what in fact is a null relationship. The empirical record, however, leads to no such conclusion. The majority of associations are positive, and the rest null, implying a positive central value.

The strongest evidence to challenge the presumption of a positive association between the two in everyday life is the three-year panel survey by Milavsky and colleagues (Milavsky, Kessler, Stipp, & Rubens, 1982). These investigators obtained repeated measures of exposure to television violence and aggressive behavior from a total of about 2,400 elementary school boys and girls and about 800 teenage males in two cities. Measures were obtained from the elementary school sample six times; from the teenage sample, five times. Respondents entered and left the sample as they entered and left the public schools that served as the principal means of data collection. Each wave contains substantially fewer persons than the total providing data over the three years, and between waves the longer the lapse the greater the attrition (among elementary school males over three months, $N = 497$; nine months, 356; two years, 211; three years, 112). The elementary school practice of day-long class groupings led to the use of the peer report emphasizing interpersonal aggression; the absence of this practice in high school led to self-report for four types of aggression, "personal" (similar to that for the elementary school sample), and "property," "teacher," and "delinquency." They report low correlations that are positive and achieve a conventional level of statistical significance between violence viewing and aggressive behavior for both elementary school boys and girls and for teenage males at both points in time. When various other factors are taken into account, such as socioeconomic status of the family and race, these correlations decrease in size and often fall below a conventional level of statistical significance, although the pattern of positive associations remains. When the investigators depart from synchronous correlations (that is, among variables measured at the same point in time) for over time inquiries in which the focus is on the association of violence viewing with aggressive behavior from three months to three years later, they report a different pattern.

Positive correlations remain more frequent, although to a marked degree only among elementary school boys and teenage males. Among the elementary school boys, they are uniformly positive and noticeably larger in size for the five of the 15 wave durations that equal or exceed two years. Several of these associations exceed the magnitude required for statistical significance when shorter time lapses led to much larger (sometimes by severalfold) samples; with such larger samples presumably some of these associations would have achieved statistical significance. Among the teenage males, the pattern of increased association with lengthening durations between waves is apparent only for personal aggression, the measure that most parallels the aggression measure for the elementary school both in content and by displaying the greatest degree of modest synchronous association with violence viewing; the correlation for the lengthiest of the four durations (one year and seven months) is insignificant. There are positive associations that achieve statistical significance among the elementary school boys, the elementary school girls, and the teenage males, but in each instance their number hovers on the border of being attributable to chance. Were there a contribution of violence viewing to the development of aggressive behavior as a permanent disposition, an over time association arguably would be expected. Arguably, then, these data give scant support to such an interpretation. Arguably, they also fail to give full health to skepticism, for the pattern can be taken as consistent with what theory and prior research suggest—some modest long-term influence on the aggressive dispositions of young males.

The investigators offer the sensitivity of the synchronous correlations to the introduction of additional variables and the failure of a sufficient number of over time correlations as failing to support the proposition that exposure to violent television entertainment contributes to aggressive behavior.

The weakness of this challenge, quite apart from the positive array of synchronous correlations that persists when other variables are taken into account (which implies that the "true" relationship bears a + sign) and the borderline significance and suggestive (if debatable perceivable) pattern of the over time correlations, is that the statistically significant synchronous correlations are equally interpretable as simply documenting the reinforcement by violent entertainment of behavior associated with those variables whose role they statistically contain. Thus, the question of a contribution by television violence to aggressive behavior remains unresolved even for their respondents. This is essentially the view taken by the sociologist Janowitz in his recent *The Last Half-Century* (1981) when he rhetorically asks whether the research on media violence and aggression does not lead to the conclusion that a substantial reduction of such content in television entertainment would not reduce the level of violence in society.

Substantiality

The meta-analysis of Hearold tabulates the average degree of association between exposure to violent portrayals and aggressive behavior as similar to that of not particularly effective social interventions in education. The meta-analysis of Andison records degrees of statistical significance for the laboratory experiments that are more often modest than strong. The surveys reporting statistically significant positive correlations typically associate slightly less than 10 percent of the measured variance in aggression with exposure to television violence. Given the presumably strong role of situational, long-term, environmental, social, and personal factors that figure in behaving aggressively, it would be implausible to expect more than this clearly modest relationship. Aggressive behavior outside of those circumstances in which it is socially approved is a persistent sore spot in social relations, and one in which the victims are unlikely to extend absolution even to those factors modestly responsible. The evidence on media violence and aggression thus does not invite dismissal on the grounds of the size of the association between the two.

Naturalism

The laboratory experiments have progressively approximated more naturalistic manipulations and measures without encountering a dramatic diminution in the frequency with which exposure to violent television and film portrayals has been followed by heightened aggressiveness. The field experiments and surveys by their very nature reflect naturalistic circumstances, and a majority report greater aggressiveness associated with higher degrees of exposure to television and film violence. The small-scale field experiment by Steuer, Applefield, and Smith (1971), for example, may be faulted because it does not distinguish aggression attributable to the exposure of individual children to violent programs from that arising out of imitation of and retaliation toward the influence exerted on one or more individual children by such exposure; but it certainly is naturalistic enough, with the manipulation employing violent Saturday morning programs, and the measure of aggressive behavior displayed in regularly scheduled play periods. The field experiments with adolescent boys in resident homes in Europe by Leyens and colleagues (Leyens & Camino, 1974; Leyens, Camino, Parke, & Berkowitz, 1975) similarly record increased observed aggressiveness in social interaction as a consequence of nightly viewings of violent motion pictures. The Belson survey extends the naturalism of the aggression associated with exposure to television violence in earlier surveys to self-reported measures of criminal acts and behavior seriously harmful to others. Thus, while many individual studies may be faulted in regard to ecological validity, the scientific record as a whole is hardly erased in implication for real social effects by its absence.

Seriousness

It has been emphasized repeatedly that the evidence is far clearer in regard to aggressive behavior than it is for criminal acts and behavior that is seriously harmful to others. In fact, it is useful to construe the evidence as varying in strength on two dimensions: the age of those involved, and the degree of social disruption, harm, and damage implied by the behavior.

The evidence is least questionable in the case of the aggressiveness of young children. This is not because positive results are more consistently produced in experiments involving younger children, for, as Andison (1977) reported, those with older subjects have a similar majority of positive outcomes, but because the circumstances of the experiment are closest to the real life circumstances of interest. The laboratory experiments which demonstrate causation largely escape the criticisms of varied artificiality and lack of generalizability when the subjects are the same age as the population of interest, the behavior of interest as expressed in play is the measure of the experiment, and the time span between exposure and measured effects is not much, if at all, different from the sequence of interest in real life, when a child views television and then turns to play.

It is a far less steady inferential step to draw conclusions about the behavior of adults from such experiments. So, too, is it a less certain step to draw conclusions about the everyday aggressive behavior of subjects of college age from the laboratory experiments in which they participate; while the populations under scrutiny and of interest are the same, the measured aggressiveness is unlikely to match that in real life and the passage of time between exposure and behavior of any consequence is likely to be much greater.

Much the same argument makes the evidence clearer in regard to aggressive behavior than for criminal and seriously harmful behavior. The behavior measured in the laboratory experiments, field experiments, and surveys far more often falls under the former than the latter label.

Yet, it would be no less than ignorant to dismiss the evidence as not pertinent to antisocial behavior beyond the tolerable. The play of children offers ample opportunity for them to harm one another. The imposition of noxious stimuli, often an electric stock thought to be painful, would be welcomed by few victims in the everyday analogue of inflicting pain when given an opportunity. Thus, the laboratory and field experiments attain such pertinence to some degree by their actual measures, as well as by the demonstration of the aspects of portrayals that can invoke changes in behavior. The surveys have often included such unesteemed behavior as starting fights and stealing among the items in their scales; the Belson data presents associations between unarguably harmful antisocial behavior and exposure to media violence; and the data of Hennigan and colleagues finds an increase in larceny as a consequence of the introduction of television. Thus, the acknowledgment that the scientific literature does not frequently document associations between such exposure and such behavior does not lead to the conclusion that it fails to deal with behavior serious in consequences.

Process and Theory

Confidence that outcomes are attributable to alleged influences is greatly increased when such an inference derives from theory and when the processes by which it presumably occurs have at least been partially explored. The proposition that media violence encourages antisocial and aggressive behavior is more credible than it would be solely from the empirical record because that record is in accord with social learning, disinhibition and cue, and arousal theory. These are not fanciful formulations unsupported by evidence. They are supported by the research on television and film violence and aggression, and by the catalogue of aspects of violent portrayals which have been found to be associated with high degrees of aggressiveness presented earlier. In the case of social learning theory, the support also derives from numerous experiments involving live actors instead of models appearing in television and film portrayals, and extends to behavior other than aggressiveness, including the reduction of phobias, deviation from stated rules, readiness to play with children of other races, liking for advertised goods, and behavior falling under the concept of "prosocial" (Atkin, 1980; Bandura, 1973; Comstock et al., 1978; Liebert, Neale, & Davidson, 1982; Rushton, 1980).

The significance of these theories is that they provide plausible and empirically verified expectations and explanations for the influence of television and film violence on aggressive and antisocial behavior. Thus, we are not left with a mere empirical linkage, but with a set of ideas about the why of behavior that makes the existence of such a linkage sensible and thereby more believable.

An inescapable question is whether arousal theory, which attributes effects to excitation resulting from exposure to violent or other stimulating portrayals, does not account for the effects initially ascribed to social learning theory or disinhibition and cue theory. It seems reasonable to assume that frequently the excitation produced in subjects has had some role in the observed outcomes. However, arousal theory does not appear to supplant the other two. First, aggressiveness has been found to be independently associated with exposure to attributes of television programming arguably arousal-producing as well as with exposure to those seemingly likely to foster the acquisition of behavior, norms, and cues, the processes to which social learning and disinhibition and cue theories attribute effects (Krull & Watt, 1973; Watt & Krull, 1974). Second, the outcomes of the experiments derived from social learning and disinhibition and cue theories are not consistently explainable by arousal. In many instances there is no reason to attribute greater or lesser excitatory capability to one or the other of the conditions (justified vs. unjustified violence, for example) or for the behavior displayed to imitate that of a violent portrayal. The psychological dynamics described by the three theories thus appear to function concurrently; all three hold.

They do concur in establishing within the laboratory experiment (as presumably in real life) prior viewer frustration, provocation, or anger as heightening the likelihood that aggressive behavior will be increased by exposure to violent television or film portrayals. This is precisely as we should expect, for the lessons of a violent portrayal are surely most applicable when a viewer is irritated, and the fact that the frustration, or provocation, and anger variously in the experiments has involved denial of playthings, insults not so different from what occurs occasionally in the flow of life, and noxious stimuli like that which the subject will have a chance to use in retaliation, does not so much place this qualification outside of as within the view reinforced by the field experiments and surveys in which such manipulations do not figure but in which exposure to violent portrayals and aggressive behavior remain associated. Frustration, provocation, and anger are merely factors which, through the three theories, make the phenomenon of aggressiveness influenced by television and film portrayals sensible and believable.

Contiguity

The laboratory and field experiments on television and film violence and aggression admittedly establish the necessary condition for causal inference of that factor said to be the cause preceding in time that presumed to be the effect. The field experiments arguably establish such a sequence in actuality as contrasted with the alleged artificiality of the laboratory setting. Yet, it is fair to ask whether such phenomena have ever been observed in everyday life while recognizing that the possibilities of replying to such an inquiry with much scientific rigor are remote, since everyday events substantial enough to be noticeable—threats, thefts, attacks, woundings, murders—are not predictable as to moment and place of occurrence and thus are not so easily captured by a research design. It might seem sensible to compare crime statistics with media violence; the two in fact do not seem to coincide (Clark & Blankenberg, 1972), although this implies no more than that the quantity of violence annually in television, films, and newspapers is not markedly associated with reported crimes and that the emphasis given to violence in the media does not reflect the degree of antisocial behavior serious enough to appear as a crime statistic, but reflects either the agenda of the media themselves as to what appears popular or interesting to emphasize, or some other social trend too obscure to have been noticed. The notion of examining crimes or publicized incidents of an antisocial character in terms of the media portrayals that precede them is not widely applicable because there are so many of the latter.

When crime, violence, or self-destruction seem to follow upon violence in the media, skepticism provides a sanctuary. The temptation is to abandon the principle of contiguity in human affairs, by which the extreme is looked upon as the exaggerated instance of what occurs on an unrecognized modulated scale in favor of the view that behavior different enough defines a different species. So, when we encounter the adoption of the human fly technique from *Topakapi* by "Murph the Surf" and friends to rob a Florida museum, the alleged attempted coke bottle rape of a San Francisco girl after a similar broomstick rape in the television drama *Born Innocent,* the immolation of a Boston nurse shortly after the broadcast of the movie *Fuzz* in which sleeping bums are set afire by a marauding gang, the frequency of Russian-roulette woundings and deaths close upon cable and pay television showings of the film *The Deerhunter* recorded by the Coalition On Television Violence (1980), the obsessive viewing of violent television entertainment before the murder of an elderly woman neighbor by a Florida teenager, and the preoccupation of an aspiring presidential assassin with the film *Taxi Driver,* we are ready—quite apart from the facts favoring or disfavoring media influence—to consign these events to minds sick or criminal, possessed, inevitably trouble- or death-prone, and thus not within meaningful sway of the media. The media seem exonerated by the seriousness of the event. And so, we rationalize away that by which we might be instructed.

Contiguity becomes a problem whose solution is perpetually rejected. Anecdotes will not do if they are too bizarre, and were they not bizarre they would go unnoticed. This does not scandalize science, for which these sequences are poor evidence, but it does raise the question as to what one might possibly want in the way of a "real life" example. In this context, *Doomsday Flight,* the Rod Serling movie that, when newly shown on television, was followed by sharp increases in airline bomb threats (Bandura, 1973), is not an oddity but a resolution.

The movie's plot is simple enough. The extortionist will reveal the location of the bomb aboard the Los Angeles-New York flight only after his monetary demands are met, and the bomb will explode if the plane descends below a certain altitude. Viewing the film itself presents not so much the story of a foiled extortion as the highly successful attempt by someone powerless to take revenge for unjust treatment by disrupting the social order. It is neither peculiarly surprising nor at odds with psychological research that the film might serve as a model for some viewers. As the captain remarks as the plane nears safety, "This is one for the textbooks!" He meant those on terrorism and airline emergencies; it has turned out to be those in psychology.

There are also the analyses by Phillips in which contiguity in everyday life is the subject of attempted capture by identifying a plausible but not pervasive kind of media content that might influence public behavior recorded in available statistics (Phillips, 1974, 1977, 1978, 1982a, 1982b). The technique is to specify a period subsequent to the mass media attention in which the level of recorded behavior can be compared to that in a matching period prior to that media attention. In effect, an experimental design is draped around the behavior of the media, turning that behavior analogous to a manipulation. Obviously, this technique imperfectly employs the experimental design as to the proper periods for comparison, for who can say until after the data have been tabulated exactly for what length of time media attention might affect public behavior, and after how much of a lag? Nevertheless, it would seem to ensure comparability of the designated periods, thereby controlling for other factors.

So far, Phillips has reported increases in recorded suicides after the publicity given the suicides of celebrities, increases in noncommercial and commercial air crash deaths after the publicity given a murderer who takes his own life, and increases in suicides after the portrayal of a suicide or suicide attempt in television soap operas. For these bizarre couplings, if indeed all of them survive methodological and statistical objections, he advances a theory of imitation and suggestibility—emulative self-destruction.

The evidence is certainly most compelling in the instance of suicides increasing after celebrity suicides. Such an effect is not only intuitively plausible, but it gains in credibility by a parallel increase in lethal motor vehicle crashes (Bollen and Phillips, 1981; Phillips, 1977), a mishap which suicide experts believe masks a number of purposeful, impulsive, or barely conscious resolutions of a bent toward self-destruction, not matched by a change in the rate of multiple car crashes and noninjurious crashes either single or multiple, mishaps which do not share the self-destructive repute of the lethal single vehicle incident. The most open to question is the soap opera-suicide association, as null is the verdict of two investigators reexamining the data (Kessler & Stipp, 1982).

The point is not to certify this series of findings but to recognize that contiguity in real life can conceivably be approached empirically, and that, as is very possibly exemplified in the case of celebrity suicides, the media may affect behavior far beyond the intentions or self-doubts of those responsible for their contents. Contiguity, then, while problematic as proof, hardly provides any basis for rejecting the support the accumulated scientific evidence gives the proposition that television and film violence encourage antisocial behavior.

IMPLICATIONS FOR PREVENTION AND CONTROL

There are three parties who conceivably might act in the prevention and control of aggressive and antisocial behavior attributable to the influence of the entertainment media. They are the federal government, the entertainment business, and the audience.

The federal government is a wholly unlikely if a not necessarily entirely impotent source for reducing the violence in mass entertainment. It has no direct way of influencing movie production and, as a consequence of cable and pay television and in-home playback and recording, increasingly fewer means of determining what can be received or displayed on a video screen. It has made few gestures to influence the content of television and radio entertainment through the Federal Communications Commission since the passage of the Communications Act of 1934. Its few such excursions have included a policy statement to the effect that increased educational and informational programming for children would be desirable, a remission of the prime time access rule that prohibits network entertainment programming before 8 p.m. in the evenings, the miscalculated *ex officio* "family viewing" experiment, and the well-known "fairness doctrine" and "equal time" provisions, by which broadcasters are required to give comprehensive coverage to public issues and equal access to competing political candidates.

It is restricted not only by the First Amendment, which the evolution of Supreme Court decisions on free speech suggests would impel the overturn of any administrative or Congressional bars on violent entertainment (Krattenmaker & Powe, 1978), but by the language of the 1934 act, which prohibits interfering in content. As Albert (1978) points out, however, the courts have been challenged, essentially on the ground that the responsibility of regulating broadcasting in the "public interest, convenience, and necessity" cannot be discharged without concern for what is broadcast. As a result, while bars against violence would probably be dismantled by the courts, stipulations to serve audiences in ways that would presumably minimize violence, such as educational and cultural offerings, might survive court challenges. Certainly, the notion of burdening any public agency with the responsibility of ruling whether a film or drama is too violent offends not only judgment, for it is improbable that any such task would be discharged sensibly or well, much less efficiently, but civic responsibility, for the popular arts can hardly be abandoned to censorship and governmental manipulation.

In one direction, the federal government should not act, and if it did it would face defeat by legal challenge. In the other, while it conceivably might act effectively, it is unlikely to do so, and its potential effectiveness is continually being eroded by technology. In this context, the periodic examination of the frequency and effects of violent entertainment on television by special task forces and Congressional hearings serves the important and useful function of regularly instructing those in the entertainment business that this is a matter of concern to many, but it cannot be expected to lead to an imposed solution.

Local communities have few effective tools, as they are limited by the First Amendment and by the proximity of communities which hold different standards. Also, the prospect of local censorship is no more attractive than that of federal censorship. Regulations and practices which encourage local outlets, whether they are television stations or theaters, to accept or reject programs and films individually also encourage the voluntary imposition of local standards and individual taste and judgment. They additionally unhappily amplify the power of pressure groups in the community, and there is no more to recommend informal censorship of entertainment by local citizens than governmental censorship.

The entertainment business is also an unlikely source of a concerted blanket reduction in television and film violence. Violence is an accepted convention of popular entertainment, and is looked upon by many as just another ingredient for concocting a compelling story, often as one upon which popular success may depend. This holds equally for those making television programs for children as for those concerned with prime time television or feature films (Baldwin & Lewis, 1972; Cantor, 1972). There is ample economic incentive for making television and film entertainment in which violence is certain to figure, as the seemingly endless lists of action and adventure serials and films document.

Violence is an expression of the legal and economic structure of American television, and is less frequent where that structure is different (Murray & Kippax, 1979). Competition among the media to attract audiences inevitably escalates whatever type of content is perceived as useful for that purpose. Theater films featuring violence have become proportionately more frequent since the emergence of television (Clark & Blankenberg, 1972), certainly in part because the theater film can be more graphic with violence, as it can with sex, than a medium directly reaching the home. Thus, violence and sexual explicitness become means in the competition with television.

Violence became a television staple with the emergence of action and adventure series in the late 1950s and early 1960s, but the number of programs featuring violence rises and falls in response to shifts in audience ratings recording greater or lesser popularity of such programs (Clark & Blankenberg, 1972). The regulation of American television, compared to that in many countries, is highly nonpaternalistic in regard to content. Competition for an audience is a key factor, because profits depend on what advertisers can be charged for reaching those audiences. As a result, entertainment is paramount, and violent entertainment frequent (Cantor, 1980; Comstock, 1980).

What the entertainment business as a whole cannot do, individuals and organizations nevertheless may undertake; and what is impossible quantitatively is not quite so intractable qualitatively. Violence has always been one of the elements with which the broadcast standards departments of the three networks have been concerned, and even though the same new technology that is eroding the potential for regulatory influence is reducing the once supreme dominance of the networks in programming, the judgment of the networks as to what is and is not acceptable remains a very important factor in the entertainment reaching American homes. Network influence is much greater than the sum of network programming at any time because discarded programming is continually recycled through syndication for broadcast by independent stations and by network affiliates during the hours when there is no network programming or when what is available through syndication is preferred to what a network offers. These in-house censors attempt to review programming from conception to execution, and attempt to eliminate elements judged to be offensive or conceivably harmful. They make no judgments on the programming schedules as a whole or on which vehicles and formats will be developed as programs, which are the provinces of programming executives, but on particular elements which fail to meet the prescribed standards of the formal codes and informal conventions under which they function. Typically, they focus on the context in which violence occurs (Schneider, 1977), and certainly they are as concerned with the appearance of harm, that is, offense to some members of the audience, as with its substance. Nevertheless, they and the decisions of programming executives are the two means by which public concern over violence is translated into programming policy.

Format is a crucial factor in the susceptibility of a program to the portrayal of violence that may contribute to behavior that is criminal or seriously harmful to others. Obviously, situation comedies may contain violent acts, as slapstick exemplifies, but usually they are free of crime and violent retribution. Thus, they are of concern primarily for the occasional dirty trick and physical slapstick that children and adults might emulate rather than for any complicity in the endangerment of life or property.

Action and adventure programs are another matter. Arguably, the more dramatic conventions are ritualized and conflicts occur in distant settings and involve the use of unavailable weapons, which is the case generally with both westerns and science fiction drama, the less likely is there to be any effect at all; arousal rises and is resolved within familiar, rehearsed patterns and there is no pertinence to the viewer's everyday life.

Dramas that are set in the present day with a degree of realism are another matter. Here, the possibility of some harmful influence escalates when the viewer is invited to side, even temporarily, with the perpetrator of violence, as violence is associated with even temporary success. Programs which focus on the disruption a violent outburst can achieve invite emulation. Those that focus on the victims and consequences of such acts do not. From the perspective of the scientific evidence on television and film violence and aggression, themes and topics that can be treated within a format such as the late *The Lou Grant Show,* which falls in the second category, take on a far less threatening cast than those police and detective procedurals in which the suspense derives from the undeniably exciting thefts, arson, blackmail, snipings, murders, and terrorism which an imperfect system of law enforcement is attempting to contain.

It should also be understood that, while programs in which violence is certain to figure are a staple of television, there is no compelling evidence that physical and verbal abuse is an important factor in program popularity. In addition to the fact that many nonviolent programs have been among the most popular over the years (Steinberg, 1980). Diener and DeFour (1978) found that, over a season, such abuse was unrelated to the audience ratings for all episodes of eleven action and adventure series, and that subjects did not differ in their liking for versions of the same *Police Woman* episode edited to be high and low in such abuse. The implication is that whatever writers, directors, producers, and executives may think, it is not this element of vicious confrontation that attracts viewers, but the story, the characters, the plot, and the exciting pursuit and satisfying resolution.

The mass media are unique among the influences on our lives because what they communicate is public, however ambiguous the meaning or effect. The audience plays a central part in what occurs, whether the arena is politics or socialization. The influence of media violence can be countered by the ways by which aggression generally is subject to prevention and control. It can also be countered by refuting its messages or inoculating those susceptible against influence.

It is abundantly clear that the mass media, whatever the topic or category of persons, have their greatest influence when other influences are mute. In the case of the mass media, instruction in modes of coping that do not involve aggressive or antisocial behavior directly counter some of the messages of violent entertainment. This intervention in the vicarious experiences provided by the media may be taken a step further. Television and film entertainment can become the subject of disassembly, with pleasure and approval made as distinct as the two different reactions they are.

Wartime heroism is a recommendation for bravery, not destruction or the use of violence to resolve conflicts. When parents consistently express disapproval of aggressive behavior, there is a much reduced association between exposure to violent television and aggression (McLeod, Atkin, and Chaffee, 1972a, 1972b). The implication is that the views expressed by these parents take precedence over and diminish any involvement of the media. There is no need to sanction violent behavior simply because it is part of a story we enjoy and admire, nor does the fact of enjoyment imply any particular degree of approval or admiration for a story. We may reject utterly the violence of a story while following that story avidly; what would be more sensible?

The media are not in the business of moral instruction. They are in the business of attracting attention, and that attention is a currency they redeem for admission fees and advertising rates. For this reason, the validity of the violence in mass media entertainment as a reference to human behavior is permanently suspect, and this is a lesson with which we must live as we attend to and sort this very violence. Success in the media marketplace bestows no value beyond itself. Popularity implies only its empirical correlates, and neither moral, aesthetic, nor other merit.

The portrayal of violence in television and film entertainment is an aesthetic and moral issue, but it should not be confused with aesthetic and moral appreciations of theater films and television dramas. It is an aesthetic and moral issue because of the social friction and disorder to which it may contribute, and thus deserves the burden of having some essential relationship to character and theme. Where this is absent or these are trivial, violence is gratuitous. It certainly does not escape gratuity by linking events or resolving a conflict. Aesthetic and moral appreciation will go far beyond this narrow subject and, depending on the point of view, may find gruesomely violent dramas admirable and nonviolent dramas repugnant.

These comments argue for a critical stance toward the media, and one that will be communicated effectively to children. In the jargon of child development, they argue for teaching children to separate fantasy from reality, for labeling clearly behavior as appropriate and inappropriate whether it occurs in the immediate environment or enters that environment through the media, and for taking the popular arts seriously.

Although the evidence is far clearer in regard to aggression, and antisocial behavior in the sense of discord, than for criminal acts and behavior seriously harmful to others, media violence appears to contribute to both. The evidence is stronger too for some influence on the young, but media violence also appears to influence adults.

Asking the right questions is essential. The primary question is whether the evidence gives us respite from or sharpens concern over the influence of media violence. The government and the entertainment business cannot be expected to substantially reduce violence in the media. In effect, a solution is left to the audience. The tools they have are those for preventing and controlling aggression whatever the source, with the addition of specifically addressing violent entertainment as such. When their efforts fail, as they so often do, the media are left with no excuse for their behavior other than the failure of society, for in being the kind of messenger they are, they have become the problem.

NOTES

1. Andison (1977) defines "moderate" associations as those involving percentage differences of 26-60 points, levels of statistical significance between .05 and .01 (+ or −), or correlation coefficients between .31 and .70, "strong" associations as those exceeding these measures, and "weak" as those falling below them but escaping the "null" category defined by 5 percentage points, significance levels .1, and correlations not exceeding .09 (+ or −). Hearold (1979) converts means differences into comparable standardized scores by calculating their ratio to a standard deviation (or an estimate thereof), and then aggregates the results for whatever body of comparisons are under scrutiny.

2. Table 3 contains six columns representing the antisocial behavior in four categories for subjects exposed to one of three *Medical Center* episodes—neutral, antisocial with punishment, and antisocial without punishment—under the condition of either high or low frustration. Milgram and Shotland (1973) do not offer hypotheses beyond the question of whether behavior might differ under one or another of these circumstances, and so they properly analyze the data for overall differences before even considering selected comparisons. Since no overall differences achieve statistical significance, they drop the inquiry.

    The work of Berkowitz and colleagues (Berkowitz & Rawlings, 1963; Berkowitz & Geen, 1966; Berkowitz & Alioto, 1973) leads to the narrow hypothesis that frustrated subjects will vary in subsequent antisocial behavior as a function of the degree to which their inhibitions against such behavior are raised or lowered by a film example. In this case, the "antisocial with punishment" version would be expected to increase inhibitions over antisocial behavior. When comparisons are confined only to subjects in the high frustration condition (the only condition in which there can be said to be any frustration at all), those exposed to the "antisocial with punishment" version engage in fewer antisocial acts in each of the four categories than those exposed either to the "neutral" or "antisocial without punishment" version. Table 3 sharply reverses the pattern of Table 2 (Milgram & Shotland, 1973), where frustration is absent; sadly, the investigators do not pursue this lead, and in further manipulations exclude frustration as a factor.

Although the precise threshold for statistical significance always remains an issue, it should also be noted that Milgram and Shotland only examine the four categories of antisocial behavior individually— "Broke into bank and stole money," "Removed dangling dollar only," "Unsuccessfully attempted to break into bank," and "Stole other items from room" — and thereby impose a higher than necessary threshold than the procedure of combining such items as well into an "overall antisocial behavior" score.

REFERENCES

Albert, J. A. Constitutional regulation of televised violence. *Virginia Law Review,* 1978, *64*(8), 1299-1345.

Andison, F. S. TV violence and viewer aggressiveness: A cumulation of study results, 1956-1976. *Public Opinion Quarterly,* 1977, *41*(3), 314-31.

Atkin, C. Effects of television advertising on children. In E. L. Palmer and A. Dorr (Eds.), *Children and the faces of television: Teaching, violence, selling.* New York: Academic Press, 1980.

Baker, R. K. The views, standards, and practices of the television industry. In R. K. Baker and S. J. Ball (Eds.), *Violence and the media. A staff report to the National Commission on the Causes and Prevention of Violence.* Washington, D. C.: Government Printing Office, 1969.

Baker, R. K., & Ball, S. J. (Eds.) *Violence and the media. A staff report to the National Commission on the Causes and Prevention of Violence.* Washington, D.C.: Government Printing Office, 1969.

Baldwin, T. F., & Lewis, C. Violence in television: The industry looks at itself. In G. A. Comstock, E. A. Rubinstein, and J. P. Murray (Eds.), *Television and social behavior.* Vol. 1. *Media content and control.* Washington, D.C.: Government Printing Office, 1972.

Bandura, A. Influence of models' reinforcement contingencies on the acquisition of imitative responses. *Journal of Personality and Social Psychology,* 1965, *1,* 589-95.

Bandura, A. *Social learning theory.* New York: General Learning Press, 1971.

Bandura, A. *Aggression: A social learning analysis.* Englewood Cliffs, N.J.: Prentice-Hall, 1973.

Bandura, A. Social learning theory of aggression. *Journal of Communication,* 1978, *38*(3), 12-29.

Bandura, A., Ross, D., & Ross, S. A. Imitation of film-mediated aggressive models. *Journal of Abnormal and Social Psychology,* 1963, *66,* 3-11.

Barnard, C. N. An Oriental mystery. *TV Guide,* Jan. 28, 1978, pp. 2-8.

Baron, R. A. *Human aggression.* New York: Plenum Press, 1977.

Belson, W. A. *Television violence and the adolescent boy.* London: Saxon House, Teakfield Limited, 1978.

Berkowitz, L. *Aggression: A social psychological analysis.* New York: McGraw-Hill, 1962.

Berkowitz, L. The effects of observing violence. *Scientific American,* 1964, *21*(2), 35-41.

Berkowitz, L. Words and symbols as stimuli to aggressive responses. In J. F. Knutson (Ed.), *Control of aggression: Implications from basic research.* Chicago, Ill.: Aldine-Atherton, 1973.

Berkowitz, L., & Alioto, J. T. The meaning of an observed event as a determinant of its aggressive consequences. *Journal of Personality and Social Psychology,* 1973, *28,* 206-17.

Berkowitz, L., & Geen, R. G. Film violence and the cue properties of available targets. *Journal of Personality and Social Psychology,* 1966, *3,* 525-30.

Berkowitz, L., & Geen, R. G. Stimulus qualities of the target of aggression: A further study. *Journal of Personality and Social Psychology,* 1967, *5,* 364-68.

Berkowitz, L., & Rawlings, E. Effects of film violence on inhibitions against subsequent aggression. *Journal of Abnormal and Social Psychology*, 1963, *66*, 405-12.

Bogart, L. *The age of television*. 3rd ed. New York: Frederick Ungar, 1972.

Bogart, L. Warning, the Surgeon General has determined that TV violence is moderately dangerous to your child's mental health. *Public Opinion Quarterly*, 1972, *36*, 491-521.

Bollen, K. A., & Phillips, D. P. Suicidal motor vehicle fatalities in Detroit: A replication. *American Journal of Sociology*, 1981, *87*(2), 404-12.

Cantor, M. *Prime-time television*. Beverly Hills, Calif.: Sage, 1980.

Cantor, M. G. The role of the producer in choosing children's television content. In G. A. Comstock, E. A. Rubinstein, and J. P. Murray, (Eds.), *Television and social behavior*. Vol. 1. *Media content and control*. Washington, D. C.: Government Printing Office, 1972.

Chaffee, S. H. Television and adolescent aggressiveness (overview). In G. A. Comstock, E. A. Rubinstein, and J. P. Murray (Eds.), *Television and social behavior*. Vol. 2. *Television and adolescent aggressiveness*. Washington, D.C.: Government Printing Office, 1972.

Clark, D. G., & Blankenberg, W. B. Trends in violent content in selected mass media. In G. A. Comstock, E. A. Rubinstein, and J. A. Murray (Eds.), *Television and social behavior*. Vol. 1. *Media content and control*. Washington, D. C.: Government Printing Office, 1972.

Commission on Obscenity and Pornography. *The report of the Commission on Obscenity and Pornography*. New York: Bantam Books, 1970.

Commission on Obscenity and Pornography. *Technical reports*. Vol. 7. *Erotica and antisocial behavior*. Washington, D. C.: Government Printing Office, 1971a.

Commission on Obscenity and Pornography. *Technical reports*. Vol. 8. *Erotica and social behavior*. Washington, D.C.: Government Printing Office, 1971b.

Comstock, G. *Television and human behavior: The key studies*. Santa Monica, Calif.: The Rand Corporation, 1975.

Comstock, G. *Television in America*. Beverly Hills, Calif.: Sage, 1980.

Comstock, G. Violence in television content: An overview. In D. Pearl, L. Bouthilet, and J. Lazar (Eds.), *Television and behavior: Ten years of scientific progress and implications for the eighties*. Vol. 2. *Technical reviews*. Washington, D.C.: Government Printing Office, 1982.

Comstock, G., Chaffee, S., Katzman, N., McCombs, M., & Roberts, D. *Television and human behavior*. New York: Columbia University Press, 1978.

Comstock, G. A., Rubinstein, E. A., & Murray, J. P. (Eds.), *Television and social behavior*. Vol. 1. *Media content and control*, 1972a; Vol. 2. *Television and social learning*, 1972b; Vol. 3. *Television and adolescent aggressiveness*, 1972c; Vol. 4. *Television in day-to-day life: Patterns of use*, 1972d; Vol. 5. *Television's effects: Further explorations*, 1972e. Washington, D.C.: Government Printing Office, 1972.

Cowan, G. *See no evil*. New York: Simon and Schuster, 1979.

Diener, E., & DeFour, D. Does television violence enhance program popularity? *Journal of Personality and Social Psychology*, 1978, *36*(3), 333-41.

Dollard, J., Doob, L. W., Miller, N. E., Mowrer, D. H., & Sears, R. R. *Frustration and aggression*. New Haven, Conn.: Yale University Press, 1939.

Donnerstein, E. Pornography and violence against women: Experimental studies. In F. Wright, C. Bahn, and R. W. Rieber (Eds.), *Annals of the New York Academy of Sciences*. Vol. 347. *Forensic psychology and psychiatry*. New York: The New York Academy of Sciences, 1980.

Donnerstein, E., & Barrett, G. The effects of erotic stimuli on male aggression toward females. *Journal of Personality and Social Psychology*, 1978, *36*, 180-88.

Donnerstein, E., & Berkowitz, L. Victim reactions in aggressive erotic films as a factor in violence against women. *Journal of Personality and Social Psychology*, 1981, *41*(4), 710-24.

Donnerstein, E., & Hallan, J. The facilitating effects of erotica on aggression toward females. *Journal of Personality and Social Psychology*, 1978, *36*, 1270-77.

Ekman, P., Liebert, R. M., Friesen, W. V., Harnson, R., Zlatchin, C., Malstrom, E. J., & Baron, R. A. Facial expressions of emotion while watching televised violence as predictors of subsequent aggression. In G. A. Comstock, E. A. Rubinstein, and J. P. Murray (Eds.), *Television and social behavior*.

Vol. 5. *Television's effects: Further explorations.* Washington, D.C.: Government Printing Office, 1972.

Eysenck, H. J., & Nias, H. *Sex, violence, and the media.* London: Spector, 1978.

Feshbach, S. The stimulating versus cathartic effects of a vicarious aggressive activity. *Journal of Abnormal and Social Psychology,* 1961, *63,* 381-85.

Feshbach, S. Reality and fantasy in filmed violence. In G. A. Comstock, E. A. Rubinstein, and J. P. Murray (Eds.), *Television and social behavior.* Vol. 2. *Television and social learning.* Washington, D.C.: Government Printing Office, 1972.

Feshbach, S., & Singer, R. D. *Television and aggression: An experimental field study.* San Francisco: Jossey-Bass, 1971.

Geen, R. G. Effects of frustration, attack, and prior training in aggressiveness upon aggressive behavior. *Journal of Personality and Social Psychology,* 1968, *9,* 316-21.

Geen, R. G., & Berkowitz, L. Some conditions facilitating the occurrence of aggression after the observation of violence. *Journal of Personality,* 1967, *35,* 666-76.

Geen, R. G., & Stonner, D. Content effects in observed violence. *Journal of Personality and Social Psychology,* 1972, *25,* 145-50.

Geen, R. G., Stonner, D., & Shope, G. L. The facilitation of aggression by aggression: Evidence against the catharsis hypothesis. *Journal of Personality and Social Psychology,* 1975, *31,* 721-26.

Gerbner, G. Violence in television drama: Trends and symbolic functions. In G. A. Comstock, E. A. Rubinstein, and J. P. Murray (Eds.), *Television and social behavior.* Vol. 1. *Media content and control.* Washington, D.C.: Government Printing Office, 1972.

Glass, G. V., McGaw, B., & Smith, M. L. *Meta-analysis in social research.* Beverly Hills, Calif.: Sage, 1981.

Goranson, R. E. Media violence and aggressive behavior: A review of experimental research. In L. Berkowitz (Ed.), *Advances in experimental social psychology.* Vol. 5. New York: Academic Press, 1970.

Hartley, R. L. *The impact of viewing "aggression": Studies and problems of extrapolation.* New York: Columbia Braodcasting System, Office of Social Research, 1964.

Head, S. W. Content analysis of television drama programs. *Quarterly Journal of Film, Radio and Television,* 1954, *9,* 175-94.

Hearold, S. L. *Meta-analysis of the effects of television on social behavior.* Unpublished doctoral dissertation, University of Colorado, 1979.

Hennigan, K. M., Heath, L., Wharton, J. D., Del Rosario, M. L., Cook, T. D., & Calder, B. J. Impact of the introduction of television on crime in the United States: Empirical findings and theoretical implications. *Journal of Personality and Social Psychology,* 1982, *42*(3), 461-77.

Hoffman, M. Identification and imitation in children. In J. F. Esserman (Ed.), *Television advertising and children.* New York: Child Research Service, 1981.

Howitt, D., & Cumberbatch, G. *Violence and the mass media.* London: Paul Elek, 1974.

Iwao, S., de Sola Pool, I., & Hagiwara, S. Japanese and U.S. media: Some cross-cultural insights into TV violence. *Journal of Communication,* 1981, *31*(2), 28-36.

Janowitz, M. *The last half century.* Chicago, Ill.: Univeristy of Chicago Press, 1981.

Kaplan, R. M., & Singer, R. D. Television violence and viewer aggression: A reexamination of the evidence. *Journal of Social Issues,* 1976, *32*(4), 35-70.

Kessler, R. C., & Stipp, H. The impact of fictional television suicide stories on U.S. suicides. Unpublished manuscript, Social Research Department, National Broadcasting Company, New York, 1982.

Klapper, J. T. *The effects of mass communication.* New York: Free Press, 1960.

Krattenmaker, T. G., & Powe, L. A., Jr. Televised violence: First amendment principles and social science theory. *Virginia Law Review,* 1978, *64*(8), 1123-1197.

Krull, R., & Watt, J. H., Jr. Television viewing and aggression: An examination of three models. Paper presented at the meeting of the International Communication Association, Montreal, Canada, April 1973.

Larson, O. N., Gray, L. N., & Fortis, J. G. Goals and goal-achievement in television content: Models for anomie? *Sociological Inquiry,* 1963, *33,* 180-96.

Lefcourt, H. M., Barnes, K., Parke, R., & Schwartz, F. Anticipated social censure and aggression-conflict as mediators of response to aggression induction. *Journal of Social Psychology,* 1966, *70,* 251-63.

Lefkowitz, M., Eron, L., Walder, L., & Huesmann, L. *Growing up to be violent.* New York: Pergamon Press, 1977.

Lefkowitz, M. M., Eron, L. D., Walder, L. O., & Huesmann, L. R. Television violence and child aggression: A followup study. In G. A. Comstock, E. A. Rubinstein, and J. P. Murray (Eds.), *Television and social behavior.* Vol. 3. *Television and adolescent aggressiveness.* Washington, D.C.: Government Printing Office, 1972.

Leyens, J. P., & Camino, L. The effects of repeated exposure to film violence on aggressiveness and social structures. In J. DeWit and W. W. Hartup (Eds.), *Determinants and origins of aggressive behavior.* The Hague: Mounton, 1974.

Leyens, J. P., Camino, L., Parke, R. D., & Berkowitz, L. Effects of movie violence on aggression in a field setting as a function of group dominance and cohesion. *Journal of Personality and Social Psychology,* 1975, *32*(2), 346-60.

Liebert, R. M., Neale, J. M., & Davidson, E. S. *The early window: Effects of television on children and youth.* Elmsford, N.Y.: Pergamon Press, 1973.

Liebert, R. M., Neale, J. M., & Davidson, E. S. *The early window: Effects of television on children and youth.* (2nd ed.) Elmsford, N.Y.: Pergamon Press, 1982.

Malamuth, N. M., Feshbach, S., & Jaffe, Y. Sexual arousal and aggression: Recent experiments and theoretical issues. *Journal of Social Issues,* 1977, *33,* 10-133.

McIntyre, J. J., & Teevan, J. J., Jr. Television violence and deviant behavior. In G. A. Comstock, E. A. Rubinstein, and J. P. Murray (Eds.), *Television and social behavior.* Vol. 3. *Television and adolescent aggressiveness.* Washington, D.C.: Government Printing Office, 1972.

McLeod, J. M., Atkin, C. K. & Chaffee, S. H. Adolescents, parents, and television use: Adolescents self-support measures from Maryland and Wisconsin samples. In G. A. Comstock, E. A. Rubinstein, and J. P. Murray (Eds.), *Television and social behavior.* Vol. 3. *Television and adolescent aggressiveness.* Washington, D.C.: Government Printing Office, 1972.

McLeod, J. M., Atkin, C. K., & Chaffee, S. H. Adolescents, parents and television use: Self-report and other-report measures from the Wisconsin sample. In G. A. Comstock, E. A. Rubinstein, and J. P. Murray (Eds.), *Television and social behavior.* Vol. 3. *Television and adolescent aggressiveness.* Washington, D.C.: Government Printing Office, 1972.

Meyer, T. P. Effects of viewing justified and unjustified real film violence on aggressive behavior. *Journal of Personality and Social Psychology,* 1972, *23,* 21-29.

Milavsky, J. R., Kessler, R., Stipp, H., & Rubens, W. S. Television and aggression: Results of a panel study. In D. Pearl, L. Bouthilet, and J. Lazar (Eds.), *Television and behavior: Ten years of scientific progress and implications for the eighties.* Vol. 2. *Technical reviews.* Washington, D.C.: Government Printing Office, 1982.

Milgram, S., & Shotland, R. L. *Television and antisocial behavior: Field experiment.* New York: Academic Press, 1973.

Murray, J. P. *Television and youth.* Boys Town, Neb.: Boys Town Center for the Study of Youth Development, 1980.

Murray, J. P., & Kippax, S. From the early window to the late night show: International trends in the study of television's impact on children and adults. In L. Berkowitz (Ed.), *Advances in experimental social psychology.* New York: Academic Press, 1979.

National Coalition on Television Violence. *NCTV news,* 1980-1982, *1-3,* entire.

National Commission on the Causes and Prevention of Violence. *To establish justice, to insure domestic tranquility.* Washington, D.C.: Government Printing Office, 1969.

Paisley, M. B. *Social policy research and the realities of the system: Violence done to TV research.* Stanford, Calif.: Institute for Communication Research, Stanford University, 1972.

Pearl, D., Bouthilet, L., & Lazar, J. *Television and behavior: Ten years of scientific progress and implications for the eighties.* Vol. 1. *Summary report,* 1972(a); Vol. 2. Technical Reviews, 1972(b). Washington, D.C.: Government Printing Office, 1982.

Phillips, D. P. The influence of suggestion on suicide: Substantive and theoretical implications of the

Werther effect. American Sociological Review, 1974, *39,* 340-54.

Phillips, D. P. Motor vehicle fatalities increase just after publicized suicide stories. *Science,* 1977, *196,* 1464-65.

Phillips, D. P. Airplane accident fatalities increase just after newspaper stories about murder and suicide. *Science,* 1978, *201,* 748-50.

Phillips, D. P. Airplance accidents, murder, and the mass media: Towards a theory of imitation and suggestion. In D. C. Whitney, E. Wartella, and S. Windahl (Eds.), *Mass communication review yearbook.* Vol. 3. Beverly Hills, Calif.: Sage, 1982. (Reprinted from *Social Forces, 58*(4), 1980.)

Phillips, D. P. The impact of fictional television stories on U.S. adult fatalities: New evidence on the effect of the mass media on violence. American Journal of Sociology, 1982, *87*(6), 1340-59. (b)

Remmers, H. H. *Four years of New York television.* Urbana, Ill.: The National Association of Educational Broadcasters, 1954.

Rosekrans, M. A. Imitation in children as a function of perceived similarities to a social model of vicarious reinforcement. *Journal of Personality and Social Psychology,* 1967, *7,* 307-15.

Rosekrans, M. A., & Hartup, W. W. Imitative influences of consistent and inconsistent response consequences to a model of aggressive behavior in children. *Journal of Personality and Social Psychology,* 1967, *7,* 429-34.

Rothenberg, M. B. Effect of television violence on children and youth. *Journal of the American Medical Association,* 1975, *234,* 1043-46.

Rushton, J. P. *Altruism, socialization, and society.* Englewood Cliffs, N.J.: Prentice-Hall, 1980.

Schneider, J. A. Letter to Lionel Van Deerlin, Chairman, Subcommittee on communications, House Committee on Interstate and Foreign Commerce, April 25, 1977.

Singer, J. L. The influence of violence portrayed in television or motion pictures upon overt aggressive behavior. In J. L. Singer (Ed.), *The control of aggression and violence: Cognitive and physiological factors.* New York: Academic Press, 1971.

Slaby, R. G., Quarforth, G. R., & McConnachie, G. A. Television violence and its sponsors. *Journal of Communication,* 1976, *26*(1), 88-96.

Slife, B. D., & Rychiak, J. F. Role of affective assessment in modeling aggressive behavior. *Journal of Personality and Social Psychology,* 1982, *43*(4), 861-68.

Smythe, D. W. Reality as presented by television. *Public Opinion Quarterly,* 1954, *18,* 143-56.

Steinberg, C. *TV facts.* New York: Facts on File, 1980.

Steuer, F. B., Applefield, J. M., & Smith, R. Televised aggression and the interpersonal aggression of preschool children. *Journal of Experimental Child Psychology,* 1971, *11,* 442-47.

Surgeon General's Scientific Advisory Committee on Television and Social Behavior. *Television and growing up: The impact of televised violence.* Report to the Surgeon General, United States Public Health Service. Washington, D.C.: Government Printing Office, 1972.

Tankard, J., & Showalter, S. W. Press coverage of the 1972 report on television and social behavior. *Journalism Quarterly,* 1977, *54*(2), 293-98.

Tannenbaum, P. H., & Zillmann, D. Emotional arousal in the facilitation of aggression through communication. In L. Berkowitz (Ed.), *Advances in experimental psychology.* Vol. 8. New York: Academic Press, 1975.

United States Congress. Senate Committee on the Judiciary. Hearings before the Subcommittee to Investigate Juvenile Delinquency. *Juvenile delinquency (television programs).* 83rd Congress, 2nd session. June 5-October 20, 1954. Washington, D.C.: Government Printing Office, 1955. (a)

United States Congress. Senate Committee on the Judiciary. Hearings before the Subcommittee to Investigate Juvenile Delinquency. *Juvenile delinquency (Television programs).* 84th Congress, 1st session. April 6-7, 1955. Washington, D.C.: Government Printing Office, 1955. (b)

United States Congress. Senate Committee on the Judiciary. Report of Subcommittee to Investigate Juvenile Delinquency. *Television and juvenile delinquency* (with bibliography). 84th Congress, 1st session, 1955. Washington, D.C.: Government Printing Office, 1956.

United States Congress. Senate Committee on the Judiciary. Hearings before the Subcommittee to Investigate Juvenile Delinquency. *Juvenile delinquency.* Part 10. *Effects on young people of violence and crime portrayed on television.* 87th Congress, 1st and 2nd sessions. June 8, 1961-May 14,

1962. Washington, D.C.: Government Printing Office, 1963.

United States Congress. Senate Committee on the Judiciary. Hearings before the Subcommittee to Investigate Juvenile Delinquency. *Juvenile delinquency.* Part 16. *Effects on young people of violence and crime portrayed on televison.* 88th Congress, 2nd session. July 30, 1964. Washington, D.C.: Government Printing Office, 1965.

United States Congress. Senate Committee on the Judiciary. Report of the Subcommittee to Investigate Juvenile Delinquency. *Television and juvenile delinquency.* 88th Congress, 2nd session, and 89th Congress, 1st session. October 15, 1965. Washington, D.C.: Government Printing Office, 1966.

Watt, J. H., Jr., & Krull, R. An information theory measure for television programming. *Communication Research,* 1974, *1,* 44-68.

Worchel, S., Hardy, T. W., & Hurley, R. The effects of commercial interruption of violent and nonviolent films on viewers' subsequent aggression. *Journal of Experimental Psychology,* 1976, *2,* 220-32.

Zillman, D. Excitation transfer in communication-mediated aggressive behavior. *Journal of Experimental Social Psychology,* 1971, *7,* 419-34.

Zillman, D., Johnson, R. C., & Hanrahan, J. Pacifying effect of happy ending of communication involving aggression. *Psychological Reports,* 1973, *32,* 967-70.

10

An Alternative to Violence: Nonviolent Struggle for Change

Neil H. Katz
with
Kathleen L. Uhler

A Member of the Polity May Need to Wheel and Deal, but a Challenger
Should be Prepared to Stand and Fight

William A. Gamson
The Strategy of Social Protest

Throughout history, human beings have engaged in collective action to achieve goals and influence behavior. These actions take many forms such as party politics and bloc voting, the formation of unions, and organized warfare. Institutionalized means to effect change are usually accepted and well known. Organized violence, though less acceptable, has received much attention from researchers, educators, practitioners, and policymakers. We devote vast amounts of material and human resources to learning and teaching the history, techniques, and principles of warfare.

Nonviolent action, another way in which collective bodies engage in struggle to bring about or resist change, has received less attention and resources. Groups in North America such as the Quakers, the Abolitionists, and the suffragists used many forms of nonviolent protest, noncooperation, and intervention to successfully achieve goals (Cooney & Michalowski, 1977; Lynd, 1970). However, American knowledge about and training in nonviolent action are a phenomena largely of the last half century.

The first writings for Americans that focused specifically on collective nonviolent struggle techniques to influence attitude and behavior were works that described and analyzed Mahatma Gandhi's campaigns in South Africa and India. Authors such as Shridharani (1939), Muste (1940), and Gregg (1943) lauded Gandhi's efforts and exhorted their readers to apply Gandhian techniques in their actions for peace and justice.

The next important period for nonviolence literature in America was the 1960s and early 1970s when nonviolent resistance became popular for waging struggle against racial injustice and United States involvement in the Vietnam War. The renewed interest in nonviolent action encouraged historians such as Zinn (1964), Brock (1970), Chatfield (1971; 1973), Wittner (1969), and Lynd (1970) to chronicle the rich, vast human history of nonviolent struggle for peace and justice in America. Along with historians, other scholars and practitioners helped focus attention on nonviolent action during the 1960s and 1970s. Psychologists, sociologists, political scientists, and activists such as Erikson (1966), Hare and Blumberg (1968), Lakey (1969; 1973), Bondurant (1965), and Dellinger (1971) all made important contributions to knowledge about nonviolent action. These works helped readers understand the psychological motivations of nonviolent leaders, the social-psychological dimensions and repercussions of nonviolent resistance, and the need for perfecting the techniques of nonviolent struggle.

In 1973, social scientist Gene Sharp published his monumental study, *The Politics of Nonviolent Action*. The benchmark contribution significantly advanced nonviolent scholarship by comprehensively "examining the nature of nonviolent struggle as a social and political technique, including its view of power, its specific methods of action, its dynamics in conflict, and the conditions for success or failure in its use [p. V]." Sharp's prodigious work catalogued and described 198 different methods of nonviolent action, divided into the three broad categories of protest and persuasion (i.e., marches, parades, vigils); social, economic, and political non-cooperation (i.e., ostracism, boycotts, strikes, refusal to obey appointed officials); and non-violent intervention (i.e., sit-ins, nonviolent invasion, parallel government). The work also refined existing theoretical knowledge on nonviolence by systematically examining the dynamics, capabilities, and requirements of nonviolent struggle. Thus, through scholarly and exhaustive research, Sharp not only helped his audience understand what nonviolent action is, but also how and why it works.

Dr. Sharp's watershed work allowed other researchers to advance knowledge about nonviolent resistance. Since 1973, American scholars such as Katz and Hunt (1979) and Wehr (1979; 1981) have used Sharp's theoretical and analytic framework and contributions to describe nonviolent struggle techniques in detailed case study approaches, to analyze protest activities to further refine theories and principles regarding the operation of nonviolent struggle, and to explore the potential use of civilian nonviolent resistance as a policy option for defense against foreign invasion and domestic usurpation. This chapter intends to continue the advance of research on nonviolent action and alternatives to aggression.

THEORY, METHODS, AND PRINCIPLES OF NONVIOLENT ACTION

Though theoretical development on nonviolent struggle is still in its infancy, Gene Sharp and other scholars have developed some general principles for doing and/or analyzing nonviolent action. By examining historical events of nonviolent struggle, these scholars and practitioners have defined and categorized nonviolent action, discussed its relationship to power, and offered criteria for improved chances of success.

Nonviolent action has been defined (Sharp, 1973) as "a generic term covering dozens of specific methods of protest, noncooperation, and intervention all in which the actionist conducts the conflict by doing—or refusing to do—certain things without physical violence [p. 64]." It is not passive, not inaction, but action that is nonviolent. Like violence, its aim is to influence behavior making it unrewarding for the opponents to do certain things and safe or rewarding to do other things. The theory of nonviolent action is based on the principle that power is pluralistic. The exercise of power depends on the consent of the ruled who, by withdrawing that consent, can control or even destroy the power of the opponent. Thus, political power is an interactive phenomenon, and power disintegrates when people withdraw their obedience and support. According to Sharp, the most effective way to do this is to strike at the six sources of power—authority (right to rule), human resources, skills and knowledge, intangible factors (habits and attitudes toward obedience), material resources, and sanctions (techniques of enforcement of obedience).

After setting forth the theory that nonviolent action can redirect power by striking at its sources and undermine obedience, Sharp distinguishes three broad categories of action through which nonviolent struggle operates. Protest and persuasion involve "symbolic actions intended to help persuade the opponent or someone else, or to express the group's disapproval and dissent." Noncooperation describes acts characeized by "withdrawal or the withholding of social, economic, or political cooperation." Nonviolent intervention occurs when the action group "clearly takes the initiative by such means as sit-ins, nonviolent obstruction, nonviolent invasion, and parallel government [pp. 68-69]."

These methods of action can lead to change in three ways: conversion, accommodation, and nonviolent coercion. Conversion involves a change of heart on the part of the opponent such that he/she willingly supports the changes desired by the nonviolent actionists. In accommodation, the opponent has not altered in belief or ability to continue the struggle, but has concluded that it is best to grant some or all of the demands at this time. Nonviolent coercion occurs when the opponent has lost the ability to continue the struggle and has unwillingly surrendered his/her position.

DYNAMICS OF NONVIOLENT STRUGGLE

In the *Politics of Nonviolent Action,* Part III, Gene Sharp (1973) "draws on the events in several significant cases of nonviolent action to construct, largely by the inductive approach, an analysis of how this technique words [p. 450]." This analysis contains useful guidelines for understanding nonviolent struggle.

After examining historical uses of nonviolent resistance, Sharp discusses some of the major requirements and dynamics that practitioners need to prepare for and follow to increase chances for success. These include preparation for nonviolent action, response to the initial challenge, the need for solidarity and discipline to fight repression, the operation of political jujitsu, mechanics of change, and the redistribution of power. In preparing for nonviolent action, the author suggests that practitioners need to pay careful attention to elements such as leadership, negotiations, timing, maintaining initiative, generating "cause-consciousness," sharpening the focus for attack, and the selection of strategy and tactics.

Sharp's research shows that, after open struggle is launched by the nonviolent activists, the initial impact usually is "a sharpening of the conflict, a polarization of the conflicting groups, a stimulation of previously uncommitted people to take sides, and an increase in the opponent's use of repression, involving the enforcement of sanctions [p. 524]." The activists need to anticipate these powershifts and maintain their morale, fearlessness, solidarity, and nonviolent discipline to fight and withstand the repression. The response of meeting violence and repression with nonviolence may bring about effects of political jujitsu—a method whereby the opponent's strength reacts against itself and ultimately becomes a source of disunity and defeat. "By combining nonviolent discipline with solidarity and persistence in struggle, the nonviolent actionists cause the violence of the opponents' repression to be exposed in the worst possible light [p. 657]." The resulting political jujitsu can produce several effects: ". . . the opponent may appear despicable; the general population may become alienated and may join the resistance; persons divorced from the conflict may show support for victims of repression; public opinion may lead to political and economic pressures; and, finally, the opponent's own agents and troops . . . may begin to doubt the justice of his policies [p. 113]." "In the long run, therefore, successful nonviolent campaigns produce a strengthened solidarity among the nonviolent militants, a growth of wider support for correction of the grievance, and a fragmentation and disintegration of support for the opponent [p. 526]."

After political jujitsu occurs, the nonviolent group may achieve concessions from its opponent either through a change in attitude (conversion), a forced change in behavior (coercion), or a voluntary change in behavior in order to minimize unacceptable losses (accommodation). Successful nonviolent struggle may result in new advantages, either through the conversion or capitulation of the opponents, or through an informal or formal negotiated settlement.

One of the most important impacts of nonviolent action is the effect of the struggle on the protest group and an alteration in the power relationship of the contending parties. Positive effects of nonviolent struggle on the contending groups include increased fearlessness, self-esteem, group unity, internal cooperation, and empowerment through learning techniques to reveal and use one's own resources. This new realization of power that people can wield to control their own lives through nonviolent action can lead not only to a redefinition of the power relationship of the protagonists, but to a pluralization and decentralization of power throughout the society.

CASE STUDIES

The writers of this article believe that comparative case studies are a fruitful way to illustrate and test some of the methods, principles, and theories of nonviolent action. For this article, two cases have been selected—one in America and one abroad—to demonstrate not only the nature and potency of nonviolent struggle to affect change, but also to present different models of nonviolence as an alternative to violence for groups waging struggle.

In the Seabrook nuclear power case study, an aggrieved, powerless, and excluded group organized itself and used sustained, effective, nonviolent action methods to gain legitimacy and credibility for its group and its concerns, as well as to gain bargaining leverage. In the Iranian revolution of 1979, oppressed people substituted effective nonviolent struggle for an unsuccessful violent campaign to topple and replace a repressive monarchy. In both cases, a combination of different nonviolent tactics and strategies were employed by "outside" groups to publicize their grievances and their goals and to provide them means to minimize reprisals against themselves, protect their organization, and retain their individual and collective self-respect.

Case I: The Seabrook N.H. Nuclear Power Protests 1976-1978

The Seabrook nuclear power controversy began when the Public Service Company of New Hampshire, the principle owner and developer of the Seabrook Nuclear Power Plant, applied successfully to state and national agencies for preliminary site and construction permits. Almost immediately after approval, opposition surfaced. The Society for the Protection of New Hampshire Forests and the Audubon Society—later to be joined in the regulatory battle by the Seacoast Anti-Pollution League (SAPL), and the Northeast Coalition on Nuclear Power—began a series of court challenges against the licensing of the Seabrook plant. Although these regulatory battles caused some construction delays, frustrated opponents of the Seabrook plant turned to other forms of action to halt construction permanently.

Two events in the winter of 1976 symbolized the change in strategy. In January, a New

Hampshire resident, Ron Rieck, occupied a meteorological tower near the Seabrook site for 32 hours in subfreezing temperatures. And in a March town meeting, Seabrook residents voted 768–632 not to allow a nuclear power plant in their town. Since home rule precedents had been upheld in other New England towns in energy related controversies, many Seabrook residents were surprised and incensed when the Nuclear Regulatory Commission ignored their vote and granted final construction permits for Seabrook Station on July 7.

Opponents of the plant immediately called for direct action. On July 9, a Granite State Alliance spokesperson said demonstrators were now "ready to vote with their feet, which is what Americans have been doing since the revolution ["Alliance Maps Action," 1976]." Nine days later, Guy Chichester, president of the SAPL, announced the formation of an alliance of approximately 30 anti-nuke groups in and around New Hampshire, to be known as the Clamshell Alliance.[1] Chichester explained that the "Clamshell Alliance was formed to reach people with information about their own interest and how they can participate to help in a direct action movement to stop the Seabrook Plant." Pledged to "use nonviolent action such as site occupation, public demonstration, and public prayer," the Clamshell Alliance desired to "stop all construction of the Seabrook Plant, assist efforts to halt nuclear plant development in New England, and let fully informed citizens decide the nature and destiny of their own communities ["N-Plant Foes," 1976]."

When the Clamshell Alliance announced its first civil disobedience action for August 1, proponents of the Seabrook plant began their counteroffensive. In a Manchester *Union-Leader* editorial, the abrasively conservative editor and publisher William Loeb called the Clamshell Alliance "environmental irreconcilables" who "don't know anything about uranium." Power Service Company President William Tallman called for a halt of the "sustained and sometimes hysterical opponents who have already cost the company and the public millions of dollars ["Seabrook Sensationalism," 1976]."

Undeterred by the attacks, the Clamshell Alliance initiated nonviolent direct action. On the first day of August, approximately 500 protestors[2] marched to the Seabrook site where land clearing had begun. While the others rallied in support, 14 men and 4 women entered the construction site. After three warnings, the 18 trespassers were escorted or dragged to police vans by Seabrook Police and Rockingham County Deputy Sheriffs and booked on criminal trespass charges ("Protestors Arraigned," 1976).

Four days later, the Power Service Company held its own groundbreaking ceremony for the $1.6 billion,[3] 40-acre plant that the Power Service Company claimed would produce 2,300 megawatts of power and 86 percent of New Hampshire's energy by 1984 (Kidder, 1978). Buoyed by the ceremonies, Loeb editorialized that the protestors were foolish to believe they could stop the plant "for the Public Service Company and the state consumers are not typical patsies and won't bow to strident fanaticisors ["Easy Target," 1976]." Ignoring Loeb's prediction, the Clamshell Alliance boldly announced that 200 demonstrators would occupy the site August 22 in "the first nonviolent mass occupation against nuclear power in United States history ("Seabrook N-Site Protest," 1976)."

On the day of the demonstration, while 1,100 supporters looked on, 180 protestors went around wire barriers and onto the construction site to plant pine trees. After several warnings by law enforcement officials, 150 state, county, and local police escorted, carried, or dragged the protestors to ten waiting school buses for transportation to the Portsmouth, New Hampshire, armory for arraignment for criminal trespass ("Protestors Arrested," 1976).

1977 Demonstration

In the fall, the Clamshell Alliance announced a large anti-nuclear demonstration for April 1977. This escalation by the Clamshell Alliance brought forth public attacks from pro-nuclear forces. During April, in different issues of the Manchester *Union-Leader*, editor Loeb referred to the Clamshell Alliance members as "anti-nuclear kooks," "anti-constitution activists," "anti-nuclear loonies," and "terrorists and revolutionaries like Nazi storm troopers under Hitler and black-shirted mobs under Mussolini ("A Sunday School," 1976)." In addition, Loeb continually attempted to link the anti-nuclear forces with the communists. He found great significance in the fact the Clamshell Alliance demonstration was scheduled for May Day weekend, said the protestors were comparable to Lenin's "useful idiots," and published an article quoting James Burnham, "an acute analyzer of communists' disinformation practices'" as stating that "the Soviet Secret Police (the KGB), had a hand in the anti-nuclear sentiment ["Who Directs," 1977]." Power Service Company President Tallman reinforced the negative stigma by pinpointing similarities between the Clamshell Alliance and the communist anti-nuclear forces in Germany. Tallman added that the Clamshell Alliance was "subversive" in calling for a government takeover of utilities, which he declared was "a primary plank of socialism and communism ["New Hampshire's Biggest Question," 1977]."

Even more inflammatory was the description of the motivation and strategy of the Clamshell Alliance. Loeb claimed that the Clamshell Alliance had planned "essentially a military maneuver, [that] might seek the unlawful destruction of lives or property ["The Real Test," 1977]." New Hampshire Governor Thomson stated that "our advance information indicated that the planned demonstration of April 30 is nothing more than a cover for terrorist activity . . . once the Clamshell Alliance illegally occupies the site they do not plan to leave alive ["Police Gird," 1977]."

The pro-nuclear leaders' incendiary accusations were answered by the Clamshell Alliance and their third party supporters. Clamshell spokespeople explained that civil disobedience was different from terrorism, and they continually stated their total commitment to nonviolence and their desire "to not see anyone hurt ["Thomson Aim," 1977]." New Hampshire State Senator Thomas McIntyre (D) criticized Thomson and Loeb for exacerbating the conflict by their "inflammatory statements." McIntyre not only accused Thomson and Loeb of excessive rhetoric, but also went further by claiming that "if violence does occur a large measure of blame will fall on those who have inflamed emotions with irresponsible rhetoric beforehand ["Demonstrators Ready," 1977]." In another split from the governor's united front, Massachusetts Governor Michael Dukakis announced his refusal to honor a "Northeast Mutual Assistance Pact" to send Massachusetts state police to Seabrook, and local police officials around Seabrook balked at sending officers to the "weekend goose chase sponsored by Thomson ["Demonstrators Ready," 1977]."

The spring demonstration went on as scheduled. On April 30, approximately 1,800 protestors arrived at the construction site to face the governor's 350 troops. After the head of the state police warned the protestors that they were trespassing, the law officials stepped aside as the marchers became occupiers and settled onto the construction site parking lot ("2000 Occupy," 1977).

On Sunday, May 1, the governor arrived by helicopter to assess the situation. Even though he had announced there would be no arrests as long as demonstrators did not try to penetrate the fenced-in area, he now informed the Clamshell Alliance that "necessary steps would be taken [unless the] occupiers vacated the premises so construction workers could arrive without difficulty the next morning ["2000 Protestors," 1977; "750 Arrested," 1977]."

The Clams met briefly and then announced they would remain on site. After Colonel Paul Doyon, commander of the New Hampshire police, warned the demonstrators one more time to depart before they would be arrested, transport buses arrived on the scene and arrests began at approximately four o'clock. The arrests were orderly as occupiers sat quietly in circles awaiting police. Most demonstrators cooperated with law enforcement officials although some did go limp, forcing police to carry or drag them to the buses. The police completed the largest mass arrest in state history by officially arresting the last of the 1,414 occupiers at 7:30 a.m. the next day ("Hundreds Arrested," 1977).

After being charged with criminal trespass, a misdemeanor, those arrested were arraigned in groups of ten in makeshift courtrooms inside the National Guard armory in Portsmouth. Most of the Clams pleaded innocent to the trespass charges "for the future of the human family" and almost all of them refused to post bail, claiming they would stay until all of them were released on personal recognizance. In the armories, the demonstrators continued their non-cooperation tactics. Clam members blocked the entrance of incoming arrestees in protest of the overcrowded conditions; they confused arraignment procedures by not answering names or drowning out the calling of names with singing; and they frustrated attempts to segregate men and women by tying shoelaces together and scrambling into each other's area.

In addition to their acts of noncooperation, the activists continued their persuasion tactics by giving "nuke raps" to the guards and questioning them about their lives and families. Some police became friendly with the protestors and aided them with vegetarian cooking needs, telephone accessibility, and the transferring of supplies and arrest lists between the prisoners and support people. Moreover, the constant "raps" and questions made many of the younger guards nervous, and they had to be replaced. To add to the state's embarrassment and misery, reporters wrote that the protestors' spirits were not weakening. Indeed, the protestors seemed to be "having a ball" in the armories at state expense as they sang, danced, skipped rope, held talent shows, practiced yoga, and discussed the evils of nuclear power. The protestors' general defiance and nonviolent action methods seemed worthy opponents to the hard line adopted by the state. On observing the protestors and their tactics, one guard proclaimed the struggle, "Showdown at Meldrinville ["They're Having a Ball," 1977]."

Although the prisoners' various acts of noncooperation were an irritant to the guards and the state, it soon became apparent that Clamshell's refusal to accept bail until all were released on personal recognizance was the key to the struggle. The prisoners were steadfast on this issue. By May 4, only 20 to 25 of those originally arrested had posted bail. The incarceration of the over 1,300 remaining protestors strained the law enforcement manpower needs and financial resources of the state. Eight hundred national guardsmen were needed for the three, eight-hour shifts. The state's cost was approximately $50,000 per day, including salary for the legal fees, sanitary and health supplies for the prisoners, and other incarceration costs. After claiming that state emergency funds were exhausted in three days, Thomson applied for national assistance to relieve the state of the crushing financial burden. Estimating that a three-week "jail-in" would cost the state $669,000, Thomson sought that amount of federal funds from the Law Enforcement Assistance Agency (LEAA), since he felt the Seabrook protest was only "the first stage of a national problem ["Thomson Asks Police," 1977]." Also, after receiving a donation from a pro-nuclear sympathizer in Washington state who claimed that "New Hampshire is doing the job for all of us," the governor sent out a national public appeal for funds "from corporations, labor unions, and rank-and-file citizens throughout America." Both of these attempts to raise funds failed. The LEAA twice turned down the governor's request for federal funds and Thomson's national public appeal netted only $6,124 ("Nuke Site Protest," 1977).

Nevertheless, Thomson was still determined to win "the battle of Seabrook." On May 5, the governor admitted that, by continuing his hard-line position on retribution, he was placing himself and the state in a precarious position, but he insisted the stakes were worth the risk. Thomson explained that "the question isn't the cost but how willing are we to see law and order prevail." "We have to see the struggle through . . . ," he claimed. "We have no other alternative." Editor Loeb gave full support to this inflexible policy. In his view, this hard line was necessary, for the battle was nothing less than a "test of the law enforcement agencies of the state ["Release Denied," 1977]."

Since the state was committed to pressuring Clam to capitulate, Governor Thomson and his allies increased the severity of sanctions levied against the protestors. They initiated procedures to withhold unemployment compensation from New Hampshire resident protestors and threatened to do the same with welfare and food stamps. Several neighboring state governors announced they would follow the same procedure. Thomson also proposed that Congress pass a federal law prohibiting protestors from interfering with construction of an energy plant, and State Senator Robert Monier (R) called for the state to "sue the protestors" since "most of them were the children of the affluent." After calling the occupation "the most well planned act of criminal behavior in the history of the state and the nation," New Hampshire Attorney General David Sauter ordered jail sentences for the arrestees on May 6, effectively depriving them of an automatic right of appeal to which they were entitled in the New Hampshire court system. Sauter defended the highly unusual move by stating that he had overheard on a citizens band radio that Clam was planning to reoccupy the site, and he needed to stop them. His unorthodox decision did not go unchallenged. In an angry editorial, the *New York Times* called Sauter's rationale "unproven" and decried his action as "smacking mightily of preventive detention." Clam lawyers filed a petition of release and asked for $30 million in damages on grounds that the protestors' civil rights were being violated ("A Power Problem," 1977).

The state's continued hard line, and the intensified efforts to crush their opponents began to bring forth responses from interested third parties and have an effect on the protestors. Many citizens and public officials agreed with the *New York Times* editors that the state should start "treating the protestors as minor offenders, not major criminals" and should start to negotiate their release, for both moral and economic reasons. On May 10, the two Republican and one Democratic Rockingham County commissioners accused Governor Thomson of "fiscal irresponsibility" for his "determination to prosecute all protestors to the full extent of the law." To protest this, the commissioners threatened "to sue the state" and passed a resolution declaring they were "considering paying the fines of the convicted protestors to limit the confinement costs [People to Pay," 1977]."

In the meantime, the Clam protestors' solidarity began to weaken. By May 9, almost half of the original 1,414 arrestees had bailed out, and, a day later, more than 100 New Hampshire resident arrestees accepted release on personal recognizance. Many of the remaining arrestees showed increasing concern for their health and the consequences of their time spent in jail.

Due to the pressure on both the state and the Clamshell Alliance to seek accommodation to end the struggle, the parties were receptive to a compromise first proposed by Rockingham County Attorney General Elredge in conversations with some arrested Clams at the Manchester Armory. Elredge's proposal called for the remaining 541 protestors to be released on personal recognizance pending their automatic appeal to the State Superior Court. In exchange, the Clams would accept a mass verdict of guilty to misdemeanor charges for trespassing onto the nuclear site rather than demand individual trials. The arrangements would be made available to those serving sentences or those out on bail, thereby meeting Clam's demand that they all be treated alike. Elredge said he and presumably the state were satisfied with the agreement since most of the arrested protestors had already served twelve days awaiting trial, and his main concern was to relieve the financial burden of the state and the physical and emotional concerns of the national guard. On May 12, without much dissent, Clam accepted the offer ("Protestors Freed," 1977).

Although the protestors were exhausted from the struggle, they were exuberant in their claims of victory. They stated they compromised "only on procedure, not on principle," and that the sustained and skilled use of nonviolent tactics had broken the state's hard line. They had effectively demonstrated the power of nonviolent civil disobedience, and next year they "would return with 25,000 protestors." The Clamshell Alliance's main opponent, Governor Thomson, claimed he didn't capitulate, and that the state had taught the protestors a lesson in law and order. However, his victory claims were dwarfed by the state's heavy economic and political losses. Total cost for the demonstration and incarceration was estimated at $500 thousand. In addition, the governor and the Public Service Company also suffered public relations and political defeats. The demonstrators were front page news in New Hampshire newspapers for almost three weeks, and the Seabrook protest was the Associated Press' number two regional news event of the year. The Clamshell Alliance received free national publicity for their organization and ideas. Thomson's political opponents, as well as many citizens, felt the state overreacted to the protestors' misdemeanor crime; and, by adopting a hard-line nonnegotiable stance, the state suffered an embarrassing and humiliating defeat when it was forced to back down. Moreover, the state had underestimated Clam's strength, commitment, and organizational ability, and had made tactical errors in misrepresenting their motivations and intended actions. Typical of much third party opinion was a *New York Times* editorial by Tom Wicker. Claiming the Clamshell Alliance had a "legitimate protest," Wicker stated that Thomson's actions "blackened the state's good name" and "probably gave new spirit and unity to the national anti-nuclear movement ["A Tale," 1977]." Even Frank Shants, manager of special projects in the Public Information Department for Public Service Company, claimed that "The Clamshell Alliance won the event [Shants, 1978]."

To counteract these developments and Clam's announced intention to reoccupy, Governor Thomson and the Public Service Company made several personnel and planning changes. State Attorney General David Sauter was replaced by his assistant, Thomas Rath. The governor appropriated funds for a civil disobedience planning seminar on how to deal with mass arrests and sent law enforcement officials to observe a nuclear power protest at Barnwell, South Carolina. The Public Service Company hired consultants from the Operation Service, Inc., firm to help them with public relations and tactical strategy. And Frank Shants began spending much more time and energy on the Seabrook campaign (Shants, 1978; Rath, 1978).

The Clamshell Alliance also began planning for the next confrontation. After holding an evaluation conference in May and a two-day information conference in September, the coordinating committee decided at a November conference to make good on their threat to "reoccupy and restore" the Seabrook site the following June with members willing to risk arrest and internment for an indefinite period of time.

1978 and the Rath Agreement
The new attorney general, Thomas Rath, was given major responsibility by Governor Thomson to develop a new strategy to deal with the proposed 1978 confrontation. Rath first redefined his role. Instead of serving as an ally of the governor, Rath publicized himself as an independent "catalyst for compromise and negotiation" who "would stand squarely in the middle" of the competing parties and protect each of their rights. According to Rath, the key to compromise and negotiation was for each of the parties to agree to a definition of these "rights," and then to negotiate a compromise plan which would not violate them. Rath allowed that the Public Service Company "had a right, as long as they are in possession of a valid construction permit, to proceed with construction at the Seabrook site . . . without hindrance or interference from outside forces . . . and without the loss of a single man-hour of work." "The citizens of the Town of Seabrook and the County of Rockingham," Rath believed, "had a right to

continue their normal affairs in their normal fashion without hindrance or interference by outside forces and . . . without a heavy expenditure of funds to see that the laws of the state are
upheld." To meet some needs of the Clamshell Alliance, Rath stated that "people who hold
views in good conscience contrary to actions taken by the courts and regulatory agencies in
connection with this project, have rights guaranteed to them by the state and federal constitu-
tions to assemble peaceably and to speak freely so that their position might be known publicly
["Newsbrief," 1978]."

To develop a plan that would respect these rights and competing interests, Rath first met
secretly with the governor's office, top law enforcement officials, and the Public Service Company. In these talks, Rath proposed that the state and the Public Service Company offer a portion of the Seabrook site to the Clamshell Alliance so that they could hold a legal anti-nuclear
rally and alternative energy fair the weekend of June 23-26. In turn, the Clamshell Alliance
would agree to four demands: 1) insure that the demonstration would be nonviolent; 2) not
enter the fenced-in area; 3) not interfere with the access road for construction workers; 4)
leave the site at an agreed upon time ("Clamshell Occupation OK'd," 1978).

By May 11, the Public Service Company and the governor's office had agreed to Rath's
proposal. The next day, Rath startled both the Clamshell Alliance and the general public by
presenting his proposal to the Clamshell Alliance for its acceptance. Since the Clamshell Alliance had expected only to "open communication links" at the meeting and had "no idea they
would be involved in negotiations as such," they were unprepared to give Rath an answer to
his proposal. Realizing that they had previously decided to "establish a permanent presence
on the site" until construction was stopped, Clam negotiators announced they would have to
bring the Rath proposal back to their constituents for feedback ("Nuke Strategy Aired,"
1978).

On June 4, the Clam coordinating committee considered input from their local groups on
the Rath proposal. At a meeting which lasted until 2 a.m., the committee decided to bring
back a counter proposal to the state and the Public Service Company. This proposal, presented
at a meeting on June 5, stated that the Clamshell Alliance would accept the state/Public Service Company proposal if the builders of Seabrook Station would agree to five conditions including: 1) proof of a safe means for disposing of radioactive waste; 2) an evacuation drill of
the area that summer; 3) assumption of full liability in case of an accident; 4) obeying of town
ordinances; 5) stopping construction until the above environmental, financial, safety, and
legal questions were resolved to the satisfaction of a mutually agreed upon commission
("Counter Proposal," 1978).

Although the Clamshell Alliance hoped its counter proposal would "open negotiations"
and "appear reasonable in the public eye," some of the Clams thought privately that the state
and Public Service Company "wouldn't think twice about it." Unfortunately for Clam, even
those fears proved understated. Rath lashed out at the Clamshell Alliance, calling it "irresponsible for their unfair and unreasonable demands." The Public Service Company lawyer and
spokesperson called the conditions "ridiculous," "not really a negotiating position at all," and
announced that Clam's rejection of the state's offer had sent negotiations "back to square
one." Surprised by the vehemence and finality of its opponent's rejection of the counter proposal, the Clamshell Alliance could only reiterate its intention for 5,000 members to illegally
occupy and restore the Seabrook site. The meeting broke on a devisive note—none of the
parties mentioned the need or desire for any follow-up meeting ("Clam Acts Irresponsible,"
1978; "Negotiations Fall Apart," 1978).

However, in the week that followed, there were several external and intraorganizational
developments that prompted the Clamshell Alliance to reconsider the original Rath proposal.
For the most part, the media portrayed Clam's perceived rejection as unreasonable and ac-

cused it of "bad faith" bargaining. Loeb and Thomson's contention that "all Clamshell wanted to do was cost the state money and set up a volatile situation in Seabrook" now appeared to carry more weight with the public. A Clam spokesperson admitted that "the state had pulled off a public relations 'coup.'" The authorities had appeared reasonable and conciliatory, while the Clamshell Alliance appeared unreasonable and unlawful when it rejected the Rath offer ("Compromise Limits," 1978).

As the state's position gained support with the public, Clam's enemies intensified their attack on the protestors. In editorials, articles and cartoons, the Manchester *Union-Leader* constantly depicted the members of the Alliance as communists, terrorists, and lawless mobs itching to initiate mass violence. Public officials both threatened and implemented retaliatory measures. Rockingham County Prosecuting Attorney Carlton Elredge continually advocated the use of dispersal tactics such as dogs, gas, and firehoses, and threatened that "everything up to and including bullets would be used as necessary to repel the invasion." Governor Thomson stirred up construction workers, urging them to settle their teamsters' strike in order to "unite" against the protestors, even though several construction workers had publicly announced their intentions of bringing baseball bats to the demonstration ("Compromise Limits," 1978).

Sanctions against Clamshell and its sympathizers were applied by public officials. Anti-camping ordinances were passed in one neighboring town and were being considered in another. (The use of property in both towns was critically needed by Clam for "staging areas.") Public officials started to enforce minor zoning ordinances, and the three Seabrook selectmen who governed the town appeared ready to pass a resolution "to uninvite the Clam to town," even though two of the three selectmen were against the nuclear plant ("Seabrook 78," 1978).

Pressure against Seabrook sympathizers was less direct and harder to prove but, nevertheless, had an intimidating effect. The Clamshell Alliance reported several instances of supporters having their tax assessments doubled or tripled and/or having their property lines "readjusted." Persons planning to lend the protestors land for staging areas were told they would be personally liable for any damages and subject to arrest. Clam members reported other cases of personal harrassment and infringement of rights. Members said they were followed and photographed, had their phones wiretapped, and their mail opened. Clamshell organizers also claimed the state sent in several infiltrators and "agent provocateurs" to split the protest movement ("Both Sides," 1978).

All of these outside pressures helped wedge an inner split within the Clamshell Alliance. Several of the local Clamshell supporters (known as Seacoast Clams) viewed Clam's rejection of the Rath proposal as "arrogant," since it "didn't recognize any of the law enforcement needs of the state or the security needs of local people whom the Clam relied on for camping areas, loan of vehicles, and other logistical support." Moreover, the Seacoast Clams argued, "acceptance of the Rath proposal would allow many folks, not very public about their feelings, to go on site." The Seacoast Clams were certain that the state's actual and threatened reprisals, coupled with the demonstrators' planned civil disobedience, would escalate the crisis and alienate this important growing support of "closet Clams"[4] ("Seabrook 78," 1978).

A reconsideration of the Rath proposal was also occasioned by an apparent shortage of Clams willing to commit themselves to civil disobedience. Outside of the Boston-Cambridge area, many Clamshell Alliance members attending nonviolent training sessions were indicating their preference for serving on "support teams" rather than "committing civil disobedience and risking arrest ["Seabrook Protestors," 1978]."

Reacting to the increased repression, the Seacoast Clams' concerns, and the fact that a large contingent of demonstrators might forego civil disobedience, the Clamshell Alliance decided to approach the state and reopen negotiatios. After the eighteen-acre site was informally renegotiated to provide more suitable land for the alternative energy fair, and Rath agreed on some minor logistical conditions involving safety and sanitary issues, Clam accepted the Rath proposal on June 12, a month after it was originally presented ("Clam, N.H. Agree," 1978; "Clams, P.S. of N.H.," 1978).

The dramatic announcement that the Clamshell Alliance had called off their massive, illegal occupation in favor of a lawful, peaceful rally just outside the construction site was both unexpected and controversial. Manchester *Union-Leader* Editor Loeb led the charges of those who felt the state had made a mistake in recognizing the protestors as legitimate adversaries with negotiating powers. Loeb also chided the governor for expecting Clam to live up to its end of the agreement. The editor's accusations and fears were echoed by many pro-nuclear sympathizers and Public Service Company employees, but criticisms against the state were mild compared to the fury of controversy that erupted within the Clamshell Alliance and its supporters. Many of the more active and militant Clams, especially within the Boston-Cambridge areas, were shocked and dismayed with the acceptance of the Rath proposal and accused the coordinating committee members of "selling-out" and violating Clam consensus decision-making procedures. Dissident Clams agreed with spokesperson Harvey Wasserman that Clam had been outmaneuvered by the state into abandoning its main tactic of civil disobedience, and "that the Clamshell Alliance was deeply divided as a result ["Protestors Convene," 1978]."

The Clam central office and coordinating committee devoted much time and energy to explaining their actions to fellow Clam members and the public at large. They claimed their primary motive for accepting the proposal was to continue to respect the wishes of the "Seacoast people, especially Seabrook folks." By doing so, they "would help insure a solid base and increase their grass roots support," and not be open to the charge that they were "intruders just like the Public Service Company." Clam spokespeople also justified their acceptance on grounds that "direct action includes education as well as civil disobedience." The legal rally and energy fair would be "a great opportunity to educate the public" and move the "closet Clams" to deeper and more public commitment. Rally and fair attendees would be able to "see the destruction that had already occurred in Seabrook, hear the real story of nuclear power and view demonstrations of real alternatives ("Seabrook 78," 1978).

The Clamshell Alliance's stated reasons for returning to negotiations and accepting a proposal it originally rejected were important and, no doubt, true; but they failed to deal with the fact that the state had taken the initiative away from it. Clam was now reacting to actions proposed and implemented by its opponents. Spokesperson Wasserman, and others, recognized that the state's "middle ground offer was calculated to split the movement. . . . If Clam refused the offer, they would appear unreasonable and lose the credibility they gained last year. If they accepted, it would look like they were going soft ["Protestors Convene," 1978]."

However, it was not just the Rath proposal that backed Clam into a corner, but a combination of a "reasonable offer," threatened and actual reprisals, and internal splits. The combination and interplay of these factors had weakened Clam's own and third party support. To most people, the Rath proposal seemed reasonable and fair in meeting the needs of each of the parties. When Clam rejected it and persisted in its plans for confrontation, state repression became more justifiable to many people. And although Clam claimed that its constituency would not buckle under to repression, it is likely that fear of reprisals, along with the option of a viable alternative, motivated some Seacoast supporters to threaten to pull out and some other members to disavow Clam's intentions to commit civil disobedience.

Despite the extreme controversy surrounding the Rath agreement, the weekend actions of June 23–26 went smoothly and peacefully. Approximately 6,000 protestors arrived at several staging and camping areas on Friday, June 23. The following morning, demonstrators marched in affinity groups by geographical clusters to the eighteen-acre site adjacent to the Seabrook Plant. Once on site, they pitched tents and readied the site for Sunday's alternative energy fair. The next day between 12,000 and 14,000 "closet Clams" and "onlookers" attended the alternative energy fair and heard speeches by Benjamin Spock, Dick Gregory, and others, and music by folksingers such as Pete Seeger and Arlo Guthrie. By Monday at 3 p.m., all the demonstrators had left the site. State and county inspectors agreed that the Clam had left the site much cleaner than it was when Clam arrived. Despite predictions of trouble, the Rath agreement was upheld. Even Governor Thomson admitted "the Clamshell Alliance was well disciplined. . . . The Clamshell Alliance cooperated. They kept their word ["Seabrook Invaded," 1978]."

Clam's upholding of the agreement demonstrated the members' loyalty to the organization (Katz & List, 1981), improved its image with the surrounding townspeople (Hunt & Katz, N.D.), won Clam some begrudging respect from its opponents, and began to activate thousands of "closet Clams." The agreement also served the interest of the Power Service Company and the state. Since the demonstration received only limited media coverage, neither was property damaged nor construction time lost, and state costs were minimized. Negotiations had indeed served some basic needs for each of the disputing parties, but it must be-emphasized that what made an agreement possible was the protestors' previous use of nonviolent struggle that had forced New Hampshire's pro-nuclear forces into embarrassing and costly actions. In 1978, the state and the Power Service Company decided to recognize and legitimize through negotiations a hitherto excluded protest group, after weighing the costs and benefits of continued confrontation. Through sustained, effective nonviolent struggle, Clamshell had become a "force to be reckoned with" in the nuclear power battle at Seabrook.

Case II: The Iranian Revolution of 1979

The Iranian revolution of 1979 provides another example of the use of nonviolent action as an alternative to aggression to effect change. It is surprising at first to note that the Iranian revolution, so violent in the transfer of power, was made possible by predominantly nonviolent means. The following case study illustrates how the revolution succeeded through a direct, nonviolent challenge to the shah's power. Extreme repression was unleashed in order to be assessed and then destroyed. The shah's repression generated a process that Gene Sharp has called "political jujitsu" (1973, pp. 657–65), in which the asymmetrical power positions of the monarchy and the masses were reversed. The study of the nonviolent struggle in Iran is of interest to scholars and practitioners, moreover, because it shows not only how nonviolence minimized the eruption of further violence, but also the ways in which violent means proved to be counterproductive to the goals of the perpetrators on both sides.

In Tehran on the night of February 9, 1979, combined Feydayi and Mujahidin leftist guerrilla forces assaulted and quelled Shah Mohammad Reza Pahlavi's own Imperial Guard as they attempted to put down a mutiny among the remnants of the Iranian air force. The rescued cadets joined the guerrillas in a two-day spree, opening up prisons, police stations, armories, and Tehran's major military bases. Similar events led by clergy (ulama) occurred in the provinces. This brought the transfer of power on February 11 to the coalition of Ayatollah Ruhollah Khomeini and his followers, including religious and a few National Front ministers. The victory, while in part religious-led, was a militant one, and the role of the guerrilla forces and cadets was held as decisive in both the Western and Iranian presses (Abrahamian, 1980, p. 13; Lewis, 1979). With this in view, how is it possible to interpret the Iranian revolution as a result of nonviolent action?

The Background: 1963–1975

Socio-Economics. The socio-economic policies of the Pahlavi regime, the "White Revolution" of the 1960s to mid-1970s, appeared to many, especially those outside Iran, as a great success story. Indeed, there were larger increases in Iran's gross national product, and impressive industrial, agricultural, and infrastructural projects, as well as a number of social welfare activities. But, in fact, the overall effect of these projects and changes was seen in Iran as divesting the clergy of property and power, and as contributing to a pro-Western, capitalist-type of agriculture and industrial growth. At the same time, the regime retained a monopoly over the ever-growing oil income (Keddie, 1981, p. 160; Tatro, 1978). Agricultural reform, for example, favored agribusiness, which was partly owned and operated by multinational corporations. The emphasis was on a small number of large farms which were worked with imported machinery. Agribusiness generally farmed only a small part of the land they held, and Iranian experts viewed their contributions to the economy as dangerously small (Hoaglund, 1980; Katouzian, 1978). Foreign influences continued to work against Iran's socioeconomic interests. Although the United States under President Carter may have influenced the shah concerning human rights violations, neither the U.S. government nor major American business interests wanted to see a fundamental change in Iran's orientation toward becoming an independent self-sufficient economy (Gwertzman, 1977; U.S. Dept. of State, 1976).

Attempts at modernizing Iran benefited mainly the new middle and upper classes: the technicians, bureaucrats, military, educators, and white collar workers, in general. But this left out the vast majority of Iranians: the peasants, farmers, bazaaris,[5] clergy, students, youth, and factory workers. Moral indignation and agitation increased among the less favored classes as the urgently needed social reforms of the "White Revolution" failed, and billions in oil revenue went unaccounted for. Particularly demoralizing was the shah's vastly wasteful celebration in 1971 of Iran's mythical twenty-five hundred year monarchical tradition. The celebration devalued Islam and was denounced by the clergy.

Religion. Although the Pahlavi era was one of rapid secularization in many spheres of Iranian life, the reaction of the Islamic clergy was a persistent inhibitive force. From the time of Mohammad (d. 632), politics and religion have always been essentially linked in Iran.

The Shi'i Islamic clergy of Iran (*ulama*, led by *ayatollahs*) do not intercede between the people and God, but carry out Muslim law, education, charity, and other social functions—a broader role than that of Western clergy. Their role is also charismatic and prophetic with their most highly qualified legal and theological scholars (*mujtahids* or leading *ayatollahs*), selected to make judgments on religious, political, and judicial questions for their followers to obey without question. The clergy are economically self-sufficient through direct collection of religious taxes and donations. Traditionally, the clergy has had strong ties with bazaaris, since often clergy and bazaaris come from the same families; and much clergy income is paid by bazaaris. As a corporate group, the clergy is endowed with sociopolitical power and independence (Keddie 1981, pp. 10, 31).

In the interpretation of nonviolent action in Iranian history, one looks in vain for a nonviolent tradition, per se: the *Koran* permits violent means to free the oppressed, for example. Thus, it seems that the choices of nonviolent means in Iranian history were guided by pragmatic and not principled concerns. Under the *Koran*, it would seem that the ends justify the means. Iranian actions, nevertheless, may be understood as belonging more or less to one of the three catagories of methods as defined by Sharp: protest and persuasion, nonviolent cooperation, or nonviolent intervention.

Mosques and shrines have been a major area of sanctuary (*bast*) for individuals and groups that feared governmental arrest or harrassment. Throughout the nineteenth century, the clery were appealed to by the popular as well as the wealthy classes to represent grievances before the government. Several times in this period, the clergy helped lead popular movements against a government seen as complaisant to the intrusions of foreign imperialists, namely Britain and Russia, and against the trend toward the sale of Iran's resources to foreigners. Moreover, the clergy's independent power and ties to the bazaaris made them useful allies to secular reformers in the struggle against foreign control.

Despotism, Resistance, and Repression. In early 1963, the injustice of the urgent need for land reform finally turned the clergy into an oppostional force against the shah's autocratic regime. Ayatollah Khomeini began to preach against the shah in the chief religious school in Qom. In March 1963, the school was attacked by the shah's troops; a number of students were killed, and Khomeini was arrested. Released after a short time, Khomeini continued to preach against the shah but in favor of the constitution. On June 4, the anniversary of the martyrdom of Imam Hosain, Khomeini was arrested again. When the news became known in Tehran, religious processions of mourning for Hosain turned into demonstrations of protest. The next day, demonstrations spread throughout several major cities and the university in Tehran. After heavy deployment of troops, the unarmed uprisings were suppressed in a few days with hundreds of lives lost. The shah restored order and his autocratic power by enlarging his security forces, shooting demonstrators, and arresting large numbers of clergy and political dissidents. In response to this brutal repression of traditional methods of persuasion and protest, the resistance went underground, and leftist guerrilla groups began forming in Iran in the summer of 1963 (Abrahamian, 1980, pp. 4-6; Gage, 1978).

In despotic style, the regime continued to curtail the power of the clergy, for example, with the institution of state schools, the calumniation of Khomeini in the press, and the promotion of Western ways. The bazaaris' power was constantly reduced by governmental favoring of Western imports and "modernization" or displacement of the bazaaris with Western supermarkets, department stores, and large banks (Keddie, 1981, p. 244).

The Failure of Guerrilla Violence: 1976

The two major Iranian guerrilla groups took root in late 1963: the Feydayi, who were Marxist and critical of the pro-Soviet Tudeh party; and the Mujahidin, who were Islamic and strove to liberalize the regime with nonviolent means. Almost all of these guerrillas were of the intelligentsia and ultimately took up arms as a result of social, moral, and political indignation rather than economic deprivation.

In 1970, in hopes of igniting a people's movement against the shah, the Feydayi began training in secret for armed struggle. Early in 1971, two of their sympathizers were arrested, and the Feydayi feared their plans might be revealed under torture. Thus, they hastened Iran's first major guerrilla operation in February 1971, attacking a jail in Siakal and killing three police in a vain rescue attempt. The shah reacted strongly, sending his brother to lead a large and well equipped manhunt that left several soldiers and thirty guerrillas dead and eleven captured. Despite the military failure, the "Siakal incident" sparked off five years of intensive guerrilla activity, because it showed it was possible to shake the regime (Abrahamian, 1980, pp. 3-6).

Armed robberies, assassinations, and bombings followed; but, by late 1976, it became clear to members of all factions of the Feydayi and Mujahidin (each group had split into two factions) that the heavy toll in guerrilla lives outweighed the gains (Willenson, 1975). Indeed, Amnesty International in its 1974-75 annual report declared that the Shah of Iran retained his benevolent image despite the highest rate of death penalties in the world, no valid system of civilian courts, and a history of torture which was beyond belief.

The guerrillas had failed in their attempts to ignite a people's revolution. Undaunted, however, the Mujahidin and the Feydayi saw their individual acts of violence as only one means toward revolution in a period of extreme repression. They joined efforts, although anonymously, with the clergy-bazaaris-led mass movements (Halliday, 1980).

The Success of the Nonviolent
Mass Movements: 1977–1979

There never was a popular violent movement against the shah and his regime. The revolution of 1979 was made possible mainly by the "religious opposition," that is, by those who voiced their views in Islamic terms. There were two major groups: first, those with a traditional religious education and functions; and second, those with Western or Western-style educations who united modern and traditional ideas under Islamic concepts. Among those in the first group were, notably, Ayatollahs Khomeini, Shariatmadari, and Talequani. Mehdi Bazargan, Ali Shariati, Abolhasan Bani Sadr, and Sadeq Ghotbzadeh were among the second group (Keddie, 1981, pp. 239-240).

Through the 1960s and until late 1978, numerous instances of nonviolent protest and persuasion were intermingled with various nonviolent acts of economic, social, and political noncooperation. The successes of these activities in the face of a repressive and implacable regime intensified the enthusiasm of the resisters, diminished their feelings of submissiveness, and increased their fearlessness. The result may be seen as a spiraling series of nonviolent actions or aggressions which escalated into the dramatic acts of nonviolent intervention of January and February 1979. The claim here is not that there was a centralized and conscious plan for a nonviolent people's revolution, but that, as Sharp (1973, pp. 777-840) would contend, nonviolent action, when consistent and persistent, has a force and power of its own, which culminates in the de-evolution of the opponents' power.

Protest and Persuasion. From its renewed upsurge in the 1960s, the "religious opposition" owed a great deal to the "Western infidels'" mass media technology, especially the cassette tape-recorder. Tapes of Khomeini's sermons were bought, collected, and played for groups of friends and in the mosques throughout the Iranian countryside, much as the tapes of great rock concert stars are in the West. Khomeini appealed especially to the lower classes: the farmers, peasants, factory workers, urban poor, rural youth, the more fundamental Shi'i Muslims, and the bazaaris. From the late 1960s, the taped lectures of Ali Shariati (d. 1977), a lay Muslim sociologist, did the most to prepare Iranian urban youth, academics, intellectuals, and the Mujahidin for the revolution. The ideas of Khomeini and Shariati were rarely distinguished by the masses in 1978-79, although Shariati placed more emphasis on the development of secular society.

The persuasive analyses of Khomeini and Shariati more than any others unified and prepared the masses for protest (Shivers, 1980, pp. 60-62). Through the 1970s, in particular, university students leafleted, produced underground films and newspapers, and, when assemblies were banned, gathered at the library steps to engage in corporate silence; many women students, and other women as well, returned to wearing the veil to protest the Westernization of the regime. From the mid-1970s, massive memorial processions of up to a million people took place for those killed in previous incidents and were repeated at traditional forty-day intervals.

Discontent among most sections of the Iranian population spread and a new outgrowth of opposition began in 1977 and was tolerated by the shah. The forms and timing were in large part the results of external aids, such as President Carter's human rights policy which threatened to deprive violators of U.S. arms and aid, and pressures from Amnesty International and the International Commission of Jurists to reduce torture and reform the judiciary (Butler & Martin, 1978; International League of Human Rights, 1978; U.S. Dept. of State, 1977). At this time, protest took the form of petitions, letters, and manifestos from groups of "moderates," such as lawyers, well-known writers and professors, and leaders of the revived National Front, including Shahpour Bakhtiar, the shah's last prime minister.

Besides pressures from world opinion, the shah may have tolerated criticisms in 1977 since he knew he was gravely ill with cancer and wished to leave his minor son and Queen Farah with some cooperation from the "moderates" of Iranian society (Gage, 1978).

Nonviolent economic, social and political noncooperation. Once the door was open to protest in 1977, it was not to be shut. There were frequent strikes by factory workers, university students in general, and woman students, in particular.

From his exiles in Iraq and France, Khomeini issued taped directives calling for strikes and boycotts, and the conversion of members of the armed forces (Albert, 1980, p. 22; Shivers, 1980, pp. 65-66). The control Khomeini was able to exercise while in exile over his opposition forces in Iran was noteworthy.

In late summer, 1978, the massive religious-led politicoeconomic strikers began the most crucial nonviolent stage of the revolution. The strikes started in the oil refineries of Tehran, Bandar Shahpur, and, soon, in Ahwaz. Strikes then spread through the government and remaining oil industry, so that by late October oil production had fallen to 28 percent of its former level. Large wage settlements were refused. By the time the military arrived, few public services were functional. Strikes increased and attempts to reimpose censorship were met by press strikes (Kandell, 1978; Keddie, 1981, p. 251). The religious-led strikes culminated in a continuing general strike which lasted until the end of the revolution in early 1979 and virtually paralyzed the economy.

Most importantly, the use of military force posed severe problems. First, by the fall of 1978, the soldiers were emotionally worn down by the kindness of Khomeini's followers and co-opted by the widely based grievances against the regime; they were refusing to fire into crowds and some were fraternizing with the people. Second, the shah still hoped, although unrealistically, to regain popularity by concessions, and did not wish to alienate more people by massacres. Third, the shah wished history to regard him as the great benefactor of Iran. Fourth, the military and secret police (SAVAK) were not trained for crowd control—another sign of the shah's lack of reality (Pahlavi, 1978; Sanders, 1978; Willenson, 1978).

By late 1978, segments of the military were in open mutiny, and the resulting inability of the government to retaliate violently made possible the final and most dramatic nonviolent actions of the people's revolution in February 1979.

Nonviolent Intervention. In January 1978, the shah demonstrated the degree to which he miscalculated the strength of the religious opposition when, reportedly at his instigation, an article was published in a leading newspaper violently attacking and slandering Khomeini. The following day, theological students in Qom staged a massive protest and sit-in. This was broken up by security forces and seventy people were killed, making it the bloodiest incident since 1963. The move by the shah, which was calculated to weaken the religious-led opposition, created the opposite effect or, "political jujitsu," in that dissent intensified in his opponent's camp, and the last of the uncommitted bazaaris were won over to the side of the clergy. The clergy and bazaaris, sensing their new power, organized massive memorial demonstration for those killed, and these were held ritually at forty-day intervals throughout 1978. The government at first dared not risk outlawing these mourning gatherings, and so the demonstrations grew in intensity with cries of "Death to the shah" being heard for the first time. Moreover, banks, shops, and cinemas were attacked and destroyed, since they symbolized dependence on the West. It is important to note that human life was spared, even of those considered enemies, except for a few rare incidents at the high point of late revolutionary fervor (Keddie, 1981, pp. 242-244).

In the early fall of 1978, however, repression became worse than ever in reaction to the millions of demonstrators who were now marching in every major Iranian city. Martial law was declared in the early morning of September 8, so that many did not hear of it. Later in that day, now known as "Black Friday," hundreds of thousands of unarmed demonstrators were fired on in the streets of Tehran. In one location alone more than 3,000 were killed, including 700 women (Albert, 1980, p. 19). After this, attempts by the shah to accommodate the opposition were totally ineffective ("Shah mollifies the mullahs," 1978).

In January 1979, Bakhtiar, the newly appointed prime minister, vainly attempted to defuse the opposition with several concessions, including the release of all political prisoners, the announced dismantlement of SAVAK, a cut-off in oil sales to Israel and South Africa, and the "temporary" departure of the shah to Egypt on January 16 ("Shah compromises," 1979). On January 18, soldiers opened fire on anti-Bakhtiar demonstrators in Ahwaz; but Khomeini urged continuation of demonstrations in spite of a recent ban, preservation of public order, and conversion of the armed forces.

This was the nadir of the Pahlavi regime. Ironically, while "Rome" was burning and the shah was vacationing, secret negotiations for a peaceful transition of power were being carried out by a coalition of all parties involved: Barzargan on behalf of Khomeini with the United States, SAVAK, and the army chiefs of staff. In the end, key generals saw that the cause was lost and did not fight (Apple, 1979a; Markham, 1979).

It soon became clear that Khomeini himself could effect an orderly transition of power, and this he did with two acts of nonviolent intervention. First, on January 13, from Paris, Khomeini announced the creation of a "dual government" in Iran, the Provisional Revolutionary Council, to replace the present "illegal" government. Second, soon after his triumphant return to Iran, Khomeini appointed Barzargan as the "real" prime minister on February 5. Bakhtiar resigned on February 11, even as the power was being effectively transferred to Khomeini at the conclusion of two days struggle between the Imperial Guard and the guerrillas along with remnants of the military forces (Apple, 1979b; Gage, 1979).

CONCLUSIONS

Nonviolent action made possible the Iranian revolution of 1979 and minimized the eruption of further violence. Consider the following:

1. Even the guerrilla groups: the Feydayi, the Mujahidin, and their factions, admitted by late 1976 what everyone else knew—that violent actions had failed to ignite the necessary "peoples' revolution." Furthermore, the guerrillas admitted implicitly that nonviolent actions were a stronger revolutionary force than violent actions when they joined the clergy/bazaaris-led mass movements, although anonymously, to contribute toward the tasks of education, mobilization, and crowd control. The guerrilla groups further demonstrated by their words and deeds that violence was not a necessary means, although for them a perfectly justifiable one, to achieve the revolution. Fortunately, the availability of successful nonviolent methods deterred the guerrillas from continuing in their use of violent options.

2. The clergy/bazaaris-led mass movements of 1977-79, especially those which defied a ban, were the nonviolent challenge that served to unleash the extreme repression of the Pah-

lavi regime. Having assessed the nature of the force as primarily the army composed of brother Iranians, Khomeini set about immediately, as it were, to "destroy" it. Even as troops were firing into unarmed demonstrators, Khomeini issued directives from exile calling for the conversion of the army. It was this direct confrontation of nonviolence with violence that brought about political jujitsu, shaming soldiers and breaking their will to fire into the crowds. The resulting mutiny from late 1978 to early 1979 undoubtedly prevented much violence from occurring before and during the revolution.

3. It is a fact that guerrilla violence against the Imperial Guard on February 9, 1979, precipitated the effective transfer of power from the monarchy to Khomeini and his followers on February 11. From the case study, it may be seen that the condition of mutiny which made possible this militant success could only have been brought about by predominantly nonviolent means. The guerrillas, who were late-comers to the nonviolent movement, simply broke discipline, since there was no directive from Khomeini to attack the Guard. It seems probable also that a peaceful transfer of power would have taken place anyway without this act of violence, given the presence of Khomeini in Iran, his overwhelming popular support, and the secret negotiations for a peaceful transfer which were going on at that time with all sides in the conflict. The guerrillas merely hastened Bakhtiar's resignation, which was imminent. In the end, a greater violence than the loss of the Imperial Guard had been averted through the masses remaining unarmed and continuing to convert the soldiers, and with the soldiers choosing political noncooperation by mutiny. By electing nonviolent methods, the masses and the army averted the greater violence that was within their power—attempted revolution by military coup or civil war.

4. The Iranian revolution of 1979 should be characterized according to the means which created the sociopolitical conditions that made the challenge to Bakhtiar's power effective: nonviolent persuasion through the tapes of Khomeini and Shariati; nonviolent protest through unarmed mass demonstrations; noncooperation through general strikes and mutiny; and nonviolent political intervention with Khomeini's establishment of dual government.

DISCUSSION OF CASE STUDIES

In both the Iranian and Seabrook situations, one can recognize many key principles of nonviolence—the need for preparation, the expectation that the initial challenge(s) will bring repression, and the necessity of meeting that repression with steadfastness, courage, and increased solidarity, militancy, and nonviolent discipline. When this happened in Seabrook and Iran, political jujitsu effects took place—the breaking of ranks among the pro-nuclear forces in Seabrook and the conversion of the army in Iran. These developments in turn brought about changes in power relationships. Negotiations with the protesters occurred in Seabrook and a change of leadership was effected in Iran.

These two cases of successful actions demonstrate the potency of nonviolent struggle and confirm some general propositions advanced by nonviolent scholars. A more detailed analysis of the two campaigns together might help us understand some of the variations and potential of this technique and highlight important research questions that need to be addressed.

Asymmetry and Redefinition of Power

Advocates of nonviolent action contend that nonviolence, like violence, can be employed to alter power imbalances. In Seabrook, the protest group initially lacked great numbers, access to decision makers, and the capability of applying strong sanctions to its opponents. Initially, the state and the Power Service Company dealt with the protesters by ignoring their concerns, ridiculing their wisdom and motivation, and repressing their actions. From 1976 to 1978, the Clamshell Alliance rapidly built up its cadre of protesters and increased its ability to embarrass and hurt the state and the Power Service Company. By the spring of 1978, government and local leaders decided to acknowledge the shift in power and recognize Clamshell as a legitimate party to negotiations.

In Iran, the power differential was acute. The monarchy had sustained its power through ruthless suppression of dissent. The 1906 constitutional provision guaranteeing the clergy decision-making power was ignored, the 1963 unarmed demonstrations were met with brutal government violence and exile of the demonstration leaders, and the government easily squashed leftist guerrilla attempts to overthrow the monarchy through violence. However, a larger, more organized and disciplined nonviolent movement was able to take advantage of the government's overreaction during "Black Friday" (Sept. 1978), and show, through successful memorial demonstrations, the uncontrolability and vulnerability of the shah's regime. Wanton violence, unleashed against obviously unarmed people, had shamed soldiers and begun to weaken their will to fire into the crowds. The resultant mutiny of the army effectively reversed the power differential and made possible the replacement of government leaders.

Jujitsu

In both cases, political jujitsu took effect as the opponents' force worked against them and caused disunity among their supporters. In Seabrook, Governor Thomson and editor Loeb attempted to discredit the anti-nuclear forces by depicting them as "irreconcilable idiots," "lawless mobs" and "terrorists." When these characterizations proved untrue, the state and the Manchester *Union Leader* lost credibility. In addition, Thomson's and Loeb's insistence on "teaching the protesters a lesson" by adopting hard-line positions on the 1977 jail-in, alienated some of the state's critical supporters and was costly in terms of money, prestige, and public relations. The desire not to suffer these losses a second time led the state to seek accommodation in 1978.

In Iran, the political jujitsu effect was even more dramatic, clear-cut, and critical. Though government repression had successfully maintained power in the past, numerous acts of nonviolent protest, persuasion, and noncooperation were organized by the grievance group in the 1960s and 1970s. These nonviolent acts increased the resolve of the protestors and their commitment to nonviolent discipline, and began to wear down the resistance of the army. The shah's January 1978 slandering of Khomeini, the resulting massacre at Qom, and the brutal killings of "Black Friday" exposed the naked terror of the shah's regime and caused third parties to support the rebels and the shah's allies to defect. The remainder of the uncommitted bazaaris joined the clergy in acts of overt defiance, and members of the army defied orders and joined the protesters. Power was effectively transferred after relatively minimal government opposition in January 1979.

Methods and Consequences

During the Seabrook campaign and the Iranian revolution, a variety of nonviolent methods were used. In Seabrook, traditional efforts to stop construction of the Seabrook plant proved futile and the Clamshell Alliance was formed with the expressed purpose of using direct action, including civil disobedience. Initial symbolic witness actions and small-scale demonstrations were followed by mass noncooperation and civil disobedient actions in 1977 which proved damaging to the state and the Power Service Company. The protestors' effective use of a "jail-

An Alternative to Violence 293

in" demonstrated their persistence and solidarity and greatly increased the costs to the state. The state's fear of a repetition of Clam's successful mass civil disobedience led the governor to adopt a new strategy in 1978. By doing so, the state and the Power Service Company recognized the legitimacy and credibility of the protesting group, but seized the initiative from Clamshell and backed it into substituting marches and rallies for nonviolent obstruction. This de-escalation of tactics carried both benefits and burdens for Clamshell.

In Iran, the Khomeini-led movement used only nonviolent methods in order to distinguish it from the guerrilla violence practiced by the Feydayi and Mujahidin. The religiously inspired protesters engaged in nonviolent persuasion through disseminating tapes and recordings of Khomeini and Shariati, nonviolent protests through unarmed mass demonstrations, noncooperation through general strikes and mutiny, and nonviolent political intervention with Khomeini's establishment of a parallel government. In general, these methods were used in a successive, escalatory pattern which gradually built up the numbers and spirit of resistance and increased the amount of disruption and damage to the government.

Mechanisms of Change

The Seabrook and Iranian case studies demonstrate how nonviolent struggle can operate successfully through different mechanisms of change. The mechanisms are at least partially determined by one's goals, tactics, and relationship to the opposition and third parties.

Accommodation best describes the mechanism of change that occurred in Seabrook to bring an end to the 1978 crisis. Although the 1978 demonstration did not bring about a resolution to the anti-nuclear campaign, it did signal a watershed in the struggle. By seeking accommodation instead of trying to ignore or crush their opponents, the state and the Power Service Company granted legitimacy and credibility to the protestors' organization and cause. The Clamshell's successful nonviolent actions in 1976 and 1977 had hurt its opponents economically, politically, and psychologically. The state's use of repression, intimidation, and clever negotiation had taken its toll on Clamshell's enthusiasm for civil disobedience. Thus, by the spring of 1978, after weighing the probable costs of enduring or continuing confrontation against the probable costs of making concessions, each of the protagonists was ready to seek accommodation. Neither of the combatants changed its attitudes on the issue, but each party opted to alter its behavior and accept the Rath agreement. This settlement offered an alternative to a highly explosive situation brought about a deescalation of tactics, and allowed the protagonists to "save face" and achieve some of their goals.

In the Iranian situation, change could not come through accommodation. On the one hand, Iranian rulers mainly followed a strategy of trying to crush the opposition. When the shah and Bakhtiar finally made concessions, they were viewed as insubstantial and too late. On the other hand, Khomeini would never accommodate on religious principles. His goal was a restructuring of Iranian society which, by necessity, meant a change in government.

Since both sides pursued complete victory and chose militant tactics, change could only come about through coercion. Even though secret negotiations were taking place, the shah was forced to abdicate, Bakhtiar forced to resign, and the die-hard army generals forced to cancel plans for a military coup.

It is noteworthy that the Iranian case highlights the interplay of coercion and conversion. Although the conflict was officially resolved through nonviolent coercive force, the mechanism that allowed the rebels to win was the conversion and mutiny of the army. The majority of the army was either neutralized or converted to Khomeini's side. This, in effect, evaporated the shah's ability to enforce sanctions and continue the confrontation. Since he had pursued a strategy of total victory or total defeat, the loss of his enforcers forced him to abdicate.

FURTHER ANALYSES AND RESEARCH

The Seabrook and Iranian case studies confirm Gene Sharp's major propositions explaining the dynamics of nonviolent struggle. However, closer examination of these historical events reveals complicated and diverse conditions and responses that contributed to the successful operation of this technique. Moreover, in examining two successful nonviolent campaigns, one notices differences in the requirements for effectiveness for this technique. The questions that are raised by this research need to be systematically analyzed to help scholars and practitioners expand and refine nonviolent principles and methods.

The following are some points of inquiry from our research:

1. *Effects of Third Parties on Jujitsu*—In both cases, third parties served as catalysts for disunity among the opposition. In Seabrook, public officials and commentators criticized the state's hard line in 1977. This, in turn, opened the way for some divisiveness from within the pro-nuclear forces' camp. In Iran, world opinion concerning human rights violations had a decisive effect on the shah, making violent repression less acceptable to both himself and his followers. More research is needed on ways to capitalize on the use of third parties.

2. *The use of counter-nonviolence by opponents and the significance of maintaining initiative*—In Seabrook, the pro-nuclear forces switched strategies and adopted a conciliatory, nonviolent posture in the 1978 campaign by offering the Rath proposal to the demonstrators. This not only allowed the state and the Public Service Company to appear "reasonable" and "fair," but it also took the initiative away from Clam. This maneuver, at least temporarily, changed the dynamics of the struggle. In Iran, the shah's attempts at conciliation backfired. Reforms and concessions by the government only convinced the rebels of the vulnerability of the shah, and fueled their passion for defiance and victory. Additional research is necessary on the effects of counter-nonviolence and the loss of initiative.

3. *Need to keep violence from being legitimized*—Social conflict theorist Charles Tilley (1978) has discussed the need for grievance groups to "avoid situations in which they appear to be dangerous, unyielding, unresponsive radicals against whom repression without restraint becomes a welcome and legitimate enterprise." Clamshell fell into this trap when it initially rejected the Rath proposal. Clam appeared "unreasonable" and "unlawful" and the state was quick to escalate its repression with minimum censure. To some extent, the same phenomenon occurred in Iran when the leftist guerrilla groups attempted to overthrow the government with violence but were stopped by even greater counter-violence with minimal public outcry. More attention needs to be placed on the effects of violence against protesters at different stages in a struggle.

4. *Effect of de-escalation of methods by the protest group*—Gene Sharp and other nonviolent theorists write about the need for being able to escalate the militancy and potential costs of nonviolent methods and move from protest and persuasion to noncooperation to intervention. The Rath agreement forced Clam to de-escalate its tactics in 1978, and replace its planned mass civil disobedience actions with marches and rallies. Public Service Company official Frank Shants (1978) believed the de-escalation would hurt Clam in the future for "if they revert back to breaking the law they'll take a public relations nosedive." If Shants' contention is correct, protest groups need to be more aware of the damages of their reversal of tactics. On the other hand, in Iran, marches and rallies proved to be effective up to the revolution, along with strikes, mutiny, and dual government. It is important to note that these marches were ac-

companied by sabotage, which intensified their impact, so that the effect, while technically a de-escalation of methods, strategically, and more significantly, escalated the costs of the struggle.

5. *Role of Negotiations in Nonviolent Struggle*—In the Seabrook campaign, the role of negotiations was crucial in meeting the needs of each of the disputants. The Clamshell Alliance engaged in a struggle to be recognized as a legitimate bargaining adversary, yet seemed to lack training in negotiation skills and suffered as a result. More attention needs to be placed on effective negotiation strategies in preparing for nonviolent struggle.

6. *The Effects of Sabotage*—According to Gene Sharp, sabotage need not be a violent action, but it does escalate risks. During the phase of general strikes and mutiny in Iran in 1978, peaceful memorial demonstrations often turned into riots where property which symbolized Western imperialism was destroyed. Although there was extensive property damage, it could be argued that the riots were a form of nonviolent protest. In any event, further research on nonviolent sabotage might strengthen the justification of those who claim to be nonviolent in principle and choose to protest through destruction of symbolic public property, i.e., MX missile nosecones and draftcards.

7. *Role of Leadership*—In the Iran situation, the leadership role and decisions of Ayatollah Khomeini were critical in sustaining dedication and discipline for the nonviolent protests. The Clamshell Alliance had an explicit commitment to function as a leaderless, democratic coalition, making decisions by consensus. The advantages and disadvantages of these two approaches need to be carefully examined.

8. *Commitment to Nonviolence*—In its founding statement, the Clamshell Alliance affirmed its commitment to nonviolent action. Among its members there were people for whom nonviolence was viewed as a way of life (principled nonviolence) and others for whom nonviolence was a means to an end (pragmatic nonviolence). In Iran, the rebellion was religiously inspired, yet tied pragmatically to nonviolence: under the teachings of the *Koran*, Khomeini could have ordered a violent campaign at any time. Questions for further research arise here: since a purely pragmatic commitment to nonviolence serves, in effect, as a continual threat to do violence if need be, isn't the pragmatic commitment to nonviolence actually a strategy of psychological violence? And does this implicit threat increase or decrease chances for successful nonviolent action?

FUTURE OF NONVIOLENT STRUGGLE

There is no doubt that nonviolent action is a potent, yet neglected form of struggle. Historians and other chroniclers of events have largely ignored the vast, impressive history of nonviolent struggle. Furthermore, by romanticizing the dramatic and heroic acts of violence for good causes, they have been unwilling (or willing) accomplices to building and perpetuating the myth of violence as the only significant form of combat (Katz, 1973; Sharp, 1973). Scholars have failed to compare violent and nonviolent techniques in terms of time, casualties, successes and failures, adequacy of preparation, and requirements for struggle. By their choices, historians and others have not only influenced how the past is viewed but also how the present is lived.

If scholars and practitioners want to promote the feasibility of nonviolent struggle as an alternative to violent aggression to bring about desired social change, they will need to continue to develop and refine their work and training in nonviolent alternatives. Important attempts are now being made to convince government leaders, educators, citizens, and social change activists that nonviolent action has been a significantly effective struggle technique in the past; is worthy and susceptible to research, study, and use in the present; and has considerable potential for the future. More attention and resources need to be applied to the further development of this technique in our schools, research institutions, and training centers. We might be able to destroy destructive myths about methods for waging conflict, and make contributions to lessen human suffering, by promoting knowledge about and skills in nonviolent struggle as an alternative to submissiveness or violence for groups who are perceived as powerless and yet want "to stand and fight" against war, tyranny, and oppression.

NOTES

1. The Clamshell Alliance was named for the numerous clam beds in the waterways near Seabrook Station. The Clamshell Alliance also referred to themselves as "Clamshell," "Clams," or "Clam."
2. As in most mass demonstrations, there were conflicting reports on the number of people attending. For this chapter we used the average from the different reports.
3. Originally, the plant was estimated to cost $800 million. By 1976, the estimate had risen to $1.6 billion. By 1978, estimates had soared to $2.6 billion.
4. "Closet Clams" was the name given to local people who supported the goals of the Clamshell Alliance but had heretofore not gone public with their views.
5. "Bazaaris" is a collective term inclusive of merchants, shopkeepers, and small bankers.

REFERENCES

Abrahamian, E. The guerrilla movement in Iran, 1963-1977. *MERIP Reports,* March-April 1980, *86,* 3-21.

Albert, D. H. Twentieth century Iranian history: A chronology. *Tell the American people: Perspectives on the Iranian revolution.* Philadelphia: Movement for a New Society, 1980.

Alliance maps action against nuclear plant. *Manchester Union-Leader,* July 10, 1976, p. 14.

Apple, R. W., Jr., Moslems and army in Iran hold talks on nation's future. *New York Times,* Jan. 21, 1979, pp. 1 & 7. (a)

Apple, R. W., Jr., Iranians turn to their past: Islamic fervor at root of drive against Shah. *New York Times,* Feb. 12, 1979, pp. 1 & 12.

Bondurant, J. V. *Conquest of Violence: The Gandhian Philosophy of Conflict.* Berkeley: University of California Press, 1965.

Both sides getting ready for Seabrook. *Boston Globe,* June 8, 1978, p. 3.

Brock, P. *Twentieth Century Pacifism.* New York: Van Nostrand, 1970.

Butler, D., & Martin, P. Shah cracks down. *Newsweek,* May 22, 1978, p. 42.

Chatfield, C. *For Peace and Justice: Pacifism in America 1914-1941.* Knoxville: University of Tennessee Press, 1971.

Chatfield, C. *Peace Movements in America.* New York: Shocken Books, 1973.

Clam acts irresponsible. *Manchester Union-Leader,* June 6, 1978, p. 1.

Clam, N.H. agree on Seabrook rules. *Boston Globe,* June 17, 1978, p. 3.

Clams, P.S. of N.H., state reach accord. *Manchester Union-Leader*, June 17, 1978, p. 1.

Clamshell occupation OK'd with limits. *Boston Globe*, May 13, 1978.

Compromise limits Seabrook rally plans. *Boston Herald-American*, June 18, 1978, p. 5.

Cooney, R., & Michalowski, H. *Power of the People*. Culver City, Calif.: Peace Press, 1977.

Counter proposal from the Clamshell Alliance, *Manchester Union-Leader*, June 5, 1978.

Dellinger, D. *Revolutionary Nonviolence*. Garden City: Anchor Books Inc., 1971.

Demonstrators ready for today. *Manchester Union-Leader*, April 30, 1977, p. 12.

Easy target? Time will tell. *Manchester Union-Leader*, August 6, 1976, p. 19.

Erickson, H. *Gandhi's Truth: On the Origins of Militant Nonviolence*. New York: W. W. Norton, 1966.

Gage, N. Iran: Making of a revolution. *New York Times Magazine*, Dec. 17, 1978.

Gage, N. Army withdraws its support for Bakhtiar; Iranian prime minister reported to resign. *New York Times*, Feb. 12, 1979, pp. 1 & 8.

Gamson, W. *The Strategy of Social Protest*. Homewood, Ill.: Dorsey Press, 1975.

Goldstein, A. P., Carr, E., Davidson, W., Jr., & Wehr, P. *In Response to Aggression*. New York: Pergamon Press, 1981.

Gregg, R. *The Power of Nonviolence*. Philadelphia: J. B. Lippincott, 1943.

Gwertzman, B. U.S. says six nations curb human rights. *New York Times*, Jan. 2, 1977, pp. 1 & 14.

Halliday, F. Interview with Mujahidin, Feydayi and Kurdish leaders. *MERIP Reports*, Mar.-Apr. 1980, *86*, 16-17.

Hare, A., & Herbert, H. *Nonviolent Direct Action, American Cases: A Social Psychological Analysis*. Cleveland: Corpus Books, 1968.

Hoaglund, E. Rural participation in the revolution. *MERIP Reports*, May 1980, *87*, 3-4.

Hundreds arrested in N.H. atom protest. *New York Times*, May 2, 1977, pp. 1 & 24.

Hunt, J. P., & Katz, N. H. Nonviolent protest and third party opinion: A study of the June 1978 Seabrook, N.H., anti-nuclear power protest. Unpublished mss. available from authors.

International League of Human Rights. Report on Iranian justice system. *New York Times*, Nov. 24, 1978, p. 6.

Kandell, J. Iran premier quits: Rioters challenge army rule by Shah. *New York Times*, Nov. 6, 1978, pp. 1 & 18.

Katz, N. H. History of human struggle re-examined. *Politics of Nonviolent Action, Peace and change: A Journal of Peace Research*, 1974, *II*, 61-63.

Katz, N. H., & Hunt, J. P. Nonviolent struggle in Albany, Georgia. In Severyn T. Bruyn and Paula M. Rayman (Eds.), *Nonviolent action and social change*. New York: Irvington, 1979.

Katz, N. H., & List, D. Seabrook: A profile of anti-nuclear activists. *Peace and Change: A Journal of Peace Research*, 1981, *VIII* (3), 59-71.

Katouzian, M. A. Oil versus agriculture: A case of dual resources depletion in Iran. *The Journal of Peasant Studies*, 1978, *5* (3), 347-69.

Keddie, N. *Roots of revolution: An interpretive history of modern Iran*. New Haven: Yale University Press, 1981.

Kidder, T. The nonviolent war against nuclear power. *Atlantic Monthly*, Sept. 1978, *9*, 70-76.

Lakey, G. *Nonviolent Action — How It Works*. Lebanon, PA: Sowers Printing Co., 1969.

Lakey, G. *Strategy For A Living Revolution*. New York: W. H. Freeman, 1973.

Lewis, P. Iran's elite army guard was routed by civilians. *New York Times*, Feb. 13, 1979, p. 8.

Lynd, S. *Nonviolence in America*. New York: Bobbs-Merrill, 1970.

Markham, J. M. Two sides in Iran take conciliatory steps: Contacts reported. *New York Times*, Feb. 5, 1979, pp. 1-2.

Muste, A. J. *Nonviolence in an Aggressive World*. New York: Harper and Co., 1940.

Negotiations fall apart on Seabrook protest. *Boston Globe*, June 6, 1978, p. 7.

New Hampshire's biggest question. *Boston Herald-American*, Beacon Section, May 1, 1977, pp. 19, 20, 23, 26-30, 31, 34.

NEWSBRIEF: A capsule of current news items concerning the company and the industry. Public Service Company of New Hampshire, June 19, 1978.

N-plant foes in Clamshell. *Manchester Union-Leader*, July 19, 1976, p. 36.

Nuke site protest aid denied. *Manchester Union-Leader,* May 19, 1977, p. 1.

Nuke strategy aired. *Boston Herald-American,* May 12, 1978, p. 1.

Pahlavi, Shah Mohammad Reza. Nobody can overthrow me—I have the power. Interview ed. by D. Mullin. *U.S. News and World Report,* June 26, 1978, pp. 37-38.

People to pay protestors costs. *Manchester Union-Leader,* May 10, 1977, p. 13.

Police gird for N-site violence. *Manchester Union-Leader,* April 27, 1977, pp. 1 & 12.

A power problem in N.H. *New York Times,* May 7, 1977, p. 24.

The protestors are arraigned. *Manchester Union-Leader,* August 3, 1976, p. 1.

Protestors arrested: Seabrook injunction ignored. *Manchester Union-Leader,* August 23, 1976, p. 1.

Protestors convene near nuclear plant. *New York Times,* June 25, 1978, p. 18.

Protestors freed under new plan. *Manchester Union-Leader,* May 13, 1977, pp. 1 & 23.

Rath, T. Interview. Concord, N.H., June 23, 1978.

The real test on Saturday. *Manchester Union-Leader,* April 27, 1977, p. 13.

Release denied: Supreme court refuses P.R. appeal. *Manchester Union-Leader,* May 6, 1977, p. 1.

Sanders, S. W. Can the shah depend on his armed forces? *Business Week,* Nov. 27, 1978, p. 58.

Seabrook invaded. *Manchester Union-Leader,* June 24, 1978, p. 1.

Seabrook N-site protest still on. *Manchester Union-Leader,* August 21, 1976, p. 14.

Seabrook protestors drop occupation plan. *Boston Globe,* June 13, 1978.

Seabrook sensationalism. *Manchester Union-Leader,* July 24, 1976, p. 1.

Seabrook 78: A handbook for the occupation/restoration (Second Supplement), June 24, 1978.

750 arrested at nuclear plant site. *Washington Post,* May 2, 1977, pp. 1 & 8.

Shah compromises. *Time,* Jan. 8, 1979, pp. 24-26.

Shah mollified the mullahs. *Time,* Sept. 11, 1978, p. 31.

Shants, F. Interview. Manchester, N.H., June 23, 1978; July 15, 1978.

Sharp, G. *The Politics of Nonviolent Action.* Part 1. *Power and Struggle;* Part 2. *The Methods of Nonviolent Action.* Part 3. *The Dynamics of Nonviolent Action.* Boston: Porter Sargent, 1973.

Shivers, L. Inside the Iranian revolution. *Tell the American People: Perspectives on the Iranian revolution.* Philadelphia: Movement for a New Society, 1980.

Shridharani, K. *War Without Violence.* New York: Harcourt, Brace, 1939.

A Sunday school picnic it is not. *Manchester Union-Leader,* April 29, 1976, p. 1.

A tale of two governors. *New York Times,* May 13, 1977, p. 27.

Tatro, N. B. Untitled. Supplementary material from *New York Times* News Service and the Associated Press, August 23, 1978, p. 15.

Thomson aim: No violence. *Manchester Union-Leader,* April 29, 1977, p. 1.

They're having a ball. *Manchester Union-Leader,* May 4, 1977, p. 12.

Thomson asks police to help defray costs. *Boston Herald-American,* May 4, 1977.

Tilly, C. *From mobilization to revolution.* Reading, Mass.: Addison-Wesley, 1978.

2000 occupy nuclear power plant site in New Hampshire: Vow to stay. *New York Times,* May 1, 1977, pp. 1 & 26.

2000 protestors encamp at site of nuclear plant. *Washington Post,* May 2, 1977.

U.S. Department of State. Department testifies on human rights in Iran. *Bulletin,* Oct. 4, 1976, 75, 429-37.

U.S. Department of State. Report on Iran. *New York Times,* Jan. 2, 1977, p. 1.

Wehr, P. Aggressive Nonviolence. In Arnold P. Goldstein (Ed.), *In Response to Aggression.* New York: Pergamon Press, 1981.

Wehr, P. *Conflict regulation.* Boulder, Colo.: Westview Press, 1979.

Willenson, K. Teheran ambush. *Newsweek,* June 2, 1975, p. 35.

Willenson, K. The army holds. *Newsweek,* Sept. 25, 1978, p. 49.

Who directs the anti-nuclear power activity in the U.S. *Manchester Union-Leader,* April 18, 1977, p. 32.

Wittner, L. S. *Rebels Against War: The American Peace Movements, 1941-1960.* New York: Columbia University Press, 1969.

Zinn, H. *SNCC: The New Abolitionists.* Boston: Beacon Press, 1964.

11
Terrorism
Richard G. Braungart
and
Margaret M. Braungart

January, 1968. Guatemala. Upon returning from lunch, the commander of the 34-man U.S. Military Advisory Group (MAAG) and the commander of MAAG's naval section were killed by gunfire from an automobile. The next day the Rebel Armed Forces distributed leaflets taking credit for the attack and accusing the United States of being responsible for Guatemalan army killer teams that murdered thousands of leftists. [Mickolus, 1980, p. 81]

March, 1971. Buenos Aires. The president of Fiat of Argentina was kidnapped, whereupon Fiat agreed to pay a $1 million ransom and rehire 250 workers fired in an industrial dispute. The government refused to release 50 prisoners, launched a hunt for the kidnappers, and surrounded their hideout. Just before the soldiers attacked, the terrorists carried out their threat to murder the victim. [Dobson & Payne, 1982, p. 236]

March, 1972. Uruguay. The Armed Popular Front (FAP) claimed credit for robbing $5,000 from the Israeli Bank of Uruguay. The FAP said in its communique it would fight "Zionist capitalism" and would kill "the two strongest figures of Zionism" in Uruguay unless the bank met its demands for money. [Mickolus, 1980, p. 305]

July, 1972. Northern Ireland. On Bloody Friday, 22 bombs exploded in Belfast within 8 minutes of each other. Eleven people were killed and 130 persons were wounded. The Irish Republican Army (IRA) claimed credit and military action against the IRA intensified. [Mickolus, 1980, p. 333]

December, 1975. Austria. Six members of the Arm of the Arab Revolution (thought to be a cover team for the Popular Front for the Liberation of Palestine or PFLP) attacked a ministerial meeting of the Organization of Petroleum Exporting Countries (OPEC) in Vienna. They seized 70 hostages, 11 of whom were oil ministers. During the shoot-out with police, 8 persons were wounded and 3 were killed, including one terrorist. The leader of the attack was the famed Venezuelan terrorist known as Carlos. Armed with Beretta model-12 machine pistols, Chinese grenades, plastic explosives, fuse wires, batteries, and detonators, the group demanded the return of one of the wounded terrorists who had been taken out of the building, the publication of a political manifesto over Austrian radio and television, a bus to take them to the airport, where a DC-9 was waiting, and rope, scissors, and adhesive tape. One rescue attempt failed when a car with two armed Israelis crashed outside the building. The Austrian government capitulated to demands for a flight out of the country, and 42 of the hostages were herded onto the DC-9 which flew first to Algiers, then to Tripoli, and on to Baghdad where several passengers were released. The next day a ransom of millions of dollars was alleged to have been paid to Haddad of the PFLP. The terrorists surrendered and hostages were released in Algiers. The terrorists did not appear to be arrested, so the Austrian government demanded extradition which was refused. Carlos and his girlfriend from Paris reportedly moved into the Albert Hotel. [Mickolus, 1980, pp. 570-73]

1970s. The Palestinian group Black September has been responsible for: the assassination of the Prime Minister of Jordan, the injuring of the Jordanian ambassador to London, the sabotage of a Dutch gas plant, an abortive attempt to hijack a Belgian Sabena airliner at Lod International Airport, the infamous attack on Israeli athletes at the Munich Olympics, attacks on Israeli embassies in Bangkok and Nicosia; the killing of two American and one Belgian diplomats at the Saudi Arabian Embassy in Khartoum. [Alexander, 1977, p. 188]

1979. Talladega County, Alabama. Nine members of the Ku Klux Klan were convicted during the year of Federal charges of taking part in a campaign of racial terrorism. One Klansman admitted impersonating an FBI agent in order to "arrest" a white man who had had black visitors in his home. The man had been flogged. Others fired rifles into the homes of black leaders and racially mixed couples. The state of Alabama charged three other hooded terrorists with the flogging of a white woman who had consorted with blacks. [King, 1980, p. 154]

April, 1980. Evanston, Illinois. A resident of the Chicago suburb noticed nine Hispanics in jogging suits trotting in and out of a van parked on a tree-lined, lakefront street. The resident called police who found the joggers were members of the Armed Front for National Liberation (FALN) a terrorist group demanding Puerto Rican independence. Police found the joggers heavily armed with an arsenal of arms and explosives in the van. [Associated Press, 1981, p. B-11]

January, 1981. Gainesville, Florida. Officials at the University of Florida found 13 examples of anti-Semitic graffiti on campus. After the wife of the university president spoke out forcefully against such bigotry, she received a telephone threat. "This is the Florida-side organization of Hitler," the caller said, "I am going to kill you." [Alpern, 1981, p. 41]

October, 1981, New York. Members of the May 19 Coalition [a radical group named for the birthdays of Ho Chi Minh and slain black leader Malcolm X] robbed a Brinks armored car in Clarkstown, New York. Three members of the group jumped out of a van behind the armored truck and a fourth sprang from a nearby bench. All opened fire and a Brinks guard died immediately while two other guards were wounded. Bags containing $1.6 million dollars were grabbed. At a roadblock, the gunmen leaped from the back of another van and fired automatic weapons, leaving two police officers dead and one wounded. Chases, searches, and shoot-outs followed with police ending in the arrest of five members of the Weather Underground, a fugitive Black Panther, and two other men with long police records. [Kraft, 1981, p. A-2]

BACKGROUND AND SCOPE OF TERRORISM

Freely mixing together political, criminal, and psychological elements, each of the above incidents represents an act of terrorism—using, or threatening to use, violence and destructive aggression in order to make a political statement by shocking or intimidating some wider audience. Essentially a form of unconventional warfare, terrorists attempt to gain power and recognition through fear and anxiety. Terrorism may be perpetuated by either a government (state terrorism) or by individuals and groups acting in opposition to a government (substate terrorism). Practiced by both the political left and political right, terrorists rely on some higher ideology or raison d'etre to justify their use of violence, and in the process, means-ends relationships become twisted and convoluted (Braungart & Braungart, 1981; Carlton, 1979; Friedlander, 1979; Kupperman & Trent, 1979; Paust, 1977; Shultz, 1980; Shultz & Sloan, 1980; Singh, 1977; Wilkinson, 1979b).

In recent times, terrorism has captured public attention, not only in daily news reports but as a captivating topic for thrillers in journalism, books, and movies. The terrorist is today's anti-hero, as tales intermingling fact and fantasy travel from continent to continent. The cast of characters in any terrorist incident is a large one: the terrorists, the crisis managers, the often hapless victims, and the viewing audience. Reactions to terrorism are seldom unemotional, and the perspectives range from all terrorism is evil, criminal, and psychopathic to terrorism is one means of establishing claims to justice, to "seek new societies, and to release frustrations that cannot be meliorated through normal political channels [Horowitz, 1977, p. 296]." Much of the world appears to be caught up in a whirlwind of fascination and revulsion over terrorism. It is one of the dark sides of human behavior which is calculating and intentionally cruel. Whether committed by or against the state, the moral and psychological question remains: how can terrorists commit atrocities that sacrifice other human beings, all for the sake of politics? And why has there been such a rash of terrorist incidents in recent times?

It is to these questions that this chapter is devoted. In order to gain a perspective on terrorism we will first present a rather extensive historical treatment, which not only describes the nature of terrorism in history but gives a flavor of the mentality of some of its foremost perpetrators. Terrorism is always justified by the terrorist, and it is an intriguing aspect of the human psyche to see how it is accomplished. As we entered into the late 1960s, the world witnessed an unprecedented rise in terrorism (Alexander, 1980; Alexander & Finger, 1977). We will describe a number of the trends and patterns in the escalation of contemporary terrorism, and then attempt to explore some of the social and psychological roots of terrorism—why such an increase in terrorism in recent years, and what kinds of persons are drawn into terrorist activities? The purpose of the first part of the chapter is to provide a background of information which can be brought to bear on understanding the multifaceted nature of the problem.

The second part of the chapter concerns the prevention and control of terrorism. This is in no way an exhaustive treatment of how to handle terrorism, for, as over two decades of research, speculation, discussion, and a growing number of experiences have indicated, there is no panacea for controlling terrorism. Hampered by the lack of a clear international legal framework and the tendency for terrorists to circumvent preventative measures, what we are often left with is the dilemma of how to manage and hopefully contain each terrorist incident that occurs. Complicating many terrorist incidents is the problem of the victim, who is a mere pawn in the terrorists' power plays, yet long after the siege is ended, it is often the victim who suffers the greatest emotional costs. And while we might wish for some kind of cookbook advice on the best way to handle the terrorists' aggressions—and, for that matter, the victims' aggressions as well—what we have learned is that each terrorist incident is a highly volatile and unpredictable social situation, with its own particular mix of personalities interacting at a given moment in history. The outcome of each incident depends heavily on human flexibility, astute social judgment, imagination, and the ability to communicate, which are not skills that can be taught easily but are more the product of a genuine understanding of history, political sociology, and human behavior. In this chapter, we offer some of the insights that have been developed thus far in coping with the problem of terrorism, but the hope is that readers will be stimulated to see new ways to better handle the problem.

Historical Origins

Historically, the term "terrorism" originated during the French Revolutionary Jacobin dictatorship which used terror-violence as a technique for political repression and control (Friedlander, 1977, 1979). During this tumultuous and violent time, the Committee of Public Safety, controlled by Robespierre who—despite his professed love of humanity and his fanatical intent to establish a French republic that was based on justice—closed churches and vociferously ferreted out any traitors. Thousands of royalist sympathizers and nobility were imprisoned, summarily tried, and guillotined. As one Jacobin explained, "What constitutes the Republic is the complete destruction of everything that is opposed to it [Wallbank & Taylor, 1961, p. 122]."

Governments, of course, have been major perpetrators of terrorism in history, either to control and repress their own populations or to gain objectives against foreign states that could not be attained through conventional warfare. Friedlander (1979) characterized state terrorism as a combination of personality and ideology: "Nazism and Stalinism were personifications of the evil genius of their leaders, but they could not have succeeded without a disoriented, terrorized citizenry [pp. 64–65]." Arendt (1958) used the term totalitarian to describe regimes that rely on terror for their power. The regime believes it can govern without consensus and substitutes terror for law. Classes are transformed into masses, the one-party system is a mass movement, and the center of power is shifted from the army to police. Far from being lawless, however, the totalitarian regime justifies its violence and atrocities in some higher authority:

> [i]t is more obedient to these suprahuman forces than any government ever was before, and that far from wielding its power in the interest of one man, it is quite prepared to sacrifice everybody's vital immediate interests to the execution of what it assumes to be the law of History or the law of Nature. [Arendt, 1958, pp. 461–62]

The "guilty" are those who stand in the way of some natural or historical process, and are declared unfit to live—dying classes or decadent people.

The Nazi and Stalinist regimes are notorious examples of totalitarian regimes. Yet, state terrorism is by no means a relic of the historical past. As Grenier (1982) said of the twentieth century experience: "Counting the dead by the tens of millions, it would appear that, in the twentieth century more human beings have perished at the hands of their own rulers—particularly those resolved to transform mankind—than have died fighting in all our wars [p. 32]." Gastil's (1981) survey of nations indicated that 61 nations in 1981 were "not free" (based on 7-point scales assessing civil liberties and political freedoms).

Despite the historical origins of the term terrorism and its persistence as a global problem today, it is substate terror or terrorism against the state that has received the most attention in recent times. There is a growing body of academic literature on terrorism, the great majority of which is addressed to substate terrorism. And it was substate terrorism to which former Secretary of State Alexander Haig referred when he declared early in the Reagan administration, "International terror will take the place of human rights in our concern [Taubman, 1981]." A perspective on contemporary terrorism can be gained by examining the historical roots of terrorism. It seems that many facets of modern-day terrorism are not new, although the nature and scope of terrorism have changed over the centuries, becoming more prevalent, widespread, complex, and perpetrated for a greater variety of reasons.

Most of the early studies of substate terrorism, as Laqueur (1977, 1978, 1979) pointed out, revolved around the issues of tyrannicide—whether it was justifiable to kill a tyrant. Insight into the motivations behind tyrannicide can be found in the writings of Aristotle, who re-marked that, while hatred and contempt were motivations for tyrannicide, there also are those who wish "to acquire, not a kingdom, but a name [Laqueur, 1978, p. 12]." These early acts of terror or violence for political purposes were generally carried out by an individual wielding a dagger.

Laqueur (1977) traced "group terrorism from below" to the *sicarii*, a religious sect involved in the Zealot struggle in Palestine (AD 66-73). Concealing short swords under their coats, the group often attacked in broad daylight by going into the thick of a crowd to murder. The *sicarii* also were credited with burning the public archives and graineries, destroying the house of a high priest, and sabotaging Jerusalem's water supplies. Not unlike the varying viewpoints about terrorism today, to most observers in the days of the *sicarii*, their acts were criminal and they were hoodlums hiding behind a cloak of ideology; yet to others, *sicarii* were seen as heroes, protesting against the rich and fighting to reject priests as intermediaries.

Religious zeal also fueled the fires of terrorism during the Crusades. After themselves com-miting atrocities in the name of "God's will" in order to eject the Muslims from the Holy Land, the early crusaders brought back tales of a fanatical Muslim sect known as the Assassins. Their name translated into Arabic means "hashish eaters," no doubt referring to their practice of performing acts of violence while under the influence of cannabis. Too few in number to openly confront their enemies in warfare, they attempted to defend their religious autonomy against suppression by a carefully planned campaign of terror. In order to overthrow a corrupt order and assure their religious salvation, Assassins stabbed the unrighteous (Laqueur, 1977; Schreiber, 1978). As Schreiber observed, far from being moral outcasts, "these early terrorists considered themselves honorable and even good men [p. 32]." Moral justification for vio-lence has long been part of the terrorists' mentality and rhetoric.

During the sixteenth and seventeenth centuries, a popular vindication for tyrannicide was drawn from the Bible, "They that live by the sword shall die by the sword," as those who con-sidered themselves to be acting as instruments of either the "popular will" or "God's will" at-tempted to assassinate tyrannical kings or other political figures (Friedlander, 1979; Laqueur, 1977, 1978). Another type of terrorism during this time was piracy. International action was taken to combat pirates, who from the sixteenth century onward were declared *hostis humani generis* (common enemies of humanity) and outlaws of the high seas. An act of piracy was legally designated as "an offense against the law of nations." However, according to maritime law, a ship has freedom of the seas as long as it flies under a national flag. Not surprisingly, abuses of the law existed, and state sponsorship of terrorism was evident in such cases as the Elizabethan Sea Dogs which, sailing under the protection of the British flag, carried out acts of piracy against the Spanish fleet, Britain's arch-enemy (Freidlander, 1977, 1979).

The nature of terrorism changed during the nineteenth century, as the philosophy of the dagger gave way to the philosophy of the bomb, and the roots of modern-day terrorism were planted. Such changes in the structure and form of terrorism can best be understood within the larger historical context of those times. In Europe, the French Revolution had fueled the spirit of individual freedom, nationalism, and democracy. Technological and industrial inno-vations were accompanied by the growth of a prosperous and more powerful middle class. At the same time, a growing mass of workers began to resent their poverty and yearned for greater control over their life situation. The age of romanticism gave way to social criticism. Reacting against the excesses of industrialization and laissez-faire capitalism, socialism took root, which in its early form was a kind of enlightened humanitarian idealism espoused by a small group of theorists. Subsequently, however, socialism took a variety of forms: utopianism, advocating socially planned or communal societies; Christian socialism, grounded in "the Gos-pel in action"; anarchism, based on the repudiation of authority and complete freedom for the individual; and Marx's "scientific socialism," or communism (Wallbank & Taylor, 1961).

It is Marx and Engel's writings (1955) that have stirred many a revolutionary into action, in the nineteenth century as well as today. As they argued in their *Communist Manifesto*:

> Every form of society has been based . . . on the antagonism of oppressing and oppressed classes. . . . The modern labourer . . . instead of rising with the progress of industry, sinks deeper and deeper below the conditions of existence of his own class. . . . And it here becomes evident that the bourgeoisie is unfit any longer to be the ruling class in society, and to impose its conditions of existence upon society as over-riding law. [p. 22]

They conclude:

> The Communists openly declare that their ends can be attained only by forcible overthrow of all existing social conditions. Let the ruling classes tremble at a Communist revolution. The proletarians have nothing to lose but their chains. They have the world to win. Working men of all countries, unite! [p. 46]

In the late 1800s, the seeds of modern revolutionary and nihilistic terrorism germinated, especially in Russia. Under the Tsars, Russia remained isolated from the modernizing forces in Europe, but at the same time the Russian government was involved in its own brand of international terrorism in the Balkan area, urging the "liberation of the Slavs" from the corruption and cruelty of the Ottoman Turks. According to Rapoport (1977), the Tsarist Balkan "intrigues" of assassinating Turkish officials were more for the objectives of publicity and provocation than just murdering the enemy—objectives later adopted by the Russian revolutionaries and anarchists, such as Nechaev, Bakunin, and Kropotkin.

From a different direction, another inspiration for nineteenth century Russian substate terrorism came from the German, Karl Heinzen, whose provocative essay entitled "Murder" was first published in 1849 (Laqueur, 1978). Arguing that murder is an unavoidable instrument in the achievement of historical ends and that history does not condemn the act of murder itself, Heinzen declared "motive is the important question." He concluded his essay: "The European barbarian party has left us no other choice than to devote ourselves to the study of murder and refine the act of killing to the highest possible degree [Heinzen, 1978, p. 64]."

By the late 1800s, the Russian revolutionaries themselves gave full voice to the use of systematic terror, advocating the employment of the atrocity to make a political statement. One of the foremost proponents of the atrocity was Bakunin (1978) who extolled that the present generation must:

> produce an inexorable brute force and relentlessly tread the path of destruction . . . it is considerably more humane to stab and strangle dozens, nay hundreds, of hated beings than to join with them to share in systematic *legal* acts of murder, in the torture and martyrdom of millions of peasants. [pp. 67-68]

Another celebrated Russian revolutionary, Nechaev (1978) also propounded the use of terror-violence to achieve political ends. According to his "Catechism of the Revolutionist":

> The revolutionary enters into the world of the state, of class, and of so-called culture, and lives in it only because he has faith in its speedy and total destruction. He is not a revolutionary if he feels pity for anything in this world. . . . The guiding principle must be the measure of service the person's death will necessarily render to the revolutionary cause. [pp. 70-71]

Villainy and hatred can be useful, Nachaev advised, since they can help to incite popular rebellion.

Marx and Engels, along with a number of others, took issue with Bakunin in particular and condemned terrorism as a tactic. At the First International (an international organization of workers founded by Marx) in London, Marx led the majority view, arguing that the state should institute a classless society; while Bakunin, the anarchist leader, opposed the extension of the state in any way (Laqueur, 1977, 1978; Wallbank & Taylor, 1961).

Radical Russian revolutionary theory moved into terrorist practice with two organizations (Friedlander, 1979): Peoples Will (1870s) and Socialist Revolutionary Party (1890s), which dedicated themselves to "the transformation of Russian society and government by assassination politics [p. 24]." The Socialist Revolutionary Party further declared its intention to "serve as a means of propaganda and agitation which will display itself before the eyes of the whole people . . . and which will bring alive other revolutionary forces [p. 24]." The assassination of Tsar Alexander II in 1881 and First Minister Peter Stolypin in 1911 rallied the forces of counterterror, one of the most violent of which was the Union of Russian Men—a reactionary group protected by the Tsar and dedicated to combatting radicalism by murder, torture, and bombing. The group carried out these terrorist atrocities not only against their enemies but against members of their own group as well (Friedlander, 1979).

The notion that terrorism and mob violence may be the swiftest way to bring about social change appealed to many radicals throughout the world in the late 1800s. One of the most vociferous and vitriolic of these was the anarchist-agitator Johann Most, whose newspaper, *Freiheit* (written in German and published in London and New York) spurred its readers to embrace terror tactics and spelled out ways to carry them out (Friedlander, 1979; Laqueur, 1978; Trautmann, 1980). Most, dubbed "The Wild Beast" because he "looked like a bulldog ready to bite anybody who crossed him," said of himself, "I was in rebellion before I was out of diapers (Trautmann, 1980, p. xxi]." Born in Germany, Most experienced a cruel and bitter childhood, became involved in leftist activities in Germany, Switzerland, and London, and finally emigrated to America where he spent most of his energy attempting to radicalize the citizenry. Although his ideas were not original, he has been characterized as "the voice of terror," with his newspaper touted as the "loudest, lustiest, and longest-lived radical journal of its day [Trautmann, 1980]."

Johann Most [1978] was a strong proponent of propaganda by deed: "Everyone knows, from experience, that the more highly placed the one shot or blown up, and the more perfectly executed the attempt, the greater the propagandistic effect [p. 100]." Although reputed to be kind to animals, Most was not exactly fond of people: "The average man in the street has something ape or parrot about him. This explains why it is that hundreds of thousands go around cutting their own throats by squawking to others what those cunning mind-warpers have proclaimed [p. 103]." Human vilification was his special forte, "The swells and other fat-faced philistines who, though one can read the stupidity on their faces, feel, in their positions as exploiting parasites and state-protected robbers, as happy in this stage of unfreedom as pigs in muck [p. 103]."

The anarchists' propaganda by deed became part of political life in Italy, France, Spain, the United States, and in France it was declared (Maitron, 1978),

A terrorist era did begin in 1892. . . . The reason is simple. . . . It was to avenge . . . the victims of police brutality on May 1, 1891 that Ravachol planted his bombs. Once raised to the status of martyr for anarchy's sake, Ravachol inspired avengers who, martyrs in their turn, engendered new terrorists. [p. 97]

Spanish terrorism was both agrarian and industrial and, from the 1890s through the 1920s, streetfights, strikes, and assassinations occurred, with the radical left battling the Spanish military. Terrorism in the United States was primarily industrial, such as the Molly Maguires and bloody forays between workers and police. One of the most dramatic terrorist incidents that occurred in the United States during this time was the Haymarket bomb explosion in Chicago in 1886. A lock-out and strike against McCormick Harvester Company escalated into a bloody riot, whereupon police killed and wounded several demonstrators. The following day when police moved in to break up a meeting to protest the police brutality, a bomb was thrown, killing 6 policemen and injuring 67 others. "The demonstrators suffered casualties two or three times as great [Lens, 1966, p. 169]." Although the bomb thrower was never found, a Cook County judge maintained that "those who incited the deed by word or action were equally guilty with those who committed the actual murder," and he sentenced eight anarchists to either life in prison or death (Morison & Commager, 1962, p. 235).

The politics of assassination had become a way of life by the turn of the century. From 1881–1912, ten national leaders became the victims of the terrorist-assassin: President Garfield of the United States, Tsar Alexander II of Russia, Lord Cavendish the Chief Secretary of Ireland, President Carnot of France, Premier del Castillo of Spain, Empress Elizabeth of Austria-Hungary, King Umberto I of Italy, President McKinley of the United States, Premier Stolypin of Russia, and Premier Mendez of Spain [Friedlander, 1979].

The spirit of nationalism and imperialism that had dominated the European world since 1870 was countered by nationalist-separatist movements in the 1890s. According to Friedlander (1979), one of the first such efforts occurred in 1893 when the International Macedonian Revolutionary Organization (IMRO) in Resna cried "Macedonia for the Macedonians." Given assistance for the movement by Bulgaria, the IMRO conducted a series of guerrilla skirmishes against the ruling and repressive Turkish government. In 1903, a Macedonian uprising was severely crushed by the Turks, who then proceeded to burn over 200 Macedonian villages, leaving over 70,000 homeless. The memory of this Turkish atrocity still hovers in the air today. A decade later in Ireland, the notorious Irish Republican Army (IRA), which grew out of the Sinn Fein in 1916, waged its war of terrorism against British intimidation and counter-terrorism—a guerrilla war which has lasted up to the present time.

From the early twentieth century to the 1960s, terrorism has been associated with nationalist-separatist movements and right- or left-wing ideological struggles. During this period, terrorism became more complex and took on an increasingly international flavor, full of state-sponsored intrigues. In the early part of the century, the Russian Pan Slavic ambitions for the Balkans conflicted with Germany's economic interests and Austria's defensive concerns in the same area, resulting in a series of wars. Quarrels arose over the spoils of war, and a number of major European powers aligned themselves with one power or the other in order to protect some special interest. For example, Germany supported Turkish interests in the Balkans, while France allied itself with Russia against its old enemy, Germany. Supported by the Serbian government and covertly backed by Tsarist Russia, one terrorist group in this tinder box was the secret Black Hand or Union Death Society, whose constitution declared, "This organization has been created with the object of realizing the national ideal: the union of all Serbs. . . . This organization prefers terrorist action to intellectual propaganda. . . . This organization bears the name 'Union or Death' [Wallbank & Taylor, 1961, p. 429]."

On June 14, 1914, in Sarajevo Bosnia, a young assassin trained by the Black Hand fired into the automobile of the heir to the Austrian throne and killed Archduke Francis Ferdinand and his wife. Triggered by this incident, the complicated alliances and support involving a number of nationalist powers led to a series of ultimatums and World War I. As Friedlander

(1977) observed: "Princips's shots were more explosive than he ever dreamed. A Greater Serbia would be created by the Treaty of St. Germain (1919) under the name of Yugoslavia, and, omnious for the rest of the twentieth century, self-determination in the guise of national liberation movements would become literally a license to kill [p. 35]."

Following World War I, terrorism on the right began to escalate, especially in Europe. When the Central Powers lost World War I in 1918, a number of rightist counterrevolutionary paramilitary organizations formed in Germany. One of the most active of these was the *Freikorps*, with over a quarter of a million men, which eventually provided the nucleus of the German *Reichswehr* (Friedlander, 1979). Some of these *Freikorps* groups were terroristic, and, as Laqueur (1977) noted, were more nihilistic in their ideology than conservative. According to one of their members, we "killed whoever fell into our hands, we burned whatever could be burned. . . . The march into an uncertain future was for us sufficiently meaningful and suited the demands of our blood [Laqueur, 1977, pp. 72-73]." Another rightist group was the Rumanian Iron Guard, described by Lacquer (1977) as full of young idealists who embraced religious revival, sacrifice, martyrdom, the Deed, and "the ethical value of force [p. 73]." The theme of death permeated their slogans and songs, but whether they actually intended to displace Rumanian authorities and seize power is uncertain.

The situation became increasingly polarized in the 1920s and 1930s in Central and Southern Europe especially. Street battles between left and right contributed to the undoing of democratic governments, and fascism gained in its appeal to restore order. From 1919 to 1934, there were several major political assassinations, the most dramatic of which were the twin slayings in Marseilles of King Alexander of Yugoslavia and French Foreign Minister Barthou, with at least four governments reputed to be involved (Friedlander, 1977; Laqueur, 1977). As a result, a conference was called by the League of Nations to deal with the problem of international terrorism. The Geneva Conference in 1937 resulted in two Conventions: the Prevention and Repression of Terrorism, and the Creation of an International Criminal Court. Not all governments were supportive, however, and the two conventions were never ratified or enforced (Evans, 1979; Friedlander, 1977).

Terrorism was by no means limited to Europe or North America, and prior to World War II, terrorist-violence erupted in China, India, and the Middle East. Several political leaders were assassinated, and in the 1930s and 1940s, the Muslim Brotherhood, Young Egypt, and Israeli groups including the Irgun, carried out systematic terror attacks against their enemies, which Laqueur (1977) dated as ushering in the era of urban terrorism. Moreover, in Latin America, a new terror tactic was introduced on February 21, 1931, when the first recorded skyjacking occurred in Peru against a Pan American pilot. Ironically, the pilot was not only the first to be hijacked but was hijacked again in 1961, becoming the first pilot to be hijacked twice (Mickolus, 1980).

After World War II, terrorism became a significant part of the twentieth century experience (Friedlander, 1979). Inspired by the Resistance movements of World War II, in the 1950s nationalist-separatist and anticolonial movements implemented the ideology of terror on a global scale. In the late 1950s, world attention focused on the Algerian anticolonial struggle and Castro's revolutionary guerrilla campaign in Cuba. Terrorist activities were a key aspect of these struggles. However, the Algerian rebels tended to favor the tactics of bombings and murder, while Castro's guerrilla forces preferred kidnapping and hijacking (Mickolus, 1980).

The 1960s have been cited as a watershed in the escalation of terrorism. Student and youthful unrest permeated every continent; and, while most of their activities were nonviolent, such as demonstrations and sit-ins, there were also revolutionary extremist groups which advocated terror-violence (Braungart, forthcoming). For example, the Weather Underground, which split from the Students for a Democratic Society, declared in 1974, "By beginning the armed struggle, the awareness of its necessity will be furthered . . . no less true in the U.S. than in other countries throughout the world." And in the name of black and Third World peoples, the Weather Underground claimed credit for a number of bombings (Laqueur, 1978, pp. 173–175). Another youthful extremist group that espoused urban terrorism was the Baader-Meinhof Gang in West Germany, which asserted in one of its 1971 publications, "The urban guerrilla's aim is to attack the state's apparatus of control at certain points and put them out of action, to destroy the myth of the system's omnipresence and invulnerability [Laqueur, 1978, p. 178]."

Not unlike the late 1800s, the two major forms of substate terror in the 1960s were the more common nationalist-separatist movements fighting for autonomy and the nihilist groups which were hell-bent on the destruction of the system. Nevertheless, there are some important differences between the revolutionaries and anarchists of the late nineteenth century and the modern-day terrorist. The nineteenth century terrorist has been characterized as more driven by love than by hate and more positive in his ideological orientation, with visions of a better world. By comparison, for many of today's terrorists, there is no grand vision of a better society, their goals are often unrealizable and their activism serves primarily to give meaning to otherwise empty lives and to provide an outlet for their free-floating aggression, boredom, and confusion (Kupperman & Trent, 1979; Laqueur, 1977). Another major difference is that most of the nineteenth century terrorists were what Laqueur (1979) described as "desperately poor people" who implemented a kind of homemade brand of terrorism. Today's terrorism, however, is big business, with some of the current terrorist organizations resembling multinational corporations, including budgets of millions of dollars and pension funds (Dobson & Payne, 1982; Laqueur, 1979; Schreiber, 1978). The scope of modern terrorism has expanded to the point that Alexander (1980) declared, "We have entered an Age of Terrorism."

The beginnings of transnational terrorism have been dated at 1968, with a conscious decision by Palestinian groups to attack targets outside Israel. On July 22, 1968, the Popular Front for the Liberation of Palestine (PFLP) hijacked an El Al airplane at Lod Airport on its way from Rome to Tel Aviv. Two Palestinians and one Syrian threatened to blow up the plane with grenades; they pistol-whipped the navigator, and fired a shot into the cockpit. The plane was ordered to land at Algiers Dar al-Bayda Airport, whereupon the terrorists demanded the release of Arabs from Israeli jails. The Algerian government became involved in negotiations and allowed non-Israeli passengers to go but held the remaining passengers and crew at a barracks near the airport. Soon, a number of Arab nations jumped into the negotiations, each making demands—Iraq wanted a MIG-2 plane returned; Egypt wanted Israel to withdraw from the Sinai; Jordan asked for the old city of Jerusalem; and Syria demanded the Golan Heights. The International Federation of Air Line Pilots' Association and several European airlines threatened to boycott Algeria. On September 1, Algeria released the hostages and flew them to Rome. At the same time, 16 Arabs captured prior to the 1967 war were released from Israeli jails. The PFLP justified the hijack on the grounds that El Al had flown military spare parts during the war and therefore was a legitimate target. Not only was this event one of the first transnational incidents, but because the Algerian government aided the skyjackers in obtaining their demands, set a precedent for subsequent incidents, such as the attack on Entebbe Airport (Mickolus, 1980, p. 94). According to Russell, Banker, and Miller (1979), the entry of the PFLP into transnational terrorism was less the result of increased skills and resources than it was a decision to use criminal tactics (kidnap for ransom, extortion) against Israel (its enemy) at its weakest point (in a third country).

Recent Global Trends and Patterns

The number of terrorist incidents and the breadth of terrorist operations accelerated from 1968 onward. Recent trends in terrorism have been identified with the aid of the ITERATE data (International Terrorism: Attributes of Terrorist Events), which were first collected in 1968 (Central Intelligence Agency, 1981; Mickolus, 1977, 1980). By and large, "domestic" terrorism is more likely to occur in developing countries, whereas about half of the "transnational" incidents were in Western advanced nations. The increase in international terrorism, however, has not been at a steady linear rate (see Fig. 11.1).

Peak years (and number of incidents) for international terrorism were 1972 (648), 1978 (850), 1979 (657), and 1980 (760). From 1968-1980, the geographic region with the most international incidents of terrorism was Western Europe (2,206), followed by Latin America (1,446), the Middle East (1,382), and North America (673). The major types of terrorist attack, in order of likelihood, during this 13-year period were: explosive bombing (2,371), threats (1,008), incendiary bombing (753), letter bombing (470), assassination (443), and

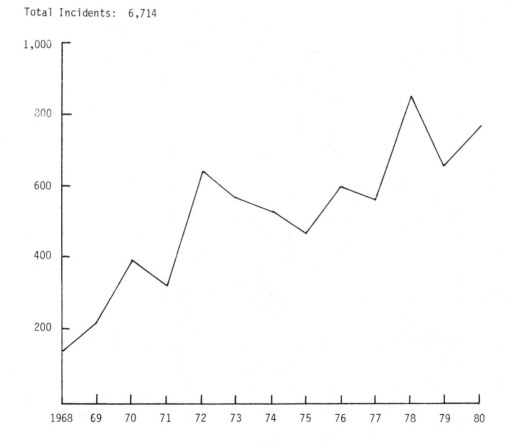

Fig. 11.1 International Terrorist Incidents, 1968-1980.

Source: Central Intelligence Agency, *Patterns of International Terrorism: 1980* (Springfield, Va.: National Technical Information Service, 1981), pp. 1-2.

kidnapping (401). Over the past decade, however, there have been some changes in the type of attack employed in these international terrorist incidents (see Fig. 11.2). For example, explosive bombings increased at a steady pace until 1974 and leveled, whereas letter bombing peaked in 1972 and declined sharply after 1973. Kidnapping was popular in 1970, 1973–1975 and dropped off after 1978. On the other hand, terrorist threats reached a high point in 1973, declined through 1974–1975, but increased markedly in 1978. Assassinations increased slowly over the decade and in 1980 were the third major category of attack.

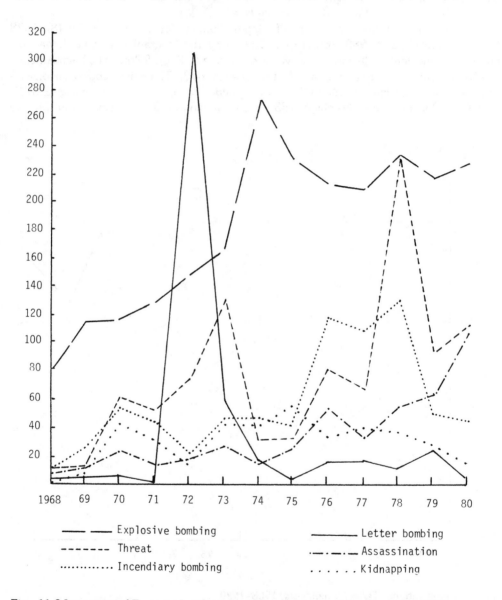

Fig. 11.2 International Terrorist Incidents By Major Category of Attack, 1968-1980.

Source: Central Intelligence Agency, *Patterns of International Terrorism: 1980* (Springfield, Va.: National Technical Information Service, 1981), p. 8.

Victims of international incidents were, in order of likelihood, North American, Western European, or Middle Eastern. Of the international attacks on American personnel and facilities, diplomats and business people were almost twice as likely to be targets when compared to American military, government officials and property, or private citizens. In 1980, some changes occurred in the pattern of victimization, particularly with regard to nationality of victim: although the United States was still the most popular target of international terrorists, citizens and installations of the USSR were the second most frequent target, followed by Turkey, Iraq, France, Iran, and Israel. The most disturbing statistic is the increase in the number of terrorist incidents that resulted in injury or death since 1968, with bombings and assassinations accounting for over 65 percent of the casualties; and, in 1980, a sharp increase occurred in the number of terrorist attacks resulting in casualties, most of which happened in the Middle East or Western Europe. The terrorist groups most responsible for these lethal incidents in 1980 were Iranian government operatives, Armenian terrorist groups, and the Muslim Brotherhood of Syria. Another change in the recent pattern is that, although American business people have been the most likely victims, in 1980 attacks on American diplomats surpassed those on businessmen. Most of these attacks on diplomats occurred in Latin America, with about 30 percent of these telephone or letter threats. A third change that has been identified is that the number of international terrorist incidents that were state-supported increased markedly in 1980, over half of which were assassinations or assassination attempts, and likely to be lethal rather than injurious. These state-sponsored incidents were frequently the work of a Middle Eastern government and transpired in another Middle Eastern nation against a Middle Eastern diplomat (Central Intelligence Agency, 1981).

From 1968–1980, there have been some notable differences in the activities of left- versus right-wing terrorists. In general, right-wing terrorism has been most often domestic rather than international. Compared to the left, however, when the right has been involved in international terrorism, their terrorism has been less publicity seeking but more destructive of select targets, with little concern about mass casualties. For example, right-wing terrorists were responsible for a bomb explosion at the Munich Oktoberfest in 1980, which killed 12 and injured over 200 persons. And despite the publicity given to the left in Italy, a good number of the terrorist casualties have been attributable to right-wing terrorism. One of the worst incidents occurred in 1980 in the Balogna railway station when a bomb placed by the neofascist Revolutionary Armed Nuclei exploded, killing 80 and injuring 200 (Central Intelligence Agency, 1981).

The domestic terrorism in the United States has for years been associated with right-wing groups such as the Ku Klux Klan and American Nazis. Then in the 1960s, extreme left-wing groups such as the Weather Underground, Black Panthers, and Symbionese Liberation Army actively employed terror tactics (Kupperman & Trent, 1979; Wolf, 1979). Extremist political rhetoric has cooled considerably—although some wild-eyed splinter groups still exist. One of the most active terrorist groups in recent times in the United States is the Armed Forces of the Puerto Rican National Liberation Army (FALN), which has claimed responsibility for a number of bombings. According to Kupperman and Trent (1979), the real terrorist threat in America today is more likely to come from foreign terrorists acting out their grievances and seeking publicity for their causes in the United States.

Contemporary Terrorist Organizations, Strategies, and Tactics

Although by definition all terrorist groups rely on violence or the threat of violence to achieve their political ends, several different types of substate terrorist groups can be distinguished primarily on the basis of their goals. The largest category of terrorist groups are those involved in nationalist-separatist movements seeking an autonomous nation-state. For these groups, terrorist activites are directed at a colonial or incumbent regime, with some of the most visible and active groups in this category being: the Popular Front of the Liberation of Palestine, or PFLP (nationalist and Marxist, fighting against Israel and for the complete liberation of Palestine); Irish Republican Army-Provisional Wing, or IRA-Provos (dedicated to the destruction of British rule in Ireland); Ejercito Revolucionario del Pueblo, or ERP (revolutionary Marxist-Leninist group determined to overthrow capitalism in Argentina in particular and in South America in general); and Basque Nation and Freedom, or ETA (fighting for liberation from Spanish and French rule and for the establishment of an independent Basque Socialist State) (Dobson & Payne, 1982; Mickolus, 1980; Wilkinson, 1979b).

A second, but far less common, type of terrorist group are ideological extremists and nihilists, which may come from the neofascist far right or neo-Marxist and anarchist far left. These are the true believers of some confused ideology which are dedicated to destruction and violence. Some of the most notorious groups in this category are: the Baader-Meinhof Gang or Red Army Faction (West German, anarchist, antibourgeois); the Japanese Red Army, or Sekigun (Japanese, revolutionary socialist and nihilist who are pro-Palestinian and anti-American); Red Brigades (Italian, Maoist or anarchist); and Weather Underground (American, revolutionary and anti-imperialist with extremely small membership). Although their membership is miniscule and there is little evidence of popular support, these groups often claim to be struggling against capitalist imperialism and waging a people's revolution (Dobson & Payne, 1982; Mickolus, 1980; Wilkinson, 1979b). But, as Wilkinson (1979b) described, "Far from speaking the language of the working classes, they live in a kind of fantasy world concocted from vulgar neo-Marxist slogans and the half-baked and dangerous ideals of Sartre and Marcuse [p. 107]." Their activities are more criminal than political—like gangs of bandits rather than any serious political movement (Wilkinson, 1979b, p. 107). As Rapoport (1977) observed, for these groups "Lacking standards to judge the political significance of particular atrocities, they are left only with the value of the act itself. Atrocity becomes a substitute for revolution [p. 55]."

A third kind of group is the issue-oriented group that may resort to terrorism when they become extremely frustrated over the lack of responsiveness within the system, sometimes described as "soft-terrorism" (Dobson & Payne, 1982; Russell et al., 1979). Although terrorism may be a thinkable tactic, such tactics are usually abandoned quickly and do not represent a major modus operandi for the group in general. For example, a group of animal lovers, as part of their protest against whaling, planted a bomb that sank a Cypriot ship in Lisbon. In another case, a group of British scientists sent through the postal mail a sample of earth said to have been infected with the highly lethal anthrax as part of their protest against chemical war research (Dobson & Payne, 1982, p. 175).

The organization of terrorist groups in general tends to be small, with some groups divided into cells of 4 to 8 persons having a leader and link person to higher ranks. The small unit has been found to work the most efficiently. Terrorist groups are knowledgeable, ruthless, and dedicated; and, for most of their members, terrorism becomes a way of life. With a great need for funds, weapons, and ammunition, sponsorship by friendly groups or governments is invaluable to the terrorist group. What terrorist groups lack in numbers, they attempt to compensate for in effect. Although they cannot expect to win by using physical force against the armies of nations, they can hope to tip the scales in their favor by the symbolic impact they can have. The goal of much of substate terrorism is to gain attention in some dramatic and threatening way which will intimidate, harass, and embarrass authorities. In the terrorists' attempts to discredit and break the spirit of the opposition, the victims (hostages, diplomats, government officials, corporate executives, or innocent bystanders) are mere pawns in the larger power play. Another purpose of their activities is to achieve stability and avoid entrophy within the ranks of the group itself. Thus, the terrorist event is staged and played out not only for the government and the public, but for members of their own group as well (Kupperman & Trent, 1979; Laqueur, 1977; Redlick, 1979; Russell et al., 1979; Shultz, 1980; Wilkinson, 1979b).

The strategy of terrorism is to create a sensation through violence or threat of violence in the hope of capturing the attention of the media and public, and then coerce the authorities into making concessions (money, freeing political prisoners, achieving political demands). The importance of the media to the terrorist cause should not be underestimated—it is a key factor, as Carlos Marighella's didactic little *Minimanual of the Urban Guerrilla* advises: "The war of nerves or psychological war is an aggressive technique, based on the direct or indirect use of mass means of communication and news transmitted orally in order to demoralize the government [Alexander, 1980, p. 90]." Terrorism has been described as theater and a spectator sport, and it succeeds if it can have a strong psychological impact on a wide audience (Cooper, 1977; Friedlander, 1979; Laqueur, 1977). One of the terrorist strategies—especially when the media are recording—is to appear the underdog, even losing a few battles with the more powerful forces of opposition; the trick is to make the victimizers look like victims (Schreiber, 1978). Getting the audience to doubt itself and its government is "step number one" in a game where the means are justified by the ends (Alexander, 1977; Cooper, 1977). As Weisband and Roguly (1976) summarize:

> For the terrorist, the path to legitimacy is through one's reputation for resilience, for self-sacrifice and daring, for brutality, and, above all, for effective discipline over words and actions. The terrorist is his own torch and bomb; he ignites the flames of national passion and, if possible, of political sympathy, and he does it by violating universal human sensibilities. It is the credibility that violence produces whenever it appalls that renders terrorism horrifying yet powerful and, if successful, self-legitimating. [pp. 278-79]

The challenge to authority may be direct or covert (bombing, extortion), but the objective is to make conditions worse through destruction and disruption, although, after the harassment and violence are finished, there may not be any systematic plan for replacement by terrorists—after the revolution, what? Surprise, novelty, and shock value are prerequisites of the terrorist incident. It is the terrorists' best hope that government will devise some poorly conceived response (overreaction is preferred) which will weaken the government's perceived legitimacy and effectiveness and result in greater destabilization.

Terrorism can either be selective, focusing efforts on a specific target (installation or persons), or it can be random where the victims are unlucky bystanders. Besides terrorism against the state, terrorism may be practiced against one's own members or potential supporters to prevent them from assisting the government in any way (Beloff, 1979; Lebow, 1980). Admittedly, terrorist activities are not likely to engender widespread popular support, but by provoking a spiral of violence and counterviolence, they weaken moderation and compromise in favor of polarization and radicalization. Stress and uncertainty are high, which can give the terrorists increasing leverage and power. Yet, rarely has a group using random terror come into power. According to Laqueur (1977), the groups that have been the most successful were those that: (1) were combating colonial powers which could not control their possessions; (2) were issue-oriented; or (3) had powerful outside protectors. Undoubtedly, terrorist groups have also been successful in aggravating international relations by kidnapping diplomats, using a state as a base without approval, acting out grievances in a state other than their own, or finding a haven in a nation where they will not be punished or extradited (Evans, 1979).

Each terrorist group has its own characteristic style of operation. For example, the IRA does not kidnap or hijack, whereas the Italian Red Brigades favor kidnapping, and when they shoot, they tend to shoot at the legs. Jenkins (1980) indicated that the preferred style of a terrorist group depends upon some of the following factors: (1) the composition of the group, (2) the resources of a group, (3) size of the group, (4) culture, which determines group actions and ideology and influences victims and targets, (5) the idiosyncrasies of a leader or key members, (6) group style of decision making, and (7) situational context. For example, with regard to situational context, the Rand Corporation found that in seizing hostages, terrorist groups operating in their home territory with outside support tended to conduct conventional kidnappings, whereas groups that did not have much underground support were likely to seize buildings, making themselves as well as the occupants hostages in a hostage-barricade situation (Jenkins, 1980).

SOCIAL AND PSYCHOLOGICAL ROOTS OF TERRORISM

Social Causes of Terrorism

The question why there has been such an increase in terrorism over the past decade has been partially attributed to changing social conditions and the structure of societies which have not only facilitated the growth of terrorism but also made the job of the terrorist easier. Perhaps one of the most fundamental reasons for the increase in terrorism is modernization. The pace of social change has accelerated both in developed and developing nations, and any time change is rapid, society is destabilized. In general, modernization increases competition among groups for resources, intensifies group aspirations, and exacerbates the gap between expectations and achievement (Redlick, 1979). As Wilkinson (1979a) explained, "social mobilization, education, and increased opportunities of political participation enhance aspirations while the already inadequate levels of production, employment opportunities, and governmental and administrative resources cannot keep pace with fresh expectations and needs [pp. 62-63]." Broadening the range of political modernization and political participation increases the potential for civil violence unless there are institutional channels available for peaceful participation (Wilkinson, 1979a). But there is a Catch-22 situation involved here, since the rapid pace of social, economic, and political modernization undermines traditional political institutions, making it all the more difficult to create broad-based political support (Huntington, 1968). Under rapid social change, norms are altered, sanctions are often weak, and the law is flouted—conditions that facilitate alienation, criminality, deviant behavior, and ultimately terrorism.

Modern social structures and patterns of urban life—such as urbanization, bureaucratization, technological innovations, and secularization—have made life increasingly variegated and complex. But in a world of massive organizations and institutions, the individual appears to count for little, with few opportunities to answer back or make his or her feelings known. Kupperman and Trent (1979) level specific criticism at multinational corporations and international organizations such as OPEC which have had a powerful influence on international and domestic affairs, yet often diverge from the interests of nation-states and human populations. Not surprisingly, as societies have become more massive and alienating for the individual, a number of persons and groups have turned away from the larger organizations and developed a stronger awareness of their ethnic, linguistic, and religious group membership. The politicization of reference group ties promotes terrorism as groups with different and conflicting value systems vie for power. The revolution of rising expectations, relative deprivation, downward mobility, status inconsistency, entitlement, and hedonism are social trends that lower the threshold of frustration, as one group perceives it is losing ground relative to another group's more advantaged position in society. As the disadvantaged group finds the inequality or imbalance intolerable, it is likely to press vigorously for social change. The appeal of terrorism is that it offers a quick, dramatic, and simple solution.

Advances in communication technology and media flow have been cited as important factors related to the proliferation of terrorism on a global scale (Alexander, 1977; Redlick, 1979). As Redlick (1979) explained, increased communication flow strengthens interpenetration and interdependence, exposing people to a wide variety of ideas and lifestyles. The effect is to increase awareness about one's position in society relative to other groups, perhaps enhancing feelings of deprivation and the desire for social change. For example, in the 1950s, French Canadians became more aware of colonial struggles, especially in a progressive review, *Cité Libre;* and, according to Redlick (1979), they began to yearn for what other formerly occupied nations in Asia and Africa had achieved.

With communication satellites and instantaneous media coverage, the propaganda by deed and psychological warfare of terrorists can have a far-reaching impact on a worldwide audience. Terrorism requires few people and resources to have an effect, and the media is one of the most important tools to publicize their cause. Similar to the advertising industry, the terrorist hungers for publicity in his quest for attention, recognition, and legitimacy (Alexander, 1977).

Another contributing cause to terrorism is the ethos of violence which permeates almost every culture today. Keniston (1968) argued that what the issue of sex was to the Victorian world, the issue of violence is to this generation. The experience of the concentration camps demonstrated that even so-called civilized and advanced nations are capable of barbarities which stagger the imagination. And the atomic bomb "provided the concrete imagery for the collective terror of the world. Germany had shown that the civilized nations could do the unthinkable; Hiroshima demonstrated how simple, clean, and easy (from the point of view of the perpetrator) doing the unthinkable could be [p. 249]." As Schreiber (1978) observed, "Moral justification for violence is part of the modern rhetoric of world politics, whether articulated by nations who have the 'right,' in international law, to wage war, or by relatively obscure groups who arrogate such rights to themselves [p. 33]." Television, of course, has brought the violence of politics, crime, and human relationships much closer to our personal experience. And, as over two decades of sociological research has demonstrated, what comes across the screen are a good number of aggressive role models who often appear to be rewarded for their violent behavior. These role models may well influence human behavior, particularly children's behavior and especially those children who have few other socialization experiences or significant others in their lives to counter what they experience vicariously on the screen.

Violence has not only been accepted as a way of modern life, it has been glorified and romanticized, especially by some of the authors whose works are revered by terrorists. The writings of Mao, Che Guevara, Franz Fanon, Herbert Marcuse, and Carlos Marighella espouse the notion that history is on the side of the oppressed and violence is justifiable as well as laudable (Kupperman & Trent, 1979; Redlick, 1979). These writings have not only inspired many a terrorist but serve as one means of linking different leftist-minded terrorist groups around the world. The flavor and mentality of terrorist thinking can be seen in Fanon's *The Wretched of the Earth* (1968) which argues, "Violence alone, violence committed by the people, violence organized and educated by its leaders, makes it possible for the masses to understand social truths and gives the key to them [p. 147]." Reminiscent of Johann Most are some of the Marighella's statements in his *Minimanual* (1978):

> Men of the government, agents of the dictatorship and of North American imperialism principally must pay with their lives for the crimes committed against the Brazilian people. . . . We are in full revolutionary war and that war can be waged only by violent means. [p. 162]

The job of the terrorist has been facilitated in a number of ways, thanks in part to recent technical innovations. Terrorism has become more threatening, frightening, and lethal due to the number of weapons for destruction which the military-industrial complex has presented the world. It seems that terrorists as well as governments have been joining in the supermarket selection of weaponry. A dramatic escalation in individual weapons are the PGMs (precision-guided munitions) which are portable, and can launch missiles with trajectories corrected in flight. Designed to be used against tanks and aircraft—and of potential use by the terrorist against cars, trucks carrying radioactive materials or chemicals, pipelines, or transformer banks—these weapons have been made available to terrorists by certain supportive nations and actually have been employed. For example, a RPG-7 (Soviet weapon) was used in an attack on El Al Airlines at Orly Airport in Paris in 1975, and there have been other documented examples as well.

Then there is the growing arsenal of weapons for mass destruction, of which nuclear weapons have generated considerable worry and controversy. As Kupperman (1979) observed, "It would be foolhardy to believe that a small, dedicated group could not build an inefficient atomic bomb, yielding between a few hundred tons and a kiloton in TNT equivalents, but this would not be a trivial challenge [p. 8]." The nuclear weapons or material needed to build a nuclear device could be stolen from government installations or from nuclear power plants.

Further into the "never-never-land" of weaponry for destruction are the chemical (nerve agents, botulinal toxins) and biological weapons (viruses, or more probably the highly lethal *Bacillus anthracis* which produces pulmonary anthrax), the sheer threat of which could cause widespread panic, and the use of which could produce thousands or millions of casualites. Exacerbating the problem, of course, is the fact that societies are becoming ever-more vulnerable to disruption through their water systems, complicated electrical and fuel systems, communications, and computers. These developments in weapons technology have increased the stakes of the terrorists' game and intensified the fear that they can inspire around the world (Dobson & Payne, 1982; Kupperman, 1979; Kupperman & Trent, 1979; Mullen, 1980).

A reasonable question is how could terrorists manage to gain access to these destructive weapons? Stealing is one way, and has been a key topic in the control of terrorism; but, for many terrorist groups, there is no need to steal. The weapons are provided by some outside nation interested in keeping terrorist antagonism against an enemy state at as high a level as possible. Providing weapons, funds, and safe-havens for terrorists has been a part of "unofficial" international politics since the Balkan wars prior to World War I. State support for terrorism is undoubtedly an important reason why terrorism continues to grow and is not a simple matter of control. For example, the Soviets began supporting the Palestinian Liberation cause in 1968, but not so much because of sympathy for the cause itself, rather they feared a pro-Chinese Arab Middle East and felt they must counter the Chinese support given the Palestinians in 1964 (Laqueur, 1977). It is not only governments that have given terrorists what they need. An added factor is private support such as Irish-American support for the Irish Republican Army and Provos, Jewish-American support for Israel and Israeli policies, and expatriate Arab support for the Palestinians. Profiteering by individuals, such as the 20-ton explosive shipment to Libya involving an ex-CIA agent is, of course, an age-old means of support for terrorism. Terrorism is not likely to find itself without some sources of support, weapons, or funds in the near future.

The job of the terrorist has also been made easier by advances in transportation and communications which have facilitated linkages among a diversity of terrorist organizations in all parts of the world. Terrorist groups have joined together to coordinate activities—meetings, finances, training, weapons, combat material, organizational support, and false documents. Two terrorist groups in particular have been at the forefront of coordination: the ERP and the PFLP. Training camps are available where a number of different terrorists go to be educated, as Kupperman and Trent (1979) described:

> Palestinian terrorist camps in Lebanon, Syria, Libya . . . have trained revolutionaries from Western Europe, Africa, Latin America, Asia, and North America in terrorist techniques. Such groups have included representatives from America's Weathermen and Black Panthers, the Irish Republican Army, the Turkish People's Liberation Army, the Eritrean Liberation Front, Japan's United Red Army (URA), and West Germany's Baader-Meinhof Gruppe. But the Palestinians have not restricted their training to leftists. They have also recruited German neo-Nazis, presumably on the basis of shared anti-Semitism. [p. 22]

The cooperativeness and shared sympathies among terrorist groups have resulted in some complicated strategies and tactics of offensive attack. One type is the attack by proxy, where one group carries out operations to advance another group's cause. The most infamous example here was the Lod Airport operation on May 30, 1972, which was conducted by three Japanese anarchists of the United Red Army. Acting on behalf of the Palestinians, the Japanese terrorists used Czechoslovakian weapons provided by Italian terrorists and managed to kill or wound over 100 persons, most of whom were Puerto Rican Christian pilgrims with no link to the Israeli-Arab conflict (Kupperman & Trent, 1979; Alexander & Kilmarx, 1979). Or, attacks may be coordinated, as in the following case (Alexander & Kilmarx, 1979):

> Three Pakistanis, describing themselves as members of the Moslem International Guerrillas, a group known to be active in the Philippines and Indonesia, seized a Greek freighter in Karachi on February 2, 1974, and threatened to blow up the ship and kill its crewmen unless two Black September [Palestinian terrorist group] terrorists, who were sentenced to death for an attack on a crowd at Athens Airport, killing five people and wounding 53, were freed. Subsequently, the Arab guerrillas were deported from Greece to Libya and freedom. [p. 49]

A third form of cooperation is the joint attack where several different terrorist groups join together to fight alongside their "brothers," as in the raid on the OPEC headquarters in Vienna. Led by Carlos, the attack was carried out by a combined squad of PFLP members with West Germans and Venezuelans and Carlos' girlfriend Gabriele Kroecher-Tiedman, a Baader-Meinhof member (Alexander & Kilmarx, 1979; Mickolus, 1980).

One of the controversial topics in terrorism is the extent to which these linkages among terrorists portend some kind of international conspiracy that is backed by the Soviet government. The official Soviet position is that "terrorism is counter-revolutionary" and is criminal, not a Marxist-Leninist movement (Fried, 1980). Claire Sterling's sensational book *The Terror Network* (1981) described a number of terrorist groups in various parts of the world ultimately tied to the KGB. The academic literature is less sensational, but a Soviet connection is assumed to exist. Clutterbuck's (1979) analysis of the Soviet connection is fairly representative of a number of experts in the area of terrorism: "It is a mistake to look for the KGB behind every revolutionary movement, but it is also a mistake not to realize that they will exploit any opportunities that exist [p. 61]." Clutterbuck added that outsiders, of course, can only exploit conflicts that already exist in a society. Laqueur (1979) concluded that, in general, the Soviet Union considers terrorism to be a "messy business," although it provides support to various terrorist groups through Cubans or East Germans. And while *Time* magazine reported that some senior U.S. intelligence officials contend that international terrorist forces are "spurred by the Kremlin," Fried (1980) noted that the Soviet counterpart to *Time* called *Novoye Vremya (New Time)* reported to its readers that international terrorism may be backed by the "CIA and other NATO sabotage and espionage organizations [p. 36]." To date, the role that the United States has played in backing terrorist operations has not been much of a topic of discussion in the terrorist literature.

Psychological Characteristics and Motives of Terrorists

Although certain social conditions have facilitated the rise of terrorism, most people exposed to these conditions have not chosen to become terrorists. The questions remain: what kinds of individuals are attracted to terrorism; what traits do they have in common; what motivates someone to sacrifice innocent bystanders for the good of some cause; and is there such a thing as a "terrorist personality"? Perhaps the most common characteristics that terrorists share are that they are likely to be young, male, and single (Laqueur, 1977; Lebow, 1980; Shultz, 1980). Many terrorists also have had at least some university education, which gives them the confidence and intellectual skills to carry out their activities (planning tactics, propaganda, and publicity, and outwitting authorities). The leaders of the terrorist groups in particular are often college educated. As Thorup (1980) reported, media images to the contrary, most of the Palestinian leaders are not deprived persons living in a refugee camp but are university graduates, perhaps with graduate degrees, who speak several languages. Laqueur (1977) made the distinction that members of nationalist separatist movements, especially the rank-and-file, tend to be young people from lower-class backgrounds, whereas ideological and social revolutionary groups appeal to young people from upper- and upper-middle-class homes. Thus, the social class composition of the IRA, Palestinian, and Basque terrorist groups differs considerably from that of the Red Brigades, Baader-Meinhof Gang, and Japanese Red Army. The Irish fighting for a homeland against the British are somewhat perplexed by the affluent nihilist urban guerrillas of Europe (Dobson & Payne, 1982).

Members of these ideological groups reject their bourgeois backgrounds and identify strongly with the struggles of the Third World, particularly the mythology of Che and Fidel. As one jailed Baader-Meinhof member expressed: "We didn't feel German anymore but a kind of fifth column of the Third World [Kupperman & Trent, 1979, pp. 25-26]." As another example. Baader-Meinhof member Susanne Albrecht, who is the daughter of a wealthy Hamburg lawyer and accused of engineering the killing of her godfather, is quoted as explaining to a friend, "I'm tired of all that caviar gobbling [Brandon, 1977]." Lewis (1978) observed that members of these ideological groups tend to respond more to abstractions than to human experience, and their membership is drawn from the ranks of the philosophically rather than economically discontent.

In attempting to uncover the layers of motivation behind terrorism, initial consideration should be given to the objective life situation of the terrorists (a group denied a homeland, a repressed and discriminated-against group, a group of restless and bored thrill-seeking bourgeois youth) and the ultimate objective(s) of each terrorist incident (to seek revenge, to vent personal aggression, to discredit and humiliate officials, to gain publicity and fame). In order to understand terrorist behavior, it may be necessary to analyze the personal historical experiences of the terrorist and how these have been perceived and interpreted at the subjective level. The life-cycle literature in psychology suggests that the kinds of historical-cultural-social experiences an individual has as he or she comes of age strongly influence the development of values and behavior and tend to provide the filtering screen for the perception and interpretation of later life experiences. Growing up Catholic in Northern Ireland has presented a specific kind of personal historical experience for adolescents—battling in the streets, family hatred for Protestant and British, attending funerals for "heroes" who have died nobly fighting for a homeland, and hearing stories about what atrocities happened to those that betrayed the cause. For Croatians, Basques, Israelis, Palestinians, Irish Catholics and Protestants, what has been provided is a unique kind of learning experience that socializes the members of each birth group into war and hatred, which partially explains why some of these wars of liberation and separatist movements have been so persistent over the years and decades.

A second factor motivating terrorists may be their desire for personal notoriety and status. Gaining public attention and making a name for oneself have been admitted motives of political assassins, in particular. For example, Arthur Bremer, who shot at Governor Wallace, had originally decided that he wanted to assassinate Richard Nixon, who was president at the time. Bremer stalked Nixon, yet claimed he was "not more or less angry with the President than he was with the anonymous pedestrians on the streets of Milwaukee whom he had earlier considered killing [Clarke, 1981-82]." Bremer kept a diary, which began with his pursuit of Nixon on April 4, 1972. After being frustrated in his intent to kill Nixon in Canada, he wrote in his diary:

> But I want em all to know. I want a big shot and not a little fat noise [the mayor of Milwaukee]. . . . I'm as important as the start of WWI. . . . I just need a little opening & a second time. [Clarke, 1981-82, pp. 102-03]

And when Bremer finally decided to drop Nixon as a target and focus instead on Wallace, he lamented in his diary:

> I won't even rate a T.V. enterobtion [interruption] in Russia or Europe when the news breaks—they never heard of Wallace. If something big in Nam flares up I'll end up at the bottom of the 1st page in America. The editors will say—"Wallace dead? who cares." He won't get more than 3 minutes on network T.V. news. [Clarke, 1981-82, p. 103]

Another force motivating the terrorists is their cognitive mindset. They appear to be attracted particularly to simplistic and violent solutions, glorifying in the antirational and spontaneity (Becker, 1980). Many terrorists unreflectively embrace some kind of ideology which not only binds together terrorist group members but provides a justification or rationalization for their violence as well. The atrocities that are committed are done in the same noble cause—a necessity to achieve the given ends. As Wilkinson (1979a) says, ideologies create and legitimate aspirations and expectations and equip militant minorities:

> to act in the name of the masses. . . . If an ideology tends to sanction violence or even to encourage and glory in it, then this inevitably strongly influences the nature of its adherents' collective response to anger, rejection, or opposition. [p. 62]

The psychodynamics of embracing some given ideology appear to weaken the link to humanity. By intellectualizing, the terrorist removes him- or herself emotionally and thus needs not feel personally responsible for what is done. Responsibility is diffused throughout the group and rests with some authority. As a result, the terrorist sees little relation between an act and its consequences. The value of life or death then becomes determined only by ideology, political considerations, or the terrorists' gain. For example, the Armenians are still avenging the Turkish slaughter of over a million compatriots in 1915, and since 1973 have assassinated 21

Turkish diplomats and carried out numerous bombings and assaults around the world. Following the recent assassination of a Turkish consul in Massachusetts, a woman claiming to be from the Justice Commandos of the Armenian Genocide called the Associated Press office in Beirut saying, "This is our style. We demand justice for the Armenian nation. We shall strike again [Essoyan, 1982]."

As part of the belief structure of terrorists, human qualities are erased and people become mere objects in the larger scheme of things. The enemy is stereotyped into some lower form of life, often relabeled or vilified in some disparaging way—"capitalist pigs," "Yankee warmongers." This dehumanization of the enemy provides the basis for inhumane and cruel acts, similar to the war experience of many soldiers. As one Vietnam veteran testified, "It wasn't like they were humans. We were conditioned to believe this was for the good of the nation, the good of our country, and anything we did was okay. And when you shot at someone you didn't think you were shooting at a human. They were a Gook or a Commie and it was okay [Schreiber, 1978, p. 143]." Or, as Bernadine Dohrn exuded over the Manson family killings, "Dig it. First they killed the pigs, then they ate dinner in the same room with them, then they even shoved forks in their stomachs. Wild [Rapoport, 1977, p. 56]." In national liberation and separatist movements, propaganda and the media are often employed to degrade and reinforce stereotyped images of the enemy, as Alexander (1977) demonstrated in his article "Terrorism and the Media in the Middle East."

The perception, thinking, and social judgment of extremists have been found to be highly rejecting, with only a narrow range of options considered to be acceptable (Sherif & Hovland, 1965; Sherif, Sherif, & Nebergall, 1965). In one study of student activist groups in the late 1960s, both the extreme right- and left-wing groups tended to reject more political positions then they accepted, with a tight consensus within their ranks about what is and is not acceptable political ideology. A much wider range of political positions was represented within the ranks of moderate youth political groups (Braungart & Braungart, 1979). Another study of these same activist groups reported that the tendency to distort objective political facts was much greater among extremist groups when compared to moderate political groups (Braungart, 1979). What these two studies suggest is that when dealing with persons who embrace an extremist political position, whether left or right, perceptual distortion of reality might be expected to be high with a tendency to find few political positions acceptable, to reject most, and to allow little diversity of opinion within the ranks of the group. Compromise, on ideological grounds especially, is likely to be difficult, if not impossible.

One of the appeals in attaching oneself to a bigger-than-life belief structure is that part of the self is relinquished for the good of some cause. The self is transcended, as the terrorist gives over his or her life to the group. Rooted in existentialism, themes of self-sacrifice and redemption overcome the triviality of life, and one's existence gains special meaning (Fromm, 1973). As Beloff (1979) observed, the political goals may not be clear nor may terrorists even expect to see their goals realized; what is important and exciting is being part of the action and feeling that in some small way, one is making a contribution to achieve some important objective.

By and large, the terrorist does not identify with conventional society or any major group within it, but instead foregoes the socializing influence of the mainstream to identify with some extremist group (Fried, 1980). The rejection of tradition allows the terrorist to break through the bonds of society. Contemptuous of society, with a mission to change conditions by any means necessary, the terrorist can more easily commit atrocities. Symbolic or ritual attempts are often made first by the group to socialize the neophyte terrorist. Skill training is one aspect of the terrorists' educational indoctrination, but another part of the training may be deeply psychological. As far back as the days of the Russian revolutionaries, Nachaev suggested the need to transcend humanity in order to become instruments of the higher cause. All terrorists are expendable, and he advised treating one's comrades as chattel (Rapoport, 1977, p. 56). Rostypin urged indiscriminate bombings or unmotivated terror because these activities obscure the victim's humanness which helps to break society's hold on the terrorist (Rapoport, 1977).

Extreme efforts are sometimes made within the terrorist group to enforce conformity and to "overcome inner layers of resistance [Rapoport, 1977]." Fear of punishment by the group is no doubt a major consideration in "motivating" individual group members to continue participating in the group and carry out orders to conduct atrocities. For example, Japanese police arrested a unit of the Japanese Red Army when it was discovered that 8 out of the 14 members had been tortured or killed for "offenses of a bourgeois mentality [Rapoport, 1977, p. 57]." A technique for enforcing discipline and conformity within the ranks of the IRA was described by Dobson and Payne (1982): "From 1973 until 1978, its kangaroo courts ordered no less than 677 'punishment shootings.' Ninety-nine percent of these were in fact 'kneecappings' in which punishment is inflicted by shooting the victim in the back of the knee [p. 32]." In order to facilitate the ability to be cruel, some groups design specific learning experiences for their members. For, as Marighella advised (Schreiber, 1978), the terrorist act must be executed with the greatest "cold bloodedness, calmness and decision [p. 31]." In order to test a member's commitment to the group and break down barriers of resistance, the Weather Underground in the United States were reported to have demanded that some members eat pet animals, defecate on tombstones, or commit acts of homosexuality (Rapoport, 1977).

The terrorist's willingness to sacrifice not only others but him- or herself for the cause indicates a suicidal theme. The terrorist, no doubt, sees the willingness to die as altruistic suicide having social significance and meaning—similar to the Kamikaze pilots of World War II. On a psychological level, however, the suicidal theme inherent in terrorism has been interpreted by the psychoanalytic camp as rooted in destructive aggressive impulses which may be turned against others and/or oneself. Erich Fromm (1973) coined the term "malignant aggression," which he defined as "biologically nonadaptive and non-phylogenetically programmed aggression. . . . [Man] is the only primate that kills and tortures members of his own species without any reason, . . . and who feels satisfaction in doing so [pp. 4-5]." Malignant aggression may take several forms, according to Fromm, but most prevalent are sadism ("the passion for unrestricted power over another sentient being") and necrophilia ("the passion to destroy life and the attraction to all that is dead, decaying, and purely mechanical"). Well-known sadists and destroyers of the recent past are Stalin, Himmler, and Hitler—certainly notorious for their state terrorism. Fromm describes the necrophilia character whose answer to life's problems is like the Queen in Alice in Wonderland: "Off with their heads!" They are unable to see options that do not require distrust, nor do they recognize the futility of force in the long run. Never do they employ sympathetic effort, construction, or example. Fromm offers an example of a general in the Spanish Civil War in the 1930s whose favorite motto was "Long live death!" Necrophilia is evident in dreams (filled with images of corpses and death), unintended actions (representing a preoccupation with death and destruction), and language (filled with words of destruction, feces, and a penchant for toilet humor).

At the core of the terrorist psyche is hatred, which may originate from: (1) frustrating objective life circumstances, such as being denied a homeland, civil rights, or life chances by some authoritarian and repressive enemy; and (2) one's own abusive, loveless life history, such as the case of Johann Most. Fried (1980) offered the example of one delinquent German boy whose hero was Stalin. The boy really had very little notion of what Stalin had said or done, but he chose Stalin as a role-model because Stalin was hated and feared by all the people he knew—the same people who had rejected him as a boy. Whatever the root, hate appears to act as a primary energizer for the terrorist to commit cruelty and violence (Maurer, 1978).

One of the most frequent questions about terrorism is whether there is a certain personality type that is predisposed to terrorist behavior. Psychologists and psychiatrists have offered a range of views about the existence of a personality type that characterizes the terrorist. Fromm (1973, pp. 288–289), for example, roots much of aggressive destructiveness in sadomaso-chism, at the core of which is "the passion to have absolute and unrestricted control over a living being." Sadism is a syndrome where living beings are viewed as objects or "things." Because the sadist feels impotent and powerless, he or she compensates by appearing at times submissive and cowardly. Sadists are stimulated by the helpless and are afraid of life; they do not like unpredictability or surprises. This personality type is likely to institute a highly repressive, and what Arendt has termed, "evil" style of totalitarian leadership.

Rather than just speculating about a "terrorist personality," some psychologists and psychiatrists have been hunting for a constellation of personality traits that describe the terrorist. After reviewing the literature, Jenkins (1980) outlined a common psychological profile of terrorists, who tend to be: true believers, uncompromising, impatient, seek immediate gratification, and are "risk seekers" fascinated with firearms. The terrorist may fear anonymity, suffer from deprivation, feel powerless, and perceive that self-esteem and masculinity are under constant assault. It has been suggested that the terrorist may try to produce in his victims the same feelings that he has suffered (Fried, 1980; Jenkins, 1980). At a conference on terrorism, Becker (1980) was asked if there is a personality type that is tempted to terrorism? He answered yes—the terrorist is likely to be introspective or moody, emotionally volatile, exhibitionist, exceptionally egocentric, the "would-be artist with no acknowledged talent" who is overly domineering or overly submissive. Others maintain there is no single personality type involved in terrorism; rather, different personality types are drawn into various kinds of terrorist activities. For example, skyjackers appear to have a specific personality type resembling the Icarian and Satanic syndromes (Fried, 1980).

Although a number of persons may share personality traits such as these, most neither join terrorist groups nor perform terrorist acts. Fried (1980) suggested the important issue here is why some persons merely fantasize grandiose antisocial behavior whereas others act on it. The existence of a so-called terrorist personality type has been questioned and criticized—as Bell (1980, pp. 201–202) observed, there seems to be great faith and little evidence in the existence of the "terrorist mind." Issue has been taken with any attempts to pinpoint a specific personality type, arguing that much of human behavior has to do with reinforcement, structural and cultural conditions (Aston, 1980). It has even been argued that almost anyone has the potential to become a terrorist, with no such phenemonon as a predisposed personality type. What appears important is individual experiences and development "in a society in which people are becoming progressively less capable of communication on the emotional level [Fried, 1980]." A middle-ground position in the debate over the existence of a terrorist personality—some, undoubtedly, psychologically disturbed, whereas others are relatively "normal" and motivated to join terrorist groups for political and/or criminal reasons (Fried, 1980; Friedlander, 1979).

This contention raises another question: how can a so-called "normal" person participate in acts of cruelty? One answer is that the norms of the social situation may disintegrate and become so bizarre over time that to participate in atrocities becomes a form of "conventional behavior," as is occurring today in Northern Ireland and the Middle East (Lebow, 1980). Secondly, studies of crowd and lynch-mob behavior indicate that when the situation becomes emotionally charged, individuals may submit their personalities to the will of the crowd or group leader, no longer monitor their own behavior, and thus perhaps participate in group-sanctioned atrocities that they would never commit alone.

What has been learned from the Nazi experience is how easily cruelty can become legitimized, and work-a-day people can leave their happy family life, go to their jobs of exterminating whole groups of humanity, and return home each evening to love their families. Some of the now-classic experiments in social psychology have corroborated the tendency to behave in cruel ways, especially when: (1) involved in competitive group struggles (the Sherifs' famous Robbers Cave experiments); (2) conforming to a specific role model (Zimbardo study of prisoner-guard behavior); (3) acting under orders (Milgram experiment where the majority of subjects, under orders from the researcher, administered high voltage shocks to a "learner" whenever he or she made a mistake); and (4) when identity is anonymous (Zimbardo experiment where cruel behavior was more likely among anonymous subjects). Zimbardo (1979) has interpreted some of these social psychological studies as indicating that "evil deeds are not simply the actions of evil people, but rather reflect the impact of evil situations on good, well-meaning individuals [p. 707]."

It is simple and somewhat reassuring to believe that people who commit horrendous acts such as terrorism are mentally ill; and, while the ranks of terrorist groups do no doubt contain a certain percentage of genuine classifiable psychopaths, other types of people participate as well (Fried, 1980; Lebow, 1980; Storr, 1978). They commit their acts of atrocity for a number of reasons: it is their job; they want to show their loyalty to the group; they are emotionally aroused and overwhelmed by hatred and rage; they will be rewarded if they go along with the terrorist group but severely punished or killed if they fail to participate. As Friedlander (1979) suggested, "When people take to terrorism even for idealistic motives, they may not only become corrupted by their own methods, they also find themselves in the company of people who were corrupt from the start [p. 64]."

PREVENTION AND CONTROL OF TERRORISM

Whatever the perspective on the relationship between personality type and terrorism, Bell (1980) pointed out that terrorism has the potential to bring out the worst in everyone. A crucial aspect is how to respond to terrorism—how to prevent it or, if it should occur, how to minimize injury and bring about an end to the incident as quickly and safely as possible. One of the puzzling aspects of terrorism is the lack of a legal framework to deal with international terrorists. Another aspect of responding to terrorism is how to prevent it, which includes placing physical or psychological barriers between the terrorists and targets and the role of the media in the terrorist event. With an increasing backlog of international experience from which to draw, there is a growing body of knowledge about handling the terrorist incident through various forms of negotiation and responses. The best defense against terrorism is predicated on a thorough understanding of its background and context, including its history, group organization and strategy, social roots, and psychological motivations.

Legal Debate and International Response

The legal problem of handling terrorism is less confusing when terrorism is of the domestic variety than when it is international or transnational. A global problem implies the need for a global solution, but there is as yet no viable international legal framework to deal with terrorism. Obviously, the problem of international terrorism is a threat to human life, and Jenkins (Carlton, 1979) warns that if terrorism continues along its present course where military-power relationships are altered in favor of some group that obeys no government, "We will enter an era of international warlordism in which the people of the world and their governments are subjected to extortion demands of many small groups [p. 228]." Also, terrorism has complicated and aggravated international relations, such as when diplomats are kidnapped or murdered; governments refuse to extradite or punish terrorists against another state; terrorists use a state as a base of operation without the state's approval; a citizen from one country is seized in another country, and the citizen's government bypasses authorities of the state where the seizure occurred and negotiates directly with the terrorists; and nationals from one country go to another country to conduct terrorist activities against a third country (Evans, 1979).

The obvious place to attempt to institute some kind of policy and legal framework to deal with international terrorism is the United Nations. And, in fact, in 1972, the United States endeavored to get the United Nations to adopt conventions against terrorism, arguing that innocent victims suffer and the fabric of the international order is weakened. However, a number of Third World and communist states challenged the proposal on the grounds that legal action against terrorism might interfere with movements for national liberation, and if such laws existed they would be used by imperialist colonial powers to justify the repression of any group seeking the right to self-determination and liberation from an oppressor. The United States countered that it is extremely difficult to determine the "causes" of terrorism and that popular or just causes do not justify immoral methods. The thrust of the argument was that certain activities—basically criminal in nature—should be prohibited, regardless of their political coloration (Evans, 1979; Fields, 1979; Friedlander, 1979; Green, 1979; Rubin, 1977; Tharp, 1980).

Although the United States and many Western nations have condemned terrorism from a humanitarian perspective, much of the rest of the world views terrorism as a political issue of national liberation and development. The justifications for the use of violence appear endless; every country is violent, so change by violence is the only alternative; in the quest for national liberation, no one is innocent in the corrupt world, and civilian casualties must be expected; because terrorists suffer and die as they attempt to correct the course of change and history, so others must suffer too for the noble cause (Evans, 1979; Friedlander, 1979; Kupperman & Trent, 1979; Thorup, 1980). As Friedlander (1979) observed, "There is . . . no indication that Third World nations have abandoned their position of viewing terrorism, when carried out by national liberation movements, as not only lawful but laudable [p. 38]." Another complication in trying to devise some kind of international policy or law is that many nation-states recognize that they want the right to grant asylum to persons accused of committing political offenses (Evans, 1979; Kupperman & Trent, 1979).

Given the difficulty of developing a workable legal framework, many have suggested pursuing multilateral and bilateral treaties. Another suggestion has been to formally recognize the illegality and inhumanity of state terrorism as well; and perhaps, if state repression and terrorism declined, substate terrorism would decrease as well (Friedlander, 1979). In a seminar sponsored by the Royal Services Institute for Defense Studies in London, it was suggested that the international community should view terrorism as Holland does: a fight against terrorism is a fight against crime, irrespective of the political reasons given to justify terrorist behavior (Thompson, 1979). Yet, as Evans (1979) pointed out, although the view in much of North America, Europe, and Japan is that violence has its origins in criminal behavior, mental illness, or alienation and bitterness toward society, it cannot be denied that self-determination and national liberation movements remain at the root of most of the international terrorism today. In American history, the Boston Tea Party is seen by Americans as a heroic act of courage as the disaffected colonialists attempted to demonstrate their disgust for Britain's unjust taxation and repression; but, to the British, such criminal destruction of property was akin to terrorism. One country's rebel may be another nation's terrorist. At the moment, with the international morass in creating, much less enforcing, a legal structure to combat substate or state terrorism, one alternative for controlling terrorism is to take measures at the preventive end.

Prevention of Terrorism

In general, barriers—either psychological or physical—are erected which make it difficult if not impossible for terrorists to operate. Target hardening is an important topic in handling terrorism, and may be as simple as installing fences, locks, thick concrete walls; hiring guards and receptionists; and installing hidden cameras. From recent experience, the most notable targets that need to be protected are diplomatic and military installations, energy systems, multinational businesses, computer networks, and water supplies (Alexander & Kilmarx, 1979; Kupperman & Trent, 1979; Shultz, 1980).

A specific area for concern in preventing terrorism has been the recent movement into nuclear energy, which may offer a highly vulnerable and dangerous potential target for terrorists, either to sabotage or steal nuclear material for their purposes (Beres, 1979; Kupperman, 1979; Kupperman & Trent, 1979; Mullen, 1980). Blocking terrorists' access to weapons is a major preventive action; but, in a society such as America where almost any kind of weapon is readily available to anyone for a price, it is unlikely terrorist bank robberies, shoot-outs with police, political assassinations, or hostage taking and kidnapping at gunpoint will lessen. This is not to say that if we had gun control terrorists would not be able to obtain and employ guns, but with gun control their job would at least be made more difficult. Lacking gun control, one alternative in controlling terrorism is to tag weapons (Kupperman & Trent, 1979). With growing ties between terrorist groups and organized crime, it has also been suggested that sustained pressure against organized crime might lesson or inhibit terrorist activities (Clutterbuck, 1979; Russell et al., 1979).

At the preventive end also is the need to develop greater knowledge and awareness of terrorism among some of the terrorists' likely targets, such as diplomats, military personnel, and business people. Marighella, in his *Minimanual*, pointed out the advantages of victimizing corporate executives which can provide the terrorist with both media exposure and ransom money. Estimates are that more than $145 million have been paid as ransom to terrorists between 1970 and 1978 (Shultz & Sloan, 1980). As a result, terrorist prevention seminars and simulation exercises have been instituted for target groups.

Potential targets and their families have been urged to be more attuned to the possibility of terrorist attack—being watched or followed, unusual phone calls or requests at the front door, anything suspicious or out of the ordinary. Precautions which are urged include changing routes and times to and from work and, in general, becoming less predictable in one's behavior (Kupperman & Trent, 1979; Pizer, 1980). If the situation appears especially dangerous, likely targets are advised to keep a low profile and perhaps use armored cars and wear bulletproof vests. Increasing the general awareness of the public may also have pay-off value in preventing terrorism. For example, an alert airline passenger spotted a man who had entered the cabin from the landing ramp rather than through the proper gate. When the man sat in a nearby seat, the passenger noticed a six-inch hunting knife strapped to his hip. The passenger quietly reported the occurrence, and security officers were able to arrest the man before takeoff without incident (Schreiber, 1978). In the area of controlling crime, it is well-known that the most effective means is less through increased police protection than it is through an informal system of community residents who are alert to and report suspicious behavior or criminal activity.

There is a price to be paid for strong preventive measures: if society is to be secure against terrorism, then individual rights tend to diminish as attempts are made to protect the larger community (Horowitz, 1977; Kupperman & Trent, 1979; Schreiber, 1978). Much depends on the climate of public opinion in terms of how much security is acceptable. For example, West Germany has tighter security precautions at major airports than does the United States. It is questionable whether Americans would tolerate armed guards in pairs carrying automatic weapons with bayonets as they roam gate areas glaring at each passenger as he or she heads for the plane; and before boarding the plane every man, woman, and small child may be physically searched, after already having gone through the usual checkpoints of personnel, x-ray, and metal detectors. Apparently to the West Germans, who have had more than their share of nihilist terrorist activity, such tight security measures are considered a necessary part of everyday airline travel. Security measures, after all, are not only to discourage terrorist attack but also are symbolic, assuring public safety. Yet, vigorous target hardening in one area may only to serve to drive terrorists to another form of activity (Schreiber, 1978). The terrorist clearly has the advantage of the offense.

A fundamental issue in the preventive and control of terrorism is the role of the media. Terrorism requires few resources to have an impact; and, in modern societies, terrorist activities have been greatly facilitated by international communications technology and the media. Terrorism is theater, and as Laqueur (1977) said, "the media are the terrorists' best friend." The terrorist is well aware of media influence and hungers for publicity, either for himself or his cause. Consequently, terrorist operations are becoming largely symbolic, primarily directed toward a mass audience.

Media coverage is a reward to terrorists and presents problems in crisis management. It is not just a one-way relationship, however. As Cooper (1977, p.150) noted, it is a mutually beneficial association—the terrorist uses the media, just as the media uses the terrorist. Television, radio, newspaper, and magazine personnel have been known to interfere with operations, harass the relatives of victims, and put added pressure on authorities which may affect negotiations. For example, during the Hanafi episode in Washington, D.C. in 1977, the media made telephone calls to the terrorists during the siege which tied up communications between police negotiators and terrorists. In addition, by giving the incident on-the-spot television coverage, unwittingly the media provided the terrorists with certain intelligence information. In one instance, some of the people in the B'nai B'rith Building had evaded capture and barricaded themselves in a room on a different floor. The gunmen were not aware of their presence. However, when a television reporter saw a basket being lifted up to the fifth floor window where the people were waiting to be rescued, he gave it immediate live coverage. "The gunmen were probably informed of the TV reporter's scoop by their fellow Hanafis who monitored the news media outside the captured buildings. Fortunately the gunmen did not break through the door (Alexander, 1980, p. 92]." There has even been collusion between media representatives and terrorists. For example, a photographer from *Der Spiegel* went with the Baader-Meinhof Gang as they attacked a house in Hamburg, West Germany, and a number of similar cases have been reported between the British or American media and the IRA (Cooper, 1977).

Not all effects of media coverage have been negative. Sometimes what terrorists really want is a forum to publicize their cause, and by publicizing the incident, the "trigger finger" relaxes. For example, in 1976, a group of Croatian exiles hijacked a TWA jet in the United States, forcing it to fly to Montreal, London, and then Paris. All along the way, the group dropped leaflets proclaiming their cause, demanding radical changes in American policy toward "occupied Croatia," and saying that they would use as little violence as necessary to achieve their demands. The hijackers were frightening in appearance and apparently armed with plastic bombs, yet they behaved politely toward the passengers. Thirty hours later, the episode ended in Paris when the Croatians gave themselves up for extradition. One hijacker reportedly tore apart the cotton fluff in his fake bomb saying, "That's show biz [Schreiber, 1978]."

The media have been helpful in establishing a link between authorities and the public in many incidences. As Alexander (1980) reported during the 1977 South Moluccan incident in Holland, "Daily news releases containing bits of information on details not crucial to developing strategy and tactics satisfied the public appetite for information, as well as conveyed an image of official responsibility and effective crisis management."

In a democratic society, the right of free press and the public's right to know are valued; and so, while press censorship might be an expedient way to remove the rewards received for coverage of terrorist events and make the authorities' jobs easier in the negotiation process, it is generally agreed that repression of news would erode trust in the media and threaten its credibility (Terraine, 1979). As Clutterbuck (1979, p. 70) advised, there is no use trying to stop the media from doing its job and recording the news, so what authorities might as well do is help them record it. In all probability, the media will tend to depict the truth, which often is on the authority's side. There is no escaping the consequences: if the message the terrorist wants or demands is broadcast, then the victory goes to the terrorist; if it is suppressed, then the terrorist has won just the same (Cooper, 1977, p. 50).

In general, the media must be willing to see itself as part of the problem as well as part of the solution. Media personnel have to be careful not to provoke or exploit the terrorist incidents. Other suggestions have been to at least wait until the incident diffuses before releasing coverage. Removing sensationalism, providing less front-page coverage, and focusing more on accuracy than emotionalism have all been recommended (Terraine, 1979).

Intervention and Negotiation

If the terrorist incident cannot be prevented, it must be handled effectively. It then becomes the job of the crisis team to control and contain the episode, which requires a precise tailoring of the response to the nature of the threat (Kupperman, 1979). At issue in handling the terrorist incident is whether the government should respond by counterassault, a no-concessions policy, or negotiations. Few experts in the area of terrorism in fact recommend either the counterattack or no-concessions approach. The dramatic counterassault has the potential for doing more harm than good, and a greater number of deaths of hostages have occurred by police action than by direct terrorist killing (Miller, 1979). It has also been suggested that tactical units such as SWAT (Special Weapons and Tactical Units) have been overplayed and exaggerated by the media. As Clutterbuck (1979) argued:

> The government and its security forces have one great advantge: the overwhelming majority of the people detest violence, and the more clearly the truth is presented to them on the media, the more they will turn against the terrorist and support the rule of law. [p. 70]

What is needed is a civilized response to an uncivilized action or provocation. At the same time, government needs to be perceived as acting to restore confidence. A policy of legitimate toughness but not overreaction is required. As an example, the Chicago police responded to the disruption of the 1968 Democratic Party convention with such force against not only young people but reporters and anyone else in their paths that what was fostered was the image of a paranoid, brutal Establishment that hated young people (Schreiber, 1978, p. 129). The Yippies and the manipulative celebrities of the student movement had successfully provoked just the kind of response they had originally wanted. Overreaction, in general, plays into the terrorist trap. As another example, in the early 1950s in Algeria, the attempts of antico-lonial radicals had failed to arouse public opinion against French colonialism. Although most Algerians did not care for the French presence, they accepted it. However, once the radicals resorted to blowing up buses and marketplaces in Algiers, they managed the response they wanted:

> Suddenly the native Algerian police force disappeared from the streets of Algiers, to be replaced by special forces of grim-faced European Frenchmen, swinging their riot sticks and inspecting people who attempted to board the buses. Now the proof that had been lacking was obvious to every Algerian. In spite of earlier French protestations, Algerians were not considered to be like Frenchmen when it mattered; they were colonials, and when a crisis arose they were not to be trusted—even to police their own people—but were thrust into the background while Frenchmen, the privileged and dominant class took over. . . . [These events] were decisive in marshaling the support of rank-and-file Algerians that eventually led to the nation's independence. [Schreiber, 1978, p. 131]

In a similar vein, security forces must be cautious about using their weapons. If they make a mistake and kill an innocent bystander, the sympathy engendered again plays into the hands of the publicity-seeking terrorists. Some of the newer weapons are impressively powerful, but their use can backfire, as in an incident in Northern Ireland in 1977 where the British antiter-rorist squads were issued Armalite rifles to fight Irish terrorists. The weapon is so powerful that a bullet "that killed a soldier in August 1977 passed through him and seriously wounded a young girl [Dobson & Payne, 1982, p. 2]."

Should the terrorists episode require negotiations, considerable background information is needed along with negotiating skills such as patience, sound judgment, and the ability to com-municate. The terrorists situation is highly volatile and unpredictable, and one useful training technique has been to simulate terrorist incidents, encouraging the actual participation of dip-lomats, military, police personnel, and business executives. These simulation exercises not only provide preventive "up-front" training but also generate "on-the-spot" data about possi-ble reactions and problems that may be encountered in handling a variety of different situa-tions as well. Based on observations from a series of these simulations, Sloan (1980) identified different stages of the siege along with expected patterns of behavior. The first stage is what he calls "it can't happen here syndrome," or the tendency to deny the threat. This is likely to be followed by a period of shock and immobilization where guidelines often break down. Next, there is a tendency to feel impelled to take action which may impede effective negotiations. The most dangerous period is the initial phase when provocative actions could well trigger an escalation of violence which no one really intended. As the terrorist incident continues, the early feelings of excitement are often replaced by boredom and fatigue—a new problem per-iod, since effectiveness in negotiation may be lessened. Sloan suggests "going slow" and keeping a routine, even when nearing some kind of resolution (negotiated or forced) to the terrorist situation. He also suggests the need for clear lines of authority and simple guidelines between police and media.

Crucial to the crisis team is intelligence information about the terrorist group with whom they are negotiating. What do the terrorists want from the situation, and perhaps what do they realistically expect to gain? What is the composition of the group, the leadership of the group, and the style of decision making within the group? What resources, reserves, and support does the group have? Knowledge of social psychology may also aid in the assessment and handling of the situation. For example, it is likely that the terrorists, as well as the crisis team, feel uncertain and impelled to act, particularly in the early stages of the siege. Under such conditions the probability of violence is enhanced. It is generally agreed that time may be one of the crisis team's best allies, with the likelihood of violence tending to decrease with the passage of time. In general, the terrorist situation has a greater potential for cruelty and violence when: terrorists are anonymous; responsibility is diffuse; terrorist group norms and values are extreme, rigid, distorted, and favor violence; terrorists feel personally threatened and defensive; all options are closed off to the terrorists except violence; the terrorists view themselves as outsiders in a hostile society and are filled with hatred and rage; and they are nihilistic and suicidal. Thus, whatever can be done to intervene and change these characteristics may reduce the potential for violence. For example, attempts might be made to structure and clarify the situation, get to know the names and personalities of the terrorists, and keep the situation calm to alleviate threat and defensive overreactions. It may also be characteristic of terrorist groups that they are so concerned with group solidarity and presenting a united front that critical thought and diversity of opinion are blunted—what has been termed "groupthink."

What is generally recommended is careful planning and flexibility in handling terrorist encounters. Pursuing a course of negotiation not only is likely to save lives but it also gains time to assess the terrorist situation and develop a plan of action. As Rabe (1979) pointed out, by negotiating, the interaction between terrorists and authorities enters at a less threatening level, yet room is left open for the escalation of force if necessary. As part of crisis management, computer programs are being developed to aid the crisis team in rapid searches for available options for response (Janke, 1979; Kupperman, Wilcox, & Smith, 1979; Shultz, 1980). Law enforcement agencies need to be kept at strength, and to be able to coordinate their activities with all the different groups involved, including the media (Alexander, 1980). Kupperman and Trent (1979) advised that the planning take place at two levels, which involves decoupling the (1) primary terrorist incident from its (2) secondary psychological effects on society. Even with the best of an assortment of contingency plans and computer programs, it is crucial for authorities to be astute and flexible enough to shift gears—it is essentially the government's job to "out invent" the terrorist (Kupperman & Trent, 1979; Russell et al., 1979).

The negotiation process requires behavioral know-how and tactical skills. Communications must be developed and kept going until the terrorists surrender. The ability of the negotiator to establish rapport is essential. Sloan (1980) suggests that the most effective negotiators tend to be individuals who can listen, can relate to the feelings of others without losing objectivity, are difficult to provoke, are patient, do not take themselves seriously, and can maintain a sense of humor. It is sometimes recommended that the negotiator not hold a position of authority. The police sergeant may be better able to relate to terrorists than captains. An added advantage is that the sergeant does not have the authority to make decisions and so can only act as a go-between for terrorists and decision makers, which buys a certain amount of time and slows down the action somewhat.

In the negotiating process, in all probability the terrorists, in order to save face, are going to need to feel they are coming away with something, particularly if the safe release of hostages is involved. Yet, only token concessions should be granted and never weapons or additional hostages. It is possible, perhaps, to substitute achievements for stated objectives, such as allowing publicity then convincing the terrorists they have achieved a propaganda victory, so it is no longer necessary to continue the siege (Geraghty, 1979). Denial of any real gain is one deterrent to terrorism. Hardening of positions is likely to occur when the government projects the image of vulnerability or terrorists feel a loss of credibility. Thus, the negotiator needs to be firm yet open to communication. In some negotiation situations, a ritualization process occurs between police and terrorists: the terrorists communicate their grievances, the police display their authority, the talk continues, and the game plays itself out.

There is a general consensus that terrorist incidents should be handled, for the most part, by the police and not the military. As Mengel (1978) argued, "[once] the military begins to intervene directly . . . a certain loss of tradition and democratic norms and values has taken place and . . . the possibility of later encroachments into the civilian sector becomes more likely [p. 413]." One of the problems, of course, is that the police in a particular locality may not be knowledgeable or effective in combating terrorism, and so some have suggested developing special police units. However, as a cautionary note, Horowitz (1977) worried about having a built-in structure to anticipate all types of terrorism, which has the potential also to destroy critical thinking, pluralism, and dissent.

At this point, it begins to look as if the terrorist holds the advantage, but there are some constraints against all-out violence on their part as well. Jenkins (1980) commented at a conference on terrorism that, to date, terrorists have been operating below their technological ceiling. Although they have a variety of weapons at their disposal—conventional, nuclear, chemical, and biological—there are some limitations to their use, not the least of which is the high risk posed to the terrorists themselves. A number of terrorists have died or have been wounded making or planting even the simplest of homemade bombs, including the terrorist who was placing the bomb at the 1980 Munich Oktoberfest when it exploded. Some of the more complex means of destruction require sophisticated know-how, skills, and training; and attempting to disperse chemical, radiological, or biological agents is highly challenging and unpredictable (Kupperman, 1979). Few terrorist groups would launch an operation when the risks greatly outweigh the costs (Kupperman & Trent, 1979; Russell et al., 1979).

Victims of Terrorism

Besides the terrorists, the audience, and the government officials involved in the terrorist incident, a fourth group of participators are the victims. Two considerations that are pertinent here involve prevention and coping. As suggested earlier, diplomats and corporate executives, in particular, are prime targets for kidnapping, hostage taking, and assassinations. First, it is essential to be prepared, including having affairs in order at all times (wills, insurance, contingency plans with family) and constantly being alert for suspicious signs. Pizer (1980) reported that half of the kidnappings of corporate officials occurred while they were in their cars traveling to or from work, and another third occurred outside their homes or offices. On hindsight, many executives and diplomats remembered there were signs that they were under surveillance (followed in cars or on foot, someone lurking outside home or office, strange telephone calls, or strangers making contact with the family under some pretense).

Once captured, it is reasonable to expect victims to be scared, shocked, and confused (yet relatively few hostages have been killed). The victim's fear is intensified, of course, if there is violence or threat of violence and pain. Victims are advised to calm down, assess the type of terrorists and group situation, avoid clashes or complaining, and try to get to know the captors as human beings. The hostage needs to appear relatively passive and nonthreatening. Coping is usually facilitated by finding and maintaining anchors to the outside world (time, date, events, remembering family). Evidence gained from concentration camp and POW experiences suggests that another functional coping mechanism is feeling that one must survive in order to bear witness (which also facilitates a feeling of objectivity in some captives) and to testify.

Hostage taking and kidnapping involve a dynamic psychosocial process that occurs over time between victim and captor (Ochberg, 1979; Schreiber, 1978). There are several psychological phenomena that are relevant here, one of which is the stress reaction. As an adaptive response to the threatening situation, the victim becomes emotionally and psychologically aroused which involves a number of biochemical changes in the body. As the situation continues, the body works to resist the disturbance (partially by increasing secretions of the adrenal cortex and anterior pituitary), and initial signs of physiological disturbance appear to be alleviated—although in actuality, disturbing stimulation continues. However, the body cannot maintain resistance by elevated levels of secretions for too long; and, with extended stress, physiological dysfunction may occur in the form of breakdown or disease. For example, all of the school children taken hostage by the South Moluccans in 1977 developed gastroenteritis during the first week of captivity (Aston, 1980, p. 74).Ochberg (1980) noted that one of the problems with victims in the terrorist situation is that the arousal accompanying stress cannot be discharged through normal flight or fight responses, and thus both external and internal stress is compounded. With knowledge of the general adaptation syndrome, however, victims may be able to exert some control over the response. What is often crucial is to recognize that one's perception and attitude toward the situation will strongly affect body response to stress. At the initial stages of the siege, victims could work to keep their arousal at moderate rather than highly elevated levels, and as the situation continues, attempt to reduce stress by employing relaxation and cognitive control techniques.

A second psychological phenomenon related to the victim-captor situation is transference—a term originally applied to the patient-psychiatrist relationship—which involves an emotional identification or bond that may occur between captive and captor. Though the bond may be mutual, and it could be that the terrorist might form a strong attachment to the captive, it is more likely that it will be the victim who experiences transference, partially based on the victim's strong dependency on the captor for everyday needs. The transference phenomenon in terrorism became evident during a 1973 bank robbery in Stockholm, Sweden. The robbery turned into a six-day hostage-barricade situation. The crisis situation itself facilitated transference since captor and hostages shared a common fate as they awaited police reaction outside the bank building. One of the female hostages and the captor named Olsson became sexually intimate, and it was noted that when some of the other hostages had contact with police negotiators, they acted hostile and mistrusting, appearing to be more concerned about what would happen to Olsson, "their captor." Even after surrender, the hostages reported feelings of loyalty and affection for Olsson which he easily reciprocated. The hostage with whom he was intimate refused to testify against him, and they continued their relationship when Olsson was imprisoned (Miller, 1980; Schreiber, 1978). Emotional attachments that may develop between terrorist and hostage have been labeled the "Stockholm syndrome" (Miller, 1980; Ochberg, 1979; Schreiber, 1978).

Another well-known incidence of Stockholm syndrome occurred in the Patty Hearst case, where early in her captivity she engaged in sexual activity with one of her captors, and later when left in a van during a bank robbery, she did not drive away. A less famous occurrence, but indicative of how strong the victim response can be, took place in another kidnapping incident in Shade Gap, Pennsylvania. As police closed in on the kidnapper and victim in a wooded area, the kidnapper began hurrying to escape. Far behind him was the victim trying to keep up with the captor; yet, all the victim had to do was turn around and run the other way to freedom (Miller, 1980). The Stockholm syndrome has the potential to increase hostages' chances for survival, but law enforcement personnel have learned that during the hostage situations they cannot necessarily rely on victims for help or even expect the victims to help themselves (Aston, 1980).

Transference is not limited only to victim and captor relations, and may occur between terrorist and negotiator as well. Again, the development of transference may facilitate a peaceful solution to the terrorist episode, but the negotiator needs to be aware of its occurrence and may need counseling after the siege is ended. Transference is also likely to take place between the terrorist group members and their leader. The leader may fulfill the role of a parent surrogate, and under conditions of external danger the emotional identification of group members with their leader can be extremely strong, to the point that members become highly sensitive to the leader's demands and may react with disappointment or depression to any slights or lack of commitment (Miller, 1980). The key to controlling the terrorist group in this case may be to gain the trust of the leader.

Following the terrorist incident, many victims—and perhaps negotiators—experience at least some, if not severe, psychological aftereffects (Ochberg, 1980). The effects tend to become evident from several weeks to a month after the episode. Common reactions are anxiety, grief reactions, phobias, and nightmares (particularly death imagery). Some victims turn to alcohol or drugs, and some may become depressed. Such behavior may be transitory or intense, and even pathological. In the long run, Ochberg (1980) reported, many victims become stronger after the experience, developing a fresh lease on life and feelings of mastery. Other former victims may react by not thinking about it, going on with life as they did before— often the more "nonpsychologically minded" types. Yet, other victims remain affected for considerable time.

Surviving after the terrorist incident as a former hostage appears to be problematic, especially in the United States. There is an unfortunate cultural tendency to be more concerned with the offender than the victim and to "blame to victim," which only feeds the victim's tendency to feel guilty for having survived or that he or she should have done something differently. In Israel and the Netherlands, by contrast, hostages are treated as heroes. Left stranded in the United States, victims often react similarly to victims of natural catastrophes (Thorup, 1980). As Miller (1980) observed, "A greater public understanding of the impact of the crisis on the hostage would be an act of kindness that would make the hostages' entrance back into society less difficult [p. 100]."

THE FUTURE OF TERRORISM

For a number of reasons, there is not likely to be any rapid demise of terrorism. First, as long as terrorism is supported financially and in other ways by nations throughout the world, it can be expected to thrive, and perhaps escalate by coming to replace the more costly traditional forms of conventional warfare. The Balkan wars early in this century clearly demonstrated the volatile situation that can take place when major world superpowers back terrorism and align themselves with one terrorist group or another to either bolster their interests in some geographic region or carry out surrogate warfare against another nation. Such a powder-keg may be ready to explode in the Middle East today.

To date, the Soviets have not been highly cooperative about endorsing an international legal framework to deal with terrorism, and a key issue has been their support for terrorist groups in all parts of the globe. However, now that terrorist attacks against Soviet citizens and installations have increased sharply since 1980, it may be in the Soviet's best interest to work more toward discouraging terrorism, rather than explicitly or implicitly encouraging terrorist operatives. Jenkins (1981) advised that the time is propitious to seek an international agreement which reasserts diplomatic immunity and sanctions the diplomatic isolation of nations that fail to extradite or prosecute terrorists who seize embassies or attack diplomats. Given the current international context and its own recent experience as a growing target of terrorism, the Soviet Union, or any other country for that matter, might find it awkward to openly oppose conventions that bolster diplomatic immunity. It is in the best interest of all countries to seek the end of terrorism. However, should the United States continue to point its finger at the

Soviet Union rather than the terrorist groups themselves, irrespective of their sponsor, then the terrorists will get off free and remain unaccountable for their deeds (Jenkins, 1981).

A second reason terrorism is not likely to decline is that it has become big business, with growing links to organized crime. Criminality is predicted to become a significant component of terrorism, to the point that the political trappings may eventually disappear (Clutterbuck, 1979). Another new twist to terrorism may be a growing tendency to see individuals who are not actually members of a political terrorist group use terrorist tactics as a means of gaining attention, such as the recent case of a Sri Lankan national who hijacked a jet to protest his wife's threat to divorce him.

There is also expected to be an increase in terrorism from the political right, which, as some recent terrorist episodes have demonstrated, can be more callous and lethal than that on the political left. Nations must always take care never to put aside democratic principles and embrace terrorist tactics such as occurred in Nazi Germany, Fascist Italy, and Stalinist Russia. If nihilism—from either the right or left—becomes more widespread in the future and terrorist destruction more devastating, then the escalation of countermeasures could create a spiral of violence and repression with disastrous consequences that no one really intended.

One important question is whether terrorists will resort to more powerful weapons of mass destruction. To date, those groups that are the most extreme in their orientation are small, and their ability to acquire such weapons is questionable. It is also doubtful at this point in time that any terrorist group would gain much by the use of highly destructive weapons. The threat of mass destruction to the population probably rests less on the activities of terrorists than on the growing number of nation-states obtaining nuclear devices, reactors, and the technology of mass destruction where the danger of accident or misuse is always a possibility.

The future of terrorism depends heavily on the course of national and subnational self-determination and international relations. Alienation is a precipitating factor for terrorism, and should the situations within nation-states worsen and alienation become more widespread, we may expect to see an increased reliance on terrorism. If the numbers of frustrated, bored, and unemployed or underemployed youths continue to grow, recruitment into terrorist organizations will be relatively easy. Another danger sign is that society will become numb to violence, so that individuals will no longer count for much and violence gradually will be escalated to achieve its desired effects. Admittedly, security of vulnerable facilities is not strong, and as technology becomes more destructive and centralized, and society less effective in its planning, the terrorists' job is made easier. The conditions of society have much to do with not only the existence of terrorist groups but also with the symbolic impact such groups can have. In the long run, the surest solution to terrorism is to strengthen the social, political, and economic fabric of societies throughout the world and to be more attentive to the needs of all their members. It is out of human indifference and ignorance that some of the worst crimes against humanity have occurred.

REFERENCES

Alexander, Y. Terrorism and the media in the Middle East. In Y. Alexander & S. M. Finger (Eds.), *Terrorism: Interdisciplinary perspectives.* New York: John Jay Press, 1977.

Alexander, Y. Terrorism, the media and the police. In A. D. Buckley & D. D. Olson (Eds.), *International terrorism: Current research and future directions.* Wayne, N.J.: Avery Publishing Group, 1980.

Alexander, Y., & Finger, S. M. (Eds.) *Terrorism: Interdisciplinary perspectives.* New York: John Jay Press, 1977.

Alexander, Y., & Kilmarx, R. A. (Eds.) *Political terrorism and business: The threat and response.* New York: Praeger, 1979.

Alpern, D. M. Again, anti-semitism. *Newsweek,* February 16, 1981, pp. 38-41.

Arendt, H. *The origins of totalitarianism.* Cleveland, Ohio: The World Publishing Company, 1958.

Associated Press. FALN regrouping in U.S. despite anti-terrorist efforts. *Syracuse Herald-Journal,* December 11, 1981, p. B-11.

Aston, C. C. Restrictions encountered in responding to terrorist sieges: An analysis. In R. H. Shultz, Jr., & S. Sloan (Eds.), *Responding to the terrorist threat: Security and crisis management.* New York: Pergamon Press, 1980.

Bakunin, M. Revolution, terrorism, banditry. In W. Laqueur (Ed.), *The terrorism reader: A historical anthology.* New York: New American Library, 1978.

Becker, J. The international scientific conference on terrorism, Berlin. *Terrorism: An International Journal,* 1980, *3* (3/4), 191-202.

Bell, J. B. The international scientific conference on terrorism, Berlin. *Terrorism: An International Journal,* 1980, *3* (3/4), 201-202.

Beloff, M. Terrorism and the people. In Royal United Services Institute for Defense Studies (Ed.), *Ten years of terrorism: Collected views.* New York: Crane, Russak, 1979.

Beres, L. R. *Terrorism and global security: The nuclear threat.* Boulder, Colo.: Westview Press, 1979.

Brandon, H. The German terrorists have a bond; it's hatred. *New York Times,* October 30, 1977.

Braungart, R. G. Historical and generational patterns of youth movements: A global perspective. In R. F. Tomasson (Ed.), *Comparative social research* (Vol. 7). Greenwich, Connecticut: JAI Press, forthcoming.

Braungart, R. G. The utopian and ideological styles of student political activists. Paper presented at the annual meetings of the International Society of Political Psychology, Washington, D.C., May 1979.

Braungart, R. G., & Braungart, M. M. Reference group, social judgments and student politics. *Adolescence,* 1979, *14,* 135-57.

Braungart, R. G., & Braungart, M. M. International terrorism: Background and response. *Journal of Political and Military Sociology,* 1981, *9* (2), 263-88.

Carlton, D. The future of political substate violence. In Y. Alexander, D. Carlton, & P. Wilkinson (Eds.), *Terrorism: Theory and practice.* Boulder, Colo.: Westview Press, 1979.

Central Intelligence Agency. *Patterns of international terrorism: 1980.* Springfield, Va.: National Technical Information Service, 1981.

Clarke, J. W. Emotional deprivation and political deviance: Some obervations on Governor Wallace's would-be assassin, Arthur H. Bremer. *Political Psychology,* 1981-82, *3* (1/2), 84-115.

Clutterbuck, R. Terrorism: A soldier's view. In Royal United Services Institute for Defense Studies (Ed.), *Ten years of terrorism: Collected views.* New York: Crane, Russak, 1979.

Cooper, H. H. A. Terrorism and the media. In Y. Alexander & S. M. Finger (Eds.), *Terrorism: Interdisciplinary perspectives.* New York: John Jay Press, 1977.

Dobson, C., & Payne, R. *The terrorists: Their weapons, leaders and tactics.* (Rev. ed.) New York: Facts On File, 1982.

Essoyan, S. Slain consul ignored advice to protect self. *Syracuse Herald-Journal,* May 5, 1982, p. A-7.

Evans, E. *Calling a truce to terror: The American response to international terrorism.* Westport, Conn.: Greenwood Press, 1979.

Fanon, F. *The wretched of the earth* (C. Farrington, Trans.). New York: Grove Press, 1968. (Originally published, 1961.)

Fields, L. G., Jr. Terrorism: Summary of applicable U.S. and international law. In Y. Alexander & R. A. Kilmarx (Eds.), *Political terrorism and business: The threat and response.* New York: Praeger, 1979.

Fried, R. The international scientific conference on terrorism, Berlin. *Terrorism: An International Journal,* 1980, *3* (3/4), 219-38.

Friedlander, R. A. The origins of international terrorism. In Y. Alexander & S. M. Finger (Eds.), *Terrorism: Interdisciplinary perspectives.* New York: John Jay Press, 1977.

Friedlander, R. A. *Terrorism: Documents of international and local control.* Vol. 1. Dobbs Ferry, N.Y.: Oceana Publications, 1979.

Fromm, E. *The anatomy of human destructiveness*. New York: Holt, Rinehart and Winston, 1973.

Gastil, R. D. *Freedom in the world: Political rights and civil liberties 1981*. Westport, Conn.: Greenwood Press, 1981.

Geraghty, T. Ten years of terrorism. In Royal United Services Institute for Defense Studies (Ed.), *Ten years of terrorism: Collected views*. New York: Crane, Russak, 1979.

Green, L. C. The legalization of terrorism. In Y. Alexander, D. Carlton, & P. Wilkinson (Eds.), *Terrorism: Theory and practice*. Boulder, Colo.: Westview Press, 1979.

Grenier, R. The horror, the horror. *The New Republic*, May 26, 1982, pp. 27-32.

Heinzen, K. Murder. In W. Laqueur (Ed.), *The terrorism reader: A historical anthology*. New York: New American Library, 1978.

Horowitz, I. L. Transnational terrorism, civil liberties, and social science. In Y. Alexander & S. M. Finger (Eds.), *Terrorism: Interdisciplinary perspectives*. New York: John Jay Press, 1977.

Huntington, S. P. *Political order in changing societies*. New Haven: Yale University Press, 1968.

Janke, P. The response to terrorism. In Royal United Services Institute for Defense Studies (Ed.), *Ten years of terrorism: Collected views*. New York: Crane, Russak, 1979.

Jenkins, B. M. The international scientific conference on terrorism, Berlin. *Terrorism: An International Journal*, 1980, *3* (3/4), 246-50.

Jenkins, B. M. *International terrorism: Choosing the right target*. Santa Monica, Calif.: The Rand Corporation, 1981.

Keniston, K. *Young radicals: Notes on committed youth*. New York: Harcourt, Brace and World, 1968.

King, W. The violent rebirth of the Klan. *The New York Times Magazine*, December 7, 1980, pp. 150-60.

Kraft, S. Terrorists were pushing 40 and their luck: Mistakes and clues led to capture of radicals. *Syracuse Herald-American*, October 25, 1981, p. A-2.

Kupperman, R. G., & Trent, D. M. *Terrorism: Threat, reality, response*. Stanford, Calif.: Hoover Institution Press, 1979.

Kupperman, R. G., Wilcox, R. G., & Smith, H. A. Crisis management: Some opportunities. In R. H. Kupperman & D. M. Trent (Eds.), *Terrorism: Threat, reality, response*. Stanford, Calif.: Hoover Institution Press, 1979.

Kupperman, R. G. The threat: Some technological considerations. In Y. Alexander & R. A. Kilmarx (Eds.), *Political terrorism and business: The threat and response*. New York: Praeger, 1979.

Laqueur, W. *Terrorism*. Boston: Little, Brown, 1977.

Laqueur, W. (Ed.) *The terrorism reader: A historical anthology*. New York: New American Library, 1978.

Laqueur, W. The anatomy of terrorism. In Royal United Services Institute for Defense Studies (Ed.), *Ten years of terrorism: Collected views*. New York: Crane, Russak, 1979.

Lebow, R. N. The origins of sectarian assassination: The case of Belfast. In A. D. Buckley & D. D. Olson (Eds.), *International terrorism: Current research and future directions*. Wayne, N.J.: Avery Publishing Group, 1980.

Lens, S. *Radicalism in America*. New York: Thomas Y. Crowell, 1966.

Lewis, F. The terrorists: Less a sign of revolution than of decay. *New York Times*, April 30, 1978, p. E-1.

Maitron, J. The era of the attentats. In W. Laqueur (Ed.), *The terrorism reader: A historical anthology*. New York: New American Library, 1978.

Marighella, C. From the "Minimanual." In W. Laqueur (Ed.), *The terrorism reader: A historical anthology*. New York: New American Library, 1978.

Marx, K., & Engels, F. *The Communist manifesto* (S. H. Beer, Ed.). New York: Appleton-Century-Crofts, 1955.

Maurer, M. The Ku Klux Klan and the National Liberation Front: Terrorism applied to achieve diverse goals. In M. H. Livingston (Ed.), *International terrorism in the contemporary world*. Westport, Conn.: Greenwood Press, 1978.

Mengel, R. W. The impact of nuclear terrorism on the military's role in society. In M. H. Livingston (Ed.), *International terrorism in the contemporary world*. Westport, Conn.: Greenwood Press, 1978.

Mickolus, E. F. Statistical approaches to the study of terrorism. In Y. Alexander & S. M. Finger (Eds.),

Terrorism: Interdisciplinary perspectives. New York: John Jay Press, 1977.

Mickolus, E. F. *Transnational terrorism: A chronology of events, 1968-1979.* Westport, Conn.: Greenwood Press, 1980.

Miller, A. H. Hostage negotiations and the concept of transference. In Y. Alexander, D. Carlton, & P. Wilkinson (Eds.), *Terrorism: Theory and practice.* Boulder, Colo.: Westview Press, 1979.

Miller, A. H. Responding to the victims of terrorism: Psychological and policy implications. In R. H. Shultz, Jr. & S. Sloan (Eds.), *Responding to the terrorist threat: Security and crisis management.* New York: Pergamon Press, 1980.

Morison, S. E., & Commager, H. S. *The growth of the American republic.* Vol. 2. New York: Oxford University Press, 1962.

Most, J. Advice for terrorists. In W. Laqueur (Ed.), *The terrorism reader: A historical anthology.* New York: New American Library, 1978.

Mullen, R. K. Subnational threats to civil nuclear facilities and safeguards institutions. In R. H. Shultz, Jr. & S. Sloan (Eds.), *Responding to the terrorist threat: Security and crisis management.* New York: Pergamon Press, 1980.

Nechaev, S. Catechism of the revolutionist. In W. Laqueur (Ed.), *The terrorism reader: A historical anthology.* New York: New American Library, 1978.

Ochberg, F. M. Preparing for terrorist victimization. In Y. Alexander & R. A. Kilmarx (Eds.), *Political terrorism and business: The threat and response.* New York: Praeger, 1979.

Ochberg, F. M. Victims of terrorism. *Journal of Clinical Psychiatry,* 1980, *41* (3), 73-74.

Paust, J. J. A definitional focus. In Y. Alexander & S. M. Finger (Eds.), *Terrorism: Interdisciplinary perspectives.* New York: John Jay Press, 1977.

Pizer, H. Executive protection: The view from the private security sector. In R. H. Shultz, Jr. & S. Sloan (Eds.), *Responding to the terrorist threat: Security and crisis management.* New York: Pergamon Press, 1980.

Rabe, R. L. The police response to terrorism. In Y. Alexander & R. A. Kilmarx (Eds.), *Political terrorism and business: The threat and response.* New York: Praeger, 1979.

Rapoport, D. The politics of atrocity. In Y. Alexander & S. M. Finger (Eds.), *Terrorism: Interdisciplinary perspectives.* New York: John Jay Press, 1977.

Redlick, A. S. The transnational flow of information as a cause of terrorism. In Y. Alexander, D. Carlton, & P. Wilkinson (Eds.), *Terrorism: Theory and practice.* Boulder, Colo.: Westview Press, 1979.

Rubin, A. P. International terrorism and international law. In Y. Alexander & S. M. Finger (Eds.), *Terrorism: Interdisciplinary perspectives.* New York: John Jay Press, 1977.

Russell, C. A., Banker, L. J., Jr., & Miller, B. H. Out-inventing the terrorist. In Y. Alexander, D. Carlton, & P. Wilkinson (Eds.), *Terrorism: Theory and practice.* Boulder, Colo.: Westview Press, 1979.

Schreiber, J. *The ultimate weapon: Terrorists and world order.* New York: William Morrow, 1978.

Sherif, C. W., Sherif, M., & Nebergall, R. E. *Attitude and attitude change: The social judgment-involvement approach.* Philadelphia: W. B. Saunders, 1965.

Sherif, M., & Hovland, C. I. *Social judgment: Assimilation and contrast effects in communication and attitude change.* New Haven: Yale University Press, 1965.

Shultz, R. H., Jr. The state of the operational art: A critical review of antiterrorist programs. In R. H. Shultz, Jr. & Sloan (Eds.), *Responding to the terrorist threat: Security and crisis management.* New York: Pergamon Press, 1980.

Shultz, R. H., Jr., & Sloan, S. International terrorism: The nature of the threat. In R. H. Shultz, Jr. & S. Sloan (Eds.), *Responding to the terrorist threat: Security and crisis management.* New York: Pergamon Press, 1980.

Singh, B. An overview. In Y. Alexander & S. M. Finger (Eds.), *Terrorism: Interdisciplinary perspectives.* New York: John Jay Press, 1977.

Sloan, S. Simulating terrorism: An analysis of findings related to tactical, behavioral, and adminstrative responses of participating police and military forces. In R. H. Shultz, Jr. & S. Sloan (Eds.), *Responding to the terrorist threat: Security and crisis management.* New York: Pergamon Press, 1980.

Sterling, C. *The terror network: The secret war of international terrorism.* New York: Holt, Rinehart and Winston, 1981.

Storr, A. Sadism and paranoia. In M. H. Livingston (Ed.), *International terrorism in the contemporary world*. Westport, Conn.: Greenwood Press, 1978.

Taubman, P. U.S. tries to back up Haig on terrorism. *New York Times*, March 29, 1981, p. 4.

Terraine, J. Terrorism and the media: Seminar report. In Royal United Services Institute for Defense Studies (Ed.), *Ten years of terrorism: Collected views*. New York: Crane, Russak, 1979.

Tharp, P. A., Jr. The laws of war as a potential legal regime for the control of terrorist activities. In A. D. Buckley & D. D. Olson (Eds.), *International terrorism: Current research and future directions*. Wayne, N.J.: Avery Publishing Group, 1980.

Thompson, R. Terrorism and security force requirements: Seminar report. In Royal United Services Institute for Defense Studies (Ed.), *Ten years of terrorism: Collected views*. New York: Crane, Russak, 1979.

Thorup, O. A., Jr. Terrorism: Prevention, negotiation, or capitulation?—A panel discussion. *Pharos*, 1980, *43* (2), 20-26.

Trautmann, F. *The voice of terror: A biography of Johann Most*. Westport, Conn.: Greenwood Press 1980.

Wallbank, T. W., & Taylor, A. M. *Civilization: Past and present*. Vol. 2. (4th ed.) Chicago: Scott, Foresman, 1961.

Weisband, E., & Roguly, D. Palestinian terrorism: Violence, verbal strategy, and legitimacy. In Y. Alexander (Ed.), *International terrorism: National, regional and global perspectives*. New York: Praeger, 1976.

Wilkinson, P. Social scientific theory and civil violence. In Y. Alexander, D. Carlton, & P. Wilkinson (Eds.), *Terrorism: Theory and practice*. Boulder, Colo.: Westview Press, 1979. (a)

Wilkinson, P. Terrorist movements. In Y. Alexander, D. Carlton, & P. Wilkinson (Eds.), *Terrorism: Theory and practice*. Boulder, Colo.: Westview Press, 1979. (b)

Wolf, J. B. Domestic terrorist movements. In Y. Alexander & R. A. Kilmarx (Eds.), *Political terrorism and business: The threat and response*. New York: Praeger, 1979.

Zimbardo, P. G. *Psychology and life*. (10th ed.) Glenview, Ill.: Scott Foresman, 1979.

12

Aggression Prevention and Control: Multitargeted, Multichannel, Multiprocess, Multidisciplinary

Arnold P. Goldstein
and
Harold R. Keller

We have sought in this book to offer a comprehensive statement regarding the prevention and control of aggression. While a great deal is known, much remains to be learned. In this final chapter, we seek to urge upon the reader three paths along which such growth of understanding and effectiveness of outcome might ideally proceed. The first concerns heightened attention to the prediction of aggressive behavior. Our second focus portrays an optimal approach to the multilevel measurement of aggression. Finally, we offer what we believe to be an especially heuristic overall research strategy—again, designed to maximize our ability to gain useful knowledge regarding the prevention and control of aggression.

PREDICTION

The prediction of aggression has not been fully addressed elsewhere in this book, and we wish to do so here because predictive effectiveness can serve as a significant enhancer of prevention and control efforts. When its timing and target are satisfactorily anticipated, steps may be developed and instituted which minimize or even eliminate the likelihood of overt aggression actually taking place. Yet, high levels of accurate prediction have proven difficult to obtain. On a broad, macrolevel of inquiry, it has been satisfactorily established that aggressive criminal behavior consistently correlates with such demographic and related variables as past criminal behavior, age, sex, race, socioeconomic status, and drug or alcohol abuse. But such group-focused, actuarial probabilities are of modest value at best in predicting the overt behavior of a given individual or individuals.

Some have posited that successful prediction might follow from accurate identification and use of childhood predictors of adult aggression. Many such possible predictors have been suggested; very few have been empirically examined to the point of successful cross-validation—especially for purposes of predicting individual behavior. Hellman and Blackman (1966), as

338

have numerous others, suggest enuresis, pyromania, and cruelty to animals be used for such predictive purposes. Based on surveys of mental health professionals, Goldstein (1974) concluded that a largely agreed upon constellation of childhood predictors of adult violence were maternal deprivation, poor identification with father, enuresis, pyromania, cruelty to animals, and abuse by one or both parents. Empirical predictive studies are not totally lacking, however. Lefkowitz, Eron, Walder, and Huesman (1977), in their impressive longitudinal study *Growing Up to Be Violent*, report such statistically significant childhood predictors of aggression at age 19 as (1) aggression at age 8 (the best predictor), (2) father's upward social mobility, (3) low identification of the child with his/her parents, and (4) a preference for watching violent television programs. McCord (1979) reported as statistically significant predictors: (1) lack of supervision during childhood, (2) mother lacking in self-confidence, and (3) chronic parental aggressiveness. And Wolfgang, Figlio, and Sellin (1972) found number of residential moves, lower IQ, mental retardation, and fewer school grades completed to be reliable childhood predictors of adult aggression. Thus we see that the potential array of useful childhood predictors of aggression is rather modest and, as we shall see, of limited utility when employed in attempts to predict overt aggression in the individual case. Findings reported are part untested speculation, part untested consensus, and part empirically identified postdictors of potential interest and usefulness, but largely awaiting predictive cross-validation.

Efforts to predict the overt aggression of any specific adult or groups of adults by means of other characteristics of such adults have generally yielded largely unsatisfactory outcomes. In his definitive work in this domain, *The Clinical Prediction of Violent Behavior*, Monahan (1981) critically reviewed the five major investigations which have sought to examine the utility of psychological test and interview data for predicting aggression. The outcomes of these predictive efforts are summarized in table 12.1. It is clear from this table that clinical prediction of adult aggression yields a dismaying number of mispredictions. False positives, i.e., predicted to be aggressive but no actual aggression ensuing, are very high across all five studies. Monahan (1981) comments:

> [the] best clinical research currently in existence indicates the psychiatrists and psychologists are accurate in no more than one out of three predictions of violent behavior over a several-year period. . . . [p. 47]

Monahan (1981), while correctly interpreting the research examined in his monograph as indicating our general inability to accurately predict individual aggression, nevertheless succeeds in pointing in hopeful directions in addition to urging further research examination of the demographic aggression-correlates and perhaps certain of the postdictively identified childhood and adult behavioral predictors noted above. The following paths are suggested by him.

1. Make base rates of violence a prime consideration. Monahan (1981) quite rightly notes that if the base rate of aggression in a given population is low, prediction of its occurrence is especially difficult. Perhaps, therefore, predictive efforts should focus mostly upon populations who have displayed such behavior earlier, e.g., high base rate populations.

2. Obtain and utilize information of valid predictive utility. More information often does not mean better prediction, and may mean worse. Crucial here is the *demonstrated* relationship between the predictor and criterion (aggressive behavior). As Monahan (1981) notes: "Focusing on a limited number of relevant and valid predictor items is more important than an exhaustive examination that yields much irrelevant and ultimately confusing information [p. 88]."

3. Make predictions based upon all relevant information. Attempt to include and properly

Table 12.1.   Validity Studies of the Clinical Prediction of Violent Behavior

STUDY	PERCENT TRUE POSITIVE	PERCENT FALSE POSITIVE	PERCENT TRUE NEGATIVE	PERCENT FALSE NEGATIVE	NUMBER PREDICTED VIOLENT	NUMBER PREDICTED NONVIOLENT	FOLLOWUP YEARS
Kozol et al. (1972)	34.7	65.3	92.0	8.0	49	386	5
Steadman and Cocozza (1974)	20.0	80.0	—	—	967	—	4
Cocozza and Steadman (1976)	14.0	86.0	84.0	16.0	154	103	3
Steadman (1977)	41.3	58.7	68.8	31.2	46	106	3
Thornberry and Jacoby (1979)	14.0	86.0	—	—	438	—	4

Source: Monahan, J. *The clinical prediction of violent behavior.* Rockville, Md.: National Institute of Mental Health, 1981.

weight negative indices as well as potentially counterbalancing positive factors that would tend to decrease the individual's propensity to aggression.

4. If possible, make combined use of person and situation variables in attempting to predict aggressive behavior. Until very recent years, the effort to predict aggression was almost entirely based on the use of personality, psychometric, demographic, and related information about the potential perpetrator as the predictive base (the personological model). In recent years, consistent with a parallel move toward person/situation interactionism in personality theory in general, increasing efforts have taken place to factor in situational, environmental information when attempting to predict aggressive behavior. Among the situational variables possibly predictive of the inhibition or facilitation of aggression are characteristics of one's family, peers, and job; the availability of intended victims; the availability of weapons; and the availability of alcohol.

We have in the foregoing discussion of the prediction of aggression touched upon potential predictors of demographic, longitudinal, concurrent, clinical, actuarial, and situational types. Monahan (1981) leaves us in his monograph, as we too wish to end consideration of this topic, with a list of questions advantageously used by interviewers in seeking to discern accurate predictive answers of these several and diverse types. These questions appear in table 12.2.

While Monahan's (1981) insights and recommendations represent a substantial step forward in our thinking about—and perhaps also our eventual ability to predict—overt aggression, our cumulative level of knowledge relevant to this predictive goal currently remains clearly inadequate. A great deal of predictor-identifying and prediction-testing research remains to be conducted. Perhaps such efforts will yield personality, demographic, situational, and other predictor information of use to this all-important task. Until such information is available, however, efforts to thwart or reduce aggression will of necessity occur primarily at a later point in the sequence of events which culminates in overt aggressive behavior, closer in temporal proximity to the aggressive act itself.

Table 12.2.   Questions for the Clinician in Predicting Violent Behavior

---

1. Is it a prediction of violent behavior that is being requested?
2. Am I professionally competent to offer an estimate of the probability of future violence?
3. Are any issues of personal or professional ethics involved in this case?
4. Given my answers to the above questions, is this case an appropriate one in which to offer a prediction?
5. What events precipitated the question of the person's potential for violence being raised, and in what context did these events take place?
6. What are the person's relevant demographic characteristics?
7. What is the person's history of violent behavior?
8. What is the base rate of violent behavior among individuals of this person's background?
9. What are the sources of stress in the person's current environment?
10. What cognitive and affective factors indicate that the person may be predisposed to cope with stress in a violent manner?
11. What cognitive and affective factors indicate that the person may be predisposed to cope with stress in a nonviolent manner?
12. How similar are the contexts in which the person has used violent coping mechanisms in the past to the contexts in which the person likely will function in the future?
13. In particular, who are the likely victims of the person's violent behavior, and how available are they?
14. What means does the person possess to commit violence?

MEASUREMENT

Measurement of aggression, for purposes of enhancing our understanding of its nature and evaluating its prevention and control, requires the same multilevel approach as does prediction. Measurement of any given phenomenon is related, first of all, to an underlying conceptualization of that phenomenon. At a theoretical level, conceptual approaches to understanding aggression range from biologically-based theories such as Freud's psychoanalytic theory (1920/1955, 1933/1964) and ethological theory (e.g., Lorenz, 1966; Tinbergen, 1968) to drive theories (e.g., Berkowitz, 1962, 1974; Dollard, Doob, Miller, Mowrer, & Sears, 1939; Miller, 1941) to social learning theories (e.g., Bandura, 1973, 1977; Baron, 1977). It is apparent that, just as in personality theory in general, theoretical considerations of aggression have largely moved away from exclusively personological models to person-situation interaction models. These more recently developed models incorporate personological variables along with situational and task variables, as well as the potential interactions among those sets of variables. As will become clear, this more complex, interactional model is in our view central to the goal of adequate measurement of aggression.

Considerable amounts of research have focused upon the linkage between personological variables and aggressive behavior. Employing a wide variety of measures with groups of people, relationships between personality measures and test signs of disposition to aggress have been shown, but with little direct linkage to the actual occurrence of aggressive behavior (as indicated in the previous section). While the amount of research is growing, considerably less is known about the linkage between settings and aggressive behavior, or about person-setting-behavior linkages. Theory and research in ecological and environmental psychology can be helpful here. In addition to personological and setting variables, changing life tasks as one develops, while conceptually related to diverse settings with which we interact and to developmental personological variables, might fruitfully be viewed as an additional and separate set of variables pertinent to this multidimensional picture of aggression. Changing task demands as we assume new roles (e.g., spouse, parent, worker, unemployed) can interact with other personological variables (e.g., coping skills) and with setting variables (e.g., available social supports, presence of a difficult child) to result in the inhibition or disinhibition of aggressive behavior. These task-behavior and person-setting-task-behavior linkages need to be examined conceptually and empirically. Any measurement system for understanding aggression or for evaluating the efficacy of control and prevention strategies must take into account this diverse set of personological, setting, task, and behavioral variables, and their interaction.

Cone's (1978) taxonomy of behavioral assessment, based upon a person-setting interactional model, provides a useful framework for describing the kind of measurement needed in this area. He presents a three-dimensional taxonomy consisting of behavioral contents, methods, and universes of generalization (see Fig. 12.1). Behavioral contents refers to motoric acts (publicly observable events), cognitive contents (private events including thoughts, images, reported feelings), and physiological contents. Methods of assessment or measurement are ordered along a continuum of directness. That is, methods are ordered with respect to the extent to which they measure the relevant behavior at the time and place of its natural occurrence. Measurement methods include interviews, self-reports, and ratings by others (about past events) at the most indirect end of the continuum, and self, analogue, and naturalistic-observation at the most direct end. The third dimension refers to the domains across which we wish to generalize about a given phenomenon. Specific universes of generalization include scorer generalization (interrater reliability), item generalization (referring to how representative a set of responses is to a universe of similar responses), generalization across time,

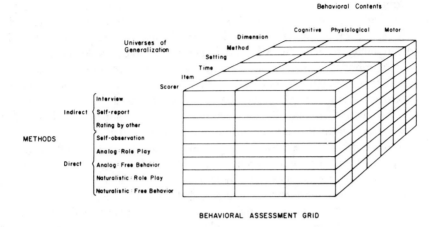

Fig. 12.1.   Cone's Three-Dimensional Taxonomy of Behavioral Assessment

Source: J. D. Cone, "The Behavioral Assessment Grid (BAG): A Conceptual Framework and a Taxonomy." *Behavior Therapy*, 1978, 9, 882-88.

setting generality (to determine the degree of setting specificity or generality of a particular set of behaviors), method generality (referring to the consistency of measuring a given behavior across methods), and dimensions generalization (referring to the comparability of data on two or more different behaviors, which allow us to understand response classes or response clusters).

Consideration of all three of these dimensions is essential to our understanding of aggression and to the measurement of intervention efficacy. While our most immediate concern might well be with observable motoric acts of aggression, cognitive and physiological concomitants of aggressive behavior—the other two facets of Cone's (1978) behavioral contents dimension—cannot be ignored. These cognitive and physiological concomitants may be antecedent to, concurrent with, and/or consequent to aggressive acts. For example, one's cognitive attributions concerning the behaviors of others in a particular setting may serve as an inhibitor or disinhibitor of aggression. With respect to measurement methods in the area of aggression, Cone's second dimension, it should be noted that a major concern with the validity of the commonly used rating scales (self or other) is the degree of behavioral specificity of the items. In addition, social desirability and other response bias and motivational considerations are relevant considerations to the use of rating scales of aggression. While analogue observation, at the other end of the methods dimension, is a procedure in which an investigator experimentally arranges conditions to maximize the likelihood of aggressive behavior in order to observe its relationship to other variables of interest, its usefulness is limited by the extent to which the results are related to aggressive behavior outside the laboratory setting (method and setting generality).

The most frequently used laboratory analogue procedures for measuring aggression have been questioned on these external validity grounds (Bornstein, Hamilton, & McFall, 1981; Edmunds & Kendrick, 1980). Such procedures include providing subjects an opportunity to aggress verbally and directly against another individual (e.g., Wheeler & Caggiula, 1966), allowing physical attack on inanimate objects (e.g., Bandura, Ross, & Ross, 1963), allowing direct physical aggression against others (though with padded swords and other similar "harmless" objects; e.g., Diener, Dineen & Endresen, 1975), and leading subjects through deception to believe they can cause physical injury to another through use of a shock device when in fact harm is impossible (e.g., Berkowitz, 1962; Buss, 1961; Taylor, 1967). The lack of method generality associated with most of these traditional psychological measures of aggression was an important consideration leading away from strictly personological models of aggression and toward person-setting models. Naturalistic observation often has the problem of reactivity to the presence of an observer, given the negative social sanctions for many forms of aggressive behavior. Certainly, direct measurement of aggression in the settings of concern provides the most powerful procedure for determining treatment efficacy. The problem of reactivity can be dealt with by directly observing behaviors highly correlated with aggression (dimensions generalization). The work of Burgess (1979), cited in the chapter on child abuse, illustrates this well. He demonstrated through direct observational procedures a clear relationship between particular parenting styles and actual abusive behavior.

The universes of generalization, Cone's third dimension, has particular relevance to research on the efficacy of prevention and control strategies. Much of our intervention research is limited by the failure to demonstrate the effects of interventions beyond the intervention setting to the daily living settings of the individuals (i.e., method and setting generality). All prevention and control research must include extensive follow-up measurement to determine maintenance and transfer effects (i.e., generalization across time, setting generality, and dimensions generality). Table 12.3 suggests a set of sources illustrating aggression measurement along Cone's three dimensions.

Measurement consistent with this three-dimensional framework, therefore, involves use of multiple methods with multiple responses and response levels within multiple settings. Such

Table 12.3. Sources Illustrating Measurement of Aggression Along Cone's Dimensions

METHOD	SOURCE	BEHAVIORAL CONTENT(S)
Interview		
Conflict Tactics Scale	Straus, 1979	Motoric, Cognitive
Self-Report		
Buss-Durkee Inventory	Buss & Durkee, 1957	Motoric, Cognitive
Anger Inventory	Novaco, 1975, 1977	Motoric, Cognitive, Behavioral
Conflict Tactics Scale	Straus, 1979	
Rating Scales		
Aggression Rating	Olweus, 1977	Motoric, Cognitive
Child Behavior Checklist	Achenbach & Edelbrock, 1981	Motoric, Cognitive
Analogue Observation		
"Aggression Machine"	Buss, 1961	Motoric
	Hokanson, 1961; Hokanson & Burgess, 1961	Motoric, Physiological
	Gentry, 1970	Motoric, Physiological
	Berkowitz, 1962	Motoric
	Taylor, 1967	Motoric
Naturalistic Observation	Strain & Ezzell, 1978	Motoric
	Wood et al., 1977	Motoric
	Burgess, 1979	Motoric
	Friedman et al., 1981	Motoric

Universes of Generalization (General Sources)		
Cronbach et al., 1972	Karoly & Steffan, 1980	Drabman et al., 1979
Goldstein & Kanfer, 1979	Cone, 1979	

measurement applied to the understanding of aggression allows for the convergence of information in the formation, testing, and strengthening of hypotheses. In addition, it allows the evaluation of unanticipated components of problems and the evaluation of unanticipated effects of interventions to prevent or control aggression. Certainly, multiple measurement research and evaluation ultimately requires complex research designs and multivariate analysis procedures. Sufficient numbers of individuals are necessary to carry out such multivariate and other between-group designs in prevention and control research. However, the eventual need for large numbers of research participants need not inhibit investigators and agency practitioners from carrying out intervention programs and systematically examining their efficacy. In recent years, the power and utility of single-case designs for evaluating interventions has been enhanced considerably (Hersen & Barlow, 1976; Kazdin, 1980; Kratochwill, 1978). While such designs were developed within the context of behavioral models, they are applicable to evaluation of prevention and control interventions from any conceptual orientation. Kratochwill (1977, 1978) in particular has described how practitioners can use these designs within the context of their own practice. Collaboration between researchers and practitioners in the area of aggression control and prevention can be greatly enhanced through use of these strategies, perhaps sequentially combined with the more complex multivariate procedures.

FUTURE DIRECTIONS

The contributors to this book have collectively presented and examined literally dozens of procedures designed to enhance our ability to prevent or control overt aggression. A few have been but little more than enthusiastic speculations, most have had a reasonable basis in systematic observation or empirical demonstration, and a small number rest on a foundation of quite substantial evidence. Hormonal, behavioral, psychodynamic, educational, sociological, criminal justice, mass media, political, architectural, organizational, and several other classes of preventive or controlling interventions have been put forth. How is the reader, the program developer, the on-the-line intervener to be aided in choosing from among this substantial array of alternatives? Our best answer to this conceptual and operational dilemma can conveniently be introduced by reproducing here a newspaper editorial one of us recently authored (Goldstein, 1982). It highlights our belief that complexly determined behaviors—most certainly including aggressive behavior—will yield only to complex solutions, and not the "big fix" or "one true light" so often unsuccessfully sought and promoted in American social problem solving efforts.

NEEDED: A WAR ON AGGRESSION

More than 11,500 of our countrymen were killed by bullets in 1981. Such lethal statistics are well-known by now, as are the tiny comparative homicide figures in so many other countries—48 people in Japan, 52 in Canada, 8 in Great Britain, 42 in West Germany. Since 1900, three-quarters of a million U.S. civilians have been killed by privately owned guns. Yet in spite of the occasional glimmer of hope that a community-supported gun control effort such as Morton Grove can inspire, effective regulation of America's 200 million firearms seems as far away as ever.

Our overall crime rate has largely stabilized in the last few years, but at unacceptably high absolute levels. Two especially aggressive crimes—forcible rape and aggravated assault—are exceptions to this trend and continue to increase. Other crimes are also becoming more violent. In 1967, for example, one of five robbery victims was physically injured during commission of the robbery. In 1977, the comparable injury statistic was one in three.

Rates of violence in America's schools are also staggering. The spitballs, occasional student backtalk, and infrequent fistfights of but a few decades back have been replaced by pistols, knives, chukka sticks and even sawed-off shotguns. In a typical recent year there were 110,000 assaults on teachers, 9,000 rapes, 600 million dollars in damage to school property from vandalism, 20 million thefts, and 400,000 acts of property destruction. From 1950 to 1975, the number of students in America's 84,000 schools increased by 86 percent, while school arson grew by 859 percent.

Conclusive research evidence from several sources exists, and has existed for a number of years, indicating that televised portrayals of violence do, in fact, increase the frequency of real life violence by many viewers—including the 25 young men who have shot themselves to death during the last two years playing Russian roulette after seeing such behavior in TV showings of The Deerhunter. Still the 1980s have seen neither a decrease in the number or intensity of such depictions, nor an increase in the frequency with which alternative constructive behavior is enacted.

It is not only America's streets, schools and mass media that are increasingly violent and dangerous—so too its homes. Spouse abuse, child abuse, and an especially nasty behavior unamusingly called "granny-bashing" are more and more with all of us today.

What is to be done about aggression in contemporary America? There is a tendency in our country to hope for, seek, and expect to find the big solution to our social problems, the one program or breakthrough which will dramatically wipe out poverty, cancer, crime, aging, and so on. Such breakthroughs are exceedingly rare and their likelihood diminishes as the problem's complexity grows.

Stated simply, aggression in America will diminish the more we plan and intervene in many ways, on several levels, simultaneously. We need a many-fronted war on aggression. Violence in the family will diminish as parents-to-be are regularly given training in parenting skills, as police are taught constructive means for resolving family disputes, as a national network of shelters for battered wives becomes a reality. Johnny will continue to assault his teacher all over America until and unless he is exposed to moral education or similar values exploration opportunities in school, and given explicit training in aggression management techniques.

It would also help a lot if for some reasonable proportion of the average 27.6 hours per week that Johnny watches television, he sees nonviolent solutions to interpersonal conflict, cooperation rather than selfishness, marital understanding and not marital abuse, empathy, caring, sharing and, in general, the best in human behavior, not the worst. His teachers must be taught how to select and use more, effective techniques for classroom discipline, not including corporal punishment—now legal in 47 of our 50 states and effective mostly in teaching youngsters the violence-increasing lesson "might makes right." The climate and organization of our schools must be made more open in their communication channels, more participatory in their governance, more readily a target for students to identify with, and generally both more firm and more fair in their daily operation.

Violent crime, too, will yield only to multiple solutions. Ideally, application of these solutions will occur prescriptively. We must match our interventions to the behaviors and personalities of individual offenders, and give up the hunt for a single, panacea solution to criminal violence. With few exceptions, the several solutions to violent crime instituted and dropped in rotation as "failures" over the past several years were not failures at all, but rather prescriptive successes. Each worked with some delinquents, some adult prisoners, some parolees, but none worked with all. Total diversion from the criminal justice system, shorter sentences, longer sentences, indeterminate sentences, community corrections, behavioral rehabilitation, graduated release programs have each yielded their partial victories. Our first task is largely a diagnostic one, to determine which felon, which delinquent, which offender is optimally to be treated in which way. Such work has but begun. [Goldstein, 1982]

It is our view, then, that aggression may yield in a multifronted war, one in which complex solutions are identified and utilized—especially solutions involving multiple interventions prescriptively selected and judiciously combined. Concretely, how is this war on aggression to be waged? We urge that it be multitargeted, multichannel, multiprocess, and multidisciplinary.

Multitargeted

Consistent with a systems or ecological perspective on aggression, our urging of a multitargeted stance toward its prevention and control requires that the interventions selected be at diverse *levels* of potential impact. Operationalizing this view with regard to the problem of school violence, Goldstein, Apter, and Harootunian (1983) described combinations of procedures useful for *simultaneous* intervention at the pupil, teacher, school administration, local school board, and larger societal levels. Terrorism, the Braungarts suggest in chapter 11, may yield most readily to simultaneous political, social, criminal justice, and mass media intervention. Child abuse, according to Keller and Erne (chapter 1), is optimally to be countered not only with interventions designed for abusing parents themselves, but those aimed at relatives, parent aides, educational systems, and other arenas capable of helping generate needed social support systems. Which specific procedures should optimally be selected from the cafeteria of interventions which constitutes this book, to intervene at which levels, with which aggressors, is the prescriptive question of primary importance, a question whose answers—or even asking—have rarely occurred.

Multichannel

Within levels of intervention, we would recommend procedures utilized should be selected to fit or correspond to aggressor channels of accessibility. Early chapters, for example, suggest that in addition to likely factors operating at other levels, juvenile delinquency may have multiple roots associated with the youngster himself—deficiencies in moral reasoning, impulsivity, a limited repertoire of means for responding to instigating stimuli, deficient interpersonal skills, a tendency to seek out and emulate antisocial models, low levels of guilt, high levels of attention-seeking behavior, and so forth. Thus, characteristics of his immediate or larger environment aside for the moment, it is clear that there are many qualities of the youngster himself which potentially contribute to his overt aggressive behavior. A multichannel perspective suggests that each of these aggression-enhancing qualities may be a fruitful channel for a complex attack on aggressive behavior. In this limited example, for instance, moral education, prosocial skill training, efforts designed to enhance reflectivity, provision and encouragement of constructive peer associations, and reward (e.g., attention) paid for appropriate rather than antisocial behaviors are each—singly and especially in combination—appropriate intervention possibilities.

Multiprocess

In addition to intervening at diverse levels (multitargeted) and with procedures aimed at the diverse roots and concomitants of overt aggression (multichannel), optimal interventions will be responsive to the fact that acts of overt aggression—as with all behavior—are the result of several simultaneously operating and often conflicting processes—inhibition, disinhibition, response acquisition, discrimination, generalization, and others. It follows, therefore, that our interventions are all the more likely to be successful when, responding to the fact of such multiprocess antecedents, the interventions too are multiprocess. As a concrete example, marital disharmony is less likely to occur or persist when each of the parties involved simultaneously is taught how to dispute anger-arousing self-statements by self-instruction and reduce physiological arousal by deep muscular relaxation (e.g., inhibition); learns how to use previously acquired more desirable interpersonal behaviors (e.g., disinhibition); or learns such behaviors for the first time (e.g., response acquisition); and learns and applies the behaviors over time and setting where and when they are (e.g., generalization) versus are not (e.g., discrimination) appropriate.

Multidisciplinary

Concern with levels, channels, and processes lies at the heart of a complex, prescriptive strategy for the prevention and control of aggression. In addition, and as a direct extension of a levels X channels X processes viewpoint, it is requisite for its success that this strategy also be multidisciplinary in perspective. The complexity of aggressive behavior; its multiple physiological, psychological, social, and political roots; its diverse supportive network of antecedents; its dependable and often substantial presence through the lifespan; and all else that makes human aggression tenacious and enduring, demands that no potential doors to its prevention and control be shut and, more affirmatively, that all perspectives be mined for what they singly and jointly may have to offer.

This book has sought to be an exemplar of such an affirmation. The Syracuse University Center for Research on Aggression is multidisciplinary because we believe aggression will yield most readily when the artificial borders of academic disiplines are breeched, ideas permitted to more fully intermingle, and new concepts at the interface of disciplines encouraged to emerge and be scrutinized. It is in this spirit, and toward the goal of identifying, examining, and disseminating increasingly more effective interventions for the prevention and control of aggression that this book has been offered.

REFERENCES

Achenbach, T. M., & Edelbrock, C. S. Behavioral problems and competencies reported by parents of normal and disturbed children aged four through sixteen. *Monographs of the Society of Research in Child Development*, 1981, *46* (Serial No. 188).

Bandura, A. *Aggression: A social learning analysis*. Englewood Cliffs, N.J.: Prentice-Hall, 1973.

Bandura, A. *Social learning theory*. Englewood Cliffs, N.J.: Prentice-Hall, 1977.

Bandura, A., Ross, D., & Ross, S. A. Imitation of film-mediated aggressive models. *Journal of Abnormal and Social Psychology*, 1963, *66*, 3-11.

Baron, R. A. *Human aggression*. New York: Plenum, 1977.

Berkowitz, L. *Aggression: A social psychological analysis*. New York: McGraw-Hill, 1962.

Berkowitz, L. Some determinants of impulsive aggression: Role of mediated associations with reinforcement for aggression. *Psychological Review*, 1974, *81*, 165-76.

Bornstein, P. H., Hamilton, S. B., & McFall, M. E. Modification of adult aggression: A critical review of theory, research, and practice. In M. Hersen, R. M. Eisler, & P. M. Miller (Eds.), *Progress in behavior modification*. Vol. 12. New York: Academic Press, 1981.

Burgess, R. L. Child abuse: A social interactional analysis. In B. B. Lahey & A. E. Kazdin (Eds.), *Advances in clinical child psychology*. Vol. 2. New York: Plenum, 1979.

Buss, A. H. *The psychology of aggression*. New York: Wiley, 1961.

Buss, A. H., & Durkee, A. An inventory for assessing different kinds of hostility. *Journal of Consulting Psychology*, 1957, *21*, 343-49.

Cocozza, J., & Steadman, H. The failure of psychiatric predictions of dangerousness: Clear and convincing evidence. *Rutgers Law Review*, 1976, *29*, 1084-1101.

Cone, J. D. The behavioral assessment grid (BAG): A conceptual framework and a taxonomy. *Behavior Therapy*, 1978, *9*, 882-88.

Cone, J. D. Confounded comparisons in triple response mode assessment research. *Behavioral Assessment*, 1979, *1*, 85-95.

Cronbach, L. J., Gleser, G. C., Nanda, H., & Rajaratnam, N. *The dependability of behavioral measures.* New York: John Wiley, 1972.

Diener, E., Dineen, J., & Endresen, K. Effects of altered responsibility, cognitive set, and modeling on physical aggression and deindividuation. *Journal of Personality and Social Psychology*, 1975, *31*, 328-37.

Dollard, J., Doob, L. W., Miller, N. E., Mowrer, O. H., & Sears, R. R. *Frustration and aggression.* New Haven, Conn.: Yale University Press, 1939.

Drabman, R. S., Hammer, D., & Rosenbaum, M. S. Assessing generalization in behavior modification with children: The generalization map. *Behavioral Assessment*, 1979, *1*, 203-20.

Edmunds, G., & Kendrick, D. C. *The measurement of human aggressiveness.* New York: John Wiley, 1980.

Freud, S. Beyond the pleasure principle. *Standard Edition.* Vol. 18. (J. Strachey, Ed. & trans.) London: Hogarth, 1955. (Originally published in 1920)

Freud, S. Why war? *Standard Edition.* Vol. 22. (J. Strachey, Ed. & trans.) London: Hogarth, 1964. (Originally published in 1933)

Friedman, R. M., Sandler, J., Hernandez, M., & Wolfe, D. A. Child abuse. In E. J. Mash & L. G. Terdal (Eds.), *Behavioral assessment of childhood disorders.* New York: Guilford, 1981.

Gentry, W. D. Effects of frustration, attack, and prior aggressive training on overt aggression and vascular processes. *Journal of Personality and Social Psychology*, 1970, *16*, 718-25.

Goldstein, A. P. Needed: A war on aggression. Syracuse Post-Standard, May 18, 1982.

Goldstein, A. P., Apter, S. J., & Harootunian, B. *School Violence.* Englewood Cliffs, N.J.: Prentice-Hall, 1983.

Goldstein, A. P., & Kanfer, F. (Eds.) *Maximizing treatment gains.* New York: Academic Press, 1979.

Goldstein, R. Brain research and violent behavior. *Archives of Neurology*, 1974, *30*, 1-18.

Hellman, D., & Blackman, N. Enuresis, firesetting, and cruelty to animals: A triad predictive of adult crime. *American Journal of Psychiatry*, 1966, *122*, 1431-35.

Hersen, M., & Barlow, D. H. *Single case experimental designs: Strategies for studying behavior change in the individual.* New York: Pergamon Press, 1976.

Hokanson, J. E. The effects of frustration and anxiety on overt aggression. *Journal of Abnormal and Social Psychology*, 1961, *62*, 346-51.

Hokanson, J. E., & Burgess, M. The effects of three types of aggression on vascular processes. *Journal of Abnormal and Social Psychology*, 1961, *64*, 446-49.

Karoly, P., & Steffan, J. J. (Eds.) *Improving the long-term effects of psychotherapy.* New York: Gardner Press, 1980.

Kazdin, A. E. *Research design in clinical psychology.* New York: Harper & Row, 1980.

Kozol, H., Boucher, R., & Garofolo, R. The diagnosis and treatment of dangerousness. *Crime and Delinquency*, 1972, *18*, 371-92.

Kratochwill, T. R. N = 1: An alternative research strategy for school psychologists. *Journal of School Psychology*, 1977, *15*, 239-49.

Kratochwill, T. R. *Single subject research: Strategies for evaluating change.* New York: Academic Press, 1978.

Lefkowitz, M., Eron, L., Walder, L., & Huesman, L. *Growing up to be violent.* New York: Pergamon Press, 1977.

Lorenz, K. *On aggression.* New York: Harcourt, 1966.

McCord, J. Some child rearing antecedents to criminal behavior in adult men. *Journal of Personality and Social Psychology*, 1979, *37*, 1477-86.

Monahan, J. *The clinical prediction of violent behavior.* Rockville, Md.: National Institute of Mental Health, 1981.

Novaco, R. W. *Anger control: The development and evaluation of an experimental treatment.* Lexington, Mass.: Lexington Books, 1975.

Novaco, R. W. Stress inoculation: A cognitive therapy for anger and its application to a case of depression. *Journal of Consulting and Clinical Psychology*, 1977, *45*, 600-08.

Olweus, D. Aggression and peer acceptance in adolescent boys: Two short-term longitudinal studies of ratings. *Child Development*, 1977, *48*, 1301-13.

Steadman, H. A new look at recidivism among Patuxent inmates. *The Bulletin of the American Academy of Psychiatry and the Law*, 1977, *5*, 200-09.

Steadman, H., & Cocozza, J. *Careers of the criminally insane.* Lexington, Mass.: Lexington Books, 1974.

Strain, P. S., & Ezzell, D. The sequence and distribution of behavioral disordered adolescents' disruptive/inappropriate behaviors: An observational study in a residential setting. *Behavior Modification*, 1978, *2*, 403-25.

Straus, M. A. Measuring intrafamily conflict and violence: The Conflict Tactics (CT) scales. *Journal of Marriage and the Family*, 1979, *41*, 75-88.

Taylor, S. P. Aggressive behavior and physiological arousal as a function of provocation and the tendency to inhibit aggression. *Journal of Personality*, 1967, *35*, 297-310.

Thornberry, T., & Jacoby, J. *The criminally insane: A community followup of mentally ill offenders.* Chicago: University of Chicago Press, 1979.

Tinbergen, N. On war and peace in animals and man. *Science*, 1968, *160*, 1411-18.

Wheeler, L., & Caggiula, A. R. The contagion of aggression. *Journal of Experimental Social Psychology*, 1966, *2*, 1-10.

Wolfgang, M., Figlio, R., & Sellin, T. *Delinquency in a birth cohort.* Chicago: University of Chicago Press, 1972.

Wood, D. D., Callahan, E. J., Alevizos, P. N., & Teige, J. R. Communication: A behaviorally based logbook. *Journal of Applied Behavior Analysis*, 1977, *10*, 706.

Author Index

Plotkin, R. C., 26
Plummer, I. L., 161
Pogrebin, L. C., 49
Polakow, R. L., 13
Polister, P. E., 26
Pollio, H. R., 180
Polk, K., 69
Pollock, C. B., 4, 6, 25
Pomeroy, W. B., 107
Potts, D. A., 12
Powe, L. A., Jr., 263
Preble, M., 168
Prescott, S., 43
Price, C., 26
Price, R. H., 86
Prinz, R., 168

Quilitch, H. R., 180
Quinney, R., 90

Rabe, R. L., 329
Rabkin, J. G., 114
Rabon, D., 184
Rachman, S. J., 137, 180
Rada, R. T., 87, 107, 110, 111, 112, 124,
    145
Rappaport, A. F., 321
Rapoport, D., 168, 178
Rasmussen, D., 168
Rathbone-McCuan, E., 15
Raths, L. E., 218
Rawlings, E., 242
Ray, R. S., 180, 188
Rayner, R., 180
Reage, P., 127
Rector, M. G., 71
Redbill, S., 1
Redlick, A. S., 11, 313, 314, 315
Reese, N. M., 184
Remmers, H. H., 253
Rest, J. R., 216, 217, 225
Reynolds, N. J., 180
Rhode, N., 168
Richards, P., 67
Richmond, A. E., 24, 103, 104
Richmond, J. B., 101
Rigler, D., 4, 5, 6
Rincover, A., 191
Risley, T. R., 180, 191
Roberts, D., 246
Robin, A. L., 168
Robinson, M. N., 127
Roeser, T. D., 70

Roguly, D., 313
Rose, E., 13, 24, 149
Rose, S. D., 165, 168
Rosenbaum, A., 18, 43, 44, 47, 55, 57, 122,
    162, 165, 167, 168, 170
Rosenbaum, C. P., 161
Ross, C. J., 1, 23
Ross, D., 1, 24, 26, 242, 343
Ross, S. A., 8, 25, 242, 343
Roth, F., 14
Rotter, M. J., 121
Rounsaville, B., 41, 54
Rounsaville, B. J., 43, 56
Rubel, R. J., 66, 67, 78
Rubens, W. S., 257
Rubin, A. P., 165
Rubin, K. H., 220
Rubin, M. E., 324
Rubinstein, E. A., 243
Ruma, E. H., 234
Rumsey, M. G., 118, 119
Rumsey, J. M., 118, 119
Rundle, L., 229, 230
Rushton, J. P., 260
Russell, C. A., 161, 313, 330
Russell, R. K., 325
Rutherford, E., 220, 232
Rutter, E., 52
Rutter, M., 76, 78
Rychtarik, R. G., 184

Sackett, G. P., 20, 27
Sahler, O., 3
Sajwaj, T., 191
Saklofake, D., 161
Saltzstein, H. D., 232
Sameroff, A. J., 4, 6, 13
Sanday, P. R., 130
Sanders, N., 13, 161
Sanders, R. W., 15, 179
Sandler, J., 12, 14
Sandler, O., 13, 20, 27
Sardino, T. J., 52, 162
Savino, A. B., 13, 15
Schachter, B. S., 235
Schaeffer, B., 3
Schafer, W. E., 69, 180
Scharf, P., 233
Scherl, D. J., 108
Schneider, C., 6, 25, 26
Schneider, F. W., 14
Schneider, J. A., 220
Schreiber, J., 303, 325, 326, 327, 330, 331

Subject Index

About the Contributors

Steven J. Apter
Special Education
Syracuse University
Syracuse, New York

Margaret M. Braungart
College of Health-Related Professions
S.U.N.Y. — Upstate Medical Center
Syracuse, New York

Richard G. Braungart
Department of Sociology
Syracuse University
Syracuse, New York

George Comstock
Department of Public Communications
Syracuse University
Syracuse, New York

Diane Erne
Alliance Child Abuse Coordinating Agency
Syracuse, New York

Barry Glick
New York State Division for Youth
Syracuse, New York

Arnold P. Goldstein
Department of Psychology
Syracuse University
Syracuse, New York

Diane Goldstein
Department of Psychology
Syracuse University
Syracuse, New York

Berj Harootunian
School of Education
Syracuse University
Syracuse, New York

Neil H. Katz
Program in Nonviolent
    Conflict and Change
Syracuse University
Syracuse, New York

Harold R. Keller
Department of Psychology
Syracuse University
Syracuse, New York

Allan Mazur
Department of Sociology
Syracuse University
Syracuse, New York

Patricia J. Morokoff
Medical Psychology
Uniformed Services University
    of the Health Sciences
Washington, D.C.

Kathleen L. Uhler
Department of Philosophy
St. Bonaventure University
Olean, New York

Deborah Zimmerman
Department of Psychology
Syracuse University
Syracuse, New York

Pergamon General Psychology Series

Editors: Arnold P. Goldstein, Syracuse University
Leonard Krasner, SUNY at Stony Brook